P9-EEJ-196

A LIFE IN LETTERS, 1914–1982

✴

A LIFE IN LETTERS, 1914–1982

Gershom Scholem

Edited and Translated by Anthony David Skinner

HARVARD UNIVERSITY PRESS

Cambridge, Massachusetts, and London, England / 2002

Published with the cooperation of the Franz Rosenzweig Center
for German-Jewish Literature and Cultural History at the Hebrew
University of Jerusalem.

Illustration on title page: Gershom Scholem, 1974 (detail).
Photo by Judah Passow. Reproduced with the permission of Technion,
the Israel Institute of Technology; and Network Photographers Ltd.,
on behalf of Judah Passow. Photo courtesy of the Jewish National
and University Library, Jerusalem.

Library of Congress Cataloging-in-Publication Data
Scholem, Gershom Gerhard, 1897–1982
[Correspondence. English. Selections]
A life in letters, 1914–1982 / Gershom Scholem; edited and translated by
Anthony David Skinner.
p. cm.
Includes bibliographical references and index.
ISBN 0–674–00642–9
1. Scholem, Gershom Gerhard, 1897—Correspondence.
2. Jewish scholars—Correspondence.   I. Skinner, Anthony David.   II. Title.
BM755.S295 A4 2001
296′.092—dc21
[B]   2001051521

EDITOR'S FOREWORD

Gershom Scholem himself was the editor of several collections of letters. Together with Theodor Adorno, he brought out a two-volume edition of Walter Benjamin's correspondence, which included a large number of his own letters. Years later Scholem published his extensive correspondence with Walter Benjamin from the 1930s. Since Scholem's death in 1982, C. H. Beck Verlag in Munich has published five volumes of his correspondence (edited and annotated by Itta Shedletzky and Thomas Sparr), incorporating materials that Scholem deposited at the Jewish National University Library of Jerusalem. The present edition of letters draws from all of these sources, and also reproduces a number of other, hitherto unpublished letters.

Naturally, a single volume of letters can present only a small fraction of the total. I have chosen letters—both Scholem's own and those from friends, colleagues, and family members—best able to capture his "self-portraiture." I have weighed and balanced each letter, now admitting, now excluding, according to the biographical, literary, or philosophical qualities of the individual document. Owing to its sheer size and its availability in English, I have left out most of his correspondence with Walter Benjamin and Hannah Arendt. Likewise, this edition gives no special privilege to scholarly letters directly pertinent to Scholem's scholarship; the "harmless and useless details" that animate his descriptions of everyday life in Germany, Palestine, and Israel often tell us more about him than one of his detailed analyses of, say, a seventeenth-century religious text.

The letters are organized chronologically, according to major periods of his life. Each part begins with a short introduction highlighting pertinent historical events, intellectual trends, and other relevant background material.

I have sought to present Scholem and his correspondents as they wrote, with a minimum of editorial intrusion, the primary aim being coherence and readability, not exhaustive academic commentary. Most of the letters explain themselves. Sometimes they don't, often for the simple reason that they refer to names, institutions, ideas, and even places once part of a thriving, now vanished, German-Jewish world. Similarly, many of Scholem's letters to friends and family were destroyed or lost during the war or in exile; only from the responses and comments of his interlocutors can his own comments be gleaned. I have added brief footnotes wherever letters allude to obscure people, events, and literary texts. To supplement the annotations, I have also appended a bibliography of Scholem's writings in English. Most of the letters in this edition include the name of the city in which the letter was written, as well as salutations and closings. Only where the original German lacks such details have I omitted them.

Throughout the correspondence, Scholem mostly used the formal *Sie* in addressing friends and colleagues. This was due partly to middle-class social conventions at the time, and partly to Scholem's own very Prussian character. His nearly exclusive use of *Sie* made the informal *Du,* when he used it, a highly significant detail. Scholem used *Du* with family members. He also adopted the *Du* form with Benjamin after they had known each other about a year. Only very rarely did he ever extend the circle beyond that. He employed *Sie* with most of his close friends, such as Werner Kraft, George Lichtheim, George Steiner, and Theodor Adorno. He used *Du* in a few letters to Hannah Arendt—but after she began publishing her writings on the Eichmann trial, he promptly reverted back to *Sie.*

One final note on the translation. All translators confront the perennial tension between literal accuracy and sense. I have chosen to lean toward the latter. These letters were written between friends or acquaintances, with no thought (or at least, in Scholem's case, no immediate intention) of publication. Rarely do they contain important philosophical formulations. But they do express a great deal of emotion, which often does not come across in a literal translation. I have sought to communicate their feeling and rhythm, to render the sentiments contained in the original German. My approach also relates to the audience for whom this volume is designed. I have prepared this selection not for Scholem scholars, who can read the originals, but for general readers interested in the drama of this great life.

Many people helped bring this book together. Above all, I wish to thank Dorothy Harman, who as early as a decade ago began to work with Harvard University Press, the Jewish National and University Library, and the Leo Baeck Institute to plan this book. Maria Ascher, of Harvard University Press, helped tighten and polish what began as a rather rough draft. I thank her for her extraordinary skill, her sense of language, and her fine taste. Finally, I would like to express my gratitude to Paul Mendes-Flohr, Amos Elon, and Steve Aschheim for their insightful comments and criticisms.

CONTENTS

Introduction
1

I. A Jewish Zarathustra, 1914–1918
5

II. Unlocking the Gates, 1919–1932
85

III. Redemption through Sin, 1933–1947
205

IV. Master Magician Emeritus, 1948–1982
343

Notes
499

Selected Bibliography
533

Chronology
535

Index
539

A LIFE IN LETTERS, 1914–1982

INTRODUCTION

Selection and abbreviation themselves constitute a kind of commentary,
and to a certain extent even an appreciation of the subject.
—GERSHOM SCHOLEM (1897–1982), *Major Trends in Jewish Mysticism*

IN 1930 BETTY SCHOLEM wrote to her son Gershom about a
disturbing experience: while traveling through Mussolini's Italy she had
had her purse snatched, and when she'd reported the robbery the local
police had enraged her by asking her to supply her mother's maiden
name for the crime report. The response sent by Gershom, then living
in Jerusalem, is revealing. "Why did you so resent the fascist officials for
what was no doubt their innocent curiosity in your family tree? [. . .]
Don't you know that such harmless and useless details can be of the
greatest importance for future researchers? If someone should someday
ask whether Scholem really lived or was perhaps only a mythical figure
(a thunder god [*ein Donnergott*]), then that scrap of paper in the police
files could illuminate a way through the jungle. The report that his
mother was named Betty will confirm his existence, as will this statement
(or some other one) concerning his maternal grandparents."[1]

Clearly Gershom Scholem, though only thirty-three, already realized
that his intellectual legacy would one day raise perplexing biographical
questions. In his study of Jewish mysticism (the Kabbalah), Scholem
nearly single-handedly turned a hitherto obscure and even despised
world of thought and belief into a legitimate arena of scholarly interest.
In directing the light of critical scholarship onto this hidden tradition,
however, he both clarified one mystery and created a new one: Gershom
Scholem himself.

Many years later one of Scholem's students, a Hungarian Jewish scholar by the name of Josef Weiss, began to probe the identity of his teacher. Weiss naturally did not question his teacher's existence; that much he knew. In an essay he published in a local Tel Aviv newspaper in 1947, on the occasion of Scholem's fiftieth birthday, he asked why Scholem's "very lively personality" and highly charged voice rarely penetrated his "seemingly dead scholarship."[2] What Weiss called his mentor's "impersonal anonymity" was particularly striking, given the fact that Scholem had begun his scholarship during World War I; finished his doctorate in the revolutionary climate of the early Weimar Republic; matured as a scholar during the British Mandate period in Palestine; and published his first major works while the Nazis reigned in Germany, a new world war was devastating the European continent, and European Jewry was being destroyed. Scholem also firmly rejected the idea that a historian can deliver a purely "objective" account of the past. Behind scholarship, he asserted, must stand a "philosophy" and a "perspective."[3] The scholar must take a stance, make a decision, pick out from history an angle suitable for his deeper needs.[4] But if so, where had his own moral voice been during that time of colossal destruction?

Weiss found an answer in a source suggested by Scholem's letter to his mother in 1930: his private life. Weiss claimed in his 1947 essay that those with a glimpse into his teacher's "singularly sculpted personality" could decipher his philological and historical studies as "Scholem incognito."[5] He went on to compare Scholem to a medieval painter who "paints his own face" onto a figure in a crowd. The master "camouflaged" himself in his scholarly compositions; he used a painter's techniques to recast personal concerns into a different era and even to portray himself in historical garb.

Scholem applauded his pupil for finding a code that would enable readers to decipher his work at last. "It's a very nice and audacious essay," Scholem commented in a letter to a close friend, Hugo Bergmann, for the inquiry into the "form of camouflage I practice when I do what is called scholarship" shows "that my pupils have learned something from me."[6]

Few other scholars of Scholem's caliber have openly admitted the intimate relationship between their personal life and their work. Nor have many been so diligent in preserving every "harmless and useless detail" in order to "illuminate a way through the jungle" for future researchers. Scholem left thousands of pages of diaries and unpublished manuscripts, carefully organized into an archive. Personal correspondence had a particular significance for him. In his diary he once described a personal letter as "second in power only to the Bible. It, too, works like an act of revelation."[7]

Scholem was one of the great letter-writers of the twentieth century, and not just in the sheer volume of his correspondence. The vast body of letters—some 16,000 extant missives in all—documents the man, his thought, and his times. They trace how the catastrophic events that overwhelmed European civilization after 1914 found a direct echo in his studies on the Kabbalah. Both his life and his work were preoccupied with the themes of exile, redemption, catastrophe, and return.

PART I A JEWISH ZARATHUSTRA, 1914–1918

A family outing, Schierke im Harz, Germany, 1913. Back row, from left: Arthur, Betty, Reinhold, and Gerhard. In the foreground are two unidentified friends. *Inset:* The four Scholem brothers, 1904. From left: Reinhold, Erich, Werner, and Gerhard. Both photos courtesy of the Jewish National and University Library, Jerusalem, Gershom Scholem Archive (Arc. 4o 1599).

Oh, my friend! You can gather from all of this that I find myself in the advanced stages of Zionism, a Zionism of the most intimate kind. I measure all things against Zion—which is why it should come as no surprise that I rank many things as too small and too crooked.

—Letter to Harry Heymann, Berlin, November 12, 1917

IN SEPTEMBER 1914, Gershom Scholem and his brother Werner exchanged a number of letters. Most of the debates and ideas mentioned in their letters have long since been forgotten, drawn as they were from a now vanished arena of conflicts, ideals, and visions. Socialism, anarchy, Socialist revisionism, the uncompromising purity of doctrine; betrayal and fidelity; youth and utopia; history and progress—all these subjects figured into the correspondence between the two brothers. Werner believed in the possibility of a better, more just world and directed his energies toward the cause of the working class and a future universal liberation, as laid down by the iron-clad principles of Marxism; Gershom looked to myth and "Zion." Werner believed that "liberation of the working class must come through the workers themselves"; his younger brother, that the Jews' "liberation or revolution" would come through the "Land of Israel."[1]

But these early letters do more than show how ideals considered sacred by one generation can become utterly foreign to another. Setting aside the specific contents of the dreams they uphold, the letters testify to precocious talent stirred by lofty ideals. It was also wartime, and the brothers' talk of revolution, anarchy, and myth attests to the speed at which the well-ordered world of their parents was quickly unraveling.

At the time of Gershom Scholem's birth in 1897, the German-Jewish middle classes had good reason to feel that their place in the world was auspicious. It was the Age of Progress, for nearly thirty years of German unification had given them a new, muscular, wealthy society. German factories were outproducing their English and French counterparts. It was only a matter of time, thought the middle classes, that German political and military power would follow suit. With little exaggeration, one could add that no single group was benefiting more from the new Reich than the Jews.

Scholem would later caricature his parents' generation as comprising "prosperous owners of factories that produced bathtubs or sausage skins."[2] German Jews tended to be urban, educated, and well-to-do, and they sent their children to the best schools. The Jews of Berlin, in particular, were concentrated largely in medicine, dentistry, law, publishing, marketing, and light manufacturing. Middle-class Jewish life was centered in the city's newer sections to the west, where rents were high and the air was clean. Walter Benjamin, a fellow Berlin Jew who would play a seminal role in Scholem's life, said of his Berlin suburb that it gave him a "splendid feeling of bourgeois security."[3]

Ideologically, German Jews were masters at navigating between the bright promises of the future and the more archaic hazards of prejudice still lurking in the shadows. They instinctively shunned extreme positions; with a sharply honed sense of the possible, they gravitated toward positions of compromise. They shied away from joining Jewish groups and almost never spoke out in public as Jews. "Education and readings were oriented exclusively toward Germany," Scholem later recalled. Middle-class Jews "emphasized over and over . . . that we belonged to the German nation." They were also great believers in liberalism. Quoting the poet Heinrich Heine, Scholem described how in his circle many believed that "the mission of the Jews" would be fulfilled with the arrival of the "worldly savior"—namely, unlimited technical progress.[4]

It was within this safe world of peace and prosperity that sociologists first coined the term "generational conflict," as the children of prosperity began to suspect their parents of having paid too stiff a price for success. In their opinion, affluence had blinded their parents to the loftier dimensions of human existence.

Fin-de-siècle Germany, and particularly Berlin, bred a host of reform movements, youth clubs, back-to-nature groups, and mystical sects. The largest youth movement was the so-called Wandervögel, whose members sang songs and carried backpacks as they wandered through the hills, mountains, and farmlands of the German-speaking world in search of an "authentic" past of castles and ancient battle sites. To escape from the manacles of bourgeois society, they sought meaning in poetry, myth, religion, literature, and their own raw youthfulness. They also dreamed of an ideal New German: heroic, pagan, simple, pure, unencumbered, and dynamic, breathing the sacred German dust raised by striding, wandering feet. The New German was close to nature, honest, faithful, often nude—and, above all, young.

Moreover, the New German wasn't a Jew, which helps explain why some young Jews became enormously interested in socialism as a universalist antidote to exclusionary nationalism, bigotry, and injustice. The majority of young Jews, however, opted for a more direct route around the chauvinism of the German youth movement: that of imitation. The plethora of Jewish youth groups that sprang up at the time—sports clubs, fraternities, hiking associations, and so on—tended to mimic Germanic ones in both form and content.

The Zionist youth movement was one among many. It had little in common with Theodor Herzl or the annual Zionist congresses held in Europe's finest gilded halls. Like other youth associations, its members came from the privileged middle class and as such prided themselves on being radical, antibourgeois, uncompromising, and determined to "return" to lost, enchanted territory abandoned by their parents. The largest Zionist Jewish youth club, Blau-Weiss ("Blue-White"), consciously modeled itself on the Germanic Wandervögel. Its members pursued "authenticity" in dueling uniforms, riding boots, and fraternity caps, and more often than not with a beer in hand.

One of the most powerful cultural impulses for Jewish renewal came from Martin Buber, who spearheaded a so-called Jewish Renaissance. This he did largely through a number of best-sellers that made him a cult figure among the progeny of bankers, merchants, and factory owners. Buber's books *Die Geschichten des Rabbi Nachman* (The Tales of Rabbi Nachman; 1906) and *Die Legende des Baalschem* (The Legends of the Baal Shem; 1908) were as popular as the works of Hermann Hesse, Stefan George, and Thomas Mann. Written at the time of a general discovery of exotic art (African, Polynesian, Asian) and the newly awakened interest in myth and mysticism, they transformed eastern European Jewish folklore into an idiom attractive to the younger generation. Under the Hasidic *shtreimel* (fur cap) Buber discovered subterranean, hidden, esoteric powers, a creative pathos, and something mystical, rebellious, and healthy—precisely the qualities young Jews most longed to find. His more theoretical writings introduced into the general vocabulary of Jewish youth the term *Erlebnis,* which literally means "inner experience," but in fact a good deal more. *Erlebnis* refers to something profound and personal, a strata of experience deeper than mere knowledge and more permanent than social norms. Today we would say *Erlebnis* is akin to a person's true "identity." For Buber it also operated as a historical identity, allowing an "alienated" young person to "feel, in the pre-existence of his Self, the continuity of his Self's unending past."[5]

Coteries of Buber disciples emerged throughout Germany. A particularly dense concentration of votaries with talent and conviction formed among the German-speaking inhabitants of Prague—a number of whom, such as Hugo Bergmann, Max Brod, Hans Kohn, and Robert Weltsch, would later play an important role in Scholem's life. Bergmann and Brod even managed to drag their childhood friend Franz Kafka along to their meetings. But forever on the skeptical fringe, Kafka could never muster the requisite faith. *Erlebnis* remained out of his reach.

The Scholem family was typical of many German-Jewish families, the line of upward mobility being almost invariably straight and direct. Gershom's grandfather, oddly named Scholem Scholem, broke with his Orthodox upbringing and changed his name to Siegfried, in honor of Richard Wagner's famous operatic hero. While Siegfried remained caught somewhere between traditional and modern Europe, his son Arthur, a self-declared atheist and "modern man," grew up with both feet firmly set on Germanic soil.[6]

And like the heads of so many other middle-class Jewish families, this law-abiding, tax-paying patriot became the target (in his case a rather amply proportioned one) of filial rebellion. The two oldest sons, Reinhold and Erich, fell in readily with their father's wishes, trotting along the path prepared for them. Both joined him in the family printing business. It was with the two youngest sons, Werner and Gershom—who in those days was called Gerhard—that rebellion began to stir. Arthur's unremitting pressure on his sons to be "responsible," "respectable," and above all employable nurtured in these two an unusually strong strain of zealotry. Betty, their mother, did her best to smooth over conflicts and to mediate between the sides. This suited her well because she was both better educated and more culturally ambitious than her pragmatic husband. A woman of great talent, she tried to keep tensions from breaking out into full-scale warfare. She had her hands full.

Werner rejected "bourgeois" values altogether and dreamed of a political career situated somewhere on the extreme left. These socialist leanings set him on a collision course with his father. When he joined the Social Democratic party in 1912, the rupture appeared irreparable.

Gerhard, the youngest, was the most driven and talented child in the Scholem household. He loved books and ideas far more than the printing business. His early favorites were Nietzsche, Hölderlin, and Stefan George. But he discovered the most "tremendous echo" of his childhood in 1912 when he read Buber's first books on Hasidism and his *Drei Reden über das Judentum* (Three Speeches on Judaism). He later recalled how the voice speaking from Buber's books was "promising, demanding, fascinating, uncovering hidden life beneath the frozen official form, uncovering hidden treasure." The books "demanded that young people be an additional link in the chain of hidden life, that they be heirs to a sublime and hidden tradition of revolt and uprising."[7]

In this search for an "authentic" self, beyond the pale of class and family, Scholem began a diary to document his dramatic changes. In 1913 he began scribbling agitated reflections into dozens of notebooks— jottings which he variously described as "out of the workshop of the spirit," the "metaphysical stories of a physical *Ich*," and "marginalia to a daily book of *Erlebnis*." The sixteen-year-old began his first entry with a bold reckoning of his family heritage. "I know of no famous rabbis among my ancestors." One great-grandfather had run a kosher eatery on Klosterstrasse in the old city of Berlin; Gerhard's grandfather on his father's side had founded his own printing house; while Betty's father had been a physical giant, the head of a synagogue, and a man with a preference for "big-breasted" women. Arthur, the first thoroughly secular man in the family, hardly figured in this genealogy.[8]

By the summer of 1914 Scholem had gone over to Buber with full sails. When referring to his new teacher, he spoke of the "quiet loneliness of holy ecstasy." In his own words, the teenage Scholem now preached "Hasidism, mysticism, Buber, socialism as a new religiosity"; he experienced "spiritual explosives"; and he bathed in something "new and unimaginable" that liberated him from the "thousands of threads and chains" tying him to state, family, and society. In the purest Buberian diction, he sensed a complete unity between himself and the "movement" of other young Jews, both forming a single *Erlebnis*. To one childhood friend he described Zionism as "revolution," a "leap," a "tremor," a way to experience "past generations."[9]

Scholem also threw himself into the study of Hebrew. Buber once described the "essence" of the Jewish "renaissance" as the attempt to "reconnect" to "our ancient past at the high point of our race," which meant for him the "restoration of the Hebrew language."[10] Scholem agreed. So as his peers sat in cafés, flirted, or wandered through forests, he spent much of his free time in the neighborhood of Berlin known as the Scheunenviertel, home to mostly Orthodox eastern European Jewish refugees, where he looked for Hebrew books sold in stores, thrown into old bags and sold on the street, or even stuffed haphazardly into sacks and offered for free. He acquired the sacred wares as his ticket back to Judaism. He also took Hebrew lessons with Orthodox rabbis. There was hardly a synagogue he did not know, a kosher restaurant he did not frequent, a rabbinical scholar he did not consult.

Scholem later described the years of World War I as the most "decisive time" in his life. In 1914 he was still an adolescent, uncertain of his place and task in life. Within four years he would discover his true "destiny."[11]

The middle classes enthusiastically welcomed the outbreak of war. Radicals, avant-garde writers, and Expressionist painters volunteered their services. Zionist rebels reacted no differently and followed in the goose step of their Christian peers. Buber described it as a "stupendous event" and cheered it on, albeit more in spirit than in the flesh (the frail, five-foot-tall, thirty-five-year-old philosopher had little to contribute to the actual fighting).[12] Heinrich Margulies, one of his young admirers, wrote in the leading Zionist newspaper of the time, the *Jüdische Rundschau:* "We went off to war not in spite of being Jews, but because we were Zionists."[13]

Most members of the Scholem household duly joined in the general martial mood. Reinhold and Erich both volunteered. Werner predictably broke ranks when he followed the leaders of a negligible faction of the socialist movement, Karl Liebknecht and Rosa Luxembourg, in opposing the war. Werner dismissed it as a bourgeois ruse designed to

undermine socialist internationalism. The fact that the majority of socialists supported Germany's entry into the war only proved that they had
fallen victim to a heretical "revisionism." Arthur Scholem naturally responded with screams and threats. The conflict ended only after Werner
was drafted into the army. In June 1916 he even emerged as a hero in
his father's eyes after he was wounded in the foot in Serbia. The reconciliation proved brief: the convalescing Werner took part in an antiwar
demonstration organized on no less an occasion than the kaiser's birthday. He was arrested and charged with treason, as well as with what the
authorities called "insulting the majesty" of the kaiser.

The present edition of Scholem's correspondence begins with letters
exchanged between Werner and Gerhard in September 1914. They
clearly indicate the extent to which the younger brother wished to follow the elder's rebellious example. At seventeen Gerhard was just below
the draft age. The atmosphere of marching armies and a vast continent
of massed troops only reinforced his faith in Zion. In the middle of
August, two weeks after Germany invaded Belgium, Arthur and Betty
Scholem took him on a trip to the Swiss Alps. Gerhard took his visions
along with him. There was a "storm in the high mountain peaks!" he
announced in his diary.

> A black wall of clouds looms threateningly over a glacier. Shreds
> of fog fly and break apart against the crags. The snow in the distance
> sparkles in a strange darkness, like the ocean swallowing up the last
> beams of sunlight before a hurricane strikes. [. . .] In the valley
> below and in the mountains above, the wind howls. Humans crawl
> out before the storm like Adam before the voice of God. Water
> gushes down from heaven as in the days of the Flood. [. . .] A wild
> army stalks above my head, and the God of the mountains rises up
> in the storm. "You lonely creature, why do you stand here?
> Doesn't the thunder call you to repent? Won't the spirits and the
> elements wage war against you for disrupting them and spying on
> them in their battle?" No, I will not retreat! For I have come here
> because of the storm. For you are the chaos now; out of you alone
> shall the Eternal Will bring renewal. God can be found only in
> danger.[14]

Three weeks later, on another stormy autumn evening, he recorded
a meeting he had had with members of the German Wandervögel,

whom he lauded for their "boundless youthful passion for romanticism and their magnificent desire for destruction."[15] That diary entry recounted his melancholy reflections on the state of the Jewish *Volk*. "Once upon a time," he wrote, "there was a people that had no happiness on earth and no sky could cause it to shine. This people had once been young, long, long before. Yes, young. The rustling of native forests and the radiance of the stars in its own skies were at work within it. But someone cursed this nation"; and this "heavy curse" forced it, stripped of "youth," to "abandon its soil and venture out into foreign lands and to other gods, to new stars." The entry continues with reference to a "new generation" embarked upon a desperate search "for its youth and for its homeland."[16] The young Scholem vowed to help direct the search; he, a self-styled Jewish "Zarathustra," set out to be the secular prophet who could lead young people to this promised land. "And what is so marvelous about Zarathustra?" he asked himself. "Regardless of what one thinks about the ideals it proposes, [Nietzsche's] book is surely a new Bible. Indeed, to write something of the sort is my goal. Yes, that's it. To compose a Jewish Zarathustra—that's my plan.[17]

In early 1915 Scholem's hostility to the war became more active when he joined Werner on his visits to clandestine meetings in a restaurant in the Berlin suburb of Neuköln. He liked what he heard and promptly translated it into his own idiom. After he took over the leadership of a small Zionist group in Berlin by the name of Jung Juda ("Young Judah"), he publicly attacked "Zionist revisionism."[18] His dream of creating a "Jewish Zarathustra" also changed, now taking on the form of critical Hebrew philology and textual scholarship.

Throughout most of 1915 and 1916 he urged friends and fellow members (names that appear in his early correspondence: Harry Heymann; Edgar Blum; Erich Brauer and his sister Grete—who was also Scholem's first love; Aharon Heller; and Meta Jahr) to abandon Europe for the Land of Israel.

Together with Erich Brauer, he published a Zionist antiwar underground paper with a run of 50–100 copies. It was called *Blau-Weisse Brille* (Blue-White Spectacles) and was printed surreptitiously in his father Arthur's printing house. "A true Zionist," Scholem announced in his paper, "must abandon Europe and its political and cultural concerns because Jewish national interests do not coincide with those of Germany. [. . .] We want to draw the line between Europe and Judah: my thought is not your thought, my way is not yours. We do not have great numbers of people for you to throw freely into the furnace like Moloch. No, we need men who have the courage to think Jewish thoughts as their ultimate thoughts."

All of this activity soon landed him in trouble. Once the school authorities realized what he was up to, they expelled him. Arthur Scholem's outrage took the form of a registered letter. It was delivered during the family breakfast, and demanded that his son leave the house.

Gerhard's diary describes the feverish nightmare he had soon afterward. In the dream, his father slowly "strangled him" while the rest of the family sang carols around the Christmas tree. "Wipe out these lice swarms! Rip off their heads," he scribbled down after he awoke.[19]

The expulsion from home only stiffened Scholem's plans to make his way to Zion. For half a year, from the spring of 1917 to the fall of the following year, he lived in a hostel named Pension Struck which was filled with eastern European Jews, many of them Hebrew speakers. There he met an unknown Hebrew prose master named Czaczkes, better known by his *nom de plume,* Agnon. When they met, the young Scholem felt as if he had seen a messenger from a distant and enchanted world. He called him one of the "most perfect incarnations [. . .] of all the mysteries of Jewish existence."[20]

New acquaintances, in turn, strengthened his belief in the power of Hebrew. He now believed that the Jewish youth movement could succeed in its deeper tasks only through the intense study of Hebrew texts. Another Russian Jew by the name of Zalman Rubaschoff (who later Hebraized his name to Shazar and became the third president of the State of Israel) introduced him to a hidden and radical Judaism in the form of Sabbatai Sevi and Jacob Frank, heretical figures from the seventeenth century and the eighteenth century, respectively.

At the time, Scholem also began to construct his own Jewish philosophy of history, which was just as subversive to German-Jewish liberalism as his emigration plans. He drew his inspiration from Walter Benjamin, whom he first met during the summer of 1915 at a discussion group on "the meaning of history." In the course of the evening, both Scholem and Benjamin rose to challenge the main speaker's assertion that history has no meaning. What most impressed Scholem was Benjamin's use of what he assumed were "Jewish ideas," for Benjamin contrasted the liberal fiction of eternal "progress" with the "Messianic kingdom." Two weeks later, after Scholem received a formal invitation for a visit, they had their first meeting, which initiated a series of discussions on history and philosophy. Benjamin, who was five years Scholem's senior, went on to become the single most decisive influence on his life and thought. It was he who first hammered away at the cult of *Erlebnis* Scholem had picked up from Buber. And as Scholem confessed in a letter to his future wife, Escha Burchhardt, he considered Benjamin to be the "only one who truly loves me."[21]

During 1916 the two friends met often. In October Benjamin left for Munich, after being granted a military exemption due to bad eyesight. He stayed in Bavaria for eighteen months, until the army reexamined him and pronounced him "fit for light field duty." The final call-up arrived in January 1917. What kept him from service, however, was a series of severe attacks of sciatica, which he most likely brought on himself. By the spring he was pronounced, once and for all, unfit for duty. On a doctor's suggestion, he left for a spa in Switzerland with his new wife, Dora Kellner.

Meanwhile, Scholem was having his own difficulties with the military. In June 1917, while still living in the Pension Stuck, he received draft orders to join the infantry. He followed Benjamin's strategy of doing his utmost to get an exemption. By July he was already under psychological observation. During meetings with doctors he would let out long screams while, like a caged animal, refusing to look anyone in the eye. He was soon diagnosed with dementia praecox and allowed to return to Berlin. In January 1918 doctors classified him as "permanently unfit for active duty; not to be reexamined."[22] They informed his father that his "psychopathia" was in part a result of domestic conflict, an opinion that led Arthur—perhaps also softened by his own weak heart—to offer his son what Gerhard described to his friend Harry Heymann as "peace without annexation."[23]

For the duration of the war, Scholem was freed from service to the Fatherland and could devote himself to Hebrew, Zion, and Walter Benjamin. He began this period at the University of Jena, where he studied philosophy and mathematics for six months. From there he went to the University of Bern, in Switzerland, to study mathematics, theoretical physics, philosophy, Arabic, and the Hebrew Bible. His parents agreed to the move after he convinced them that the cures available in Bern would improve his health.

The truth is that he left for Bern to be close to Benjamin. In the spring of 1918 Scholem settled in a village called Muri, just outside Bern, where he would stay for well over a year. From the beginning of May to the end of July, he lived in what he described as a "preestablished harmony" with his new friend.[24] They met every day for discussions, which "often turned to Jewish theology and the foundations of Jewish ethics."[25] They had such long philosophical talks that Benjamin jokingly suggested they found their "own academy," the University of Muri. Benjamin would serve as *rector magnificus;* Scholem, as either a lecturer or the "janitor of the religious-philosophical seminar."[26]

While Scholem was in the bucolic refuge of Muri, dramatic events were occurring elsewhere. Close friends died at the front, and the Russian Revolution broke out, fanning his hopes that the war would soon end. Once it finally did, however, dire economic conditions combined with a brewing civil war meant possible ruin for his family. When Scholem returned to Germany in August 1919, he found himself in an unfamiliar country. The kaiser had abdicated and a new government was in power. Worst of all, a terrible uncertainty had descended upon Germany.

In 1916 Scholem (using the name he would later adopt, Gershom) had lamented in his journal that "the theory of language in the Kabbalah has not yet found a worthy worker. [. . .] Oh, Gershom Scholem, how much you have yet to accomplish!"[27] Scholem's letters to friends and family (above all to Edgar Blum, Erich Brauer, Werner Kraft, and his mother) offer a fairly good portrayal of his efforts to avoid military service, his feigned madness, the move to Muri, his decision to study the Kabbalah, and his resolve to emigrate to Palestine. Far less clear, however, is what he meant by "the theory of language in the Kabbalah," and even blurrier are the shape and content of the intellectual strategy that would prove strong enough to support, with minor adjustments, his work for the next fifty years.

When one of his very few female friends, Gerda Goldberg, wrote to him in the military psychological ward in August 1917 and requested a précis of his philosophy, he replied by complaining of his own meager "possibilities and abilities of expression." "My thinking has led me to adopt, as the most appropriate medium of communication, a language that is difficult to master," he told her. "The only people who can understand it are those who themselves think like me. To everyone else I remain a sealed book because they cannot make sense of my language."[28]

By "people who can understand," he meant primarily Walter Benjamin. Almost no letters to Benjamin survive from those days, though we can gather from other letters and diary entries how seminal his long conversations with Benjamin were. One letter to Escha Burchhardt describes how he "sat" in Muri and "forged" his "weapons."[29] While in Switzerland he decided to "go along with Benjamin" and to devote himself to the "theory of language in the Kabbalah."[30]

Benjamin was already a mature scholar when they first met. He was a writer, a bibliophile, and a man with wide-ranging literary tastes (including a love of detective novels that would prove contagious). And Benjamin loathed Buber and his notion of *Erlebnis* because it implied that the person with "experience" could stand in stunned authenticity before himself, reveling in his naked originality. For Benjamin, experience was primarily historical; that is, he believed that a person "experiences" something only as a member of a linguistic, cultural tradition and not by dint of pure desire. Far from arising in the contemplation of the self, experience is grounded in a tradition that bears upon one's contemporary circumstances. Benjamin was intrigued by the interplay between tradition and the contemporary moment.

Doing philosophy or history meant, for him, registering the shifts of past truths as they are exposed to the living present. Moreover, every creative act renews tradition by making it speak to the present. Benjamin was thus preoccupied with words, texts, ever-changing human culture, and the ability of the historian to bend these to conform with his contemporary cultural and political needs. He also believed that "listening" to largely forgotten and despised sources (what he called in 1914 the "most endangered, slandered, and mocked creatures and thoughts, buried deep within each present moment")[31] could release unexpected revolutionary powers. Language, the repository of tradition, contained for him all of humanity's hopes; it becomes a "key to realms of hidden knowledge," both in the past and in the future. "All higher language," he held, "is a translation of lower ones, until in ultimate clarity the word of God unfolds, which is the unity of this movement made up of language."[32]

Scholem absorbed Benjamin's thoughts on tradition and language with unbounded enthusiasm. His major intellectual epiphany occurred in October 1916, when Benjamin wrote him a long letter which would eventually form the basis for an essay entitled "Über Sprache überhaupt und über die Sprache des Menschen" (On Language as Such and on the Language of Man). The abstruse deliberations it contained left a deep impression on Scholem. After he finished reading the letter, he recorded a vision in his diary. "First I stand somewhere on the flat earth, while Benjamin is in heaven. And then what he has expressed approaches me. Suddenly [. . .] I find myself in the center, where things are no longer difficult for me and I can wholly identify with his views and further develop them."[33] He described how "the divine court" held a special session about him in heaven. "Afterward they sent an angel to ask my wishes. Because of my proper metaphysical metamorphosis, the angel appeared in the form of Benjamin. [. . .] I wished for *order* [*Ordnung*]. In a second session, in October, it was decided to grant me my desire gradually and to give me, during the winter, some words of true godly science: to reveal the Torah, or the Teaching [*Lehre*], from which I can expand and build."[34]

To judge from Scholem's diaries and letters, he quickly absorbed the lessons of Benjamin's essay and began to reinterpret his Jewish "ideas" according to Benjamin's method. He transcribed and typed them up, and gave copies to friends. Particular terms that appeared in this piece now became permanent features of his new vocabulary. He wrote to Werner Kraft that, when he tried to translate it into Hebrew, he felt overwhelmed by a series of "miracles."[35] He now mocked Buber's notion of *Erlebnis* and denied that it could reveal the secrets of being.[36] From then on, he tailored Judaism to fit into a larger philosophy of language and history. Judaism became synonymous with what he later called "the unbroken spirit of language."[37]

Soon after receiving Benjamin's letter on language, Scholem speculated in his diary that the "philosophy of language" was the "disguised heart of Judaism,"[38] at work whenever the Torah was studied. Of the Kabbalists, he said that they regarded the "genuine search for truth as essentially the study of language, for one searches the roots of letters, the 'divine alphabet,' for the spiritual powers that lie within them." "The messiah," he added, "will be the last, and first, philosopher of language: he will deduce Judaism from its language."[39]

Such speculation placed Benjamin in the illustrious company of mystics, and the same applied to Scholem himself. He spoke of a "lifetime" project of "rebuilding Zionism anew."[40] His dream of being a leader and a prophet equipped with radical solutions was now directed to the quiet work of scholarship and to a historical–philological analysis of traditional Hebrew sources. The Torah no longer consisted of the books of Moses, but encompassed everyone and everything that had a part in the "unbroken spirit of language." The individual was bound to the nation by textual tradition and commentary. By uncovering old and hidden connections among books, words, and styles, the commentator could illuminate the nature and sense of the nation.

For the next fifty years Scholem steadfastly continued to regard the philological analysis of the textual sources of Jewish tradition as the key to Jewish renewal; such analysis became, in his eyes, the only true secret science. Once Jews returned to their textual tradition, they could, he believed, use it as a compass to guide them through the modern world. One might say that he invented an "existentialist philology" in which a close examination of texts reveals the dialectical nature of tradition and ultimately the self-expression of those engaged in it. The philologist comes to resemble a detective in a novel. A detective looks for fingerprints, a displaced glass, a slightly skewed picture frame, or a tampered lock as signs of a clever thief; the philologist analyzes a seemingly traditional religious text packed with timeless truths and seeks out the dusty traces, clues, variations, and ruins in order to find signs of creative interpreters living in history.

Scholem chose to study the Kabbalah because it best illustrated for him the utopian powers of interpreters. Long dismissed by liberal Jews as an unfortunate aberration in the otherwise rational history of Judaism, Scholem found in it a radical history with fresh new readings of tradition, by men of piety who responded to times of crisis and disaster with new and revolutionary interpretations. Scholem's Kabbalists did not flee history on a magic carpet of words, but fully engaged in the events of their time by bending and twisting tradition to address persecution, war, and chaos and to articulate an undying faith in Zion.

Scholem's initial insights into the power of scholarship crystallized during a time of war and chaos—a conjunction that was not insignificant. Philosophy, he realized, was not a purely intellectual science cut off from history. In Scholem's view, philology does more than merely uncover the hidden dialectic of history. The good philologist produces

.✳.

1914

TO WERNER SCHOLEM

Berlin, September 7, 1914

Most honored brother,

It may surprise you to get a letter from me, of all people. How awful—a letter from the mama's boy! A fanatical Jew! But everything has its reasons. Over the past three months I've often thought about writing you, and you'll discover the reasons below. The time has come to open up. Yesterday I read your letters from August, and "behold, they found pleasure in my sight." To be sure, I think rather highly of you anyway, though my respect has now increased a notch or two.

After the patriotic position the Party has taken vis-à-vis the war (I will avoid making any judgments and leave it at that) and after hearing from you face to face, I never would have thought that you could be so rational as to refuse to volunteer and that, in general, you would respond to this mass murder (otherwise dubbed a "cultural war") with such reservation. [. . .][1]

The aim of this letter, however, is to express to you not my respect but something quite different. That is to say, I'd like some information from you that you'll no doubt be able to provide. Here, I've been unable to find it.

Despite the fact that I can go along with the Erfurt Program, I still don't call myself a Social Democrat—for the simple reason that you are "organized."[2] I don't care much for any kind of organization. An organization is like a murky sea that collects the lovely flowing streams of thoughts, which are never allowed to escape again. "Organization" is a synonym for death—and not only among the Social Democrats! This is true for all such "isms," even if it takes a particularly frightful form among socialists. The Social Democrats desire such beautiful things

a new reading based upon new experiences.[41] And it is
philologist becomes a "ventriloquist," or at least a good no
lem considered the *Zohar*[42] to be the Jewish *Nibelungenlied,*
the perfect material from which to forge his own philosophy
and Jewish renewal.

.⁜.

1914

Berlin, September 7, 1914

Most honored brother,

It may surprise you to get a letter from me, of all people. How awful—a letter from the mama's boy! A fanatical Jew! But everything has its reasons. Over the past three months I've often thought about writing you, and you'll discover the reasons below. The time has come to open up. Yesterday I read your letters from August, and "behold, they found pleasure in my sight." To be sure, I think rather highly of you anyway, though my respect has now increased a notch or two.

After the patriotic position the Party has taken vis-à-vis the war (I will avoid making any judgments and leave it at that) and after hearing from you face to face, I never would have thought that you could be so rational as to refuse to volunteer and that, in general, you would respond to this mass murder (otherwise dubbed a "cultural war") with such reservation. [. . .]¹

The aim of this letter, however, is to express to you not my respect but something quite different. That is to say, I'd like some information from you that you'll no doubt be able to provide. Here, I've been unable to find it.

Despite the fact that I can go along with the Erfurt Program, I still don't call myself a Social Democrat—for the simple reason that you are "organized."² I don't care much for any kind of organization. An organization is like a murky sea that collects the lovely flowing streams of thoughts, which are never allowed to escape again. "Organization" is a synonym for death—and not only among the Social Democrats! This is true for all such "isms," even if it takes a particularly frightful form among socialists. The Social Democrats desire such beautiful things a new reading based upon new experiences.[41] And it is here that the philologist becomes a "ventriloquist," or at least a good novelist. Scholem considered the *Zohar*[42] to be the Jewish *Nibelungenlied,* and as such the perfect material from which to forge his own philosophy of Judaism and Jewish renewal.

and their aim is to liberate men, yet they go about it by squeezing people into organizations! What irony! After thirty years of party politics, of legislative squabbling and strife, the socialist idea now survives only among outsiders, heretics, "imperfect socialists." Why? Sometime you'll have to ask Marx, the Organization, and the "misery of philosophy"! Yet they all want such beautiful things! Look at me or Proudhon if you want a historical illustration of this.[3] You follow me, I trust. [. . .]

In brief, I need you to clarify the following points as precisely as you can: (1) your relation to anarchism and (2) the reason for your rejection of anarchistic ideas. [. . .] This leads me to my second question, one I assume you have often enough posed yourself—namely, your position on "good" and "evil." I would very much like to know whether you consider morality as something real—that is, inherent in us—or something invented. It is vital to know this, to ascertain both your position on anarchism and the deeper foundations of socialist ideas. [. . .]

Perhaps you have already heard of the mystical sect among us Jews, the Hasidim of Galicia, who preach (or preached!) socialism *sans phrase*. They stood for unity and myth, and myth is life. Since no one believes in the soul any longer, socialism naturally does not have one. But I am eager to know whether it has a myth, just as the Jews have the legends of the Nazarene, the Baal Shem, and Jehovah, or the Buddhists have their perfect Arhat.[4] And since I cannot find answers to these questions in books, I have turned to you. Much depends on your answer; I anxiously await it. I believe in socialism and in the direction it's taking. I believe in the will to happiness, though I don't believe that you or we can bring it about. Martin Buber in his *Three Speeches* used a parable to speak about happiness: Before the gates of Rome sits an old beggar and waits. He is the Messiah. . . . And for whom is he waiting? "He is waiting for you."

Greetings from Gerhard S.

FROM WERNER SCHOLEM

Hannover, September 8, 1914

Dear Gerhard,

Your letter did not surprise me nearly as much as you may think, since I've been expecting it for some time. Every thinking Jew somewhere along the line becomes a socialist—which you now are, since you stand on the foundation of the Erfurt Program. [. . .]

As for me, my position vis-à-vis this [war] madness has been the same from the first day, because I know quite well that the insane politics adopted by Austria in the Balkans makes it just as guilty for the war as czarism—with Germany, as always, limping loyally behind, according to its idiotic *Nibelungen* code of honor. France is completely innocent, not to mention Belgium. In the end, however, they're all scoundrels. The reason I did not obediently answer father's letter demanding I volunteer for the army, but instead evaded it, lies in the fact that I'm terribly tired and ill at the moment and have no desire to be thrown out of the house. You can see from this that I, too, am gradually equipping myself with a commonsensical *Weltanschauung*. Perhaps I will yet become a junior partner in "Arthur Scholem: Printer of Stationery and Lithographs." [. . .]

Having made these remarks, I'll now try to follow your lead into the more rarefied heights of the mind. Before I start, I wish to point out that I may not always be completely successful, for intellectually I've gone to seed. Aside from a logarithmic table, I haven't touched a single scholarly book since May. There are various reasons for this. You can call it stupidity—I don't care.

1. The question of organization. I hate organizations. You've no idea how right you are with your simile of the murky sea. But what can we do about it? [. . .]

2. The relations to anarchism. There's no greater contrast than the one between socialism and anarchism. While Social Democracy places the state over the individual, anarchists stress the sovereignty (Oh my, a foreign term!) of the individual. [. . .]

3. Reason for my rejection of anarchism. Marxian socialism teaches historical materialism, which is, as well, the spirit that infuses the Erfurt Program. To put it crudely, it holds that things make man, not the other way around. Which means that economic motivations—above all, class conflicts—rather than ideals, are the driving forces in history. [. . .]

4. Socialism and morality. Of course, the large majority of party members don't give a damn about these issues, and even our literati have little to say about them. That said, our position has been formulated in a book you must read right away: Kautsky's *Ethics and the Materialistic View of History*.[5] It articulates my own position. According to Kautsky,

those of us who follow historical materialism naturally do not believe in an innate morality. As such, the ethical stance of Marxism rejects out of hand all fixed notions of good and evil. It is irreconcilably opposed to Kant's moral law, and it views all reigning moral laws as merely an ever-changing mirror of the times. The only moral law it recognizes is a "social drive," which is already at work in animals and which finds its highest expression in socialism. [. . .]

5. Myth? Your last question is confused and struck me as entirely opaque. Maybe I'm too simpleminded to grasp it. What is a myth? Only peoples or, ultimately, religions can have fables and gods. They cannot have worldviews. When all is said and done, socialism has adopted Life itself as the true embodiment of its ideas. So if this is what you mean when you speak of myth, then it's Life you're speaking about—as is the case with Hasidism. Of course, our books have nothing to say about such mystical things. Economic conditions demand socialism, and so it will come; and its by-products will consist of the ennoblement and liberation of man. Whether it will bring perfect happiness to every individual, I can't say. One can well doubt it. In any case, it will offer a higher level of culture than capitalism and its world wars. This is the only thing we know for certain. Just in passing, what do you mean by "truth"?

Martin Buber is a coffeehouse anarchist, and I can't stand the sort of mystical parables you gave me. What is all this supposed to mean, anyway? Happiness is inner peace for one person, stormy longings for the next. In general, it's different for everyone. Most people see a full belly as their greatest happiness. Rubbish! I won't break my head over it, and I suggest you don't either. [. . .]

W.

TO WERNER SCHOLEM

Berlin, September 23, 1914

Dear Werner,

I have finally roused myself enough from my indolence to reply to your letter. It's a nasty business having to make one's way through the Berlin schools these days. Orders from above require that all students over the age of sixteen be "pre-drilled" for the military. In the coming days I, too, will have to prepare myself for all sorts of physical exertion.

It's bleak. Father can't stop sneering at me because I've shown myself to be such a "coward," lacking even the slightest noble stirrings of the heart. I have arrived at the famous end of the road with him—something you should be familiar with. I'm anxious to see how things develop at Neue Grünstrasse 26.[6] Notwithstanding all of the screams and arguments, however, these quarters are vastly preferable to yours.[7] [. . .]

As I launch my remarks, the only expression that comes to mind is, "My ways are not your ways, your thoughts are not my thoughts." I haven't a clue how I can begin to give you a reasonably clear picture of what I think; where I come from; why, "despite and not because of" my total rejection of philosophical materialism (perhaps later I'll say something about historical materialism), I have taken up with socialists rather than the Social Democrats; and why I claimed to support the Erfurt Program. [. . .]

Dear Werner, I do not believe in the philosophy of history—whether it be Hegel's (that is, Marx's), Ranke's, or Treitschke's, or (for all I care) even the negative form of it preached by Nietzsche.[8] In other words, I believe that if history produces laws at all, either history or the laws are worthless. At the very most, I think that only anarchism can be of some use if you really want to prove something through history. [. . .]

For good reason, I don't think anything in this world of ours can be proven, with the exception of non-Euclidean geometry and differential equations. *Nothing* is provable. Indeed, it would be awful if we could "prove" everything. Ugh! [. . .] Least of all can our feelings be explained, not to mention be fully proven (that is, it can never be conclusively demonstrated that we had to feel a certain way and not otherwise). Despite all of Herr Wundt's best efforts, this simply cannot be done.[9] What we feel is our innermost, most personal possession, it is our *experience* [*Erlebnis*]. But experience, which *from start to finish* is not what happens around us but that which occurs within us, does not belong in the sphere of causal laws—that is, it cannot be proven. And here comes the great conceptual leap! There are experiences not only of individuals but also of the masses, just as there is a social or national psychology alongside an individual psychology. [. . .]

For the time being, I'd like to postpone any discussion of anarchism—otherwise this letter will be too long. Now onto *the main question,* that of myth! Well, my dear Werner, perhaps I'll discuss the issue the next time I write, if I can ever bring myself to put my thoughts down on paper—thoughts you've never heard of because I have gone off in a direction you can't even imagine. The doctrine of myth has become the main pillar in the intellectual structure I'm busy conceptualizing. It was only naturally that the word "myth" baffled you so. But we'll have to go into this some other time!

Any more questions? What do you think of Zionism, after all of your rude disappointments? Is it still so deplorable? Next to socialism, of course, Zionism is a good example of the teaching of myth. [. . .]

Regards, Gerhard Scholem

1916[10]

TO ERICH BRAUER[11]

Oberstdorf, Switzerland, June 21, 1916[12]

Dear Brauer,

[. . .] At the moment I'm doing nothing but building myself up again. It's as if God, myself, and Zion were alone in the world, and as a result I'm not forced to engrave my ideas in stone any sooner than necessary. Here I build my Zionism into a structure strong enough so that I can erect my entire life upon it without any fear that it could collapse. Already I'm certain that when I return I will be able to speak with you more forthrightly than before, because now everything will prop up this building of mine. I'm also trying to do now what I had earlier attempted in Berlin—namely, to direct myself where I must go with the most absolute extreme power of desire. One of my starting points is the notion of permanently staying in the fast lane—in short, remaining in movement. We want our inborn spectacles—the blue-white spectacles—to guide us in being doctrinaire amid danger, equipped with the final one-sidedness that does not allow for any "both this and that." (In particular, not "both German and Jewish"! I think you understand what I mean.) [. . .]

Best regards, Gerhard Scholem

TO MARTIN BUBER[13]

Oberstdorf im Allgäu, June 25, 1916

Dear Herr Doctor,

Since I am not quite certain whether you will be hearing from Herr Benjamin soon, I want to inform you, as promised, of the result of our conversations about *Der Jude.*[14] At the worst, you will have two versions of the issue.

I need not repeat to you the course of the conversations, along with all the loud cannon shots that were fired. Suffice it to say that, for the time being, Benjamin has arrived at a point from which a literary statement (which is all that could be expected from him, since he could not contribute to any substantive discussion) is not possible for him, and, what is more, not even permissible. The very idea of a "journal" in itself seems to him objectionable; but especially the promotion of living Judaism through such a journal proves, from his point of view, unthinkable and incomprehensible. It seems that he is inwardly wrestling with Judaism and that this struggle must be waged and decided in private. [. . .]

TO MARTIN BUBER[15]

Oberstdorf im Allgäu, July 10, 1916

Dear Herr Doctor,

[. . .] To describe to you the part that Heinrich Margulies has played in my life, I must briefly tell you the story of my expulsion from school, a Berlin *Gymnasium.* It is extremely complicated and distinctly odd, and I shall have to leave out a great deal.

In January last year, I was on the verge of promotion to the graduating class. The terrible psychological collapse of that generation of young people, a collapse that first began showing its true effects in December 1914 and thereafter, had driven my friends and me to ever more intense introspection and outrage against the general confusion. The great question for us, of course was our position on the war, a question that was continually kept alive by the famous wave of volunteering among many groups. The Jews in the upper classes of my school were all Zionists; we stuck closely together and made no bones about our views. Then on February 5 there appeared that article which climaxed in the staggering sentence: we were marching off to war not despite the fact that we were Jews but because we were Zionists!!! At the time, it threw me into an insensate rage in the most literal sense, for I lashed out against the others without restraint. We—about twenty of us—sent a furious statement of protest to the *Jüdische Rundschau* in which, with one voice, we clarified *our* position in a few extremely unequivocal sentences. [. . .] In my incredible stupidity I took this statement along with me to school, where some of my schoolmates wanted to sign it. In some mysterious fashion, either by chance or espionage (for, unknown to me, I was being spied on at the time), a few superpatriotic fellow students learned what was going on and what was in the letter. A bitter trial lasting four weeks—the documents are on file at the Berlin district school board—was conducted against me as the ringleader and three friends as "misled" followers. In the course of it, some magnificent circumstantial evidence of my "anti-national" ideology was produced, and conviction was much facilitated by my open advocacy of Judaism and my propaganda directed against the youth regiment that had expelled all its Jews. But, as I said, this phase is extremely difficult and complicated. The upshot was that they got rid of me. In order to avoid an unpleasant fuss, they promoted me to the graduating class and gave me an excellent final report card, but with "Conduct: Unsatisfactory." [. . .]

All this has in no way influenced my views. Of course, we merely fought all the more bitterly against the confusion thereafter. For the rest, I have every reason to be grateful to the school for throwing me out, for this year, which would have been a very dreary one, has become precious and blissful for me like no other before it. [. . .]

FROM ERICH BRAUER

Berlin, July 15, 1916

[. . .] I met your brother with the wounded foot.[16] I didn't recognize him very clearly. Among other things, he'd had to have his hair shaved off. Between you and me, he did not give me the impression of being a particularly logical man or one with firm convictions. I may be wrong, but I had the feeling that his socialism was somewhat snobbish. It seemed clear that for us Zionism is something very different from what socialism is for him. Beyond this, I do not *believe* that he can be as *Jewish* as we are—even if he presents himself as such. Judging by the state of his Judaism, I consider his present condition to be thoroughly cockeyed. Do you agree?

TO ERICH BRAUER

Oberstdorf im Allgäu, July 17, 1916

Yadidi[17] (*When,* oh when, will you understand this?!)

Dearest friend,

I can answer you promptly because the weather, to my great ire, has again taken a senseless turn for the worse. The fact that I doubtless have a larger burden of correspondence than either you or Heller[18] (my list has fifteen to twenty people on it) does not hinder me from answering you courteously and without delay. By the way, I find it extremely puzzling that I haven't heard a word from Harry Heymann, even though I've written to him. What's he up to? Have you heard anything from Pick?[19] With the exception of my friend Blum, all of those in the field pursue me with a stubborn silence. And we have to sign them up for *Blue-White Spectacles!* You seem to be the international traffic bureau for radical Jewish youth, so think of me and keep me informed about our soldiers in the field! [. . .]

I hear that you Berliners now get only 200 grams of meat per week to "eat" (though you can hardly call it that)—news which takes away all of my desire to return. I would prefer to move on to Heidelberg in the winter, where more alluring voices beckon. By now you must have completely wasted away with hunger. Send me a self-portrait! [. . .]

Present circumstances convince me more than ever of the need for an immediate issue of *Blue-White Spectacles,* edited by all of those who have something to say—such as you, my brother, Heller, and myself. This should be enough for three volumes! [. . .] *BWS* has not changed in the least; it's only become more focused. I know precisely what I want, and I believe I now have a great deal to say. Take the following, for instance, which I produced in spirit (and partly on paper).

Manifesto of youth: Ideology II

What is radicalism? To mention only the most important related themes: the attempt to draw boundaries; revolution; the necessary spiritual condition of youth; Buber and us; and notes on the Jewish movement. Besides the above, there are numerous annotations: "On the dogmatism of youth," "Marxism and Revisionism among youth," "Hebrew," and the like. I have thought a great deal and have much to say! So let's do a little work now! It will of course be easy to come to some agreement with my brother, if you refrain from exercising a pro-war censor. We must open up our big mouths once again! Don't fall asleep! For the past fourteen days I've been in a truly ecstatic state for our cause!

I consider your opinion of my brother unjustified, and on crucial points. For even if everything were as you say, you should not forget *one thing:* that he is *on the right path.* He left us four years ago, and now he's returning again. He wrote me that, once the war ends, in order to play an active role he will have to take a *close* look at the Jewish movement. His Judaism is "remediable" because he is not smugly content with himself, which is something I can't say for many "Zionists." The more you work on him—and in the course of time I intend to win him *fully* over to our side—the more he will consciously turn to the *one* way. I know, for instance, that he has gone through a religious change; I know that he wants to raise his children *Jewish;* and I'm convinced that he will soon arrive at the Hebrew language. *My brother and I basically see eye to eye on things.* We both have a truly honest ideal of a "movement" and of "radicalism." You are *without question* mistaken about his socialism. I know this for certain; and precisely *because* I know this, I also know it will lead him to Zion. [. . .]

Gerhard Scholem

FROM EDGAR BLUM[20]

From the Front, September 28, 1916

Dear Scholem,

Only now can I answer your letter from September 5 (I can't write much, just as I cannot read the few books I have with me). We lead a dismal existence here, going from one reserve to the next, and from there into the trenches, and then back again to the reserves. Rarely do we spend more than three days at the same spot. We find ourselves on a somewhat precarious position southwest of Lusk, where the Russians have time and time again launched new and good forces in order to break through. This month they've attacked three times, and in each case their special attack strategy has succeeded in totally breaking through our lines. But for no good reason, they've allowed themselves to be driven back each time—it's unbelievable. [. . .]

FROM SIEGFRIED LEHMANN[21]

Berlin, Undated

Dear Herr Scholem,

Recently I've met a number of people to whom you have, without any reason, made disparaging remarks about the Volksheim. [. . .] I would like to point out to you that poking your head into the rooms of the Volksheim on your monthly visits gives you no right whatsoever to criticize its work. By chance you once stumbled into a lecture I was giving and, as you have admitted, had the opportunity to hear only the *concluding part* of it!!! And then you have the nerve to talk so high and mighty!! [. . .] Until now I have considered you somewhat immodest. [. . .] Now I am forced to add "seriously superficial" to this diagnosis.

TO SIEGFRIED LEHMANN

Berlin, October 4, 1916

Dear Herr Lehmann,

I came to the Volksheim on Saturday evening to speak with you, but no one was around. Your letter arrived today, and its tone seems to preclude any personal discussion between us. I had entertained only slight hopes for a personal rapprochement from such a discussion, though I did have great hopes for clarification. I will now at least express a number of things in writing for the sake of the matter itself.

It seems to me that you do not appreciate, or refuse to see, the deep and substantial opposition dividing us, an opposition that lies behind the stance I have taken. I have never had any personal prejudices against anyone who works at the Volksheim. The fact that I developed a prejudice against you after listening to you speak for half an hour has its foundation in my manner of seeing things. There must be some reason I have sensed in you what I have never found among the great majority of German Zionists, with their confused and reprehensible ways: in particular, the impression of a lack of morality—a morality round as a bullet, self-anchored and unassailable from the outside. A full treatment of your letter, which word for word unfortunately only confirmed my opinion, demands more than these much-needed personal remarks (I say "unfortunately" because I would prefer to change my opinion and see you as someone truly ordained by Zion).

From the beginning, both before and during my absence from Berlin, I had the *most positive* views possible of the Volksheim. In *Der Jude* I even expressed the exaggerated hope that a youth movement could arise out of it—if people directed themselves from the perspective of Zion. On the first day after my return, a discussion I had with an enthusiastic follower and assistant of the Volksheim caused me to have serious and substantial misgivings. In addition, I realized that the literary documents of the founder did not fall into line with my own views. Then I arrived at your lecture and heard your comments on Marxism and the renewal of Jewish religiosity. Without exaggeration, those thirty to forty-five minutes constituted the most appalling and terrible experience I've had in the field of Zionism. Here in writing it seems to me rather pointless to try to prove this to you, particularly since you are so absorbed in this experience [*Erlebnis*]. It seems grotesque to even say so, but those present in the room fell into an *aesthetic ecstasy*. With the most unbelievable arrogance, your letter referred to those thirty minutes as an argument *against* me, though in truth they are the strongest proof against you and *for* me. Some ten days later, you sought to defend yourself vigorously against me with the accusation of irreligiosity, something I had already anticipated. I fear, however (and the opposite would please me greatly), that you still fail to see what a deep-seated and entirely revolting immorality it is—and I ask you once again to take this harsh accusation absolutely literally—to attempt an interpretation of Jewish religiosity (which is precisely what you did) before a society of fifty people, some of whom really know something, but most of whom lack elementary knowledge of Hebrew and haven't the foggiest notion of either the Jewish conception of "Torah" or of the totality of mysticism. And you did not improve matters by declaring at the start of your lecture that you do not understand anything about the *subject*. Nor does it help when you use the term "irreligious" to describe someone who honestly goes to great lengths to understand these things and who knows that to do so demands an unusual amount of Jewish *knowledge*. Buber certainly has this—and he is one who could instruct you with greater authority than I on the immorality of aesthetic profundity and the ignorance that leads to pretentious bragging about religiosity. You, however, do not. [. . .]

As if additional proof were necessary, what followed proved that the conclusions I drew from this experience were terrifyingly correct—conclusions about you and those who see these things as the deepest foundation of the Volksheim. All of the Volksheim people I spoke to were extraordinarily delighted with your lecture, etc., etc., which only made it abundantly clear that you and your ilk have great powers of confusion. I predicted to Fräulein Halle,[22] whom you must know, precisely what would occur on that Saturday evening when the discussion took place. Sure enough, everything played itself out just as I had told her. On that evening you did everything in your power to avoid the demands I had made of you (and I did so because I have made the same ones upon myself). You proved that you do not do my work; you do the work of laziness that is under the illusion of greatness. Everything would have been completely fine had I said at the time, "Okay, we want to read a Hasidic book; I will translate it for you and we will then 'interpret' it." But on that evening I encountered such childish naïveté and insolence among your aspiring pupils that I knew quite well I could not work with those people, who believe they can learn the Torah in six weeks of *prattle* (a word whose most pregnant sense stems from Kierkegaard)[23] and who consider it the essence of the Volksheim.

The "essay," which I have not heard of, doesn't change a thing. For I am simply incapable of constantly making an un-Jewish and spiritually repugnant separation between things that strike me as forming a unity— namely, between a theory that could be abominable and a practice that could be good. (And this is the way a number of people have tried to defend you, or rather the Volksheim. They abandon you while characterizing the teamwork as good.) Someone can have "false" opinions, yet do "good" work; but no one can be in a state of confusion, yet perform clearly defined acts. No act can be internally "good" while the one who performs the act is "bad." Taking Zion and Berlin as spiritual principles, one can and indeed must work from the perspective of Zion, just as one can perhaps work from the perspective of Berlin; *but one cannot and must not work from the perspective of Berlin as if one were doing so from Zion.* If you were a Zionist, we would have to come to some agreement, for there is no Zionist alive with whom I cannot reconcile myself; and if you were a Berliner, I could freely debate with you; but being what you are, and given the way you use the language of Zionism, I can only view you as twisted to the core. It used to be that in Zionist youth clubs, when someone wanted to kill some time, he (harmlessly!) danced; now he works in the Volksheim—and this is *absolutely despicable*. The young Zionist today turns God, Zion, and the Torah into a game and guards himself against the possibility that someone will come and seek out the holy. He carries Zion around in his addled mind and in profuse speech, but when someone comes and makes demands, he takes leave of it in his heart. [. . .]

The "superficiality" you diagnosed in me can now indeed be revealed as a complete farce. "Stop, thief!" calls out the man who stole the goose.

Herr Lehmann, your hue and cry is, "Hah! This irreligious one, this superficial one, this immodest one!" At least I've been humble enough to join in on a conversation only when it was necessary and permitted! Do I have to be the first to demand of you an honest self-reckoning? [. . .]

TO SIEGFRIED LEHMANN

Berlin, October 9, 1916

Dear Herr Lehmann,

In glancing through your letter I was astounded time and again by the spirit you gave it. Once again, I'm dumbfounded to discover insulting expressions in much of what you wrote—especially after you forced me to repeat my accusations (as I did, and in a purely descriptive manner, avoiding all possible bombast). This you can by no means justify. [. . .]

I fully understand how you could have arrived at the view that I consider the Talmud, or Jewish scholasticism—however concocted— as the primary source of religious investigation. But you are completely mistaken in this view of yours. [. . .] No, the true difference between us lies elsewhere. It lies in the fact that I have, in fact, come to comprehend the totality of Judaism in its *total* sense and I know that, internally, the *totality* of Judaism contains certain essential *ingredients*. [. . .] And this includes the creation of most *post-biblical Judaism (basically the pharisaic literature, massively deepened and its truth expanded through the Kabbalah), without which the soul of Judaism, its creator, can never be grasped and enriched* and without which the Jewish notion of God (it's foolish to speak this way) is unthinkable. This creation, Herr Lehmann, is in truth the decisive development of the notion of God that you believe cannot be found in the Talmud. In response to your demand, I will point out only a few aspects here: *the concept and reality of the Torah; the Jewish understanding of "Teaching"; the unimaginably deep and true Jewish notion of "Tradition" that we are bound to realize in actuality.* It's no accident that the great Christian Kabbalist Fritz Molitor entitled his extraordinary book on the Kabbalah *Philosophy of History; Or, On Tradition!!!* Herr Lehmann, a book on Jewish mysticism from a mystic with the title *On Tradition!!!* Indeed, he who has the Word has Judaism; but you cannot understand this word if you do not know the text; and you cannot comprehend the Torah if you don't know it; and you cannot "experience" if you do not know God's work, God's actions. God's actions, however, constitute the "Tradition," the Torah. And the Torah is not just the Pentateuch. The Torah is the essence and integral of all religious tradition, from Moishe Rabbenu to Israel Hildesheimer—and, if you are a Jew, Herr Lehmann, to you yourself.[24] And according to the true words of the mystics, the Torah will be perfected in the days of the Messiah. The innermost comprehension of the Torah as the true living soul of Judaism is the primary requirement in order for a valid renewal—validated by God—to be possible. I quote "in Hebrew." But according to the words of the prophets, the Torah goes out from Zion; and this is something I understand intuitively—namely, that the inner point of departure for the Torah must be Zion, *Zion taken as a religious symbol;* that Zion, both internally and externally, is the innermost center of the Torah; that he who calls himself a Zionist must strive not for an experience but toward the Torah, toward life; and that the Zionist can hear the words of God only from Jerusalem. Isaiah 2:4. This means to me, Herr Lehmann, that, when directed at Jews, the living word of God cannot be comprehended in the German language. Only from the innermost soul of Hebrew can the inner form of Judaism be understood. Hasidic words—like the words of the prophet, not in their manner but in their essence—have a soul, and this soul is somehow *tied up with the magical form of the language itself.* Translation only distorts them at their core. I am astonished that I'm forced to waste words with you over the magic of language. [. . .]

Shalom, Gerhard Scholem

TO EDGAR BLUM

Berlin, October 26, 1916

My dear Blum,

[. . .] Seen objectively from the outside, this war business has now really grown into something completely unpredictable; viewed subjectively from within, however, the precise opposite has happened. Its duration has openly unmasked all of its stupidity and madness, far more than any argument presented by those with some sense in their heads. This has in turn made people totally indifferent to the war. With the exception of those actively opposed to it, indifference is the best response. Among us, for instance (meaning me and my friends), the war simply does not exist. We take note of it, and all of our people are out fighting in it; yet from the perspective of Zion, this world war is invisible. Since from the center of our souls we cannot see it, no one can force us to waste our time on it. We labor with our entire beings; and as long as we are not called up for duty, we will continue to ignore it. This war no longer exists for Zionists of the first order like ourselves.

Over the summer I've given a lot of thought to Buber. What had been already determined during the winter has now unmistakably revealed itself: that I am and must be *against* him from the very essence of my being. It has become utterly transparent to me that Buber, despite all of his Jewishness, is ultimately not a Jewish figure but a modern one. Not only is his philosophy of history wrong, it's even *demonstrably* so. Since returning to Berlin, I've had "experiences" with a number of "Buberians" that have shown me quite clearly how dangerous and ruinous this way is. Instead of Zion, it leads to *Prague*.[25] [. . .]

Best greetings, Your Gerhard Scholem

FROM WALTER BENJAMIN[26]

Munich, November 11, 1916

Dear Herr Scholem,

I'm very grateful that you supplied me with the information so quickly. A week ago I began a letter to you that ended up being eighteen pages long.[27] It was my attempt to answer in context some of the not inconsiderable number of questions you put to me. In the meantime, I felt compelled to recast it as a short essay, so that I could formulate the subject more precisely. I am now producing a fair copy of it. In this essay, it was not possible for me to go into mathematics and language— that is, mathematics and thought, mathematics and Zion—because my thoughts on this infinitely difficult topic are still quite far from having taken final shape. Otherwise, however, I do attempt to come to terms with the nature of language in this essay and—to the extent I understand it—in its immanent relationship to Judaism and in reference to the first chapters of Genesis. I await your judgment on these thoughts, certain that I will benefit from it. [. . .]

TO HARRY HEYMANN[28]

Berlin, November 12, 1916

With God's help

My friend and comrade, beloved by God and by men, Haim the son of Joel Heymann, peace and blessings! O my friend!

Thank you very much for your letter. I perceived in it the gradual preparation for a reconquest of the spiritual battlefield, because you appealed to me courageously on the most extraordinary matters. In passing, I notice that I am writing in German. Your letter arrived *opened,* so I assume it is forbidden to write in a foreign language. As a consequence, you'll have to make do with a translation.

You were in fact on the mark when you surmised that I had no interest in your military adventures (as long as you're not ill!). They're all part of a world that's far away from me. I only hope that you can get out of it with as few scratches as possible—unlike my poor friend Blum, who died on November 1, his twentieth birthday.[29] His death has deeply depressed and affected me. He was my only friend from childhood. I knew him for seven years, and we wandered together in the realm of the spirit, where nobler wars than this one are waged. We influenced each other. I'm indebted to him for fundamental insights in mathematics. He was truly a genius. In Jewish matters, too, he was always on the move, and even on the battlefield eagerly studied Hebrew. His death is so horrifying that I'm unable to offer his mother even half a word of comfort. I feel that I'm my friend's spiritual heir. I feel obliged to accomplish the things he has been prevented from doing. If it were necessary for me, this would spur me on to stronger intensity in my work. "His soul is tied up in the bonds of the living."[30]

[. . .] Until the beginning of the semester, and generally in my free time, I will exclusively focus on Judaica. Owing to reflections I had over the summer, I'm now studying S. R. Hirsch more than anyone else, in particular his book *Der Pentateuch.*[31] I now appreciate the unsurpassed greatness of the man. Above all, I've thrown myself into the theory of language; I have thought, think, and will think long and hard over it. [. . .] Finally, I'm reading Hebrew, Hebrew, and more Hebrew. I spend my time in old kabbalistic books, the supposedly "ludicrous commentators." I'm also studying Bab Mezia in the Talmud with Bleichrode, and reflecting on the Hebrew language.[32] If you were to come here to listen to what I have to say (even though you would probably rather not, since thinking has fallen out of fashion these days), I could go on for months about my new thoughts *(hidushim)*. To sum up, my mind is incessantly occupied with Zion: in my work, in my thoughts, when I'm taking walks, and even when I dream. I dreamed recently, through some strange association, that you deserted from the army. Oh, my friend! You can gather from all of this that I find myself in the advanced stages of Zionism, a Zionism of the most intimate kind. I measure all things against Zion—which is why it should come as no surprise that I rank many things as too small and too crooked; that things which may sound lovely and harmonious in Berlin ring hollow; or that numerous corpses litter the field, including that of Siegfried Lehmann. [. . .]

All the best to you, G. Scholem

1917

FROM ARTHUR SCHOLEM

Berlin, February 15, 1917

I have decided to cut off all support to you. Bear in mind the following: you have until the first of March to leave my house, and you will be forbidden to enter it again without my permission. On March first, I will transfer 100 marks to your account so that you will not be left without means. Anything more than this you cannot expect from me. It would therefore be a good idea for you to turn to the officials in charge of civilian service. They can offer you paid employment commensurate with your abilities.

Whether I will agree to finance your further studies after the war depends upon your future behavior.

Your father, Arthur Scholem

FROM ARTHUR SCHOLEM

Berlin, May 12, 1917

I have received your letter, and note that your delusions have by no means lessened. If I were a nineteen-year-old with two strong arms, I would be ashamed to accept handouts.

You would not need to beg from me if you'd taken my well-meant advice and accepted some stable vocation back in February. You still have time to do so. The War Office can offer all sorts of employment opportunities. This will teach you what gainfully earned bread tastes like. And real work will do your arrogance a world of good. What you call work is nothing more than a game. No doubt the people who must come up with money to support your literary activities and discussion groups are secretly angry about it. Money is something very concrete, and those people who busy themselves merely with abstractions consider earning it indecent.

[. . .] I still do not know if I will give you any extra money once you've been drafted into the military. This will depend upon the reports I receive regarding your behavior. But if you come out with any of your anti-German attitudes, I will break off all contact between us—just as I did with Werner, though unfortunately too late.

Your father, A.S.

TO KÄTE SCHIEPAN[33]

Berlin, June 6, 1917

Dear Aunt Käte,

Thanks once again for the money. At the same time, I regret that you've forced me to turn to additional sources of help. [. . .]

Now onto the main issue at hand. I'm sorry that I must firmly reject your suggestion, even though—as you well know—I understand and acknowledge your efforts at mediation. I won't hide from you the reasons for this.

Given my father's letter, I see no reason whatsoever to enter into personal contact with him. Though someone may have told my father that *I* wanted to speak with him (or at least that's what he says), I know *precisely* what he means by an "agreement." He has already described to all sorts of people the terms he will "dictate" once he bestows his grace upon me. The main condition (and Uncle Theobald's denials can't hide this from me) is the repression of my Zionist activities. As things stand now, I do not believe there's any hope of an *honest* agreement with my father (which would be merely a reconciliation that still bore the germ of the old disease). Moreover, after everything that has happened recently (for instance, even if you don't want to believe it, you know that my father has insolently boasted of having me spied on), I can't see any use in having a discussion with my father, for the simple reason that *I cannot guarantee reasonably calm negotiations.* Such an encounter could lead to an ugly eruption of the very bitterness that he systematically bred into us. Such a scene would serve no one's interests. I see no reason why I should stupidly walk into something with such irreversible consequences, especially because I *unfortunately*—and not unjustifiably—suspect that such a discussion would place me at the mercy of my enemy's whims.

Recent experiences have proven to me that, at least for the time being, I must live *without* my father. The only way I could foster a decent relationship between us would be by refusing to crawl before him in the dust in the most degrading manner, which would merely feed his hunger for power through more "forced" humiliation. [. . .]

At the same time, you're surely of the opinion (or at least have been until now) that I should by no means return home. My father, for his part, spreads the word that he—as he puts it—"would allow himself to speak to me only after he led me home on a bridle." [. . .] I would rather not enter into negotiations whose aim is not understanding, but humiliation by means of a bridle.

Once again I want to emphasize how much I appreciate *your* friendly intentions. I hope that these somewhat negative lines will be as kindly received as they are intended.

Sincerely yours, Gerhard

FROM WALTER BENJAMIN

Dachau, June 30, 1917

You are expecting this letter to contain a review of the new translation.[34] I'm sorry I can't get it to you at the moment, because we're in a fury of packing. Finally I'm on the verge of taking a decisive step to deal with the paralysis and pains that have totally worn me out recently. The doctor has insisted that I take a one-month cure in Switzerland, and, all difficulties notwithstanding, yesterday we received the travel passes. [. . .]

TO AHARON HELLER

Allenstein,[35] July 5, 1917

My friend Aharon,

I'm lying in bed. In the past few days I've fainted a number of times. My nerves are all on edge, and I can't write much because of my hand. It trembles terribly. On top of this, my letters may be censored, so I have to be cautious. [. . .]

TO WERNER KRAFT[36]

Allenstein, July 5, 1917

My dear Herr Kraft,

I just received your letter and was quite astonished by what it contained. Yet I assume that the enclosure was in fact meant for me, and I may even understand Benjamin's intentions. If it's all right with you, I will keep it. Or do you want it (or the card) back? (By the way, I fully share my friend's opinion of detective novels! The older ones distinguish themselves with an important idea and a great purity of spheres. To my mind, Ricarda Huch's detective novels are awful.)[37]

Herr Benjamin wrote to me today saying that you are interested in his essay on language and that I should send you a copy. Unfortunately, I find myself temporarily in the jaws of Moloch (though the chances of improvement are good). All my things are stored with friends in Berlin, so I can't get to them. If I take a vacation or even return to Berlin, I will immediately send you my copy. I suggest that you make yourself a copy, which would be to your advantage in a various of ways. I also ask you to forgive me for the delay in sending it, something I really regret. (At the same time, I ask your forgiveness for the impossible handwriting of these lines—I'm sitting in bed recovering from a nervous attack.) [. . .]

Best regards, Your Gerhard Scholem

TO AHARON HELLER

Allenstein, July 8, 1917

Dear Aharon,

I'm sending you and all the members of Jung Juda the hasty news that yesterday I was examined for the second time by the military physician. As soon as there is room, I'll be transferred to the sick bay's mental ward, now full to overflowing. Until that point (there may be a long delay), I will not have to perform any duties. I don't have to do anything but sweep the barracks and stand around. [. . .]

Gerhard Scholem

TO WERNER KRAFT

Allenstein, July 14, 1917

My very dear Herr Kraft,

I assume you're completely in favor of the openness with which you discussed the mysterious story of the letter and detective novel. I will try to explain the situation as best I can.

Both Benjamin and myself have an interest in the most important detective novels—those which have nothing in common with the Ullstein series, but which, at their best, are characterized by an unapproachable purity of spheres. My hunch is as follows (and the possibility of error is naturally very great, which would turn this entire story into something truly inexplicable).

Walter Benjamin is a man of unusual circumspection in everything pertaining to his personal life and to politics. After I was suddenly drafted and he left for Switzerland, he wanted to drop a hint to me (or at least this is how I interpret it) as to how we could establish communication, even under prevailing circumstances that seriously hinder discussions of great personal importance to me. To do so, he came up with a certain plan. And how else could he bring the plan to my attention, other than the way he chose? He could write about me to you or to some other acquaintance. So he chose you. Given the substantial risk that the letter could end up in the wrong hands, it was impossible for him to send it, with all the necessary instructions, directly to me here in the army. Nor did he want to write to you *directly.* For this reason, he chose what looks to you to be highly puzzling comments on particular features of the genre of detective novels. Naturally, he wrote in such a way as to make every unwitting reader think you're involved in a lively correspondence over such issues, free of any other intention. At the same time, at the very beginning of the letter [. . .] he gave you a clue to the riddle by telling you to send *me* the letter because I'm greatly interested in Ricarda Huch. Now, as you must have noticed, the letter has nothing to do with Ricarda Huch, nor am I particularly interested in her (something you of course did not know, though it tipped me off). It was thus expected that you would sense this and pass the letter on to me. There was nothing more to fear in sending it in this way, primarily because it was signed only with a *first name.* [. . .]

This is the story, in my opinion. Walter Benjamin acted with the greatest caution and discretion. I hope that I more or less hit the mark with my explanation. You can tell that he's obviously learned something from detective novels, even though, given the great investment of effort and your own puzzlement, it may not have been worth the trouble. Who can say?

By the way, please don't take me for a detective because of the above; as with Walter Benjamin, my business lies elsewhere. I've merely tried to clarify what seems highly baffling, so you won't have any doubts concerning a man whose utter purity is absolutely beyond question. [. . .]

With best regards, Your Gerhard Scholem

TO ERICH BRAUER

Allenstein, July 15, 1917

Dear Erich,

Today I nearly forgot to write to you. All sorts of things muddle up my mind in this place. Today is the second Sunday of the quarantine. At least today the divisions were once again led out in closed groups. They're not allowed to enter the city, go into taverns, or meet with civilians. Though they're required to "take walks," they're forbidden to pick blueberries. So they race around like mad sheep in the forest, spouting their smutty talk (with the junior officers leading the way) and amusing themselves in all sorts of ways. Today I got out of this by telling them I had postal duty. As a result, I managed to remain in the barracks. [. . .]

Only on one very melancholy point can I report something new about my life. Ever since my illness freed me from service and I was assigned to mail duty, my comrades (those close to me in the barracks) have developed a rabid hatred of me, though earlier I got on with them very well. They're quite aware of what's wrong with me (they themselves repeat the most outlandish things that His Nibs, the lieutenant, has been saying about my mental condition), but the fact that I have it better than they do is ample reason for them to insult me and to show off their power and barbarian strength in the routine tasks at which, as you can imagine, I am so inept. Only now do I know beyond a shadow of doubt something I have never felt with such force: that, in the long run, living with such people is *absolutely impossible.* The only thing that prevents them from pushing things to an extreme is their raw fear that, in the midst of a paroxysm, I would beat someone half to death. Our corporal, who's basically a decent sort, is likewise deeply afraid of my seizures, and this prevents him from unleashing the fellows on me. You simply cannot imagine the horrible vulgarity of the Germans, who know how to disgust a person after just a few minutes. You can't speak to them rationally, for they're not mentally equipped to think clearly. They interrupt you after every third sentence. The heavy footsteps of anti-Semitism are always thumping behind my back. But on this point I've made an experiment, and now everyone prefers to keep quiet around me. In the courtyard of the barracks, where all of the soldiers and officers were gathered, some guy began to utter a slur. In a burst of rage, I beat him to a pulp. These Krauts, however, have endless means at their disposal, and a major clash is imminent—though I'm not afraid of it in the least. The outcome can only be to my advantage. [. . .]

Your friend, Gershom Scholem

TO AHARON HELLER

Allenstein, July 17, 1917

Dear Aharon,

Since entering the military, I haven't felt as much joy over anything as I felt over your letter. I see we have absolutely the same desires (and most of the time even say so using the same words), and this gives me the comforting feeling that even now, with all of the external pressures brought on by the draft, the Berlin chapter of Jung Juda cannot be equaled.[38]

I copied your letter by hand and sent it back to you. In view of its importance, I had it sent special delivery. Now on to a few comments.

I am in *complete* agreement as to the main extension of the program. As far as I can tell, the ethical side of Zionism (or the "improvement of the heart") was always a subject of extreme importance for you. It was in fact a mistake on my part not to emphatically raise the issue. I wrote the letter after a severe nervous attack and was not at the height of my powers. I can't think of a single Zionist—one unencumbered by quotation marks, of course—who would not agree with all of the things highlighted on page three. That goes as well for your last point about sexual relations. We must all realize that to build what *we* want requires a bit of asceticism (in *all* things!) Here in the military I've had to learn in the most terrifying fashion what sexual impurity does to people. We are simply doomed if we strive to attain the kind of "national fitness" that turns these Germans, my fellow recruits, into a "healthy" *Volk*. Obscenity blocks every possible access to the holy in this place. As I have written to you before, it's better to obtain greatness and purity in Exile (if this is even thinkable) than to endure pagan abomination in Eretz Israel.[39] If we want to be holy (even though one cannot become holy—holiness is a state of being; the only question is whether or not holiness is *visible,* as with the *saddik*),[40] we must bind ourselves together in isolation. These days, any community that does not arise out of isolation is a fraud. It has not yet overcome *galut;*[41] instead, it carries its strongest poison around in its heart.

[. . .] My health isn't so bad. I have a lot of time on my hands, since they declared me too *crazy* to work in the mail service. Today and tomorrow I have toilet duty, meaning that I will have to sit on a stool for two to four hours a day and make sure that everyone washes their hands with carbolic soap (as I've already written, we are under quarantine). Otherwise, I'm free to do what I want, which is of course wonderful. By the way, there is no hope of getting discharged. At best, they'll declare me unfit for duty and send me to Warsaw, where they'll get some use out of me. The people in the office here have promised that I can work censoring Hebrew documents. [. . .]

All best from your friend Gershom Scholem[42]

FROM WALTER BENJAMIN[43]

Zurich, July 17, 1917

Dear Herr Scholem,

Allow me to say a few words concerning your translation of the Song of Solomon. I unfortunately do not have the text in front of me now and could not read it in its entirety during my recent grueling stay in

Dachau. Nevertheless, these limitations are less important than my ignorance, not only of the Song of Solomon but also of Hebrew. Consequently, what I say cannot be more than an aperçu, but I think I am
on relatively firm ground in what little I do have to say.

What distinguishes the second from the first translation is its thorough
and conscientious application of *critical methodology*. The revision is me-
thodically based, and at the same time is only methodical. And, if I might
allow myself a conjecture, this is because, in the medium of the German
language, your love for Hebrew can manifest itself only as reverence for
the nature of language and the word as such, and thus only in the application of a proper and pure method. This means that your work will remain apologetic, however, because its proper sphere does not include
the expression of love and reverence for an object. In principle, it would
not be impossible for two languages to inhabit the same sphere. On the
contrary, this is the foundation of all great translation and is the basis of
the very few great translations in existence. In the spirit of Pindar, Hölderlin discovered the congruent spheres of German and Greek: his love
for both became *one*. (I am not sure, but I think it is almost possible to
accord equally high praise to George's Dante translation.) Nevertheless,
you are not as close to German as you are to Hebrew, and therefore
you have not been *called* to be the translator of the Song of Solomon.
[. . .]

TO AHARON HELLER

Allenstein, July 25, 1917
Military Reserve Hospital I

Dear Aharon,

I finally landed in the military hospital, but not before the downright
stormy events of the past few days cost me one last seizure, the day before
yesterday. It's a lot better here than I imagined it would be. Despite the
constant observation, within limits you can move around freely. You
can rest the entire day; you can do what you please; if your nerves hold
out, you can even cogitate. All of the doctors here are supposedly Jews.
The hospital is small—about seventy men. We're all alone in one large
building. The food is somewhat better than in boot camp. For the moment, I will establish my kingdom here—and this might turn out to last

quite some time. In any case, the devil will have to take me lying down, if they try to send me back to the infantry. [. . .]

Best regards, Gerhard Scholem

FROM WALTER BENJAMIN

St. Moritz, July 31, 1917

Dear Herr Scholem,

We haven't heard from you in quite some time, nor you from us. We arrived a week ago and have been spending our time in this lovely landscape with magnificent weather. But it seems to be taking a turn for the worse, and the lake in front of my window (a wonderful alpine lake) now has the poison-green color that presages a storm. As far as my illness allows, we take long walks and recuperate. In periods when I'm unable to work, I begin having all sorts of thoughts. You'll be hearing about them soon. Meanwhile, we hope you are well. Write soon. On each and every morning, my wife and I send our greetings.

P.S. What's happening with your father?

TO WERNER KRAFT

Allenstein, August 3, 1917

Dear Herr Kraft,

Extremely repellent circumstances have joined forces with near total exhaustion to prevent me from responding to you as quickly and in as much detail as I would have wished. After a number of incidents, I finally landed in the military hospital a week ago. I'll remain here at least until August, perhaps longer, and in the meantime my final military status— insofar as anything final exists now—will be decided. I need and am also enjoying total rest. Since there's no treatment in this place, when I can, I spend my time daydreaming. I would have enough time to write to you in detail, but even writing requires an extraordinary effort— something you will notice from my handwriting. I must beg your indulgence. In fact, I had intended to send you an elucidation of the text on language,[44] but in the past few days I've found a way to make the essay available to you. The woman who is keeping it for me will locate it among my papers and eventually type up copies. If I write about it at all today, it will be only briefly. By the way, the letter on language you have already read is not a copy; it's the original.[45] It was never sent to me. I received instead a paper introducing key concepts in the philosophy of language, which Benjamin and I—to an ever-increasing degree and from different angles—both consider seminally important as the true foundation of every philosophy. The work is a polemic against the reigning conception of language, and subsequently (in the second part) a discussion of the first chapters of Genesis and on what the Bible has to say about language. (This second part I consider unsurpassed.)

Naturally, absolutely fundamental elements are still missing from the work—for instance, a discussion of the nature of symbols in language (which Benjamin will no doubt deal with in a second essay) and the theory of signs and of script, which in my opinion lead to the deepest levels possible, for they raise the most decisive questions for mathematics and the philosophy of religion (to wit, whether the spiritual essence of the world is language and script—a proposition which I, according to my notion of Judaism, tend to affirm). But the essay "merely" set out to accomplish an unspeakably important task: to clarify terminology and to prepare the broadest possible groundwork for a theory that will be able to locate all of the problems of language and see them in their natural order. [. . .] The first section raises the questions: What is language and what is the language of mankind? What does a language communicate? The second section then introduces a few fundamental problems connected to a notion [. . .] of great importance for all theories of language: the notion of the *language of God* as it appears in biblical *revelation*. Problems relating to naming, proper names, and the source of abstractions in language are hinted at. The great question arises: Did human language suffer an original sin? And what was the nature of it? The essay concludes with a discussion of the theory of signs.

I believed that I grasped it, since my own reflections went in the very same direction as Benjamin's. But I fully made it a part of myself only after first trying to translate it into Hebrew, which I succeeded in doing for large sections of it. As Benjamin himself has clearly noticed, the paper's great strength is its immanent relation to Judaism. This was also proven by the wonders I encountered in translating it.

It is certainly possible that for you the problem of language may take on a very different aspect. Still, I think that for you too the essay may correspond to personal experiences, even if the spirit of the mighty science that blows through its entirety—and that arises from these very foundations (which we call the doctrine of order)—remains for you alien and far afield. For me (and, from my perspective, I do not know whether I can say "unfortunately"), the aesthetic sphere remains [. . .] so totally inaccessible and even invisible that I cannot possibly imagine where aesthetic orders exist in the world. Perhaps you can explain this to me in detail.

In general, you should never forget that linguistic questions can nowhere be so easily answered (and posed) in an antibourgeois manner as with religion, and for this reason the greatness of the coming philosophy must lie [. . .] in the fact that it succeeds in gaining this perspective *without* religion as well. I would like to expand on these thoughts for you; but since I don't have any idea whether this is at all of interest to you, I will end at this juncture, where you can easily become acquainted with my thinking. I should really tell you something about myself, for otherwise you will no doubt misunderstand a number of things. Whether this is permissible or not, I do not know. The direction of my education is surely astonishing to you. You are no doubt unacquainted with both of the things that form the immutable center of my life: Zion and mathematics, in their own spheres. Perhaps at some point I will be allowed to introduce you to them.

In similar fashion, my preoccupation with Hebrew and reflections upon the foundations of mathematics have driven me to meditate upon the nature of language. I have thus been devoting time to the study of three theories of language that have developed within the Jewish tradition—and as you may know, this has been utterly decisive for me. Like my own thinking, all three developed out of the same general problem—namely, whether the spiritual essence of the world can be expressed (in *one way* or another, which doesn't *yet* imply that everything is knowable, since pure actions, for example, also have an expression and a language). This is a question that the much-maligned rabbinical Judaism has tacitly, though no less clearly, affirmed. And it has done so in the most penetrating way, through its literature and through the eminently profound notion of "commentary." [. . .]

Best regards, Your Gerhard Scholem

TO GERDA GOLDBERG

Allenstein Military Hospital, August 6, 1917

Dear Gerda,

I must beg all of your indulgence, both for the delay in getting back to you and for the content of my answer itself.[46] You can see from this address that I am no longer in those barracks where I experienced so much horror in the past several weeks, but in the military hospital, or rather the mental ward. Here, fateful decisions regarding my relationship to—or within—the army will be made. Since the minimum period of observation is six weeks, I will remain here until the beginning of September. I'm completely idle. From morning till evening I enjoy a rest so perfect that, thus far, not even visits have disturbed it. I am sadly in the *most* dire need of rest, owing to the highly unstable condition of my psyche. For days on end I'm often unable to think, to read, or to write, which is why I haven't written sooner. You understand it's precisely because of the extraordinary importance of the issues involved that a sketchy description would horrify me—and in my present state this is all I am able to give in writing. Please take this into account. I know perfectly well that my abilities have been greatly reduced. If my immediate environment did not preclude it, I would invite you here for the holidays, when I'll be free the entire day. Dialogue in particular reawakens my addled spirit, and I could really use some discussion as therapy. In fact, I may even extend such an invitation as soon as I have the hope of obtaining permission to leave the base (the option is open to a "well-behaved lunatic"). Give it some thought, since we could then discuss these questions truly in depth! I've no chance of getting a furlough from here, because my psychological state is undergoing observation. At the very most, I can make a foray into the city.

By the way, I have exclusively Jewish doctors, which correlates with an indescribable hatred of Jews here, greater than in other military hospitals. More than this I have nothing personal to report.

So you insist on hearing something about my philosophy. You're certainly right to do so, since such a discussion will considerably simplify things between us. But I cannot yet give you my philosophy, for the simple reason that I don't quite know it myself. And (for the time being!) the philosophy I do have will appear to outsiders as terribly obscure. My possibilities and capabilities of expression are unfortunately very meager;

and now, more than ever, the direction of my thinking has led me to adopt as the most appropriate medium of communication a language that is difficult to master. This explains why nearly the only ones who can understand it are those who themselves think like me. To everyone else I remain a sealed book because they can't make sense of my language. I believe that only very gradually, after progressively clarifying and systematically developing my thinking, can I eliminate this flaw— if I can indeed get rid of it, rather than have it clinging to me forever. With this in mind, it simply makes no sense to present my philosophy to you, in all its murkiness. Today I'll limit myself to individual points mentioned in your letter. I regret that I'm unable to address them all now (for instance, what I think about the nation, a topic unfortunately so tied to my own manner of expression that, in my present state, I can't hope to say anything about it in a letter.)

What is the Torah? I see it as the following. (1) The principle according to which the order of things is fashioned. Now, Judaism views this principle as the language of God, which is also—even primarily— recognizable in the traditions of men (and it is here that the concept of "tradition" acquires its particular importance, as a complement to that of "doctrine"). (2) Consequently, within Judaism (to which we owe the concept of tradition) the Torah signifies the network or embodiment of Jewish traditions, from earliest antiquity to the age of the Messiah. [. . .]

The Torah has an internal relation to what I call history. My views on *language* lead me logically to a view of the Torah which is very close to traditional Judaism's view. And what about the question of your atheism? I've already explained to you that I do not consider this to be the primary *problem*. More important than belief in God is whether you accept the Torah—which is to say, whether we make a *law*, or a metaphysically grounded *imperative*, an integral part of our lives because we submit ourselves unconditionally to a principle. I can offer no personal opinion on this question, for I do not have a relationship to God that is founded on belief (in the Christian sense). We Jews are in no way believers.

What is important for me is that we should submit our lives to laws— and not those of a "law book" but rather the deep laws of the spiritual world which I sense are active in Zionism. My entire wisdom is that we should not live as *heathens*. The heathen lives intensively; he enjoys himself to the hilt. This is precisely what we reject. [. . .]

I'm sorry, but I must redirect the question of culture back to you.

It's up to you to determine *how* culture is to lead to the Center. Insofar as it has a culture, the twentieth century is essentially a culture of intensive life, meaning that it stands precisely upon those spheres of Torahlessness that seem to me to forbid access to the Center once and for all. The Jew is not (inwardly) adapted to these modern conditions. When his creative powers awaken, they are directed toward Zion. We have had a relationship with Europe only to the degree that Europe has acted upon us as a destructive stimulation. I must ask you now to please explain to me how, say, the real *synthesis* of the Jewish spirit with that of Europe has revealed itself.

It is very difficult to answer the crucial question, "Where did the evil way of the Jews begin?" *Perhaps I can say it most clearly through what I've said before:* when Jews started to live *intensely;* when they no longer wanted to be *holy* (it could be that the sin began only in the innermost reaches of their hearts); when they were seized by the confused belief that a *synthesis* was possible between the decisive commands of a foreign spirit and their own. Since the days of Moses, our history has been one long original sin. The servants of God have had to battle against it time and time again—in Palestine just as much as in Russia or Germany. [. . .]

There is *one way to solve the Jewish question* [. . .] *and that is to live holy lives.* More than this, I do not know—nor do young people such as us, who stand at the crossroads, need to know anything more. We will have to make great sacrifices [. . .], for we have to win back our purity. We will not be prophets, but we will know that we are situated where the law directs us, and the justice that we seek is attainable only through *denial.* He who *cannot* deny himself cannot help himself. He also cannot be helped.

Take all of this in the spirit in which it was given.

Yours, Gerhard Scholem

FROM WERNER KRAFT

Ilten, August 8, 1917

Most esteemed Herr Scholem,

My deepest thanks for your detailed letter. I only regret that you are not doing well, and am all the more sorry because I'm completely unable to help—unless being aware of others who are suffering and empathizing with you provides a certain comfort.

I must admit I don't have much positive to say in response to your equally matter-of-fact and enthusiastic remarks. We seem to be speaking to each other across an abyss—one that I, at least (in my present psychological state) feel incapable of bridging. I will try in a few words to give you the reasons for this.

[. . .] If I'm not mistaken, you are a scientifically minded man. For a number of very complex reasons, I continue to be the very opposite of this. What is *decisive* here is that I am incapable of presenting my free artistic nature as fully equal to science. Why? I am extremely unsure of myself, and a short time ago even had to jot down (trembling) the same truth that led Goethe to write his *Werther:* "I am a value." Even today, this vaguely implied conflict makes me incapable of all scientifically based activity—though thoughts have come to me that surely have occurred to no one else and that, being things which arise naturally, bear witness to the true accomplishments of our time. But I don't want to go into these things. In a particular context, I've had to write things about Judaism that you of all people would be incapable of writing. I feel boundless adoration for German art, Goethe, and our contemporary Rudolf Borchardt; I hate Martin Buber with all my heart. Shall I go on? I cannot. No one would be happier than I if you could overcome this chasm between us. [. . .]

TO WERNER KRAFT

Allenstein, August 11, 1917

Dear Herr Kraft,

I am answering your letter directly. Your letter deeply moved me, all the more so because I am now able to share news with you that has kept me in a constant state of bliss for the past two days. It's news that will certainly please you no less, seeing that it is the only possible remedy for me. After only fourteen days here, I've been told by the doctors that I'm to be released as soon as possible and that they will do everything in their power to prevent me from being re-conscripted. You can perhaps imagine what effect this information has had on me. The formalities of release will take some time (you can safely continue to send your letters here; in the worst case, they'll be forwarded to me). In any event, I will certainly be free by September.

I fantasize all day about what I'll do now. I'll make the serious decisions in Berlin, where I will stay for a couple of weeks. If at all possible, I'll spend the winter at a small university—unless I can go to Switzerland, which could do just as much good for my health as for my studies. In any case, I will be able to *work* once again. I view my release as a victory earned through spiritual exertions that have cost me dearly. I can easily comfort myself with the well-known fact that psychiatrists do not need much research zeal to pronounce someone crazy. Anyway, from the standpoint of the war I *am* crazy. Had the doctor only read the previous letter I wrote to you—and who can say that he *didn't*—he would easily have had enough material to declare me unfit for service. I also hope that perhaps a personal meeting between us now lies in the realm of the possible. You can now safely count on getting the essay on language.

Let me say a few words in response to your confessions. It seems to me that the chasm you see yawning between us arises for the most part from the fact that you haven't yet decided once and for all whether to have a relationship with things that for me are of the utmost importance. This is only temporary; in one way or another, you will be forced to enter into a relationship to these things. Take, for instance, what you said about Judaism. I think I have an idea of what Judaism is all about, and therefore implore you to believe me when I say that, based upon what I know, Buber is inherently anti-Jewish. How did you come to see him as the representation of Jewishness, whose most essential categories he despises or suppresses? *As a Jew and a Zionist* I reject Buber as decisively as you do. What, then, does your hatred of Buber prove against Judaism? Of course, since you know nothing about Judaism you cannot establish a relationship with it. [. . .] Judaism makes the highest demands on someone who wants to look into it *seriously*. "Getting to know it" presents nearly insurmountable difficulties to those who do not possess (like Walter Benjamin, as far as I can tell) a tremendous intuition for it, which is to say an eminently positive relationship with it. If it is a concern of the ultimate importance, it cannot be any other way. Moreover, the complete inner certainty that it is precisely *this* has guided me through all of my initial years of study. I confess that I've never had such a central relationship with any other thing; it has commanded my full attention from the time I began to work and think for myself (to wit, from the age of fourteen). The confrontation with German culture which presents so many Jews with such painful dilemmas has never been a problem for me. Nor has the absolutely un-Jewish atmosphere in my home been able to change this. I have never found or sought out values whose legitimacy was rooted in the German essence. Even the German language, which I speak, disappears for me completely when compared to Hebrew, which my children will speak and which I myself have begun to learn. [. . .]

Sincerely yours, Gerhard Scholem

TO HARRY HEYMANN

Allenstein, August 14, 1917

Dear Haim son of Joel,[47]

[. . .] I don't want this letter to be a chronicle of my experiences in the military over the past two months. Perhaps we'll have an opportunity to discuss this later. At the moment, I have but *one* single thought: soon I'll be free! Listen and be amazed! Though I was supposed to stay here for six weeks, after fourteen days the doctors called me in and again inquired about a number of issues. They then announced, in the friendliest tones, that I was "of course" entirely unfit for service and that they would expedite my release as much as humanly possible—which they admitted could happen only after an unavoidably long wait. I've been pushed to the head of the line. To be precise, this is the *last* station for those who are three-fourths insane, epileptics, and to a lesser extent total lunatics. From here, *everyone* gets released. In the next two to three weeks I'll be granted a vacation pending my final release, along with the permission to wear civilian clothes. As far as the military is concerned, I'll be furloughed to the home of my parents. My father will of course behave with the greatest caution, since I'll be returning mentally ill. He has already offered me peace without annexation. The chief physician said they'd decided to release me after determining that I had been living for years in a visionary state and that this had rendered me completely unsuitable for *all* military duty. (By the way, I've already gone on strike—otherwise I wouldn't have ended up here. I ask you for *Stika* on this!)[48] He told me that under no circumstances would I be called up once again. Orders are that those released with my symptoms should not be drafted again, for bad experience has shown that they would only put the discipline of the army at serious risk. Physically I've never felt better—I'm nearly bursting with health.

What do you say Heymann, my friend! (By the way, keep sending your letters to this address. I won't be getting out terribly soon, and in any case everything will be forwarded.) In the winter I'll be able to *work* once again. I won't be squandering my youth in these odious circumstances, and I can celebrate my twentieth birthday wearing civilian clothes. Where? In any case not in Berlin, where I won't find the peace and quiet needed for complete recovery of my health. I'll have to go *immediately* to another university. I am debating between Heidelberg and Jena. Externally, the situation here in the hospital is quite good, even though I have to admit I've occasionally felt absolutely dreadful. Is my Zionism a product of my visionary condition, too? [. . .]

All the best, Your Gerhard Scholem

TO AHARON HELLER[49]

Allenstein, August 15, 1917

My dear friend Aharon,

I have the distinct pleasure to inform you that the day approaches which will take me back to Berlin. [. . .] We can discuss a number of things then. So instead of revealing to you truths about Eretz Israel, I'll report to you on the true nature of my illness, as well as the means and methods I used to liberate myself from bondage. You've probably guessed that I was never really sick; it was all a colossal fabrication. At the beginning of this strange business I was in fact so healthy that I had no idea what to do. I thought about it and discovered a way. Now I will leave the army as a "lunatic." [. . .]

Warmest greetings from your friend, Gershom[50]

TO WERNER KRAFT

Allenstein, August 19, 1917

Even if I have too little power to help, I wanted to respond promptly because I cannot endure silently watching you slide into that terrible abyss—a danger we *must* avoid at all cost and against which one can never be warned urgently enough, even if it doesn't do any good. I very much want to speak with you in person. Maybe I would have more success that way; I know from similar cases of boundless tragedy how powerless the written word can be against despair. But rest assured that I write these pages in holy earnestness and with all the reverence I can muster. You certainly have said this to yourself before, perhaps even more often than I have, but I still want to repeat that the Spiritual Center is stronger than violence; that for us there is no other weapon against devilish brutality, injustice, and disorder than to overcome them by focusing on what is essential. Of course, under these circumstances one can also say that magic plays a part in true conquest. In the past weeks, I've learned that there is no greater bulwark against my environment than purity. To triumph over the military, you must recognize its deepest flaw. Human violence is a great disorder, but equally so is the deep impurity of all the spheres and men that are, without support, swept up into its orbit. He who begins at the roots cannot fall victim to despair. *Why* shouldn't you use the power that lies in your own hands? *What* sort of weakness hinders you from doing so? The military surely doesn't merit any pity, nor it is possible that you are too weak to focus on spiritual things. You must *realize* that the military can do nothing against you. You *mustn't* even consider entering into a coalition with violence, not even with a wink of the eye or impure speech. How could you then fail to be secure in your own order of things! It was precisely Zionism that equipped me for this ultimate effort. I have passed securely before the abyss of madness. A *single conscious thought* (that *I will be needed,* that *not a single Jewish soul* shall be sacrificed) literally drove me on and kept me upright when the moment of truth quite literally arrived. How should it be any different with you? [. . .] I know that Zion, where God dwells, is more than this militant spirit. I'm convinced that you know the same. It may be that with you the knowledge is latent—I can't say for certain, because I don't know you well enough. You must allow it to become active. If it's at all necessary, it surely won't be difficult.

I beg you to spend the entire day just thinking those thoughts that, as you've told me, no one has ever thought before. Direct your entire power to them, and keep in mind that it is better to be a lunatic in a Prussian mental ward than to nurse madmen back to Prussianism. [. . .]

With warm regards, Gerhard Scholem

FROM WALTER BENJAMIN[51]

St. Moritz, September 1917

Dear Gerhard,

Permit me to combine my commemoration of your battle and victory with our shift to a first-name basis. In spite of all the pleasure your last letter gave me (and which, as you can see, I am answering right away), I experienced an almost painful sensation at the thought that we won't be together. Is it really impossible? I am convinced that, in a certain respect, in the very circumstances of our existence we have reached an *equality* whose primary color is no doubt gratitude and which would hold the promise of an extremely productive and splendid collaboration. Another reason I wish we could be together is that my wife and I are totally isolated here. Wouldn't it be possible for you, through some modest enterprise, to earn a modest amount of money (in francs) which, added to your monthly income, would guarantee a modest but healthy standard of living? How long would we otherwise have to wait before seeing each other again? [. . .]

FROM BETTY SCHOLEM

Berlin, September 21, 1917

My dear child,

[. . .] If you don't go to stay at the boarding house, which is what I still consider best for you, at least take advantage of the lunches there. Otherwise you'll float entirely in the air on an empty stomach.

Beware of the soap: it's a bandit that takes more than it gives. Since I myself have no soap made with fat—the kind that lathers and dates from peacetime—I can't offer you any. Makes sense, doesn't it? So be a man and wash yourself with war soap! [. . .]

You can write to Werner as often as you want—just be careful what you say. He can write only one letter a week, on Sundays.[52] He said I could visit whenever I pleased. So I set off right away, with very little sleep, and all worked up. I arrived, opened the door—and I wasn't allowed in. One must make an application in writing. The excursion completely wore me out. [. . .]

Kisses, Your mother

Berlin, November 16, 1917

Dearest child,

Your agitation is completely unnecessary, lacking all foundation! We did not fight the diagnosis but welcomed it, because now you won't be called up once again and can remain free of burdens. And this is what counted. Otherwise, we wouldn't have felt comforted by Dr. Liebermann's opinion, which is wrong. But what difference does it make? The main thing is that his diagnosis has freed you for good. Dr. Meyer has also written to say that he made his medical report with the express purpose of getting you free, but that you are *completely healthy.* There is no danger for you in studying, though naturally within limits. You're a nervous person, after all. Don't throw yourself immediately into a hundred seminars. [. . .] Do you remember Herr Gersing, who spent the afternoon with us? We've printed a number of his books, on the nerves and suchlike topics. He may never have passed his exams, but he has a great deal of knowledge and universal erudition, and is for us as solid an authority as a doctor from the outside. Yesterday Father described your letter to him and told him the entire story. Since he's used to observing people closely, he remembered you precisely. He said that there's no trace of any mental disease in you! So don't imagine things. Just be healthy. George and Käte, too, said that you are healthy. In the military, everyone who doesn't fit in is declared mentally ill. [. . .]

Kisses, Mum

November 28, 1917

Dear Herr Scholem,

[. . .] I now have the opportunity to make a new request, this time for a transfer to a different military hospital in a university town. At least there I can salvage my period of military service by attending some lectures.

I'm deeply interested in hearing more about your relationship to Hölderlin.[53] I've given some thought to the issue lately. In particular, I've thought about accusing you in a roundabout way of knowing too little about the German heart. At the same time, your enthusiastic knowledge of Jean Paul, which I probably couldn't match in ten years, really puts me to shame.[54] Still, at least for now I think my accusation is correct. [. . .]

TO WERNER KRAFT

Jena,[55] November 30, 1917

Dear Werner Kraft,

[. . .] With the possibility of peace in the offing, something entirely new and unimaginable has appeared on the scene. You can only imagine how much I set my heart on the offer made by the Russian revolutionaries. If their efforts meet with success, the kind of blessings that will be heaped upon these men (whose best comrades in Germany sit in prison) will be simply unfathomable. I've never read such a humanly moving and authentic political tract as the document on the Bolshevik Revolution. And I don't believe that such a document has ever before appeared in history. The most amazing thing of all is that *each and every* one of us can place his signature upon these things. [. . .]

My dear Kraft, when will you finally show some consideration and send me the elegy you promised! In today's mail I'm also sending you some extremely beautiful things. Such as Walter Benjamin's review of Dostoevsky [. . .] and something you've surely forgotten all about: the essay on language (typed up with diligence and self-denial by a female friend of mine). Walter granted explicit permission for me to give it to you. A thorough study of it may spur you to write an additional piece— say, on the relation between language and symbols. I must reserve the third part, on language and mathematics, for myself. But all three of us could organize a competition for authorship of a second part. The winner will receive permission to touch the stars with a crown on his head and to call himself the "Master of Language" *(Baal-laschon).* [. . .]

Gerhard Scholem

FROM WALTER BENJAMIN[56]

Bern, December 3, 1917

Since receiving your letter, I often feel solemn. It is as if I had entered a festive season and I must venerate revelation in what was disclosed to you. For it is surely the case that what came to you, you alone, was meant just for you and reentered our life for a moment. I have entered a new phase of my life because what detached me with astronomical speed from everybody and pushed even my most intimate relationships, except for my marriage, into the background, now emerges unexpectedly someplace else and binds me. I do not want to write you any more more today, even though this is meant to be your birthday letter.

Yours, Walter Benjamin

TO HARRY HEYMANN

Jena, December 4, 1917

Truly, "I am the man who has suffered misery under the rod of your wrath."[57] I'm now composing the mildest and meekest letter, gentler than David's reproach to Jonathan.[58] Oh, holy Bimbaum—how you personally feel like a target for blows and think up all kinds of disgusting possibilities in your dark soul! As the prophet says, "An abomination is he that choseth you." But we should finally come to some kind of peace by entering into negotiations for a general armistice—for why should we be any worse than the German government? The events of the past days have stirred my interest for the first time. I hope and impatiently wait for the day when these people, whose best friends in Germany (and not only here) sit in prison, will bring peace to the world. It could be that you feel yourself more confirmed in your views than we could ever dream of being, though the West doesn't seem to want peace right away. Jews, who see things rather more humanly than others, consider every day to be holy. Nor would it even be an obstacle to peace if Eretz Israel remained Turkish after the conclusion of a general peace! Let me tell you, I've been reading nationalist German newspapers for some time now and it's unimaginable how those miscreants do their best to undermine the peace. And this after three and a half years of war! [. . .]

Best regards, Gerhard Scholem

FROM WERNER KRAFT

Hannover, December 15, 1917

Dear Scholem,

[. . .] I have not succeeded in bringing order to my chaos, despite all the noblest powers of the heart. I even accuse myself of purposely strengthening our relationship, knowing full well that I cannot follow you into the lofty realms of your enthusiasm. I have failed to establish any connection to Judaism whatsoever, and am worlds away from all philosophy. Instead, my feelings succeed one another pell-mell: now a state of mind that sends me deep into the lowest reaches of humiliation, now a boundless confidence in myself. [. . .]

Incidentally, for the longest time I have wanted to ask you whether Walter Benjamin's friend was a Jew or not. In either case, it's an issue of the utmost significance.[59]

TO HARRY HEYMANN

Jena, December 28, 1917

My friend Haim and the man Heymann, peace and blessings![60]
My dear friend,

I had so much to do around the end of the semester that I could not write. Moreover, between the twenty-second and yesterday I had two female guests from Berlin.[61] Finally I can now write once again to thank you for your two letters and your birthday greetings. I also want to answer your letter from the sixteenth.[62] It's been lovely here. There's a deep blanket of snow, and things would be utterly perfect if only my room had some heat. Unfortunately it doesn't. I couldn't ask for a lovelier region, and my guests and I have been marching around in it. Now they are gone and I can tackle the mountain of correspondence that has piled up on my desk from all fronts and regions. It's your luck to be the first. I regret to say that I'll have to start off with a piece of unpleasant news: today I received orders to appear before a military examination in Jena on January 14. I'm terribly nervous about what could result. If they have my papers, meaning the psychologist's report, I have nothing to worry about. But it could just as easily happen that they will try to start everything all over again. In one way or another, this would certainly be a disaster. I dare not be optimistic. Pray for me!

With stars such as Troeltsch, Simmel, and Gundolf sparkling and chattering,[63] your university course seems to have been quite an illustrious affair. I hope you can soon pursue this agreeable occupation permanently. I'm really delighted that you have developed an interest in philosophy, the heart of my life. What stimulated your interest? You ask about an introduction to philosophy. There are only two ways. You could begin immediately with a major work of philosophy. Over the past 2,000 years, there have been two texts in particular that have presented the central questions of philosophy in a truly and absolutely grand fashion. By this I mean Plato's *Theaetetus,* a work of a mere one hundred pages whose magnificent contents can give you an infinite amount. Perhaps even more shattering is Kant's *Prolegomena to any Future Metaphysics* (which Reklam has published in two volumes). If you weren't in the army, I would direct you straight to his *Critique of Pure Reason,* though for a complete novice it's exceptionally difficult and as such won't be as helpful as the shorter though splendid excerpt contained in the *Prolegomena.* He who reads the Prolegomena and still has no use for philosophy should stay away from it. It's a perfect litmus test. [. . .]

TO WERNER KRAFT

Jena, December 28, 1917

Dear Werner,

For the past couple of weeks my correspondence has come to a total standstill and I have not written a single letter. Why? [. . .] Above all, because I have not been in the right mood. I've been thinking a great deal about you. I would even like to invite you to Jena—that is, if something completely absurd and superficial did not stand in the way. The coal has run out, which is the reason I'm writing this letter in the community house rather than my unheated apartment. [. . .]

Your last letter caused me *enormous* concern. I again plead with you not to lower your powers of resistance. Your condition has become so critical that it requires all of your effort and conscious labor to avoid reaching a potentially tragic point—and you know what this would mean. For me, standing by your side to constantly lift and strengthen your courage is a source of supreme happiness. [. . .]

My brother is going to Hannover tomorrow to get married.[64] I feel I should go with him, though a severe shortage of cash prevents me from making such a long trip. In one way or another, though, the two of us must see each other soon! I'll remain in Jena until the end of January. If by then you haven't been able to come here, then we'll have to see if we can meet somehow in Hannover.

My answer to the query in your last letter is that Walter's friend is in fact a Jew, and this seems to be one of the main reasons Walter's Judaism has taken possession of him in such a positive manner. I also believe that such a relationship between a Jew and a non-Jew would have been impossible. *All* other things might be possible, but the inherent distance between German culture and Judaism clearly precludes a shared life in any proper sense. Only a miracle could bring about such a friendship, and such a wonder has rarely, if ever, occurred: namely, a Jewish Gentile. [. . .]

Sincerely yours, Gerhard

1918

TO HARRY HEYMANN

Jena, January 15, 1918

Oh, boy! Just imagine the scene. Yesterday morning at around eight, 150 of us—those fit for garrison duty, along with those declared temporarily unfit—were herded into the community center of Jena in order to undergo a war fitness experiment. There was wailing and gnashing of teeth. To my great delight, once my turn came and I entered into the review room (in a dubious condition), I noticed right away that my file, thick and fat, was sitting on top of the shelf. I was afraid it had remained in Berlin. My delight grew when the clerk read aloud, "Med. I/15" (the correct and awful digits). The doctor responded by looking at me with a *very* compassionate gaze. He picked up my file and paged through it for a couple of minutes, along with a major. The two of them must have been satisfied, for they stopped examining me. After a couple of minutes, they promoted me from "temporarily unfit for use by the recruiting authorities" to "permanently unfit for war service: not to be examined again." This was my final review, and I've been stricken from the review list. Among the 150 in the room, I was the only one who managed this. Try to imagine the expression on my face. Without any worries, I can now concentrate upon the perplexing problem of where and how I will spend my summer vacation. [. . .]

TO HARRY HEYMANN

Jena, March 1, 1918

My good friend,

As of today, you've spent two years in that famous kingdom familiar to all Babylonians—the one that stands in intimate connection to the land of no return.[65] I will not allow this deeply melancholy anniversary to pass without offering you my token of commemoration. As you can see, you have not been forgotten. After the most recent attempts by the *Germanim*,[66] my hopes for a rapid end to the war have slipped far below zero; I simply do not fathom how anyone can still claim that the *altera pars* are responsible for the continuation of war. A written statement is unnecessary, however; you can figure out for yourself my opinions on these affairs. [. . .]

Among other things, two days ago I delivered a lecture on the development of the Talmud in front of a rather large crowd in Erfurt. I tried my best to explain the spiritual foundation of the text in as clear a manner as possible (which is not without its use for a lot of people). Beginning with an internal metaphysical concept (constituting the spiritual essence of the Talmud) in connection with the historical development, I wanted to elaborate on the gradual and necessary formation of the Talmud. The idea of the lecture is surely not a bad one, and I'll continue to give it some thought. As you may know, a number of my eastern European acquaintances like to get together in Erfurt. One is a Bolshevik, or very nearly so, and the others are Zionists. In Heidelberg I met the most perfect incarnation of the truest and deepest essence of Judaism, in the form of a Russian Talmud scholar. [. . .]

I think I must have written to you that I did a translation of the Lamentations, though it's different from my accursed translation of the Song of Songs.[67] I made it a linguistic philosophical study. What are you up to, old man, besides training to throw hand grenades!! Recently I heard a magnificent, infinitely deep soldier's expression: "to sit inside the ass of eternity." Do you know it? Write soon to this address. A warm Shalom.

Your Gerhard Scholem

TO GRETE BRAUER

Jena, March 7, 1918

Dear Grete,

I can't tell you what an effort it took to write you this letter; I only know that it has precipitated a crisis that will either bring perfect purity to my life or else shatter it into pieces. This letter caused me such physical distress that I traveled to Halle just to post it; I couldn't have done it from here. It's a very good thing I wrote it, though. You may gather from what I write now that the few words in your letter released me from the enormous tension that was tearing me to shreds. I still cannot speak with you as is ultimately necessary, and I have no doubt that even now the most vital things can be said only in silence (and not in writing; I would have to look you in the eye). Yet despite everything, I address myself to your heart. Without question, you will grasp a number of things that I cannot openly express. As amazing as it seems, the more you are surrounded by walls and locks, the more certain I become in reaching into the center of your loneliness, directly and immediately. I ask for only one thing, Grete: take every word that I say in complete and utter earnestness. I'm not playing a rhetorical game with you. Keep in mind how sacred language is to me. Perhaps you would understand me better if you yourself were not largely the object of these words and the meanings that lie within them (and now I will not speak about any-one else *at all*). There is no one else in the world with whom I can discuss you, and for this reason I must necessarily turn to you.

You already have in your hand the most important evidence of my condition. I wanted to speak with you when I gave you the Lamenta-tions. But then I did something I cannot justify and which prevented me from understanding my own mute desires. I was, at the time, in the same state I'm in now—one can even say that it's gotten worse, because the colossal contradictions that push me to make a decision have mean-while increased.

Dear Grete, bear in mind that I cannot write everything that I need to. Since entering the military, as early as April or May of last year, I've been filled with agitated emotions that have placed my entire life under their command, forming the real center of my life in a way I never imagined possible. Shall I name the three inexhaustible sources of these emotions? I myself am the first, and I need not add how this enabled the two other sources to open themselves to me. And these sources flowed from my friend Walter Benjamin and from you, quite literally the only people who have ever affected the very center of my being. I won't discuss Walter here. I will point out only that our absolutely and wholly positive relationship forms one side of the ever-growing contra-diction that has compelled me to speak. If comparisons can be drawn in such matters (which is in fact impossible; they're two wholly different spheres that complement each other), then one would have to conclude that the things I owe to you are more important. I trust you understand me. In the deepest sense, it is the pure power of your *existence* rather than some comment or the like that has kept me healthy during this entire time and has single-handedly prevented me from being consumed by the glowing embers—through which I have lived and in which continue to exist, since everything I am describing here has served to only intensify them. You are just as old as Walter, yet the age disparity between us affects me very differently from the one that exists between me and Walter. Herein lies the reason I have *always* been ill at ease with you outwardly, while in truth (inwardly) there was no one else I could speak to with such immediacy. I've never done anything but take from you; I can't say what I have given in return. You made me good. I was simply incapable of having bad thoughts any longer. I am now unable to speak about these things at any length. All of this should simply explain to you why you have the power to heal my existence, which has fallen ill because of a terribly serious mistake. Since I arrived in Jena, I've fallen into my present state. [. . .] I fell into the condition manifested in my Lamentations. You'll grasp the deepest meaning of the Lamentations when you read them as a *confession* of my state—as it no doubt is. You will appreciate the stubbornness of my condition from the fact that in the past few days I've continued to work on the translation, hoping for further results. If I do not free myself soon from this atmosphere, I will never get out. I'm pouring out my troubles to you, Grete. What else can I do? You can return to me my language by not refusing me your being. [. . .]

Regards, Your Gerhard

FROM GRETE BRAUER

Berlin, March 11, 1918

Dear friend,

I'm sorry that what I have to tell you I can't say face to face, without the mediation of a letter. I have no choice, however, so I won't go on without admitting how hard it is for me. Things must be clear and open between us. Even if knowledge of the truth is painful to you, there must be no misunderstanding. I can't help it; I'm compelled by some inner law and am unable to free myself. You failed to consider in your letter that it may not be in my power to be there for you and to give you what you ask and hope for. [. . .] Please understand me, this is not something that depends upon my will. I can't, even if I wanted to with all of my power. The reason lies in a different sphere, over which I have no control. I want to continue being your friend, as I have been until now. But I cannot give you any more. I have full confidence that you will be strong. And when you think about me, consider one thing: that I too live under a burden that often seems impossibly heavy.

Grete

FROM LUDWIG STRAUSS[68]

Berlin, March 15, 1918

Dear Herr Scholem,

I cannot say much about your translation of the Lamentations and the accompanying essay. I compared it with Luther's translation and noticed that it has the effect of a completely different work. It has become clear to me, based on my own knowledge of the Luther translation and now the impression of the original produced by your translation, that the Lutheran Lamentations present us with something bourgeois and Germanized (reaching into the content itself), which in turn demonstrates the utter necessity of your translation. Luther's otherwise extraordinary work of poetry doesn't contain a trace of "lamentation" in your sense of the word. Your translation, taken as a work of German literature, seems to me really quite lovely—and deeply moving, to boot.

I agree with everything in your essay that I could understand. It makes sense to me to characterize the nature of language in the Lamentations as language's outer boundary. I can grasp the metaphysical meaning you attach to this without calling this "knowledge." A number of things remain obscure for me, such as when you speak of the mystical laws of the people.

TO LUDWIG STRAUSS

Jena, March 24, 1918

Dear Herr Strauss,

[. . .] The comments you made on the Lamentations pleased me greatly. [. . .] The theme continues to occupy me. If I could, I would add to the essay a number of fundamentally important chapters (or rather sketches, since the essay is more of an apodictic table of contents). Above all, I would include something on the definition of silence from the (metaphysical) perspective of the philosophy of language, where natural silence and refraining from speech are a world apart. Furthermore, I would add one on the relationship between lamentation and music [. . .] and another, nearly separate essay on the nonacoustic, visible lamentations of nature (for instance, the expressions of dogs, landscapes, and the like). Walter Benjamin has already thought and written very profound things about this.

I have but a single important comment to offer you regarding the mystical laws of the people. I take Tradition to be the only absolute object of mysticism, which is the reason I call the mystical laws of the people genuine mystical laws. This statement—which you can find in the essay—no doubt requires a more exhaustive and expansive formulation than I provided. You should recall that the essay attempts only to give a linguistic philosophical definition of lamentation as succinctly as possible. Like hacking through a jungle. I believe I have done so *in nuce*. [. . .]

A warm Shalom, Your Gerhard Scholem

TO ESCHA BURCHHARDT[69]

Jena, March 24, 1918

Dear Escha,

Even though I haven't said so expressly, you will have gathered from my silence that I'm not doing well. When your last letter arrived I was entirely incapable of reading it. I've had a difficult time since my return from Heidelberg three weeks ago. I traveled to Berlin with your unread letter in my pocket. There, in the course of two days, a terrifying explosion finally liberated me. Now I need absolute solitude in order to regain my health and to become a human being once again. I have finally read your *very* sincere letter. Astonishingly, it corresponds with what I myself have just been through and have thought. My relationship to most people (in truth, to everyone—with two exceptions) has been inwardly untenable because it has been built upon a lie. Only *very* good people have the power and greatness to extricate themselves from such a flaw *all by themselves*. [. . .]

Your Gerhard Scholem

March 30, 1918

[. . .] I have read your essay, the one you sent my wife, three times. The third time, we read it together. My wife plans to thank you for it herself. I personally owe you special thanks because, without your knowing that I wrestled with the same problem two years ago, you have made a significant contribution to clarifying it for me. Having read your essay, I now see the problem as follows: on the basis of my nature as a Jew, the inherent code, the "completely autonomous order," of the lament and of mourning, became obvious to me. Without reference to Hebrew literature, which, as I now know, is the proper subject of such an analysis, I applied the following question to the *Trauerspiel* in a short essay entitled "The Role of Language in *Trauerspiel* and Tragedy": "How can language as such fulfill itself in mourning and how can it be the expression of mourning?" In so doing, I arrived at an insight that approximates yours in its particulars and in its entirety. At the same time, however, I wore myself out to no avail studying a relationship whose actual circumstances I am only now beginning to divine. [. . .]

Just a short word on your translation. We—my wife and I—have the same thing to say about it that we previously said about your translation of the Song of Solomon. In the final analysis, your translation (of course, I am unable to judge its relationship to the Hebrew, but I have total confidence in you in this regard) has the character of an academic study in terms of its relationship to German. The issue in your translation is not, as it were, to save a text for the German language, but rather to relate it to German in terms of what is correct. In this respect, you have not allowed yourself to be inspired by the German language. [. . .]

TO WERNER KRAFT

Jena, April 8, 1918

Dear Werner,

Thanks for the two packages that arrived today. [. . .] I saw in them a copy of the letter Benjamin once wrote to you after our conversation about Judaism. Back then, he read the contents of the letter aloud to me. I recall with amusement how, as he told me, you responded to the conversation by claiming that only a woman could have stimulated his turn toward Judaism. Even now when I think about it, I have to laugh. Haven't you ever given him a more intelligent answer than this? How unbearably painful it is for me, especially now, not to be together with Walter Benjamin, when the two of us could devote ourselves to such great things! And now more than ever, after the terrible past three months. [. . .]

Gerhard

TO WERNER KRAFT

Jena, April 13, 1918

Dear Kraft,

[. . .] On Thursday, April 11, Dora Benjamin gave birth to a son. I can't begin to describe the thrilling and (I don't know why) *healing* effect the news had on me. I can't stop thinking about it. Today I organized a quiet celebration for myself, in the good clothes I very rarely wear. The entire world around me was festive. To congratulate the parents for the child is not actually correct; instead, I congratulated the child for the parents. [. . .]

With best regards from your Gerhard

TO ESCHA BURCHHARDT

Muri (near Bern), June 21, 1918

Dear Escha,

Thank you so much for your letter. You are of course correct when you noticed something constrained in my first card (now I no longer remember a thing I wrote). Whether this constraint has now subsided— or whether I've simply become more relaxed here—I can't say. You'll have to decide for yourself, if possible, on the basis of this letter. I did not arrive in Switzerland as unburdened as I'd hoped. When I sit here alone in my attic room, I'm overcome by sad memories—for which I paid a heavy price last year. Here, I am for all practical purposes completely alone. Besides my friend and his wife, I have no one here, and

I can really burrow into myself. I can work, think, take walks, or cry, just as I please. Now I know—after various experiences—that I left my childhood behind when I departed from Germany. Or you could perhaps say that sometimes I stir up waves like the sea, and, as with the ocean, there is no one to watch. Just as well. I can only wait humbly and see what will come of all of this commotion. I'll become as hard as granite—which is the only way to avoid being consumed in flames. My room can put up with a lot . . . The landscape stretches out before me; its quietness and compactness do wonders for me. I live in a village. I see no houses at all, and a wheat field is outside my window. I take flight into the countryside when I'm not doing well. This is the first time in my life I have had this stupendous opportunity. [. . .]

TO AHARON HELLER

Muri, June 23, 1918

Dear friend,

I can tell you openly the reasons for my reticence, if you haven't already guessed. I didn't want to write to you, in particular, until I could be fully open. Silence is better than writing a letter that would have inevitably given you a false impression of me. I should tell you directly why I was unable to speak frankly. Never before have I been in such desperate shape, inwardly, as in the period following my arrival here— or rather, since I began to come to grips with myself. Agreeable external circumstances allowed me to endure this all alone (which is the reason I haven't tried to establish contact with Erich Brauer, beyond a failed attempt during my first days here—I didn't want to irk him with all my misery). I see no one other than Walter Benjamin and his wife. I sit completely withdrawn in my attic room above the fields—like Agnon's Torah scribe, minus his peace of mind.[71] For weeks I have feared the worst, and I feel crushed by a tormenting uncertainty about whether my recovery, obtained through Herculean efforts and at the most exacting price, will prove permanent. Here, of course, I can do whatever I want: I can work, think, take walks, or cry. And I assure you that I have made particularly intense and despairing use of the first two. I also know quite well that I would be defenseless if my genius (I cannot use a lesser word for it) were to let me down. I now live as I did last summer, which is all the more terrifying since I must now fend off real, not feigned, madness. The only thing that keeps me going, in a grand and masterful way, is the indescribably magnificent landscape around me here. To show it my gratitude, I have invested my best efforts in philosophically coming to grips with the essence of a landscape, an undertaking that for me seems to have enormous value. If all goes well, I'll end it with a commentary on Psalms 104 you will find astounding. [. . .]

With warm regards from your Gerhard Scholem

TO ESCHA BURCHHARDT

Muri, July 23, 1918

Dear Escha,

I have devoted this evening to you and to both of your letters (I can't say when they were posted, since you are not in the habit of dating them). They have waited impatiently for an answer that has just come to me.

I will gladly help you from afar in whatever way possible, particularly given that you are one of the few people (even this is an exaggeration) I would like to encourage with my solidarity. It may well be that you are now in much need of it. [. . .]

Don't worry about the fact that you never seem to answer my letters. To tell you the truth, I almost never expect a reply from the letters I write, and almost never get one!! There is also something else at work here. My letters seek not to elicit a reply, but to be absorbed into your wordless silence—or, if you'll allow me to use the most appropriate expression, into your love. I hope that your life, which is invisible to me, is the reply. You may laugh or write me off as conceited, but I know perfectly well that you have to love me in order to write me a perfect letter. To date, the only letter I have ever received (I am still young) which I regard as a perfect answer and perfect letter was a ten-line missive from the friend I am now together with here.[72] [. . .]

Currently, I'm quite busy at the University of Muri, where my work won't end until August 15;[73] the semester in Bern already ended a week ago. We study Cohen two hours a day.[74] [. . .] In addition, I'm working on the Book of Isaiah for six to eight hours daily, in the most comprehensive fashion. I can already give a truly philosophical seminar on it. The most tremendous things have come to me in *every* respect—regarding not only Isaiah (this least of all, since the procedure here is that at the beginning one can just ask questions), but primarily the things that come to mind through it—above all, lamentations; the philosophy of the Hebrew language (oh, if only someday these things could be the focus of my worthy labors!); and philology, of which I have in fact developed an extraordinary conception and which should be discussed only with the greatest reverence. Philology is truly a secret science and the only legitimate form of historical science that has existed until now. It is the greatest confirmation of my view of the central importance of Tradition, though of course in a new sense of the word.

Your Gerhard Scholem

TO ESCHA BURCHHARDT

Bern, Weissensteiner Strasse 87, October 26, 1918

Dear Escha,

[. . .] All I have to say about my life and work here is how tranquil and diligent they are. Take note of my address! The heating is bearable, mostly because the weather is rather warm now. My situation still remains somewhat precarious; I'll probably have to move out in the next few weeks, and I have no idea if I'll find a decent apartment. The university has been closed (that is, hasn't reopened) because of an outbreak of influenza. Though I still don't believe it, they say it will reopen at the beginning of November, in which case I'll have to busy myself with a lot of mathematics. I'll be studying Greek with the wife of my friend, a most exciting prospect for which I've already done the necessary spadework. I also read mountains of books, thick and thin, on Jewish scholarship. I'm considering making the acquaintance of a famous local Jewish scholar to see if I can profit from him. Otherwise, I continue to live as I always have. My friend is writing his dissertation, and we often discuss the issues involved in it. I know no one else besides my friend who has become such a teacher to me, owing not only to the ingeniousness of his mind, but also to the sterling purity of his existence. Not only has the past half-year liberated me from what is negative, after the torment of last winter—it's also been positively redemptive. [. . .]

Gerhard Scholem

FROM BETTY SCHOLEM

October 31, 1918

Dear child,

I can't tell you much, since censorship is still flourishing. I can only refer you to the newspapers, which at least speak clearly. Since all of our allies have fallen away, one hopes that peace has come closer, and from this perspective I'm very happy about what happened in Vienna.[75] Here, we've all been felled by the flu. Perlstein and the manager, too, so that father must do everything himself. The times are really quite nerve-racking—I've bitten my fingernails down to the quick. Irma had a love affair, and Aunt Grete has been crying.

Kisses, Mum

TO LUDWIG STRAUSS

Bern, November 1, 1918

Dear Herr Strauss,

[. . .] I live in total isolation here and never meet up with the local "Zionists." Benjamin, his wife, and a member of Jung Juda are my only acquaintances.[76] For this reason, I'm working well and with a great deal of joy. I've begun to learn Greek. Since an outbreak of influenza has temporarily kept the university from opening, I have a lot of time for Jewish studies. I still think I'm on the right track. As always, I remain completely absorbed in the literature of lamentation.[77] I have translated and worked through all of the biblical lamentations with the exception of Job (in particular, I should draw your attention to Chapter 1 of Joel and Chapter 3 of Job), and am now able to elaborate my views on the subject with ever more precision. I have now discovered medieval poetry, which is immeasurably more beautiful and poignant than the modern sentimental babble of Canan and the like (in modern literature I

think only prose is possible).[78] Among medieval works, I found songs
of lamentation of unheard-of power—for instance, those of Abraham
ibn Esra on the destruction of the communities during the time of the
Almohads and others.[79] Reflecting on the system of rules in the genre
of lamentations leads me ever deeper into fundamental problems concerning the philosophy of history—precisely the spot where I end up
in all of my other studies, such as those on the Bible; the philosophy of
religion in the Middle Ages, Cohen, and Hirsch; rules of pronunciation;
and, last but not least, the Kabbalah.[80] The essential categories of Judaism
are becoming more and more evident to me. I have come a great distance
in the past half-year, and I at least know for certain what it's all about.
This is a good beginning. Above all, I am preoccupied with three ideas,
along with their corresponding categorical connections (the first and perhaps final task of a Jewish thinker is to systematically establish internal
links between them)—namely, the ideas of doctrine, messianic time, and
justice. I've worked especially diligently on the last, and I think I have
uncovered a great deal. Not only can I define "justice" systematically,
but its relation to "canon," "doctrine," and "messianic time" has also
become far less foggy. The most decisive things flow from all of this.
[. . .]

Sincerely yours, Gerhard Scholem

FROM BETTY SCHOLEM

Berlin, November 11, 1918

Dear child,

What happened was no laughing matter. On Saturday, father and I
were on the Schloss Bridge when we suddenly found ourselves in the
middle of all the shooting. Well, I got my legs into gear! [. . .] After
everything seemed to quiet down, I went with your father to see a bit
of the revolution. As soon as we innocently arrived at the Lustgarten,
shots rang out from the Schlossplatz. The shots rapidly grew into the
powerful rattling of machine-gun fire. Everyone panicked and ran across
the Schloss Bridge, with the two of us in the middle of the pack. Can
you imagine that this should happen to me! My bones are still shivering.
Yesterday the situation still appeared ominous, as if the Independents

could seize control of the government and set up an autocracy.[81] Thanks to the energy of the Workers-and-Soldiers Council, however, an agreement was reached and events can now unfold without a civil war breaking out. Today the situation already looks better. The general strike planned for today will allow all of the workers to participate in the assemblies, but tomorrow everyone will return to work. All of our workers showed up for work as usual, but at noon your father sent them away to attend the assemblies. Hermann's printing house is protected by the authorities because it prints food ration coupons and money—which means that we're protected, too. The red placard of the Workers-and-Soldiers Council hanging at the entrance to our shop says, "Communal Institution! To Be Protected!" Soldiers with red armbands stand near the doors. All organizations and institutions have been smart enough to side with the new government, so that it can, by hook or by crook, maintain public order and, above all, prevent hunger. We thought the difficult times were behind us. Now it seems they've just started. The conditions set by the armistice are truly inhuman. But since they were imposed prior to the kaiser's abdication, one can only hope they'll be made less stringent for the Republic. [. . .]

Kisses, Mum

TO ESCHA BURCHHARDT

Bern, November 23, 1918

My dearest Escha,

Your letter took a mere three days to get here and was not held up by the censor, so it seems that communication has become significantly simpler and faster. If they check mail only for thousand-mark notes, you can write with a good conscience as long as you please. That surely won't be banned. [. . .]

There is a crystal-clear difference between my position on the war and my position on the revolution. I confess that I participate in neither; still, I rejected the war from the start, whereas with the revolution I at least look on as a spectator. There's no doubt that it has historical justice on its side, and as such I take it into my field of vision—nothing more than this, though also nothing less. And I will consider it my duty not to abandon my "benevolent neutrality" so long as the new order does not impinge on the role of the spirit. More I cannot do, for the simple reason that this revolution (even if it naturally has something messianic about it) is not identical to the theological one. *Joining* this revolution is something I would regard as the greatest task of all. [. . .]

Your Gerhard

FROM BETTY SCHOLEM

Berlin, November 29, 1918

My dear child,

[. . .] We are transferring to you the equivalent of 1,100 marks, or just over 750 francs. It's your birthday present, with 5 francs earmarked for gingerbread. Oh, my precious son! Don't carry the mammon openly for every thief to see. Put it in the canton's bank. Our sincerest congratulations that you have reached the age of legal accountability—and eligibility to vote.

It's become awful here in Berlin. [. . .] The supplies have all run out— all eaten away. We live literally from hand to mouth. Food supplies have not yet appeared on the black market. Only cigarettes, and then only in bulk quantities.

Kisses, Mum

FROM BETTY SCHOLEM

Berlin, December 11, 1918

My dear child,

The birthday card you sent on the twenty-fourth finally arrived on the fourth of December—the first piece of mail to arrive unopened. Your wishes that the situation would soon improve couldn't have been further off the mark. The total chaos we have here can scarcely get any worse. No one commands, no one obeys. Conditions are miserable. The only surprising thing is the way the sense of order among the population keeps the minutiae of public life from falling apart. Things somehow continue to run. I'm deeply disillusioned with the Social Democratic party. Gone is my earlier belief that it is politically mature enough to govern; it vacillates as much as the old regime, or even more. In no time at all, Herr Müller from the Executive Committee deluded himself into thinking he was some kind of Caesar. A handful of Spartacans now threaten to completely disrupt all economic life, which would only bring everything to a grinding halt.[82] A dictator would then eventually appear on the scene; in our case, this means the Entente, and we in Berlin fully expect enemy occupation. It's really hopeless. A few days ago the Spartacus people staged a massacre on Chaussee Strasse, and of course they tried to shift the blame. They drive around with machine guns, and the government's so weak that it permits this!! Right-wing parties have been distributing leaflets inciting Jew-baiting, a time-honored trick to divert popular outrage. The blockade has been tightened to such an extent because of the measures taken by Marshal Foch that we no longer get a thing from the neutral powers, and so we're facing hunger. What do people in Switzerland say about acts of revenge against an innocent people? As always, the big shots have all slipped away and the little man gets strung up. Reinhold is still stationed near the bridge to Cologne, on this side of the Rhine. Every day or so he telegraphs us. On November 30, Erich was released from the Ammunition Unit and was enlisted right away by the War Ministry's Department of Economic Demobilization.[83] [. . .]

Kisses, Mum

PART II **UNLOCKING THE GATES, 1919–1932**

Scholem in Palestine, 1924. Courtesy of the Jewish National and University Library, Jerusalem, Gershom Scholem Archive (Arc. 4o 1599).

The rumor has recently begun to circulate around Munich that, using black magic, I can create mice and elephants. For now, however, I can conjure up only flawless texts no one can top—and with *white* magic, which is something completely permissible and free of sorcery! By the time I take my exams, though, I hope to work up to bigger things by creating camels and the like! In any event, I would recommend the greatest caution in any future dealings with me!!

—Letter to Betty and Arthur Scholem, June 14, 1920

SCHOLEM WAS STILL IN SWITZERLAND in April 1919, when his mother Betty wrote him a note suggesting that he stay put, far from the upheavals of postwar Germany. "Enjoy yourself in this terrifying world," she counseled. This was the first sign of a long collaboration between the gifted son and the keenly observant and articulate mother. Chaos had broken out in Germany: bread lines stretched around city blocks, rebellious soldiers filled the streets, and political unrest baffled people long accustomed to law, order, and good behavior. Betty must have felt that her son's plans to leave Germany were not so farfetched after all.

By the time Gerhard returned home at the end of the year, the revolution had already crested and a new democratic republic in Germany was established, though never firmly.[1] Putsch attempts and economic decline continued to polarize society, and Jews more often than not were caught between the factions, clinging to a rapidly shrinking liberal center.

The conflicts of the day ran directly through the Scholem family. Like most soldiers who fought on the front lines, Reinhold was aghast at what he saw when he returned to Germany. Much of the blame, he thought, rested with the socialists and revolutionaries. He promptly took up membership in the right-wing, nationalistic Volkspartei and began to proclaim the virtues of the "German Idea"—a common conservative shibboleth which he used to attack the supposedly effete "coffeehouse socialists."[2] Werner and his wife responded to the "new Germany" by becoming committed Communists. It goes without saying that the ensuing family feuds took a heavy toll on Arthur Scholem's already failing health.

Weimar Germany brought more than political imbroglios; it also produced an extraordinary cultural flowering. It was the Germany of Kurt Tucholsky's stinging satires and of political cabaret. Bertolt Brecht and Kurt Weill transformed German drama, while the Bauhaus made its mark on city planning, architecture, and industrial design. In literature, the exoticism of the prewar period assumed a different and darker tone. Avant-garde writers took less interest in the savagery of "primitive" peoples than in the violence of "civilized" Europeans.

For Jewish intellectuals in particular, the new order offered more room for movement than the far more rigid *Kaiserreich*. Those with talent, drive, and luck had a relatively unencumbered path to the stage, the feuilleton page, the silver screen, and the bestseller lists. And many Jews turned to Jewish themes in their work. Germany's popular literary journal *Die Weltbühne* published tales based on the Talmud, with catchy titles such as "Akiba's Wife" and "The Rabbi and the Robber," written by Moritz Heimann, the chief editor at Fischer publishing house. The Kabbalah grew in literary appeal, owing to its associations with the occult. The illustrious German publisher Ernst Rowohlt brought out Josef Kastein's *Sabbatai Sevi: The Messiah of Ismir*. The story reads like a novel, with a gripping narrative and alluring chapter titles ("The Prophet and the Whore," "Tumult," "Echo," "Catastrophe," "Death Shivers"). Another publisher, the patron of avant-garde literature Kurt Wolff, made a small fortune from a bestseller called *The Golem*, by Gustav Meyrink. A film based on the life of the legendary Rabbi Loew of Prague brought audiences flocking to cinemas throughout Germany.

Scholem paid little attention to the "Jewish awakening" within the cultural avant-garde. His literary tastes were on the conservative side; he preferred the German writers Jean Paul and Paul Scheerbart. Pleasure reading consisted mostly of detective novels, a lifelong habit he had picked up from Benjamin. When he did take notice of "Jewish" modernism, he usually panned it for lack of philological seriousness. The single exception to this rule was his exuberant appraisal of Franz Rosenzweig's *Stern der Erlösung* (Star of Redemption; 1921). His critique of

Ernst Bloch's *Geist der Utopie* (Spirit of Utopia; second edition, 1920) was more in accord with his standard line: instead of following the long, weary, and very lonely path into Hebrew and Jewish texts, Bloch, he charged, had taken the easy way out, a short-cut to Judaism.

Scholem had his own revolution to carry out and was impatient with those who spoke in the name of Judaism but were unwilling to pay the stiff price it demanded. And carrying out his revolution would require far more knowledge and better-honed instruments than the perfunctory bit of Jewish scholarship he had picked up on his own and in Berlin's Scheunenviertel. He needed to study. As he half-jokingly explained to his mother in 1919, he first planned to become "Gershom" (changing his name from Gerhard), "then a Jewish philosopher, and finally an angel in seventh heaven."[3]

Upon his return to Germany, Scholem enrolled as a student at the university in Munich, intending to write his dissertation on the Kabbalah's theory of language. He chose as his topic a critical edition of the oldest extant kabbalistic text, the *Sefer ha-Bahir*.[4] Even Arthur liked the idea—so much that he gave him a monthly stipend. Compared to Werner's communism, his youngest son's career choice seemed to him the paragon of responsibility.

Scholem arrived in Munich at a stormy time. A brief revolution had erupted in 1919, and ended only after the German army invaded the city to "restore order." "Order" in this case was a right-wing purge, with thousands of deaths and arrests. A young corporal who took part in the suppression, Adolf Hitler, embarked on a political career with beer-house speeches denouncing the Weimar Republic and its Jews.

But Scholem hardly noticed. With civil war still in the air, he pored over kabbalistic manuscripts housed in the city library. In his free time he often strolled through the city's gardens and spoke Hebrew with the novelist S. J. Agnon, who was also in the city at that time.

Many of Scholem's prewar friendships did not survive his change in lifestyle. With all his powers devoted to preparing for his journey to Zion, he ceased to be interested in those who had no desire to follow him. A broken heart brought on by his unrequited love for Grete Brauer led him to Escha Burchhardt, with whom he read in Hebrew—as a kind of first date—Moses Maimonides' dense philosophical tract *Guide for the Perplexed*, originally written in Arabic around 1190.

Scholem's career quickly took off. Besides translating passages from the Bible and short stories by Agnon, he published two theoretical articles: the first, "Lyric of the Kabbalah?" (written in German), was published in 1921 in Martin Buber's *Der Jude;*[5] the second, "A Reply to Mr. Lev on the Method of Studying the Hebrew Language" (written in Hebrew), was published in 1922 as a letter to the editors of the journal for the Jewish university students' movement.[6] In early 1922 Scholem's dissertation on the Kabbalah won him high praise and he received his degree *summa cum laude.*

In the spring of 1922 Scholem returned to Berlin as a success story. On the strength of his dissertation, his Munich professors immediately offered to sponsor his *Habilitation,* which in the German academic system was the final step in the long road toward a professorship. This naturally delighted his pragmatic father. Embarking on such a career path, Arthur pronounced, would cure his son of his "youthful foolishness."[7]

What he failed to notice is something the German philosopher Hans-Georg Gadamer grasped many years later: in *Buch Bahir,* the book based on his dissertation, Scholem approached his topic not with the "skeptical distance" of the professional "deciphering something foreign," but with a "shocking degree of identification." The Kabbalah had seized the "researcher's imagination and sharp reasoning with an unrelenting grasp."[8]

If Arthur had read "Lyrik der Kabbalah?" he would have realized that solid scholarship was his son's first step to Zion, not a ticket to a German academic career. As the article put it, only within the Hebrew-speaking community in Palestine was it now possible "to see things from within" and to "rebuild the entire structure of scholarship in light of the historical experience of the Jew who lives amid his people."[9]

After completing his dissertation Scholem spent several months back in Berlin, where he prepared for emigration. He also taught a course on the history of Jewish mysticism, under the auspices of the city's Jewish Adult Education Program. In his free time he engaged in long personal conversations with Benjamin, who had also returned to Berlin.

Before leaving Germany, Scholem went to Frankfurt for the summer of 1922. One of Buber's disciples, Ernst Simon, invited him to teach a course at Franz Rosenzweig's Freies Jüdisches Lehrhaus (Free House of Study). Like most other Jews in his circle, Rosenzweig came from a household where Judaism had lost all content. Rich, handsome, and endowed with astonishing intellectual talents, he seemed destined for success in the German academic world. But like Scholem, he set out to rediscover Judaism instead. Simon, too, had been brought up in a rich assimilated Frankfurt family; he turned to an exploration of his "Jewishness," and then became a follower of Buber, during the war. By 1922 he had mastered Hebrew, adopted Orthodox tradition Jewish practice, and developed a close relationship with Rosenzweig. At the Lehrhaus, Scholem lectured on Agnon, the book of Daniel, and the Kabbalah. He also led small seminars based on readings from Jewish mystical, apocalyptic, and midrashic texts.

The final push that impelled Scholem to leave Germany came from Escha Burchhardt and Hugo Bergmann, both of whom had already settled in Jerusalem. Bergmann emigrated in 1920, following Buber's old dream of establishing a Jewish university. Like Buber, he believed that Jews needed a university because the Jewish genius needed a home, so he took his own substantial genius to Jerusalem. But he had to content himself with building a national Jewish library, since there was little money available. Escha began working as an assistant to Bergmann, whom she strove to influence on Scholem's behalf. Bergmann liked what he heard and offered Scholem a fictitious appointment to help him secure a residence permit from the British.

In February 1923 Scholem shipped to Palestine his 2,000-volume Hebrew library (including 600 volumes of kabbalistic texts), along with his volumes of Scheerbart and Jean Paul and his collection of detective novels. He followed his books several months later. When he arrived in Jerusalem after the two-week journey, he found temporary lodging in the Bergmann home.

Scholem never looked back after he left Germany—an understandable reaction, in view of the economic situation there. His departure coincided with the height of the great inflation, which wiped out his family's savings. The printing business stayed afloat only because Arthur Scholem got a contract to print money—a thriving enterprise when new bills, needing ever more digits, lost value overnight. Werner was continuing to be another source of worry for Arthur's weak heart. In 1922 he became a Communist deputy to the Prussian Diet, where he slavishly defended the Moscow party line. Two years later he was elected to the Reichstag as its youngest member. His sharp tongue, now exercised before the nation, made him a well-known public figure. For those belonging to the small Nazi party, Werner embodied everything they thought was wrong with the Republic.

Throughout the 1920s, Betty kept Gershom abreast of family gossip and the various political changes in Germany. She reported to him on family picnics and outings, funerals, marriages, births, the improving German economy, the nasty Berlin weather. At the beginning of 1925 Arthur died of a heart attack; Reinhold took over the business. Werner got himself expelled from the Communist party and began to study law. After 1929 Betty's main subject was the economic crisis in Germany and how it drove the family into bankruptcy, robbing them of business, home, car, security. Throughout these years she also faithfully sent Gershom a steady supply of marzipan and pork sausage, scarce commodities in far-off Jerusalem.

The other primary correspondence Scholem maintained with his contacts back in Germany was with Benjamin. He provided details concerning his life in rustic Jerusalem, and Benjamin did the same regarding his own far less sedentary existence, which shifted between Berlin, Paris, and Capri.

Scholem considered the years 1923–1928 a time of complete openness and trust between them. He continually urged Benjamin to learn Hebrew and settle in Palestine. Benjamin coquettishly kept his friend's hopes alive, but in truth he never earnestly entertained any such plans. In 1925 he gave up on an academic career after his professors at the University of Frankfurt rejected his *Habilitation* as incomprehensible. This failure left him with few options other than a career as a freelance writer and critic. For the next several years he traveled across Europe, wrote for various newspapers and journals, and published a number of works. But the lack of a steady income kept him in a state of insecurity and anxiety.

Enter Zionism. In 1927 Scholem returned to Europe on a research trip. The two met in Paris to discuss Benjamin's future. Scholem showed up with Judah Magnes, an American-born pacifist rabbi and the chancellor of the Hebrew University, whom he hoped would provide his friend with the financial help necessary to allow him to study Hebrew. In the course of the conversation, Benjamin confided to Magnes that he could no longer find a focus for his linguistic, philosophical ideas within German or French. He needed to find "texts of canonical importance" so that he could, through commentary, "develop his philosophical thoughts." Through his friendship with Scholem, he continued, it had "become ever clearer" that in order to "arrive at an entirely new level" he would have to devote himself to Hebrew and Hebrew scriptures. Calling himself a "metaphysician," he informed Magnes and Scholem that he now wanted to study Hebrew texts and to make the "religious world of Judaism a central object of his own work." In the words of his enthusiastic friend, "it was a living confession testifying to the chances of a new birth for the Jewish people and Judaism."[10]

Benjamin got the stipend, announced his imminent departure for Palestine, then postponed it. He repeated the cycle of promises and retreats until he finally sorted out his financial problems. In the meantime, he fell in love with a Communist from Riga, a woman named Asja Lacis. By 1929 Scholem no longer had any illusions about his friend's professed intention of moving to Palestine.

In his letters to his family and Benjamin, Scholem not only responded to what they wrote but also offered descriptions of his own life in Palestine. He had a lot to recount. The country was a backwater of the British Empire, still awakening after four hundred years of Ottoman somnolence. English civil servants built roads, organized an efficient postal service, and did their best to get the economy moving. Still, there was little they could do about the searing summers, the droughts, and the raw wet winter cold that easily invaded the unheated apartments. Nor could they keep a lid on the political unrest that constantly threatened to boil over.

Shortly after arriving in the city, Scholem married Escha. They moved into an Arab-built house just outside Mea Shearim, a neighborhood filled with pious Jews who mostly considered Zionism the work of Satan and did their best to keep it far from their world by insulating the quarter with a high stone wall. Scholem chose to live there because he had heard that a number of Kabbalists still practiced their ancient tradition; some even engaged in "practical Kabbalah," a form of magic. The sight of a six-foot-tall secular German intellectual and Zionist combing the neighborhood's crooked streets in search of secrets from the survivors of an ancient tradition was no doubt an odd one. Nevertheless, he gradually won their trust because of his zealous devotion to their sacred books. He described himself as "the snake that crawled over the walls of Paradise."[11]

He and his bride soon fled to the secular neighborhood of Rehavia, the home of the city's intellectual caste. Bergmann proved a good friend when he offered to turn Scholem's fictitious job at the library into a real one. Bergmann had found the right man for the job. Scholem knew Hebrew books and loved to gather as many as he could. The job paid the bills and gave him ample time to pursue his own studies, which he carried out with boundless energy.

Such dedication to his work earned him a unique place in the small Zionist society of Jerusalem. For the most part, the Polish and Russian Zionists composed a Spartan caste of militantly secular men and women characterized by khaki shorts, callused hands, and contempt for their pious and weak ancestors. Scholem—dressed as if still in Berlin (tie, gray suit, polished black shoes) and well fed on a steady supply of German sausage and marzipan—was no brawny Super Jew. Moreover, he loved the holy books most Zionists spurned. Chaim Nachman Bialik, the greatest living Hebrew poet of the time and a resident of the pioneer city of Tel Aviv, admired the twenty-six-year-old for combining so many contradictory talents and passions; he considered Scholem the leading candidate to find "the lost key to the locked gate of the temple" of Jewish mysticism.[12] Agnon, who had by now also settled in Jerusalem, paid him a supreme compliment when he endowed a fictional character with Scholem's scholarly features and habits. Dr. Ginath, as the character was named, seemed to approach his crumbling and obscure manuscripts with scholarly distance and objectivity, but in truth he looked to them to find his own "Faust III."[13]

Scholem's career flourished after the founding of the Hebrew University on Mount Scopus in 1925. The university finally got off the ground after Judah Magnes convinced the millionaire Max Warburg, scion of a great Hamburg banking family, to donate half a million dollars for the cause, an enormous sum at the time. Magnes, its first chancellor, offered Scholem one of the first positions at the young university—and in the field of Jewish mysticism to boot, the first chair of its kind in history.

Scholem entered into a phase of remarkable productivity, publishing a torrent of essays in Hebrew journals and newspapers and delivering public lectures on topics ranging from the Kabbalah in seventeenth-century Palestine to the Baal Shem Tov. Back in Germany, Kurt Wolff published two of Scholem's books (*Das Buch Bahir,* which was based on his dissertation, and *Bibliographia Kabbalistica,* a bibliography of works on the Kabbalah). A variety of German journals and newspapers helped spread his reputation by feeding his articles (such as "Alchemy and Kab-

balah," "An Unknown Mystical Text of Moses de León," and "A Kabbalistic Explanation of Prophecy as Self-Encounter") to a market hungry
for Jewish esotericism.

In addition to his many other commitments and relationships (teaching, writing, Escha, two cats, his circle of friends), Scholem became a
member of a political group. It was his first—and last—such involvement. The self-declared "anarchist" grew into a good bourgeois liberal
proclaiming the virtues of tolerance, compromise, reasoned debate,
moderation. After so much rebellion, he finally became a good German
Jew. Bialik called him a *yekke.*[14]

In other words, Scholem navigated his way into the political middle-
of-the-road. And for good reason: the stormy realities of Palestine
quickly freed him of whatever illusions he had brought with him from
Berlin. Violent Arab opposition to Jewish colonization began in earnest in 1920. Many Zionists responded in kind. Zev Jabotinsky, the
charismatic leader of the militant faction, called for a "Jewish legion"
that would provide for self-defense. The Socialists, led by David Ben-
Gurion, rejected Jabotinsky's doctrine of brute power, though only tacti-
cally. They, too, were prepared to take counter-measures against hostile
Arabs.

The worst rioting occurred in 1929, after an incident at the Western
Wall in Jerusalem ignited latent tensions and hatreds. Muslim religious
leaders spread rumors that the Jews planned to destroy the mosque built
on the site of the ancient Temple. The small number of British forces,
who at first watched helplessly as Arabs attacked Jews, were subsequently
overwhelmed by the violence. The disturbance reached a terrible high
point in Hebron, with the massacre of sixty Jews in a synagogue. Troops
eventually quelled the rioting, though bayonets could not slay the poi-
sonous mistrust left in its wake. The Jews were stunned both by the
depth of the hatred that the violence revealed and by the failure of the
British to respond. Now the Socialists followed Jabotinsky's exhortation
to build—as he famously put it—an "iron wall" of defiance against Arab
opposition.

This set the stage for a full-scale conflict. Scholem warily observed
the growth of militancy among his fellow Jews. What disturbed him
even more was the place that tradition and the Bible came to play in
Jewish nationalism. Secular Zionists began to discover how effective
myth could be when used for political ends. Jabotinsky spoke of the

"Kingdom of Israel," and of the "tradition handed down at Mount Sinai" as an instrument in the "active service of liberation"; Ben–Gurion
identified with Joshua and the "conquerors of the Land."[15] Such language opened Scholem's eyes to the many dilemmas involved in trans-
forming a liturgical language into a national one. In a letter he wrote in
1925 to Rosenzweig, he mockingly described Hebrew's "spectral degra-
dation" into the Yishuv's "phantasmagoric Volapuek."[16] Its old messianic powers had vanished, leaving a "vestigial, ghostly language."[17] Hebrew, a language he had long associated with redemption, was ill-suited
for use in military marching orders.

The disturbances convinced Scholem of the need to seek a common
Jewish-Arab solution to the thorny issue of political sovereignty and
popular representation. Along with a number of other mostly Germans
Jews, including Ernst Simon, Hugo Bergmann, and Hans Kohn, he
helped found Brit Shalom ("Covenant of Peace"), a group which declared itself prepared to give up the dream of a Jewish state and of a
Jewish majority in Palestine in order to achieve a binational Jewish-Arab
government. Bergmann called their group "the last flicker of the humanist nationalist flame, at a historical moment when nationalism became,
among the nations, an antihumanist movement."[18]

1919

FROM BETTY SCHOLEM

Berlin, January 7, 1919

My dear child,

At the moment I cannot come up with a longer letter, but at least I can get this postcard off to you. These days are turbulent beyond belief, with constant putsches and riots. Who knows what we have yet to go through. Machine-gun fire rattles while I write!! The Spartacus people have occupied all of the newspaper offices. Your father has just told me that a regiment of the Guards has gone over to their side. In the past few days, they've been agitating for a general strike. Yesterday our workers walked off the job at 10:00 a.m. in order to join in the street demonstrations. This morning they all showed up, and after half an hour their spokesman, a Spartacan, again asked for a day off to demonstrate.

(January 9) The workers held a meeting after your father flatly turned them down, and the older and more rational ones, in particular those who had just returned from the front, well-nigh beat the life out of the Spartacus people. With a vote of everyone else against four (the four Spartacans in the shop), they decided against a further strike. I wrote the beginning of this letter on Tuesday afternoon. I had stayed home because I'd invited Richard and Fritz Pflaum[1] for dinner, and wanted to show off the house all spruced up. Then suddenly the underground and the trams were shut down, and a terrible gun battle broke out on Wilhelm Strasse by the Brandenburg Gate, so that the Pflaums quite understandably feared coming. How were they to get to Grunewald and eventually return home?! [. . .]

On Monday, when I took a walk with Reinhold through Old Berlin to show him the Ephraim House, Nikolai Church, Kroegel, City Hall,

Kloster Strasse, Marien Church, and so on, we kept coming across parades of people demonstrating. They marched in unison, of all things. And why not? They did so for the simple reason that they had all served in the military! [. . .]

Kisses, Mum

FROM BETTY SCHOLEM

Berlin, January 13, 1919

My dear child,

This past week has been incredible, bizarre beyond belief. It now seems that the Spartacans have been all but driven out. Their reign of terror was horrific. Our good old standard clock atop the Spittel Market took a bullet in the dial and heart. Two bullets flew through the shop of our local butcher, ripping a hole in his spleen—luckily the spleen sitting on his shop counter. On Saturday afternoon I went with Dr. Meyer (who wanted to watch the revolution; nothing I could say could keep him from it) down pitch-dark Wall Strasse until we arrived behind the colonnade on Leipzig Strasse. Everything was dark as coal; Leipzig Strasse was entirely hidden by the night; Beuth Strasse was blocked; Dönhoff Square echoed with the sound of shots; everywhere there were ghost-like groups of people. Well, we turned around at once and made our way back. In the evening *Vorwärts* was taken and the Spartacus people vacated the Mosse and Ullstein buildings.[2] Yesterday afternoon we went to take a look at the *Vowärts* building. It looked awful. Shells had ripped through the building from the roof to the cellar. The neighboring buildings and those across the way also look terrible. [. . .]

Your father sends his greetings. He has no time to write. He and Reinhold work without interruption now—there is so much to do! Times are good for the printing business: handbills, proclamations, and placards follow each other in furious succession. [. . .]

Kisses, Mum

FROM BETTY SCHOLEM

Berlin, January 22, 1919

Dearest child,

Our situation is becoming ever more dreary. Dr. Meyer can provide you with plenty of stories about Berlin. There was an attack on the Anhalter train station (of all places) while we were there. Hand grenades shattered the windows of the office where the doctor was peacefully haggling for a ticket. He'll tell you how terrifying the situation was and how courageous I was and how comforting the old official was who assured us that just the day before three people had died in that very hallway. Every day brings a new drama. The electrical plants have been on strike since yesterday, ergo no light. Since morning there has been no power. [. . .]

Kisses, Mum

FROM ERICH BRAUER

Berlin, February 20, 1919

Dear Scholem,

[. . .] The Orthodox pose the old question: What is the position of Zionism with respect to the Torah? Berger replies precisely as you always have: according to him, Zionism will submit to the will of the people.[3] Surely you don't mean "today's people," which is his sense, but instead what we might call the "historically developed people." This, however, is only a deferment of the problem rather than a solution. Moreover, the way Berger answers the question is obviously false. For instance, he says that "if the people demand a struggle against capitalism, I would fight against capitalism." But what if the people demanded the exact opposite—which is precisely the case in the Torah? There are many things in the Torah you may not like. But what would you do if the people demanded it? The phrase "will of the people" is rather vacuous.

Brauer

TO ERICH BRAUER

Bern, February 28, 1919

Dear Erich Brauer,

[. . .] What you said about the relationship to the Torah, at any rate, does not correspond to my own. As I wrote to you, there is *authority,* or rather spiritual authorities, in a *community.* (A community being *not* just any social conglomeration of people, but something that deserves the name. In my opinion, community is the highest thing that exists. It may well never thrive in Palestine; it may be able to flourish only in Zion.) Let us assume that in a proper community, there might still be discord among the inhabitants. In this case, I could not exempt myself from the community's judgment of actions (and actions are the only relevant concern of ethics) unless I wanted to *deny* the community as such. The messianic or theocratic society surely rests upon certain things that form the *criteria* for its existence, whether or not we know what all these things are. I might, of course, decide that a certain community's rules (such as those that permit sexual impurity or murder) contradict the criteria for a community (as a possible authority), in which case this community could not require me to act in any specific way. And since it would not be a community, I would be responsible only for myself. Now, as for the Torah in particular, my views must certainly be no mystery to you. I have always, unambiguously, declared myself to be a skeptic in terms of the concrete manifestation of the Torah today (and I have very specific reasons for this, chief among them being the "unavoidable bending of the rules").[4] Though I don't know if it's of any use, I am always prepared to be convinced one way or the other. And this *concretization* of the Torah (and not what one can call the Torah itself, which is a spiritual power; this sounds silly, and I won't bind myself to the expression—the Torah is an agent, a mediator between realms, an agent through which something breaks and appears: in particular, the idea of the just life and of history) can be an object of dispute only if the theocratic community is an authority for me and, as far as I'm concerned, for everyone who considers himself a part of it. At the moment, I cannot explain why I must reject the statement "There are many things in the Torah that you yourself perhaps cannot go along with"—because for me this is not what it's all about, and, on close inspection, I can't even make sense of the statement (when, that is, I use the term "Torah" as I understand it). Conceptually, we must make more careful distinctions than people do today. Of course, the expression "will of the people" is empty or even false. And so long as the messianic realm has not come—or has not sprung up out of my own research—I will not accept any sort of authority over my actions besides those that we erect on an anarchistic and free basis. [. . .]

Shalom to you, Gershom Scholem

TO BETTY AND ARTHUR SCHOLEM

Locarno, March 21, 1919

Dear parents,

I am very happy. After the semester ended, I went to Locarno [. . .] with a friend who was here for a couple of days. Only four weeks remain of the vacation; the semester begins on the twentieth of April. I'll stay here in Locarno for ten days, and after that I'll return to Bern. I'm doing splendidly. You can't imagine how lovely it is here. I'm constantly reminded of Easter seven years ago, when I was with Father in Lugano. It's quite warm, with occasional snow. We've been amusing ourselves a great deal. I did not gamble at the casino, but my friend won a small fortune—so much that it covered the entire evening for all three of us! Once we went on a marvelous canoe trip, and suddenly a storm came up. After much lively effort, we found ourselves stranded on the shore not far from the bay. I had to swim to land to fetch help, and after running for ten minutes I met a three-man rescue team sent out to bring us home dead or alive! These have truly been wonderful days. The Gotthard is still completely blocked with snow. [. . .]

Gerhard

TO WERNER KRAFT

Bern, April 10, 1919

My dear Werner,

It's certainly been a long time since I wrote you a decent letter, though I've been intending to do so ever since I received yours of March 18. I'm just getting around to it now because Escha Burchhardt, one of our comrades and a friend of mine, was visiting me between the first and the thirty-first of February (maybe I wrote to you about this already, though perhaps not—I can't recall). I dropped everything while she was here, and I was totally incapable of writing letters. I had been together with this girl only once before (last February in Heidelberg), which made those weeks a true thrill for me. We lived together the way I would like to live with all of my friends. She stayed in my room and I slept with Erich Brauer (who has meanwhile left Bern). You can imagine how little studying I got in. We learned a lot of Hebrew together and discussed all sorts of things. She's quite an extraordinary girl, completely and utterly pure, free of warps. It was good for both of us, and we parted grudgingly. We had truly beautiful Sabbaths and maintained an orderly Jewish home. [. . .]

By the way, Walter has now finished his dissertation (on the Romantic conception of art criticism) and is now polishing the final version. Afterward he'll have to study for his examinations, so that by the summer he'll have his doctorate. Everyone involved is convinced that his main adviser won't understand the work any more than you do Chinese— even though it's crystal clear. I can be with Walter only very rarely, and this for deeply personal reasons. I feel the need to stay for a spell within an exclusively Jewish circle, even if it's made up of only myself and my books, or in an anarchistic community with other humans. [. . .]

I have the following to report regarding my brother.[5] So I far as I can tell, he is most likely of little direct interest for you; he understands nothing of the things that most concern you. Personally, I would counsel you to go and see how he behaves one of these days—that is, whether he disappears into a cloud of pure phraseology. I hope he doesn't, since I hold his wife in the *highest* esteem. I think you could discuss your own poetry with him. When you go (Linden, Nieschlag Strasse 26) you just have to ask for him, when he's not making some speech. Incidentally, you should know of him through the press. He's supposed to be the roaring lion of the Independents for the entire province. He is (at twenty-three!!) the chairman of the Linden Independent Socialist faction and of the workers' council in Hannover to boot, and editor of the *Volksstimme* in Braunschweig. Moreover, he can be of some help if you are now interested in socialism. Naturally, he is a "Communist." [. . .]

Best regards (from Walter and Dora Benjamin too), Gerhard

TO BETTY AND ARTHUR SCHOLEM

Bern, April 26, 1919

Dear parents,

[. . .] I have decided to remain here for the summer after all, on account of my studies. Since the interval will be so short, I would prefer to spend my time here with a couple of people rather than in Geneva or Lausanne, where I would hardly have anyone to speak with. It may be that Herr Benjamin, who sends his regards, will be taking his examinations, and of course I'll have to be here for support. Do I have a specific study plan this year? In the most general terms, my plans are as follows. I intend to devote myself to scholarship, and more specifically to philosophy and two of its related fields—mathematics and Judaic studies. So I want to obtain as decent a training in these disciplines as possible. Here I can pursue only philosophy and mathematics. If one can plan so far in advance, I would like, if possible, to do my doctorate in philosophy (as a major), with mathematics and oriental (Semitic) languages as minors. [. . .] This seems to me to be a rather good combination, considering the way my mind works, which makes me much more receptive to philology, philosophy, and mathematics than to the experimental sciences. [. . .]

I hope that my plans seem reasonable to you—sufficiently so to gain your support. Even if it isn't necessary to say so, I'd like to make it clear that I *do not* base these plans on the intention of living off your generosity in the future. Even if I will not immediately become a professor in Jerusalem, when the time comes I have no doubt that I can earn enough to support a simple life. My dual mastery of German and Hebrew, for instance, will always make me a good translator. (If you wish to see how well I'm faring, take a look at the May edition of *Der Jude,* which contains my translation of a long article.)[6] I apologize for this silly bragging, but I can find no better way of showing off my talents to practical people like the two of you than by telling you the truth and by showing you how the people who count have the highest regard for me as a translator, even if I have published very little. I get lots of offers, which I mostly turn down because I want to spend my time studying. I agree to translate only those pieces with which I'd like to have my name associated. But this is all chit-chat!! I merely wish to say that I am not shamelessly building my plans upon your money—and given the present situation,

you could rightfully claim that nothing may be left of it in three
years. [. . .]

Gerhard

FROM BETTY AND REINHOLD SCHOLEM

Berlin, April 29, 1919

Dear child,

[. . .] No, we have nothing against Locarno or a vacation. In any
event, the terrible monetary situation has put a time limit on your Swiss
sojourn. In the long run, this cannot go on. We have completely given
up on our plans for a trip to Switzerland. With an exchange rate of 280,
we cannot afford such adventures. [. . .]

The strikes continue to take their course. Your father sits from morning till evening on the arbitration board. Salaries climb inexorably; no
one wants to work any longer. There has been no meat for three weeks,
not even on the black market. It's a lovely mess we're in. Write soon
and tell us about your shopping excursions.

Many greetings to my Zionist brother!—Reinhold.

Kisses, Mum. Jewish is good! But what is it?

FROM LUDWIG STRAUSS

Berlin, June 2, 1919

Dear Herr Scholem,

[. . .] Welt Verlag, where I'm working, plans to publish a Jewish
library series to disseminate inexpensive volumes (of around eighty-five
pages) of selections and entire pieces taken from Jewish literature and
literature on Jewish themes. Among others, the first of the series will
include Mendelssohn's *Jerusalem,* Herder's *Spirit of Hebrew Poetry,* selections from Flavius Josephus, and excerpts from the memoirs of Mendele
and Kottik (in Kaufmann's translation). I would appreciate it if you
would allow us to include your translation of biblical lamentations in
the series. You wrote that you've translated a number of other passages
from the Bible, besides lamentations. I already have the lamentations. I

would be grateful if you could send those others to me as well. Your collection of lamentations will be printed in a manner worthy of it, and I'm convinced that its publication could really make some waves. It would be very kind if you could give me suggestions as to which pieces from old and new Jewish literature would be worthy of inclusion in the series. One of the first books I'd like to publish is on the "landscape of Palestine"—an anthology of portrayals of the land in Palestine, both in translation and in the original. Maybe for this anthology you could give me some tips on works I'm unaware of, especially in the field of Hebrew literature.

LS

FROM BETTY SCHOLEM

Berlin, June 8 (Whitsunday)

My dear child,

[. . .] Yesterday we had another general strike, as a change of scenery. Streetcars and trains stopped running. There was also a strike in our firm because, I am sorry to say, we have a hothead in the worker's council. [. . .] We're afraid that on Friday there will be more rioting in the wake of Rosa Luxemburg's funeral.[7] [. . .]

Kisses, Mum

TO LUDWIG STRAUSS

Bern, June 13, 1919

Dear Herr Strauss,

I received your letter of June 2 only yesterday. I am replying promptly with the hope of encouraging you to do the same, or even to better me. [. . .] Your request puts me in an awkward position, mostly because your lack of clarity makes it difficult for me to come to a decision. Certainly, I've never heard of Welt Verlag and know nothing of the conditions under which it operates, or the rights and duties I would incur if I published with the house. I would therefore be grateful if you could send more precise details regarding your suggestions. Independent of these concrete issues, however, I cannot deny that I'm inclined against publication—both because of a theoretical concern as to the maturity and purity of my present knowledge regarding the lamentations, and because I am uncertain whether it is permissible to print these songs without at the same time printing a longer fundamental, theoretical work. [. . .]

Yours, Gerhard Scholem

TO META JAHR[8]

Munich, July 1, 1919

Dear Meta,

[. . .] In answer to your provocative query (don't be offended, you'll soon see why) as to whether I already knew that Agnon had married Esther Marx, I must tell you cheerfully that I certainly did (and how could I not!). I've also been vested with the authority to baldly deny it before the *entire world.* During her last visit here, Esther Marx, the woman you refer to as Frau Czaczkes, disputed the marriage with such a thoroughgoing Agnonesque style that I had no choice but to assume it was true—the marriage, that is!! You can make of this what you will; everything else is open to interpretation. In passing, I hold Fräulein Marx in the highest esteem. She knows Hebrew even better than Fräulein Burchhardt, who admittedly knows nothing. She's quite capable, that is. She even denied the marriage in the very same Hebrew in which the wedding is said to have been conducted. Besides this, she's wise, and whenever I encounter this *mida* it fills me with *yira*—which according to the Kabbalah is even more important than *chochma* itself.[9] I am rarely filled with *yira,* and women always have *chochma.*

You'll gather from the previous sentence that I have become a *makubel*[10] who spends his days penetrating this primordial forest of ruins. These ruins, too, exist. It's an extremely remarkable matter and I would have a great deal to say about it if I were speaking with you face to face. But my health is sadly worn thin; in the most literal sense it hangs in the balance between two eggs, rotten from the inside. This means that I am not in the kind of tip-top working state I would like. At least I'm learning Hebrew as much as I can. Four times a week I study the talmudic tract *Katuba,* on the question of how a man goes about getting a wife, and many other things that we must prepare ahead of time. The teacher, a Dr. Ehrentreu who is an old man and a dyed-in-the-wool Lamdan,[11] speaks only when we come up with something stupid. We're learning a lot this way, especially because there are only four of us. Besides sorcery and black magic, the other bit of systematic learning I'm doing is to continue work on the book of Jeremiah with Fräulein Burchhardt (with all sorts of commentaries and Jalkut,[12] Maimonides' *Mishna Torah,* and finally the Kabbalah). [. . .]

Your Gerhard

FROM ARTHUR SCHOLEM

Berlin, August 1, 1919

Dear Gerhard,

Many thanks for your friendly card from the twenty-fourth. I am pleased to hear that you are in good health and thus fit to work, at least if one can judge by the copy of *Der Jude* that was sent me. I passed it on to your mother, who will be able to muster the necessary insight to appreciate the abstruse differences between Halachah and Aggada.[13] Sorry to say, it's all over my head. The main purpose of today's letter, however, is to sound out your intentions for the coming semester and the more distant future. Given this exchange course you're currently taking, I can no longer finance your Swiss sojourn. Unless you can come up with some alternative suggestion, *faute de mieux* you'll have to return to Germany. I assume you already know the direction your life will take and in which discipline you will, in the near future, get your doctorate. I need to know these things in order to make future preparations for the family budget. You take up a handsome share of it.

Father

TO BETTY SCHOLEM

Munich, November 23, 1919[14]

Dear Mother,

[. . .] This will be brief, because I have little to report about myself. A lawyer helped me get a residency permit for three months (as a disabled ex-serviceman, until February 15), which means that I can now buy food. [. . .]

What will become of Gerhard Scholem?

First, he'll become Gershom Scholem,

Then he will (hopefully) become Dr. Phil.,

Then a Jewish philosopher,

Then an angel in Seventh Heaven.

Yours truly, Gerhard

FROM REINHOLD SCHOLEM

Berlin, November 25, 1919

Dear Gerhard,

My warmest birthday greetings! I hope your stay in Munich will show you that the German Idea is still alive and kicking and has not been drowned out by the resonant phrases of coffeehouse socialists. It now seems as if the Independents and other such luminaries have passed their peak—above all in Munich after the days of the Council Republic.[15] I would be very interested if you wrote me about the political happenings among students. There, too, the Russian and Bavarian Jews have given us a bad name. Has anti-Semitism flared up at the university?

What else are you up to in Munich?

Enjoy your birthday in the hopes of better times—or the Messiah or whatever else you want to call it. This has absolutely nothing to do with Judaism; it's a universal and human concern.

Sincerely yours, Reinhold

Reserve Lieutenant and Member of the German Volkspartei

TO BETTY AND ARTHUR SCHOLEM

Munich, December 6, 1919

Dear parents,

Many thanks for the warm birthday greetings and the delightful gifts. They all arrived on time. The package reached me a few days earlier (a comrade of mine just left for Berlin with a mission to bring greetings to Neue Grünstrasse). I liked everything, but the pigeon had unfortunately gone rancid and couldn't be eaten. Last night I went to the local opera house to hear *The Magic Flute*. It was the only thing in town and cost a small fortune, but it was really beautiful. [. . .]

By the way, I want to thank the M.d.V.L.d.R.X.Y.Z. for his ridiculous letter, which just goes to show how "the reaction rears its head."[16] I don't know anything about student politics, other than the fact that everyone disagrees with everyone else and that a quite vulgar anti-Semitism hovers over the place. I didn't participate in student council elections, because they're a farce. [. . .]

1920

TO WALTER BENJAMIN

Munich, February 5, 1920

Dear Walter,

In the past few days I've read a large part of Bloch's *Spirit of Utopia.* I expect a great deal from your review, and I hope that it will make the virtues of the book clear to me.[17] I don't doubt there's something there. By the same token, I have to say I've discovered some highly suspicious things in it. Let me voice my complaints loud and clear, since you've already discussed the book's faults in esoteric language. This will enable us to determine if we see eye to eye. In what follows, I will focus mainly on the section (which I totally reject, to the extent that I understood it) entitled "On the Jews" and "On the Shape of the Non-Constructed Problem." I have the impression that, using inadequate means in the worst possible sense, Bloch has committed a border violation leading him into territory which should be kept to an absolute minimum in such a book. With a sorcerer's flourish (and take care—I know the source of this magic!), he makes claims about the historical development of Judaism, about history, and about Judaism per se that clearly bear the terrible stigmata of Prague (which means Buber, in my book). No matter how you look at it, even the phraseology stems from Prague. There's no such thing as this "Jewish generation" Bloch has discovered; it exists only within the spiritual kingdom of Prague. Under no circumstances should he be allowed to use a historical-philosophical method in which testimony and witnesses (and the author of the book is one such witness who speaks out loud and clear) are conjured up from German Jewry and from the Jewish-German and German-Jewish way of life to testify to the living, bright, and dark heart of things—and not, let's say, to (Jewish) demonism and demonology. Time and again, the only thing he pulls off is ontological proof of the existence of the devil. It's evident that Bloch openly despises philology; but this seems most serious when his historical-philosophical observations do not in the least conform to philological demands (prejudice in the choice of sources!!). More suspicious still is when he believes that, for his aims, he can forgo philology altogether and can mix sources indiscriminately. With well-nigh magnificent incoherence, Jewish categories (among many others, the wretched misunderstanding of the "name of God"—*Kiddush haschem*—stemming from *Das Buch des Judentums*)[18] are hurled into a discussion for which they are totally unsuited, and this naturally leads to as many misunderstandings as it solves.

Your Gerhard

TO BETTY AND ARTHUR SCHOLEM

Munich, March 19, 1920

My dear parents,

Have you survived the past week?[19] I hope nothing has happened to you—please send me some word soon! The situation here has been quite turbulent. In Munich, too, there were incitements for a pogrom, and I had a fistfight with an anti-Semite on the street. Now everything has returned to normal. Only the printers are on strike. The same with you? [. . .]

Sincerely, Gerhard

TO BETTY AND ARTHUR SCHOLEM

Munich, March 29, 1920

Dear parents,

I'm puzzled and somewhat uneasy about the fact that I haven't heard a word from you two. The entire city of Berlin seems to have gone dead. Please drop me a line to let me know how you've weathered the recent turmoil. I'll get a few days of holiday soon. I'd like to rest a bit, and I don't plan on studying anything besides Greek vocabulary. If possible I'll make a short excursion either to the lakes or to the mountains. I haven't yet seen a thing in the area.

Incidentally, though I'm not going to Berlin yet, I will have to travel there in the summer or fall in order to consult library materials which are unavailable here. I'll have my hands full then.

As always, father's monotonous and recurrent concern about the purpose, or lack of purpose, of my "sport" (meaning my studies) remains unjustified. Already there's a circle of men who do not dismiss what I do as a sport; on the contrary, they regard it as very necessary. The "Cultural Minister of Palestine" (I'm acquainted with the Under-Secretary) holds an opinion different from father's. Naturally, one must have more ability than a wretched statistician or a high school teacher. When all is said and done, the most you can do is ensure that your powers do not disappear. I don't mean to say that I would never allow such a thing to happen or that I ideally apportion every minute of the day. Yet despite my weakness, I strive to do just this. It's *dai la' mevin*— meaning it's enough for those who are prudent.

Please send the money. I find myself in desperate straits. [. . .]

Greetings to everyone, Gerhard

FROM WALTER BENJAMIN[20]

Berlin, April 17, 1920

Dear Gerhard,

You are the last one in your family to receive my attention during my stay in Berlin. I have already consulted with your brother Reinhold and used the opportunity this occasion offered to chat with your father. [. . .] In the course of a conversation we had, your father succinctly pronounced you a genius—he should know. But may God preserve every father from having such a genius. If you add to this that he then felt it necessary to explain what the Jews call *tachles*,[21] you can imagine the direction the conversation took. Your father struck me as being *very* content and spoke most kindly of you. [. . .]

TO ERICH BRAUER

Munich, June 6, 1920

Dear Erich,

I am now a full-fledged doctoral student and am finally doing Semitic studies with Hommel. It looks as if my work will be evaluated by three professors who are said to mutually encourage one another!!! The dissertation will be a vast foundational philological-philosophical monograph on an early kabbalistic text from around the year 1230, an important work for the development of the Kabbalah. Nothing worthwhile that's any longer than four pages has been written about it. Meanwhile, I have become a Kabbalist, pursuing textual criticism and even more mysterious things in the local library with the help of a marvelous Spanish manuscript. [. . .]

Your Gerhard

TO BETTY AND ARTHUR SCHOLEM

Munich, June 14, 1920

Dear parents,

[. . .] The weather lately has been a bit mean-spirited, though still bearable, and I'm concentrating on getting my work done. I have a lot to do. We'll have to negotiate over printing the dissertation, but let me first get it behind me and then bring you together with a publisher. At the moment, this is all laurels in advance. The only thing that's clear is how much work I have ahead of me. The rumor has recently begun to circulate around Munich that, using black magic, I can create mice and elephants. For now, however, I can conjure up only flawless texts no one can top—and with white magic, which is something completely permissible and free of sorcery! By the time I take my exams, though, I hope to work up to bigger things by creating camels and the like! I recommend the greatest caution in any future dealings with me!! [. . .]

From Gerhard

TO ERICH BRAUER

Munich, December 14, 1920

Dear Erich,

[. . .] You no doubt would like to know what I am up to. I'm being downright respectable and almost overly industrious. Once again I'm participating in a math colloquium on number theory, which is a science that makes the greatest—and oddest—impression on me. In mathematics, there's certainly nothing like it. In one seminar we're now studying

the basic principles. To round off my entire philosophical career, this
winter I'm also attending a lecture by a professor of theology on the
"philosophy of mathematics," a topic he knows absolutely nothing
about. I have my hands full with Judaic studies. At the moment, I'm
surrounded by six manuscripts of *Das Buch Bahir*. I've ordered a photograph of an old Latin translation from the Vatican in Rome, and will
"decorate" my study with my analysis of it—though it is so exceptionally
difficult to decipher that I have to spend a fortune to get a readable copy
from Munich's best Renaissance paleographologist, who's the only one
around who has proved capable of reading it. Anyway, it's taught me a
lot, even about Hebrew paleography. Yesterday I found in one of my
sepharim the formula for the seven-mile leap![22] But it's obviously not the
right one. Kabbalah studies and their methodology are almost the only
things to which I give any serious thought. [. . .]

To top it all off, I am studying—along with Fräulein Burchhardt and
another of the *bachorim*[23] (someone I like very much, a most capable
former Blue-Whiter from Kattowitz)—Bartinora's commentary on the
Mischna Bab Mezia, which incidentally is such a magnificent tractate
that it surprises even me. Because we've been working so hard, we're
now taking a break for the Christmas holidays. We are also studying the
Guide for the Perplexed,[24] which we're going to read from the beginning,
in twice-weekly sessions, and see how far we get. I have already mentioned that I'm also busy waltzing my way through books of magic,
investigating the meanings of the Sefirot.[25] I'll be writing a review essay
for *Der Jude* on a number of recent books on the Kabbalah, some of
which are quite useful. In any case, they're unquestionably superior to
the utter rubbish I mentioned above. Finally, in the evening I've been
correcting Straussen's translation of Agnon's *Ha-nidach*.[26] This sums up
my daily work on Judaica. On Saturday mornings the Catholic professor
of theology A.T. delivers his lecture on Talmudic literature. According
to the old tried and true method, I've taken it upon myself to challenge
the friendly old man through pedantry. He has no idea what he's talking
about—surely no more than Grete or Freund, even if he believes a priori
that he can "read the Talmud." In order not to undermine his authority—and one should not undermine authority in front of the goyim—
we have used scholarly demeanor to drive all of the non-Jews out of
the lecture hall. It became too difficult for them. Now the professor
himself has to learn diligently, and it was he who got me the Vatican

manuscript I mentioned. The man speaks Aramaic with an Upper Bavarian accent, which makes for a friendly change in mood. I'm learning southern Arabian inscriptions with Hommel, which will also lead to Ethiopian. Hommel, by the way, is a proper ignoramus. [. . .]

Yours, Gerhard Scholem

FROM WALTER BENJAMIN[27]

December 29, 1920

Dear Gerhard,

I have surmised the reason for your having remained silent for so long. I wrote to the Gutkinds even before I had come to a decision, purely because of my agonizing indecisiveness.[28] In response I received their rebukes soon after receiving your letter of the eighteenth. I replied to these rebukes yesterday. As you will see, my reply also contains my coming to terms with your letter. Because I am unable to improve on what I have already said, there is no better alternative than to copy and send you what I wrote the Gutkinds:

"When your letter arrived, the dilemma that had caused me to suffer for weeks had been resolved, and, after reading your letter, I thought about it once again and reached the same conclusion. No, there is no other way. I am unable to devote myself to things Jewish with full intensity before having derived from my European apprenticeship what may result at least in some chance of a more peaceful future, family support, and so on. I must admit that I have been spiritually ready to turn away from things European and begin a lengthy new apprenticeship approximately since the time of my Ph.D. exams. But I also know that the difficult decision I have nurtured for such a long time will leave me the choice, made freely and calmly, of when to carry it out. As it is, it is true that, as Scholem wrote, the older you are, the more difficult it is to make such a choice, and age can ultimately turn it into a catastrophe, even in the most favorable case. Even if it is a purifying catastrophe. But the decision that has been so long in coming and is firm also has a *settling* effect. Moreover, it will probably be a matter of no more than two years *at the most.* During this time, I intend to carve a project out of the complex of ideas floating in my mind, and write a book on it. This project— although it is important to me—can be defined and limited. The prospect of starting in on Hebrew is *overwhelming*. It is therefore impossible to say something like: I will first learn Hebrew for one or two years, and tackle the project only after that. You will have to acknowledge the clear reasons for my decision. So I ask you, please do not postpone your own studies, but wait for me with your heart."

Only now, while writing this, do I see the extent to which these lines are addressed to you. The only thing left is to add my promise that, after completing this project, I will truly not allow myself to be detained by anything that may come up. [. . .]

Yours, Walter

1 9 2 1

TO FRANZ ROSENZWEIG[29]

Munich, March 7, 1921

To Franz Rosenzweig, on the translation of the prayer said at mealtimes.

In my opinion, your translation is seminal. For quite some time I have grappled with the problem of whether one can find within the German language some realm of inner balance and meaningful density that could be related to the truly hymn-like movements in our language of prayers, a realm in which sober objectivity and symbolic power announce themselves with equal dignity. As for myself, I have not succeeded in finding a solution. Let me elaborate, albeit briefly, on the essential reason I have not stumbled upon your solution. I have given especially careful thought to the various problems, both theoretical and practical, involved in translating the hymns—even though solving these problems cannot help in translating even a single line of a run-of-the-mill prayer. It seems that you have discovered such a realm. In any event, the almost blessed richness of your translation—if I may say so—and its profound harmony, plus a quality that points to something beyond expression, along with the nonmetaphorical uniformity of your stance (something which I regard *without any hesitation* as the legitimate seal over the abyss of the religious agitation of our wretched people and which you, perhaps without consciously setting out to do so, established in your words) indeed prove that such a realm exists in the German language and has not yet vanished, even in contemporary Germany. I need not emphasize to you the enormous miracle I see in the possibility of translation, one that flows in and out of the heart of religious matters. The reason your translation has proved to be fundamentally problematic and closely related to the language of R. Hallo,[30] however, is the downright puzzling and highly systematic tendency to adopt the language and terminology of the church. In this translation the strictest, clearest, and most worthy Jewish elements seem to be eliminated; the true moral aspect of our language, the *haznea lechet*,[31] is banished; and language gets transformed, for no reason, into the nuance-rich colorfulness and demonic ambiguity of the terminology of salvation. You have tried to convey the utopian precision and chastity of Hebrew into a realm in which, out of utter theological necessity, something perforce must be sacrificed—even though no one has yet demonstrated that in German this is largely unattainable. But only in the language of the church does it fail to be clearly expressed—because of the destructive affinity that many (though not all) religious expressions have with the language of the "Old Testament." [. . .]

FROM FRANZ ROSENZWEIG

Frankfurt, March 10, 1921

Dear Herr Scholem,

[. . .] Only someone who is inwardly convinced of its impossibility can be a translator. Naturally I'm referring not to the impossibility of translation per se [. . .], but to the impossibility of achieving the particular translation on which he works. The *specific* impossibility is in every case different. In my case its name is Luther. And not only Luther, for he is merely the point of passage in which the most ancient and most contemporary writers are briefly bound together; but, to be more exact, Notker—Luther—Hölderlin.[32] There is no such thing as a simple linguistic fact. The German language became Christian through these three names. He who translates into German must in one way or another translate into a Christian language.

Franz Rosenzweig

FROM ARTHUR SCHOLEM

Berlin, March 12, 1921

Dear Gerhard,

I am hereby sending you best wishes for your birthday. I've also sent you one hundred marks, to be spent enjoying an evening at Pension Apel. I'm very busy these days, and my heart has been drawing unpleasant attention to itself by starting to bang once again. I'd like to take another electric cure as soon as I can. It did me so much good at the beginning of the year.

I have not heard much from you, and I would very much like to know if your doctoral thesis is in full gear. I only hope that it will be more readable than your critical commentary on the lyric of the Kabbalah, an essay chiefly remarkable for the time-span it dealt with.[33] In any event, your study shows an inverse relationship between the amount of knowledge pumped into it and the clarity of its expression—and I must sadly admit that it cost me great intellectual effort and a number of tries in order to negotiate those lengthy periods of time. In fact, though it pains me to have to confess this, I was unable to comprehend the work, which has been described as having such beauty. Perhaps the problem is solely mine. But in my opinion, the many recipients of *Der Jude* (volume 1) who received your piece as an inducement to subscribe have been wrongly characterized as being "in the bag."

When I ask myself how I would write a critique of your review from the standpoint of the (unfortunately still undefined) "man on the street," I would say: it's a pity that all this scholarship should have been used so idly, and a double pity that such productive powers and intellectual labor should have been expended so uselessly. These are merely opinions! With all due respect, and with allowances for my hobby-horse, it's hardly worthy of presenting the outlook and being the life task of an intellectually distinguished man.

And so I return once again to your birthday. It is my quiet wish and strong hope that during the coming year you may finally grasp how important it is, in these difficult times, to have both feet planted solidly on the ground. This would prevent you from being driven about aimlessly by every wind in the sky of ideas. Three cheers for Hebraica and Jewish studies—but not as a career! Take my word for it: if you don't change course you will experience a bitter shipwreck, and who knows whether you'll be able to reach safe harbor. Those arms of yours are, after all, not very strong. I therefore wish only the best for you!

Sincerely yours, Father

TO ROBERT WELTSCH AND HANS KOHN[34]

Munich, July 30, 1921

Dear Sirs,

Some time ago I received a written statement, with your signatures, which I took to be an invitation to contribute to the planned sequel to *Das Buch des Judentums.* [. . .] I have concluded that you are fundamentally mistaken when you consider my work closely allied to your own endeavors. This error is perhaps caused by my reserve in openly declaring my views. At the same time, I find it quite astonishing, given the exceedingly precise and unambiguous public statements I have made against the movement you push (or which pushes you) and against the group that you—rightly—consider the guardians of the "ideas of 1913."[35] [. . .] Simple honesty compels me to point out the total and principled discord between us, at least insofar as I am able to assess the situation. Notwithstanding the respect, honor, and affection I feel for some of the people whom you count, or who count themselves, as members of the unified group you hope to create, I think it fitting to mention these things before you decide whether you want to invite someone into your house who so totally rejects your ideas and views them as alien. For my part, I must ask myself whether I can make use of this hospitality. Since I cannot tell you in person what I feel I must (and this would clarify things the most), you will have to forgive me when I sketch out the central points in a few sentences.

Not only does my systematic notion of Zionism strictly disqualify as irrelevant, if not pernicious, the expression *"revolutionary* Zionism" you so often employ; in reality, it disqualifies the entire political sphere in which the revolution is rightly regarded as essential. Even if Zionism were a revolutionary undertaking, it would have to exercise double or triple caution in avoiding such terminology, which only gives license to empty minds to swagger and boast as they like and, with their prattle, to compromise and endanger the most vital affairs of our people. The impurity of this terminology has allowed a loquacious clique of *galut* literati to extol themselves as "young workers" and to overcome with a few clever phrases the distance between them and Palestine (a distance that stems not from ignorance but from reverence for what occurs there). Such impurity is inherently obscene. Added to this is the real reason driving it all—namely, the fatal "modern" conflation of religious and political categories that desecrates both, turning them into a game that someday is bound to turn violent. [. . .]

I in fact pledge my allegiance to an utterly nonrevolutionary notion of Zionism—or one that can be labeled revolutionary only with deep and nearly indecent irony, since it refers to a stratum where there are no revolutions. I do not think that the task of Zionism has any essential relation to social problems. In other words, I am convinced that *if* the rebirth of the Jewish people succeeds, it can do so even in the worst capitalist state, just as it could flounder in a socialist one. Nor do I know a thing about the revolutions of the spirit that you demand. Instead of the upheavals you lay claim to, I know only the deep continuity of the Teaching[36]—which has obviously faded from Zion, though Zionists haven't noticed this. [. . .]

With best regards, Gerhard Scholem

FROM WALTER BENJAMIN[37]

November 27, 1921

Dear Gerhard,

[. . .] The Angelus has been assigned the place above our sofa.[38] Everyone was pleased with him. Just as before, he disdains to whisper suggestions—like the oracle. [. . .]

What I still have to report—something the Angelus has learned as well—is that I was delighted, albeit silently, with the slight allusion to my "Task of the Translator" that I believe I discovered in the original version of your "Lyric of the Kabbalah?" To be specific, the allusion is that, in your words, the true principles of translation have already been established "often enough." I no longer found this thin reed of an allusion in *Der Jude*. [. . .]

Yours, Walter

FROM WALTER BENJAMIN[39]

December 2, 1921

Dear Gerhard,

This letter of congratulations will begin with the blessings of the Angelus and the loud acclamation of the subjugated peoples who surround my writing throne.[40] For these peoples have recently been placed under my supervision, since being settled in the wardrobe of the Ethnological Institute of Muri to their general satisfaction (see "A New Procedure for Settlement," *Publications of the Muri Academy*). Even I am finally being taken seriously as someone who offers congratulations, which I hope to prove by means of my enclosures and best wishes. These are chiefly meant for your successful completion of the *Bahir,* to which I hope to see a *summa cum laude* attached like a dog's little tail wagging to announce its friendliness. They are also meant for the well-being and prosperity of the fertile fields of Hebrew, which are subject to the Angelus, their liege lord. [. . .]

Yours, Walter

1923[41]

TO SALMAN SCHOCKEN[42]

Berlin, September 8, 1923

Dear Herr Schocken,

I am writing to you on the eve of my departure from Berlin—heading for Munich and thence to Trieste after Rosh Hashanah. From there, on the fourteenth of September, I will make my way to Jerusalem. Unexpected circumstances, hopes, and plans have all contributed to the decision to expedite my trip in this unusual manner. I had thought I would leave much later. Be that as it may, my trip is taking place under auspicious conditions—I've even managed to talk my entire personal library into joining me in solidarity. It's already swimming toward Hamburg. [. . .]

With the greatest respect, Your Gerhard Scholem

FROM BETTY SCHOLEM

Berlin, September 21, 1923

My dear child,

[. . .] I had hoped—in vain—to hear parting news from Europe while you were still in Trieste. You could have sent a card. I only hope one will arrive from Alexandria. Always bear in mind that I'm waiting to hear from you! Please give me a detailed description of the trip, tell me if you managed to negotiate the border-crossings and luggage, and let me know how your money is holding out. [. . .]

The shipping company sent the container from Berlin to the Hamburg harbor at the proposed rate, an altogether decent price of 290 million marks. The only things still to come, and which are still unknown, are the transfer charges and the shipping fees to Palestine. Meanwhile, the currency gyrations have assumed truly grotesque forms. Bread prices now apply for only a few hours, and other prices don't apply at all. Everyone charges what he wants. It's a miracle that we managed see you off in a dignified way. The most recent proposal here is for a currency dictatorship that supposedly could bring everything under control. But it's totally hopeless; no one can do a thing against the rampant greed and profiteering. Just be glad, my child, that you've escaped this witches' cauldron. [. . .]

Kisses, Mum

FROM BETTY SCHOLEM *(mailed with the following letter, from Arthur)*

Berlin, October 9, 1923

My dear child,

We received your detailed letter[43] on the fourth of October with great joy. Keep up the good work! [. . .]

So you had a lovely and interesting trip! All of us are *extraordinarily* interested to hear about it. It's only a shame you saw so little of Egypt, though since you now live so close you can of course still go. We were greatly relieved that the amount of money you had sufficed. It was impossible to give you more. We only hope you're able to earn a salary soon. We're not in the least worried about your livelihood. Just be glad to be where you are. Here it has become simply terrible. I can imagine that outside Germany people must have the strangest notions about this place. The reality is even stranger. When you left, the brand of sausage I gave you cost 12 million marks; today it's up to 240 million. All prices have risen at this pace, often even faster. The collapse of the economy is complete. No one can buy a thing, and the unemployment rate has thus been on the rise.

You'll be glad and interested to know that we've been printing money—for the government printing house, of course. A general rapture prevails on the shop floor, since the threat of unemployment hangs over everyone. [. . .]

Kisses, Mum

FROM ARTHUR SCHOLEM

Berlin, October 9, 1923

Dear Gerhard,

I have just returned from a meeting of the commission in the Reichstag, where I spoke as an expert on matters of health insurance. After I finish these lines, I will drive to the Ministry of Labor to display my wisdom there as well. I am not doing so badly, though climbing the stairs has become ever more difficult. Your new niece Irene is a very nice child and earns a lot of cheers—at least from her two grandmothers. Reinhold's boy is in high spirits and babbles back everything one says. He climbs over everything and has already gotten his first bump on the head. It comes with the territory.

Mother has already written you about the business. Printing is now such a hot field that I could pay your shipment bill, a total of thirteen pounds. I have young friends who long for your postage stamps. Do a good deed and include in your letters a few you're able to collect. I hope things continue to go well for you.

Sincerely, Father

FROM BETTY SCHOLEM

Berlin, October 15, 1923

Dear child,

We have not yet received your second letter. Hopefully, it'll arrive this week. Conditions have taken a catastrophic turn here. Notice that this letter cost 15 million cash; it will be 30 million beginning the day after tomorrow—and this price will most likely last a mere two days at most. Now you can get things done only with billions. To ensure that next week's payroll will keep its value, the boys bought dollars on Friday at the (ridiculous!!) exchange rate of 1.5 billion to 1, and they'll re-sell them on Thursday in order to pay people. For the time being, this week's pay will be 8 billion, though we've had negotiations today because the workers are demanding twice that much. The bread ration card has been done away with, and a normal loaf of bread now costs 540 million; tomorrow, surely twice as much. The streetcar fare is 20 million (tomorrow it'll be 50!). My God, you probably don't have faintest notion of this million-fold witches' Sabbath. You must know that we send women's magazines to Frau Jacques Meyer. A few days ago her husband sent us a bank check for over 5 million. When we went to the bank here in Berlin to pick it up, it cost 40 million in transfer fees! I ask myself if the neighboring Swiss are indeed so ignorant of our circumstances, or if they just *act* that way! This small anecdote can illuminate everything. If throughout the world there is such little understanding of our plight, how can we expect that anyone will come to our aid? It seems inevitable that we will lose the Rhine and the Ruhr, that Bavaria will break away, and that Germany will once again fall apart into minuscule petty states. [. . .]

The Communists made their weekly visit to Erich's. Little Edith was delightful and charming.[44] She explained to everyone how she went to the hairdresser on Monday to have her hair washed and her bobbed hair set. Werner said that she would take dance lessons and attend a charm school and that he would look for a better apartment, but that he first wanted to wait for the revolution (planned for November 10!). They and his friends had to go to lunch. They ate a rabbit for 1.75 billion. Erich mentioned to me how extremely amusing, but also quite pathetic, it was to hear those politicians speak.

Kisses, Mum

FROM REINHOLD SCHOLEM
(mailed with the following two letters, from Erich Brauer and Betty Scholem)

Berlin, October 23, 1923

Dear Gerhard,
    Congratulations on the job![45]

Reinhold

FROM ERICH BRAUER

Berlin, October 23, 1923

Dearest friend,
    I just paid a visit to your parents. I read your letter of October 9,[46] and I congratulate you with all my heart! Oh, how lucky you are—and how wretched *we* are. Your letter was so descriptive that I immediately understood something about life in Jerusalem. It's precisely the way I

more or less imagined it to be. One needs only the right amount of decisiveness (and naturally the proper talents). There's nothing new to report from here; we all make our way, twisting and turning, through Germany's ruins. I'll write soon in more detail. My best greetings to Jerusalem, Escha, and yourself.

Yours, Erich Brauer

FROM BETTY SCHOLEM

Berlin, October 23, 1923

My dear child,

Your letter from the ninth brought enormous joy. We no longer have to worry, now that you've set yourself up by obtaining a position and a certain degree of satisfaction. It's an incomparable stroke of luck to earn a living by doing what is also the substance and aim of your life. Thus, our warmest congratulations! Anyway, dealing with books is far preferable to dealing with other people: books—unlike humans—mostly give reasonable answers when queried. [. . .]

It's lucky we're in the business of printing money. Once again, we have 130 workers. With the exception of the money presses, the few customers able to pay such fantastic prices do not require much effort. By contrast, the boys are busy day and night with the money transactions. They are now more bankers than book publishers. They have to watch like a hawk in order to plan properly and to prevent the billions of paper marks, which are now their business, from disappearing into thin air. You can't imagine how things have become! In three days the dollar has gone from 10 billion, to 18.5 billion, to 40. Bread: 900 million, 2.5 billion, 5.5 billion. The collapse has been total. Here and there plundering has flared up, but not much. The despairing women are far too weary; they put up with everything. *Until now* there has been no unrest, though for weeks we've expected it to break out at any time. [. . .]

Kisses, Mum

Jerusalem, the holy city that will be erected once again

19 Cheschwan 5684 [October 29, 1923]

My friend,

I have now been in this country for six weeks, and am writing only to reassure you and promise that as soon as I've managed to crawl out from under all of my many burdens I will write again, and in detail, about the things that interest you. Don't think that I've forgotten you or any other of the friends whom I met in Frankfurt.

Meanwhile, I now have something to be congratulated for: a wife named Escha. At the moment she's in the hospital (with jaundice, a very common disease here, threatening all of us), which is the main reason I haven't been as free to write as I would like. This you can surely understand. I'm busy at work and will write you about it in detail, along with very concrete "intentions." I've been hired as a specialist, an "expert" in Hebrew literature, at the National Library. [. . .]

Yours, Gershom Scholem

FROM ARTHUR SCHOLEM

Berlin, November 1, 1923

Dear Gerhard,

I have read your letter with its somewhat timid announcement of your engagement to Fräulein Burchhardt. I am not nearly as surprised as you, in your naïveté, seemed to think I would be. I was certain about this particular daughter-in-law, and I even offered to bet your mother that the girl would have you in her pocket in short order. As has happened more than once in my life, I got it right.

So I wish you every happiness in your marriage. You seem to think I have something against Fräulein Burchhardt. This isn't true. She comes from a good home, which I consider so important that I can't raise the least objection to your marriage. She will also be just as clever as my other *Schnuere*.[48] How you'll run a household on such a small salary is your business. You cannot count on financial help from either set of parents—at least, not from me. [. . .]

FROM BETTY SCHOLEM

Berlin, November 2, 1923

My dear child,

[. . .] I was at Reinhold's on Friday evening—all of the uncles send their regards. The interest was colossal, and Max described the enormous appreciation you have stirred in Zionist circles. A leading Hebrew novelist told him that you are the hope of Palestine. Now, my son, go and fulfill this hope!

I'll respond one by one to the items you list in your letter. Unfortunately, I can't return to you the nine pounds for the household appliances. I showed the list of things you wanted to Erich instead, who told me to get dressed and go to Lademann at once. "The dollar is now at 80 billion marks; tomorrow it'll be at 300 billion." Erich is my rod and my staff. He did not allow me to run around; at Lademann he bought only the things on the list, paid the billions, and now sends his love. We could buy neither a vegetable knife nor a vacuum cleaner. The first was far too expensive; and, as for the second, the only model they had was electric. [. . .]

Kisses, Mum

FROM BETTY SCHOLEM

Berlin, November 20, 1923

My dear child,

[. . .] There were *no* pogroms in Berlin. But anti-Semitism has penetrated and poisoned the people to such an extent that from all sides you can hear curses against the Jews—completely in the open, and with a lack of embarrassment that has never before been seen. [. . .]

Kisses, Mum

1924

FROM BETTY SCHOLEM *(mailed with the following letter, from Arthur)*

Santa Margherita Ligure, January 22, 1924

My dear child,

[. . .] Do I have time to write my memoirs? Aside from the fact that a few contemporaries and ancestors would not come off so well, these days I have less time than ever. The more I seek peace and quite, the louder my day becomes; the more my sons leave the house, the more their progeny return home! [. . .]

We just ran into Gerhart Hauptmann on the wharf, with his beautifully groomed Goethe-head. He was accompanied by his son Benvenuto, with his brown Christ-curls, and by a lovely young woman. In addition to such live celebrities, there are a number of marble statues perched on stone pedestals along the magnificent street bordering the bay. At ever-varying distances, Garibaldi, Columbus, Cavour, and Victor Emmanuel emphatically stake out their right to the sea. And when another statue of Garibaldi appears, you know that a new neighborhood has begun. [. . .]

Kisses, Mum

FROM ARTHUR SCHOLEM

Santa Margherita Ligure, January 22, 1924

Dear children,

What can I add to your mother's lovely feuilleton? At most, the report that the view of the Mediterranean stirs the appetite for Jaffa and the surrounding landscape. We'd like to put off the trip until next year, though. Are there even hotels in Jerusalem and Judea? I recall having heard that Cook's always does its tours with their own tents, toilets, and other such necessities.

Adieu—off to eat!

Best, Father

FROM BETTY SCHOLEM

Berlin, March 24, 1924

My dear child,

The bank assures me that the letter with instructions to pay you the equivalent of 50 dollars—which amounts to 11.5 pounds—was sent on Wednesday, March 19, to your agent in Jaffa (or Haifa?). In any case, you will finally be in possession of the money and you can pay the oppressive customs taxes. I'll send you more if I can, though at the moment no one in the family has any hard currency in the bank. Our trip swallowed everything, and now there is nothing more to buy. We're also out of cash because the business capital all vanished during the inflation. With the new currency firmly in place, the customers are now returning, so that the acrobatics over salaries and payments have started all over again. It's a dance I know quite well, and I've even performed it myself. But I won't forget you. As soon as I have something to give I'll get it to you, so that you'll finally be free of the taxes. [. . .]

Regarding our trip, I still want to tell you about Arthur Hirsch.[49] We arrived in Zurich on the first day of the holiday, and he was very happy, saying that he was completely at our disposal. This allowed us to have a decent conversation at last. You interest him enormously. He literally cried over the apostate of noble mathematics; he said that he had always hoped to see you in the service of this majestic goddess and that you would achieve the fame denied him. I told him you'd taken some mathematics books with you, and he saw in this a glimmer of hope that the goddess may one day be able to pull you back into her temple! He spoke for six hours with the fellow you'd sent as your messenger, until his wife showed up around nine o'clock because she thought someone had dragged off her husband. Then he spent an additional six hours, or even longer, vainly trying to grasp the essence of your Kabbalah book. He was honestly sad, and spoke of the great hopes he had had for you— such a "mathematically gifted young fellow"! He was elated by the news of the other aspects of your life—your job and above all your marriage. He called this the cleverest thing you could do with your life, and ended by sending his warmest regards to your and your wife.[50] [. . .]

Kisses to you both, Mum

FROM BETTY SCHOLEM

Berlin, April 8, 1924

My dear child,

The registered letter arrived only on Friday. Of course, it was opened in Munich to see if there were any Egyptian pounds to confiscate. The stamps and the rolls of film are undamaged and complete. I took them directly to Scharzlose's, and he promised to have them developed by three P.M. today. [. . .]

I'm sending you, via book mail, an edition of *Vorwärts* containing a political caricature of your brother. Your father brought two copies so that I could send you one and you could thus give us your opinion. We find it marvelous; it skillfully captures his characteristic expression and the look of his ears. I must confess that I'm almost proud. Being caricatured is part of a politician's job! Last week I got together with him and Emmy. This was the first time I'd seen him since the trip, for he's now a big shot with lots to do. He was able to devote two hours to his mother, owing to a canceled conference. During this time, though, he also had to buy a blazer—not the latest thing in fashion but a rather inconspicuous one, suitable for a defendant of the people! We then went to Beudke's. Last winter he went to Moscow for six weeks, and he told me fantastic things about that utterly Asiatic city with its mixture of a hundred different tribes. It seemed to me that he spoke slightly less nonsense than before, meaning that he appears to have matured a bit.

Kisses for now, Mum

FROM BETTY SCHOLEM

Berlin, May 5, 1924

My dear child,

[. . .] The Reichstag elections took place yesterday. I talked Martha[51] into voting for the Democrats and, with our united power, we helped a couple of dwarfs win in Berlin. The German Nationals (read: anti-Semites) and the Communists made the most gains. The Communists went from sixteen delegates to sixty. Werner got elected in Potsdam district II. He's finally found a career for himself! The old proverb really sums it all up: "Oh, with how little wisdom is the world governed!" [. . .]

Kisses, Mum

FROM BETTY SCHOLEM

Berlin, June 3, 1924

My dear child,

[. . .] We now come once again to Werner, whose name has been daily plastered all over the papers. Enclosed is a copy of the *8-Uhr-Abendblatt.* I wanted to have a couple of tickets to the opening of the Reichstag, but Werner said that was impossible. Most likely I wouldn't whistle and make the necessary volume of noise, which is the reason his party has to give the tickets to someone more reliable! When the young Bismarck was called up, Werner screamed, "Woe to you that you're a grandson!"[52] All of the newspapers and parties took notice of his heckling call, though I don't find anything particular clever in it. It hits too close to home.

Now onto something grotesque. Uncle George says that his Christian practice in the Sebastian neighborhood has almost completely faded away, thanks exclusively to Werner's public appearances!!! I let out a mocking laugh and asked him if he hadn't ever heard of anti-Semitism! No, he replied, his patients are not "anti." The dumb goyim simply don't know whether the Communist Scholem is his father, his son, or even he himself. And for this reason they prefer to have nothing more to do with him. [. . .]

A thousand greetings.

Kisses, Mum

FROM WALTER BENJAMIN[53]

Capri, June 13, 1924

Dear Gerhard,

[. . .] I began this letter yesterday in a café, where I was sitting near Melchior Lechter, whom I met here a few days ago. A friendly, very sophisticated old gentleman with the round, red face of a child. He walks on crutches. In the course of time, especially since the Gutkinds left, I have gotten to know one person after the other here in the Scheffel Café Hidigeigei (except for its name, there is nothing unpleasant about it). In most cases, with little profit; there are hardly any noteworthy people here. A Bolshevist Latvian woman from Riga, a Christian, who performs in the theater and directs, is the most noteworthy. [. . .]

Today is the third day I have been writing this letter. I spoke with the Bolshevist woman until 12:30 and worked until 4:30. Now, in the morning, under a cloudy sky with the wind coming from the sea, I sit on my balcony, one of the highest in all Capri, from which you can look far out over the town and onto the sea. By the way, it is striking how often people who come here for a very short time cannot make up their minds to leave. The grandest and oldest incident of this kind involved the emperor Tiberius, who on three occasions started returning to Rome only to turn back before reaching his destination. The weather here also does not make for conversation, something I would like you to convey to Escha. Since I have been here, it has rained four times at the most, and then very briefly. For a short time now, I have again had a little money, and once I have managed to come to terms with my conscience I will go to Naples—maybe even as far as Paestum.

I will enjoy looking through a travel guide to Palestine. I intend to do this as soon as I have the opportunity. Until then, however, do not worry about anything in your letters being incomprehensible. Whatever I do not understand when I get one of your letters, I will understand later, and it will be all the more enduring for that. You say very little about Safed. Isn't there still a school there devoted to the study of the Kabbalah? I imagine all sorts of things about the considerable number of incredible types whom you seem to run into there, as I gather from your vivid descriptions—I imagine above all that, even in much of Palestine, things proceed in a very human and a less Jewish fashion than someone who is ignorant of Palestine might imagine. [. . .]

Yours, Walter

TO FRITZ HOMMEL, PRIVY COUNSELOR

Jerusalem, July 18, 1924

Most honored Sir,

[. . .] I am sending you all of my scholarly publications that have thus far appeared here in the old-new Hebrew language—in particular the second, which has uncovered the direct relationship between the Kabbalah and Sufism and which should be of general interest to those studying the history of religion. I hope this will give you some idea of my work here.

I am the director of the Hebrew division of the Jewish National and University Library, which itself serves to prepare the way for a great academic undertaking that will be closely connected with the rebuilding of this land by Jewish hands. It is a serious position, replete with scholarly tasks and prospects. I have ample free time for scholarly pursuits, insofar as the climate here allows me to make use of my time. I must confess I have been grieved by the sobering events and circumstances that have done no little damage to the reputation of the University of Munich, both here and elsewhere outside Germany.[54] They have also convinced me that Jewish scholarship and its disciples must temporarily give up the hope they once placed in Munich. It is better for me to build my life on a foundation and in a context that promise, despite shortages and obstacles, to develop securely and steadily in all areas of life, and where young people like myself are free of the spiritual tensions and torments inevitably associated with life in Munich. Please forgive these personal remarks! [. . .]

Your faithful pupil, Gerhard Scholem

FROM BETTY SCHOLEM

Berlin, September 2, 1924

My dear child,

We did not receive any letter from you last week. In the interim, Uncle Katz gave a fright to his entire family. One evening he became so ill with intestinal bleeding that it seemed as if he would die any moment. But George got him on his feet again. The cause is still a mystery. This week he'll leave for Karlsbad. You have to pity the old man. His children aren't happy with him either, because he's devious beyond belief and a loudmouth to boot. I experienced this myself when he exclaimed to me the other day, "Hah, now I'll tell you something that'll anger and annoy you! Werner took some blows during the constitutional celebration."

"First of all," I replied, "this does not anger me in the least; second, I'm not annoyed by it; and third, where did you get your information?"

"I heered it."

"And who told *you* this? You don't even know Werner, and he's not even in Berlin!"

"Ah," he said, "so now ya see what kinda nonsense da people speak!'"!! Isn't this closing remark fabulous? But the prattle that *he himself* speaks doesn't bother him in the least! [. . .]

Kisses, Mum

FROM WALTER BENJAMIN[55]

Capri, September 16, 1924

Dear Gerhard,

[. . .] [Hugo] Bergmann is probably not back from London or America yet. Is there anything new you can tell me about the status of the plans for the university? I had already received the news of de Haan's murder.[56] But what is almost more terrible than that is what you have to say about the effect this event has had. I recently spoke with a Russian Jew from the Kiev area, a farmer who came directly from Palestine. I do not remember his name. He did not look like just any Tom, Dick, or Harry and attracted my interest since he firmly believed he had seen me in Palestine. He has also seen you and heard of you, though he's never spoken with you. [. . .]

Yours, Walter

FROM BETTY SCHOLEM

Berlin, September 22, 1924

My dear child,

[. . .] You speak of memoirs! This isn't as easy as you think. I have often asked myself whether I shouldn't begin to write a history of the family, and just as often I've realized how impossible it would be. Or I would have to limit myself to simple data, without the wider context or ironic embellishments. If I felt the need to call someone a larger-than-life monster, the relatives who may have known him would strongly disagree, and as a result *I'd* seem like the villain! Or should I just tell the same old stories that everyone has already swallowed and digested? Should one immortalize what, with hindsight, can only be portrayed as balderdash? For instance, contemporaries mainly see that Grete Borchardt chews cigarettes and tells lies. Yet she's an inestimably valuable person—capable, energetic, smart, pleasant, replete with kindness, and inexhaustibly cheery. *I* don't see your grandfather Scholem's character merely as black, but rather as pitch black. Still, maybe he was white?! De mortuis *nil,* nise bene! And you can't even open the really secret closets. [. . .]

Good night and kisses, Mum

TO WERNER KRAFT

Jerusalem, December 17, 1924

Dear Werner,

[. . .] My life here is very quiet. I don't have much to say about my own convictions regarding the situation in this country. Concerning the fate of the Zionist movement, I have unconditionally committed myself to the sect with apocalyptic views. You can't possibly imagine the sorts of worlds that bump into each other in this place. For thinking minds, it's an open invitation to go overboard. And even if you don't want to make some kind of "public appearance," you necessarily assume a theological pose, sometimes in the most ridiculous forms—now a messiah, now a labor union leader, now in still stranger costumes. You can get away with all kinds of remarks about the new Palestine (if I make myself clear), especially bad ones—and how could it be otherwise, given this unimaginable collision between the various types of creativity released from the four corners of heaven and earth? But it seems to me a brute fact that this occurs here more often than elsewhere. Personally, I suffer catastrophically from linguistic conditions that escape rational description. If I write a study about this someday, you'll be the first to know.

While the literati are as bad here as elsewhere—as Jewish literati tend to be—they are not as cunning as the ghosts you described. In this country (and here is a phenomenon that the Zionist phase will be able to bring to full blossom) they are but one thing and one thing only: stupid.

Astonishingly dumb, I assure you. The phenomenon of *primal,* aboriginal (not to confused with original) Jewish stupidity is quite clearly unknown in the Diaspora. This is among the strongest impressions one gets in this country. I kid you not. In this apocalyptic place, and only here, you meet the utterly amazing phenomenon of Hebrew-speaking philistines. You also can run into the last of the Kabbalists.

You asked about Benjamin. In November he was still in Italy. I don't know if he has returned to Germany, though I assume so. He was in Capri for half a year.

From your Gerhard

FROM BETTY SCHOLEM

Berlin, December 21, 1924

My dear child,

[. . .] We were all interested in what you wrote about the creation of the university. No one can stop you now from "striving." On top of this, we're all totally convinced that you know precisely what you want. [. . .]

Our plans for our trip to Palestine are already completely set. Carrying them out depends on the rentenmark,[57] and on your father's health. But I'm sure that if we scraped together the money to make the trip, he'd muster the necessary strength. [. . .]

FROM WALTER BENJAMIN[58]

Berlin, December 22, 1924

Dear Gerhard,

[. . .] I hope someday the Communist signals will come through to you more clearly than they did from Capri. At first, they were indications of a change that awakened in me the will not to mask the actual and political elements of my ideas in the Old Franconian way I did before, but to develop them by experimenting and taking extreme measures. This of course means that the literary exegesis of German literature will now take a back seat. This exegesis is at best essentially meant to conserve and to restore what is genuine in the face of expressionistic falsifications. As long as I do not manage to approach texts of a totally different significance and magnitude from a stance that is appropriate to me, that of commentator, I will generate a "politics" from within myself. And in view of this, my surprise at the various points of contact I have with radical Bolshevist theory has of course been renewed. It is really a shame that I still do not anticipate producing a coherent written statement about these matters and that, until I do, I may remain the object of your speculations on the elective affinity between Walter Benjamin and Werner Scholem. [. . .]

Yours, Walter

1925

FROM BETTY SCHOLEM

Berlin, January 12, 1925

My dear child,

[. . .] Honestly, Gerhard, I'm nearly shattered! We are very sorry that you see anything hostile in our comments on Zionism or on Jewish matters in general! What one hears and reads here is often negative. We write as we do precisely *because,* unlike you, we cannot judge what we read. And we believe *you* when you tell us that it isn't so! You should assume that we repeat the things we hear out of interest, not hostility. We have no greater desire than to see you happy over there, to see you fulfill your dreams. It's the furthest thing from our mind to want to offend you the way you seem to be offended. You know perfectly well that I've never made a wisecrack about Zionism and have never considered Zionism to be a joke! It's just extremely difficult for us to remain close to you through letters. In total innocence we write you about everything we think might interest you. Mostly you're in a good mood and it works. But as soon as a mosquito bites, you get hot under the collar and you don't want to discuss a thing. [. . .]

Kisses, Mum

TO ERNST SIMON

Jerusalem, January 24, 1925

Dear friend,

Even though I have no expectation of receiving a reply from you (unless it's in the form of a lead article in a newspaper), I'm sending you a letter once again, for the very human reason that the literary appearance you recently made among my Jerusalem neighbors and through which you assumed such a prominent place has given rise to a great deal of unpleasant and even pessimistic reflection (and, if nothing else, I demand at least clarification). I felt my spirit so provoked by the *Jüdische Wochen-blatt*[59] (I have been a reader of it for some time now) that you must excuse me when I write so openly and say things as if you were standing before me, even if no discussion ensues from of it. In the worst case I am simply wrong—though if I am right, you would surely not want to shelve my warnings. [. . .]

Your newspaper has three basic faults: it is inane, unclear, and "intellectual." If these accusations anger you, I would ask you to take a look at an issue after putting it aside for six weeks. At least for you, my dear friend, *Der Israelit* can't be salvaged (I read it and can prove it): it is clearly and massively stupid and transparent.[60] In itself this does not particularly bother me. It's this crazy Schlegelism staring out from every corner that is not in the least amusing. [. . .] I have no idea what kind of human sensibility these *Kindertotenlieder*[61] for Sabbath afternoons, this horrible Schlegelism with Torah sauce (God forgive me), are meant to serve. When you first turned to me for help, I immediately unsheathed a fragment from an essay I wrote for *Der Jude* to send you. As soon as I caught sight of the mess, however, Gustav Landauer (blessed be the memory of the just)[62] appeared to me in a dream ("May God forgive you for this!") and I withdrew my cooperation.

I think you should come *as soon as you can*. If I may still speak of it in these terms, coming here would do wonders for the things we have in common. The *galut* will eat you alive; you cannot expose yourself to this without paying a price. What you are doing now clearly makes no sense at all, though with your talents it's very seductive (I promise that you can study here too, if you have the talent). You write extremely high and deep, yet what you write is as tepid as a woman (that is, one who writes).

A Ba'al Tschva[63] must take care not to become a hybrid. Don't offer your prayers through a lead article, and don't allow Harry Levy[64] to experiment with the Kingdom of God—because such things will avenge themselves. *Ki col oese elle lo ynake.*[65]

Yours, Gerhard Scholem

FROM BETTY SCHOLEM

Berlin, February 9, 1925

My dear child,

Your father is no longer with us. It was impossible for you to see him one more time. After his lung infection three years ago, he himself lived in perpetual readiness for this and considered his days numbered. How many times I virtually had to force him to have something new made! So often he would say, "Oh, I've got enough for the couple of weeks I have left!" I still can't believe that he's dead, that he will never return to us. He had just gone to the shop, as cheerful as always—or rather, as cheerful as he ever was during the past year. I'll try to give you a detailed description of his last days. I wrote to you about our trip. Your father was completely fit in Kiel. On Sunday we drove to the sluice-gates in Holtenauer, which interested him a great deal. He had so much curiosity—everything in life found an echo in him. That afternoon we stayed in our lovely hotel room and rested, and in the evening we went to the municipal theater to see a comedy that amused him no end. On Monday afternoon we drove home, since at nine A.M. Tuesday your father had a meeting at the Reich's Arbitration Office, where the conflict between the doctors and the national insurance administration was finally brought to an end—to no one's satisfaction, of course. Father did not come home to eat lunch but didn't mind this, because for him meetings were the spice of life. I saw him for only half an hour, over coffee, and then he left for the bank (he took the car, since he no longer walked even the shortest distances by foot), where the purchase of the estate was on the agenda. Around eight P.M. he came home for dinner. Reinhold wasn't home, and we discussed the matter all evening. Father complained time and again about the child; he was attached to him with all his heart. Wednesday morning he had such an amusing time with his friend and barber, Kramer, that I could hear the laughter all the way from the bedroom. The next morning he drove to work and at eleven A.M. he returned to the bank, where three fellows from Freudenholm came to pick up the money from the purchase. Father refused their invitation to eat at Kempinsky's and returned home. "Oh," he said, "there was no way I was going to let the big shots pay for me. I'm not even supposed to drink wine, so why should I go to Kempinsky's? I'd rather eat with you!" I'm glad he didn't go; otherwise, I would have suspected that he'd died from drinking wine. We again had coffee together, and then he sat down on the sofa feeling quite tired. I told him he should stay home instead of going to the shop. He didn't want to. "You know well enough," he said, "that I prefer being on the go. I have all sorts of things to finish." With that he left, at around 3:45.

Shortly afterward Werner phoned and said he had the afternoon free, so we made a date to meet at the Café Bellevue on Potsdamerplatz at 4:30. Being used to letting people know exactly where I am, I told Martha where I was going. Werner and I had scarcely exchanged a few words when Erich appeared, completely beside himself. "Father is dead," he said. [. . .]

Your father didn't own anything valuable. He had a large gold pocketwatch and a gold wristwatch. Choose which of the two you want. Werner will take the other—he doesn't care which. It's your pick. [. . .]

Your mother

FROM BETTY SCHOLEM

Berlin, April 6, 1925

My dear child,

On the first of April I received your postcard; also the offprint on alchemy and Kabbalah sent March 24. Uncle Hans took it with him to read and will return it to me. My siblings were here at the time. It is such a beautiful piece of work! Isn't it a bit too scholarly for me though?

Today I'll send you some newspapers articles commemorating the opening of the university.[66] The papers of all of the political parties have shown a great deal of interest in it. I hope you'll write us a detailed letter about your impressions of the celebrations and what you did. [. . .]

Kisses, Mum

FROM BETTY SCHOLEM

Berlin, April 26, 1925

My dear child,

[. . .] Today is Election Sunday. The signs are inauspicious for a good voter turnout—there's a miserable rain falling. I hope it won't rain this way in the other German states. Hindenburg's candidacy is frightful rubbish, but no one knows what will happen.[67] On Friday evening at the Georgens' we listened to the radio—we heard the speech that Grandpa

Hindenburg delivered in Hannover and the one given by Marx in Nuremberg. The technology itself was far more interesting than the phrases of the candidates. [. . .]

We've commissioned the construction of a family gravesite. As we were in the process of buying the plot, Reinhold suddenly arrived and said that he too wanted a place in our family garden and paid for a third of the plot—on the spot and in hard currency. (I put the money away for my trip to Palestine.) Our site is right next to the entrance of the cemetery, around the corner from Aunt Katz and just opposite Richard Pflaum. All of them found their resting place there early in life, scarcely over sixty. Aunt Angress will be eighty-five tomorrow; I don't begrudge her a day! But just think, if I could have had your father for twenty-three more years! We'll make the large back wall out of yellow sandstone, and two steps will lead up to a balustrade surrounding it. We've decided to inscribe only your father's name and his birth and death dates. This is what he wanted. How often he made snide remarks when he saw entire novels written on the stones at Weissensee! We won't have a Hebrew inscription. There's no point to it. No one reads it, and *you* will be visiting your father's grave very rarely. [. . .]

Kisses, Mum

FROM WALTER BENJAMIN[68]

Frankfurt, May, 20–25, 1925

Dear Gerhard,

I am again sitting in Frankfurt during one of the endless waiting periods into which the local academic enterprise is divided, if not dissolved. My formal application for the *Habilitation* has been before the college faculty for a week. My chances are so slim that I put off my application until the last possible moment. [. . .]

At a party a few days ago I met Professor Horowitz, with whom you, of course, have spoken in Palestine.[69] I was unable to speak with him at length, but little of what he had to say about the inauguration of the university was close to the information in your report. Your revelations really interested me, especially your remarks about the conflict between the socialist settlements and American financial supporters. I will always be grateful to you for any additional reports that consider events from this point of view. It it also important to me in every sense to hear how you will judge further developments as you await with apprehension the effects of intense capitalist colonization. Your observations on the "seemingly dead" transmitted language which, as the Hebrew living and being transformed in the mouths of the new generation, threatens to turn against those who speak it, are not clear to me in every respect.[70] [. . .]

Yours, Walter

TO ERNST SIMON

Jerusalem, September 2, 1925

Dearest friend,

[. . .] Please confirm whether you got the offprint of my article on Abraham Ha-Levi.[71] I am now busy writing extremely obscure essays, placing my trust in the kind of immortality that comes to those who are not read, only praised. This remains the case, that is, until someone begins to raise questions—just as I am doing with regard to the blessed Steinschneider.[72] In my memoirs I will let loose against him. I've already issued a warning!

My Hebrew book on two kabbalistic brothers who lived around 1260 will soon go to press. It's a shame I'll have to pay for it myself. I'll sell it door to door, which probably means a trip to Europe. When you read my books, you can correct the numerous typos.

You know that I came to Palestine without many illusions. After two years, I can now assure you that I unfortunately have even fewer than before. We are in God's hands on this boat—and we surely have no other. We can no longer expect much help from history. No one should foster the illusion that what happens here and will occur in the future (after the open retreat from everything to do with human *tikkun*)[73] has the slightest thing in common, *in substantia et essentia,* with Zionism, in whose name your faithful servant is here. In the battle between the building up of Palestine *coûte qu'il coûte* and Zionism, the latter is hopelessly outgunned. The honest question consequently arises: What is the best way to support the cause of those who have paid the price of the Zionism which they now betray? [. . .] The Zionist movement is now almost entirely preoccupied with dressing the recent *aliyah* in Zionist garb.[74] I consider it God's just punishment for the misuse of the *haluz* that the most conniving sharks and the seven streams of hell now pour in upon us from Lodz. And if they get baptized into *haluzim,* then the saying fits: "And they shall devour Israel with open mouth."[75] Zionism abdicated long ago; the only question the Zionist should now ask is where he really belongs.

You must have heard that the government recently passed a new naturalization law which, to judge from the Hebrew text, represents the most unimaginable baseness. You should write something publicly about this. We are completely at the mercy of the English (and believe me, you have to see it to believe it). If I do something the government doesn't like, it can revoke my Palestinian *natinut!!!* This means *natin* until countermanded!!![76] And we have to accept it; we have no other choice, because we have nothing. I must confess that when I read this announcement, everything went black. Today the law is of course directed against the Communists; tomorrow I may be the next victim. A week ago the Palestinian office of the Agudat Israel opened up across the street from my house. It's a collection of sharks who make me despair about this religion of theirs. But *these people* won't be able to bury Zionism either.

Pardon me for these gloomy outbursts. Indeed, there's nothing to laugh about. And so your devoted servant lashes out in writing against the government, while sending his best regards.

Yours, GS

FROM WERNER SCHOLEM
(mailed with the following letter, from Betty Scholem)

Berlin, October 4, 1925

Dear Gerhard,

Mother tells me you've gotten a position as professor at the university in Jerusalem. I congratulate you on this important breakthrough! At the moment, I find myself in a rather precarious position. The death of the Communist party is close at hand, but before this happens they want to give the boot to everyone who refuses to go with Noske.[77]

All the best, Werner

FROM BETTY SCHOLEM

Berlin, October 4, 1925

My dear child,

This brings me such colossal joy! Congratulations on your success, which you've been so quick to achieve. If your father were alive, he would be delighted. All the boys send their greetings and wish you all best. I immediately told everyone who's interested, and of course boasted that you are only twenty-eight years old. The news was a sensation at the Friday night dinner at the Maxens'. Write to me in detail about your responsibilities and whether you will stay at the library. I assume so, since you wrote that you would like to get a one-year leave from your position there. [. . .]

I'm curious to know whether the marzipan arrived fresh and still tasty. The postage cost nearly four marks, and I don't know if it was worth it.

Theobald and his wife are also firmly intending to visit you in the spring. They said that when the Theilhabers were in Palestine for four to six weeks (I'm not sure precisely how long), they needed 1,600 marks apiece. The two of them are planning to spend about the same. I can't spend more than 4,000; I'm no maharajah. In Palestine I'd like to live very simply; otherwise, I'll never manage to visit you. Hete[78] nearly laughed herself to death when she heard your suggestion. Do you really think that Theo will spend 8,000 marks for such a trip? So, my child, please come up with a more reasonable proposal! You can't base your estimate on the prices charged by the best hotel in town. I can do without such luxury! In general, I thought it would be possible to simply rent a room and eat when the occasion arose. It will work out!

Kisses, Mum

FROM BETTY SCHOLEM

Berlin, October 12, 1925

My dear child,

[. . .] We're eager to print the translation of your inaugural address, and are looking forward to its arrival. Please don't say that I took "basically no notice" of it!!

I often hear about the reputation you enjoy. Edith has a cousin who has lived in Haifa for years. Recently he came to Berlin and visited us. It was only here that she heard she was the wife of a Scholem. "Is your husband by any chance related to Dr. Scholem?" He, the cousin, has never met you—he knows you only through hearsay. But he became enthusiastic when he told us what a superstar you are. [. . .]

Kisses, Mum

TO ERNST SIMON

Jerusalem, "built upon its own heap . . ."[79]

December 22, 1925

Dear Simon,

[. . .] We're doing well. As a "professor" I can enjoy 50 percent of my freedom, which is nothing to scoff at. I am working a lot. I have some serious personal reservations vis-à-vis the Institute of Jewish Studies, and I can't deny that I consider Klausner's appointment in the apparently "harmless" field of *toldut sifrut* a highly questionable blunder, motivated by the purest cowardice (or in the long run by fear).[80] I've heard him speak; yesterday I went to hear him lecture again. Take my word for it— it's obscene to allow such a second-rate hack to teach at the University of Jerusalem. In view of all this, at least I can be happy that people leave me in peace.

You'll soon get to read a small piece of my immortality: a printed version of my inaugural address. I had the terribly embarrassing task of speaking after Klausner gave an unbelievably stupid and pompous lecture. That's life. God's sun shines upon all sorts of beasts.

I read an interesting article by Rosenzweig in *Der Morgen*. Do you still see him? Send him my greetings when you get the chance. Incidentally, I'm of the *keen* opinion that he hit the nail on the head when he admitted not being the best interpreter of his own work. It's really *most* curious that his book hasn't been mentioned in the Hebrew literature— not a syllable. Often I must fight back the temptation to write a few words about this in Hebrew. And especially now that the *classic work on Jewish Satanism* has appeared: Goldberg's *Reality of the Hebrews*[81]—a book that I highly recommend to you. I've been unable to say a good word about Hirsch since reading it.[82] The Orthodox should actually be forced to say what they think about such satanic work, which concedes everything to them. Rarely have I had such fun as with this polytheistic Torah commentary (so similar to excellent detective novels!). It ultimately tells you how the devil reads the Bible—if he's snooty enough to try.

But back to Rosenzweig. To my utter amazement, I read in the latest edition of the *Jüdische Rundschau* a truly hellish promotional blurb concerning a Bible translation "undertaken" by Buber and Rosenzweig. I was flabbergasted, even though I saw it coming—flabbergasted at the very possibility that such authors could reap this kind of praise. I fear the absolute worst from this translation. After working through the entire text, I consider Rosenzweig's translation of Judah Ha-Levy really quite poor (Rosenzweig is without question the driving force behind the Bible project). The annotations are all that redeem it. But by the time you get to them, they've lost their sense. I have always been of the secret opinion that the last *xenia*[83] the Jews would be required to provide before, or during, their exit from Germany would be a Bible translation. Will this be it? [. . .]

Yours, Gerhard Scholem

1926

FROM WALTER BENJAMIN[84]

Berlin, January 14, 1926

Dear Gerhard,

I had been meaning to write to you for a long time. Your letter to Dora just arrived today. She plans to answer you herself. I believe I am at liberty to reveal that she was very pleased to get it. A more detailed report on Stefan will most probably be included in her letter. He is of course learning Hebrew now—but probably not much is accomplished in his elective courses, and the only thing he really likes are the Bible stories, which are taught by another teacher. Speaking of this, I would really like you to tell me whether you know of a Jewish anthology (with German text) that I could go through with Stefan. I read aloud to him for a few hours, if not every day, then certainly every week, and in doing so I wander aimlessly through a fairy-tale edifice, something urged upon us by our books. Instead of this, I would like to read Jewish history or stories to him, something that, in the final analysis, would also be more appealing to me—regardless of my imminent involvement with problems relating to the fairy tale. But I do not know whether there is anything that would meet such vague goals. There has recently been a flood of festivities, for Stefan too—Hanukkah (after that, Christmas at my parents') and Dora's birthday—and he received more gifts than his still rather sparsely furnished room can hold. Naturally he has had his own room for a long time now; Grete has the room next to the kitchen, in which my brother used to live. In a few days he will be marrying a likable young woman, a friend of my sister, whom he trained to be a Communist. His Christian in-laws, therefore, have a doubly bitter pill to swallow. By the way, has your brother Werner been expelled from the party, as you once seemed to predict? [. . .]

Yours, Walter

FROM ERNST SIMON

January 1, 1926

Dear Scholem,

[. . .] Erich Fromm mentioned in passing that you had asked indirectly through Frau Theodor whether he wanted to take over your job at the library. One year of unpaid training, and then he would get the job you had vacated because of your position at the university. It's possible that I could take it up around Pesach,[85] assuming that the report is accurate and hasn't been distorted on its way through the grapevine. [. . .]

As for the translation of the Bible, I consider it *very* good—beyond all of my expectations (though I, too, am wary of the Judah Ha-Levy translation). The blurb in the *Rundschau* was indeed "hellish," as you so lovingly described it. Right after I saw it, I phoned Frau Rosenzweig and asked her to relay my outrage to her husband. I then repeated this in person, but he denied that it was a "blurb"; it was a publisher's advertisement, and you cannot dictate a particular use of language to a publisher. [. . .] The upshot is that I agree with you. Yet *despite* the blurb and the occasional pomposity and a number of individual anomalies, it's a good translation. Taken as a whole, I think of it as a Jewish Luther-Bible. I know what I'm talking about, and I also know that you'll hold it against me in the event (which is likely) that you arrive at an opposing viewpoint.

Sincerely yours, Ernst Simon

TO ERNST SIMON

Jerusalem, January 1926

Dear friend,

I'll answer you according to the questions raised in your letter.

There is nothing that can be done concerning the situation at the library. I don't have any idea whether I'll be leaving. I'm still director of the Judaica section of the library. [. . .] The matter with Fromm was merely a provisional inquiry. In the real world, you wouldn't have a chance to earn a salary at the library next year, since it doesn't pay a thing. (Where should it get the money?)

I wasn't in the least happy with your reply to my observations about the new *targum*.[86] Meanwhile, I've read both excerpts printed in the *Frankfurter Zeitung* and the *Jüdische Rundschau*. I await the book. In my opinion, the excerpts have an *unmistakable false pathos* without the slightest trace of the Luther Bible. Luther had a fine and genuine sense for the musical pitch of language; and in this regard Buber and Rosenzweig are totally off key—to say nothing of the wild pretentiousness of their language. You call this "good," but you'll *atid atah latet et ha-din*.[87] [. . .] If I were better acquainted with Buber, I would grumble to him too. I'm deeply disappointed that such barber-shop German has suddenly raised its head again. [. . .]

Yours, Gerhard Scholem

FROM BETTY SCHOLEM

Berlin, February 2, 1926

My dear child,

Last Wednesday I did not get a letter.

With only fourteen days before the steamship departs, I heard from Cook Tours that the Dutch lines have definitely reserved a spot for me. Hopefully I can travel with this ship, since the large East Asian lines are cheaper and better than the smaller Mediterranean ones. In any case, Cook wrote to Marseilles and there are two ships I could take, one leaving on the second of March and the other on the ninth. In one way or another, I will make it. [. . .]

Werner came to have dinner with me. On top of suffering from an inflamed liver and gallbladder, his political position has become precarious. The group that he and his friends squeezed out of power has now returned, following a sudden shift of wind coming from Moscow. This time they've thrown *him* out of the saddle—using the typical political devices of character assassination, fact-twisting, and insults. He has not chosen a very easy life for himself. [. . .]

Mum

TO MARTIN BUBER[88]

Dear Dr. Buber,

It took a long time for me to get around to looking over all of the Genesis translation you sent me and to thanking you with a good conscience, albeit belatedly. As you can easily imagine, I have thought about problems of Bible translation for so long and so intensively that your and Rosenzweig's undertaking has evoked a very lively response in me. Until quite recently I struggled with the translation of those parts of the Bible in which I had a special interest (at least as regards my responsiveness to them) and with my harmful doubts about the translatability of these things to such an extent that, if you will permit someone who has been defeated by this problem to tell you this, I can only send you my best wishes for the success of your project—even in areas where I still have my doubts. I do not believe that it can be useful for you, a man who has received such distinct inspiration from the text as it presented itself to you, to reencounter as "criticism" misgivings that have probably arisen in you a hundred times. In your translation, I admire the magnificent objective clarity. In it, I find the best expression of the way in which you, in your own way, so unmistakably respond to the Bible. *What fills me with doubt* is the excessive *tone* of this prose, which leaps out almost uncannily from the particular phrasing (this word is wrong; I mean the *niggun* of your translation).[89] [. . .]

I am planning to attempt a coherent presentation of the thoughts stirred by your translation in a Hebrew debate with another reader, Agnon. If it materializes, we shall certainly present you with a transcript.

All of us here are very sorry that your trip to Palestine did not work out this time either. I had thought it was a sure thing, and I had hoped to be able to speak with you about the university and everything connected with it. Surely our present test-tube situation is rather unhealthy. I could also tell you quite a bit about my own plans and ideas about the nature of my work and activity within the framework of the university. At bottom, it seems to me that everything revolves around the language question—a problem which, I fear, is partly responsible for your not coming and so many other negative conditions. Your not coming: not as a tourist but as a citizen.

I am not giving up hope of seeing you soon. I, to be sure, shall certainly not come to Europe this year.

Sincerely yours, Gerhard Scholem

FROM BETTY SCHOLEM

National Hotel, Cairo; Friday, May 7, 1926

Dear children,

[. . .] Early this morning, around six, Ali turned up with the car and we went to the Pyramids. The car stopped at a respectful distance, so as not to ruin business for the camels. The truth of the matter is that you could just as easily do the entire tour of the Sphinx and the Cheops Pyramids by car, given the smooth and hard road that has already been beaten into the earth. Anyway, I made myself comfortable on the kneeling camel. When the beast rose up into the air with me on him, I went pale from fear. "Madam, I am here for you," scolded Ali. And so I sat on it like an ape, though I got used to it quickly and was able to marvel properly at the ancient wonders. The desert ride lasted forty-five minutes. Ali insisted that I climb at least four of the 475 steps of the Great Pyramid, and four other fellows also tried to drag me up. They surrounding me picturesquely, only to take on an expression of disdain because I didn't have a camera to snap a picture of them. [. . .]

Kisses, Mum

TO ERNST SIMON

Jerusalem, May 12, 1926

Dear Simon,

[. . .] Contrary to your assumption, not only did I sign the declaration against the legion (which has generated a flood of slander against us all, true to the dictum: "Who asked you?"), but I am the one who more or less composed it.[90] Practically speaking, I cannot see what—as you supposed—I should have against the others who signed it. That they pay homage to a less catastrophic view of history than mine? At least these men have a heart, even if they are absolute fools (as is Rabbi Benjamin). For all that, *irbu c'mohem b'israel.*[91]

I've decided that I will take leave of philology and return to the realms of (still far from comprehensible) thought, even if—to quote my friend Walter Benjamin—I will fall apart in the process. My attempt to provoke a philosophical debate over fundamentals of the Kabbalah among the people sitting in my lectures has until now failed, owing to their absolute inability to think. [. . .]

Yours, Gerhard Scholem

FROM WALTER BENJAMIN[92]

Paris, May 29, 1926

Dear Gerhard,

As you can already gather from the format, I am gearing up to write a long and detailed letter. Nevertheless, I confess that I am somewhat uneasy at barely being able to respond to your most urgent questions. For this very reason, I would like to make my unworthy effort to do so right at the outset. It is basically very difficult for me to have to give a hypothetical account of myself, since my book on these matters (should it ever materialize) has not yet matured. What there currently is of it increasingly seems to be giving signs of attempting to leave the purely theoretical sphere. [. . .] If I were to join the Communist party someday (something that, in turn, I am making dependent on one last twist of fate), my stance would be to behave always radically and never logically when it came to the most important things. Whether it would be possible for me to stay in the party would be determined simply through experimentation. What is more interesting and more debatable than whether I will join the party is how long I would stay a member. The brazen weapons of certain irrefutable insights (such as, for example, that materialist metaphysics or, indeed, even the materialist conception of history is irrelevant) may in an emergency achieve just as much in practical terms, and perhaps even more, acting in concert with Communism rather than against it. If it is true, as you claim, that I have actually gotten "behind some principles" that I knew nothing about in your day, I have gotten "behind" this one above all: anyone of our generation who feels and understands the historical moment in which he exists in this world, not as mere words, but as a battle, cannot renounce the study and practice of the mechanism through which things (and conditions) and the masses interact. [. . .]

Yours, Walter

FROM BETTY SCHOLEM

Berlin, November 8, 1926

My dear child,

I'm starting this letter in the morning. The last time the post went out, I began the day with a headache and in the evening I had a concert, the result being that I had no time for you. This time I don't want to wait until the last minute!

I replied to your letter from October 22 the day it came (the twenty-seventh), so here I can only repeat what I wrote: that I fear I'll see you drown someday in kabbalistic manuscripts—two hundred all at once. You work much too hard. Even cheap detective novels would be too weak an antidote to keep your spirit in balance! [. . .]

Kisses, Mum

FROM BETTY SCHOLEM

Berlin, December 7, 1926

My dear children,

[. . .] Werner was expelled from the Communist party, along with the others who refused to bow to the dictates from Moscow. He will keep his Reichstag seat as long as the parliamentary session lasts, for the simple reason that it belongs to him and not to the party. The moment the Reichstag is dissolved or new elections are called, he will be left high and dry. This won't be such a catastrophe as long as his wife has a good job. He now intends to study law, and the boys want to support him. But is he cut out for it?! With his pessimistic nature, his lack of self-confidence, and his famous name, it is *not* at all certain he can succeed. But what else can he do? If his own party's paper refuses to hire him as a journalist, then newspapers of other political persuasions certainly won't print his articles. The boy has a real cross to bear. Yesterday evening he left for Moscow, summoned before the bar of the highest party tribunal. I hope he can reach some agreement with that rabble. I simply do not understand why, beginning with the Social Democrats, he has always opposed his own party.

1928[93]

FROM WALTER BENJAMIN[94]

Berlin, January 30, 1928

Dear Gerhard,

This letter may well turn out to be interminably long. You should view it as chain lightning, to be followed in a few days by a long, rumbling clap of thunder in the form of an imposing package of books. How long you will have to wait for it will be a direct function of the distance from the eye of the thunderstorm to the Holy Land. May the package find a resounding echo in the alpine valleys of Your Excellency's head!

It simply would not have done to write yet again to "announce" the publication of my books. And luckily it was the end of January before both of them were available. Now I can simply say, "Here they are." In your role as protector of the university library, you will receive at the same time a second copy of both works and, in your no less important role as protector of my career, a third copy of the *Trauerspiel* book with an inscription for Magnes.[95] [. . .]

Now that the way ahead is clear, nothing would be more obvious for me than to make the decisive move to commit myself to Hebrew. I am free, but unfortunately in the twofold sense of the word: free of obligations and of income. If you and Magnes are currently engaged in serious discussions about me, explain to him how things stand: that I need a stipend, or, to express it better, security, if I am now to jump off the cart that, although slow-moving, is traveling the career path of a German writer. And if things get to the point where he asks you for a figure, tell him 300 marks a month for however long an accelerated course of study would take. He himself will be best able to estimate the duration of such a course of study, predicated on my total independence from other ties and interests. [. . .]

Yours, Walter

FROM BETTY SCHOLEM

Berlin, January 31, 1928

My dear child,

You're being very stubborn when you insist on composing your letters on a typewriter. I got your marvelous-looking missive of January 19 on the twenty-fifth. I sympathize completely when Escha says she's tormented by the click-clack of the machine; the very thought of it makes my eyelids flutter.

We read about your three-year appointment. You can't imagine how delighted I am by your financial security. If I may remind you, however, you already received my congratulations two years ago when you ordered a list of books in anticipation of this appointment. [. . .]

It's really dreadful to get a list of everything we *should* send you, followed by a hue and cry because we sent the wrong thing. I really must finally break my habit of sending you things. If one of your cabinets falls apart, a carpenter can no doubt fix it; I can't send you thirty marks to replace it. I have to say no for once—otherwise, there will be no end to it. You earn a decent salary, after all. You can buy your own filing cabinet, instead of constantly nagging me for one. I bought two *sausages* for you today with my last penny. They'll be off to you tomorrow. Leave me in peace for a while!

If I had sent you filing cards as printed material, they would certainly have arrived dog-eared and crumpled. Then you would *surely* have ranted and raved and asked why we hadn't put them in the cabinet. There's no cure for an irritable temperament.

Two ties, two books, a towel, and more sausages are on their way. I haven't even managed to say a thing about the family or myself; I've done nothing but respond to your screams, to the point that it brings tears to my eyes. Oh, son! [. . .]

Kisses, Mum

TO BETTY SCHOLEM

Jerusalem, January 31, 1928

[. . .] This week another book of mine will be published—small but beautiful, and in the most elegant print. Forty pages. Once again it's a bibliography, and as such indigestible for the average reader. It will appear in honor of Martin Buber's fiftieth birthday.[96] [. . .]

We are most offended by your sausage comment; Escha in particular has developed a strong sense of honor about these matters. Of course we're prepared to send money in advance for the things we request, but we're also aware that doing so would significantly hamper your natural instincts toward generosity. [. . .]

TO BETTY SCHOLEM

Jerusalem, March 7, 1928

Dear Mother,

[. . .] Today is Purim, a holiday always associated with a great deal of excitement. Escha made me happy by giving me the crepes, chocolates, and cream cakes I wanted. A rather tasteless carnival is underway here, and outside there are absurd numbers of masks moving about. Yesterday something big happened: the midgets got married.[97] We all went to the wedding: the Cohns, Dr. Bergmann, and Agnon. Escha was forced to sit with the bride under the huppa.[98] The Yemenites sit under it for hours. The bride, wearing a silk dress, a veil, and a garland made of orange blossoms, looked simply fabulous. Next to her, Escha looked like a massive hen who had hatched a small, gaudy chick. The groom looked serious and solemn and newly dressed up. Surrounding us were the colorful Yemenite masses. The orchestra played "The Little Doll," and a few of the more up-to-date boys and girls danced to modern music. [. . .]

Your devoted son, Dr. Gerhard Scholem

FROM BETTY SCHOLEM

Berlin, March 27, 1928

My dear child,

[. . .] Once again I am really concerned about Werner. You know his pessimistic way of speaking. Well, he now claims that once the Reichstag is dissolved he'll be immediately arrested because of what happened in 1923.[99] It still has not been laid to rest, and he and a dozen other Communists continue to be held responsible. If he's arrested he won't be able to pursue his studies. The boy bears a cross. You can only pity his wife, who has been very ill. Despite Käte Schiepan's impassioned warnings, she had a doctor (a "comrade"—for her, the highest authority!) install some sort of contraceptive device. But Käte is no Communist and supposedly does not have a thorough grasp of such matters. Then she wound up terribly maltreated, and Käte was beside herself over her stubbornness. People are stupid and there's not a thing you can do about it. [. . .]

Kisses and adieu, Mum

TO BETTY SCHOLEM

Jerusalem, April 13, 1928

Dearest Mother,

The salami arrived, along with the Ben-Jehuda dictionary. Many thanks. Escha stored them away for a couple of days because of Passover, though this evening I hope I can start in on them. Max Brod[100] is in town at the moment, and there have been a number of receptions for him. We've been real Epicureans lately. [. . .]

Faithfully, Your son Gerhard

Dear Mother,

Rest assured that this man, your son, mercilessly exploits me and I'm not happy about it. It occurred to me long ago that, in his mind, a woman exists to serve.

Give yourself a treat.

Escha

TO BETTY SCHOLEM

Jerusalem, April 25, 1928

[. . .] The book on alchemy, my dear mother, which you couldn't bring with you because of your hurried departure from Germany,[101] is of extraordinary importance for my studies and I implore you not to forget about it. A thousand thanks for *The Castle* and *The Trial.*[102] [. . .]

To broaden my horizons, I am now reading *Gentlemen Prefer Blondes,* in the English original. I still prefer brunettes, but I'm learning some exquisite slang.

I wish you all the best and greet you on behalf of Escha, who has a stomach ache and sprawls idly on the sofa because of the sudden arrival of warm weather.

Your obedient son, Gerhard

TO BETTY SCHOLEM

Jerusalem, May 10, 1928

Dearest Mother,

[. . .] My constant begging bothers Escha. She has issued a warning by referring to Heine's biographers, who have criticized his uninterrupted *schnorring* among his relatives. But I'm not like Heine. I place full trust in the unerring instincts of future generations, who will be able to follow the track of purest joy (mine in receiving, yours in giving) running between the lines of our respective letters. Who at the moment is thinking about publishing our letters anyway??

Speaking of literature, dearest mother, what on earth prompted you to compare your gifted son with Richard Pflaum?[103] I don't deny that he may have been a talent worthy of affection—but as a writer, wasn't he largely a comical figure? In general, I don't hesitate to admit there's a certain ridiculous element in my character, but as a writer I am inclined to forbid the comparison. I thus read your words with puzzlement. Try as I might, I could not find the *tertium comparationis.* [. . .]

Your obedient son, Gerhard

TO WERNER KRAFT

Jerusalem, May 10, 1928

Dear Werner,

[. . .] It's a real shame I didn't see you in Germany. I'll be staying put in Palestine this year—feeding sumptuously, as it were, on what I found during last year's visit. I'm not yet thinking about what I'll do next year. In this I follow Karl Krauss's maxim: "We'll just have to see what happens."

In Berlin I gave instructions to have a small publication sent to you: an alphabet book for philosophically inclined children.[104] I hope you got it, because I couldn't give my brother anything more than "Podbielski Strasse" as the address. Even though I don't want to get myself involved in competition with lyricists, for the first time in my life I've also written an article without footnotes.[105] If only for this deeply symbolic reason, I'll send you a copy as soon as I get my hands on an offprint. I expect it to arrive any day. It's an article in Buber's *Der Jude*—a journal which I cannot assume will be of any interest to you, even if I value certain things about it.

It seems rather doubtful that your knowledge of Hebrew would be sufficient for you to read my other cheap novelistic accomplishments. Maybe one of these days you'll pick up a bit and can study the conditions of this language here on the spot.

Many greetings to you and your wife.

Warmly, Gerhard

P.S. Long ago (this is an answer to a question you posed in an earlier letter!) I read Kafka's *The Trial* and *The Castle*. I own all of his books, and cannot deny that I had a long discussion with Max Brod, who was here three weeks ago. I consider *The Trial* an absolutely magnificent work. It is the first retelling of the book of Job that a human being— naturally a Jew—has managed to produce. Rarely have I been so moved.

By the way, Brod is crazy about commentary on Kafka's books. You'd be doing yourself a service if you told him what you thought. Brod truly delighted me when he (like many people here) claimed that I bear a remarkable similarity to Kafka. Lord, how I loved to hear that!

FROM WALTER BENJAMIN[106]

Berlin, May 24, 1928

Dear Gerhard,

I am enclosing a copy of my vita and the exposé I am sending to Magnes in London today. I hope you will find it satisfactory. You will see from my letter to Magnes that nothing is happening with Paris and

I do not know myself if and when anything will happen this year.[107] I am finding it difficult to leave Berlin. First, there is my room—specifically, a new one, because at the moment I am not living in Grunewald but in the heart of the Tiergarten (In den Zelten), in a room into which nothing but trees peer at me through both windows. It is wonderful and, in addition to everything else, only ten minutes away from the National Library, the other focal point of the ellipse that keeps me here. My work on the Paris arcades is taking on an ever more mysterious and insistent mien, and howls into my nights like a small beast if I have failed to water it at the most distant springs during the day. God knows what it will do when, one of these days, I set it free. But this will not happen for a long time; and though I may already be constantly staring into the cage in which it does what comes naturally, I let hardly anyone else have a look inside. [. . .]

I have firmly put an autumn visit to Palestine on my agenda for the coming year. I hope that Magnes and I will have reached an agreement about the financial terms of my apprenticeship before then. Thank you so much for your invitation. I would naturally be very happy to stay with the two of you for a few weeks, if this can be arranged. [. . .]

Yours, Walter

FROM WALTER BENJAMIN[108]

Berlin, August 1, 1928

Dear Gerhard,

My trip to Palestine is a settled matter, as is my intention to strictly observe the course of study prescribed by Your Hierojerusalemitic Excellency. Let me moreover vow that the awestruck undersigned will be able to read the alphabet common to the country before he sets foot on the soil of Eretz Israel. On the other hand, in return for some donations to the authorities, he intends to take advantage of the assistance of public scribes at first. According to the reports of travelers, these scribes exist in the Orient and can be found everywhere, especially in the neighborhood of Mea Schearim in Jerusalem.[109] With the help of such a scribe, he plans at the very start to direct a request to Professor Magnes for a

partial stipend, whether for one or several months, leaving the amount
the undersigned will receive to Magnes' judgment.

So much, dear Gerhard, for the official part of this letter. Now to
the pertinent details. First the date of my arrival. It may have to be de-
layed until mid-December. This will depend first of all on whether I
can make up my mind to complete the Arcades Project before I leave
Europe. Second, on whether I get together with a Russian woman friend
in Berlin in the fall. [. . .]

Yours, Walter

TO BETTY SCHOLEM

Jerusalem, September 6, 1928

Dearest Mother,

[. . .] The chief purpose of this letter is to convey warmest wishes to
you and the rest of the family for a happy new year. All the best for the
new year!!! *L' shana tova ticatevu.*[110]

As my New Year's gift, I would very much like the Strack–Billerbeck
commentary to the New Testament, *volume 3,* bound in the same format
as the previous volumes. May I once again send a general list of things
for gradual purchase? You yourself wrote that autumn was coming and
that your sojourn in the countryside won't last much longer. The season
is drawing to a close, and marzipan, chocolate, sausage, and goose fat
are thus once again drawing near to me. I forgot to add that the aforementioned reference work was published by Beck in Munich.

Your obedient son, Gerhard

FROM WALTER BENJAMIN

Berlin, September 20, 1928

Dear Gerhard,

[. . .] I agree that it would be better not to approach Magnus about the
Palestinian stipend until I have really begun intensive Hebrew lessons. In
this regard you are completely right. I do not, however, want to make

it contingent on my arrival in Palestine. I will most certainly come for four to five months. But precisely because I will be there for such a long time, the date of my trip is still not easy for me to pin down; it can just as easily be January instead of December. In any event, living with you will be of the greatest importance at *every* stage of my Hebrew studies. According to our agreement—and I mean its spirit, not just the letter— Magnes will surely realize that I am expecting the grant from the time I actually begin the real studies and make them the focus of my work. [. . .]

Walter

TO BETTY SCHOLEM

Jerusalem, October 4, 1928

Dear Mother,

Many thanks for the warm and lengthy letter. I see you're touring the world again. Being so good-natured, I applaud this wholeheartedly. I'm writing to you at your fancy Viennese hotel with the hope that this letter will reach and amuse you. Vienna is a target for us, too, in the near future: for me as a locus of scholarship, for Escha (who, like all woman, is superficial) as a locus of sightseeing. We'll just have to see. In any event, we certainly won't end up at your hotel. Your son Rein-hold must have planned something extraordinary for his anniversary, seeing that he is so resentful toward his wife for clinging to him. Has he calmed down again?

We don't treat our cats like that, and we don't give them away. Re-cently we had six: the older one; one from the first marriage; and four newborns from the second. We took a trip to my brother-in-law's for five days, and when we returned we found that the one from the first marriage had died under mysteriously circumstances. Now we have only five cats left. We really mourned the little kitten. We'll probably keep one of the new kittens—black as a raven, this time—which should make a good impression. This is the way we are! It's name will be Schem-hurisch[111] Scholem. [. . .]

Your faithful son, Gerhard

FROM BETTY SCHOLEM

Auf dem Semmerling, October 7, 1928

My dear child,

I can't bear this Vienna, so I sit up here in order to catch my breath. First things first. We left with the car early on the morning of Wednesday the twenty-ninth. It was a marvelous drive. I can hardly describe the pleasure it gave me! [. . .] On the third day of the trip we followed the Danube, through magnificent countryside. We drove through Linz and then took a look at the famous monastery of Melk, a fantastic building overlooking the river. In the evening we waltzed our way into Vienna. We had to drive more than an hour through dreadful suburbs until we finally saw the center, the royal city. It's a superb scene with wonderfully beautiful Baroque palaces. These people certainly could build! But we also find ourselves breathing concentrated gasoline fumes. I, for one, cannot endure the air, and my energies began to flag as soon as I set out to walk the streets. [. . .]

Warmest kisses, Mum

TO BETTY SCHOLEM

Jerusalem, November 8, 1928

My dearest Mother,

[. . .] The news that you printed my essay is both surprising and de-lightful.[112] Is the type still set up? [. . .] This study is of the *utmost importance* to me. And if it appears in such a beautiful and dignified form, it will first and foremost enhance my reputation. In addition, I can eventually sell it to utopians and the like, just as I did with *Alchemy and Kabbalah.* I'm sure you understand me and will make all of the appropriate arrangements.

Warm thanks in advance for the birthday present. I've made Escha's wish-list public as well and hope it'll be a grand birthday. I'm hereby confirming the arrival of the sausage. [. . .]

Your obedient son, Gerhard

1929

TO WERNER KRAFT

Jerusalem, February 27, 1929

Dear Werner,

[. . .] I read your remarks on Kafka in the *Weltbühne,* along with the woman's response. I have no idea what this woman means by "mentally ill," though the issue seems to revolve around it. Authoritative Kafka experts (such as Hugo Bergmann) also assure me that Brod's description of Kafka in his last book hits the mark, all the way down to the demonic details. It must be true, given the fact that Kafka's friends had until the end a deep and abiding mistrust of Brod. Brod's depiction of the mood around Kafka seems wonderfully successful. Ultimately, the service Brod has done in this case is so great that we can easily forgive him five bad novels—even though, surprisingly enough, they are not nearly as bad as one would expect.

Your Gerhard

TO BETTY SCHOLEM

Jerusalem, March 4, 1929

Beloved Mother,

You've no doubt wondered why there haven't been any letters from your truest and youngest son. I have frivolously surrendered myself to pleasure. My sister-in-law Tescha (given this name because it rhymed with "Escha") has just arrived and turned our lives topsy-turvy. During prime letter-writing time we went to a carnival with Tescha in Tel Aviv (a city built on sand, though it's still standing). Dressed like a Persian Jew, I attended a rather raucous ball. I found myself amid the jubilant masses. You must have read in the paper how the Graf Zeppelin dropped confetti from the sky. Confetti did not fall on me, though I saw the Zeppelin directly over Cohen's chocolate shop. It passed over the city of Tel Aviv, made a couple of turns, performed some short, easy maneuvers, signaled with its lights, and then vanished. [. . .]

Your obedient son, Gerhard

FROM WALTER BENJAMIN[113]

Berlin, March 15, 1929

Dear Gerhard,

I was delighted to hear that you will probably not come to Europe. This may make it possible for me to begin my trip to Palestine even before the fall.

I spoke to Buber yesterday. I explained the situation to him in detail and learned that Dr. Magnes is not here at the moment but is expected back in a few days. I will turn to him. Robert Weltsch has already left for Palestine. Buber told me that he recommended me as someone to give lectures at the School for Jewish Youth. For the time being, however, I more easily see myself sitting at one of its desks than standing at the lectern.

Optime, amice, you ask about what might lie hidden behind my essay on Surrealism. (I believe I sent it to you in its entirety. Please let me know if you have received it). This work is, in fact, a screen placed in front of my Arcades Project—and I have many a reason to keep secret what goes on behind it. But I will nonetheless reveal this much just for you: the issue here is precisely what you once touched on after reading my *One-Way Street*—namely, to attain the most extreme concreteness for an era, as it occasionally manifested itself in children's games, a building, or a real-life situation. A perilous, breathtaking enterprise, repeatedly put off over the course of the winter, not without reason—also because of the terrible competition with Hebrew—thus sometimes paralyzing me, and, as I have discovered, it was just as impossible to postpone as it is to complete at this time.

I will consequently *a tempo* take up Hebrew and at the same time make enough progress on the Arcades Project that I can again put it on a back burner in Palestine without any harm coming to it. The best thing would be for it to come to a sudden conclusion. But I am unable to count on that. I will write to Magnes as soon as I have started my lessons. [. . .]

Yours, Walter

FROM BETTY SCHOLEM

Berlin, April 22, 1929

Dear child,

[. . .] By the way, the local paper carried a picture of the carnival in Tel Aviv; it appeared, as well, in the illustrated supplement to the Sunday editions of the large newspapers. Palestine never quite disappears from their field of vision. Koestler wrote an article in "Aunt Voss"[114] on the ancient synagogue at Beth Alpha. He was taken there by an archeologist from the Hebrew University. [. . .]

Warmest kisses, Mum

TO BETTY SCHOLEM

Jerusalem, April 24, 1929; Eve of Passover

Dear Mother,

You see that I got the letter earlier than you thought. I thank you heartily for granting me absolution for my delinquency in writing during Purim, when the Graf Zeppelin tried in vain to target me with its confetti. Apropos of the Zeppelin, yesterday someone in Tel Aviv found an unopened bag of confetti on the roof of his house. It's being exhibited to the dazzled masses at the Middle Eastern Fair in Tel Aviv. [. . .]

One day, earlier this week, I had just decided to go to the movies when I saw a car waiting in front of the house. It took me to see Max and Felix Warburg (the famous Jews from Hamburg and New York). We discussed Judaism, Zionism, and so on. The gentlemen were most charming. I also had some successes in my role as an Elder of Zion. Max W. is one of Reinhold's colleagues—a member of the German Volkspartei.[115] Unlike Reinhold, though, he strives hard to find a relationship to Zionism. [. . .]

Your faithful son, Gerhard

TO BETTY SCHOLEM

Jerusalem, August 22, 1929

Dear Mother,

[. . .] There's a bit of confusion now that the Jews are squabbling with the Arabs.[116] I assume the *Vossische Zeitung* has played up the news that Herr von Weisl was put under arrest for two hours.[117] You are a shrewd woman, and I hope you won't think that we're all slaughtering one another. Half of the clamor in your press over there will be in honor of the noble knight von Weisl. I say this to give you some perspective.

Escha has her hands full. She's now one of two people standing in for the director, who's overseas. She has thus taken on a haughty persona, and I come off badly next to her. Since I have an honorary position at the library, she claims that, as an employee, I am temporarily her underling. This does not suit me in the least. No woman, or least not mine, should be allowed to have a career.

Your faithful son and his wife, Gerhard and Escha

FROM BETTY SCHOLEM

Zernsdorf,[118] August 27, 1929

Dear children,

You can just imagine how much the alarming reports coming out of Jerusalem have shocked us. I wanted to send a telegram, but then it occurred to me that you surely would have cabled if everything was fine. I trust you'll write me a full account of what happened, and I only hope that the newspapers exaggerate. "Hundreds of dead" sounds awful. Don't the Wygattners live in Talpioth? Is it possible that fifty children at once could have been killed in Hebron? I keep telling myself that it's like Berlin in 1919, when none of the rumors of supposed bloodbaths proved correct. But I imagine there is something to the reports and I eagerly await word from you! Won't these riots prove a major setback to the Zionist cause? It's a fearful story, and I'm going out of my mind with worry. [. . .]

Jerusalem, August 29, 1929

Dearest Mother,

I've telegraphed my sister-in-law asking her to phone you and assure you that we are fine. I hope she did it. These past days have been exhausting and upsetting. It all began at the Wailing Wall, where the Muslims have been claiming ever more rights—that is to say, they are stressing ever more loudly that the place belongs to them, as it legally does. Muslim chicanery stirred up the Jews, who then foolishly trumpeted their own claims. As a result, the Muslims accused the Jews of wanting the Mosque of Omar for themselves. With such a slogan it was easy to induce the population of a number of villages, and to a lesser extent city dwellers, to join an armed uprising against the Jews. We saw all this and knew that the situation had become serious; but we never thought it possible that on a Friday, as demonstrations threatened, the Arabs would stand in the middle of Mea Schearim in broad daylight armed with clubs and knives. I was at home, and Escha was still at work in the library. When I heard the news I went downstairs, though by that time the attack had already been repelled. The Arabs could not get very far, because the Jews and the police luckily had pistols, while the Arabs had none. Just think that this all took place two minutes from my apartment, in the heart of Jerusalem. Naturally, we haven't been able to relax since this happened. While the immediate danger was averted, the general situation remained uncertain and communication was poor. The government, which at first hesitated to forbid all demonstrations, now shied away from calling up a sufficient number of soldiers. What saved us, then, was the relatively small number of weapons in Arab hands, along with the Arabs' lack of military experience. In the future, England will have to station far more soldiers here. There were numerous attacks throughout the country. Everywhere the Arabs were repulsed, at the cost of many lives. A terrible pogrom took place in Hebron, where Jews and Arabs live together. Many Jews were either murdered or cruelly abused. It's said that, all told, 110 Jews died throughout Palestine and many more were wounded. You can just imagine what Jerusalem looks like. The entire city is full of soldiers from various regiments. Until yesterday, gun barrels still protruded from most cars. Today is better. The Jews have left nearly all of the outlying areas and the mixed Arab-Jewish neighborhoods. This goes for nearly all of our friends, who live in those parts because the modern apartments are all in the newer parts of town. We had a lot of luck with our apartment. [. . .]

Yours, Gerhard and Escha

FROM BETTY SCHOLEM

Berlin, September 2, 1929

My dear children,

Your letter from the twenty-second eased my mind a bit. I was of the opinion from the start that the whole thing was just media hype. But there must be something to the reports if England sent out warships! Or were they sent out by the newspapers? In any event, I've cut out articles from *Voss* and *Tageblatt* and will send them to you. It's urgent that you read them and tell me what's fact and what's fiction. [. . .]

Were there also attacks on the university and the library? I eagerly wait your next letter and expect to be *completely* informed on the situation. Palestine is now our only topic of conversation. Max heard somewhere that a protest meeting was announced in the *Rheingold,* to be presided over by Julius Berger.[119] But what in the world does "protest" mean? What do the Arabs care if a couple of Jews in Berlin stage a demonstration? [. . .]

Kisses, Mum

TO BETTY SCHOLEM

Jerusalem, September 5, 1929

Dearest Mother,

Since the typewriter is being used, you'll get a handwritten manuscript this time! We received your letter of August 27 and completely understand your anxiety, which was in this case more or less justified. Things here were most unpleasant, though the *Voss*'s reports from London were exaggerated and above all badly informed. They were completely different from the reality. But it was bad enough. You must read the next edition of the *Jüdische Rundschau* to get an accurate picture. It's not true that there were "hundreds of dead" in the first days of the uprising. Still, 130 Jews died; 70 were brutally murdered in Hebron. No one can tell the total number of Arab dead, since the villagers take the bodies and bury them right away so that no one can find out where the attacks originated. But casualties among the Arabs were certainly many times greater than those of the Jews, because once the situation became worse, the Jews, left in the lurch by the government for three days, had to defend themselves and they didn't play around. In addition, at that point the military (regrettably much too late) began to take extremely severe measures against the plundering villagers. Sefad, with its lovely hotels, will without question be a ghost town for the next couple of years. But in general (with five or six exceptions, which will cost the Arabs a damn fortune), the Zionist positions were undamaged in the places where young people were willing to shoot, and the Arabs knew it. Aside from a completely unsuccessful attack on Beth Alpha, nothing happened in the most important areas of settlement, such as the agricultural regions of Judea and Samaria, the Emek, and the Jordan Valley. Remarkably enough, during those wild days one of the most influential Arab sheikhs, who eight years ago made a peace pact in which he solemnly pledged to stop attacking the Jews (a pledge which at the time kept him from a fifteen-year prison sentence), kept his word. This alone was enough to protect the orange plantations, where enormous sums have been invested. Not a single shot was fired there. Alas, there is a bit of honor left in the world. It must be said that, generally speaking, the Arabs' woes have grown substantially after the pogrom in Hebron, which has put them in a terrible light in world opinion (they did not attack Zionists, the ostensible target, but murdered Talmud scholars, students, women, and children). The English commander fully intended to use his firepower to reduce Hebron to rubble because of what happened in the city. Even without this, the city is finished. No Jew will go there any more, and the Arabs will have to pay a frightfully high price. Already they're coming to the Jews with offers!!

Of the eighty-four houses in Talpioth,[120] seventeen were plundered, mostly in the outlying areas; four were totally destroyed; the others were undamaged. Nothing happened to the Wygattners' place, though *Agnon's* house was nearly totally plundered. The villages that took part in the violence were surrounded by the army and searched. The English made a terrible mistake when they evacuated Talpioth. It could have been defended with only a few weapons, but they forced the Jewish self-defense groups to leave. In the meantime, most people have already returned.

We should be safe in the coming years, after this trial of strength. Not only will the British military remain stationed here, but the organizers of the Arab revolt have taken notice that, when push comes to shove, the Jews are stronger than they expected. During the attack on Mea Schearim, a couple of minutes from us, the Arab police stood by without raising a finger. Yet two or three people struck back and managed to fend off the wild assault, so that the Arabs did not repeat it.

Similarly, the university survived intact, even though very ugly crowds gathered up there. The Arabs not only believed that we had a great stockpile of weapons and munitions, but apparently also feared the uncanny potential of the Chemistry Institute; and as a result, not a single shot was fired at the buildings. Believe it or not, in reality we only had three (legal) weapons for both of the campuses (the library up there has already been completed). We bluffed our way through the crisis with great skill.

The real bitterness here is aimed not against the Arabs, who were clearly stirred up and fanaticized through absurd lies, but against the English, whose bureaucracy played dirty. The Arab camp, oddly enough, feels the same way. The fact that the government first armed English citizens and government officials, and then, after a few days, confiscated the weapons from Jews (including high-ranking Jewish officers among the English forces) has created great resentment. You can't imagine what kind of effect this has had. [. . .]

Your faithful son, Gerhard

FROM BETTY SCHOLEM

Berlin, September 17, 1929

Dear child,

[. . .] When I got home I found your detailed letter from the fifth. Everyone read it with the greatest interest. We all think the situation is bad enough, even if the agricultural areas were luckily untouched. Quite enough has been destroyed in the realm of facts and ideals. People here have become darkly pessimistic about Zionism in general. I don't agree with them. One setback can never hold back such a development. Back in 1926 you told me that the Jews had organized their own self-defense. It seems to have worked during this catastrophe, which would have been much worse without it. [. . .]

Kisses, Mum

TO ROBERT WELTSCH

Jerusalem, September 22, 1929

Dear Dr. Weltsch,

We have been asked to express our opinion on the Haganah,[121] now that the events of recent weeks have given us an opportunity to observe the Haganah's activities and we've been able to discuss them in detail with the leaders responsible. We feel obliged to clarify our own position on the Haganah to you and to the others who support the ideas of Brit Shalom.[122] We wish to stress that we do not want to judge what has happened in the past; we wish to focus only on what, in our view, is crucial: the present situation and that in the near future.

All of us who were here during those critical days can attest that the Haganah's actions must be judged positively.

1. It was completely under the control of its leaders, and its discipline proved valuable in a critical situation. Unfortunately, this was not the case with a large portion of the Yishuv.[123]
2. It acted purely defensively and attacked only when absolutely necessary.
3. Not only did it refuse to take part in any revenge or terrorist activities, but we are convinced that it actively countered such tendencies in the strongest possible way. [. . .]

We have no doubt that during those critical days only the existence of a well-disciplined Haganah prevented a catastrophe of much greater proportions than the one which in fact took place. We were able to draw this conclusion during the first difficult days, from the most unmistakable evidence.

Furthermore, we have become convinced that in the future the Haganah's leadership will face the Arab problem with the greatest understanding. At the very least, anti-Arab tendencies are neither represented nor supported in its ranks, and the Haganah decisively rejects Revisionist schemes.[124] Naturally we are of the opinion that, now more than ever, Brit Shalom must represent a firm policy of mutual understanding as the only positive way to solve the problems entailed in developing this country. Nevertheless, given the present situation, we believe it is impossible to protect the life and property of the Yishuv without an armed militia— a militia independent of the authority of England and, in its crucial decisions, answerable to and controlled by the responsible institutions of the Yishuv. In fact, we agree with the Haganah that, under the existing circumstances, only an invisible and illegal organization can fulfill this task. And it can do so without causing damage because the danger of provocative action, which is a concomitant of everything military, can best be kept to a minimum precisely within this organization and through the decisive good will of its leaders. While there were ample opportunities to do the exact opposite, in the past weeks the Haganah has proven its good will to such an extent that we are convinced it deserves a great deal of moral credit from our circles as well.

Given the prevailing psychological and political conditions, we are acutely aware how difficult it will be to achieve a viable political arrangement with the Arabs while securing our defenses against the kind of attack we have experienced. To us, however, there appears to be no other way.

Naturally, we cannot say anything certain about the behavior of the Haganah in the future. But we have reason to believe there will be no change in the overall factors that have determined our present opinion.

With friendly greetings, G. Scholem, E. Simon, H. Bergmann

FROM BETTY SCHOLEM

Zernsdorf, October 9, 1929

My dear child,

Now that Palestine has disappeared from the pages of the daily newspapers, we assume that peace and quiet have been restored and that your life will return to normal. Hete Scholem recently made some hopeless comments. She said she could not possibly imagine any fruitful common life with the Arabs so long as both sides carry revolvers (either hidden or in the open) and stare at each other with suspicion. My experience, however, is otherwise: in life, things never succeed as wildly as people think they will—yet neither are the setbacks quite so bad as people fear. Things mostly take a middle course. [. . .]

Kisses, Mum

1930

TO BETTY SCHOLEM

Jerusalem, January 30, 1930

Dearest Mother,

[. . .] So you insist on getting a political report from me. Oh, Mother, I would really rather not. No gentleman likes to speak politics with a lady (the exception is Escha, who is a master politician). Anyway, I've been doing little else since those eventful days in August, from morning until evening. To top it off, you allowed my brother Werner to attach an insulting and suspicious remark to one of your letters.[125] Forget it! The situation has become a bit more relaxed since the terrible Commission of Inquiry left the country. It was here for months, day in and day out, forcing Jews and Arabs to hurl their accusations at each other. Of course, nothing has been forgotten—or will be forgotten, for a long time to come. Peace and quiet have been fully reestablished, and development has by no means been interrupted. On the contrary, people are busy building and planting, even if this can continue for an extended period only after conditions here normalize. The hornets' nest Dr. Bergmann finds himself in at the moment isn't so bad.[126] I for one always stand up for him proudly. We belong, after all, to the same political group that's striving for a clear and rational policy of accommodation with the Arabs. This has unleashed some unseemly reactions around us; but you know how bellicose a race we Scholems are. Besides, given the circumstances here, there's no doubt that the Cassandras have raised their cry too soon. We're optimistic. [. . .]

Sorry I can't send you my celebrated Hebrew article on the Arab question, printed in a local workers' newspaper. You'd have trouble understanding it anyway, written as it is in highly dignified, and polemical, Hebrew. Dr. Bergmann has become more famous in Israel through a couple of commonsensical essays than he ever could have become through a lifetime's work in the library. He's one of the "best-hated" men here—though on this score he's no competition for our chancellor Dr. Magnes, who's been a pacifist for ages!!

Your son, Gerhard

TO WALTER BENJAMIN

Jerusalem, February 20, 1930

Dear Walter,

[. . .] Given that your last letters elucidated matters of acute importance between us in such an unmistakable way (particularly the first, which made me quite uneasy), it would perhaps be good if we clarified where we stand. Three years ago you claimed, and I agreed, that you had arrived at a point where a fruitful dialogue with Judaism seemed the only way to make positive progress in your work. This insight, which seemed so certain to us both, led me to take the course I in fact did, with the aim of allowing you to realize your plans. After three years, the question now is this (and it seems to be answered by your location and activities): Haven't you long since abandoned the view that you once set out and explained to Magnes? *In actu,* you prove that the kinds of questions you now address, and the position you have achieved (or I'm sure will achieve) as an extraordinary literary critic, place you well beyond the pale of the Jewish world we were thinking of at the time. It will be good if we can achieve clarity on this point, if only so that I do not find myself in an awkward position here in Jerusalem. For I cannot continue, year after year, to maintain that you are on the verge of doing something, when in reality—as has become ever clearer to me—you will never actually do it. We both know all too well, from long experience, that with you internal constraints bring external ones to the fore. Isn't it obvious that the hesitations which for twelve years now have affected your position on these things (though in each period of your life, they've taken on different spiritual or physical forms) are so fundamental that it would be better if we realized your life actually lies outside the Jewish world, instead of allowing ourselves to cling to illusions about a dialogue with Judaism which will never take place but which we've viewed as our common cause for nearly fifteen years? Given your present interests, it's become clear that you'll surely find other causes. It's also become clear that the comment you made three years ago—to the effect that other than devoting yourself to Hebrew, the only course left for you as purified action would be to leave literature and enter pure party politics—now appears exaggerated and wrong; nor does your presumptive position as the only true critic of German literature *require* the study of Hebrew. I hope these comments will force you to face up to yourself—and I have the impression, which you can scarcely deny, that you don't like to do this, certainly not with any enthusiasm. What's more, I hope you will explain your position with the same clarity I have striven for in my dealings with you. I believe I have the right to expect this. Whatever happens, we will at least not deceive each other about our private apocalypse—the divergence in our paths. Certainly I'm the kind of man who could understand, calmly and even sympathetically, if you were to tell me that, at least in this life, you no longer envision a true confrontation with Judaism, beyond the bounds of our friendship. Sometimes I think you take more account of my feelings than of your own when you speak about these things; as paradoxical as it may sound, I really consider this an accurate summary of your position in many situations. And if I weren't suffering in this situation, I wouldn't feel the way I do about you. Sometimes I say to myself: Because of his friendship with me, Walter hesitates to make a clear assessment of his situation and avoids "getting to the heart of the issue," comprehending it. But I assure you this should not be a valid reason, either morally or symbolically. For me, it is much more important to know where you really are and where you will someday want to be—since given the way you have constituted your life, it's certain that you'll always end up in a different place from the one you intend. Even if I'm completely wrong in what I have said (of course I don't believe I am—though the course of your life over the past ten years has provided many occasions for such errors, even among your friends), it's better that I have finally said it. Even more, I wish that the crisis in your external life—which I've had to glean from hints in your letters, without of course having the power to do anything to help—will at least shed light on where you belong and where you stand.

This letter was conceived in the spirit of friendship and written with my entire heart.

Your Gerhard

TO EDITH ROSENZWEIG

Jerusalem, February 20, 1930

Dear Frau Rosenzweig,

I've taken the liberty of enclosing herewith three copies of a speech I gave at the university's memorial service. It's entitled "Franz Rosenzweig and *The Star of Redemption*." [. . .]

I was ill prepared when I first read *The Star of Redemption,* shortly after it appeared. I vividly recall the terrible difficulties I had in freeing myself from its influence. Shortly before I read it, I had just finished Eduard Strauss's book against Zionism—a strange but highly significant work, painful and stimulating in every respect (and I'm sure it remains so, even though I haven't reread it since). What I saw as the work's pietistic tendencies greatly irked me. When I began to read *The Star,* in particular the way in which it challenges Christianity, those tendencies suddenly seemed to enter into a powerful historical-philosophical connection. This, to my mind, made the debate with these tendencies an imperative. However positively others may view it, the mystery of this connection was at the very least a difficult test for me. Only much later was I able to solve it. The immediate power with which *The Star* took hold of me (and repeatedly keeps doing so—for instance, in the introduction to Part I, the meta-ethic, and the entire second part) derived from a guarantee contained in the third part, a section that remained obscure and problematic in my mind. Specifically, it stemmed from the guarantee of a secret connection that the third section seemed to provide between its own most provocative positions. That is to say: between, on the one hand, the paradox of a mystical epistemology, taken in its strictest and most precise sense and introduced with a hefty polemic against the mystics; and, on the other, the overpowering theological paradox of a confrontation between Judaism and Christianity that ended in a theological *non liquet!* Returning to my speech, I fell into an abyss of incomprehension, and in front of people who naturally had never read *The Star of Redemption.* But I allowed it to happen. At the same time, I can't conceal the fact that there's something in the book which has deeply and (as is demonstrated most recently by this letter) often occupied me. I am convinced that the time will come in which a confrontation between Christianity and Judaism will be necessary, and in a more catastrophic sense than the one alluded to in the book (at least to my mind, for I was unable to penetrate the vehement background to that chapter) under the rubric of "anticipation." I don't know if many other readers of *The Star* have noticed the obvious and by no means accidental silence with which *The Star* meets those central concepts of Judaism that have not developed from the category of "anticipation" (justice, etc.), and how the book makes them visible only indirectly, through a dialectic which simultaneously pushes them into some mute positive sphere. This would be the point at which a Jewish discussion of the book would have to begin. And if not now, with the living writer (a discussion which, for whatever reason, I failed miserably to initiate and perhaps, at least for me personally, was doomed to fail), then with his immortal genius. I've often thought about making *The Star* the subject of a seminar at the university. I've recently given a lot of thought to the possibility of such an arrangement and to the things that could grow out of it. However paradoxical (in Rosenzweig's sense of the term) the course description may sound, we would discuss *The Star* as a work of mystical theology (in my sense of the term)! But in such an undertaking, I would and could make full use of the "amnesty" that the "New Thinking" offers to those who wish to interpret the author using the Kantian notion of *Anweisung*.[127]

TO MARTIN BUBER[128]

Jerusalem, February 27, 1930

Dear Dr. Buber,

Under separate cover I sent you today a copy of the talk about Rosenzweig and his book that I gave at the university. I hope it will reach you safely. [. . .]

There is more in my heart about Rosenzweig than I was able to say here; the day may come when people will study and discuss this book as they do *The Guide for the Perplexed.* Ernst Simon always says that Rosenzweig cared greatly about a Hebrew translation of his *Star of Redemption*—its being "saved" by being put into that language. But this was easier with the *Guide.* To translate the *Star* takes more doing and is not possible without a critique. There are pages in it that are not translatable, at least not in this generation. The very fact that the philosophy of language is tied to a substantially different language places a great burden on the Hebrew language, and I cannot imagine anyone who could undertake this translation without completely rethinking entire portions— something that cannot be done, of course. These are difficulties that are bound to become quite apparent in the translation of your own writings (such as *I and Thou*) as well.

[. . .] It was my intention to travel to Europe this year, and I hoped to be able to visit you, but my work does not permit me to get away.

Because of the August disturbances we were unable to do any serious work for three months; contemplating their meaning did not permit it. And I am very sorry that I cannot even discuss my studies with you. For the first time I have dealt with the Lurianic Kabbalah in my seminar. Will you come to see us? Your visit seems to keep getting postponed.

Sincerely, Gerhard Scholem

FROM WALTER BENJAMIN[129]

Meineke Strasse 9, Berlin; April 25, 1930

Dear Gerhard,

I am once again rereading the last page of the letter you wrote on February 20. And I must once again put off giving a definitive answer to the question it asks. Not, to be sure, for much longer. And not without telling you that in one respect—that of our relationship—it is insoluble in its alternative form. I have come to know living Judaism in absolutely no form other than you. The question of my relationship to Judaism is always the question of how I stand—I do not want to say in relation to you (because my friendship for you is no longer contingent upon any decision)—in relation to the forces you have touched in me. But whatever this decision may depend on, it will be made soon—however much it is embedded, on the one hand, in circumstances that seem totally alien to it and, on the other hand, in that procrastination which has been stretched to the limit and which is second nature to me when it comes to the most important situations in my life. Having begun to loosen the extremely tangled knot of my existence in one place—Dora and I have since gotten a divorce—this "Gordian knot," as you once justifiably called my relationship to Hebrew, will also have to be unraveled. [. . .]

Yours, Walter

TO MARTIN BUBER[130]

Jerusalem, May 22, 1930

Dear Dr. Buber,

[. . .] I think it is quite likely that I shall write something about Rosenzweig again, though not right away, but I could do so only from an entirely different perspective—namely, from that of the third part of his book. Once the hieroglyphics there have been interpreted, they will probably turn out to be exciting enough. I wrote Frau Rosenzweig about this a few months ago. To be sure, a historical viewpoint would be required for it—let us say frankly, the viewpoint of Zionism, which has in recent times threatened to become unreal. I do not know whether you share my feeling, but there would be no use in denying that the countenance of the Zionist cause has darkened in catastrophic fashion for us (and by this I mean the people who at bottom are alone in bearing the Brit Shalom). After all, the gloomy insights that we have had do not extend to the political question of the Arabs but concern the physiognomy of a cause that in a historic hour is of necessity assuming definite form—and to have devoted a life to this cause threatens to prove to have been a dubious undertaking. The torment of this condition, which Ernst Simon may demonstrate to you more clearly than I am able to do here, is reaching the limits of endurability. After all, we have to realize that our interpretation of Zionism does no good if someday (and there is no mistaking the fact that the decisive hour has come) the face of Zionism, even that which is only turned inward, should prove to be that of a Medusa. To be sure, this is the moment for whose sake many of us, and certainly I myself, are here. We believe that it would be unbearable to have to realize that our cause has failed without our having participated. The frightful inner condition, the complete demoralization that are revealing themselves to us here leave us hardly any hope that something can still be done. After all, historic hours do not return, and there is no making up of anything that has been lost for the regeneration of Judaism during the past six months. But if a definite and fixed image of Zionism becomes historical in our time, where shall we stand and how will it be possible to have discussions that will proceed no longer on the basis of a living power but from the magical double of a stage peopled by ghosts—discussions in which even the saddest of all questions, the question of blame, will assume a fearful but justified and genuine and ineluctable actuality? I believe I have given you a rough idea of the situation in which we live here, and it is certainly not the situation that would justify a critical examination of Rosenzweig, which needs a different atmosphere.

It is already very late and this letter must go out, and thus I hope to write you about other things when another opportunity presents itself.

In three weeks I shall also be able to send you my new book about the Kabbalah manuscripts in Jerusalem.

Sincerely yours, Gerhard Scholem

TO BETTY SCHOLEM

Jerusalem, August 28, 1930

Dearest Mother,

[. . .] As usual, there's nothing new to report from here. Escha works. We both do. We are also active in a political group, not to be confused with Knopp's historical association in Wilhelm Busch (whose works you could give me as a gift).[131] Such things occupy a large part of our hurly-burly life here. In terms of the heart, we have each other—not to mention the cats, those genuinely enchanting creatures. Our friends still consist of the same old crowd: Bergmann, Hans Kohn, Fräulein Lasker, and so on. This afternoon we sat with Professor Fodor in the neighborhood's new café, famous for its whipped cream. This café is a trap I have laid for Escha's virtue, and I lure her into it as often as possible. Right next to it is a real German bookstore, where your son can browse and borrow books. All of this is across the street from the Zion Cinema. You can't have forgotten the place, but you wouldn't recognize it any longer. It's undergone a thorough renovation, and the roof now can be folded back on nice summer evenings. When were the summer evenings anything but lovely? [. . .]

Your faithful son, Gerhard

TO BETTY SCHOLEM

Jerusalem, September 18, 1930

Dearest Mother,

[. . .] You wouldn't believe our afternoons. Doctor's orders have turned Escha into a *perpetuum mobile.* In the afternoons, after she has returned from school and has eaten and rested a bit, she must spring up again and wander around Jerusalem. Like Kant did in his day, she always takes the same route. Often, though not always, I agree to meet her on

Zion Square (the square I described to you), just to give me the feeling that I have a wife. So you see how much our afternoons have changed. You'll be astonished when you visit in the spring. [. . .]

You seem to have only imperfectly fulfilled your voting duties. Even here, so far away from the action, we're caught up in the excitement. Heil![132] All the best.

Your devoted son, Gerhard

P.S. All the newspapers here report that German Jews are trembling at the prospect of what may come.[133] It is feared that those who can will spirit their money out of the country as fast as possible. Is there anything to this? There are not only evil Arabs in the world; there are also evil Germans. The correspondent for the *Berliner Tageblatt* runs through the cafés here with supposedly terrifying telegrams. What do you expect!

FROM BETTY SCHOLEM

Berlin, September 30, 1930

My dear child,

[. . .] The results of our election must look much worse outside Germany than they do here. Here there's a great deal of resignation, though this is due more to the economic crisis than to fear of anti-Semitism. It would do wonders to calm the situation if the newspapers were all banned for three months. The sort of nonsense and lies they come out with is detestable. The *Tageblatt* is even worse than the *Voss.* [. . .]

All the best, Mum

FROM BETTY SCHOLEM

Berlin, October 6, 1930

My dear child,

[. . .] Reports that "the Jews are fleeing to Switzerland with bag and baggage" are of course a big fat newspaper hoax. Most likely, *not even a single Jew* has left. And why should they? There hasn't been a single pogrom. Even the new Reichstag won't be any different from the old one. If only the newspapers would stop printing their lies! Erich was in

the Rhineland and Eifel for eight days shortly before the election. He
didn't even notice any special election propaganda; at most, he saw a
couple of tame placards. The German people are so stubborn! But conditions here are really miserable. [. . .]

Kisses, Mum

FROM BETTY SCHOLEM

Pensione Maja, Merano, Italy; October 21, 1930

My dear child,

[. . .] I traveled in true luxury (but when don't I?) and had a sleeper
all to myself. Grete met me here and attended to me as if I were her
child. The butler took the baggage; and since he was an old local, familiar
with all the ins and outs of the city, we took the streetcar. From the
tram station we had to walk down a small street. It was 6:30 and everyone
was returning home for dinner. We were making small talk. Suddenly,
some man grabbed for my purse, which I regret to say hung loosely
around my arm. I instinctively pressed my arm tightly against my side,
but he must have torn away the handle. Then he disappeared into a dark
alley. I of course let out a scream. We were immediately surrounded by
a crowd, and automobiles with powerful headlights came from the Via
Roma—but at the very instant it happened, no one was near me! Had
I been alone, without Grete, no one would have believed that I'd been
robbed of my purse. They would have said I'd lost it. I never carry much
money with me; I had only the fifty-four lire I'd put into the bag at the
Brenner Pass. I kept my spare eyeglasses and my luggage keys somewhere
else. Losing the passport is the only really unpleasant thing. I was questioned for quite a while by the prefect. "Please, my dear lady, what was
your mother's maiden name?" This made me furious and I asked him,
shouting, whether I would get my purse back if the mighty Italian police
had my mother's name from a hundred years ago in their files! If I sent
an account of my experience to the *Berliner Zeitung,* no one from Berlin
would ever again venture into that robber's den! After that, they did
their best. They lined up four vagrants in front of me, and I was supposed
to pick one out. Needless to say, I couldn't recognize the robber. This

witness's main testimony: "I believe he wore a hat." Grete insisted it was a cap. [. . .]

Kisses, Mum

TO BETTY SCHOLEM

Jerusalem, October 30, 1930

Dearest Mother,

We received your first letter from Merano with the greatest joy. The petty assault was easily *the* sensation for us. Of course, I dramatized the scene somewhat; my mind, overheated with detective novels, demands juicy fodder. But in my capacity as a son, I was also pleased that the robber was only a pickpocket and wasn't carrying a revolver. The shock was therefore mild, and easy for me to overcome. It's highly commendable that you weren't carrying a lot of cash in the stolen bag. I attempted to use this as an object lesson for my Escha. She protested by saying that *no one* with any brains travels with more than the absolute minimum in his bag, she least of all. But there's something I find less easy to understand: Why did you so resent the Fascist officials for what was no doubt their innocent curiosity about your family tree? If that was indeed all they wanted. Don't you know that such harmless, trivial details can be of supreme importance for future researchers? If someone should someday ask whether Scholem really lived or was perhaps only a mythical figure (a thunder god), then that scrap of paper in the Merano police files could illuminate a way through the jungle. The report that his mother was named Betty will confirm his existence, as will this statement (or some other one) concerning his maternal grandparents. I, your son, would be more than pleased if the bags of all my Kabbalists, or of their mothers, were stolen—assuming that some nice orderly police department could be found that would use the opportunity to take careful notes on all of the genealogies. [. . .]

1931

FROM BETTY SCHOLEM

Berlin, January 6, 1931

My dear child,

[. . .] I received your Christmas letter—it arrived on January 1, as a New Year's greeting. The sausage will, I hope, follow on the heels of the marzipan bread. It went out on the following Tuesday. [. . .]

Now I come to my trip. Good news. Yesterday, after Erich made the rather painful amputation of Egypt, we reserved the tickets at Cook's. [. . .] Through Cook's we ordered the following: passage to Constantinople and reservations at the "Hôtel de Londres, Constantinople" (the latter required a deposit). We'll take a ship to Beirut, and on the return trip we'll go from Haifa to Trieste. In Beirut we'll stay at the Métropole. We have no plans for the journey from Beirut to Jerusalem. Erich wrote down the departure times for the train, which agreed with the information you gave us. We'll see whether it isn't better with a car! Most likely!! Or most certainly!! Do you think it's necessary to book advance reservations with Cook's for Damascus, too? [. . .]

Kisses, Mum

TO BETTY SCHOLEM

Jerusalem, January 15, 1931

Dear Mother,

[. . .] My dear mother, don't get caught high and dry! It'll be tight with 2,500 marks. You haven't given sufficient consideration to the fact that a tourist, even if he just wants to chat, remains a tourist. Our home is pleasant enough; but on occasion you'll surely want to sit in a café, go to the cinema or the theater, or attend a cabaret. You won't be so indolent as to stay stuck within four walls just because they don't cost anything. You also can't think that we poor civil servants making do with reduced salaries can afford such a high standard of living. Now and again you'll want to invite us out. [. . .]

Your obedient son, Gerhard and Co.

FROM BETTY SCHOLEM

Berlin, March 2, 1931

My dear child,

Now everything is a piece of cake! Cook's has taken care of the rooms, numbers of beds, and hotel reservations in Istanbul and Beirut, and our dates are now firm: we depart from Berlin on Saturday the fourteenth of March and arrive in Jerusalem on the thirty-first. [. . .]

We're all great fans of architecture and archeology, and we hope to make the most of this trip. Hete has even prepared herself with a lecture series on Egypt, while Erich has had Baalbek and Damascus on his mind for weeks. In Jerusalem we want to take a look at that old stone.[134] Last time there were many things I failed to see, so I'm going to make up for it now. You sabotaged the Garden of Gethsemane. These things, after all, have nothing whatsoever to do with a foreign religion. They are simply a part of history. [. . .]

Kisses, Mum

FROM BETTY SCHOLEM

On the good ship Carutio, May 2, 1931

Dearest children,

Now I have three fine days behind me.[135] The sea has been blue, and smooth as a mirror. You notice the ship's movement only when writing, which explains my scrawl. But things look very suspicious this evening: no full moon and no stars in the sky. The water slaps up in the glass, and the ship's attendant says that heavy winds are on their way. He should know. Maybe I have only a brief stay of execution, so I should use it to tell you about how I've been faring. [. . .]

My neighbors at the dining table are eastern European Jews who come from Manchester. They smuggled their son on board (he lives in Haifa), and he even joins them for meals. When I heard about this during the second course, I had to stop eating and broke out in laughter. The father knows you from your work on the Kabbalah. He instructed me, "Tell ya son dat a Zionist from Manchesta sez hello." Nice people. The wife shares a cabin with me. The other woman in the cabin is (along with her husband) a missionary from Canada who was in Palestine for

a year trying to convert the Arabs. What people do to make ends meet!
[. . .]

Kisses, Mum

FROM BETTY SCHOLEM

Zernsdorf, June 10, 1931

My dear child,

[. . .] Your bathroom quite rightly has been lauded; it really signals
a mighty step forward. Just as Erich and I constantly praise the beauty
of Jerusalem, I tell everyone how you now live in tip-top conditions.
Then everyone asks the seemingly natural follow-up question: whether
we want to live there. They still imagine the country as a sort of Hotten-
tot kraal and listen with astonishment when I describe your comfortable
European lifestyle. [. . .]

The boys tell me that twelve million inhabitants in Germany live off
the state: four million unemployed and the rest pensioners, war invalids,
invalids who are also pensioners, and other hungry stomachs. And this
doesn't even take into account the parasites receiving sick pay or living
off professional associations! Compared with these enormous sums
which society has to come up with, the reparations play hardly any role
at all. Even if the Allies canceled all of our war debts, we'd still be in
the same hot water. Try as we might to blame our economic debacle
on the reparations, no one will believe our belly-aching so long as we
still build tanks. [. . .]

Kisses, Mum

FROM BETTY SCHOLEM

Zernsdorf, July 28, 1931

My dear child,

[. . .] Last night the boys came to Zernsdorf with the nightmarish
news that they fear losing everything: the house and the business. Our
customers have been dragged under due to the collapse of the bank.
Everyone has been scared off; business is dead. On Saturday Erich was

happy to get a 500-mark contract with Ultra-Phone; on Monday the company went bankrupt. [. . .]

I'll keep you abreast of the news (as I have over the past eight years). And rest assured that I, for one, won't lose my composure. If I run out of money, I'll live more simply. Whatever I do have I'll use to help Werner, who has been pulled into all of this. I'll give you more details the next time I write. For now, my eyelids are drooping from fatigue. Here in Zernsdorf everything's as beautiful as always—despite it all. This we still own!

A thousand kisses! Mum

TO BETTY SCHOLEM

Jerusalem, July 30, 1931

Beloved Mother,

We're grateful for your report on the recent events. We, too, follow everything with great attention in the press; after all, it concerns us intimately. As things look now, our budget will be cut *once again* around 20 percent, so you can imagine how little is left. We sit here high and dry, as it were. I hope that meanwhile you've cobbled together some way of paying the salaries. At the end of the day, all the other firms are in the same boat; and not every shop in Germany can simply go under. In any event, I must wait to see what will become of my portion of the inheritance, and I only regret that we did not save our property before this all started. But this was not provided for in the will. Or as Escha's uncle somewhat naïvely said, "No one could have predicted that such a thing could happen." Only foreigners did; otherwise Germany, with its high interest rates, would be swimming in money. [. . .]

Your devoted Gerhard

FROM BETTY SCHOLEM

Zernsdorf, August 4, 1931

My dear child,

Your letter of the twenty-second arrived on the thirtieth. Meanwhile, you should already have received two letters from me describing the terrible situation. Technically, I'm in no position to give you a *complete* picture of the collapse, which you'd need in order to really understand what's happening. The year 1930 was still a good one. We were a bit in the red; but given more or less normal business, we still hoped to make it up eventually. We never would have taken such a long trip if we'd had an inkling that such a crisis lay ahead!! It hit us like a catastrophe. An enormous fall in the demand for price tags caused our debts to swell. Just as all business came to a halt, the bank failed; so there was no one to speak to. The banks went into a government holding company, which showed no interest in the debts of "customers." All of this happened at once. It looks as if we'll lose everything. It's cold comfort to know that the entire commercial sector is in the same position and that more shops are going under than staying afloat. Since everywhere you look there's desert, you see no chance to plant anything new. The situation is desperate. [. . .]

I cannot continue to maintain my own house and household—this much seems certain. A pity, isn't it? My mama, hardly a wealthy woman, at least died in *her own* apartment. Of all the possible alternatives left to me, moving in with Erich seems the best. Hermine is leaving on the first of September, and Martha will move into her room.[136] As long as we can still keep the house, I want to stay in my own apartment. For now, the rent of 170 marks is still easy to come up with. Martha helps with the cleaning, and for lunch I go upstairs. I make my own breakfast, and evenings I'm mostly out. As an innocent victim of Germany's crisis, I will have to place my existence upon the famous "other basis" and enjoy the last good thirty years of my life like a fine-tasting stew.

Even though *at the moment* things aren't so bad that I have to give up the household, they could reach that point at any time. I'll ask you now if you could use anything, because it takes two to three weeks to get a letter back from you. Selling things amounts to giving them away. I'll let Werner have what he can take; other things can be stored in the attic of the Fregehaus. It's impossible to send furniture to Palestine, isn't it? Shipping and taxes are expensive, and who can pay them? You must bear in mind that we have *nothing*. [. . .]

With kisses, Mum

TO BETTY SCHOLEM

Jerusalem, August 5, 1931

Dear Mother,

I received your last alarming letter, and I hope a better one is en route. It may well be that my business training is too meager for me to fully grasp what's happening. I'm sorry you've had such a stressful time. Having said this, and despite the dangers of getting myself further involved in unpleasant affairs, I ask you to please give me a clearer picture. Why would my brothers reject financial help from the family while continuing to accept it from the Darmstadt Bank if the bank offered it? What's going to happen to my money if the firm is liquidated? Is it really more of a moral risk to accept money from Reinhold's family than to endanger all of ours? You must know full well that my situation is anything but rosy and that the danger of losing the foundation of our existence is quite real. At least Werner has already gotten a part of his inheritance; and you will always somehow manage as long as my brothers are around. But it will be difficult for me as a scholar to exist at all without this support. This entire misfortune has arisen because father made out his will like a feudal knight who sees his manor as the embodiment of the family's honor, of its glowing reputation. The money, down to the last penny, was to remain in the firm. When anyone wants to get to his inheritance he finds it inaccessible, tied up for years in the firm at a low rate of interest. So long as the firm prospers, this might be good; but as soon as business sours, all the money pumped into it doesn't seem to help the firm, and the entire family is swept into insecurity. [. . .]

Yours, Gerhard

TO BETTY SCHOLEM

Jerusalem, August 19, 1931

[. . .] I'm still in the dark, even though I asked you more than once to clarify my legal position in this dilemma. Am I a creditor in the firm? Do I have any claims or duties? I hope I won't have to make any practical use of this information, but I still would like to know.

A most astonishing thing happened to us. It goes without saying that we haven't told or even written to anyone about how dangerous your situation has become, for the simple reason that (according to my frankly simplistic view of things) bad rumors about a wobbling firm can easily push it over the edge. Out of the blue, Heinz wrote to his wife in a free and easy tone that you have totally collapsed and that my inheritance has been completely lost. He wanted her to offer his condolences. This was the first scrap of information I've received from the extended family (via a distant and perhaps not altogether authentic member) on the fate of my inheritance. [. . .]

Your dutiful son, Gerhard

FROM WALTER BENJAMIN

Berlin, November 3, 1931

Dear Gerhard,

[. . .] If sometime in the near future you were to come to Berlin for ten or twelve days, you'd most likely stumble across countless curiosities—no fewer than most people see in Moscow.[137] But here the sights are gloomier, seen both from an overall point of view and from my own. The economic system in Germany has as much firm ground under its feet as do the high seas, and the emergency decrees crisscross one another like the crests of waves. Unemployment is about to make a revolutionary program just as obsolete as the economic and political programs already are. For, according to all appearances, the National Socialists have practically been delegated to represent the masses of the unemployed. Until now the Communists have failed to make the necessary contact with the masses and hence to find possibilities for revolutionary action. The mammoth size of the army of the unemployed means that representing the workers' interests must become the task of the reformer. And it's likely that the Communists can address these issues no better than the Social Democrats. Because of this, the mere fact that someone still has a job in a factory is enough to turn him into a member of a workers' aristocracy. Meanwhile, an enormous group of pensioners with inherently microscopic concerns has apparently developed from within the ranks of the unemployed: an idle petty bourgeoisie who spend their time gambling and lazing about and whose days are characterized by the same philistine precision that animates the lives of small-time gamblers at summer resorts.

I've taken a break from writing to reread your description of the situation of Zionism. I do so with the greatest sympathy and, I believe, with as much understanding as you could hope for. For my part, at least, I view your lines as a kind of historical document. It should surprise me that your detailed accounts do not always reflect my agreement with your position. Still, I can imagine that by means of these questions we could achieve a surprising understanding in other, apparently unrelated areas which have remained a sore point between us for some time. I urge you to tell me as much as you can about your experiences in these matters, whether by writing letters or by sending documents.

1932

TO BETTY SCHOLEM

Jerusalem, January 8, 1932

Dearest Mother,

Today I can tell you with great joy that the university administration has approved my request for a vacation. Now that all problems have been resolved, apart from the most serious one of money, I will be on my way at the beginning of March. I'll make my journey and trust in God. Should my pound-sterling carpet be pulled out from under me in the middle of the trip, I'll have to tell the English consulate to send me on as a ward of the state, devoid of means. I'll be going to Germany in any case. There I'll have a first-hand look at your life.

[. . .] The sausages, my loving mother, did not and will not arrive. Please lodge the strongest complaints! It's simply impossible that sausages should arrive on every single other occasion, yet willfully refuse to come when they are sent for my birthday! There must be an investigation, if need be through a private detective. [. . .]

Faithfully yours, Gerhard

FROM BETTY SCHOLEM

Berlin, February 9, 1932

My dear child,

[. . .] I think it's an awful idea to travel to Germany in times such as these, with all this tension, political contamination, and anti-Semitism in the air. Some of Erich's friends were at a hotel in Neustrelitz, and the waiter who served them wore a swastika! In passing, it seems that Bavaria, boycotted by north Germany in general and Jews in particular, has completely changed its tune and has now begun to fawn sweetly upon outsiders.

Kisses, Mum

FROM BETTY SCHOLEM

Berlin, March 10, 1932

My dear child,

[. . .] I hear that you're building a house together with Dr. Bergmann in Rehavia. (This is where Professor Fodor lives and where the Cohns have a boardinghouse, isn't it?) I am happy beyond belief. The fact that you're moving into your own house is, to me, a comforting sign that you consider conditions there to be secure. Palestine made a powerful impression on me last year. I scarcely recognized Jerusalem, the city on a hill. [. . .]

Warmest kisses, Mum

FROM BETTY SCHOLEM

Berlin, March 18, 1932

My dear child,

So I can now send my greetings to you in Europe![138] I hope the trip went well and that you avoided getting seasick! [. . .] Since traveling interests me so much, you must give me a detailed report of your trip! Two days from Port Said to Naples is terribly quick. I don't understand *at all* why you can't spend *a single day* in Naples. Because you want to spend three months in Rome and you're so anxious to immerse yourself in manuscripts! Allow me to cite Goethe, whose collected works (which have been advertised in the newspapers like a second-rate movie) we just bought at Wickel. As Goethe said so aptly: "Parchment—is that the sacred fount / From which you drink, to still your thirst forever?"[139] Why, my son, why don't you take a long walk along the gulf, where the magical island of Capri is bathed in elegance and where all the gods of beauty are set free! [. . .]

Kisses, Mum

TO BETTY SCHOLEM

Rome, April 19, 1932

Dearest Mother,

Please forgive me for taking so long to respond. [. . .] I'm so absorbed in my work that I have little time to write. At the moment I am utterly content—which may sound rather out of step with the mood of the times. You know how much I like to work. Here in Rome I've discovered a mountain of things directly related to my research, some of which are also of the utmost significance. The time slips away, and the hours I am in the Vatican, from 8:00 A.M. to 6:30 P.M., fly by as if on wings. [. . .]

Oh yes, the *house,* dear mother! I must confess I forgot to mention it. I nearly fell over from shock when you wrote that you'd heard about it from another source. The first reason I forgot may be psychological. Since my money is tied up with you, it is not my house at all, but in fact Escha's. While you were in Jerusalem, all of my timid attempts to induce you to pitch in to build it (which would have been a great help) failed miserably. The upshot is that, besides what we could borrow, the only money we put into it came from Escha's inheritance. That's life. With 200 pounds more we could have built a much nicer home. As it is, we must cut *all* corners and cannot even pay for stone, but have to use concrete. An additional reason is that, to spare myself the headache, I'm scarcely at all involved with it. Escha and Lottchen Cohen are doing it all. With the exception of my library, which will be very lovely, we are not "villa owners" but poor, small-time proprietors. Oh, if you'd merely lifted your little finger to help us!!

Your obedient son, Gerhard

FROM BETTY SCHOLEM

Berlin, April 28, 1932

My dearest child,

[. . .] It's a total fabrication to say that the house slipped your memory because it's not yours, but Escha's. I've noted your feeble explanation with benevolence. I am awfully sorry I couldn't give you anything for your house. When I returned last year, I immediately found myself in a catastrophic situation and couldn't even get to my own money. My money and my claims are just as frozen as yours. Hopefully someday everything will thaw out again! You're in better shape than any of us, and it really takes a load off my shoulders to know I don't have to worry about you. My other sons sit heavily upon my shoulders. So keep in mind that everything that concerns you is also of interest and importance to me. Don't make it sound as if I don't care in the slightest what happens to you! [. . .]

The 170 supporters of Hitler in the Prussian parliament don't make life any easier. Do the Italian newspapers take any notice? [. . .]

Many greetings and a kiss, Mum

TO BETTY SCHOLEM

Rome, May 1, 1932

Dear Mother,

[. . .] You ask what people here think about Hitler. This is an easy one: the entire press without exception (needless to say, not without a wink from above, as is always the case here) is pro-Hitler, with a vengeance. You won't find a single word about the real situation in the *Voss.* They simply keep their readers in the dark about everything (that Passarge is, after all, a reptile).[140] It goes without saying that the support here for Hitler has nothing to do with anti-Semitism (which plays a minor role—the Italians couldn't care less about it) but instead is a function of his anti-French policies. You should have seen the commentaries on the disbanding of the SA groups[141] and on the elections. People here not only reckon with a Germany under the dictatorship of Hitler, but actually hope for it. [. . .]

I would like to order the following books—and don't be shocked because they're by Franz Kafka, a writer you don't care much for: *The Trial* (Kurt Wolff Verlag); *Posthumous Writings* (Gustav Kiepenheuer Verlag). [. . .]

My warmest greetings to everyone, Gerhard

FROM WALTER BENJAMIN[142]

San Antonio, Ibiza; June 1, 1932

Dear Gerhard,

[. . .] I must say that the news about your small house is sensational, as is the news of Noeggerath turning up, but in a completely different way.[143] Let me extend you my most sincere congratulations! If I had a *broche*[144] to recite over the house, it would contain the wish that it, along with its books and its friends, may outlive the next world war. All on its own, it will of course probably be able to resist the end of the world coming in the form of taxes, bankruptcies, and so on. I think I have now effectively countered your suspicious grumblings about the absence of manuscripts and will close with most sincere regards.

Yours, Walter

FROM BETTY SCHOLEM

Berlin, November 15, 1932

Dear children,

[. . .] Nothing new to report. None of Herr von Papen's lovely speeches can bring new jobs out of the woodwork,[145] nor will the situation improve if people are kept busy with elections. There's already talk of dissolving the Reichstag, largely because Papen can't stomach the idea of a hundred Communists. The transportation strike lasted five days, and the strikers got nothing from it. Our Friday evening at Lene's suffered because of it. Only Erich and Edith made the half-hour pilgrimage to Kreuzberg; it was much too far for the others, including myself. A certain Herr Berger-Son was there as well. I've often heard about his enormous muzzle. He said that strikers in Neukölln had piled four trains one on top of the other. Sure, sure, said Erich. "Three I can imagine—but how did they stack the fourth upon the third?!" [. . .]

Sunday I had a very amusing time at Werner's. I completely reject his educational maxims—his most recent fad of always telling the truth just as much as his earlier system of always hushing everything up.

Reinhold, who's terribly despondent, was just here for an hour. There's nothing that can be done. Contracts for price tags have shrunk so much that the factory is hardly utilized at all. Since Theobald made the merger primarily to do price tags, the future looks truly bleak. Reinhold's visits always make my heart heavy. What has become of the boy!

Warmest kisses, Mum

FROM BETTY SCHOLEM

Berlin, November 20, 1932

Dear children,

[. . .] Reinhold comes to see me by himself sometimes. I feel so sorry for him. He's a defeated man. On top of this are the business worries. After fruitless efforts, Herr von Papen is being pushed to the side. Today I read in *Voss* that Hitler will become chancellor after all. But he won't be any different from the others. It's almost gotten to the point where I couldn't care less. [. . .]

Warmest kisses, Mum

TO BETTY SCHOLEM

Jerusalem, December 28, 1932

Dear Mother,

[. . .] The crate finally arrived. I only had to pay duty on the carpet, at ten piasters a kilo. It weighed seven kilos. The transportation from the docks to Jerusalem was pricey by comparison. In such situations our fellow human beings give you a total fleecing. [. . .] The rather threadbare carpet immigrated to my bedroom, where it now serves as a bedside rug. It makes the room look quite stately. The small patterned red carpet that you earmarked as Escha's birthday present was annexed by her in advance. It lies in the reading corner. [. . .]

This week I went on a trip to Tel Aviv to raise funds for a Jewish academic organization. I was only away for one day, but I used the opportunity to visit a so-called children's village not far from Tel Aviv.[146] It's an institution that would interest you. If, as we hope, you can find the energy and opportunity to visit us, you'll certainly see something like it. The children are not only raised and educated in a kind of rural educational community; they themselves do most of the agricultural labor and craftwork, some of which is truly complicated. There are girls and boys of all sizes, from all walks of life, and from all of the country's various regions and social strata. The houses are lovely and the climate magical. You find things there that are otherwise hard to come by in Palestine: a river, a large swimming pool, and a forest. At the very least, it's something new to see.

Otherwise nothing new to report. The first tourists are already arriving little by little. We live in peace and entertain a lot of guests, without of course feeding them. [. . .]

Yours, Gerhard

PART III **REDEMPTION THROUGH SIN, 1933–1947**

Scholem with his second wife, Fanya Freud, in their library, 1937. *Inset:* Betty Scholem in Sydney, Australia, 1939. Both photos courtesy of the Jewish National and University Library, Jerusalem, Gershom Scholem Archive (Arc. 4o 1599).

∴✦∴

Something I noticed last Sunday: there's so much German spoken on the streets (and in Tel Aviv it's even more conspicuous than here) that yours truly has a strong inclination to withdraw back into Hebrew. Sadly, I've already driven one female interlocutor to tears with an analysis of the dream world in which German Jews have been living. Given my opinions on things here, I never dreamed until now that I could, on top of everything else, also earn the reputation of being an extreme chauvinist. This is perhaps the proper revenge of the *genius loci*.

—Letter to Walter Benjamin, June 15, 1933

IN THE SUMMER OF 1936, Benjamin was living as an exile in Paris, Werner Scholem languished in a Nazi prison camp, and rioting and violence threatened to spin out of control in Palestine. As the world around him became more threatening, Scholem retreated into his study. "I sit in Jerusalem and work as best I can," he informed Benjamin. "I've written a number of studies, including an extensive essay on mystical nihilism in the ghetto. It should interest you, though I wrote it in Hebrew. I wrote a brief summary of it for the *Schocken Almanach,* which should find its way to you somehow after it comes out.[1] Now I'm doing a bit of work on my history of the Kabbalah. I have so much in my head, yet it all goes so slowly! Still, I'm happy that I can take up my work again."[2]

Scholem had by this time become a famous figure in Jerusalem. Elsa Lasker-Schüler, among the most celebrated poets in Weimar Germany and now stranded as a refugee in Palestine, described him as "the Kabbalist of the Holy City."[3] But Scholem's work was not a flight into magic or into a quietist's tranquillity. Through his scholarship, he responded to the terrors of the time with more than impotent tears or a raised fist; the essays and books he composed on the mystical imagination celebrated vibrant creativity during times of disaster. While European Jewry was being decimated, Scholem uncovered the creative core within Jewish life that, throughout history, had always generated renewal.

Hitler exploited economic collapse to present himself as the savior of Germany. Populist economics served as a vehicle for bringing his crude nationalistic rancor and crazed racial theories into the mainstream. His vision of a strong new Germany was seductive, and his list of foes who ostensibly hindered its realization—the French, the Communists, the unions, and above all the Jews—was so broad and amorphous that it allowed him to cobble together a large following. His largest financial and political backers—industrialists, old-style conservatives, and Prussian aristocrats—shared his hatred for leftists and labor unions, and entertained the illusion that they could use this firebrand to smash them, then dispose of him like a spent bullet casing. Yet with his diffuse agenda and ad hoc nostrums for problems ranging from unemployment to national hygiene, few liberals and leftists took him very seriously. Among the Scholems, only Werner paid much attention to him.

The Reichstag fire in late February 1933 changed everything: within two weeks, the enabling act had given Hitler his dictatorship. If the Austrian corporal had learned one lesson from his service as a front-line soldier, it was the primacy of surprise attacks to catch slumbering opponents off balance. The Nazis used a constitutional mechanism (Article 48, which allowed the federal government to declare a state of emergency) to orchestrate their swift, brutal, skillfully executed revolution. In May, labor unions were banned; in July, political opposition itself became illegal; in April, racial laws banned "Semites" from working for the government and universities. In the course of time, the government purged Jews from hospitals and the legal profession. The Sturmabteilung (SA) instigated wild boycotts of Jewish shops, accompanied by random beatings. Many Jews were forced out of their jobs; others left the country; some took their own lives. German-Jewish life, like the Golden Age of Spain, began to slip into a dark age. A thousand years in Germany appeared to be a tragic illusion, doomed from the start, as if all of the Jews' earlier belief in Enlightenment, culture, and the rights of man were but mirages in a harsh and savage landscape.

The change in regime struck the Scholem family particularly hard. Like the bulk of Germany's Jews, Betty, Reinhold, Erich, and their families opted to stay put and wait it out. If their days were numbered, there was no way they could tell—the atmosphere was characterized more by confusion and mixed signals than by unambiguous signs of doom. Intimations of ruin mixed with equally strong signs of hope. And the two poles alternated with such furious speed that no one, not even the darkest pessimist, could clearly see into the future. Gershom, the Zionist, was no more a prophet than Reinhold, the German nationalist. "The streak of rotten luck that's been dogging you for two years is bound to change," he assured Betty in his letter of April 20, 1933. He urged her not to lose hope. He told her not to leave Germany unless she had no choice.

The real problem was Werner, whose notoriety as the "Red Scholem" lived on in the minds of the Nazis. In February 1933 they imprisoned him; then they freed him for a month; then they locked him up again, this time for good.

With the exception of a journey to the Vatican Library in Rome, Scholem followed the vicissitudes of his family and friends from distant Palestine. He saw his friend Benjamin only once more—briefly, in 1938. They maintained their friendship through a long series of letters, which he would publish more than forty years later. George Steiner has perceptively noted that the letters (of which 128 survived the war) document the way in which "two masters of the spirit and of language" devoted their best efforts to making sense of devastation.[4] The correspondence reached a zenith in their debates on the interpretation of Kafka. Given their divergent starting points, one should not be surprised that they came up with very different readings. Scholem, gainfully employed as a distinguished professor in Jerusalem and an eyewitness to riots, political terrorism, assassination, and fanaticism, was loath to accept revolutionary slogans or solutions. His Kafka did not present a world utterly devoid of meaning, value, and law; truth was merely hidden, encased deep below the surface. Thus, commentators should continue to grope in the dark in pursuit of lost yet existing truths. Benjamin, cast adrift by events beyond his control, was by contrast a good deal more attuned to apocalyptic upheavals—and to radical messianic solutions. In Benjamin's view, Kafka described a world devoid of meaning; it was up to human beings, and them alone, to create their own truth and meaning.

An equally gripping story—one of most remarkable testimonies of everyday life in Nazi Germany—is presented in Betty Scholem's letters to her son. These letters expose the brute facts that made Kafka such an important writer among German Jews during the Nazi regime. It's a story of people slowly falling into a trap; of the collapse of a world; of panic and misunderstanding; of hopes raised, only to be dashed by indifferent or malicious bureaucrats. It's a tale of exile and fragmentation. But what links Betty's detailed descriptions of the hapless efforts to free Werner, the transfer of family furniture to Palestine, and her interest in her son's Kabbalah studies—what binds all the elements together into a single and poignant tale—is a mother's deep love for her children.

Scholem began the Hitler years at a high point. In 1933, with the aid of Hugo Bergmann, he and Escha completed building a house in Rehavia, a bucolic neighborhood in Jerusalem with a high concentration of *yekkes* (Central European Jewish refugees). His letters from those months are happy ones. No place on the entire continent was so clean and orderly; nowhere were the coffee and pastries so good, the shopkeepers so helpful, the workers so diligent as in their quarter. The tall, spindly figure became a virtual landmark of this transplanted piece of Central Europe. Agnon, who set his last and greatest work, *Shira,* in the Rehavia of the 1930s, once again used Scholem as a model for one of his protagonists: Dr. Weltfremd (which might be translated as "Dr. Starry-Eyed").

A number of Scholem's old acquaintances arrived in Palestine in the course of 1933. His friend from the World War I years, the poet Werner Kraft, joined Elsa Lasker-Schüler, Hans Jonas, and the many other displaced Weimar intellectuals who gave Jerusalem a cosmopolitan flair. A wave of professionals also began to arrive from Germany. Bankers and lawyers often worked as construction workers, and surgeons drove dump trucks; others had to sell the pianos, cars, and appliances they had brought with them, so that they could pay for overpriced apartments. In time, as the economic situation improved, a sense of optimism grew among the immigrants. Capital and skills from Germany helped create a boom. German importers sold good Cuban cigars. Restaurants, concert halls, and cabarets transformed the city.

For Scholem, the most immediate effect of mass immigration was the impact it had on the university. After he became a full professor in 1934, he worked hard to expand and improve the humanities faculty so that it could accommodate a massive influx of new students. He pressured Buber to join him from Germany; he fought some appointments while pushing others; he helped found journals; and of course he continued to write and to teach.

Meanwhile, big changes were underway in his personal life. His decision to share a house with Bergmann proved ill-considered. In 1936 the Kantian philosopher managed to pry the blue-eyed Escha away from Scholem—who promptly married a young woman named Fanya Freud, one of his former pupils and a distant cousin of Sigmund Freud.

Political developments also weighed heavily upon him. Brit Shalom failed to bring mutual understanding between Arabs and Jews. In fact, the group found itself locked in a terrible conflict of interest. Most of its support came from recent immigrants from Germany, but in 1936 this wave of immigration triggered a new round of anti-Jewish rioting. With the arrival of tens of thousands of largely liberal and educated Central European Jews, Arab nationalists felt the demographic balance shift and feared losing control of Palestine. This made any further immigration a *casus belli*. Arab leaders used every means at their disposal, including indiscriminate violence, to urge the British authorities in Palestine to put an end to Jewish immigration. Unorganized rioting turned into a well-orchestrated uprising. The Zionist leadership fought back. What had been mere castles in the air—the dream of a Jewish state—began to take on tactile proportions as a band of Zionist mavericks and revolutionaries formed into a tightly organized, homogeneous ruling elite of pugnacious fighters, union leaders, and party bosses. The liberals lost.

In divided and tumultuous Palestine, split along ethnic, religious, and linguistic lines, all hope of dialogue was dashed. Brit Shalom disbanded, and Scholem returned full-time to his quiet study in Rehavia. Henceforth, his political and social beliefs were expressed less often as proclamations than as hints and suggestions carefully concealed in his work. In the midst of a world turned suicidal, his work became more esoteric and hence more personal, with his deep, humane convictions camouflaged behind an exacting philological apparatus.

This fusion of scholar and political-social ventriloquist is most visible in the interplay between Scholem's correspondence and his published works of the 1930s and 1940s. During the long years in which he followed the plight of friends and family, Scholem managed to produce some of his most important works. He matured into one of the greatest scholars and writers of his day by developing a style and literary strategy skillfully tailored for a time of unremitting gloom.

Some of his best works were published by Schocken Verlag in Berlin. Salman Schocken, his old friend and patron, managed to distribute hundreds of thousands of books within Nazi Germany (Kafka's collected works stand out in particular) because his firm operated within a Jewish cultural ghetto. The censors failed to notice that Schocken's presses produced a torrent of materials whose contents violated state-imposed boundaries. As Ernst Simon described it, the company's strategy was to use "an insider language that the enemy rarely understood, Jews almost always." Its books "contained answers to questions that at the time of publication could be posed only in whispers, in *camera pietatis*."[5]

Scholem, by now a master of secrecy and subterfuge, became one of Schocken's leading writers. He contributed translations of both poetry and prose; an anthology of the *Zohar* entitled *Die Geheimnisse der Schöpfung* (The Secrets of Creation); numerous articles for the *Schocken Almanach;* and his first major works on the history of the Kabbalah.[6]

His single most important, and most controversial, piece of writing appeared in 1936 under the title "Redemption through Sin."[7] It was his clearest statement to date of his dialectical view of history. The essay, written in Hebrew, was also a literary masterpiece akin to a great detective novel.

"Redemption through Sin," while traversing the familiar terrain of philology, bibliography, and translation, also ventured into the more speculative realm of intellectual biography. Scholem chose as his subject Jacob Frank, a second-generation follower of the seventeenth-century mystical heretic and false messiah Sabbatai Sevi. Scholem characterized Frank as a sexual pervert and cynic, a demagogue, and a man of "corruption lacking all scruples." Yet he saw Frank's life as a noble, if misguided, rebellion against the indignities of Jewish history and the "sordidness" of exile. Frank, he said, had "placed the redemptive power of destruction at the center of his Utopia."[8] For instance, Frank had demanded what Scholem called a "Jewish legion" (the phrase was a transparent allusion to the organization founded by the Revisionist leader Zev Jabotinsky) to liberate Palestine from the Arab infidels and to restore it to its rightful owners. Frank, like the rough-and-tumble Zionists Scholem knew so well, had "desired to turn believers into the virtual opposite of the ghetto

Jew: soldiers, with whom he hoped to realize, in one way or another, a Jewish territorialism."[9]

In the course of the essay, Scholem identified a dialectical "cunning of reason" that, among Frankists of the eighteenth and nineteenth centuries, had transformed the "priceless pearl" buried within Frank's messianic nihilism into a positive force for emancipation. The old immorality had disappeared, leaving as its purified core the "longing for freedom" and "dream of a universal revolution and renewal of the world." Later Frankists had come to support the Jacobins in France, and Frank's nephew had been an adviser to the governor of revolutionary Paris; in southeast Europe, where most of Frank's disciples had lived, they had "secretly desired the overthrow" of oppressive regimes.[10] Scholem maintained, though, that the thrust of their revolution had not been overtly political; rather, it had consisted in the new and creative ways they had "returned to the sources" of tradition. They had "perused" the Bible, Midrash, and the *Zohar* for fresh readings and meanings. The contemporary message of Scholem's essay was clear.

The peace and quiet Scholem enjoyed through much of the 1930s also allowed him to complete a project he had been discussing since World War I but had never found the time to write: a history of the Kabbalah. He finally got his chance to work on it in 1938, when the Jewish Institute of Religion, based in New York, invited him to give a series of lectures. The lecture format, along with a generous stipend, gave him his first opportunity to formulate his "dialectical" philosophy of Jewish history for a broad public audience. The lectures served as the basis for his book *Major Trends in Jewish Mysticism.*

Scholem, speaking in heavily German-accented English, characterized Jewish mysticism as "the attempt to discover the hidden life beneath the external shapes of reality." The chain of reasoning was simple. In however concealed a fashion, the best commentators and exegetes of Jewish texts have always responded head-on to their existential historical circumstances—though not by relying upon old interpretations, whose "prejudices and values . . . arose out of very different conditions and reflections." Because each generation must respond to very different conditions, there can be no authoritative line, no absolute truth. "Forces whose value was once denigrated will appear in a different and affirmative light. Forces which were not considered important enough for seri-

ous scholars to research will now be raised from the depths of conceal-
ment. Perhaps what was once called degeneracy will now be regarded
as a revelation, and what seemed to [scholars] to be an impotent halluci-
nation will be revealed as a great and vibrant myth."[11]

This was nowhere truer, Scholem continued, than in Jewish messianism, whose very utopian and radical character is best revealed during
times of catastrophe, when the relatively stable canon becomes suscepti-
ble to constant revisions and upheavals. "Jewish messianism," he asserted, "is, in its origins and by its nature—this cannot be sufficiently
emphasized—a theory of catastrophe. This theory stresses the revolutionary, cataclysmic element in the transition from every historical present to the messianic future." His primary example of this was the creation
of the "Lurianic Kabbalah," a movement that grew up around a charismatic figure named Isaac Luria in Galilee a generation after the Jewish
expulsion from Spain in 1492. Luria's teaching taught Palestinian Jews
to live and thrive in a shifting, tragic, unpredictable world.[12] Given the
fact that Scholem compared the events of 1933 with those of 1492, the
lecture series can also be read as his own attempt to apply the principles
he articulated to the tragedies of his time.

Betty Scholem stayed in Germany until 1938, when she emigrated
to Australia to join Reinhold and Erich, who had settled there a year
earlier.

Scholem returned to Palestine after he had completed his New York
lectures. The outbreak of the war a few months later cut him off from
old friends and family. Battles in the Mediterranean closed down the
sea lanes, making correspondence with Europe and America impossible.
Word from his mother and brothers, who now ran a small shop in Australia, was sketchy. Scholem first heard rumors of Benjamin's death in
October 1940. At the same time, he learned indirectly of Werner's fate:
the Nazis had murdered him at Buchenwald.

In Palestine, life returned to normal after the British defeat of Rommel's forces at El-Alamein in 1941. For the remainder of the war, the
country served as an important base for the British military. This, in turn,
ignited an economic boom. Work was plentiful, and the land became a
peaceful island far from the terrible theaters of war. In time, the sea lanes
opened up again, allowing Scholem to correspond with his mother in
Australia and friends in America. And by that time he had good news

to share with distant friends and family: he had been elected dean of the humanities faculty.

Scholem's two most important wartime acquaintances were Hannah (Stern) Arendt and Theodor Adorno, both of whom were also friends of Benjamin's. Arendt had met Benjamin in Paris after fleeing Nazi Germany, and had met Scholem during his research trip to Europe in 1932. She ended up in New York in 1941. Adorno had first met Benjamin in 1923 but became close to him later through the Institut für Sozialforschung (Institute of Social Research) in Frankfurt, which Adorno co-directed with Max Horkheimer. The two of them reestablished the institute in New York after the rise of Nazism in Germany.

Adorno was the first to confirm the rumors of Benjamin's death. He also resolved, together with Scholem, to save Benjamin's works from loss and obscurity. No one knew precisely where Benjamin was buried; it was said that his grave lay somewhere near the French village of Port Bou, on the border with Spain. "The place is beautiful," wrote Scholem years later; "the grave, apocryphal." As early as 1942 Scholem began to gather together Benjamin's literary estate—including scattered correspondence, for a separate volume of letters.[13]

Tragedy did not hinder Scholem from continuing his scholarly work. In 1941 Schocken Books in Jerusalem published his *Major Trends in Jewish Mysticism*. The volume was dedicated to Benjamin: a man of "genius" with the "insight of the Metaphysician, the interpretive power of the Critic, and the erudition of the Scholar."

✳

1933

FROM WALTER BENJAMIN[1]

Berlin, January 15, 1933

Dear Gerhard,

[. . .] I am very eager to receive your open letter "Jewish Faith in Our Time."[2] At the same time I wish to thank you very much for sending me your "Kabbalah." Though no judgment can arise out of the abyss of my ignorance in this area, you should still know that the rays emanating from your article did force their way even down there. Otherwise, however, I have to content myself with gossamer-thin esoteric knowledge—at the moment, for the purpose of a radio play about spiritism. I am about to cast a glance over the relevant literature, not, to be sure, without having constructed, slyly and for my private pleasure, a theory on these matters which I intend to put before you on a distant evening, over a bottle of burgundy. [. . .]

FROM LAMBERT SCHNEIDER[3]

Berlin, January 26, 1933

Dear Herr Scholem,

By this time, you will have received a letter from Herr Schocken stating that Schocken Verlag is interested in your research into the Kabbalah. Herr Professor Buber spoke with us about your work plans, and we have passed this information on to Herr Schocken, who has a great deal of interest in it. We are pleased, for our part, to establish contact with you. We do not know if the information Herr Buber gave us concerning your plans is definitive. He mentioned to us the following five publications:

Development of the Kabbalah (including the *Zohar*);
Introduction to the *Zohar* (a systematic and historical overview);
Theology of the Kabbalah from a historical perspective—that is,
    a kind of history of kabbalistic ideas;
The history of kabbalistic literature;
A summary lexicon of the language of the *Zohar*. [. . .]

Sincerely yours, Schneider

FROM BETTY SCHOLEM

Berlin, February 7, 1933

My dear child,

The flu is going around, and "Heil, Hitler!" can be heard in every shop. But first to your letter from January 26, which arrived on February 4. It was the anniversary of your father's death, and Reinhold drove me out to Weissensee. We picked such a terrible time—it was snowing, stormy, and cold—that I couldn't spend even two minutes at your father's grave. The weather's always bad here. If I hadn't yet noticed the kind of horrible climate we're stuck with here, it would have dawned on me at Weissensee. [. . .]

Business hobbles along. [. . .] Hitler's appointment brought a new shock.[4] Theo told me yesterday that not a single new contract came in all last week. People are gripped by fear again. Some are even buying canned food, thinking that a famine will break out! Last Monday I saw *Faust,* and during the intermission I looked down into the Gendarme Market. I saw a vast torchlight procession moving toward the Linden.[5] An hour later, during the second intermission, they were still marching. (Where did the Nazis come up with 20,000 torches so quickly?) Otherwise, everything's calm. There are certainly no more swastikas around than before. [. . .]

Kisses, Mum

FROM BETTY SCHOLEM

Berlin, February 14, 1933

My dear child,

[. . .] Went to Werner's for dinner on Sunday. His beloved jeremiads are now in full swing. He considers the political situation to be extremely grave, and draws from it the most disastrous conclusions for himself. If he were still a member of the party, it would certainly be even worse for him! I had a good time in spite of this gloom and doom. The stuffed squabs were delicious. [. . .]

Your card from the second arrived on the tenth. Ludwig[6] wrote about Palestine in two short and very beautiful chapters, and showed a lot of understanding for the mission of the pioneers. He called the chapters "The Pathos." Again, it's a lovely book. A travel book full of clever observations, persuasive because it's true rather than flashy.

Kisses, Mum

FROM BETTY SCHOLEM

Berlin, February 20, 1933

Dear children,

[. . .] A trip in a car is far from being daredevilish![7] The best trip of my life was our drive to the Gardasee, which gave me so much pleasure. It was the most beautiful example of seasoned tourism you can think of. And now the little car has been sold and is gone; the garage has been rented out.

With us here, political changes appear first of all as a shock to business. This is, unfortunately, an old experience of ours. Business came to a standstill after Hitler became chancellor. Some people even canceled contracts retroactively, and Annchen Sussmann bought, of all things, a sack of flour! Phiechen asked whether it wouldn't be wise to put something by. "Of course," replied Erich. "A clever thing to do would be to get yourself fifty loaves of bread." Each change in the cabinet almost automatically raises the specter of strikes and food shortages. Hitler blabbers incessantly on the radio, without saying anything positive. Though the ban on newspapers that only prattle is very positive indeed. There has also been a mass dismissal of republican-minded civil servants, from top to bottom: district magistrates, high police officials—they're all being given the boot. Since all of these people will be entitled to full pensions, our civil service budget will only balloon again. Newspapers are not allowed to complain, even mildly. An Ullstein publication, a supplement of the *Berliner Zeitung,* was banned because it carried an article in its economic section claiming that the prevailing conditions here have thrown the stock market off! And the highly respected Catholic paper *Germania* also got closed down, even though it was closely allied with Herr von Papen. It goes without saying that the same fate befell the Communist papers. Soon we won't have any other newspapers but the Nazi ones. Hitler does things with violence. For the time being, the Jews have nothing to fear. There are few Jews in the civil administration and the civil service, and special laws won't be enacted so quickly. [. . .]

I went to see a marvelous production of *Faust II,* magnificent and sublime. It lasted from 7:00 to 11:45 P.M., and I sat through it without the least effort. I treated myself to a good seat: second balcony, first row.

We're buried in snow, and with a bit of imagination I can envision the clouds surging up over the white rooftops to be mountains. It's beautiful, even if the cold is awful. Why don't I live in Santa Margherita, by the blue sea?!

Warmest kisses, Mum

FROM BETTY SCHOLEM

Berlin, February 28, 1933

Dearest child,

Today I'm so upset I can't even write. Last night Werner was arrested again! You must have read that some lunatic set the Reichstag on fire, something so idiotic you can even imagine it was a contracted job. The government responded by arresting all former Communist members of the Reichstag and regional parliaments, along with the Communists' attorneys and lawyers—who are not even Communists but who only defended them in court! A harsh wind is blowing. Werner and Emmy were with us on Saturday evening. He even said that, if he were denounced, it wouldn't surprise him if they locked him up. We did not believe they could do a thing against him—and Emmy agreed with us. He was, after all, thrown out of the party seven years ago and hasn't been in the least politically active since he began studying. [. . .]

Early this morning at around 4:45 a guard and two others appeared, and, as no one opened the door when they rang, they opened it with a picklock. Lovely, isn't it? They searched the house for an hour, even the child's room. They found *nothing,* for the simple reason that Werner did not have anything forbidden in the apartment. But they had orders, so they took him with them anyway. Someone at the police station very politely informed Emmy by telephone, "That's right, Herr Scholem is here and you can speak with him early tomorrow morning, not to-day."

This entire business might also be just an election maneuver. Who can say anything about ruses of destructive politics? Things look terrible for us. Business, too, is completely dead. "Come back after the elections," the customers all say. This election has strangled everything.[8]

I can't tell you how worried I am—simply beside myself. I still can't stop crying. Emmy smelled danger and wanted Werner to spend Saturday night somewhere else. He just laughed at her. Then came this fire at the Reichstag, poisoning everything. [. . .]

Goodnight and kisses, Mum

TO BETTY SCHOLEM

Jerusalem, March 2, 1933

My precious mother,

[. . .] You mustn't under any circumstances compare this plan with your sweet memories of driving to the Gardasee.[9] Driving through the heart of Europe is very different from driving through the Balkans, not to mention Asia Minor—with their numerous cold mountains and snowed-covered roads, and their lack of proper highways, gas stations, repair shops, or decent inns. It's a relief to know that the plan was just a passing fancy, so we don't have to worry night and day about whether you've had an accident in Serbia or Turkey.

I'll supposedly be able to hear Hitler on the radio this evening. Listening to the radio here normally amounts to hearing terrible clatter and whistles and other awful noise. We sum up this racket as the sound of the world, which to us is no more harmonious in Palestine than in the rest of the world. We're hoping for clear weather so the reception will be good. We're following your rapidly developing political situation with sympathy—as much as we can, given the enigmatic, or at least badly translated, telegrams. This morning in particular, between a quarter to nine and a quarter to ten, you'd be interested in listening. At this time a university bus will drive up the mountain, packed full of youngsters who are partly from Germany and partly interested in Germany. They've all read the newspapers and are now properly prepared to pour out what they know. [. . .]

P.S. At the Ruppins', in Zion.[10] I just heard Hitler's speech at the Sports Palace. Now I need say no more! It was as if the glorious days prior to 1914 had returned. At the end, there was a mere symbolic announcement that the Reichstag would be transferred to Potsdam, which is without doubt precisely where it belongs.

Faithfully yours, Gerhard

FROM BETTY SCHOLEM

Berlin, Sunday evening, March 5, 1933

Dear child,

I'll begin by telling you that Werner was released late this morning and came here for lunch. He knows something about legal procedures: immediately after his arrest he submitted a statement to the chief of police in which he provided proof that he was a member neither of the party nor of the parliament. He also wrote to Emmy on February 28, though the letter arrived only yesterday at noon. Werner was very composed and didn't understand our excitement in the least. He said that it's happened before and that he'd experienced far worse things during four years of war. [. . .]

On Friday the police appeared at Siegfried's.[11] Erich led them around and they inspected what was being set in type and printed. The members of the patrol were polite and well mannered, and took only a copy of the *Jüdische Rundschau* with them. They were searching for illegal presses because the Communist press has been outlawed. We have to be careful, since the latest emergency orders suspended the paragraphs on personal freedom, privacy of mail and telephone, and so on. Foreign newspapers can inform you better than I can. The streets are quiet, nearly empty of people.

The turnout for today's election was enormous—the radio says 90 percent. Erich and his visitors are sitting in the front room listening to the results. I've excused myself. It's enough for me to hear it in the morning. [. . .]

Warmest kisses, Mum

FROM BETTY SCHOLEM

Berlin, March 19, 1933

My dear child,

[. . .] You wrote that you want precise information! I must refer you to the newspapers. Caution is the order of the day, and no one is allowed to pass rumors around. But this isn't necessary, since the facts speak for themselves. Lawyers and teachers have it the worst: they can be completely barred from their professions. Jewish doctors have already been shut out of the hospitals, and the national medical insurance is probably next in line. Still, the government won't directly interfere with their private practices. [. . .]

I myself am really quite calm. I'm not the only one in the world I have to think of, however, and my concern for my children and grandchildren has nothing to do with paranoia or an overactive imagination, which are not something I incline toward. It's a real stroke of luck that you're out of harm's way! Now, suddenly, I want to see everyone in Palestine!! When I only think of the outcry heard among German Jews when Zionism began! Your father and Grandfather Hermann L. and the entire Central Verein beat themselves on the breast and said with absolute conviction, "We are Germans!"[12] And now we're being told that we are *not* Germans after all! [. . .]

The streets are utterly quiet, at least in the sections of the city I frequent. But the Tauentzien, with its elegant shops, is full of the usual hustle and bustle. The number of people holding swastika boxes and collecting money has increased, though I've never seen anyone make a donation. I go there often because I like to meet with my gossip group at the Wittenbergplatz. I then complain about events as we sit on the silver terrace of the K.d.W.[13] I know quite well, of course, that *we* still have it good as long as we can sit undisturbed and blabber at the K.d.W. [. . .]

Warmest kisses, Mum

TO WALTER BENJAMIN

Jerusalem, Undated (ca. March 20, 1933)

Dear Walter,

[. . .] This year I have to restrict myself *in puncto* to Jewish philosophy (of the Middle Ages). Beginning in October I'll probably give a seminar on it—that is, if my position is approved this summer. My appointment to full professor in Jewish philosophy and in the Kabbalah has at last been formally proposed, after a long fight. [. . .]

I dare not even think what we would experience here if in fact Germany bars Jews—including those who already have positions—from pursuing university careers (something I consider wholly possible). There's apparently a great deal of uncertainty, both here and in Germany, about whether we can expect a large wave of immigrants from Germany. To a certain extent such immigrants are already very visible in Tel Aviv, and the government here would by no means be averse to seeing ten or fifteen thousand German Jews, instead of Jews from Poland or Romania, receive the hotly contested certificates—that is, immigration papers for Jews without means (the papers are issued every six months, according to the job market, by the government and are given to the Zionist bureau, which is responsible for distributing them). At the moment, there's a lot of room in Palestine for workers; but none for academics, who now come in great numbers with every ship, especially from Germany. Fourteen architects and engineers recently arrived on one vessel. We soon expect doctors from the city hospitals, lawyers, and professors. Under these circumstances, the only professors who will have any luck here are teachers of Hebrew. [. . .]

Gerhard

FROM BETTY SCHOLEM

Berlin, Monday, March 27, 1933

My dear child,

Your letter from the sixteenth arrived on the twenty-fourth. Many thanks!

Werner is continuing to work undisturbed, both with his attorneys (four socialists, two of whom are Communists) and with the office of the Attorney General. What will happen in the future is totally uncertain and does not depend upon the individual.

The government is taking the strictest measures against the atrocity stories, of which *at least* 99 percent are pure lies. But such lies spread when the press is not allowed to write as it sees fit. The fables now going around are ghastly. [. . .] Last Monday I went to see Traude Zucker. She was stirred up like a witch's brew! This old rumor-monger whispered to me straight off, "My dear Betty, pogroms are on the way!" "How do you know?" I asked. I don't doubt that among the people randomly and unjustly arrested some have been beaten, and for them it's terrible. The situation in the courts is awful, and horrible things happened in Breslau and Gleiwitz. Perhaps the agitation has been greater and more justified in smaller cities. But here in Berlin it's quiet—this no one can deny. Not a single shop has been plundered. Not one of us or of those we've spoken to has been a witness to the insult or abuse of Jews on the street or on public transportation. So you should wait until things happen before you talk about it. Nothing can be either done or prevented through a preemptive outcry.

Enough reasons for worry remain, even if everything is calm! Business is slow and difficult. We don't know if the state office for geology and the German Geological Society, customers for twenty years, will continue with us. Geology is an exclusively Christian field; it seems that Jews had no part in the creation of the world. Werner, of course, paints everything black.

You've no doubt read about the "moderate" speech Hitler made in Potsdam. I sat and listened to the whole thing, from 10 A.M. to 2 P.M. Many people were incredulous: "How could you listen to it!" We live in Germany, and *yes* I consider it important to listen. It really concerns all of us! Granted, what the government does is much more important than what it says. In any case, the speech hardly had a soothing effect.

Mass dismissals affect a great many Social Democrats. I think they must have more to worry about than we Jews do. [. . .]

Warmest kisses to you both, Mum

FROM BETTY SCHOLEM

Berlin, April 2, 1933

My dear children,

I hope that my missing letter from March 23 has arrived. Recently I've been writing *every week.* There may be delays because there's most likely random censorship of the mail.

Yesterday's boycott,[14] whose significance you've no doubt gathered from reading German newspapers, took place in absolute calm and without a single incident. Many shops did not even open; others closed soon after they opened! It was characterized by remarkable discipline, and no one was harassed. No one appeared in Schoeneberg, nor was there a sign posted on the shop. Two boys showed up on the doorstep of my little Katen,[15] of all people, and politely informed her that she had to close. Hedwig Hirsch and I were there at the time. "Oh, you mean," Katen replied, "that I should send my patients away?" "Of course not," said one of the boys. "Those you are treating now can stay; you just cannot accept any new ones!" The rest of the day's consultations continued as normal! For years, a businesswoman down below on the first floor has hung her sign next to Katen's. The boys put their placard there; they couldn't find any other place for it. The woman of course made a terrible fuss, and later added a small penciled note to the placard: "This concerns Frau Dr. Schiepan." But no one noticed the note, and as a result the poor merchant was promoted to being a Jew. [. . .]

Kisses, Mum

TO BETTY SCHOLEM

Jerusalem, April 5, 1933

Dearest Mother,

We received your letter from the twenty-seventh, and are very glad to hear that you're well. We hope that your migraines and other such ailments will soon pass. You shouldn't have to live with them. Have you consulted your doctor?

Our opinion of the "horror stories" that are supposedly 90 percent lies is very different from yours. Of course, it is not the horror stories that have made the deepest impression and that have led to such a large movement against the German government throughout the world. We did not take it seriously when we heard about Jewish corpses floating in the Spree.[16] We read only of reports citing mass public rapes of Jewish women and other such incidents, in *German* newspapers anyway, printed as examples of the "shameless incitement abroad." Believe me, even if stories of this sort have managed to reach Palestine, they have made no impression whatsoever outside of Germany. What's made the deepest impression, however, are the confirmed reports of the expulsion of Jews from their positions, the prevention of Jewish lawyers from appearing before the court, the restrictions on the number of lawyers allowed to practice, the plans to act against Jewish doctors, and so on—in short, things that you can read in every legal and reliable German newspaper. Outside of Germany, we know quite well that one can destroy the Jews without physical assault; one can shut Jews out of the professions that once formed the basis for their existence—and this is true even though the economic crisis long ago destroyed the important positions Jews once held, and many years after anti-Semitism began threatening the future of Jewish youth. People here now know that the government can finish off the Jews without physical attack by strangling them bloodlessly— that is, by closing down the free professions, which have been the Jews' most important source of income. No one abroad will accept from the Germans that these are emergency measures, or will believe that a great nation like Germany has been forced to use such measures against 1 percent of its population. We believe that these things are sufficient to arouse anti-German sentiment. Nor do we believe that the regime's political opponents who have fled Germany have contributed much to this sentiment. The fact that completely apolitical Jewish families have left Germany, abandoning all their possessions, suffices to convince people abroad that at least the moral pressure on Jews in Germany today has become unbearable. [. . .]

Don't forget that in Spain in 1492, there were no pogroms and no Jews were murdered; the Spanish simply tossed them out. And now (according to the official radio broadcasts, which the Germans apparently consider quite decorative and impressive) something original has been added to this formula: Jews are simply forbidden to leave Germany— which is hardly understandable, given the previous logic of "Please, just go to Palestine." Do they think we're too stupid to understand what follows from this?

Love, Your Escha and Gerhard

TO LAMBERT SCHNEIDER

Jerusalem, April 6, 1933

Dear Herr Dr. Schneider,

Please forgive me for the delay in answering your letter of January 26 regarding your publication suggestions. [. . .]

The plans I developed with Herr Professor Buber boil down to publishing my studies of the entire kabbalistic movement in stately form, essentially through two separate series. In a nutshell, the first would deal with the history of the Kabbalah and of Jewish mysticism, from its beginnings until the eighteenth or nineteenth century. To do this would entail presenting the development of the movement and its literature through a historical portrayal and an exhaustive historical and philological analysis of source materials which have remained largely unknown until now. The first and second of the five publications you mentioned would belong to this series. If I could sketch out the entire plan, the series would encompass the following volumes: (1) Jewish gnosticism in the talmudic and post-talmudic, Gaonic period;[17] (2) the rise of the Kabbalah and its history until Moses ben Nachmann; (3) the Kabbalah during the period of the *Zohar;* (4) development until the expulsion from Spain; (5) the Kabbalah in Sefad and its influences; (6) finally, mystical heresies since the Sabbatian movement, the outbreak of Hasidism, and the decline of the Kabbalah. Writing such an all-embracing study represents the scholarly aim of my life's work. In addition, there would be another series with works of a more monographic, summarizing, and intellectual-historical nature. The most important among these would be the work on the theology of the Kabbalah I already mentioned to you, along with a lexicon of the language of the *Zohar.* This study of the theology of the Kabbalah, which you suggested as the first book I should prepare, would not only deal with the historical development of kabbalistic ideas,

but would at the same time be a pertinent interpretation and confrontation of these ideas with traditional notions of Jewish philosophy and with
the so-called essence of Judaism. [. . .]

Along with a theology of the Kabbalah, I would also venture to produce a philological-historical work. In particular, I am thinking about
a lexicon of the *Zohar,* though I am still not certain whether the lexicon
should be written in German or in Hebrew. I imagine a contract between us stating that I would write specified books for your publishing
house, and you would commit yourself under certain conditions to buy
and print them. I had thought that within two years I could get one of
these books to you, but an increase in my teaching duties now puts great
pressure upon my time. Under certain circumstances, I may therefore
have to count on an extension.

I hope to hear from you soon, and I ask you once again not to take offense
at my long silence. I would also ask you to pass on the enclosed personal
letter to Herr Schocken, whose address I do not have at the moment.

With highest esteem, Gerhard Scholem

FROM BETTY SCHOLEM

Berlin, April 9, 1933

Dear children,

In the past couple of years I've calmly accepted many of the things
that have happened to me. Now I cannot digest what is happening—
and I refuse to do so. I'm completely speechless. I simply can't imagine
that there are not 10,000 or 1,000 upright Christians who refuse to go
along by raising their voice in protest. What happened first to the lawyers, who from one day to the next have had their livelihood taken from
them, can occur tomorrow to the doctors. This won't happen so quickly
to the merchants, since Christian suppliers will not give up their customers so easily. [. . .]

Everyone asks me why I am still here and why I didn't leave long
ago to be with you. Of course I hope that this refuge will always remain
for me, and for this reason I am not at all worried about myself. I do
worry about my three children here, with their wives and children, and
for this reason I cannot flee in panic from this place. Am I right? [. . .]

Warmest kisses, Mum

FROM BETTY SCHOLEM

Berlin, April 18, 1933

Dear children,

[. . .] The Seder evening at Theo's was completely overshadowed by recent events. Before the Seder, Theo gave a lovely speech and said that "Jewry will overcome this persecution, too." Jewry, no doubt—but what about German Jewry? What's especially awful about the measures taken against Jewish lawyers and doctors is that they were first instigated by their own colleagues from the Law and Medicine Chamber. A small event: The Zernsdorf bus normally stops on our street *before* the bus stop, so we don't have to walk so far. This time, someone called out to the driver as he lowered the steps for us: "So, for this pack of Jews you're making an extra stop!!" Now do you understand why I've been getting migraines?

Kisses, Mum

TO BETTY SCHOLEM

Jerusalem, April 20, 1933

Dear Mother,

We received your letter of April 9 right on time. We're quite distressed to hear that your health is not the best. You should do all you can to recover and to rest, and you should avoid dwelling unduly on your various worries and concerns, which we understand very well. We hope you'll succeed in this. You know of course that with us you will always have a refuge from all difficulties. But we do not think it right to suggest that you come—unless you have no other choice. For Palestine is a land of the young and for the young. In the long run, you will feel very uprooted here, cut off from the friends and way of life you are used to. We don't know how you'll manage with the climate, either. While you were here, you were always in a rather strange and sour mood. In any case, don't lose hope. Just think how often the most terrible circumstances can change. The streak of rotten luck that's been dogging you for two years is bound to change. We're sure that you'll have good luck again soon. [. . .]

There's nothing new to report from here. We're still getting a large stream of immigrants, whose future here is really up in the air. The country's too small to absorb a massive influx of intellectuals. The transition to agriculture is not easy, and can succeed only in rare cases where people have their own capital to work with. In short, this entire matter confronts us with the most vexing problems. And there are even more inquiries than arrivals. We've received letters from a great many of our German friends, many of whom are no longer even in Germany. Sadly, it's very difficult to offer them any assistance.

Other than this, all is well. We are healthy, and today it was really warm for the first time in ages. We planted some carnations in our front yard. Behind the house stretches a desert of stone, and it looks rather hopeless. The carnations demand constant watering by Escha, as the heavens won't do the work here. Our finances are so-so. At the moment, all of the countries that raise support for us are bankrupt. This doesn't do much to make us optimistic, but we haven't abandoned all hope. [. . .]

Forever yours, Gerhard and Escha

FROM BETTY SCHOLEM

Berlin, April 25, 1933

Dear children,

Something awful has happened again. On the night of Sunday the twenty-third Werner was arrested again, and to our unspeakable horror Emmy was taken away too. We have no idea why. He had begun very promising negotiations for his livelihood. In contrast to his typical pessimism, he was hopeful when I saw him on Saturday. He was thinking of possibly doing a Ph.D. in law, to improve his chances. We had already made contact with Dr. Meyer.[18] Since sending letters back in forth is no longer possible, he was considering going there on Sunday afternoon to get more precise information. The professor with whom he had done his teaching internship gave him an extraordinary letter of recommendation to the local professor there. Emmy was on a business trip, and he picked her up at the train station on Saturday evening at eleven. Erich very much wanted to speak with him, and went to see him on Sunday morning at ten. They were both gone by the time he arrived. They were arrested at 5:30 A.M. by police officers (not SA people) after presenting their identification papers. [. . .]

Kisses to you both, Mum

TO BETTY SCHOLEM

Jerusalem, April 26, 1933

Dear Mother,

[. . .] We are comforted in these times of injustice by Billar's latest offspring: a sweet white kitty with a lopsided black mustache. Maybe you should get a kitten of your own, to counteract the migraines. I wouldn't give your headaches such dubious nourishment—all those various encounters with more or less evil men; it's better to let them starve. We, too, have a lot pent up inside us because of our obsession with reading all the newspapers we can get our hands on. We often read Nazi papers, to obtain all sorts of information—in particular, to get to the original sources through legal proclamations and ministers' speeches. We should all take a philosophical view of events. The day may perhaps return when the Germans will realize they didn't have it so bad with their Jews after all. As an aside, it's curious how the nature of the Jewish Question fundamentally changes here. In Germany people view the Jews as foreigners, and even some German Jews have considered themselves to be foreigners. But here the Jews, who are for the most part from eastern Europe, look upon German Jews as foreigners. They see them as being more German than Jewish. I'll give you an illustration. A district court officer arrived a short time ago on one of the most recent ships. He declared to the aid committee that he's willing to do any sort of work. He expects only a minimum salary (nevertheless around 200 marks), and he's even prepared, if necessary, to sacrifice his academic title. For this gentleman such a claim no doubt represents extreme sacrifice; for the local Jews it's a joke. [. . .]

Warmest regards, Gerhard

FROM BETTY SCHOLEM

Berlin, May 1, 1933

Dear children,

Werner and Emmy have not yet been released. On this score, I have nothing comforting to report. But little Edith was granted permission to speak with her mother.

I called the police station from their apartment to find out where they'd been taken. I was given the information right away. This allowed me, on the twenty-seventh, to go directly to the station at long last and ask some questions. I was not dissuaded, even though the boys—thinking it best to wait until the two of them made contact—didn't want to let me go. All of the officials were helpful and friendly. I did not get permission to speak with Werner and Emmy, but the officials said that I could write and even promised to deliver letters and food packages for me. Still, it did not happen as easily as they said. I wandered for three hours through the offices, hallways, and stairwells of the gigantic police headquarters. At least I knew that the two were somewhere in the building. *Why* they are there no one could tell me.

On the twenty-eighth little Edith arrived from Hannover, where her mother had sent her with instructions not to write but to return at the end of the week. She was told to go to Emmy's office, where she learned where her mother was being held. The brave child then went to the police headquarters. They were humane enough to allow her a conference with her mother.

Emmy figures that a baseless denunciation must be behind everything, since there *cannot* be the slightest shred of evidence against them. The investigation into the charges is painfully slow because so many thousands have been randomly arrested. The child can return tomorrow. They even gave her hope that her mother would soon be released. She couldn't get any information about her father. We still have not received the letter that he must have written following his arrest.

That's where things stand now, and in the meantime there's nothing more to do. At the information desk I asked whether we should get ourselves a lawyer. There's no point, they told me. An attorney will get permission to speak with him only after a hearing date has been set. [. . .]

Kisses, Mum

TO ULRICH GERHARDT[19]

Jerusalem, May 3, 1933

Dear Herr Gerhardt,

[. . .] I don't need to describe to you the impression made on me by the German newspaper reports and the manifestations of the "new German spirit" in the official rallies broadcast on the radio, not to mention the news of the fate of our families and the awareness of what is happening there. It's abundantly clear that no one entertains any illusions about the significance of these historical events, ourselves least of all—those of us whose sad prognosis regarding the fate of German Jewry has not only been fulfilled, but exceeded a thousand times over. The urgent need to come to the aid of everyone who has turned to us for help, both the new arrivals and those still left in Germany, has thankfully pushed to the side (at least for a few hours) the melancholy reflections that inescapably force themselves on every Jew with a scrap of honor and self-awareness. My wife and I have often spoken about you and others. We have imagined how you might occasionally sit and reflect in front of the bookshelf you showed us in Halle. The difference between today's events and those in 1492 is only a moral one, despite their great similarity in importance and kind. Back then Jews had more substance, and there weren't any "national Spanish Jews" who still licked the boots that trampled them. At the same time, the people with power had not yet learned to demand that the persecuted deny, with fear and trembling, the very existence of persecution. We have learned a great deal about Jewish history over the past two months, and hopefully this knowledge will prove fruitful someday. Our days of remembrance will now resemble the first of April of an earlier time.[20]

The reports from my own family are quite distressing, though not by any means the worst when compared to everything we hear around us. When you first met my mother, during her visit here in October, she still seemed young and full of life. She has now completely fallen apart. Aside from all the many dire events, this psychological situation—which I needn't describe—leaves one speechless. Furthermore, we have great personal worries of our own. It's highly questionable whether we could organize a mass emigration from Germany, which would be the only means of rescue. Meanwhile, whenever they can, people send us their most precious possessions: their children, whose education can now be

conducted on an entirely new basis. Like everyone else, we now have
friends from Germany staying with us. One manages the best one can.
[. . .]

Yours, Gerhard Scholem

FROM BETTY SCHOLEM

Berlin, May 10, 1933

My dear children,

I still can't report any good news. Both are still under arrest, but neither has been interrogated even once! This means that our hands are
tied. Every third day I go to the police headquarters without first having
received permission for a conference. The official is quite friendly. Each
time, he tells me that "a few days won't make any difference"; that "as
a grandmother" I should "look after my grandchildren"; that "Emmy
will certainly be interrogated in the morning"; and that I should "come
back in three days and then perhaps something can be done." And when
I come to the office three days later, the same story repeats itself and I
get nowhere. Yesterday he asked me to drop by on Friday the twelfth.

Today I got a letter from Werner (what a marvelous correspondence,
when it takes twelve days for a letter to go back and forth). He is deeply
despondent that he hasn't yet been interrogated, since this means he can
neither clarify a thing nor get himself a lawyer. On the very first day,
he requested to see his wife in order to settle some financial matters and
to make some decisions about the children. Nothing came of it. Probably
the officials do not yet have a technical handle on the situation, so they
arrest whoever is denounced—and the masses of people affected just
have to wait! In our case there's no doubt that it goes back to a denunciation, since neither one has done a thing! It's outrageous enough to arrest
Werner, a Jew who was once politically active—but what has his wife
done?! Surely no one can have any interest in ruining this family! [. . .]

Yes, the newspapers offer a lot of reading material! Lovely speeches
on the first of May, in the universities and schools. Even the question-
naire sent out by the General Medical Council is a document from our
times. Yesterday I helped Katen fill it out. We were supposed to disclose
where our grandparents were born, where they married, and where they

died, down to the day and the hour! Strangely enough, I knew a mass of details! "Carelessly incomplete information can lead to the loss of registration." (Can the General Medical Council revoke a registration issued by the state?)

All of the children from our circle continue to attend school undisturbed, at least for now. (This of course could change any day!) Either they're the children of frontline soldiers or the percentage of Jewish students is not above 5 percent—recently they've not been counting children from mixed marriages. And where it's above 5 percent, people shut their eyes. The parents pay school fees! [. . .]

Your dispirited mother

TO BETTY SCHOLEM

Jerusalem, May 23, 1933

Dear Mother,

[. . .] We're receiving inquiries from all sides regarding the possibilities for settling here and getting a job. It seems as if the majority of our acquaintances and relatives abroad are ready to pick up stakes and leave. To add to this, people often take it badly when we can't give clear and precise information. Life is hard—none of us ever thought it possible that this sort of thing could happen. [. . .]

Many greetings and all the best, Gerhard

FROM BETTY SCHOLEM

Zernsdorf, May 28, 1933

Dear children,

On Friday I was finally permitted to speak with Emma for *ten minutes.* At least I saw her in person, which gave me a bit of comfort. I can't tell you the unimaginable effort it cost me to arrange the conference! On the twenty-fifth the children got a phone call at Klopp Strasse telling them that Werner had been transferred to Spandau and that his mother should go to police headquarters to get permission to speak with him. Under the assumption that the call came from police headquarters, I ventured there once again. But no one knew anything at the station. Since I was already there, I put up a fight until I got permission to speak to the state prosecutor, and I didn't let up until he gave me his permission. In the next room, where the gentlemen in charge of these things sat, everything began from the beginning. "No, you can't have permission. No, no." But I refused to let the commissioner off the hook. In the meantime, he attended to a number of other people. I wouldn't let loose. He was a friendly man. He did not throw me out, but finally gave me the slip of paper. Then it lasted yet another hour. I had to wait, got screamed at, and finally a female bureaucrat appeared wearing a white frock and a decent face and leading Emmy along behind her. In a large office where people were "speaking" in every corner, we could talk with a table between us. An official constantly called out to us, "Okay, wind it up!" "Stop!" Of the ten minutes three were spent crying, and then Emmy hurriedly told me what she needed. She also said that she'd already been interrogated and that both of them had been charged with high treason. In other words, based on a denunciation, they were accused of participating in Communist activities. Not a word of it is true. [. . .]

Obtaining permission to speak with Werner is impossible, because it would "prejudice the course of justice"! There are strange things in the world! I have to wait four weeks before speaking with Emmy again. By that time I only hope they'll be free. [. . .]

Warmest kisses, Mum

FROM BETTY SCHOLEM

Berlin, June 7, 1933

Dear children,

Last week I was so completely occupied with organizing Werner's household that I could send nothing more than a card. The constant writing generally demanded by Werner's case requires such effort that every day it seems I really can't go on. It's like a Hydra: a new head springs up daily. The people in Hannover now bombard me with letters asking for information. They, too, are frightened.

There are new reasons to be upset. On Monday (June 4), the second day of the Pentecost holiday, Dina[21] came to Zernsdorf with the news that Werner had phoned at around 9:30 from Spandau to say he was being released, with a number of others. A car was already waiting in front of the gate to transport them to Alexanderplatz, where they would be set free. He would be there in an hour or two and would immediately go to Zernsdorf with Hete (she was the only one he could reach; everyone else had left the city for Pentecost). Hete waited all alone until ten in the evening. Every two hours Erich telephoned from Zernsdorf, and in the evening I went into the city to wait some more.

Werner never arrived! Isn't it enough to just drive you out of your mind! Though I detest the very thought of it, I'll go to police headquarters later—maybe I can get some information.

We've heard nothing about Emmy. There's an apprentice in her office, a strapping fellow who's been a Nazi for three years now. From the start, he has made a colossal effort to help. He has constant access to police headquarters. Last week he got permission for a forty-five minute conference. He took Edith with him, but the child wasn't allowed to go inside with him. [. . .]

Adieu for now, Mum

FROM BETTY SCHOLEM

Zernsdorf, June 11, 1933

Dear children,

Last week I didn't get a letter from you; perhaps there's one on its way. In the morning we will drive into the city.

It's been a totally disastrous week. There was no explanation for the phony reports of Werner's release. We know nothing, and we haven't heard a thing from him. The office at Spandau told me that he's still there, so Erich sent him three packages of books, clothes, and food. Yesterday Martha[22] came by and announced that all three packages had been returned, marked "Addressee Released." The people at police headquarters told me that the examining magistrate in Moabit was now in charge of the case and that I should phone there. But the examining magistrate informed me that he wasn't in charge. Tomorrow we'll call him once again. Gradually I'm being left with the choice of becoming either apathetic, or wild with rage. [. . .]

Isn't it awful how Werner has squandered his life on godforsaken politics! How right your father was. He said over and over again that

Werner should first finish his studies and get his career under way; *then* he could toss as many bombs as his heart desired. [. . .]

Kisses, Mum

TO WALTER BENJAMIN

Jerusalem, June 15, 1933

Dear Walter,

[. . .] Acquaintances from Germany, along with many people I don't know, now roam this place in ever growing numbers, and both groups make increased claims on our time. Something I noticed last Sunday: there's so much German spoken on the streets (and in Tel Aviv it's even more conspicuous than here) that yours truly has a strong inclination to withdraw back into Hebrew. Sadly, I've already driven one female interlocutor to tears with an analysis of the dream world in which German Jews have been living. Given my opinions on things here, I never dreamed until now that I could, on top of everything else, also earn the reputation of being an extreme chauvinist. This is perhaps the proper revenge of the *genius loci*. From the perspective of unfolding events, the old thesis has been reconfirmed once again, and in the strangest way: that Zionism has had the greatest insights in diagnosing the Jewish condition, but the most tragic weakness in prescribing therapy. [. . .]

Gerhard

FROM BETTY SCHOLEM

Zernsdorf, June 18, 1933

Dear child,

[. . .] It's downright unpleasant here. This business about Werner's ostensible release has really finished me off. Furthermore, it seems impossible to find an attorney. Everyone we've asked has declined, after hearing the word "politics"! It's also hard to put up with Werner's despairing letters asking us to find him a lawyer and to visit him. We've done nothing during the past few weeks but try to secure permission to see him—without getting it! Werner writes repeatedly that it's ludicrous for attorneys to be afraid; nothing could happen to them! It *may* be ridiculous, but they're scared to death to represent a Communist and thereby risk losing the license they've worked so hard to obtain! Someone from the Alpine Hiking Association recommended a Deutschnationale attorney, who pledged to visit Werner first and to decide about representing him *after* the interview. But this glimmer of hope faded fast. The gentleman backed down even before their meeting. Werner waited for him in vain.

Kisses, Mum

TO BETTY SCHOLEM

Rehavia, June 22, 1933

Dear Mother,

[. . .] There's great commotion here over a terrible political assassination, this time carried out not by Arabs but unfortunately by Jews from the most extreme wing of the Revisionists. They killed the political head of the Jewish Executive in Palestine, an old friend from the days of my Zionist activities in Berlin back in 1916–1917.[23] It's ghastly. At the same time, another large wave of Germans has arrived. I'm overrun by friends and many others. The last ship brought five old acquaintances from ten to fifteen years back. One fellow I'm extremely fond of is now staying in Escha's room. In general, there's a lot of life here. People have only one problem: their financial resources from Germany. For this group at least, everything depends on them. *Everyone* thinks that by autumn the situation of Jews in Germany will be such that the masses will *have* to emigrate. [. . .]

Your son, G.

FROM BETTY SCHOLEM

Zernsdorf, June 27, 1933

My dear child,

[. . .] Werner is outraged at the "cowardly and despicable behavior" of the attorneys. He's deeply depressed in particular about a personal friend he was sure would represent him: Dr. Kaufmann, the head of the Alpine Hiking Association. Werner complained bitterly about what Dr. K. had said: that he was of course quite interested in taking the case and deeply grieved over Werner's situation, but that for him to get involved in anything political was completely out of the question. He told Erich straight out that Werner won't find anyone willing to represent him. Isn't that appalling? [. . .]

Emmy wrote that she'd had a severe gallbladder infection, though now she's doing quite well. She has a lot of time to rest. At Moabit she's under constant observation and can eat well. Both tell me that the meals are adequate; they can also buy additional food in the canteen. All they lack are things to liven up the monotony, and fresh fruit. Erich mails them whatever else they ask for, such as books and household utensils. I buy the items, and he sends them from the shop. Werner and Emmy are allowed to subscribe to newspapers. Every ten days they can receive a package of food. Selma, the maid, did this until June 7. She baked them her special cake and biscuits, which they ate for breakfast, since the black bread did not agree with either one of them. Last week little Edith brought them fresh fruit—strawberries and cherries. She had to skip school, but of course she won't be able to continue doing this. [. . .]

You must have read that the Social Democrats have now been outlawed and all of their former leaders imprisoned. Moreover, the church has been "taken over" and brought into line with a bunch of other organizations. The same goes for the theater. However serious the situation is, there are still a few things you can laugh about. [. . .]

For now, kisses, Mum

FROM BETTY SCHOLEM

Zernsdorf, July 4, 1933

My dear child,

[. . .] How could we send Edith to Ben Shemen?[24] We don't have the money for it, and without the parents' permission it's simply out of the question. One must *discuss* such matters, and to date we haven't obtained permission to speak about this. We have easily a dozen requests floating around the Federal Court in Leipzig—yet no permission has been granted. They don't even answer us! And such a question cannot be pursued through correspondence, which is very uncertain and problematic. For the time being, we haven't made any changes in Edith's education. She goes to school, and is registered as a Christian because of her mother. [. . .]

It's generally believed here that the position of the Jews will worsen by the fall! We're convinced that one profession after another will be closed off. In merchandizing this is done through laws that strictly forbid government officials to buy from Jews. All Christian firms dealing in raw materials and wholesale goods are barred from doing business with Jews. For the time being, it's still possible to manage things under the table; at the end of the day, however, we also think that most Jews will have to leave. Herr Goebbels pledged once again on the radio that he won't rest until the last Jew has gone! But where to? [. . .]

Kisses, Mum

FROM BETTY SCHOLEM

Berlin, July 9, 1933

My dearest child,

On the seventh I received the letter you sent to Zernsdorf. Now that the weather is warm, it's fabulous outside. I don't want to rub it in for Escha, but the cherries taste marvelous. Now it's Reinhold's turn to pick. Ah, it's really peaceful. God, you know how accustomed I am to taking things as they come. I could almost be happy out here in the country, if only I weren't so concerned about Werner and about what will become of us. [. . .]

Theo hasn't the slightest doubt that *all of us* will ultimately have to leave. Have you read that they're now closing in on the doctors? After the Jewish community established an information center for Jewish doctors, they arrested thirty functionaries and accused them of being an underground "Marxist" organization!! A large number of Jewish doctors have already been prevented, some even by *telegraph,* from taking patients with state medical insurance. On the first of July, all of the so-called private insurance companies "brought themselves into line" and ceased to honor bills from Jewish doctors. My sister, who has been practicing since 1906, has not yet received the ban, though she will. [. . .]

July 10, 1933

We met together around 10:30 at the prison, after I had already waited two and a half hours at the parcels receiving office. The child and Erich spoke with Emmy. We couldn't speak with Werner until about two. I had to go home and then return; Erich too. Erich says that Emmy is at the end of her wits. She cried, and we could not reason with her. "Do what Werner wants," she said. Werner, whom we spoke with for twenty minutes (ten are allowed), looks quite well, even if the basic impression he gives is one of despair. [. . .]

Mum

FROM BETTY SCHOLEM

Zernsdorf, July 18, 1933

My dear child,

Last week I didn't hear from you at all; hopefully I will in the morning! The only thing I have to report is a visit to Werner, during which the warden expressly asked us to curtail our correspondence. No other inmate gets so much mail, he said. He has to spend two and a half hours just reading the Scholem correspondence, and this won't do. I can really sympathize with him. Some days I get three letters from Werner, six to eight pages of his scrawl. And in the end the censors cut them into little pieces. We agreed to write only once a week. Speaking for myself, this takes a real load off my shoulders. As much as I feel sorry for the two of them, I couldn't have kept up the incessant writing. I can now see Emmy once every two weeks, which is at least something. The lawyer we'd placed so much hope in hasn't shown his face again. Erich wants to phone him on Monday, to get at least a yes or a no out of him. It is, and remains, a terrible disaster! Both are bearing up very badly under prison conditions. It's driving them out of their minds to think that they got arrested without even anticipating it. The government quite simply intends to destroy the Communists. We're very pessimistic and can't do a thing about it! It seems that Werner had no perspective whatever on the situation. On Thursday, the twentieth of April, he already had a visa, but he continued lounging around until Sunday. He wanted to leave in the afternoon, and then he and Emmy were arrested at five A.M. [. . .]

Kisses, Mum

TO WALTER BENJAMIN

Jerusalem, July 26, 1933

Dear Walter,

[. . .] Concerning the possibilities for you here, it seems to both of us completely out of the question that you could survive on a hundred marks a month. Not that this is objectively impossible—one hundred marks is now equivalent to seven pounds, easily enough for a simple life. But we're of the opinion that such a simple life won't do here. Added to this are the immense psychological difficulties, for we don't see any possibility that you could find work or employment even halfway suitable for you. In this country it's not good to live without work. Subjectively, it would put you in an unbearable state of mind. You'd be unable to make yourself known to the people here. The most important issue is whether you would be forced to live completely isolated here, as if on some island like Ibiza,[25] or whether you'd be able to participate in a life so different from the one you're used to. You could, of course, do your literary work here. Jerusalem offers more than Ibiza: first of all, there are people like us here; second, there are books. All of this would be splendid if one could just imagine you freely pursuing your work, which is so distinctively European. But it seems to us doubtful that you'd feel comfortable in a land in which you took no direct part. This might well leave you feeling like an outsider—a morally untenable situation in which what is vital cannot thrive *(exempla docent)*. Perhaps the only way to find out would be to give it a try. At the same time, the most elementary reflection tells us that these spiritual and moral difficulties will not exist for you in Paris. Our experience is that in the long run the only people who can survive all of the difficulties here are those who are fully devoted to this land and to Judaism. [. . .]

Gerhard

FROM BETTY SCHOLEM

Auxerre, August 1, 1933

c/o Dina Scholem, Ecole Savry no. 8, Auxerre-Jonne, France

Dear children,

Eight days ago I went into the city for a prison visit. In the evening Theo showed up, to talk me into this trip with Hete. Right away I got a German exit visa from our local police station. So, from one day to the next, I was ready to trade the ghastly atmosphere of Berlin for the freedom across the border. All of the children and siblings naturally encouraged me, and I can't do a *thing* to help Werner anyway. Early Saturday we left, with a very cheap third-class holiday pass. [. . .]

Now onto the news about Werner—details I could not reveal from home and to which you may respond *only* in a letter sent to Auxerre. [. . .] Werner and Emmy were arrested with a group of about twenty others, all members of a secret organization. For the past three years they've been seeking to infiltrate the army with Communists, with the aim of eventually overthrowing the government. It was Emmy who was involved; whether Werner knew about this or not, I can't say. In any event, she was not arrested because of *his* incriminating background, but *he* because of *hers.* A list of names most likely turned up in one of the raids or house searches. It's certain that someone denounced Emmy. Someone from her office, no less. At work she must have made some very careless comments. It is of course outrageous that Emmy remained a card-carrying member of the party after Werner was expelled and had begun to devote himself to his studies. It's an even greater injustice to her husband if in fact she was active. Both were somehow unimaginably foolish and reckless. [. . .]

We are convinced that Dr. Thurnheim will not give Emmy back her job. He is a Jew; she is a leftist. They already have such enormous problems that they've taken the name "Thurnheim" off their printed materials. It seems completely out of the question that they will endanger their reputation by having an employee who's been branded a Communist. They gave her April paycheck to Erich. Though they have discussed the situation with Erich often since then, they've said nothing more about this matter. When Emmy asked to speak with Dr. Thurnheim, he refused. One cannot blame any of us who still have some sort of income for displaying the greatest caution. Nevertheless, Emmy and

Werner are beside themselves over the "cowardice" of their friends. They sit behind bars and really fail to grasp that the Nazis are doing precisely the same things that the Communists would do if they were at the helm. [. . .]

Both are incredibly open and incautious in their letters. Werner wrote to me that when clearing out his things from his apartment I should put all of his writings in a suitcase and store them at my place—something I would have done anyway; I never would have left papers in an unguarded apartment! At the end of June, when I was in Zernsdorf, two criminal investigators appeared at the house on Alexandrinen[26] and asked about the "suitcase with writings." Edith phoned Erich, who told her to show the gentlemen the suitcase, which was stored with other cases full of clothes and linen. I had told Erich where to find the keys, though in all of the excitement no one knew where they were. So they broke open all of the cases and brought out every last hand towel. There was nothing incriminating; Werner, as he once told me, had already removed everything. But the officials took his military papers, his war diaries, his passports—and everything that, given the climate today, could easily be used against him. [. . .]

Mum

TO MARTIN BUBER

Rehavia, August 10, 1933

Dear Herr Buber,

[. . .] It pains me to hear that your ambitious plans for an educational project, which we've followed here as best we can with great enthusiasm, seem to have so little prospect of success.[27] All of us here—and I speak especially for myself—find it extremely difficult to comprehend the spiritual and moral attitude of German Jews to their own fate. This is precisely what concerns us so much. Terrible though the thought may be, it almost seems as if large segments of German Jewry have failed to grasp what is happening, and as if even more horrors must occur before they're roused. We have many sad examples of this. [. . .]

For now, warmest regards to you and your wife.

Yours, Gershom Scholem

FROM BETTY SCHOLEM

La Bourboule, August 19, 1933

Dear Son,

[. . .] Now on to the most important thing: money! In this you are completely correct, and for some time now I've been thinking of transferring some to you. Scraping everything together, I now possess five thousand marks in cash. I should be able to rescue a few thousand more, but the business has not been liquidated nor has Zernsdorf been divided up and sold. Right away I'll start transferring small sums. I'll send two hundred marks using my passport at the end of August or the beginning of September.[28] [. . .]

I can take only small sums *peu à peu* from my account. If someone goes sniffing around my bank account, I can justify the withdrawals by claiming I needed the money for Werner and his children. I don't dare take out two thousand marks at once. Please open a completely separate account for me! In the meantime, all of the money that I transfer to you must remain in cash because I don't know how I will need it. If I need to use your house as a refuge, I can build one or two rooms onto it. This seems to me an obvious solution, and it cheers me to know that an asylum will be ready for me should conditions become even worse here. *All* of us are thoroughly pessimistic. They are systematically and logically denying Jews their ability to exist. [. . .]

Mum

TO BETTY SCHOLEM

Jerusalem, August 23, 1933

Dearest Mother,

[. . .] P.S. We've been told something I don't hesitate to tell you directly, since it is no mystery to the police—namely, that you are under constant surveillance. I don't write this as a warning, and you have nothing to be afraid of. I just want to explain that a number of guests you've been expecting have noticed, and as a result have been avoiding you.

Gerhard

TO MARTIN BUBER[29]

Jerusalem, August 24, 1933

Dear Herr Buber,

[. . .] Your indication that there is a chance of seeing you here pleases me particularly; it would be an immense benefit if you were here now. Truth to tell, no matter what the basis for your intimation may be, and despite the fact that *in concreto* it may refer only to a temporary sojourn, it seems to me that if the university is now really to be expanded substantially by the appointment of colleagues from Germany, it would be of the greatest importance if someone of your moral authority worked here. The very addition of a considerable number of scholars to whom this university and its problems have hitherto meant nothing will very quickly create many serious problems, and then a man of your authority would be all the more valuble. This is my personal conviction. [. . .]

Sincerely, Gerhard Scholem

TO BETTY SCHOLEM

Jerusalem, August 30, 1933

Dearest Mother,

[. . .] Tomorrow we celebrate the birthday of Escha's cousin, who will be twenty-four. She arrived a few months ago and works as a piano teacher, a profession without many prospects here. Because she can also work as a housekeeper and, if push comes to shove, is willing to do so, she'll always be able to find a job. At the moment, she's renting a room not far from us and pays us an occasional visit. She entertains us with her Hamburg dialect. While diverging greatly from Escha's very mild one, it still reminds me of it. We're even going to make her a birthday cake. This being the young lady's first birthday away from her parents' home, we have to make it a big celebration. I've invited one of my pupils who's the same age: a cat-like young thing who someday will be able to describe herself as the world's first professionally trained female kabbalist.[30] Other than her, we've invited a number of even younger colleagues and friends, whom I don't think you met. The speeches I give and the yellow tea cart always play the central role on the evenings we entertain. You haven't seen the cart; Escha gave it to me as a birthday gift a year and eight months ago. She pushes it into the center of the circle, where it sits heavily laden and sparkling. Everyone is ranged around the outer edge of the setting sun.[31] I avoid stepping on it and don't allow anyone to sit on it (in a chair). Only the cart, which is very light, is allowed on it. I say all this to give you some idea of our social life. [. . .]

Love from your devoted son, Gerhard

FROM BETTY SCHOLEM

Berlin, September 26, 1933

My dear boy,

We really needed this sense of joy! I congratulate you from the bottom of my heart and with great delight. I'm proud and happy that your scholarly accomplishments have found such recognition through this appointment.[32] When I first opened the letter, your visiting card fell out; and as soon as I read "Prof. Dr. Scholem," I began weeping. I couldn't even read the letter. While Edith read it aloud to me, her milk boiled over on the stove. Then I got into high gear on the telephone, which we are otherwise very frugal in using. What a pleasure it is to spread good news! [. . .]

A thousand greetings and kisses, Your mother

FROM WERNER SCHOLEM

Sender: Werner Scholem, Prisoner 1660

Moabit Prison, Berlin, October 5, 1933

Dear Gerhard,

Mother has told me of your appointment as professor, and I'm writing to send you both congratulations and greetings. You have achieved something because you gave up trying to become someone in Germany. If you'd become a professor here in Germany, you might be roaming the world the way some of my friends and law teachers are. I hope you can continue to live in peace. You'll be fine so long as the Arabs aren't allowed to murder you—and for the time being, it appears that this turn of events won't happen (though it might well be expected someday). This makes me glad.

Mother has told you of my fate. I'm a dual target: a Jew and a former politician. Six years of legal studies and internship were entirely in vain. I've thus squandered the most decisive years of my life, without managing to obtain amnesty for my previous political activity. This will remind you of our conversation last year during your visit, when I predicted this would happen—and then was derided by everyone as a "pessimist"! This only goes to show how little of a pessimist I really was. I was an optimist blinded by rose-colored glasses, for it never dawned on me that anyone could make something out of nothing. After leaving the Communist party in 1926, I never could have imagined that anyone would still accuse Emmy and me of high treason. *Nemini parcetur!*[33] [. . .]

Your brother, Job

TO BETTY SCHOLEM

Jerusalem, October 19, 1933

Dear Mother,

[. . .] The division of the Zernsdorf property interests us greatly. Escha is convinced that you'll lose the cherry trees. Is this true? Once you have the means again, Escha would be very grateful if you could pay for the transport of a few large crates of books. When the time comes, she'll write you the details.

All is well with us, and we stagger from party to party. Recently Dr. Senator, a member of the Executive, held a lovely dinner in honor of the new professor.[34] Only twelve people were invited. Escha even wore a new dress for the occasion. The man of the house offered a sort of toast on my behalf. Tomorrow and the day after, we'll be celebrating day and night: it's our tenth anniversary. Apparently this is called the green anniversary. In honor of this jubilee Escha has lost around ten pounds, and now weighs approximately the same as she did at our wedding. [. . .]

This evening we'll go to see the opera *Rigoletto* for a change. For a number of years opera was more or less dead here. It's now making a comeback, since so much new talent has arrived in the country. People with the greatest experience and talent who at first perhaps couldn't find work have gradually gained a reputation. A new opera is scheduled to début every week, and will be performed on three different days in the three largest cities. Here it'll be at the Zion Cinema. This theater used to be an old wreck, but some time ago it was given a tiptop renovation. All it's lacking is a cloakroom. Everyone has to sit with his coat and hat on his lap. Otherwise, as I said, it leaves nothing to be desired.

Yours, Gerhard

P.S. Regarding Ben Schemen: it's a good school for young people who want to be assimilated into life in this country. This assimilation is precisely the task the school has set for itself, and is its primary merit. Now, since Emmy's questions reveal that she has very different plans for her child, I must vigorously counsel her against it. Under such circumstances, it makes absolutely no sense to give the child a Jewish-national education and prepare her for life in Palestine.

FROM BETTY SCHOLEM

Pensione Maja, Merano, Italy; October 23, 1933

My dear child,

[. . .] The atmosphere among Jews in Germany is one of terrible depression. It's feared there will no longer be any limits set on the government, now that it's left the League of Nations.[35] The Reichstag elections are a farce, and everyone knows it. What will become of Werner and Emmy is as uncertain as ever. There are still no formal charges against them—nothing. They sit in jail and are ruined, one way or another. [. . .] We've now heard that the arrest warrant was originally only for Emmy; they arrested Werner merely because he was there at the time. The jackass! "Well, well," said the police officer, "we thought you were in Switzerland. We gave you the exit visa." He then phoned the station. "If he's there," someone there told him, "bring him in"!! Isn't this horrifying?!

Mum

FROM BETTY SCHOLEM

Merano, October 30, 1933

My dear children,

[. . .] The papers are full of reports of rioting in Palestine.[36] One fear is that this could lead to a backlash in other countries that have accepted Jews. If even Palestine doesn't want them! How awful! The Germans may be behind it all—who knows? [. . .]

Warmest kisses, Mum

FROM BETTY SCHOLEM

Pensione Maja, Merano; Friday, November 3, 1933

My dear child,

[. . .] The German newspapers are making a big deal of it. They've published reports of street battles in Tel Aviv, though it seems to be a matter more of Arabs against the English than of Arabs against the Jews. I read in a Prague newspaper that the Arab National Council has made a proclamation which is quite reasonable—I hope it'll have some effect. What will happen if it doesn't? Is my money just as endangered over there as it is here at home because your economic existence is also uncertain? Nowhere do we have peace. I always believed that you were so safe, which was a comfort to me through all of the blows of recent times. Now you too are tottering! [. . .]

Your mother

TO BETTY SCHOLEM

Jerusalem, November 16, 1933

Dearest Mother,

[. . .] The unrest has ended. There were no street battles in Tel Aviv, though some bloody clashes did occur in Jaffa and to a lesser extent in Jerusalem between Arabs and the police. The fact that this happened is bad enough and can perhaps harm immigration. The riots, however, will have scarcely any effect on the economic security of those people who have already put down roots here. You needn't worry about yours truly. [. . .]

I wish you all the best.

Your son, Gershom

TO WALTER BENJAMIN

Jerusalem, December 24, 1933

Dear Walter,

[. . .] I'm working a great deal, and enjoying it. Among the most recent discoveries to enrich my knowledge is proof of an *Ur*-Bahir, whose remains I found last week in a manuscript from Rome. It gave me an entirely unexpected confirmation of my favorite theory of the origins of the Kabbalah. Beginning this week and continuing every fortnight, I'll be giving a series of two-hour lectures in Tel Aviv: an introduction to the Kabbalah. I'm currently preparing my notes for this. Beyond this, I'm devoting my energies to the study of Manichaean religion, and for good reason. You may not know that one of the greatest sensations in the field of history of religion recently suffered a terrible setback. The discovery of Coptic papyri containing undeniably authentic original writings by Mani and his first disciples rightly filled many souls with great expectation. But they're in terrible shape, and the only man able to conserve and thus save them in the eighteen months before they disintegrate into dust, the Berlin genius Ibscher, is deathly ill.[37] The only person who can read them, moreover, is a Russian Jew whom the Prussian government now wants to throw out of the country—in the best tradition of the ancient Germans from the great age of national migrations. The upshot of all this is that those parts not owned by the English and which contain irreplaceable treasures (the authentic letters of Mani and his books of hymns) will shortly disintegrate into nothing under the watchful eye of the Berlin Academy, the owner. Whatever else it may be, the printed report of the academy's 1933 meetings is one of the best gangster stories in recent memory. Highly recommended reading. [. . .]

Your Gerhard

Jerusalem, December 27, 1933

Much-Honored Sirs,

In what follows, I will take the liberty of expounding on the current status of the study of religion and appealing for the establishment of a chair in this field at the university. I believe that furthering the study of religion—whether the methodology be historical, systemic, or psychological—must be counted as one of the most important tasks of the humanities faculty at our university. In the development of any university, this field is typically recognized as a central pillar among the various humanistic disciplines. The university of the Jewish people, established in Jerusalem on a site rich in tradition, should be the last to overlook the fact that religion is no less significant than philosophy in the spiritual growth of humanity. It seems to me that one of the principal and most specific tasks of our university is to examine the issues and phenomenology of religion and to awaken an understanding of the historical developments that stem from these sources. There can be no doubt that here in Jerusalem the possibility for such study exists in the broadest sense and that study of this type, if concentrated in the hands of a major scholar, could provide highly fruitful stimulation not only for students, but also for the many existing disciplines that currently have no organic relationship to one another. I mean by this an academic position through which general religious studies would be taught without adherence to any particular dogma, free of theological or practical goals; and one not primarily devoted to the study of the religions of primitive peoples. In universities that have specific chairs or courses devoted to studying the phenomena of the great religious systems of India, Greece, the Near East, and Europe, a professorship in the general history of religion or in religious studies becomes all too easily and automatically a professorship in the phenomenology of the extant primitive religions. This should not be the focus of such studies in Jerusalem. For a generation which to an astounding extent seems to have lost all sense of religious reality and religious issues, it is vital that a thorough and scientifically grounded study of the general conditions and manifestations of religion seek to remedy this loss. I personally find it baffling that the university of the Jewish people strives to foster a special awareness of the dignity and complexities of philosophical knowledge, yet at the same time fails to foster in equal measure an awareness of the dignity and complexities of religious experience and knowledge. This attitude, it seems to me, bears no organic connection to the most important traditions of our people.

A wide-ranging curriculum on the study of religion could bring together subjects such as the Bible, the Kabbalah, Jewish religious philosophy, the religion of Islam, and Greco-Roman antiquity. Horizontal connections, grounded in the systemic characteristics of one of the most fundamental areas of intellectual history, would supplant the vertical separation of subjects into historical categories (Jewish, oriental, general).

More than anyone else, Prof. Martin Buber should be considered as a candidate for such a chair. He formerly taught this subject at the University of Frankfurt, a position that he has lost. There is no need for me to dwell on Buber's qualifications. But I must emphasize that hiring Buber would not only serve the specific interests of religious scholarship; it would also provide the university in Jerusalem with a figure of immense stature and formidable reputation—precisely those qualities which, in my opinion, have not as yet been granted their due importance here.

Yours respectfully, Prof. Dr. Gerhard Scholem

1934

TO MARTIN BUBER[38]

Jerusalem, February 2, 1934

Dear Herr Buber,

I hope you have received my last letter and the little volume *Conversations and Stories.*[39] I am writing you today to describe to you the situation relative to your coming here, so you may know where we stand. As a professionally interested party, I submitted a formal proposal to the faculty council that a professorship of general religious studies *(madda ha-dat ha-kelali)* be created and that you be appointed to it. I did this after Magnes had indicated that he preferred such a proposal from me to direct action by him. All of us—especially Magnes, Bergmann, and myself—fully realized that bringing this matter up for serious discussion (and I substantiated my proposal in a memorandum) would cause lively debate. I made it clear to Magnes from the outset that on this occasion a fundamental discussion about the orientation of a university of the *Jewish* people could not be evaded. I certainly need not reiterate this for *you.* In the meantime, the matter has been discussed, and in all its aspects—that is, both the general question of religious studies and your appointment in particular. I regard your coming as a cause that is worth fighting for with the utmost vigor, and I believe you are sufficiently acquainted with conditions of a personal nature to know that a clear and resolute fight is necessary. This is how things stand: after the angriest discussions in the faculty council (as a young *sheigetz,*[40] I was determined not to concede anything to the other side), a committee was appointed under my chairmanship to make proposals to the council. Thus, there will be another discussion. I am convinced that if we conduct ourselves carefully and vigorously, your appointment will go through [. . .]

We believe that the need to install your person and your personality *here,* provided that it is possible to do so, reduces everything else to secondary importance. On the other hand, we fear that under the present circumstances it may be particularly difficult for you to decide to take the definitive step that we consider especially important and fruitful, and therefore necessary, in the higher interest of the Jewish cause. I am told by Schocken and Bergmann that you have accepted an assignment in

Germany from which you may not be able to disengage yourself in a short time. Thus, if I understand the situation correctly, it may be that the offer of an appointment may plunge you into a conflict of duties. You will realize that your friends in Palestine are convinced that—in this country and in the education of the younger generation in Jerusalem—even more decisive things are at stake than in Mannheim. You must be here if you do not wish to forgo having an influence on the development of the country; anything else would be an illusion. If you remain remote from what is here, nothing of you will become part of it. [. . .]

Sincerely yours, Gershom Scholem

FROM BETTY SCHOLEM

Berlin, March 7, 1934

My dear child,

I spoke to Werner yesterday. It's heartbreaking to see how the boy sits and cries. He wails like a child that he has heard nothing from his wife. *We* are supposed to find out where she is! Speaking of which, she could of course write—but she doesn't! The officials have said that her flight has greatly worsened Werner's case.[41] There is no chance he'll be released *before* the trial. He's been sitting in prison for eleven months! Now he has a lawyer, a friend from the Alpine Association. But this fellow can't do anything either, even though he does give Werner a bit of comfort. [. . .]

Warmest kisses, Mum

FROM BETTY SCHOLEM

Berlin, April 8, 1934

My dear child,

[. . .] On the sixth I had a conference with Werner. I was hoping that he'd already received Emmy's letter and would finally calm down a bit. But the examining magistrate, who's the only person who can authorize delivery of a letter from outside Germany, was on his Easter vacation. The secretaries had already read it; they told Werner the contents and assured him that she wanted to remain faithful to him (!). Then a wild scene broke out. He screamed at the officers and called them inhuman for withholding the letter from him. He ranted and raved to the point where he completely lost his voice. It was painful to watch. Poor little Dina, who had come along with me, visibly trembled. In the end, the officials began shouting back and the whole thing turned into pandemonium! They finally began to speak kindly to him again. I must confess I'm surprised they didn't have him taken away! These people of course know his situation and must realize that he was locked up for no reason. He's now been behind bars for a year; he hasn't been interrogated for the past nine months; and the file on his case is somewhere in Leipzig. The whole affair is simply beyond belief. But his instability and his lamenting about his wife make such an unpleasant and undignified impression that nowadays when I visit him, I always go alone. I no longer take anyone with me. The assistant judge says that none of the other people awaiting trial causes such a scandal and makes such demands as Werner. As long as Emmy was in jail, he acted as if *everything* would be fine once she was free! Now she's out of prison and in safety, and he behaves a thousand times worse. And why? Because she could cheat on him! It's pathetic! [. . .]

Mum

TO WALTER BENJAMIN

Jerusalem, June 20, 1934

Dear Walter,

[. . .] The semester has come to an end and I can now pursue my work for a couple of months. I'll make abundant use of this time. Escha's sciatica has improved in the past two weeks. She now works three hours a day again, though she's far from fully recovered. Perhaps or even probably I'll write a few things in German this summer, so I'll have something to show you. I do virtually all of my writing now in Hebrew. In the past couple of days I was able to celebrate a rather unusual event: the completion of a humble 220-page essay which will be published in a journal here. It's an analysis of the development of a certain mystical terminology. I now plan to write about religious nihilism. In order to gain some security first, I've purchased a "lifetime" spot in the synagogue. This is how controversial the theme is.

Please write from Scandinavia! Send a copy of Brecht's *Saint Joan of the Stockyards*. I'll eventually pay you back.

Warmest greetings, Your Gerhard

FROM BETTY SCHOLEM

Zernsdorf, July 17, 1934

My dear child,

[. . .] Little Renate arrived in Berlin on Thursday, and the next morning I went with her to see Werner.[42] The visit went very well. It made Werner happy to see the child, and she was delighted too. She didn't even cry. Nor did she get any idea of how monstrous the situation is— we were sitting in a rather peaceful room with two smiling officials. I read Emmy's letter aloud slowly, so that Werner could take notes and write.

Since the Federal Court has been deliberating over the political cases for a year without any progress, they will now go to the new People's Court, which has not yet begun work. The interregnum, which has lasted more than four weeks, has extended Werner's time in prison. His lawyer has not been approved, and he cannot write or visit. Everything is as bad as possible and there's no end in sight. [. . .]

A warm kiss to you both, Mum

TO BETTY SCHOLEM

Jerusalem, July 28, 1934

Dearest Mother,

[. . .] It's vacation time again, and Escha and I have our trip already behind us. I don't take a real vacation; instead, every evening I hold classes for the students of mine who've stayed—if, that is, the electricity hasn't gone out, which happens fairly often of late. Many blame the amusement park that has set up shop between the Zion Cinema and

Rehavia. It's got a genuine roller coaster, and as far away as the streets of Rehavia you can hear people shouting and cheering. [. . .]

All the best, Your Gerhard

FROM BETTY SCHOLEM

Berlin, August 12, 1934

My dear child,

[. . .] An amusement park? I find this utterly appalling and downright tasteless for a city like Jerusalem. It always cheers me up to think that I've seen a slice of the Orient that still remains somewhat authentically oriental. This headlong rush to adopt the worst parts of the West and of America is really a shame, even if it seems inevitable.

Nothing new from Werner, and no better news. The People's Court did not confirm his lawyer, and no objections to the chicanery and arbitrariness of the judgment are permitted. Two weeks ago a very well-meaning official at Moabit Prison told me that Dr. Kaufmann would not be confirmed, because his activities have been too personal and he's gone "too far." He summarized the view of the examining magistrate—namely, that Dr. K. suggested or even aided and abetted Emmy's flight! Dr. K. has advised Werner not to do a thing. He is of the rosy opinion that the case pending before the Federal Court and the People's Court is, in one way or another, falling apart. He's sure that sooner or later it'll be settled! Werner and the rest of us don't share his assessment. We see no end in sight. Formal charges have not yet been filed. As soon as this happens, Werner will let the state-appointed defense attorney take over. [. . .]

Kisses, Mum

FROM BETTY SCHOLEM

Berlin, August 20, 1934

My dear child,

[. . .] For eight months I've been saying that I'm at the end of my rope, but my hue and cry does no good and this Hydra continues to grow new heads. Werner worries me terribly. He's in a miserable position. Now they've transferred him to Plötzensee, which makes it harder for us to visit.[43] At Moabit we were readily befriended by the officials. They helped me whenever they could. But the past two visits alone have shown me the difference between the two places. Plötzensee is more like a convicts' prison! When I received Werner's postcard with the news of the transfer, I was hit with a terrifying nervous breakdown. My sister had to come over, and she raised such an uproar that I didn't even recognize her. That's how angry she was. She said she'd put me away in a mental asylum if this damned obsession with Werner didn't stop! But such is life. Mary stands for all eternity at the foot of the Cross. [. . .]

Kisses, Mum

TO BETTY SCHOLEM

Jerusalem, November 21, 1934

Beloved Mother,

First and foremost, warmest greetings for your birthday! They'll most likely arrive a few days too early—but they're that much more sincere. We are sending you one pound or its equivalent in marks, so you can buy yourself a silk nightgown. [. . .]

We are fine; for once we can't complain about our health. I don't itch any longer, and Escha has both her legs back. Our garden is about to get some cyclamen, though they're so slow in coming that you could wait for them nearly forever. Besides this, new flowers are once again blossoming and old ones are gradually dying back. In front of our house blooms something quite unusual—a sort of tree or shrub that produces pure white marguerites. Everything has such a fantastic form, is so thoroughly crooked and bent, that it appears downright graceful. [. . .]

Your Gerhard and Escha

TO WALTER BENJAMIN

Jerusalem, November 22, 1934

Dear Walter,

I received your last two letters some time ago, but I was sick for a long time; and once I was able to write again, and wanted to, the semester began (four weeks ago). A lot is happening here. So only now can I thank you for your letters and answer them. From your silences and your hints, I can guess how difficult your position has become, as conditions in Europe continue to unfold along the course that's been set. I don't see how one can escape it; it's a terrifying *circulus vitiosus*. At the moment, the only question people seem to be asking themselves is which country they'll be in when war breaks out. I personally don't think this will happen anytime soon. [. . .]

Will you be staying in San Remo over the winter? Unfortunately, I have no immediate plans to come to Europe. Who knows how long it will be before I can do so again? I've gathered everything that'll be necessary for my work during my two long trips. [. . .] This means we won't have a chance to speak face to face—unless the opposite happens and it becomes possible to finance a trip for you here. That would be something to consider. I wonder whether it wouldn't be possible to arrange such a trip—say, for three to four weeks. Palestine itself wouldn't cost you much; arrangements could easily be made. The question would be whether you could find cheap transportation—a cargo ship or something like that, from Genoa, Trieste, or Marseilles. From what I've heard, a return trip on the deck of an express steamer would be even cheaper. I'd like to discuss such a trip if you think there's a chance you could come here. Think about it. The summer would be a good time for it.

We've been frantically busy, since (as I've read) a total of only *seventeen* Jewish first-year students were admitted to German universities. Even if its eventual direction remains quite unclear, a considerable stream has been arriving: many hundreds of new students fill our handful of institutes and disciplines. On paper, they amount to about a thousand—but, in reality, a large number of these don't come to us but go to the port cities to find work! [. . .]

Werner Kraft sits here rather gloomily; no one knows what will become of him. He's not very flexible, and regards the entire atmosphere here as quite alien. I made a very energetic attempt to sell him to Schocken as a valuable secretary. But Schocken took one look at him and declared him wholly unsatisfactory, though he considered Kraft's essay on Kafka outstanding. To date, this was the only opportunity I could come up with for him. [. . .]

Your Gerhard

Jerusalem, December 17, 1934

Dear Herr Spitzer,

I'd like to get directly down to business in my letter today. I will cover all of the relevant points, and then, to spare myself the task of copying the letter, would be grateful if you eventually conveyed it, along with my greetings, to Herr Dr. Schneider.[44]

During the summer break, which starts approximately on the first of July, I intend to begin my major study on the Kabbalah. I expect that within a year I will deliver a manuscript ready for typesetting. Whether or not I prove able do this in a shorter period of time depends in large measure on whether the work goes quickly for me. I intend to write a kind of rough sketch of the Kabbalah. In other words, instead of covering the various periods and relying on weighty scholarly proof and close attention to academic detail, the book will be a summary of my studies presented in the more or less deliberate style of a course lecture. It will be designed to serve as an introduction to the literary history and intellectual development of the Kabbalah. Besides rich literary historical and bibliographic details and dry facts, it will include what I hope will be a lively analysis of the intellectual world and the internal dynamics of this literature. I have also spoken with Herr Schocken about my intentions and have told him that it is not easy for me to determine its size in advance, though I suppose it will be around five hundred pages. [. . .]

So far as I can tell, the suggestions you made in your letter (dated June 19) for modifying my proposed volume of essays would result in an entirely new book. In view of the first plan described above, however, it probably wouldn't be worthwhile to do this and might (given my style of working) cost me far more time than is reasonable. As for a *Zohar* reader, I would consider it if I didn't have doubts about whether the texts are suitable for a general audience. I am prepared to do a short book of translations taken from the *Zohar*'s commentary on the first chapters of Genesis. I could deliver this to you around the fifteenth of April, 1935. Alternatively, I could prepare a more general selection of texts on the beginnings of creation. I have already begun the volume based on kabbalistic-messianic texts, though I've been finding that the material is (1) not very coherent and (2) not very accessible for a mass audience. [. . .]

Yours, G. Scholem

1935

TO WALTER BENJAMIN

Jerusalem, February 6, 1935

Dear Walter,

[. . .] We've been giving some thought to your eventual visit. I held off writing to you until I could make some definite decisions regarding my work—decisions that have some importance in this connection. I'd like to give you a picture of the situation as I now see it. From *the first of July* until the first of November, I will disappear from the world. During this time (the vacation period) I will write a book for Schocken, or at least make some substantial headway with it. The book, which I'll aim to finish, will demand my utmost concentration for a few months. It will be a sort of summary of the Kabbalah, between five hundred and a thousand pages, and will offer a concise exposé of the results of my studies over the past fifteen years. I won't have the necessary materials gathered together until the start of the vacation. I don't think there's any real sense in encouraging you to come during this time. I'll be preoccupied, and thus unable to engage you in any fruitful conversation. So it would be better if you came either directly before this time, or directly after it. "Before" means May 15 to July 1. You could of course stay longer if you wanted to, without spending much time with me—though I don't recommend this, since July is not a good time for guests. You could also come later, during the winter. [. . .]

We think that this winter (though *definitely* not in the summer) it may be possible for you to deliver a series of lectures which could earn you a few pounds in pocket money. But you could be certain of this only a short time beforehand. In Jerusalem, speaking in public in German is out of the question, unless it's just once in a single lecture. Perhaps something of a private nature can be arranged. It's best if you don't count on this as a source of income. In this country, nothing ever happens as planned. I repeat: if you decided to come in the spring, we'd try to make arrangements for a comfortable living situation, with us, the Bergmanns, or Werner Senator. If you come, say, for two months, it'll be easy to arrange cheap accommodations. We can't finance your travels within the country, though. [. . .]

Your Gerhard

FROM BETTY SCHOLEM

Berlin, March 12, 1935

Dear children,

Werner was acquitted, but instead of releasing him they've kept him in this infamous "protective custody"! Here's what happened. The trial—there were twenty-three defendants—lasted five days. I was supposed to appear as a witness on the fourth day, so I could testify that in July 1932 Werner was with me in the Tyrol. The liar who made the denunciation in the first place, the source of all of this trouble, claimed to have spoken with him at the same time in a bar in Moabit! Dr. Kaufmann, Werner's first attorney and a friend from the Alpine Hiking Association, was also summoned to testify. He claimed that during this period the two of them dedicated a new hiker's cabin in the Kufstein Alps. I showed up with Erich, my travel diary, and a stool to sit on, which was anything but superfluous since we had to wait in the corridor for an hour and a half. After Dr. Kaufmann's testimony, they decided not to call me to the stand. The Senate considered the matter settled. We greeted Werner during a five-minute recess, when the swarm of defendants appeared in the corridor. He looked completely out of place; he didn't even know any of the other defendants! Seven were found guilty. Following an amnesty, the trial of another twelve people was suspended. Four were acquitted, Werner among them. Erich went to hear the final verdict, which was pronounced on Saturday in a public session. He spoke with Werner, who said that all the defendants would be returned to Plötzensee and that he'd send word from there. I didn't write to you immediately because I wanted to see him first! Around six o'clock Emmy called from London and, delighted with the results, said he should immediately join her. I told her that Werner remained very skeptical and feared another period of protective custody. *She* thought this was out of the question. Ten minutes later one of Werner's fellow prisoners, now freed, phoned to pass on a message from Werner: they had in fact re-arrested him and we shouldn't expect him. The lawyer conjectured that because the officials didn't want to exert themselves on Saturday afternoon and Sunday, his release would come on Monday, which was yesterday. Nothing happened. We haven't heard a word from him. Of course he's written. But when will we get his letter?! The lawyer will pursue the matter tomorrow morning. And so everything begins again—

we're back to where we were two years ago. Still, I'm happy that the trial has ended with a splendid acquittal and that there's closure. I just spoke with the prison official at Moabit who was always so nice to me. He told me that I should count on protective custody, which will last at most two to three months. Afterward, Werner will finally be freed. [. . .]

Kisses, Mum

TO BETTY SCHOLEM

Jerusalem, March 17, 1935

Dearest Mother,

Many thanks for your letters from the fifth and twelfth of March. I congratulate you because of Werner. Give him my most cordial regards. Even if you don't know how long it will still take, at least now there's a provisional conclusion and a great sense of relief. Good thing it's not so easy to avoid making mistakes in details; this way, the truth comes to light. Your double case of the flu, along with this episode, has taken such a toll on you that you should give yourself some rest. [. . .]

Warmest regards, Your Gerhard

TO WALTER BENJAMIN

Jerusalem, March 29, 1935

Dear Walter,

Thank you for your last letter, which enabled me to see or to glean something of your plans. It greatly saddened me. Escha, myself, and others must of course accept that you can't come this summer. Still, it's a real pity—in particular because, as I understand your situation, it seems far from certain that you'll be inclined to come during the winter. Too many unforeseeable circumstances, related to urgent material concerns, already seem to have a large and even decisive influence on your travel plans. [. . .]

Tomorrow morning Buber arrives in Jerusalem and will stay for a few weeks. As you may have read in the papers, the Gestapo in Prussia banned him from making public appearances. This is a very mysterious thing, and the real reasons behind it remain murky. He'll stay with the Bergmanns, next door to us. At the beginning of the month, my brother Werner appeared before the People's Court. After two years of detention and four days of secret deliberations, he was acquitted, together with twenty-five others. He was immediately placed under protective custody and has vanished without a trace. No doubt they sent him to some concentration camp. The family's distress is enormous. I feel sorrier for my poor mother (who has gone though all too many dramatic twists and turns) than I do for my brother, whose behavior in times of crisis I will never understand, to the end of my days. No one knows whether he'll be kept *ad infinitum* as a special object of Gestapo hatred (like Torgler)[45] or whether his release will eventually be secured. According to what I've gathered, after they built up their case through bribing, buying, and beating "testimonies" from former members of the party, the charges against him fell apart—all through the testimony of one honest witness, an "Aryan" lawyer. [. . .]

Your Gerhard

FROM BETTY SCHOLEM

Berlin, March 29, 1935

Dear children,

Nothing has been clarified. Tomorrow it'll be three weeks. The lawyer has tried his best, without any success so far. Eight days ago I went to the Gestapo building myself. I was turned out of two offices with a casual, "We cannot help you. Good day." In a third I met a friendly gentleman who advised us to present our request in writing. Nothing can be achieved in person; only in writing is one sure to get an answer. That very evening, the twenty-third of March, the lawyer sent the petition—I spoke with him that afternoon. But he has yet to get an answer. No one can claim that all this running around does me any good. Emmy just wrote a completely despondent letter. You really have to pity her. [. . .]

Kisses, Mum

FROM BETTY SCHOLEM

Riva, Italy; May 11, 1935

Dear children,

[. . .] I'm sending you Emmy's letter, which should be of some interest to you. I consider this thing with the Quakers a pipe dream.[46] The Hammerstein story goes something like this: Werner, in his profound cleverness, persuaded General von Hammerstein's daughter to join the Communist party. When they arrested her in April 1933, she of course changed sides and did her best to wash herself clean through accusation—more specifically, by claiming that Werner had seduced her (hopefully only to Communism!). I heard about this girl only once, when Werner bragged that an aristocrat had gone over to their side. He really is a jackass of historic proportions! [. . .]

Warmest kisses, Mum

TO EDITH ROSENZWEIG

Jerusalem, Rehavia; May 29, 1935

Dear Frau Rosenzweig,

Thank you for your letter.[47] I have no intention of making a fuss about this matter, even if I found it more than a little astonishing. I think I can say I have no illusions whatsoever that Franz Rosenzweig felt "respect for me, personally and professionally." I have no reason to expect it, being someone who so fleetingly appeared in his life. Nor would the opposite surprise me, or complete indifference. *Some* criticism of me, based on a first impression, wouldn't bother me in the least. Anyway, it might be on the mark! I wouldn't even have objected to the opinion that my behavior was "beastly," no matter how unexpected such a characterization was (I haven't yet forgotten the meaning of the German word). Everyone has a right to his own impression—but it must be his impression, and not something else. No one who reads the letter can be expected to know that F.R. never saw me again during my entire time in Frankfurt in 1923. *This* is what hurt me in the letter. But I got over it a long time ago, and the entire matter should be dropped. I am not interested in any kind of public statement.

If I had given it a couple of day's thought, I never would have said anything. The volume of letters contains far too many exciting things for me to have let my ephemeral reaction eclipse my genuine one. Allow me to point out, by way of assuaging my regret, that (according to page 461) I was the only one who asked Buber for his sources and the only one who forced him to come up with a list of sources for his book on the great Maggid—insistence which rubbed him the wrong way.[48] This anonymous service of mine consoles me for behavior that at the time seemed bound up with it, in the days when I was still young and apt to draw such conclusions.

Thank you so much for the work that went into this book. Something will be learned from it.

> With warmest greetings, Gerhard Scholem

TO WALTER BENJAMIN

Jerusalem, June 28, 1935

Dear Walter,

Your last letter, written at the end of May, has been lying around for weeks now, while I've been preoccupied both with finishing the volume on the *Zohar* for Schocken and taking care of a nasty case of sore vocal cords. Today the last week of the semester begins, and in a few days I hope to start on my major study: my survey of the history of the Kabbalah. [. . .]

The need to make progress on this book and a few other factors make it extremely doubtful that I can still ask you to visit this winter, as both Escha and I had hoped. Besides my absorption in my work, there are relevant family circumstances that I cannot go into in writing. It is thus unlikely that we could take you in for two months, as you and I discussed. On the other hand, it's very likely that I will travel to Europe for a few weeks next year, if only because of my mother's seventieth birthday. [. . .]

> Your Gerhard

TO WALTER BENJAMIN

Jerusalem, August 25, 1935

Dear Walter,

[. . .] The political excitement sparked by the English–Italian crisis has reached all the way to Palestine, since the eastern Mediterranean could very possibly be a theater of war if conflict should break out. The Italians are looking for allies among the Arabs in case there's a war with the English, and they seem to be putting a lot of money into doing so. For the time being, however, things are more or less peaceful here. Did you know (I didn't!) that in the past three years the number of Jews here has doubled? This should tell you what's been happening here! Immigration has taken on legendary proportions. Every month five thousand people arrive. Even though the numerical proportion of German Jews is not very large, they stand out in the most extraordinary way. [. . .] A few weeks ago I saw your cousin's wife, Hannah Stern.[49] She's now working in Paris, preparing children for the trip to Palestine. I did not get the feeling that she was in close contact with you; otherwise she would have brought greetings from you. For this reason I didn't ask her about you. She is said to have been Heidegger's most brilliant student. [. . .]

Gershom

FROM BETTY SCHOLEM

Berlin, September 18, 1935

Dearest children,

[. . .] You've read about the new laws. The game of question-and-answer among housewives: "How old is your maid?"[50] Everyone in our circle has had to give up girls they've relied on for years. Only Hete is allowed to keep hers, the forty-six-year-old Elisabeth. Käte Schiepan, by contrast, would like to get rid of her gabbling old hag of a maid but can't fire her. Our Rosh Hashanah evening will be at Theo's (though Hete can't be there), since he has seniority. Elizabeth will bake the goose and I will set the table. There may not be a trace of New Year's hope for us, but at least there is for you! One can wish you Happy New Year with a full heart! Stay healthy and take care!! I still have the comforting prospect of going to you if I need to. This gives me some reassurance for the future. What will become of the others is more uncertain than ever.

Warm kisses and happy holidays, Mum

FROM BETTY SCHOLEM

London, October 1, 1935

Dear children,

[. . .] Goebbels, the swine, "unmasked the Bolsheviks" (!!) in a speech given at Nuremberg. In it he personally called Werner the "mastermind of *Die Rote Fahne*."[51] If after sixteen years they still keep digging up his old stupidities, how can anyone expect that he'll be freed! I brought Emmy the newspaper clippings. After she's read them, I'll send them on to you. On our last visit to him, Werner asked right away if I'd heard the radio broadcast. The prison camp listened to the proceedings of the entire Party Congress in Nuremberg, and when Werner's name was mentioned, everyone who knew him turned and looked at him. What a fabulous sort of fame! [. . .]

Mum

FROM BETTY SCHOLEM

London, October 14, 1935

My dear children,

[. . .] One day this past summer I was called from Zernsdorf to Reinhold's in order to speak with a gentleman who brought news from Werner. He called himself "Herr Schutz" and was trembling with fear that someone might spread the news that he'd said something. Every released prisoner must sign a document pledging that he will say *nothing*—good, bad, or anything else—about the concentration camp. Otherwise he'll be immediately locked up again (which is the reason you either hear nothing at all from the camps, or are regaled with mendacious horror stories). He had promised Werner to reassure us about his condition. The prisoners are treated well and humanely; the camp commandant is a decent man. He had his clerk bring him the files of all those who had been imprisoned longer than two years, and he promised to work for their release. Within a month, twenty-eight of the sixty prisoners had been freed. When this "Herr Schutz" visited us, he felt certain Werner would be free within three weeks. That was at the beginning of July, or three months ago. Surely, not a single Communist was among the twenty-eight freed. Communists to them are like a red flag to a bull. The informant is a homosexual, and as a result sat in jail four months for the purposes of Nazi "reeducation"! He told Reinhold that there had been two hundred of his ilk at the time he went in; the number has now shot up to eight hundred. Nice, huh? There's virtually nothing but homos in the camp. Revolting.

Through a whole long maze of acquaintances, Edith finally got to know a woman "at the top" who has already secured the release of a large number of prisoners. (I'm skeptical; maybe it was only *one!*) I had to write an entire novel-like account of Werner's life. Once the woman finally reached the part about his being a Communist member of the Reichstag in 1919, she gave me back my beautiful concoction. "Of course, for *this* case," she told me, "nothing can be done!" I get hives when people tell me I should write to Göring or to the League of Nations! I'm plagued with such loads of rubbish that sometimes I can't stand it. [. . .]

A warm kiss for now, Mum

TO WALTER BENJAMIN

Jerusalem, December 18, 1935

Dear Walter,

[. . .] I've recently had a frightful fit of writing, but I'm still not very happy with myself. For the past several weeks I've been alone and forced to fend for myself. Escha had to leave Jerusalem for an extended period, and is now in Tiberias recovering from sciatica and gall bladder problems. Soon afterward my Yemenite maid came down with something serious. This meant that I had to live like a student again—which isn't the best thing for my work. At the same time, Escha lost her job at the library. After Bergmann's departure (as the first rector of the university, he's now preoccupied with administrative concerns), the library's management went through a change. Her position became both superfluous and unpleasant. There's no question that the need to support two households, together with the loss of Escha's income, has delivered a fatal blow to our plans for bringing you here. [. . .]

My book on the *Zohar* has apparently been very successful with readers. Your comments were of great interest to me. I would like to be able to write an entire book on the Kabbalah in the same terse style I used for the introduction. I still have to work awfully hard at it. I want to write a particularly good book. But I've realized how much I'll have to depend on inspiration in order to do this. [. . .]

Gerhard

1936

FROM BETTY SCHOLEM

Berlin, March 1, 1936

Beloved children,

Yesterday I got the urge to travel to Palestine for a few weeks. I have no idea why I didn't come earlier—it's been five years since I visited you. We'd have a lot to talk about. Health-wise, we're more or less fit. Last night I spoke with the boys, who were in full agreement that I should leave *immediately!* Maybe the ads for cheap spring cruises awoke slumbering desires. Erich will go to the travel bureau first thing in the morning and if possible book a cabin for the beginning of April. [. . .]

Kisses, Mum

TO BETTY SCHOLEM

Jerusalem, March 7, 1936

Dearest Mother,

This is a hurried response to the airmail letter I just got, announcing your forthcoming Palestine trip.[52] Naturally, I will be delighted if you want to come, and I'll be happy to see you again. But since you asked, I must mention something that may be of some importance. Escha will most definitely *not* be here. *By no means* can you count on her being here; I will be alone. You of course can stay in our house, but you should also know that as of the first of May I will no longer have a maid, for the simple reason that I can no longer afford it. [. . .]

If you wish to bring something special with you, there are a number of possibilities besides chocolate marzipan: for instance, six really good shirts with pre-washed soft collars, size 41—but really excellent quality, gray-blue and cream colored. Or you could bring fabric for one *very good* blue suit. If you don't consider any of these within your means, then get two good, plain, dark-red ties.

I will be very happy to see you. It'll be your seventieth-birthday visit. Stay healthy, and don't do anything foolish on the way over here!

In a rush, Your Gerhard

TO WALTER BENJAMIN

Jerusalem, April 19, 1936

Dear Walter,

[. . .] The separation from Escha has created the greatest difficulties for me, inwardly as much as outwardly. I have no need to go into details to a friend like you, who's been through something similar. Actually going through the separation, after finally reaching the decision last summer, cost me nearly eight months and has, of course, decisively altered my life. The fact that it is I who demanded the divorce has placed me in a truly difficult situation, as I will need to support two households— if, that is, Escha does not remarry. The consequence was (and remains) that I've had to greatly lower my standard of living and severely cut back on, and rethink, my commitments. Here you have the naked reason why, in this situation, I could not pursue plans to bring you here. During these difficult months I would have had nothing to offer you, least of all intellectually. Meanwhile, the divorce has gone through, while everything else remains rather uncertain. For the time being, Escha is staying in Tiberias. Generally we dealt with each other in as friendly a manner as possible. If Bergmann succeeds in procuring his divorce (which is a terribly complicated matter), he and Escha will marry. [. . .]

Your Gerhard

TO BETTY SCHOLEM

Jerusalem, May 23, 1936

Dearest Mother,

[. . .] We've had days of unrest here.[53] The situation is no better than it was a week ago, even if there are no "incidents" to report. The state of siege continues without interruption. Curfew begins at seven P.M. One might think this would be conducive to work, but the necessary atmosphere of concentration and peace is missing. So we all sit sunk in our armchairs. Everyone wonders how it will all end. [. . .]

Your Gerhard

TO BETTY SCHOLEM

Jerusalem, June 9, 1936

Dear Mother,

I just got your letter from Trieste. I hope you arrive safely in Berlin and that your tale of suffering will come to a satisfactory and easy conclusion. [. . .]

The *Jüdische Rundschau* can fill you in on what has happened; I can't add anything new. The curfew still begins at seven P.M., after which we all sit around at home. Either you invite guests to spend the night, or you work alone, or you bend the rules a bit and make a dash across the street to a neighbor's. Last week was really chaotic here. There's still is a great deal of shooting in the hills at night. The gunmen shoot aimlessly and without hitting anything—out of protest, so to speak. As I write these lines, for instance, every half-minute I can clearly hear a round of gunfire ringing out from Moza.[54] One gets accustomed to the booming sounds, though it's certainly no pleasure. The semester has been almost completely lost because of the riots. Even if the unrest were to end within two weeks (something even I don't believe is possible), the semester would be over already.

Have my brothers and Theo received the Schocken deluxe edition yet?[55] I've been told that everything's been sent out. Please ask the parties involved. Theobald sent me some marvelous marzipan, for which I'm most grateful. He discovered a brand whose packaging stands up well even when shipped in summer. [. . .]

Your old son, Gerhard

TO WALTER BENJAMIN

Jerusalem, August 26, 1936

Dear Walter,

[. . .] For the past three months, we in Jerusalem have been living under a state of siege. Every night you hear more or less wild shootouts. From time to time you have to spend a few hours on guard atop a "strategic" building at the edge of the neighborhood. Otherwise you wait patiently for the latest news. There's a considerable amount of terrorism. Until now the Jews have, with great effort, successfully avoided stooping to counter-terrorism, a patently obvious and all too practical instrument. But I'm not at all certain how long this will last. A few days ago a colleague of mine who teaches Arabic literature was murdered in his study while reading the Bible.[56] You can imagine the concern this aroused. That sort of thing accustoms a person to a large share of fatalism. No one knows whether someone will toss a bomb his way or around the next corner; at the same time, you become relatively calm after hearing that most bombs never detonate or do any damage. Ten minutes before I left Tel Aviv, a bomb was thrown out of a train onto an overpass that lay on my route. There were casualties, and when my train got there it had to pass through a great crowd of people. Generally speaking, however, the city is paradise compared to the open country. There you find real pitched battles, some between British troops and Arab partisan fighters and some between Arabs and the Jewish colonies, which they incessantly attack. It'll take a long time before peace and quiet return. The policy of the English is hesitant and unclear. They fear turning either the Arabs or Jews into bitter enemies, so they've set their hopes on a diplomatic miracle. The Jews are all the more upset because, as I have said, they avoid venting their fury through real acts of violence. They prefer to "keep quiet," and for very good political reasons. In the coming political negotiations, this will have decisive importance. There's no doubt that we have a very turbulent half-year ahead of us. At the same time, immigration continues at a very high rate despite the Arabs' violent attacks, and of course in the end everything depends upon this. The world situation has created so much pressure in the direction of Palestine that one can hardly expect any serious attempt to block immigration. All nations want to get rid of their Jews, and closing the gates to Palestine is harder today than it was seven years ago. On the other hand, perhaps a setback would be good, at least for the moral side of our project. Everywhere people are asking themselves: Who supports the Arab movement? Rome, Berlin, or Moscow? Or all three? The whole situation is very opaque. Incidentally, the way in which the Communists have inspired anti-Jewish agitation is a bit upsetting. A philological analysis of the Communist leaflets sent to my home, whatever the language they use, clearly shows that they're written by German Jews who have recently arrived in the country. The colossal hatred for these groups is the result. [. . .]

Yours, Gerhard

TO BETTY SCHOLEM

Rehavia, December 4, 1936

Dearest Mother,

[. . .] I'm afraid I have some news that will disappoint you. I must inform you that I decided to marry Fanya Freud, a woman whom you know but who has been unjustly and unfortunately cast in a bad light. We acted on the decision early this morning. I wanted to marry on my birthday, but that fell on the Sabbath so I decided to move the wedding up a few days. Both my wife and I have given this matter a great deal of thought, and I hope we'll be good for each other. Meanwhile, I hope you'll show as much good will toward my wife as she in fact deserves. She sends her cordial greetings. [. . .]

Your newly married but regrettably disobedient
(thank God disobedient!) son, Gerhard

TO WALTER BENJAMIN

Pension Helena Cohn, Jerusalem; December 29, 1936

Dear Walter,

[. . .] I have left the home where I once lived; Escha, who became Frau Bergmann a short time ago, has moved back in. In this context it's only fitting to announce my recent remarriage—to a young woman named Freud from the depths of the Sarmatian forest. I can't provide you with an image of her until you meet her personally, as I have no doubt you will. In any case, at present my private life is being thoroughly transformed. We hope for the best. We still don't have an apartment and are currently living in a hotel. It's difficult for me to find something suitable because my library has grown so enormous, and as a consequence virtually immobilizes me. The largest part of it still remains in the old apartment. I don't know how things will turn out; the next few months will tell. Somehow we'll have to find a place to live. You can easily imagine what it's like, since you yourself are such a leading expert in the diasporic way of life. [. . .]

Gerhard

1937

FROM BETTY SCHOLEM

Berlin, February 20, 1937

My dear children,

[. . .] I've gone through another big shock with Werner. He was suddenly transferred to the Dachau camp, near Munich, and no one knows why. I had just received permission to visit him. But that Sunday it was sixteen degrees below freezing, and we couldn't drive on the ice-covered roads. By the next Sunday he was already gone. I really went to pieces because I was unable to speak to the poor boy again. I can hardly make a trip down to Dachau. It's unspeakably terrible. There is less and less hope that they'll free him. In Dachau he's allowed to write and receive one letter a week. [. . .]

Warmest kisses, Mum

TO WALTER BENJAMIN

Abarbanel Road 28, Jerusalem; May 7, 1937

Dear Walter,

[. . .] A deep sense of turmoil grows when you realize how little substance lies behind the alleged plans to partition Palestine into an Arab area and a Jewish state with the status of a dominion. We in Jerusalem are to become an international zone, an "irredenta." Rumors are already circulating that the university will remain where it is in order to represent the Jewish people *in partibus fidelium*. I myself wager that none of this is true, even if things look rather serious. But no one will know anything about the political recommendations until the end of June. The tension is in any case very palpable. There are pro-, anti-, and uncertain views on cantonization. I count mine among the latter.

Our apartment is quite lovely. I would like you to know that there's enough room to accommodate you. We must see if we can come up with a plan that will make use of the lodging. I have to write a book over the summer and won't be much of a host. This raises the earnest question if you would like to be our guest during the winter—say, in December or January. [. . .]

Yours, Gerhard

FROM BETTY SCHOLEM

Berlin, June 17, 1937

My dear children,

[. . .] As a result of my petition, I received a summons last week to appear before the Gestapo. The official in charge, who was most pleasant, immediately offered me a seat. "What do you wish to speak about with Werner? Couldn't you do so in writing?" he asked. I spent more than thirty minutes in his office, explaining the entire catastrophe and the kind of disruptions that occur when one sends letters back and forth to Dachau. He then told me that I should write another petition and that the file would remain on his desk until he determines what can be done. I wrote right away, yet have not received an answer. I don't even expect one. It's really futile. [. . .]

Kisses, Mum

TO WALTER BENJAMIN

Abarbanel Road, Jerusalem; July 10, 1937

Dear Walter,

[. . .] There's much to tell you! The long-awaited report by the Royal Commission was published two days ago and, as you can imagine, has aroused a great deal of excitement both here and in the rest of the Jewish world. The English government ceremoniously proclaimed it to be the foundation of its policy. You must have read in the newspapers that Palestine is to be divided once again. The issue of a Jewish state, with all of its implications, forty years after the First Zionist Congress and twenty years after the signing of the Balfour Declaration, has now entered a historically decisive and deadly serious phase. Here people naturally speak of nothing else, though for the time being opinions—my own included—remain uncertain. The report (in nearly every respect a historic document of the *highest* order, and a huge tome, to boot) has greatly disappointed Jewish expectations (which it obviously did its best to accommodate in a general way) on three or four points. These are very delicate issues and extremely crucial matters of honor. When the Zionist Congress meets in four weeks in Zurich, the position it will adopt vis-à-vis the whole infernally vexed question will depend on whether the English government compromises on these points. If this happens, the Jews will no doubt agree to the establishment of a Jewish state—and they have scarcely any choice, since the other alternative (the continuation of the Mandate, with strict limits on immigration and the purchase of land) would be even more unfavorable to them. According to the report, Jerusalem is to remain under eternal English rule for "the protection of holy sites." This wouldn't be so bad if the proposal didn't contain a recommendation (which also represents an enormous psychological blunder) to scrap the Balfour Declaration and the recognition of Hebrew as the official language within this region. Aside from the fact that Jerusalem has a large Jewish majority, any solution which involves abolishing existing rights in what is naturally felt to be *the* metropolis of the Jewish people is highly insulting. There are a number of such points. But I believe that the problems can be resolved around the negotiation table in a more or less civilized manner. The English think it important to rid themselves of the Mandate if possible, and, through a rather ambiguous and gleaming trademark called "the Jewish state," to make the Jews responsible for their own future. No one can offer any really well-founded prognosis about the future or the viability, internal as well as external, of this new state. It can just as easily be a success as a failure; all of the factors involved can go either way. What is obvious is that this will be crucial for the position of the Jews in the world. Like a number of others, I am in principle against this partition, because I consider an Arab-Jewish federation for the entire area of Palestine to be the ideal solution. But because this opportunity no longer exists for us, the only relevant question is whether we could achieve something better if we rejected the partition. The answer to this question, sadly, cannot be yes. [. . .]

I hope you will seriously consider paying us a visit. If you can't come this winter, something else may enable us to meet: I will most probably, or almost certainly, be appointed a visiting professor at the

Jewish Institute of Religion in New York (please keep this strictly confidential). The appointment will be for early next year and will enable me to spend six months over there, looking through kabbalistic manuscripts. [. . .]

Yours, Gerhard

FROM BETTY SCHOLEM

Marienbad, Czechoslovakia; July 16, 1937

My dear children,

[. . .] Once again we can't seem to agree on money, and I'm forced to write you an extra note with my calculations. I already did this *with you* before returning home from my trip in 1936! These discrepancies appear because you mix up your money with mine, dipping into it whenever you need something! Through Hete, I asked you to start a separate account. She asked and you said no, claiming that you needed my signature for it. This is nonsense! You can have ten different accounts, such as Prof. Scholem's account 1, account 2, and so on. You wrote, in addition, that you won't allow any withdrawals against the three hundred pounds. Oh, my son, as long as I have breath in my body the three hundred pounds belongs to me, and you cannot dispute this. I can make as many withdrawals as I wish! You know I have no intention of doing so, but it is my emergency fund and I can do with it as I please. I did not give it to you. [. . .]

Now it appears that you deducted twenty-five pounds from my money to buy the gift you gave me for my seventieth birthday!!! It's of course natural that my son should show his mother some attention on such an occasion, and the way you normally shirk such things is really not very pretty, my darling! It was for this reason that I was so happy to be wearing such a lovely jacket when representing you before our clan. For it always embarrasses me how little you do for me—that you're forever asking for things, even though I myself have nothing left and Werner weighs so heavily upon me! Take a good hard look at yourself! [. . .]

Kisses, Mum

FROM BETTY SCHOLEM

Marienbad, August 3, 1937

My dear child,

Yesterday I received your letter from July 27. I'll reply to your points in order of happiness! First of all, your visiting professorship thrilled me terribly and spread a sense of excitement all around the coffee table. Heinz Sussmann gave us a proper translation of the invitation—after I had already pieced together its meaning. I got a true case of lockjaw when he got to the name Stephen Wise.[57] "Do you have any idea who Stephen Wise is?" he screamed. "One should stand up and bow in reverence!" He was so completely enraptured that he kept bowing while he read. You always wanted to take a trip to America, and I'm delighted that now you can do so. Oh, how happy I am for you! [. . .]

Many kisses, Mum

FROM BETTY SCHOLEM

Berlin, October 26, 1937

My dear child,

[. . .] We went to some bookstores to inquire about travel guides to New York. The last Baedeker guide to the United States is from 1909, which makes it too outdated. It costs fifteen and a half marks. Neither Cook's nor American Express is allowed to import English guides, while German bookstores need permission from the Foreign Currency Office for each individual foreign book, and this they rarely get. I got a few brochures and maps at American Express. The people there were all very nice, though at the same time astonished that you couldn't get all the guides you need in Jerusalem. [. . .]

Mum

FROM BETTY SCHOLEM *(combined with the following letter, from Erich Scholem)*

Bodenbach, Czechoslovakia; November 21, 1937

My dear son,

We have matters of utmost urgency to resolve with you, and for this reason I bought a Sunday ticket and came here yesterday. Erich arrived today. I couldn't write the letter alone; because of the dangers at the border, I was unable to make any notes, and I was afraid of forgetting some important point I had discussed with the boys. For a variety of reasons, which I have no time to explain in detail, Erich has firmly and irrevocably decided to emigrate as soon as possible. He has already taken all of the necessary steps and filled out the relevant applications. He is taking no property; he must leave behind, for his family, everything he received from a loan against his life insurance and from the sale of Zernsdorf, after subtracting the 7,000 marks belonging to me. He needs a "security sum" of 250 pounds when he lands. I have decided to lend him the money from my account in Palestine and thereby enable him to emigrate, which is, it appears, necessary for him. This is not up for discussion; we have neither the time nor the opportunity for it. The matter is very urgent. I want to do this; and I won't be risking a penny, because the first thing he'll do after he lands will be to send back the money. That he will do so is not open to discussion either.

When I visited you a year and a half ago, I was ill and unable to talk with you about finances. You know what always happened: I would begin but couldn't continue! I'm fully aware of how ill-suited you are for coping with sudden and unexpected events. You'll probably respond to this urgent request for 250 pounds by running around the room and wringing your hands. But it's really very simple, and we're certain you can settle the entire matter with one trip to your bank. The bank will do everything for you; you need only impress upon them the need for the utmost speed. We assume that within fourteen days the entire transaction can be accomplished and the money transferred to London. This matter must be settled before the end of the year because as of February 1 you will be in America, and unreachable for months.

Mum

FROM ERICH SCHOLEM

November 21, 1937

Dear Gerhard,

Mother had already written the first page of this letter by the time I arrived! I intend to go to Australia with Reinhold. Reinhold can go with his family. He has enough money for a security deposit. But he has only enough for three people, meaning that he cannot include me. As Mother has already told you, I'm going to leave my money here for my family. I have only enough for the journey, which is the reason I must use Mother's money for the security deposit when I emigrate. [. . .]

Erich

FROM BETTY SCHOLEM

Berlin, December 6, 1937

My dear children,

[. . .] Your new tuxedo interests me greatly! Do you still have the tailcoat with the striped pants—that ageless garment? Do you have to drag along many books with you? It sounds to me like an enormously difficult task, preparing for such an excursion. Fanya will lend a helping hand! Loosen up on her chain a bit, my child. For years it was wound tightly around me. The fragments of it, however, have all disappeared. They were probably given to the Fatherland during the war!!

Mum

FROM BETTY SCHOLEM

December 7, 1937

[. . .] Listen, my son, have I ever made any "accusations"? I never do, nor have you any reason to get angry about what I said. This would hurt me deeply! I'm merely in the habit of writing the way I speak, so you shouldn't be offended. And if I say something wrong, Your Highness will let me know! It seems that in the present situation you don't have to put anything down in writing; I'm so thick-headed, I don't understand a thing anyway. Instead, I hope that at least one of us will speak with you in person. I would of course prefer to do it myself, though winter won't be a good time for me. If you decide to return via San Francisco, the South Seas, and India, I'll go to Milan or Switzerland to meet you. I'd prefer Switzerland. [. . .]

Mum

1938

TO MARTIN BUBER

Jerusalem, February 1, 1938

Dear Herr Buber,

I'm sorry that the hopes of your friends to see you here on your sixtieth birthday have not been fulfilled. From afar, at least, I send you my warmest regards. These days, it's not easy to find the right thing to wish. I can only say that I wish—on your behalf, as well as for all of us—that the difficulties which until now have constrained you in your decisions may soon be completely resolved and that you may proceed along the course for which you seem to have been born. I wish, for our sake, that over the next ten years you may effect and accomplish in our midst as much as you have in the past ten years. So much has already been done! And we have so much to thank you for in recent years! But thinking of you causes us to train our eyes upon the future, which isn't normally the case for sixty-year-olds. I wish with all my heart that in the coming year you may be granted the opportunity to take up the struggle here. Your powers in this fight are beyond question. But we are impatiently waiting to see you put them to use. This is what moves me the most when I think of you. [. . .]

Sincerely yours, Gerhard

TO WALTER BENJAMIN

Library of the Jewish Theological Seminary
Broadway and 122nd Street, New York City[58]

March 25, 1938

Dear Walter,

The flood of New York life has kept me under water so long that I'm only now reemerging. I have completed all of my lectures (with very great success) and I am now busy consulting manuscripts. This will take some time, as will my attempt to see and understand a bit of America. I'm learning a great deal here and, insofar as I can, am using the opportunity to catch a glimpse of this strange country.

I must tell you that I've already set the date for my return to Europe, where I hope we can finally get together. I'll be leaving on the twenty-third of June and will be in Frankfurt until the first of August. I will have my wife meet me there. Then I'll spend a number of weeks in Paris, Switzerland, and Italy (in the region of Merano). At the end of September I'll return to Jerusalem via Rome. This is my itinerary. The question is whether we can meet, say, between the first and the fifteenth of August. [. . .]

Wiesengrund was not on the ship, nor did he send word; I met instead with Tillich and his wife.[59] They absolutely insisted that they should bring me together with Horkheimer and Wiesengrund, whom they called close friends. This caused a little embarrassment on my part.[60] We discussed you. Tillich spoke of you in glowing terms. Of course, the picture he painted of Horkheimer's relations with you was altogether different from the one you have assumed in your various esoteric warnings. I prodded Tillich to elaborate a bit. According to him, H. has *the highest* opinion of you, though he *understands perfectly well* that with you he is dealing with a *mystic* (and, if I understand you right, this is not the impression you wanted to give him). This was not my word, but Tillich's. To come to the point, he said something to the effect that those people are neither too dumb not to know whose spiritual child you are, nor so narrow-minded for it to bother them much. They would do everything possible to help you, and have even considered bringing you here. [. . .]

FROM BETTY SCHOLEM

Berlin, September 27, 1938

Dear children,

I have rented a room in the pension where Reinhold stayed during the several weeks before he left. When I move in, I'll send you the address. For the time being I'll stay on Alexandrinen Strasse. I received your card from Rome on the twenty-sixth. I hope you've returned happily to your home.

We now need to confer seriously about what I should do. Reinhold wrote and insists that I come right away; but I should first go to stay with you because this will take a few months. I think I should not go to the boys right away, while they're still making preparations; it would be best if I went only *after* they've established themselves in business and in fact have some income, however meager. But I do want to get out of here as soon as I can, of course. Would it be all right if I waited peacefully with you before moving on? I don't know whether it's possible to make two applications at once! Perhaps it's simpler and faster to get an immigration certificate for Palestine, in which case I mustn't speak of a permit for Australia! Since *both* countries go through the British consulate, that wouldn't be possible. [. . .]

Kisses, Mum

FROM BETTY SCHOLEM

Berlin, October 12, 1938

My dear child,

[. . .] If I emigrate to Sydney and as a result cannot bring you my property tariff-free, shall I ship you the sofa and whatever else you want? I could also ship you the Korassan (the blue Persian one from my living room) and the Weinlaub box. But import duties will have to be paid. And we must keep in mind how much customs duty you'll have to pay for old clothes! Last night I read terrible news from Palestine and from Cairo. I thought to myself how *you* could easily go to an American university if a catastrophe occurs in Palestine.

Mum

FROM BETTY SCHOLEM

Berlin, October 25, 1938

My dear son,

[. . .] We're following reports of the violence with enormous concern![61] England's role in Europe is just as unclear. I am not worried about you; America is always an option! Please forgive me for taking this self-centered viewpoint—I really have the greatest sympathy for *all* those involved. Because of Werner, I've been in touch with the Hilfsverein.[62] I've had to do a great deal as a result of their recommendations—for instance, speak with Werner's earlier lawyer and write letters inquiring about the possibilities for emigration. It's a long shot. But all of us would be thrilled if it met with some success! Werner himself is allowed to write letters asking about the chances of emigrating—which was never allowed before. His last letter, dated October 16, I delivered to the Hilfs-verein. A certain Herr Loewenstein was extraordinarily moved by Werner's situation. He even knows him, for he worked for a long time in Munich and has been to Dachau. He also knew about our attempt to get Werner to Palestine in 1935–1936.[63] Both he and the lawyer consider it a step forward that they've transferred him to Buchenwald. Everything humanly possible will be done for the poor boy—but I'll remain skepti-cal until the day I see him on the other side of the border. [. . .]

Warmest greetings, Mum

FROM BETTY SCHOLEM

Berlin, November 13, 1938

My dear children,

I haven't heard anything from you since I wrote you on the twenty-fifth of October. *You* have of course heard about what we're going through here.[64] You can well imagine our sense of dread. I don't want to write about it; I assume you know everything. W.'s case now seems completely hopeless. He said in two separate letters that he hoped I'd long ago begun arranging for his emigration. Oh, Gerhard, what should I do? [. . .] He wrote that it's unlikely they'd allow him to go to England; he'd have to go as far away as possible, to some place like Australia! To get a permit for him, however, is totally impossible. It takes a year or more—and what about the costs of such a trip! I don't have such sums of money any longer! *You* should look into the matter again and see if you can do something, because I'm at the end of my rope. The Hilfs-verein seems to be closed now. For the past several days no one has answered calls at their central office. The organization can no longer do a thing.

As for me, after all of the letters I've received from the boys—and they have certainly written to you as well—I will emigrate to Australia. By hook or by crook, though, I'll stay with you as long as my health and the permits allow. The rioting doesn't scare me; I am in God's hands!

The exit permit that I applied for on the twenty-second of September has not yet arrived. Until it comes, there's no sense trying to arrange for the passport etc. Have you heard anything about the entry certificate? Is it possible to change the name to Werner's? In such a state of despair, one thinks about things that are probably completely impossible. At least the officials there will listen to *you* and won't throw you out of their office! [. . .]

Yesterday, I received a letter Emmy wrote after she received the terrifying reports. She told me to join them *at once:* that I should leave everything behind; that they're awfully worried about all of us, but I should at least get out of here right away; that I would certainly get a visa; that I can have my own room; and that she would take care of me until I could leave to join the boys. I should simply come, just as I am! Once I'm there, I can make all other arrangements! I know Emmy perfectly well. She may often be deluded and unreliable, but her willingness to help is boundless and genuine. If I had a passport, I'd be on the train today! This is what is so terrible! I'll no doubt get a British visa, yet I can get a passport *only* once I present emigration papers. She wrote that I should go to Hannover, and from there one of her relatives will accompany me to England and will take care of all of the luggage so that I won't have to strain myself. I would accept the help right away if I had a passport! I want only to get *out of here.* Agitation and fear are killing me, and I can't bear to think that I'll be unable to go to you and that they'll rob me of my last dime. [. . .]

Warmest kisses, Mum

FROM BETTY SCHOLEM

Berlin, November 19, 1938

My dear child,

Early this morning Reinhold phoned to speak with my brother about business. I also spoke with him. He told me that the permit has arrived and that he'll send it airmail next week. A detailed letter is on the way explaining how I should travel via *Canada,* together with friends of his who already have their permits (and who booked their trip long ago). I told him that I don't want to and that I prefer to travel by way of

Palestine. I couldn't say anything more. Hans got on the line again but hung up once the six minutes (106 marks) were up. This was before Erich could get to the phone. To my great sorrow, I couldn't speak with him. I wrote to you on the thirteenth (I assume that news from you is on the way, but you must answer *today's letter* by return post), saying that I need to know what *you think* I should do! Once I have crossed the border, I'll be in no hurry and would like to spend some time with you. The boys are afraid of the rioting and the long, and possibly complicated, voyage from there to Australia. [. . .] Dearest Fanya, could you please go to Cook's and ask what kind of direct line *they* offer? It's of course very important that I pay in *Berlin!* And if the two of you can't give me any information on the trip, at least tell me whether or not I should go to Palestine. *I* want to see you again! You must understand that I find myself in the most painful state of mind and that I need all my nerve just to survive. What we are experiencing and suffering is horrible. Edith[65] sits and cries here with the children; and on top of everything else there's Werner, whom I have to abandon without being able to do a thing for him. [. . .]

Just write to me. It's been so long since I've heard from you, and I worry about you because of the terrible unrest there. I haven't heard a word from you for more than four weeks —since the sixteenth of October. This is too long!

How can I manage to handle all the things weighing me down? I have no one to give me advice. My siblings are themselves falling to pieces and can't help in the least. Granted, Reinhold's friends want to relieve me of whatever burdens they can. Thank God they live close by—but at the end of the day I have to do everything alone. All will be fine if I can only travel with my health intact. There's no longer any money to speak of.

I'll wind things up. I'm upset and write nothing but nonsense. But today I offer congratulations in advance, my darling.[66] You certainly must be congratulated. How you got it right, a thousand times over!

From the bottom of my heart, Your mother

1939

TO SHALOM SPIEGEL

Jerusalem, Rehavia; January 1, 1939

From Shalom to Shalom:[67]

Like a river of peace! My dear friend, please don't think that my failure to write means I've forgotten you. Quite the contrary! You, your family, and all of our friends are stamped indelibly on our memories. If you ask why I've been silent so long, I can only reply: out of shame. Shame because I still do not have the clear and simple information you naturally expect from me: news about the fate of my book.[68] Oh, if you only knew what I've had to put up with! I am more or less certain that Schocken wants the book, though he constantly stretches things out instead of making a clear, unambiguous decision. I hesitate to write to my friends in America because I want to give them definite information, which is the reason for all of these obstacles and constraints. Every day my wife and I discuss the fact that I really *should* write to you at long last. Now Schocken has sent a letter to his two sons (whom you've probably met at some point) to get their advice and to shift the responsibility onto them! And I—why do I put up with it all? At this point I must make a shameful confession to you. I have emerged from a period of terrible exhaustion, which meant that I could not push things along as I would have under normal circumstances. I returned from my trip happy and satisfied. Then my own eyes suddenly became my worst enemies. I suffered for some time, until I was finally forced to see a doctor. I had to undergo an operation, and was on the road to recovery. Then this profound exhaustion came over me. I could not do any serious work, and I had the evil urge to draw support for these internal inhibitions from external obstacles. To make a long story short, I am only now slowly regaining my energy and beginning to work. To this point, I've been doing merely what I always do during periods of helplessness and exhaustion: feeding off yields sown in better times—that is, working on my dictionary of the *Zohar*. I have agreed to write the "Kabbalah" article for the Yiddish encyclopedia in Paris, but even this obligation I have not yet fulfilled, though the submission date has already passed. Instead,

I sit and work on the *Zohar* and on the many documents I brought with me from New York. [. . .]

Amid all this news, I haven't even mentioned the events that have hit us, and indeed what's been occurring beyond Palestine! Apropos of Palestine, I can happily say that the situation does not look as bad it did last summer. There have been bleak and somber times, but the situation now is much improved. The partition plan has gone up in smoke, and we've missed a golden opportunity; I just hope something much worse doesn't happen instead. At the same time, you should know that things aren't as bad as reported in the press. For political reasons, the government refuses to give out immigration visas. This is a fact, and by no means a cheerful one. But the government allows (I'm tempted to say it actively supports) illegal immigration, which has risen substantially of late. This would of course be impossible if the government, which knows more about it than all of us put together, did not want it. Recently (in the past two months) four thousand such immigrants have arrived from Vienna alone. They can be seen everywhere, and more are on the way. When ships land, the military helps things along by preventing all unwanted observers from approaching the shore! It's a strange world we live in. The Arabs are told, "We won't give out any more visas to Jews," while the Jews are assured, "Why all the fuss? You can bring entire legions of youngsters into the country. We'll look the other way." The unfortunate thing about all this is that the immigrants arrive without a penny to their names, and foreign aid organizations ignore them because they don't appear in the official statistics. Now we're trying to come to grips with this.

The worst thing, of course, is what's happening in Germany. Each one of us is worried about relatives. The echo and impression of the pogrom were deeper than anything that has occurred up to now. How is the mood among your people there? Have events altered the general feeling of indifference? Here we've been reading about all sorts of plans to ease immigration to America. What's happening with this? Can they give entry permits to all of the people in the country on whose behalf you've applied? For a few weeks I ran from office to office trying to secure an entry permit for my mother. I was among the lucky ones who succeeded, though it was all in vain. The doctor in Berlin determined that she couldn't tolerate the climate here, so she'll go to stay with my brothers in Australia, who have yet to settle into their new life. This causes us a considerable amount of grief and worry, since my mother is seventy-two and not in the best of health. Can she survive the hellish torments that the officials in Germany inflict on those Jews who want to emigrate? And my wretched brother is completely alone. In recent months, various people have come out of Dachau and Buchenwald (where he's now being held) and have described to me everything that happens there. All agree that the few political prisoners have no chance of release.

Your true friend, Gershom Scholem

FROM BETTY SCHOLEM

Berlin, February 7, 1939

My dear children,

Your letter from the twenty-fifth of January arrived on the thirtieth; Gerhard's enclosure with Theo's letter, on February 2. I wanted to answer right away, but we had such terrible and unfathomable difficulties with the financial bureau (though *everything* of ours is in order) that we thought we'd die of despair. Whatever can be done to make one's life more difficult is done deliberately. Today, after eight weeks, I received the clearance certificate, though still no passport! It's all so incomprehensible. [. . .]

Kisses and a thousand greetings, Mum

FROM BETTY SCHOLEM

Berlin, February 15, 1939

My dear son,

There's been *one* step forward. Yesterday—after nine weeks!—I got my passport. I needed every ounce of determination to endure it. I sat for three and a half hours at the passport office with Irene, who took care of me. We got there at eight in the morning. We were then shuffled among four different offices. They made it unimaginably complicated! [. . .]

They want to drive you to utter despair. What I suffer is nothing in comparison to poor Edith. I have no idea what has come over Erich! When I lie awake at night, useless questions dance their way into my mind and I ask myself why I didn't go to you earlier, years ago. But things weren't exactly simple with you, and then I developed this cyst! I'm completely despondent, and I can't stop crying. Do you think I'll ever get out of here? I'm awfully sorry to burden you with my melancholy letters. I hope my old self will reappear.

I can't yet say *a thing* about my departure. For Werner I made reservations with Cook's to Shanghai and sent the Gestapo three documents required for emigration, together with an application. This is all driving me out of my mind!

Kisses to you both, Mum

FROM BETTY SCHOLEM

Berlin, February 23, 1939

My dear children,

They are intent on causing us the most horrific problems until the very last minute. What kind of times are we living in! They won't let us take either silver or jewelry with us. What can one say about this! One should just thank God to be able to get out of here, naked as a jaybird. [. . .]

Many kisses from your old mother

TO WALTER BENJAMIN

Jerusalem, March 2, 1939

Dear Walter,

[. . .] My eyes are unfortunately as bad as the political situation. [. . .] What's now going on is far from good. The negotiations in London have reached such a critical point that any day an uprising could break out here against the proposed "solutions." The atmosphere here is heavy these days. The English naturally want to try pairing us with the "Czech" formula from Munich, but this will not happen peacefully. The mood here is very agitated, because the Jews feel (more or less rightly) that they've been sold out. Their willingness to respond with violence is extraordinarily strong. Of course, given the fact that the situation of the Jews is very different from that of the Arabs, this would be idiotic. Any terrorist actions by Jews could easily be repressed. Still, given the mood, one should expect such actions. If someone accepts the risk—or rather the certainty—of ruining *everything,* he can of course change the situation. But in that case nothing will remain afterward. I'm nearly certain it *won't* come to this—I'm sure there's still a chance we can see you here. Of course we're still thinking about it. It seems to me that on both sides it's nothing but a question of money. (What's the situation with your papers? Will they allow you to travel?) I must have written to you that my mother is not coming. She's leaving Berlin on the twelfth of March and going to Australia by way of London. I hope to see her on the way over, at Port Said. The main question, of course, is how she can be supported and how much money I'll need to send to Australia, where my brothers have yet to find a livelihood. If all of this weren't so unclear, I would have already begun negotiations over your future!

Gerhard

FROM BETTY SCHOLEM

Berlin, March 4, 1939

Dear children,

[. . .] I'm happy already. Soon, very soon, it'll all be done. We have our visas and the tickets for the ship. Either on Sunday the twelfth or on Monday, we'll be on our way to London. Jews are no longer allowed to travel in sleepers (!!), but I'll survive the night! This morning we took the car to the pawn shop and delivered over the silver and jewelry. What do I care! I've supplied Werner as best I could. The Jewish community, where Jewish emigration is now centralized, is also doing its best. But I don't believe the efforts will succeed, even if he were to fill out all of the applications. Their thirst for revenge knows no bounds.

I'll write from London, and I still hope to get a letter from you here. I have a tough week ahead of me. With Edith's help, I'll make it.

Kisses from your old mother

FROM WALTER BENJAMIN

Paris, March 14, 1939

Dear Gerhard,

[. . .] I was glad to see that you've set your sights on my visit to Palestine, without even knowing my current situation. As things now stand, the important question is whether it's possible for me to stay a number of months. (I don't delude myself into thinking you could finance this yourself.) Circumstances are such that among the various danger zones in which the world has distributed its Jews, France is at present the most ominous, because here I am *completely* isolated financially. [. . .]

Walter

TO WALTER BENJAMIN

Jerusalem, March 20, 1939

Dear Walter,

Your letter from the fourteenth of March just arrived. You can imagine how much it disturbed me, and for obvious reasons. [. . .] The worst is, of course, that your catastrophe with the institute[69] coincides with that of the most helpful people here. The events over the past months, together with the sudden collapse of Czech Jewry, has forced nearly everyone here to take unimaginable action for the sake of family members. Rich people have been ruined in twenty-four hours, and their families who live here must suddenly take on responsibilities they never expected. This is the case with my mother; it would have been somewhat easier for me to take care of her in my own home than to have to send a part of my salary to her in Australia (where apparently my brothers still have no means of support). It goes without saying that I want to assist you in any way I can. Helplessly, I wonder how, if necessary, I can do so. In view of the political developments, it appears highly doubtful that we could now arrange a visit for you here, though we might have all the will in the world and you might be able to get a tourist visa. *Even this* has become a question!! Let alone the financial end of things: 2,400 francs a month is fifteen pounds here—quite a sum, given our budget. I can tell you only whether it will be possible to finance your stay here for a couple of months, after the enormous commotion has eased among the families affected by the fate of Prague. So long as we ourselves have something to eat, you'll always find a meal in our home. Everything else, though, is completely up in the air at the moment. [. . .]

Your Gerhard

FROM BETTY SCHOLEM

Marseilles, March 25, 1939

Dear children,

As early as last summer, a female prison counselor told Käte that all officials had been verbally instructed to harass the Jews. Everything should be made difficult in the extreme through chicanery. Nothing should be done for them right away; things should be dragged out interminably. It took nine weeks to get my clearance certificate. I constantly had to hand in new property declarations. Each time, they told me that everything was in order and that the certificate would be sent out. Nothing happened. We would go to the office again, and they would demand a *new* declaration. Finally they took out your father's tax records and invented an excuse to demand back taxes from *me,* though I haven't had to pay taxes since 1930! Once I lost my temper and screamed at the official, "I've been running around for six weeks to get the certificate!" His reply: "Why have you been running? You should take a car!" [. . .]

Mum

FROM BETTY SCHOLEM

On board ship, April 13, 1939

Children,

[. . .] An exciting announcement: the ship will cross the Equator at 4:15! And this great moment occurs in the rain. What do you think about that? It's pouring!!! The clouds dance on the horizon; the rain comes down in torrents. There isn't much difference between this and Gleisdreieck, the spot in Berlin where you get the best view of the sky. Today we had another afternoon downpour, yet it's quite hot.

I got mail from the boys. Erich has bought a shop and hopes it was the right decision. At the moment, he's happy and thinks he'll soon make a go of it. He sells absolutely everything, and we imagine the shop to be like the store in Zernsdorf that sold bread, sausage, kitchen appliances, rat poison, and everything else. Erich has rented a small furnished apartment for Edith and the children, until the shipping container arrives. [. . .]

Love, Mum

FROM THEODOR ADORNO

New York, April 19, 1939

Dear Herr Scholem,

I'm not just being rhetorical when I say that the *Zohar* translation you sent me gave me more joy than any gift I have received in a long time. Don't read into this remark anything pretentious, because I am far from claiming to have fully grasped the text. But it's the kind of thing whose indecipherability is itself an element of the joy I felt in reading it. I think I can say that your introduction has at least given me a topological notion of the *Zohar.* A bit like someone who goes high into the mountains to spot chamois bucks but fails to see them, because he's a nearsighted city dweller. After an experienced guide points out the precise spot where the bucks congregate, he becomes so thoroughly acquainted with their territory that he thinks he must be able to discover these rare creatures immediately. The summer tourist cannot expect to glean anything more than this from the landscape, which is truly revealed only at the price of a lifetime's commitment—nothing less.

This said, I would like to make two comments, even if they should prove utterly foolish. The first is that I'm astonished at the connection between the text and the tradition of neo-Platonism. Such a connection is the last thing I expected. I had imagined the *Zohar* to be somehow the most inward and self-contained product of the Jewish spirit. Now, however, I discover that it is in some mysterious way—particularly in its strangeness—a part of Western thought. If the *Zohar* is in fact a Jewish document in some significant way, then it is such only in the sense of a mediation—and mediation, in the diaspora, has been essentially the Jewish fate. This seems to me of great importance because it brings the text into a broader historical-philosophical context than the unsuspecting person who hears the word "Kabbalah" could ever imagine. Perhaps I may be so bold as to raise the question whether the metaphysical intuitions expressed in the text aren't more graspable under the historical-philosophical aspect of the "decline" of occidental Gnosticism (as you well know, the term "decline" when I use it has no connotations of decadence) than under the aspect of a primal religious experience. You, who have made the great commentaries your bailiwick, are surely just as skeptical as I am about a "primordial experience." For philosophical reasons, I don't believe in any such thing. I cannot imagine the life of truth being anything other than something mediated. [. . .]

Sincerely yours, T. Adorno

FROM BETTY SCHOLEM

Sydney, New South Wales, Australia; May 9, 1939

Dear children (who are too lazy to write),

[. . .] *Werner:* Hans and Phiechen[70] have managed to get the clearance certificate from the finance bureau, as well as the certificate of good conduct. The passport awaits a signature. The monstrous Gestapo still has to dot a few *I*'s and cross some *T*'s, but these, as before, are the only things missing. [. . .]

Erich: [. . .] He has bought a small "variety store" (what we call a grocery—Zernsdorf has three such places) in a neighborhood filled with simple people. He works sixteen hours a day, from Monday morning to Sunday evening. No pauses, no breaks for food. On Sunday morning the store is closed for two hours while all the customers are at church, and then they start banging on the back door. He has almost everything, including jam, butter, eggs, sausage, thirty-six different types of cookie; he has cakes, bonbons, chicken feed, rat poison, colonial wares, fruit, tobacco, and sewing supplies. He also has a large refrigerator to keep ice cream (an important business in these parts) and a gas oven to warm up meat pies at lunchtime. [. . .]

Reinhold: [. . .] We live in the country, in a lovely area similar to Schandau. We have a large one-story wooden house. The shop is right next to the train station. We live off the train traffic! The back of the house is on stilts—it rests on high stone pillars—and the land drops off sharply until it reaches a wide river. On the premises there's a so-called pleasure ground (a large park with a pool and twenty-five cabanas) where the weekenders, who apparently crowd the place in summer, eat their picnics. There's also a gas station on the premises, and Günter pumps the gas.[71] The owners, a very nice couple, worked for four weeks to train Reinhold, from 8:30 in the morning until 6:00 in the evening. Everything's just like Erich's, only larger. The workload's heavier, too. But everyone is happy just to be *able* to work. [. . .]

Kisses—and write soon, Mum

TO THEODOR ADORNO

Jerusalem, June 4, 1939

Dear Herr Wiesengrund,

It was a real pleasure for me to read your letter from the nineteenth of April, which took a full four weeks to reach me. Your remark about its being such a "gift" constitutes for me a most appropriate honorarium. There is no one really equipped to read kabbalistic writings, so all that separates us is a bit of philology.

Your astonishment at the connections with neo-Platonic tradition will disappear once you cast a benevolent glance at your humble servant's most pertinent writings. If I can manage to round up a copy of my 1929 essay "On the Question of the Origins of the Kabbalah," I'll honor you with a registered letter.[72] The essay sheds light on this tradition and its relation to the Kabbalah. Of course, the strangest and most alluring thing is the fact that the most original products of Jewish thinking are, as it were, products of assimilation. All of these various questions no doubt lead to paradoxes—in other words, to dialectical connections. Though for twenty years I have sought to decipher the Kabbalah's mysteries, this astonishes me as much as it does you. What is remarkable about every rational form of mysticism lies in the relation between tradition and experience (to be on the safe side, I naturally avoid using such a dubious expression as "primordial experience"). It seems to have escaped you that Jewish mysticism, in its very name, points to this relation; for *Kabbala,* in German, translates as "tradition" and not "*Ur*-experience." From the outset the Kabbalists, including the greatest visionaries among them, always—and with awesome energy—affirmed that their insights were a species of commentary. The fact that in this case Gnosticism proves to be the unbroken thread leading through the labyrinth only shows how confounding the pertinent connections really are. [. . .]

I am greatly concerned about the fate of Walter Benjamin. I've received the most worrying reports about him from Paris. Is there any chance you could somehow put him back on his feet for a few years? I would have liked to have him here in Palestine for a longer period of time, but the attempt to put this desire into practice has hit a number of very serious snags which, unfortunately, I initially underestimated. Does the institute intend to take up his case any time soon? [. . .]

Yours, Gerhard Scholem

TO WALTER BENJAMIN

Abarbanel Road 28, Rehavia; June 30, 1939

Dear Walter,

You probably think I disappeared long ago, kidnapped by roving bands in the deserts of Arabia where I died of thirst, or somehow wounded or silenced by frequent bombings! Not even the packet containing your lovely commentary on Brecht's Lao Tzu poems managed to break the silence, though it has all the qualities capable of loosening a tongue such as mine. If you have not lost every vestige of faith in my existence, you must assume, in this case correctly, that something has prevented me from speaking—something stronger than all wishes and duties. It's really nothing physical or health-related (I don't know whether to say "thank God" or "unfortunately") but, rather, the boundless gloom and paralysis that have come over me during the past several months because of the current state of affairs. In fact, I find it impossible *not* to think about our situation—and by "our" I don't just mean those of us in Palestine. The dreadful catastrophe that has befallen Judaism, a disaster whose dimensions no one can fully grasp, and the utter hopelessness of a situation in which hope is manufactured only in order to taunt us (like the shameless "project" to send Jews to British Guyana as "colonists")[73]—all of this strikes one down and destroys one's peace of mind. I would have greatly preferred to write about the opportunities we could find for you here and about arranging for you to visit for a few months, which has preoccupied us longer than you can imagine. But I can't bring myself to extend an invitation (which, as it were, assumes a certain level of bourgeois comfort, even when one must reduce this to the absolute minimum) to live in a situation where tomorrow, or certainly at the very least the day after, there will be murder and all the things that follow from it. My long silence bears witness to nothing other than a decisive and depressing absence. You know me well enough to know that I'm not easily depressed. The past few months have done the trick. That Palestine should be turned into a showplace of civil war is a disgrace, and ultimately, for me, much more than just one more lost chance among others. After everything I have experienced over the past six years, I can no longer find any good reason to believe in a revolution that could resolve all of the tensions here. The labor movement is, as a revolutionary and political factor, deader than a doornail.[74] There is no point in fostering any illusions about this. [. . .] We'll have to face the fact that it's not going to revive in the present generation. And since there is nothing that can assume the function of Palestine within Judaism (besides empty phrases that no longer appeal to anyone), how can I come to terms with all that has happened during these years? Confronted with this darkness, I can only keep silent. The chances that Palestine will remain a vibrant colony through the next world war are endangered just as much by ourselves as by the English and the Arabs. Frightful things are coming, and I shudder when I try to imagine how it will all turn out. We live in terror. The capitulation of the English in the face of violence leads the fools among us to think that we can accomplish something only through the weapon of terror, irrespective of our particular situation. But there are too many fools around for them to stand out. Thus the present state of affairs. I never believed that the English could do much against us, so long as we did not abandon the humane foundation on which our cause rests. But we are well on the way to doing precisely this. Here you have in a nutshell the reasons for my uncommunicative silence. I am ashamed to discuss the things that preoccupy me, just as I am ashamed to act as if the situation were not in fact so threatening and so real. Therefore I say nothing. Your situation, which I think I understand quite well, is dangerous and I can't offer any logical remedy. Indeed, it may be that, in the present situation, your visit here is no longer even technically possible, meaning that they won't even allow you into the country. [. . .]

Now on to my work. I've been able to do only basic research, my state of mind permitting nothing more. I'd like to begin expanding the book I wrote in English, which means doubling it from its previous size. Schocken wants to print 450 pages. The holidays start this week, and you now know the main goals I've set for myself. Besides this, I have to write a few smaller things and prepare my lectures on Sabbatai Sevi, which after much study I will finally venture to tackle next year. For years, I've slowly been forming an image of the results of all these efforts, to the point where I can really set to work with a good conscience. [. . .]

Gerhard

FROM BETTY SCHOLEM

Sydney, November 6, 1939

My dear son and Fanya,

[. . . I just spent five days in the city. Edith had an exhibit, a kind of bazaar together with her landlords. I think she earned a couple of pounds. We still have to count up the money! I was able to give her a hand. There was an afternoon tea in her apartment, and I took charge of organizing it. A real commotion broke out. The people showed more interest in her Meissen cups than in the lovely dresses she was supposed to sell! [. . .] Yesterday evening I returned completely refreshed from the nice change of scene, but now I'm feeling quite low. Reinhold had a very poor week and a bad weekend, for the weather is still erratic. Lately it's been cold, with a lot of rain and icy wind. This is for the most part a windy country; occasionally we get a boiling hot day when the dampness and heat could kill you. I recovered a bit at the beginning, but now I've once again become so thin that all of my clothes hang loosely on me. I don't allow myself to think about Werner. One hears such terrifying things about the concentration camps. I wrote to him several times by way of Emmy and people in Berlin, but I don't know whether he received my letters. [. . .]

Kisses, Mum

TO WALTER BENJAMIN

Jerusalem, December 15, 1939

Dear Walter,

[. . .] Hopefully we'll succeed in getting our work done during the long war (or wars—the plural seems more accurate) most likely facing us. In the true sense of the term, I find myself "well out of harm's way" for the time being (but who knows for how long). Everything continues normally at the moment. To be sure, we have our material concerns— but who doesn't? In any event, we at the university are busy with the new school year, which began in November as if everything were peaceful. Instead of coming from abroad, many of our new students are locals who would otherwise have left the country to study but now can't. *Nolens volens,* the university will have to support many of the fictitious students from Poland.[75] And many young people will also enroll as students because there are no jobs for them. In addition, there are those who unexpectedly arrive from "countries that remain free" and those who got their papers in order in time. And so we hold classes as if everything were normal. I'm giving a course—for the first time—on the Sabbatian movement, lecturing to what I consider unbelievable audiences of sixty or seventy people (we have no student fees—we're a progressive institution!), while even my aristocratic seminar on the book of *Bahir* has attracted as many as ten magicians. But *pourvu que cela dure,* as Napoleon's mother supposedly said. Schocken has left for America to put our financing in order. We'll have to wait and see what happens to our salaries. Meanwhile, people work if they can. I'm filled with good intentions for the near future, and am awaiting only the decisive surge of inspiration. The prospects for my work look especially promising, because I now have an opportunity to open up something like a "Scholem school" of research.[76] Some other time I'll give you the details. I wish I could have the same success promoting the quality and importance of your work that I do promoting my own! But I haven't been slacking in this regard. Shortly before he left the country, Schocken staged an evening on Karl Kraus (he had bought the original manuscript of *The Last Days of Mankind*) and invited Werner Kraft and myself to speak. Instead of blowing my own horn, however, I read a large portion of *your* manuscript, which evoked a thunderous ovation. Everyone was truly impressed with you— in addition to the person whose impression is the only one that counts.[77] The demons are taking steps to defend themselves against you. [. . .]

1940

FROM WALTER BENJAMIN[78]

Paris, January 11, 1940

Dear Gerhard,

[. . .] The description you gave me of the reading at Schocken's soirée is truly gripping. I didn't keep it from Hannah Stern, who returns your greetings. Your report makes me thirst for revenge, since I am rather slow to see the work of demons in people's shabby behavior.[79] But if I want to slake that thirst, I will have to wait for the first things Schocken himself publishes. Hannah Stern was of the mitigating opinion that Schocken, in the depths of his soul, thinks more of Brod alone than of you and me put together. [. . .]

Yours, Walter

TO THEODOR ADORNO

Jerusalem, April 15, 1940

Dear Herr Wiesengrund-Adorno,

Last week, after a very long though apparently safe journey, your friendly package containing the latest issue of the *Zeitschrift für Sozialforschung* arrived.[80] Many thanks for thinking of me. But my sequence has a gap, since I never received the previous issue. If you have a spare copy, please be so kind as to drop it into an envelope for me! So much for the *schnorrer* section of this letter. In terms of content, I can only say that the issue truly interested me, and in a variety of ways. Lacking all prior musical knowledge, I can only say that the philosophical perspective set out in your essay—at least what I could gather of it beyond the topic of music—lies close to my own. [. . .]

I am very concerned about Walter Benjamin, who has neither sent word nor answered any inquiries since the beginning of December 1939. He wrote quite regularly after his return to Paris, and I'm extremely pleased with the offprints of his work. Please write if you know anything. These days, all avenues of communication have become so difficult—

a letter to Paris can take ten days, even thirty. Has something come up to thwart his plans once again? [. . .]

Gerhard Scholem

FROM THEODOR ADORNO[81]

New York, July 16, 1940

Today I want to write on behalf of Walter Benjamin, whose fate worries me as it does you. He has managed to escape from Paris to Lourdes, which lies in the unoccupied zone of France. His present address is 8 rue Notre Dame, Lourdes. He's in no immediate danger, though due to the developments in France it's more than justified to fear for the fate of Jewish refugees. We are therefore trying desperately, with all means at our disposal, to facilitate Walter's immigration into this country. It would be a great help if you could write a testimony about Walter Benjamin as a personality, scholar, and philosopher—if possible, with special reference to the way in which his thinking is bound up with the Jewish tradition. Could you please let us have this testimony with six copies, each of them signed by you with all your titles and degrees, on official paper, and written in English. [. . .]

FROM BETTY SCHOLEM

Como/Sydney, September 27, 1940

My dear children,

On the fourteenth we received an airmail letter dated August 2 from Arthur Hirsch, with the terrible news that Werner is dead. Arthur's brother Paul passed on the news to him, with the single addendum that "there is no precise information." I'm stunned and completely beside myself. I always believed he would be released. And now, with this as the conclusion of seven and a half years of misery, I can't pull myself together! Those monsters no doubt killed him, but we'll never find out what really happened. Werner wasn't the type to commit suicide. Until the very last, I heard time and time again from people who'd spoken with him that he wasn't doing badly. He worked as a guard and never gave up hope. The only consolation I have is to know that I never abandoned him and did whatever was humanly possible to secure his release. Conflict over Werner runs like an unbroken black thread through the past thirty years of my life. I always stuck by him, and now it's all over. [. . .]

With the start of the summer, business has picked up again. Reinhold is in a sour mood, his energies and nerves all worn thin. When a spoon clatters on a plate, he cringes as if it were a bomb. In the long run he won't be able to endure the incessant hard work day after day, the irregular meals, the lack of sleep, and everything else that goes with the job. What can you do! The doctor prescribed two medicines, *est aliquid fiat,* which can't help him in the least.

For three months now, since the seventh of June, we've received no word from you (other than the personal greetings and photographs brought by Frau Schocken),[82] though I've written four times during this period. Today's letter makes it five. [. . .]

Mum

FROM BETTY SCHOLEM

Sydney, November 10, 1940

My dear Gerhard and Fanya,

Many thanks for your letter of September 30, received on the nineteenth of October [. . .] It made me exceedingly happy to hear about you from Herr Schocken over tea. He was here in Sydney for only two days and devoted an afternoon to me. He had to turn down our lunch invitation because of an engagement to shake hands with a group of forty men. He also delivered a lecture in which he spoke exclusively about you and your research! He takes such interest in your work that he went out of his way to bring me a copy of the program of your working group, which was something special for me. He then told me about a reception that was held to honor the anniversary of twenty-five years of your research, starting with your polemics against Blau-Weiss. I asked him right away about your translation of the Song of Songs and the Psalms. My knowledge of your work is so limited! If I hadn't made such a wreck of my life here in Australia, I could at least warm myself next to the glow of your fame. Instead I sit here and face one *fatalité* after the other. Getting back to Schocken, he said that if there was one man on earth he envied, it's *you.* Your path through life, your character, and your work inspire his envy! [. . .]

Mum

TO THEODOR ADORNO

Jerusalem, November 11, 1940

Dear Herr Adorno,

Like all letters that come from America, yours dated July 16 unfortunately took ages to arrive. Letters arrive sometimes after a month, sometimes after four months. I received your plea to help Walter Benjamin a few days before I got Hannah Stern's terrible message from the south of France informing me about our friend's suicide. She told me that Walter had gotten a visa to the United States, obviously as a result of your efforts, but that he was not allowed to pass through a Spanish border town. Hannah Stern did not give me an address that would have allowed me to write to her. She wrote that she first received the news, four weeks after the event, from his sister. I assume that you have more direct information about the details, or that such news is easier to come by in New York than here. I don't have to tell you what Benjamin's death means for us and how vital it is for me to know, if at all possible, the details of the last days of his life. Insofar as present circumstances allow, it is, I believe, the duty of his friends to save his papers in one way or another and to prepare a dignified memorial for him. The events of world history are such that the destruction of a man of genius is, amid all this terrifying turmoil, scarcely even noticed. Yet there are enough people for whom this death will be unforgettable. Please tell me everything you have heard or can piece together. In the event his papers have not survived or have not arrived in New York, I am probably the only one who possesses a relatively complete collection of his writings. Perhaps the time will come when someone will make use of this invaluable legacy. I'm sure there are far more handwritten materials than published ones, and I needn't say how important I consider it to eventually bring them all together in some safe place. [. . .]

Last summer I completed my large book in English, *Major Trends in*

Jewish Mysticism, which will probably be printed here. I hope you can get hold of it. It's intended for an American audience and contains an elaboration of the lectures I held there. I will dedicate it to the memory of our friend, something I already intended to do while he was still alive. [. . .]

Yours, Gerhard Scholem

1941

FROM BETTY SCHOLEM

Sydney, April 26, 1941

Dear children,

I was delighted to receive another letter from you—or, rather, to be "presented" with one! It was sent on April 6 (postmarked April 8) and arrived speedily, on the nineteenth. I wanted to answer straightaway, but I had to help Käte manage the shop.[83] I scarcely have a free hour these days, what with all the work I have to do, partly sitting down and partly wandering around. I do it gladly so long as I can help Reinhold, though it costs me a great deal of effort not to pitch a plate at his dear wife every day. I fear someday I'll do it. More on this after I touch on Fanya's letter! My dear child, I hope that all of your infirmities (which, added up, are most unpleasant and I am very sorry to hear about them) will soon disappear and never show up again! Your buttocks are surely the least of your problems, since that part of your body can put up with a lot; but the boil in your ear sounds awful! That you're reading Fontana with such pleasure makes me happy, though. You can't be exclusively eastern European if you're so enamored of this Prussian, with his fondness for the Brandenburg nobility and his slight dose of anti-Semitism. The only books I took with me were Fontana's collected works. I've read them over and over. Tell me which novel you like the most. [. . .]

Gerhard, I'm fascinated by the news of your book and your other scholarly activities. If I could, I'd have come to hear you speak about the secrets of this world and the next! I'm enormously interested in the Messiah—though I think he should hurry up. I regret to say it, but for now the only one in charge down here is his powerful antagonist. [. . .]

FROM BETTY SCHOLEM

Sydney, July 11, 1941

My dear children,

Your letters from the nineteenth of May and the fifth of June arrived on the twenty-fifth of June. Many thanks. I wanted to send heaps of delighted congratulations to the dean at once, but I was so busy that today is the first opportunity I've had to express my joy.[84] Yes, Herr Dean, I am *very* happy for you. It's a great honor, and a scholar does well to work for the sake of such honor! Do you wear the philosophers' purple gown at dissertation hearings and university celebrations? [. . .]

I didn't know that Walter Benjamin had died. You didn't write a thing about it. His son was just a baby when we visited them in 1918 in Bern! The Jewish Welfare Society in Sydney keeps a list of all of the internees. Erich called them and they told him immediately which camp Stefan Benjamin is in. I wrote to him on July 6, and as soon as he answers I'll send him some chocolate. We've learned about a number of such cases here. Isn't it terrible that these young people who fled to the Union Jack are now being prevented from leading a normal life! [. . .]

From your old mother

TO SHALOM SPIEGEL

Jerusalem, July 17, 1941

My dear and esteemed friend,[85]

For the past year I have not had the honor of hearing from you. I don't know whether you received either my last letter (written around the time of Sukkoth) or the article that I took such great pains to send to you and to other friends. No one has answered me. Who knows what happens these days with letters and packages? Still, one doesn't despair and keeps trying. The time has come to send you words of thanks and a promise. My book is finally being printed, after I put it in what I take to be the best possible form. Printing has begun, to my great delight, and the books should be ready for shipping, I hope, sometime between Purim and Passover. God only knows when they will reach you—but this, too, will happen! A great deal of work went into the volume; I just about doubled the length of the manuscript you saw. It is a serious introduction and a guidebook to the Kabbalah, even if it does not offer a complete picture of its teaching and history. It should be of great interest to readers. [. . .]

The most important recent event is the death of my friend Walter Benjamin, who took his life while fleeing over the border from France to Spain. I'll never recover from this terrible blow. I received a detailed letter from Dr. Wiesengrund-Adorno, the only one in New York who still writes to me. I was able to surmise from his letter the awful depth of this tragedy. Benjamin was on his way to America; he had a visa, money, everything, along with a secure job at Horkheimer's institute in New York. And despite all this, he fell victim to scoundrels. It's a pity you didn't have the honor of meeting him, as I thought and hoped you would. I wanted to send him to you.

Life here proceeds along its old tracks. The direct threat to the country has been eliminated. We feel a great sense of relief after the English victory in the Egyptian and Libyan deserts.[86] The economic situation is of course bad, and in this respect there's a lot to worry about. Yet books and other things are still being produced. In this field, especially, a lot is happening. Schocken has published an almanac in Hebrew for the first time. Since he's in New York now, I hope he gives you a decent copy printed on good paper; our books are published on such bad paper that I don't dare send you one. There are a number of things in it from the "Scholem school." I'll send you an offprint of an essay on Sabbatai Sevi, which made an appearance in the almanac.[87] [. . .]

FROM BETTY SCHOLEM

Sydney, September 26, 1941

My dear son and Fanya,

[. . .] I'm still reading Heine's prose works. One of these days you really must put together a literary anthology of everything Heine ever said about the Bible, Jews, and Judaism. This would be a most interesting compilation, and of the greatest relevance! The philosophers, he said, do a lot of work for nothing. The world is one large cattle pen, though one that's not as easy to clean as the Augean stables because, during the shoveling, the oxen remain inside and the dung continues to pile up! What do you say about that! Well put, don't you think? [. . .]

Best wishes from your old mother

1942

FROM THEODOR ADORNO[88]

New York, February 19, 1942

The most important thing I have to write is that two suitcases with manuscripts and books of Walter's have reached us in New York. A friend of his, Dr. Dohmke, brought them over. He told us many things about the reasons for Walter's death, some of which sounded rather fantastic. According to Dohmke, Walter decided to take his life anyway and would have probably killed himself even if he had safely come to Lisbon. This is supposedly due partly to his fear of losing his independence and unique intellectual position he had in France (a consideration which of course is entirely baseless, since nobody ever thought of curtailing his originality in the least or of giving him any routine work), partly to an absolutely unimportant literary affair he had with a man called Krafft [*sic*], who incidentally now lives in Jerusalem (the issue is the priority of the discovery of Jochmann).[89] But all this cannot possibly explain what happened, and it remains as senseless and completely beyond any reconciliation as ever before. I made a complete catalogue of the content of these suitcases. It's much more complete in the later years than in Walter's earlier period. The most important pieces are a selection of exceedingly bold notes bearing the title "Central Park"[90] (a *double entendre* referring to the importance of these notes, as well as to his plans to come to New York), which evidently should be the nucleus for the last big section of the Baudelaire book which was never written. There are also the historico-philosophical theses of spring 1940, which you probably know.[91] There is, however, not a single trace of material from the *Passagenarbeit,* which doubtless exists somewhere. There are rumors that he has deposited this material at the Bibliothèque Nationale in Paris. There is a certain hope that they may hibernate there and that we can get hold of them after the war.[92] [. . .]

Is your book out? Please let me have it as soon as possible. The fact that you have completed a *chef d'oeuvre* is one of the very few positive things that I can find in life.

Sincerely yours, Adorno

TO THEODOR ADORNO

Jerusalem, March 27, 1942

Dear Herr Adorno,

[. . .] I'm very pained to hear that the letters I wrote you last spring have been lost. Since I kept copies, I can say that they contained a synopsis of Benjamin's literary legacy. I am of course very interested in the possibility of gathering all of his writings together in one safe spot in America, so that they can be published after the war. [. . .]

It would also be exceptionally important to compile his correspondence. In his early years, he must have had more than a few highly interesting exchanges with various people whom I know about; but these letters probably haven't been preserved. On the other hand, I can't imagine that somewhere there isn't a complete collection of his correspondence with Dora, Ernst Bloch (ugh—or do you perchance have a soft spot for this gentleman?), and others. I've saved all of the letters he wrote to me over the past twenty-five years, and assume that my letters to him will show up somewhere in his literary estate (only in three or four cases did I make copies). His letters to me number more than three hundred.[93] [. . .]

Gershom Scholem

TO DORA BENJAMIN

Jerusalem, April 1, 1942

Dear Dora,

During the past few weeks I've been thinking a great deal about Walter and about all that has been. I'm writing now to ask you (and I've wondered repeatedly whether I should) if you could set down on paper what you know about Walter's life. The importance of this dawned on me only after I myself began to ponder what I, if asked, could say about him. You must admit that—among those he left behind—after you, I'm the one who was most familiar with Walter's true self. But as the knowledge of every detail of his life becomes important, I now realize how little I know beyond the things that I myself experienced. The reasons for this are clear. Walter, as you remember, did not like to speak about himself to others, and I carefully respected this, particularly during the

period in which our friendship was closest. On top of this, I came to know him only after his decisive years in the youth movement. It would be a help if someone who knew him in those early days could write about him, both from within and from without. You are the only one who can do so, and I am also certain that you may and should. The unforgettable years 1912–1922 need to be preserved by those who have a right, as well as a duty and a calling, to do so. Of the people who were truly close to him at that time, only you and I are still alive. Let's be frank: Who knows how long we'll survive, given the apocalypse that we foresaw but that has now arrived? My dear Dora, you surely have a right to feel outraged that I'm making such a demand; I'm well aware of what happened to you.[94] But I'm still certain, if I may say so, that you of all people can find salvation through this very act of memory. It's for this reason, as well as for me and for all of Walter's future friends, that I make this request. You know the twists and turns of his life better than anyone else. You are the only one who *knew* his mysteries. Like the rest of us, you don't need to betray any confidences; you yourself know what should remain for you alone and what may be communicated to others. Walter would have turned fifty this year. Think of what you would say if you were to write something for his birthday. Do it only for Stefan, or for me. Don't forget that you are the only one who even knows the precise dates of the important events in his life. He told his story only to you. In sum, you would be doing something truly great if you were to describe those years and the people who inhabited Walter's world back then, in that period so utterly different from today.[95]
[. . .]

Warmest greetings, Your Gerhard

FROM BETTY SCHOLEM

6 Abbott Street, Coogee-Sydney; June 20, 1942

My dear son,

I'm worried because it's been so long since I've heard from the two of you. I got your last letter on February 2. I responded on February 5, February 23, March 13, and March 30, the last being the most important letter of all! Because for five months I haven't received the news I was waiting for, I myself let three months elapse between letters. It's getting harder and harder for me to write. My right eye has gotten worse, while the left one, the better one, has failed to improve. The worst part is that I can't read anything. But the newspapers don't bring me glad tidings anyway, and people fill me in on what's happening. Why don't you write to me in detail about Palestine? You're certainly permitted to do that. Here I'm dependent on word of mouth. For months I haven't received the *Hogoa-Blatt*.[96] In the last issue there was something about an attack on Dr. Simon, which is disgraceful. In an earlier letter I asked you about the sources of this harassment of Dr. S., but you never responded![97] [. . .]

Kisses to you and Fanya, Mum

1943

TO THEODOR ADORNO

Jerusalem, January 28, 1943

To the master of Los Angeles, and his wise wife:

[. . .] I would like to hear a couple of things from you. First, please tell me something about the condition and prospects of the Benjamin estate. Then, please tell me something about conditions where you are. I feel completely in the dark. What institute business has brought you to Los Angeles, on that distant coast? I see from your wife's brief note (which after more than two years gave me double pleasure!) that you at the institute are interested in anti-Semitism. I can only offer you my condolences. I regret to say that as a long-time historian I no longer think that social scientists can add anything relevant to the topic. I've become more and more convinced that only a metaphysician can contribute anything useful in this regard. [. . .]

What does Your Highness think of my book? Not even your wife, a Jewish child, has read it—even though the book, like every dialectical truth, would probably thrill her!! I had thought, in this regard, that your journal would include a review of it by the likes of Leo Strauss or Marcuse.[98] Didn't this ever cross your mind?

I am now writing a book (in Hebrew) on one of the major themes treated in my *Anglicum,* in the chapter on Sabbatianism.[99] I believe I mentioned this to you at one point in New York. Besides this, I'm doing quite well. I just finished a two-year stint as dean of the humanities faculty. Next year I won't have to sit on any committees. After the war I would like to go to America again for a year. I'm merely waiting for you to extend an invitation. [. . .]

FROM ADOLPH S. OKO[100]

December 13, 1943

Dear Dr. Scholem,

I must tell you that you have written a wonderful book, both in its contents and its architectonics. *Major Trends in Jewish Mysticism* is a creation—*eine Tat*. Accept the thanks of a reader. They come deep from the heart. Regrettably, we could not round up an adequate reader—unless we would have asked you to do the review. The current issue carries a review of your book contributed by Hans Kohn, who, however, writes around the book.[101] [. . .]

1944

TO ADOLPH S. OKO[102]

Jerusalem, March 26, 1944

Dear Mr. Oko,

It was a real pleasure to see your signature under the letter from the *Contemporary Jewish Record* dated December 13, 1943, which reached me only last week. I have often been thinking of you and wondering what you might be doing at this time. When I came to the United States six years ago you were not there, and we have lost a precious opportunity for some hearty and spirited talk. I consider this a great loss. Now I am very glad to learn that you have entered the publicistic arena again. I hope I have already identified you under your new signature in the last two numbers of the *Record* which reached Palestine. For the style is the man. It is only fair to say that I would have appreciated much more a review of my book coming from your hand, being that of a man with real philosophic intelligence and understanding—if you actually were unable to round up a so-called expert reviewer. You might have written whatever you liked about or against my book, and I would have enjoyed it much more than I will ever be able to take pleasure in the insignificant *schmus* of that everlasting *Ober-Quatscher*[103] who is known by the name of Hans Kohn. By Jove, that would have been the last man to make him write a review of my book. But in this world there is neither blushing nor shame, or whatever the right phrasing for this may be. Everybody in Judaistic America who is anybody has taken great care not to burn his fingers at my book. I was stupid enough to think my book a challenge to Jewish scholars, who have written so everlasting idiotic statements about Jewish mysticism, and I thought someone would feel obliged to answer that challenge—but all the wise men kept their peace. And as a great expert emerges Hans Kohn. I should add that I have not seen his review, as this number has not been received here; but "Der Zaddik lebt seinen Abneigungen,"[104] which constitutes a sound base for his faith. [. . .]

Do you happen to know Mrs. Hannah Blücher in New York?[105] I saw an article of hers some time ago in the *Record,* but I think that if you don't know her personally you should take the trouble to know

her. She is one of the best minds who have come over from Europe.
[. . .] She has sent me one of the two intelligent criticisms of my book
I have seen, and heaven knows why she did not print it. [. . .]

FROM ADOLPH OKO[106]

New York, May 25, 1944

This will interest you. I did not originally ask Hans Kohn to review your
book; I am, at least intuitively, too intelligent for that. I had asked Professor Irwin Edman of Columbia University to do the review—in the form
of a *causerie* or soliloquy, knowing that he could not discuss your opus
critically. But Edman was in Mexico at the time, and Kohn happened
to visit me just then. I was full of your book, and I mentioned it to
Kohn, and he entreated me to let him review it. Truth to tell, I didn't
know of any American Jewish scholar competent enough to review the
book adequately—Professor Ginzberg is a publishing rather than a writing scholar. Only you can do justice to the theme.

I know Hannah Blücher as Hannah Arendt. I fully share your opinion
of her, both as a mind and personality. She is a truly civilized being
indeed. It may amuse you to know that my first real talk with her was
about the Spinozist Count de Boulainvilliers—and G. Scholem.[107] [. . .]

I wish, dear Dr. Scholem, I could reciprocate your letter in kind.
Alas, your inimitable charm cannot be borrowed. So I can only thank
you for existing—and if you do not believe in existence, I thank you
for being.

FROM BETTY SCHOLEM

Coogee-Sydney, November 11, 1944

My beloved son,

The airmail will, I hope, bring you my birthday greetings on time,
four weeks from today. We all congratulate both of you. Stay happy
and healthy! The prospect of my visiting you has become weaker, even
if I haven't abandoned the thought altogether. Given the way this war
is being conducted, it could last another ten years—and a miracle is not
in the cards! Please think about whether I should come for a visit. [. . .]

You must have heard from Hedwig that Käte was deported some time back.[108] Hitler won't allow anyone to remain. We sent something through the Red Cross directly to Theresienstadt and gave a London address—packages are still allowed to be sent from there. I'm deeply saddened about my poor Käte. Will she survive? [. . .]

From your old mother

TO BETTY SCHOLEM

Jerusalem, November 19, 1944

Dear Mother,

[. . .] As I told you, all of us made it through the summer reasonably well. My body is only a bit weak and tired. To cure it, I spent two weeks with Fanya at a seaside resort on the Palestinian-Syrian border. Everyone was sorely disappointed that your son could swim and hence could not provide them with ammunition for bad jokes, kabbalistic cracks, and so on. It was so lovely there that I squandered the money I got from the three articles I wrote last summer instead of doing my book. Upon my return I got some sort of shot to boost my energy, and now I feel much better. Everyone agrees that I look wonderful.

I can't promise that your entry into Palestine will be easier if you become a naturalized British citizen. But I still think it's probably worth the trouble, since you just can't tell—it might make travel easier. Naturally, once the famous Jewish state has been established (which people have been talking about since Herzl but which none of you have done much to help pave the way for, as you yourself have rightly lamented), no attention will be paid to the color of the passports held by arriving Jewesses, young or old. I've placed my bets on the creation of a Jewish state, though I'm not at all sure it'll happen. In the meantime, as you know, we're heading toward civil war because our own people have set up shop and begun peddling terrorism. We've been obliged—justifiably—to clear out their stores, but this can't be done very simply without a host of casualties. [. . .]

We received your airmail letter from the twenty-second of October with the news of your sister's deportation. We'll check to see if packages can be sent from here; if they can, rest assured that we'll try to mail something. For now, it seems that correspondence by way of the Red Cross is absolutely impossible from here. But it's comforting to know that the Nazis use Theresienstadt as their so-called showcase, for display to the outside world. They give the Red Cross and others access, something which can only be dreamed of in the other deportation sites. This means that some minimum standards must be kept. [. . .]

Your devoted son, Gerhard

1945

TO BETTY SCHOLEM

Jerusalem, February 27, 1945

Dear Mother,

[. . .] With inflation running so high here, no one knows what's going to happen to prices. Will they will suddenly drop as soon as the market opens, or will they remain high? The people on fixed incomes suffer the most, as always. For this reason the packages from Erich were greatly appreciated. Those things would have cost several times as much here. If you'd like to send something else, Fanya would very much appreciate two pairs of pantyhose, size ten. They're nowhere to be found here. Over there, it seems as if they grow on trees. [. . .]

You wouldn't believe how many break-ins have been occurring throughout Jerusalem. We ourselves have escaped, as it were, with only a bloody nose. I told the booksellers of my suspicion that the antiquarian society had organized the robbery in order to get their hands on my library. If you recall the famous "fixed capital" from the time of inflation, the library is unfortunately (or, if you will, thank God) my only property, and I look upon it with as much love as booksellers do with lust. The setting sun[109] is still in its place, blessed be the name of the Lord. Although I could buy a watch for sixteen pounds, I could never manage to purchase a rug. Furniture now costs a fortune. [. . .]

In vain I've tried to remember which Jewish poet we visited together in Jerusalem. In any event it wasn't Sholem Asch, who never lived here.[110] [. . .] Probably you confused him with our friend Agnon, who writes not in Yiddish but in Hebrew, and who also writes much better prose than Herr Asch—whom I can't stand, independent of whether he's flirting with Jesus Christ.[111] This latter character, as you know, has always been in fashion among Jews. The latest result of this fondness, which is something I hope wasn't reported in your newspapers over there, occurred when the chief rabbi of Rome, a relative of our friend Meta Jahr, had himself baptized. You can just imagine the scandal. Nothing like this had ever happened before. The reason for his sudden discovery of the True Faith is as follows. When the Germans arrived, the chief rabbi behaved like a terrible coward and egomaniac. Instead of standing his ground, he went into hiding and let all the others pass through hell's fire. By the time he resurfaced and wanted to take up his old job as chief rabbi, he had lost all credibility among the Jews of Rome, who had suffered a great deal. No one wanted him back; and the upshot was this fine business. The only reason he won't become a cardinal is that he simultaneously baptized his wife. [. . .]

Your obedient son, Gerhard

Warmest greetings and best wishes to you from me as well.

Meta Flanter-Jahr

(Gerhard has ordered me to tell you that I have gotten married. As has my daughter—who looks just like me when I was eighteen and was making eyes at Gerhard.)

TO SHALOM SPIEGEL

Jerusalem, May 8, 1945

My dear friend,

I promised a long time ago to write, but I didn't keep my pledge. I neglected my letter-writing duties, in part because I was prey to a certain internal weakness but also in part because I looked forward to sending words of peace—and now I'm writing to you on victory day in this mighty cause.[112] I am alone in the house (my wife has gone to a spa in Tiberias for urgent treatment). I'm thinking back over the past six years, which came upon us like a storm bringing total devastation. It's difficult to greet this victory with a sense of jubilation, since everyone else has won; we alone have lost. And on this day of stocktaking, there are endless bitter thoughts directed at ourselves and others. Yet despite everything, something new yet at the same time old has come into the world. To be sure, the Messiah has not come and the world goes on as usual. But at least we've achieved one thing: good and evil will now be intertwined, as they were formerly, and it will at least be *possible* once again to fight *as effectively* for the good. It'll be a long time before the dark days return—the days when it was said, "For, lo, thine enemies make a tumult, and they that hate thee have lifted up their head" (I chose this psalm ages ago as my private liturgy for victory day).[113] We cannot expect anything more than this. The wrestling match will start from the beginning; and the essence of our "success" lies in the fact that it can begin at all. [. . .]

Over the summer I hope to complete my major study of Sabbatianism, which I've repeatedly postponed. I and my dear students have come up with a multitude of new things in this field! Three months ago I came across a volume in the National Library whose real character I had never recognized before. It's a 600-page work called *Sefer ha-Zoreph,* by Rabbi Heschel Zoreph (Rabbi Adam Baal-Shem) of Vilna. This was a great find, in my opinion, and I now sit and ruin my eyesight reading its minuscule print. I've amassed a mountain of materials on Sabbatianism since embarking on my "march of conquest" in this area of study! A number of things still await us, lurking in places we don't expect. Apropos of this, I recently sent you a copy of the letter I wrote to Isaiah Sonne two months ago in response to the bizarre gibes he aimed at me and at the new research into the Kabbalah.[114] I did so to let you know what I think. I didn't want to make a public rejoinder, but neither did I want to keep completely silent. I don't understand this man and his rancor. [. . .]

Yours, Gershom Scholem

TO THEODOR ADORNO

Jerusalem, July 4, 1945

My dear Herr Adorno,

Having heard nothing from you for three years, I was delighted this morning to receive the journal issue dedicated to the memory of Walter Benjamin.[115] Hannah Arendt had already told me to expect it. I interpreted the parsimonious note attached to it—"Greetings from A."—as coming from you, and wanted to convey my thanks for the package without delay. I read your essay (or at least a piece I immediately ascribed to you) on George and Hofmannsthal with enormous interest and would like to offer some comments on it. It made a great impression on me. If, as I suspect, you included it in the volume to show your indebtedness to Benjamin's way of seeing, my opinion is you've clearly succeeded. Please don't take it amiss that I, a despondent non-Marxist, initially thought your analysis gave evidence of a syndrome I had often pointed out to Benjamin (in whom it was very clearly pronounced): your anarchistic élan and tendencies, which have led you to so many deep insights, didn't seem to fit under the same roof with the method you had chosen. As I read through the piece, however, much of this impression disappeared. For if one interprets Marxism in Benjamin's sense as an esoteric method of true theology, then much can be said for the *sacrificium* demanded by the method—especially the *sacrificium* that appears to forbid the dialectical explosion of the concept of society as a sphere of immanence (a high price to pay on the part of philosophers, for whom the work of "critical theory," if I understand it correctly, contains an element of "dynamite held in reserve"). Your presentation of a specific social dialectic beyond the realm of clichés, which have plagued discussions regarding both gentlemen,[116] is extraordinarily exciting. Even more exciting to me were Benjamin's theses, which are in truth an encoded will and testament that only a poetic metaphysician like Edgar Allen Poe could come up with. Did the people over there have anything to say when they read it? Did people even read it? [. . .]

Yours, Gerhard Scholem

TO HANNAH ARENDT

Jerusalem, August 6, 1945

Dear Hannah,

The good example we vowed to give each other has quickly degenerated into a terrible standstill. Your letter from the thirty-first of March, which I received some time ago, still lies unanswered and weighs heavily upon my conscience. The reasons for this are many: health, commitments, and all manner of delays. But none of these things can exonerate me. Meanwhile, Kurt Blumenfeld[117] sauntered into my study and told me (insofar as his diffuse way of speaking allows) many enchanting things about you and relayed from you all sorts of greetings. I tried to follow carefully what he said, but this was, as you can well imagine, not easy. In general, he's very charming and now and then comes up with comments of astonishing intuition and intellectual force. But amid all this stands a total wreck of a man who has collapsed into himself, focused on himself, and who analyzes contemporary world events through a few too many tears. Still, he often remains above the standard of his friends, which should make you wonder. He appears to be completely taken with you and your husband. The other things he said about America were not cheerful.

I got your essay on minorities, though not your piece on the revision of Zionist theory, which perhaps has not come out yet.[118] Please indulge my bibliographic urges and kindly send me whatever you write. Thank God I read English better than you do Hebrew. It remains to be seen whether I'll be able to steal a copy of your dissertation from Hans Jonas. He's still a sergeant in the brigade,[119] but will be demobilized within six weeks and will move back to Jerusalem from Italy. He wrote me a letter full of heroic sentiments. [. . .]

Four weeks ago I received the Benjamin issue from the institute, along with a very laconic dedication from Wiesengrund. I thank you for this, since I ascribe it to your efforts. For years I've heard nothing from Wiesengrund, and I don't know why. At the beginning there was no end to his solemn declarations of friendship; then, suddenly, total silence. I sent him a letter right after I got the journal. His essay on George is truly interesting, though endlessly convoluted and in part even malicious in its misinterpretation. He obviously lacks something Benjamin had—namely, a feeling for poetry. In general, the technical jargon that was used so heavily by all the issue's contributors turned my stomach. I have no idea what will happen with Benjamin's literary estate. Now that the war is over, serious thought can be devoted to this. Has anyone in Paris looked into the papers that his sister had with her? (She's died in the meantime.) I spoke to Arthur Koestler about it. He may be a very gifted writer, yet as a person he's such a *mauvais sujet* and so repulsive that, after our first renewed contact, I even dropped the idea of inviting him to my home. I've met with him twice to discuss Benjamin. You know that they lived in the same house. But he cast such aspersions on Benjamin's character that I saw right away he was a fellow completely infatuated with own greatness, someone who uses others only as a backdrop for himself. At that point I gave up. My wife managed to insult him deeply. He apparently knows nothing about the literary estate. He said that Benjamin gave him half of his morphine. It's a pity Benjamin wasn't more generous, for in Lisbon your friend Koestler swallowed what he had and vomited it up again. A healthy young man! His book on the Moscow trials is the only thing I find admirable about him.[120]

You ask about my writing. I'm in the middle of a number of interesting things in Hebrew. They won't do you much good, though they will advance scholarship. Also, this coming summer I have to stay here and work on the second edition of *Major Trends,* which will probably come out next year in America in expanded form, most likely in two volumes. [. . .]

Detailed reports from Europe are now arriving here. The concrete effect this will have on the individuals concerned is of course much worse than the widespread knowledge of mass murder. The destructive impact of this information on people's minds and souls is enormous; but there is no way to avoid it, even though everyone says that ignorance in such matters is better than knowledge. [. . .]

Yours, G.S.

TO HANNAH ARENDT

Jerusalem, December 16, 1945

My dear friend,

Your letter from the twenty-second of September arrived after a considerable delay. Since then I, too, have been terribly negligent, allowing weeks to pass before sitting down to answer it. I'm making up for this now by sending you a friendly gift in today's mail, enclosed in a regular envelope. It consists of two of Walter's essays: the piece on Hölderlin's poems "Dichtermut" and "Blödigkeit," and the one on Franz Kafka.[121] (For the time being, these are just for you; but if you have the time, you might see about getting them published.) I'm sending them to you first and not to the institute because of Wiesengrund's baffling behavior (for nearly four years he didn't write, and then a few months ago he sent me the institute's memorial issue with a mere one-line inscription), and also because of your own sympathetic remarks on the mysterious way in which the institute is sitting on the literary estate, to the degree that it is in the institute's possession. As a novice in such things, I'd be very grateful if you could educate me about its legal status. Who owns the rights to Benjamin's unpublished manuscripts that are held not by the institute but by me, you, or somebody else? [. . .]

From March 1 to November 1 of next year I will take my so-called sabbatical. Originally I wanted to go to England, to wind up my archival research. After serious reflection, however, I think it's far more vital that I use this precious time to do as much writing as possible. In particular, it's more important that I finally complete my major—and long over-due—study of Sabbatianism than to wade through fifty more manu-scripts which, at the end of the day, are unlikely to yield anything very revolutionary. So I'm looking forward to a productive period, either here or (in case this proves better for my concentration) on Cyprus. Of course there's no knowing whether at the last moment politics (a topic about which you and I are probably in tearful agreement) will annihilate these noble plans with a roar of cannon fire and a hail of bullets. Still, for the time being things are much quieter than many people predicted, given the prevailing mood of intense bitterness toward England. I think I said something of the sort in an earlier letter. If the English don't do anything too provocative—and naturally no one can know with any certainty whose hands are really pulling the strings behind the scenes—my hunch is that the winter will pass without any major incidents. What counts for a lot in this, I believe, is the general feeling that the country isn't even equipped to absorb the very masses we carry on about in our resolutions. If Mr. Truman's 100,000 Jews legally poured into the coun-try tomorrow, we'd have a catastrophe on our hands.[122] While such mea-sures naturally do nothing to quench the thirst for action among our young people, they do play a considerable role in the thinking of many citizens.

Schocken has arrived and has been sitting around for a couple months without making any decisions. After two months of negotiations and discussions with me, he still hasn't made up his mind to guarantee five more years of financing for my Kabbalah institute. He comes out with a lot of high-flown nonsense. All things considered, he's not dumb; it's just hopeless to expect that the fellow will change. My complaints to him on matters pertaining to Hannah Blücher must have reached you all the way over in New York. But these days a nature formed by the world of Zwickau is beyond refashioning.[123] At some point in the future I hope to be able send to you, *gratis* and *franco,* an analysis of this remark-able character. [. . .]

Yours, G.S.

1946

TO HANNAH ARENDT

Jerusalem, January 28, 1946

My dear friend,

I received the articles you sent, as well as the issue of the *Menorah Journal*. Many thanks. I find myself in the extraordinarily unpleasant position of having to give you my opinion on the essay "Zionism Reconsidered," though I don't in the slightest wish to have a fatal falling out with you.[124] It's impossible for me to offer detailed discussion of all the many issues I could raise concerning an article which disappointed me so profoundly and which, to tell you the truth, somewhat embittered me. Please don't be offended if I express myself trenchantly.

While I basically agreed with your starting position in the first paragraph, I read the elaboration of your argument while vigorously shaking my head. In vain I asked myself what sort of credo you had in mind when you wrote it. Your article has nothing to do with Zionism but is instead a patently anti-Zionist, warmed-over version of Communist criticism, infused with a vague *galut* nationalism. You denounce Jews in Palestine for maintaining an otherworldly separation from the rest of mankind, but when these same Jews make efforts to fend for themselves, in a world whose evil you yourself never cease to emphasize, you react with a derision that itself stems from some otherworldly source. The structure of your arguments is extremely odd, and the whole displays such inconsistency of scale and perspective that I can make sense of it only by viewing it as an assemblage pieced together by someone who wishes to disavow the "reactionary" concerns of Zionism. Herzl's reactionary personality; the shameless exploitation of anti-Semitism for the sake of Zionist propaganda; the accursed theory of eternal anti-Semitism; the otherworldly sectarianism of aristocratic kibbuzim which don't give a damn about the fate of the Jewish people; the arrogance of this entire Palestinian project vis-à-vis the question of the Jewish people as a whole; the worn-out opinion that the organization of a community into a state continues to make sense in an age of international federations; the flirtation with Hitler through the transfer agreement and the scandalous undermining of the boycott;[125] and finally the utter mindlessness of Zionists toward Jewish history, a subject they should know more about—all this, my dear friend, is a lovely assortment of anti-Zionist arguments. In order to prove my claim that your essay is—*sit venia verbo*[126]—an act of political balderdash, I would really have to go into specifics. Instead I can only register my vigorous protest against your "better insights" and "self-criticism." Of course, there are many points on which Zionist politics are completely wrong, and you focus quite rightly upon these weak points. You do this, however, not from a Zionist perspective but from one propped up by obviously Trotskyite, anti-Zionist arguments [. . .]

I am a nationalist and am wholly unmoved by ostensibly "progressive" denunciations of a viewpoint that people repeatedly, even in my earliest youth, deemed obsolete. I believe in what can be called, in human terms, the "eternity" of anti-Semitism. Nor can any of the clever inquiries into the roots of anti-Semitism ever prevent it from generating new crusades in perpetually new constellations. I am a "sectarian" and have never been ashamed of expressing in print my conviction that sectarianism can offer us something decisive and positive. I don't give a rap about the problem of the state, because I do not believe that the renewal of the Jewish people depends on the question of their political or even social organization. My own political credo is, if anything, anarchistic. But I cannot blame the Jews if they ignore so-called progressive theories which no one else in the world has ever practiced. Even though I have a clear notion of the vast differences between partition and a binational state, I would vote with the same heavy heart for either of these two solutions. Yet you make fun of both with truly astonishing ignorance. The Arabs have not agreed to a single solution that includes Jewish immigration, whether it be federal, national, or binational. I am convinced that the conflict with the Arabs would be far easier to deal with after a *fait accompli* such as partition than it would be without it. In any event, I have no idea how the Zionists could go about obtaining an agreement with the Arabs, even though each and every one of us came to this country without any agreement—and if we were still on the outside waiting to enter the country, we would still be prepared to come. Unfortunately, it is by no means idiotic when the Zionist politicians declare that, given the sabotage efforts made by the British administration, there is no chance of reaching any kind of understanding, however formulated. Certainly, as an old Brit Shalom follower, I myself have heard the precise opposite argued. But I am not presumptuous enough to think that the politics of

Brit Shalom wouldn't have found precisely the same Arab opponents, who are primarily interested not in the morality of our political convictions but in whether or not we are here in Palestine at all. [. . .]

Allow me to conclude with a comment on the phraseology of "reaction," which plays a role in your thinking. The moral debacle of socialism, which is unparalleled in the history of the past generation (since fascism, as is implied in the fact that it wanted to eliminate morality altogether, had no moral idea to defend), has created such confusion over what is reactionary and what is progressive that I can no longer make any sense out of these notions. Everyone today is a reactionary, quite often for a completely defensible reason. Moreover, the willingness to go to any length to avoid falling into this category, a willingness apparent on every page of your essay, is one of the most depressing phenomena to be seen among clever Jews. It hits me each time I read *Partisan Review*, which you yourself send me. I feel free enough in my thinking not to be disturbed when I'm accused of holding reactionary opinions—opinions that can easily be demonstrated by pointing not only to my professed religious sentiments but also to my conviction that the social revolution, however desirable it may be, has less to do with the Messiah than commonly thought. I consider it abundantly obvious (and I hardly need emphasize this to you) that the political career of Zionism within this exclusively reactionary world of ours has created a situation full of despair, doubt, and compromise—precisely because it takes place on earth, not on the moon. About this I have no illusions whatsoever. The Zionist movement shares this dialectical experience of the Real (and all its catastrophic possibilities) with all other movements that have taken it upon themselves to change something in the real world. [. . .]

And if I may duly and respectfully mention this as well, the cynicism with which you used lofty and progressive arguments against something that is for the Jewish people of life-or-death importance is unlikely to persuade me to abandon the sect. I never dreamed that it would be easier for me to agree with Ben Gurion than with you! But after reading your essay, I have no doubt about this. I consider Ben Gurion's political line disastrous, but at the same time it's much more noble—or a lesser evil—than the one we would have if we followed your advice. [. . .]

Being a long-time religious reactionary, I hope for your repentance—or, as old Buber has rendered it in his marvelous style—your "return."[127]

With the warmest and most resolute conviction (resolute not to be made a fool of!).

Yours, G.S.

FROM BETTY SCHOLEM[128]

Sydney, February 17–20, 1946

My dear son,

Yesterday I received your letter from the eighth. I still have not received an answer to my letters of December 15 and January 20. On the twentieth of January I sent Fanya a pair of pantyhose, enclosed in a regular envelope. [. . .]

Once every two weeks Arthur picks me up at Erich's,[129] and in the evening Erich comes to get me in his car. It's wonderfully comfortable! On alternating weekends I spend three days in Carlton. Last week I extended it to five days owing to a case of diarrhea, which was nearly epidemic around here because of the sudden shifts in weather. Reinhold then came with his old Ford and drove yours truly back home. [. . .]

A kiss to my beloved children, Mum

FROM HANNAH ARENDT

New York, April 21, 1946

Dear Gerhard,

[. . .] If you had any knowledge of the relevant literature, you would yourself consider the claim that this article is a "warmed-over Communist critique" rather curious. Obviously, you reached such a conclusion not because of my essay but because of my work with *Partisan Review*—which is today one of the best-known literary journals here, and has nothing whatsoever to do with Trotskyism. [. . .] As for me, I have never been a Marxist (nor have I ever been "dialectical"). People here generally regard me as an anti-Marxist, which is far closer to the truth. [. . .]

I have always considered your position as a Jew to be a political one, and I've always had the greatest respect for your decision to take the political reality of Palestine seriously. To be honest, not even in my dreams did it ever occur to me that you had a Zionist worldview as a result of your political involvement. Perhaps because deep down I hoped that you didn't. [. . .]

You have no choice but to look on me with consternation, for in my case repentance can hardly be expected. And if I may say so, the Buber citation won't work very well either. The more pertinent question seems to me how we will get along after this orgy of truth-telling. I really didn't take the least offense from your letter, though I have no idea how you will respond to mine. When all is said and done, you are *masculini generis,*[130] and for this reason naturally (perhaps) vulnerable. For God's sake, despite this letter, I've never considered myself a "fanatic for truth"! For me, human relationships are far more important than "heart-to-heart talks." In this particular case you have demanded more provocation from me than is reasonable and fair. Maybe you can bring yourself to follow my example here: know that a human being is far more valuable than his opinions, for the simple reason that humans are *de facto* much more than what they think or do.

Hannah

FROM HANNAH ARENDT

New York, May 20, 1946

Dear Gerhard,

If you find yourself in Berlin, go and see Ernst Grumach, who lives at 53 Schlüter Strasse. He knows more than anyone else about the handling of Jewish libraries in Berlin because the Gestapo commissioned him for the task. Grumach is also an old friend of mine, though since 1930 I haven't had any contact with him. He's a good philologist and knows something about Judaica.

Hannah

TO LEO BAECK[131]

Zurich,[132] June 2, 1946

Highly esteemed Herr Baeck,

I am on a mission on behalf of the university, and was sent to Europe at the beginning of April. My task is to clarify the situation of Jewish libraries and book collections that fell into the hands of the Nazis and are now scattered in various places. As I traveled through London on April 12–13, I tried to reach you but unfortunately had no success. No one answered the phone; apparently you'd left on a trip. I had to continue on to Paris at once, but thought I'd have a chance to return to London to get your personal feedback on the political line which the university is thinking of pursuing with respect to these collections. Then everything got dragged out in Paris, and on top of it all we had considerable difficulty obtaining a visa to get to London. I should be heading to Germany and Czechoslovakia, but the military authorities in the occupied countries have raised large obstacles. They are following their own policies concerning the fate of these libraries, and the policies don't seem to be particularly advantageous to the Jews. In any case, they obviously view a mandate by the university in Jerusalem with the greatest antipathy. I'm not at all certain it will be possible to overcome this resistance. So far as I can tell, the American policy basically aims to return the vestiges of the Jewish collections, particularly those in Offenbach, to the governments of those countries where they originated—and not, say, to the Jewish people or their representatives. This means that a great many books will disappear back into Russia and Poland. We mustn't have any illusions about the future fate of these collections. The libraries in Germany will either remain in the American zone or will be shipped to the United States pending a final resolution. In practice, nothing much seems to have been done to carry out this policy; still, the general line seems certain.

Dr. Magnes is now in the United States, working to create a unified representative body drawn from all relevant Jewish institutions. Such a body will be able to approach the highest echelons of the American government without being hampered by competition and contradictory demands. It could request that all collections whose legal owners no longer exist or can't be identified be delivered over to Jewish institutions. The university's viewpoint in all of this is that Jerusalem should be considered the spiritual heir and successor of the central European institutions destroyed during the catastrophe that befell our people. The university makes no claims of ownership, nor does it have the slightest intention of violating any legitimate interest of persons or institutions that still exist in reality and whose reconstitution is not just a sham. The university wishes to be recognized as a trustee of these collections, and is prepared to assume all of the duties and responsibilities associated with this. We realize that everything does not belong in Jerusalem or Palestine and that equally legitimate arguments could be made for America. We hope that Dr. Magnes can come to a friendly agreement over the eventual control of these collections. [. . .]

I turn to you today to ask for your help with an aspect of this mission. It so happens that while I was in Switzerland I had the opportunity to travel directly to Prague and enter into discussions on the fate of the extensive holdings, mostly from public Jewish libraries, that had been left by the Nazis. You must be familiar with them. Apparently, these holdings consist of rather large Hebrew and Judaica collections in Prague and Pressburg that did not originate from Czechoslovakia but were transported there. In accordance with my official mission, I would like to persuade the Jewish organizations there to hand these books over to the trusteeship of the Hebrew University, without of course harming legitimate claims of ownership. We fear that otherwise these libraries will eventually be confiscated by the Czech government on some legal technicality and thus will no longer be available for the vital work of Jewish scholarship. And it is precisely the productive use of these collections, for the spiritual work within Judaism and in its most decisive centers, that has motivated us to take these steps.

I would be extraordinarily grateful if you would support the university's trusteeship of the remains of Jewish collections from Germany now in Czechoslovakia.

Sincerely yours, G. Scholem

TO SIEGMUND HURWITZ[133]

Prague, June 8, 1946

Dear Herr and Frau Hurwitz,

Everyone has left Prague for the three-day Pentecost holiday, and I'm sitting here in a hotel, feeling a bit lost and studying the catalog of 30,000 books (Hebraica) transported from Theresienstadt to Prague. The work is very time-consuming. It would perhaps be more pleasant to stroll around Prague, though that's easier said than done for a foreigner with no knowledge of the language. And you can't even buy a tour guide here in French or English! [. . .]

Yesterday I walked alone for an hour through the old Jewish cemetery. It filled me with inexpressible emotion, and I could not hold back my tears. I fear nothing will remain here but the cemetery and a synagogue, which has now become a museum. [. . .]

Yours, Gerhard Scholem

TO THE HEBREW UNIVERSITY[134]

Munich, July 29, 1946

I am writing to you shortly before leaving Munich for Berlin, where I expect to stay for some time. I shall have to decide whether or not to go into the British Zone.

To my great distress, I found out in Frankfurt that the whole Hebraica collection of the Municipal Library, the most valuable collection in Germany, was burned during an air raid on the sixteenth of March, 1944. The Judaica and Hebraica have been saved. I spoke to the newly appointed socialist director of this Municipal Library (Eppelsheimer) about the question of the initiative being taken by German authorities for the secession of these Hebrew manuscripts and part of the Judaica. He was very sympathetic and willing to consider it with his municipal authorities. To put such a proposal through would, of course, require much time. Naturally, our position with regard to Frankfurt is a relatively simple one, since all these objects were paid for by Jews.

This is not the case with regard to the Hebrew manuscripts in the Munich State Library, where the famous Code 95 of the Talmud is to be found. Whereas nothing else is left in Munich of any Jewish collection and no trace of it is as yet available, the Hebraica collection and the Hebrew manuscripts of the State Library have been saved.

I have had discussions with several people of important connections with the Bavarian government, which is the legal owner of the objects and has taken the same line as in Frankfurt. I said that it might be an important moral gesture if the German authorities, of their own free will, would turn over certain of these objects, and especially the Munich manuscripts of the Talmud, to the Hebrew University in Jerusalem as a symbolic act toward the Jewish people and as a first step toward bridging the awful abyss that has been created between the two peoples.

I have a very reliable and influential man in Munich who is willing to act as mediator to induce the Bavarian government to take steps in this direction. This is Professor Hans Ludwig Held, director of the Municipal Library. He and other people who have taken an interest in the matter are asking me, "What would be the answer from Jerusalem to such a symbolic gesture of good will on the part of the Germans?" They do not want to be "spit in the face" by a provocative answer. [. . .]

Best regards and greetings to our friends.

Yours very tired, Gerhard Scholem

TO DR. SHARP[135]

Berlin, August 4, 1946

[. . .] Only recently I have come across important information and I should like you and all those concerned among our friends to take very serious and immediate action on the following matter.

I know definitively that the most important part of the German Jewish libraries, several hundred thousand volumes, have been sent by the SS in Berlin (12 Eisenacher Strasse, office 7) for safekeeping to Schloss Niemes, near Reichenberg and Möhmisch Leipa. The names are now in the Czech language: Castle Nimon, near Liberec and Cesha Lipa.

I have talked to the man who sent the books away. This is Dr. Grunach, a Jew and a very reliable man who was forced to work for the Gestapo library in Berlin.

We have two witnesses who say that they have been to the castle after liberation and the books were still there. If these books are still there now and have not been taken away by the Russians or the Czechs or somebody else, it would be one of the, nay, the most important things in my mission, and we must include them in the action for transfer into trusteeship of the Hebrew University. [. . .]

Yours truly, G. Scholem

TO SIEGMUND HURWITZ

Jerusalem, November 1, 1946

Dear Herr Dr. and Frau Hurwitz,

[. . .] The trip through Germany was as depressing as it was interesting. There was scarcely anything cheerful to see. I traveled a lot, and my meetings with people both inside and outside the camps were quite moving. In Offenbach there are still plenty of books that will eventually revert to the Jewish people, even if the really valuable things did *not* fall into the Americans' hands. Many things were burned in the air raids— far more than I initially thought. [. . .]

Sincerely yours, Gershom Scholem

1947

TO SIEGMUND HURWITZ

Jerusalem, October 24, 1947

Dear Herr Dr. Hurwitz,

I was away for some weeks, on vacation in Naharija (according to the new diction of partition and political reorganization, it's now called "Little Yekka-stan").[136] I found your letter waiting for me when I returned on September 14. [. . .]

The question of whether I can take advantage of your invitation to Ascona[137] unfortunately depends not only on the political situation here (the birth pangs of the Jewish state?), but above all on the severe currency restrictions. I would very much like to come, together with my wife. It's doubtful, though, that we could obtain permission to go abroad by paying money (which we don't even have, but assuming we did) for a plane ticket to a company based outside the Pound Zone. But it's too early to lose sleep over this now. All eyes are naturally turned toward the negotiations at the UN. That after thirty years England would ultimately betray Zionism in classic fashion and would set everything in motion in order to liquidate it (and therefore us); and that, with one powerful *salto mortale,* a country such as Russia which until now wanted nothing to do with Zionism would emerge on the stage, alongside the United States, as its great champion *against* the land that signed the Balfour Declaration— these things should be a good lesson for political souls! Who would have expected it? The "secret" to the riddle is of course obvious: we've suddenly become kosher and interesting to the Russians *because* England has broken with us. *Timeo Danaos et dona ferentes.*[138]

G. Scholem

TO HUGO AND ESCHA BERGMANN[139]

Jerusalem, December 15, 1947

My friends Escha and Hugo,

Many thanks for your warm wishes on my birthday. And thank you, above all, for Hugo's essay. I'm not sure whether I have it in me to fulfill Hugo's demands.[140] In fact, I rather doubt it. I no longer believe in direct "messages," nor can I find among the "messengers" anyone who could have brought some blessing. I tend to believe that it is precisely this naive appeal to others—as if it were possible now, at this hour, to repeat in new and different words the truth, "He hath shown thee, O man, what is good"[141]—that lies behind the failure of such attempts, even when they're not cloaked in Buber's phony Elijah mantle. Of course, it is true that if the Jewish state is granted us and is not submerged at the outset in a sea of blood, then the question of Judaism and of Jewish tradition will be raised in its ultimate and sharpest form. Who knows what will happen, or what direction the Jews will take in their own state? I live in despair and can be active only out of despair. Sometimes I'm amazed by how quickly a man such as Magnes—whose honesty clearly far exceeds that of Buber—seems to have forgotten his quarrels with the Holy One (Blessed be He) and begins making appeals to a form of knowledge that contradicts our knowledge. Oh, how easy it is to tell *others* to rely upon God! I'm outraged each time I hear this preached.

There was great excitement here in the country. In general, it must be said not only that the members of Mapai won a great victory, but that even after the Declaration they demonstrated a large measure of understanding and praiseworthy caution.[142] The Haganah still practices the rule of "measured response," a discipline that without question bodes well for the future. Given the course of things, though, it doesn't look as if we can keep this up for long. You've no idea how much hostility the English have provoked among the population in recent weeks; it's not easy to maintain *sophrosyne*.[143]

If events continue to develop as they have, it will be doubtful indeed if we can keep up a normal academic life at the university. All manpower will most certainly be mobilized for the great trial of strength (and there will be one) after Passover. Great surprises are of course always possible. It may well be that this entire "war" will last only a few weeks—for who knows what's developing behind the scenes?

My birthday was celebrated in the shadow of these mighty events. All of my pupils sat themselves down and composed more or less proper essays to honor the occasion. My pupil Weiss occupied himself with the same question that Hugo raised—namely, which form of camouflage do I practice when I do what is called scholarship? It's a very nice and audacious essay.[144] You can see that my pupils have learned something from me, and in this respect I can't complain. I got a mountain of marzipan! [. . .]

PART IV **MASTER MAGICIAN EMERITUS, 1948–1982**

Scholem in his study in Jerusalem, 1976. Photo by Aliza Auerbach. Courtesy of the Jewish National and University Library, Jerusalem, Gershom Scholem Archive (Arc. 4o 1599).

✦

I do not claim to have any kind of mission or calling; I don't harbor the slightest illusion about the endless challenges to human behavior that are posed by terrorism; and I am enough of a Jew to bear in mind the old saying from the Mishna: don't judge your neighbor until you've been in his shoes.

—Letter to Gotthard Koschel, July 4, 1960

SCHOLEM'S REPUTATION began to spread far beyond Europe and Palestine after 1945, when *Major Trends in Jewish Mysticism* was published in America. The book united a dazzling command of the textual sources with a supple literary style to demonstrate to a large nonprofessional readership the centrality of messianic mysticism in the course of Jewish history. Many of the leading intellectuals of the day—Theodor Adorno, Hannah Arendt, and Leo Strauss, among many others—applauded *Major Trends* as a masterpiece.

Scholem's status as an international academic celebrity began in earnest in the 1950s. In 1949 he began to make yearly forays to Switzerland to attend Carl Jung's Eranos conferences, giving him a distinguished platform for his ideas. In 1957 he completed his magnum opus, the Hebrew original of a book that would later bear the English title *Sabbatai Sevi: The Mystical Messiah*. Ironically, nowhere did Scholem's name gain more renown than in his native Germany. In 1970 the illustrious German publishing house Suhrkamp Verlag began to issue a multivolume series of his essays called *Judaica*. The last three decades of his life brought many tributes and awards, including membership in the order Pour le Mérite, the highest honor the German government can bestow.

Scholem did not attain his towering stature solely because of his research into the Kabbalah; after all, few could properly assess his contributions to such an esoteric field. Perhaps more central to his fame were his autobiographical works, written in the last two decades of his life.

But even such widely read books as *From Berlin to Jerusalem: Memories of My Youth* and *Walter Benjamin: The Story of a Friendship* did not create the Scholem legend; at most, they confirmed and deepened it. A comment made by the philosopher Hans Jonas following Scholem's death comes closest to the mark: as Jonas said to Fanya Scholem, her husband's passing marked the "end of an era."[1]

In the postwar years Gershom Scholem became the living embodiment of German Jewry—of its formidable talents, as well as its tragedy and its determined survival. His prolific scholarship buoyed a world still sunk in disbelief at the monstrous effects of Nazi anti-Semitism. Against this bleak backdrop, Scholem portrayed Judaism as a living, dynamic tradition equal in power and profundity to any other. Scholem himself came to resemble many of the great exegetes he discussed in his work; his peculiarly allusive method, and the terrible context in which this allusive writing appeared, fostered a new Jewish historical consciousness that was able to absorb and overcome disaster. As a result of his international status, Scholem's views on issues ranging from the Eichmann trial to the "German-Jewish symbiosis" often set the tone for interpretations of the recent past. He coined the phrases and established the moral parameters that people needed in order to interpret what he called simply "the Catastrophe." And because he did so with such eloquence and power, he became the spokesman of a Jewry that not only had endured but that continued to flourish.

After the war, Scholem had more on his mind than fame. On behalf of the Hebrew University, he spent much of 1946 and part of 1948 in war-ruined France, Germany, Czechoslovakia, and Poland. He crisscrossed Europe, surveying the state of surviving Jewish institutions. His task was to transport Jewish libraries to Palestine. Given his extraordinary love for books and what he called his "sharp nose" *(Spürsinn),* worthy of a detective, he was ideally suited for the job. He succeeded in tracking down entire libraries and shipping them to Palestine. Success came at a price, though; he described his work of assessing the terrible losses and salvaging the remains of a once-vibrant culture as the "most bitter months of my life."[2]

Nor did returning to Palestine offer him much respite from tragedy. While Europe was slowly recovering from war, Palestine itself was descending into conflict. Arab terror and British repression marked the immediate postwar years. Often, illegal refugees from European death camps found themselves once again behind barbed wire, interned by the Mandatory forces—treatment which only fanned the hostility of Jews toward the British. An underground Jewish terrorist organization emblazoned Scholem's neighborhood with posters inciting rebellion against the Yishuv's erstwhile benefactors. There were assassinations, executions, bombings.

A civil war finally broke out in 1947. When the Arabs rejected the partition of Palestine and the British agreed to withdraw from the country, the Yishuv pursued a war of independence. Freedom was costly, however. One percent of the population died; large parts of Jerusalem were laid waste; and the entire eastern section of the city, including Mount Scopus and the campus of the Hebrew University, fell under Arab control.

Scholem, an old critic of Ben Gurion and the Labor party, applauded the birth of the State of Israel in May 1948. Yet he never ceased to exercise his right to censure, decrying "insolent boasting" and "nationalistic phrases."[3] His solid patriotism, liberalism, and basic attitude of loyal opposition resembled (albeit in a very different context) what his father's had been in Germany. Arthur Scholem had been a "German," with all the failings and paradoxes implied by this term; his rebellious son became an "Israeli."

Scholem's real passion remained scholarship, not politics. To most contemporaries, he resembled the archetypal apolitical professor. Now, with Mount Scopus behind enemy lines, he walked to the new university campus—housed principally in a converted Catholic monastery—around the corner from his house. He rarely had to leave Rehavia; and when he did, it was mostly to attend academic conferences abroad.

In 1949 he left his apartment in the care of his friends the Agnons (whose own house had been pillaged during the war) and traveled with Fanya to New York. From there—as was so often the case with German-Jewish intellectuals at the time—he went to the University of Chicago, where his friend Leo Strauss taught. On the way back to Israel he stopped off in Switzerland to attend Gustav Jung's annual Eranos conference.

During the last three decades of his life, Scholem continued to teach, travel, and generate a constant stream of publications. Teaching brought mixed rewards. As his eminence grew from year to year, so did the respect he engendered—and the fear. The exacting scholar made the highest demands on his students, and few could pass muster. "The Catastrophe," he wrote of the Holocaust, had "cut off the branch" which had upheld the Jews. The great human reservoir of Jewish talent was gone. His dream of creating a "new Jewish historiography," he confessed, "has been left behind in Auschwitz and elsewhere. It's pointless to entertain any illusions: we have suffered a loss of blood whose effects on the spirit and on scholarly achievement are simply unimaginable."[4]

Those students who did meet his high standards of quality and independence hardly fit into a "school." The "Scholem Institute of Mysticism" that he had set up in Schocken's library gradually lost its momentum. Isaiah Tishby, one of Scholem's best students, left to pursue a university career of his own; and another promising student, Jacob Taubes, was expelled from Scholem's circle because of a breach of confidence.

Disappointment and intrigues meant that Scholem found his closest friendships among members of the younger generation who shared his European culture, even if they had little sympathy with his Jewish and Zionist concerns. In 1960 he befriended Peter Szondi, a German-speaking Hungarian Jew who lived in Berlin and who was writing an article on Benjamin. Another of his young friends, the American writer George Lichtheim, lived in Palestine during the war. The two became collaborators when Lichtheim helped Scholem with the English version of *Major Trends*. After Lichtheim left for London in 1946, they maintained a stormy but close friendship. Scholem outlived his young friends. Weiss, Lichtheim, and Szondi all took their own lives.

Despite the demands on his time, Scholem completed his book *Sabbatai Sevi: The Mystical Messiah,* originally published in Hebrew in 1956.[5] Like his earlier essay on Jacob Frank, the book examines the biography of a heretical figure—in this case, the life of a pseudo-messiah who founded a vast movement in the seventeenth century—to reveal powerful subterranean currents at work within Jewish history. It shows how the figure of a melancholic apostate messiah lived on as a creative force within Jewish history.

Scholem wove a number of his favorite themes into his magnum opus. The central drama pertains to the complex relationship between Sabbatai Sevi and his faithful prophet, Nathan Benjamin of Gaza. Sevi declared himself the Messiah, then judiciously converted to Islam years later, after the Turkish sultan threatened him with death. This led many traditional authorities to denounce Sevi as a heretic, a fraud, a mountebank. But Scholem presented a different story. For the movement that Sevi triggered, known as Sabbatianism, became the single most important force in modern Jewish history until the dawn of Zionism. Indeed, said Scholem, modern Jewish history *began* with the Sabbatian heresy.

How could a false messiah play such a pivotal role in Jewish history? Scholem explains this unlikely outcome by shifting the focus from the hapless Sevi, addled by self-delusion, to Nathan, who was far more emotionally anchored and theologically astute. Nathan became the real hero of the book through his mastery of "camouflage." Unlike the melancholic false messiah, Nathan never broke from Jewish tradition but instead made the tradition speak to the tensions, contradictions, and richness of the life of his age. The book is not a story of triumphant messianism, but an attempt to make sense of—to "redeem"—loss and tragedy.

In a period enamored of psychoanalysis, the idea of a secret, hidden tradition caught on, though not in the way Scholem intended. Few could follow his subtle dialectical moves—not even one of the great Hegelian masters of the age, Theodor Adorno, who wished to see a radical and hidden "mystical tradition" in the likes of Karl Kraus, Franz Kafka, Arthur Schoenberg, "and perhaps even Freud."[6] One scholar asked Scholem to comment on the way in which the Kabbalah may have influenced Jorge Luis Borges. Another wanted to know about the Jewish mystical roots of Paul Celan (particularly his translations of Shakespeare) and Osip Mandelstam: since Benjamin had been under the spell of the Kabbalah and since Celan knew Benjamin's work, perhaps the Kabbalah had rubbed off on Celan.[7] Almost without fail, Scholem dismissed the idea of such hidden influences. They smacked, he thought, of the Jungian doctrine of the unconscious. He liked Jung and the Eranos conferences far more than the psychoanalyst's "system."

Scholem's fame grew in another way. Beginning in the early 1960s, he worked hard at getting Benjamin's works published. Together with Theodor Adorno (the official executor of Benjamin's estate), he helped edit the collected works and two volumes of general correspondence. All of Scholem's clearly nonscholarly works—*Walter Benjamin: The Story of a Friendship; From Berlin to Jerusalem: Memories of My Youth;* and *The*

Correspondence of Walter Benjamin and Gershom Scholem—dealt with his dead friend. Scholem's last detective work, completed shortly before his death, was an essay about an obscure figure named Felix Noeggerath, who had been a close friend of Benjamin's. He also did a study of Benjamin's family tree. One of the most exciting moments in his scholarly life came when he succeeded in proving an old hunch: that Benjamin was a direct descendent of Heinrich Heine.

The bulk of the letters Scholem now wrote and received turned more upon his personal life and attitudes than upon the Kabbalah. Among the changes that became apparent was the alteration in his signature. In his earlier years Scholem had used the Hebrew name "Gershom" mainly when writing in Hebrew. But after World War II this name (or the simple initial "G.") clearly gained the upper hand over the German-sounding "Gerhard," which nearly vanished.

As Scholem's fame spread, old acquaintances suddenly reappeared, while a number of the leading intellectuals of the time—figures such as Daniel Bell, Elias Canetti, Friedrich Dürrenmatt, Jürgen Habermas, and George Steiner—engaged him through letters. Perfect strangers from America and Europe began to view him as an oracle; reporters sought his opinion on war and peace; one young admirer wanted to know what he thought about Bob Dylan. But his Prussian impatience with overwrought hero-worship and psychobabble made him ill-suited for the role of guru, and he consistently refused to give any clear prophecies, to point the way, to encourage would-be disciples. "A scholar is not a priest," he said in his last Eranos lecture, "and it's a mistake to make him into one."[8] He had come a long way since the days when he had dreamed of writing a "Jewish *Zarathustra*." He now even denied, disingenuously, that he'd ever liked the book.

Perhaps the most unexpected exchange took place between Scholem and his older brother, Reinhold. Scholem had lost one of his closest correspondents when his mother died in 1946. After that date, family affairs (and thus small and revealing glimpses into his everyday life) disappear almost entirely from his letters. This changed only in the early 1970s, when he met up with Reinhold in Switzerland. They resumed a relationship that had broken off before World War I, discussing family members and even exchanging views of a more intellectual nature. The differences couldn't have been greater between Gershom and the old *Deutschnationaler,* as Reinhold continued to define himself. Yet Reinhold proved one of his brother's best critics. He rightly saw that within his brother—the ardent Zionist and famous scholar of Judaism—was a writer, biographer, and memoirist, a product of European civilization.

Scholem's letters were also full of polemics. As his moral authority grew, so did the pitch of his words. Differences of opinion often made their way into the public arena, where international attention fanned personal disagreements into acrimonious controversies. One writer, the scholar Isaiah Sonne, took issue with his work on Jacob Frank and the way in which it glorified that "Jewish Hitler."[9] Others frowned on Scholem's efforts to fit Benjamin into Jewish thought. Marxist critics charged that he had distorted Benjamin's legacy when he portrayed him as a "metaphysician marooned in the mundane."[10]

Yet these were minor skirmishes compared to the rancor generated by the question of "Germans and Jews." Scholem showed a generous latitude and even an astonishing tolerance toward non-Jews with checkered pasts. For instance, he never broke with Jung and Mircea Eliade because of their dubious records vis-à-vis fascism. One of the strangest and most moving letters Scholem received came from a former soldier in the German army, who admitted Germany's guilt while describing the unspeakable suffering he had seen among Germans exposed to Russian reprisals in 1945. It's a revealing seven-page document in which a man who suggests a relationship, however lopsided, between German and Jewish suffering nevertheless addresses Scholem as a Jew and an Israeli. He was also one of the few correspondents who truly understood Scholem. This former soldier, named Gotthard Koschel, confessed that *Major Trends* "comforted" him. It left him with the belief that all of his former Jewish friends, victims of a "crazed maniacal hatred," could "at some point take part . . . in fashioning the future." Jewish culture would continue and the talents of forgotten victims would mysteriously reemerge—as rediscovered texts, hidden thoughts, images of humanity—at some point in the future.[11]

Scholem's tone changed markedly when intellectuals ignored certain distinctions most non-Jewish Germans could no longer deny: that there is a Jewish people with a separate and unique Jewish history; and that any legitimate perspective on Jewish history—however critical of individual Jews or even of the entire people—had to respect the integrity of such "borders." The reserved scholar was capable of lashing out when fellow Jews blurred the boundaries between Germans and Jews, between culprits and victims, or when people maintained that Nazism was just a technical breakdown of civilization, a ghastly sideshow to the otherwise inspiring success story of Jewish emancipation.

The most bitter and protracted conflict he had was with Hannah Arendt. In 1944, with an essay on Kafka in *Partisan Review,* Arendt had embarked on a dazzling career of her own as one of America's premier intellectuals. She subsequently published a number of other articles, including a glowing review of *Major Trends* entitled "Jewish History, Revised." The two friends broke over Arendt's *Eichmann in Jerusalem* (1965). Scholem's critique focused on what he diagnosed as her lack of *ahavath Israel* (love for the Jewish people). Her "flippancy," the "heartless, almost sneering and malicious tone" she employed in telling the story of the Holocaust, outraged him because he thought it reflected an impassive moral distance from actions and policies that had destroyed a third of the Jewish people. This he could not forgive.

Another major controversy that is dealt with in Scholem's correspondence centered around the so-called German-Jewish symbiosis. In 1962 a writer by the name of Manfred Schloesser wrote an article about the "indestructible core of the German-Jewish dialogue." From Scholem's perspective, Schloesser depicted Nazism as volcano-like eruption that had buried a well-integrated and successful Jewry. While not denying anti-Semitism, Schloesser considered the central narrative of German-Jewish history to be one of adaptation, gradual integration, and eventual equality. The natural terminus of the historical process of emancipation was the Weimar constitution rather than the Nuremberg laws, mass expulsions, and death camps.

Scholem wrote a furious response to Schloesser's article—a response that later grew into an essay entitled "Against the Myth of a German-Jewish Dialogue," which adamantly rejected the "illusion of a German Judaism."[12] There never had been any "dialogue," according to Scholem, and this was not just because the Germans refused to listen. Jewish emancipation had simply "gotten off on the wrong foot." And because of this, when Jews spoke to Germans they typically demonstrated a "lamentable lack of dignity."[13]

✶

Scholem considered it the height of irony that someone like himself—
who had left Germany of his own volition, who denied being a "German," and who scornfully dismissed any notion of a historical "dialogue"
between Jews and Germans—should be so highly honored by postwar
Germany. In 1981 he traveled to Bonn to attend the award ceremonies
for the order Pour le Mérite, an academy that is limited to a small number
of distinguished scientists and artists. From there he continued on to
Berlin, the city of his birth, where he was a guest at a research center,
the Wissenschaftskolleg.

While in Europe, Scholem began to complain of a mysterious pain.
Tests in Switzerland and Germany came up with nothing. He returned
to Israel but the pains intensified, and he underwent further inconclusive
tests. For the first time in his life, he was too fatigued to write or to
work. He wrote his last letter on January 31, 1982. Three weeks later
he was dead.

Even though he was well into his eighties when he died, the death
of such a vital man came as a shock. Expressions of grief come from all
over the world. Flowers were sent, articles written, speeches delivered,
elegies composed. Those who mourned his loss discussed his contributions, his genius, his character. A simple query surfaced in much that
was said: Who, after all, was Gershom Scholem?

One of the most moving eulogies appeared in the *Frankfurter
Rundschau* in Germany. Walter Böhlich, an old friend of Scholem's, tried
to explain Scholem for a German mass readership. In his "long and by
no means happy life," wrote Böhlich, Scholem had devoted himself to
two major themes: first, "the most creative element" in Jewish religiosity, which he had located in its "unorthodox, heretical form"; second,
"the Germans, who would have murdered him had they gotten their
hands on him." Böhlich continued with a brief history of the Scholem
family. He began by mentioning Prussia's act of Jewish emancipation in
1812, and the four generations of Scholems who had so eagerly assimilated into German culture. But in the fifth generation a voice of "protest" had been raised. Gerhard had become Gershom and had left Berlin
for Jerusalem. It was there that Gershom, "in the attempt to save the
dying tradition of the Kabbalah, saved himself." His brother Werner had
taken another route, becoming a Communist and paying the ultimate
price for it. Werner had seen the social problem; Gershom, the religious
one. In both brothers the "non-Jewish Jew" and the "Jewish Jew" stand

"face-to-face, irreconcilable." Scholem, "who no longer wanted to be a German, nevertheless could not—and would not—completely cease being German, in his own way."

> It goes without saying that he was a typical German professor of the very best sort—living in Jerusalem, but ever a Berliner. In addition to his writings in English and Hebrew, he wrote many books in German, even if these were not his main works. And how many years he devoted to the work of his friend Walter Benjamin, whom he could not save and who was one of those "non-Jewish" Jews! Scholem could never fully leave the land of murderers. He could not forget, nor did he want to forget. He insisted that one had to speak about what happened, about what was, before discussing what could be in the future. He did not believe this because he was a historian or a philologist—and what a historian and philologist he was! He believed this because victims cannot forget as easily as perpetrators.[14]

Böhlich's tribute captured salient elements of the Scholem story. There were other such efforts. Some years before Scholem died, the *New York Times Book Review* commissioned the American novelist and essayist Cynthia Ozick to write an article on him. At first she threw up her hands. What could a "fiction scribbler" say about the Kabbalah? But instead of focusing on his work, she sought a key to unlock Scholem's personality. She probed behind what she called his "bookish distance and objectivity," the intentness with which he'd composed "volume after volume on the history of Jewish mysticism." "Is the hidden cauldron not an enticement and a seduction to its investigator? Or, to say it even more terribly: it may be that the quarry is all the time in the pursuer."[15] The words earned her Scholem's respect and friendship—and his agreement. He liked her metaphor of the quarry; he added only that the "true" answer to the mystery lay somewhere "between the lines" of all he had written.[16] Scholem made a stringent demand on his devoted readers: that they learn from him the art of philological detective work.

1948

TO ISAAC LEO SEELIGMANN[1]

Jerusalem, February 10, 1948

Dear Herr Seeligmann,

[. . .] I see from the latest reports that the most important ministries have already agreed to the transfer of books from Theresienstadt. All that's missing are the signatures of three or four ministers—a purely formal, bureaucratic procedure. [. . .] It seems that the books from the castles will be transferred just as easily. According to Dr. Muneles' calculation, in addition to the 17,000 books from Theresienstadt another 20,000 to 30,000 will come from the castles. [. . .]

Furthermore, it's possible I may have opportunities to get hold of books from Poland. I still can't go into details about this, and I ask you to treat the matter with discretion. If the rather murky reports we've received from Warsaw prove correct, it would mean an extra 10,000 volumes for the university collection. In this case—as I understand it and as I will present it before a meeting of the Library Commission tomorrow morning—the mere act of bringing in from the *galut* such a stock of books in need of processing will most likely justify the founding, as planned, of a special office; this may be needed even in the event the Offenbach plan does not work out.[2] You understand better than anyone else that the university cannot make any final decisions as long as it has nothing concrete to show for all of these transactions. Developments in America seem to show that every delay brings with it the danger of loss. Time works against Jewish interests. We can only be happy that we can finalize matters in Prague and Warsaw without General Clay's interference,[3] and in particular that we've hindered the transfer of materials from Prague to Offenbach. [. . .]

You will surely get plenty of news from others about what's happening here. The situation is far from being simple or pleasant. We'll just have to grit our teeth and wait to see how things go in the spring and summer. Our private fate will follow the fate of all of Israel; and so our mood swings with the general mood, which changes quickly and shifts from optimism to pessimism. The university has been very much affected by recent events, and work has suffered greatly. To date, there have been no direct attacks against the university; and transportation, which has been disrupted over the past few weeks, will hopefully improve in the spring. Every night some bomb explodes with a great boom. One never knows exactly where—it could be five hundred meters or three kilometers away. [. . .]

Sincerely yours, G. Scholem

TO ISAAC LEO SEELIGMANN

Jerusalem, August 3, 1948

Dear Herr Dr. Seeligmann,

[. . .] Thank you for your good wishes and your concern for us. As you know, the past few months have been very trying, particularly here in Jerusalem. If you came for a visit, you'd find us looking youthful— nothing but skin and bones. Yet having been here while it was all going on was a real treat, especially now that the whole thing is behind us.[4] It was impossible to do much work; there was always something or other to do for the mobilization. I myself was involved—as a sort of porter *honoris causa*—with a group led by the Haganah to prevent the plunder of books, which meant that I prevented myself from taking part in the corresponding looting. It was all very exciting and interesting. One of the biggest surprises of recent months was that Jerusalem could put up such a good fight, though sadly with considerable loss of men and matériel. [. . .]

The English army's bombardments of the Jewish quarter have had a severe and most unfortunate effect on the printing presses, of all things. The destruction of the *Jerusalem Post* building ruined their press and burned up the entire run of Tishby's book, his edition of Sasportas.[5] Two hundred pages had just been typeset, and these were the last of the galleys; the rest had already been proofread. The original manuscript has survived—but who can say when printing will resume? This year is out of the question. Meanwhile, Schocken has closed down his printing house, and the presses for *Ha'aretz* in Tel Aviv were seriously damaged in an air raid.[6] During the blockade of Jerusalem there was of course no electricity, so all of the printing plants were shut for months. Besides, the workers had been mobilized. Only now is it possible to get back to work, slowly and fitfully. The consequence of all this is that there won't be much literature coming out of Jerusalem this year. All the periodicals have also been suspended for the time being. [. . .]

My own book on the origins of the Kabbalah is completely finished and proofread. It's sitting in Tel Aviv, waiting for the machines to start running. I hope to see it appear by Rosh Hashanah. [. . .]

Yours truly, G. Scholem

TO MORTON SMITH[7]

Jerusalem, August 6, 1948

My dear Mr. Smith,

[. . .] The last months have been most eventful and we could go on and on telling about our experiences. It was a great time. Of course, no academic work could proceed orderly but everyone has had his fill of excitement and work, building fortifications, standing up to shelling and sniping, it was all very much (a little too much, perhaps) "Historic." I was some kind of porter *honoris causa* with the Jewish H.Q. and have spent some time on Mt. Zion when we took over the *dormitio* of the Benedictines. The good padres had fled and we had to guard the place. You would not have recognized Jerusalem these days! The shelling (very much English-made) was disagreeable, distasteful and exceedingly noisy. Some fell around our house, but no damage was done. Nobody knows whether the whole thing is going to start anew, and both sides are preparing themselves. The optimism which greeted the second cease-fire has vanished. Wirshubski is educational officer in the Haganah and Mrs. Hans Lewy, the widow, is a soldier and can be observed guarding the agency building with a sten-gun. Some of our best friends are no more; the toll has been considerable. The Samburskys are well and you may have heard the story that the Arabs have given up Safed because they were told by some of their people that the Jews had a small atom bomb. If they had asked Sambursky, they would still be there.[8]

Everybody has become tall and meager and since the end of the siege we are living on food parcels from every corner of Israel. Everybody wanted to do something for us. To which we could not object, reduced as we were in physical strength. Let us hope that the tribulations of Israel are soon over, and that we meet again in peaceful employment.

With kind regard, Gershom Scholem

TO MORTON SMITH[9]

Jerusalem, August 29, 1948

Dear Mr. Smith,

Is this a sign of better times? Letters are beginning to arrive, some of them even without delay, as did your long letter of August 17, which Mrs. Scholem and I have been reading, or should I say studying, with great interest. Your news about the other side of Jerusalem was, indeed, partially news to us. We do not get any papers from the USA, heaven knows why, and our political education and information is six months old. On the other side, for people who have to put up without the *New York Times* and *Time,* we are not doing too badly. If there actually is peace around the corner, we don't know, although we have been praying for it very whole-heartedly. But from our angle the picture does not look very peaceful, and as I am writing these very lines shells from the Arab lines are falling around our quarters, and during the last week shelling has been so heavy that—*o tempora, o mores!*—the inhabitants of the old Orthodox quarters north of Mea Shearim have had to leave and have been moving into Katamon, which you would scarcely recognize these days. The Hebrew University has taken a lot of shelling but no really serious damage has been done, and everything could be repaired in six or eight weeks (except for one or two of the laboratories), if only we could get our people there to do the repairing in peace. But this is plainly impossible under the present "truce" conditions and we will have to wait. If the war drags on as it threatens to do now, we will have to move temporarily to some place in town, but there may be few students anyhow, what with mobilization and all kinds of services abounding.

The library is not damaged, only the windows are broken (as everywhere) and some shells have landed in the walls of the building without
penetrating them. Books, manuscripts, and foremost the Smith thesis[10]
are therefore intact, though they are not, of course, in current use. [. . .]

With kind regards, Gershom Scholem

1949

Chicago, May 6, 1949

Dear Friend,

We assume that you've already moved into the apartment and feel at home, even though we have no proof of this other than your wife's handwriting on the envelope of the letter, which just arrived. How do you feel in our place? What sort of crimes did you find in the bathroom, kitchen, and library? Perhaps you've already written a story about the apartment, about the homeowners from the priestly caste, or about what happens to someone who takes a walk on Abarbanel Road at six in the evening? Or does my library prevent you from writing because you prefer to sit and dream? Sometimes we picture in our mind's eye what you're up to. Has the situation in Talpiot returned to normal? Are your books still in the sacks of the Genisa?[12]

We saw Schocken here. He's a broken and miserable man who has managed to make himself hated by everyone in America. It's really a tragedy to listen to him and to hear people talk about him. I don't think he'll be going back any time soon, though his wife is putting a lot of pressure on him to do so. He's simply afraid. It's impossible to come to any agreement with him. He lives in his own fantasy world. [. . .]

In friendship, Gershom Scholem

1950

TO MORTON SMITH[13]

Jerusalem, 28 Abarbanel Road; December 30, 1950

Dear Mr. Smith,

[. . .] As to your question concerning the Bollingen scholarship, I shall presently proceed to give you my opinion. Before Barrett, who, if I am not mistaken, is the secretary and *spiritus movens* of the Bollingen Foundation. In case you have any dealing with them, you might therefore give (if needs arise) my name as a reference without being hurt by this. We met in 1949 and 1950 at the Eranos meeting in Ascona, and he professes to be some sort of admirer of me. I might be able to help you.

I think it would be a fine idea to avail yourself of the possibility of a double scholarship such as you mention. I am not a psychologist myself, and even in Ascona (where the influence of C. G. Jung is very much felt, he himself being the moving spirit of those congresses called "Eranos") I did refrain from psychological excursions. But I felt that much could be done in this field by someone with a sound philological training and not given to the more extreme forms of psychoanalytical fantasies for which I cannot arouse much sympathy on my part. I feel that much of the amateurish character of psychological researches into the History of Religion, especially of a book of the Freudian and Jungian brand, is caused by the lack of a sound philological basis for their contentions. I am sure that somebody who would combine both modes of approach should be able to do most valuable work. [. . .]

My own work, alas, has stocked too. I have done a lot of reading and studying in oriental religion, in connection with my study of religious nihilism. Then I had to go to Europe. The matter of the Jewish books and libraries in Germany is shortly nearing its end. We have brought over quite a lot, and I hope that after this visit I will be under no further obligation to go to Germany, where I found the atmosphere in September most sticky. This time my wife did not accompany me to Europe, which enabled me to send her some parcels. In Amsterdam and Berlin I bought a lot of books and feel now well prepared for the third world war, although to tell you the truth this is no laughing matter and we are already feeling the impact of the general uneasiness. People who had accepted positions at the university cancel their plans and stay where they are, and we will have to do very largely without additional new blood from abroad. [. . .]

Cordially yours, G. Scholem

1951

TO JACOB TAUBES[14]

28 Abarbanel Road, Jerusalem; October 7, 1951

Dear Herr Dr. Taubes,

I beg your forgiveness for writing a letter so critical to our relationship shortly before your return and, so to speak, out of the blue. But with great pain and regret I am compelled by my own conscience to do so. I would have written sooner had the information I am about to convey been known to me earlier.

Not long ago a certain Herr Talmon, a graduate of our university, returned from Leeds in England. Prior to his stay there, he had never heard your name and had never met you. He spent last year as a lecturer at the University of Leeds. I learned from him that in late winter or early spring he read a number of your letters to Josef Weiss, which were shown to him by Weiss. Herr Talmon knew nothing about your relationship to Weiss or about mine to you, but was most shocked by the letters' contents. I was all the more dismayed to learn two things from his account.

First, you revealed things that you and I had said to each other in the strictest confidence, even though you made all kinds of declarations that you would pass nothing on. Apparently, you conveyed them in writing to Herr Weiss, the person in the world they were least intended for. To my great horror, Herr Talmon cited from your letters statements concerning Weiss himself as well as certain parts of his dissertation— things I had said to you during an evening conversation which I allowed myself to get dragged into, and things I now regret (for instance, that I'd learned Weiss was undergoing psychoanalytic treatment and that I claimed to have found signs of mental illness in the last sections of his dissertation).

Second, you repeatedly counseled him in your letters to avoid contacting me and to avoid writing to anyone in Jerusalem, least of all to me (because, you said, his prospects here are now hopeless, and because I persecute him, etc.), despite the fact that after various inquiries you knew I had not written to Weiss after his nighttime departure because I was waiting to see if he would get in touch with me—as should be expected, given the distressing way in which he unfortunately left the country. I can only attribute it to the active intervention of Herr Talmon and his wife that Weiss, notwithstanding all of your advice, finally got in touch with me.

While I could perhaps somehow explain the second point as a misunderstanding which, however difficult to explain, does not constitute a breach of confidence, the first point has profoundly hurt me. Of course, I am ready and duty-bound to hear your explanation, if you have one. Tell me: How can you imagine any kind of continued relationship with me after such an extreme breach of trust? Given Herr Talmon's all too persuasive account concerning the content of your letters, I have to assume that an indiscretion actually occurred. If you indeed committed a breach of trust—and I write this after discussing it with Professor Bergmann and with his full knowledge—you should anticipate what is for me the most severe outcome: namely, the need for me to sever all contact with you. For without trust my relationship with you cannot continue, and this case has shown that the absolutely necessary condition of personal trust is lacking. For you, there are no less severe consequences. Technically, of course, you can return and deliver your lectures as a research fellow without continuing to regard yourself as one of my students. In this case I would ask you to cease attending my seminars. But you should think about whether, *rebus sic stantibus,*[15] it wouldn't be better to reconsider both your return here and your stay in America. Perhaps it would be wiser for you not to return, but instead use the help your father-in-law would surely give you and build yourself an academic career over there. [. . .]

Yours truly, G. Scholem

1952

TO HANS-GEERT FALKENBERG[16]

Hebrew University, Jerusalem, 1952

Dear Herr Falkenberg,

    Three days ago I received your letter from the ninth of July, along with a number of issues of the newspaper you edit. [. . .] Let me say that I have the highest esteem for the sentiments expressed in your letters, and that I haven't the slightest inclination to underestimate or to belittle the good you wish to do and perhaps will do. I believe I can understand your situation completely, *sub specie* in particular your German duty and German task. Yet allow me at the same time to say that this task can be accomplished only by you yourself, or not at all. It is my opinion that we Jews of the present generation should, as far as possible, steer clear of issues pertaining to our two peoples which no discussion, no matter how noble and rational, can resolve. We should allow time to do its work, for the simple reason that the historical conditions of such a "dialogue" have made the anonymity of the German public (to which a Jew appeals through a German publication) something dreadful for each one of us. I can and would speak to individuals; at present, I cannot bring myself to address an anonymous collective—of any kind. This may not pertain to translations or publication of essays and books, but it certainly goes for personal, direct discussions with the German public. Since 1945 I have been to Germany three times on missions for official Jewish institutions, and it looks as if I'll go again in the next several months (to Hamburg). Each time, I returned with a particular personal impression. Even without my going into details, you will certainly understand when I say that those months were among the most difficult and bitter I have ever experienced. What evokes such enormous, almost insurmountable reluctance, in particular with regard to your invitation to write for your journal, is the difficulty of intimacy. What occurred was not just the result of murder, theft, and drunken violence. Especially in the academic arena (though not exclusively, of course), these things were not the primary problem. The professors we want nothing to do with (as fellow members of a freely chosen community) are guilty not of these things but of something even more unimaginable—and those professor include contributors to your publication. Often enough, infamy does not hesitate to disguise itself in forms of the sublime, which does not make it any less ignoble and destructive. But now these gentlemen have forgotten their own past—and I have discovered that they react with utmost astonishment when I remind them of it. This is something that only a new generation will be able to sweep clean. You belong to this generation and can hope for and do your part to bring about the restitution of things we hold in common and a reconciliation between Germans and Jews. I hope with all my heart that you will be able to help create an atmosphere in which honest words can once again have meaning and in which a Jew can once again speak to an anonymous group of German strangers without having to think about their past actions.

Cordially yours, G. Scholem

1953[17]

TO SIMCHA BONIM URBACH[18]

Adar I, 5714 (February 8, 1953)

[. . .] I was most astonished at the way you erroneously interpreted the intentions behind my research into the Kabbalah. When I said (as I still do) and then sought to demonstrate that there is something in the Kabbalah which brings out the mythological element in the Jewish soul, I never claimed this was all there was to the Kabbalah and "that's that." When you put this brief phrase into my mouth and see it as the ultimate outcome of my historical conclusions, you distort my conception of the Kabbalah as an extremely vibrant form of mysticism which despite its roots in mythology transformed itself (at its height) into an element of living Judaism, with all of the dangers entailed in this.

"That's that" appears nowhere in my writings—I have never expressed it, implied it, or taught it.

Contrary to what you allege, I am perfectly aware that an explanation of the historical meaning and development of symbols can by no means exhaust the possibilities these symbols offer as vessels for the living content of belief.

It has never occurred to me that "I have succeeded in deciphering all of the mysteries of the Kabbalah." I would never have written anything so ridiculous. I wonder where you could have found such a statement in my writings, and I regret reading such irresponsible passages in yours.

I speak about the Kabbalah as someone who tries to understand what is at work there, insofar as scholarship is able to determine this through historical criticism.

My published writings have quite often stressed the simple fact that philology and history are necessary and important for an understanding of the larger picture, which otherwise gets distorted. They are, however, not ultimate values determining the life of men. ("And that's that!") [. . .]

Respectfully yours, Gershom Scholem

TO THEODOR ADORNO

Jerusalem, May 1, 1955

Dear Herr Adorno,

I received your letter from April 5 with the good news that an agreement has been reached on the Benjamin edition. I got it three days ago,
on my return from Rome, where from the fourteenth of April I was
attending a conference for historians of religion (which was the purest
humbug). [. . .] I've now had a chance to look at some of his papers
for you, the ones that predate his departure from Germany. Enclosed is
a list of dates that may be of some use to you. After 1923 I was with
him for only a month in Paris (in August), and later in Berlin; in February
1938 I spent a week with him in Paris. If you're interested in a list of
dates based on his letters to me in the years 1923–1940, I can try to put
one together. Yet this kind of information may be of no interest to you.
Tell me if I can give you answers to particular questions. Of course,
from 1915 to 1923 Dora was with him nearly all the time. The marriage
was deteriorating as early as 1920, but until their divorce at the end of
1929—which took an extremely harsh form—they continued to be very
close, even during the last five years, when he had a liaison with Asja
Lacis (a woman I never met). Through the correspondence, I was able
to keep track of his journeys and wanderings after 1924. It goes without
saying that, in comparison to his other writings, W.B.'s correspondence
preserves much more of his year-by-year circling of the subject of Judaism; his repeated attempts to penetrate it; and the plans to bring him to
Jerusalem. You surely know that in 1928 and 1929 Dr. Magnes, the
chancellor of the University in Jerusalem, granted him a stipend to allow
him to live in Jerusalem for a year, which W.B. accepted. The events
surrounding his divorce, and possibly other things I don't know about,
thwarted those plans.

Concerning significant dates, I perhaps should have noted that W.B.
once paid a visit to Franz Rosenzweig, in December 1922 (Rosenzweig
was very ill at the time). [. . .]

Scholem

1958[20]

Jerusalem, January 13, 1958

Dear Sir,

A few days ago I received no. 112 of *Molad,* with your critique of my *Sabbatai Sevi.*[22] A number of points in your article astonished me, and I am not sure whether I could present my concerns in person with the appropriate calm. For this reason I prefer to write a brief note. I see from your words that you regard my book as a masterpiece. The stronger the praise, the greater the damage.

This is why I was initially taken aback by your words. The reader learns nothing from you about the original contribution my book makes. He does, however, become well acquainted with your contrary opinions—though not through the interpretation of documents or through arguments and counterarguments that pursue the subject at hand without affectation or an admixture of emotion.

Most of your reflections concern questions of perspective which in part have no answers. Each and every reader has the freedom to judge individual events from one or another (entirely different) methodological perspective. But there are things in your essay I'm not sure I fully understand, and other passages in which I can't tell whether statements are being made in a spirit of attack or of irony. I must confess that I do not accept ironic remarks about my work (instead of reports on the matter under investigation), in particular when they stem from differing perspectives, be they true or only apparently so.

I would like to give an example of this irony, which in my humble opinion does neither you nor the subject much justice.

You write: "The author's conclusions from his textual analysis and his precise depiction of the movement perhaps owe more to enthusiasm and overvaluation of the examined materials than to careful and exact deliberation, which elsewhere has been one of the greatest accomplishments of Scholem's scholarly system."

These words refer to my article "Redemption through Sin," in which I showed, with all possible precision, that in my view Sabbatianism *eo ipso* was a pioneer movement and that the last Sabbatians joined with the

Enlightenment and other such intellectual currents while still clinging to their Sabbatian beliefs (the latter point was based on documentary evidence and my own research). I added new materials to this in some of my later studies and in the book I wrote in English. I have repeatedly stressed that it will always be difficult to assess the full truth because those directly involved destroyed most of the relevant documents, and for good reason. This is why it is necessary to use as material proof—in addition to the historical and psychological circumstances at the time the Sabbatians lived—their own internal claims, along with the external claims of those people who knew the last Sabbatians and who tried to hide the traces of their activities in the Enlightenment camp. [. . .]

No doubt, anyone who so desires could write a wonderfully interesting book using all of the facts which appeared in my book for the first time, and could do so without adding a single new detail by presenting the entire episode differently through another view of the same facts. What would this prove? And what does it mean to include me among those who hide their opinions and suppress things between the lines, when my opinions are in black and white and when whoever wants to accuse me of something is welcome to do so? In truth, I do not believe that the followers of Sabbatai Sevi ceased being Jews merely because they got themselves mired in a complex and insoluble predicament. The fact is that I don't think you could have added a thing to this affair, other than in irony—an irony I comprehend all the less because you don't write from a position of faith, even if your readers may mistakenly think so. I deplore the inconsistency of your criticism, and not your views, which I respect—even if they are far from my own.

I deplore your comment on "the refined act of racking one's brains to find more and more Sabbatianists, and the eagerness to uncover strange acts—if possible, even stranger than those known up to now." This sentence astounds me. Who racks their brains to find more Sabbatianists? It's obvious: G. Scholem and Isaiah Tishby, for I know of no others. Your comments on the scholarly endeavors of both men are so far removed from the facts of their research that the reader is simply astonished. "Racking one's brains" is not a compliment. I don't know how anyone can study a historical phenomenon whose traces people have tried to suppress wherever possible, other than by "racking one's brains"—to wit, by ferreting out documents through archival examination and research in books. Until now, no one has done this or sufficiently understood how to do it. What right do you have to question the spiritual motives of those involved in this historical investigation—motives you know nothing about? And what about the words "eagerness" and "strange acts"? Either/or: if there are serious reasons to study the Sabbatian movement and to become engrossed in it, how is it possible to do so other than by immersing oneself in all the confusions and obscurities? I ask you to show me a page from my book, or from any of my other books, where an illegitimate enthusiasm or superfluous alacrity might determine the investigation into these questions.

If you have read my essay "Redemption through Sin," you could easily offer many serious comments about the problem of "strange acts" and all the things relating to the obverse of this movement. These connections, however, were discovered not by my critics but by me (the same goes for the entire terminology that belongs to it—demonology and so on). If you really wanted to interpret my efforts to understand Sabbatianism (as alluded to in the title of your essay)—and wished to do so correctly, in line with the author's intentions—you would have to add a page or so. For to see only enthusiasm and a racking of the brains in my relation to Sabbatianism is an accusation that does justice neither to the language of the work and its content, nor to the scholarship that informs it. But perhaps you can use the phrase "racking one's brain" for all research which, owing to the objective state of the science and the nature of the documents, requires a certain degree of detective work. In this case it would have been more appropriate to point to the need for racking one's brains instead of discrediting it in such a dismissive tone as you have done in your article.

I find myself confronted here with a phenomenon that is completely foreign to me—namely, a psychological interpretation of the factors determining the relation between a researcher and his field of study. A major part of your essay is devoted to such reflections, and I cannot understand your interest in it. Was it a bad joke that led you to write about me in such a way? Or did you think you had discovered something about my innermost soul that has not yet revealed itself to me? I can only shake my head. I am well aware that I do not understand my own true depths, and I am intelligent enough to accept this—even though I am no disciple of the various psychoanalytic methods. Yet what can the following sentence possibly mean? "The contemplative and scientific value of working on Sabbatianism compensates for the value of practicing strange acts." Is this sentence a jest or a revelation about my soul? I cannot enter into a discussion of this. [. . .]

And now a word on Judaism and the way it is constituted in the minds of the believers whose identities you have questioned. Where does this irony come from? As I see it, believers are those who are considered as such in their particular generation and who see themselves in this role, who affirm the heritage of past generations and the tradition of historical Judaism, and who feel themselves duty bound to it. It may be that this definition sounds empirical, but there is no other. Your reference to "Elijah, the prophets of Baal, and the like" is doubtless nothing but further irony and mockery, as you are surely aware. But are your readers able to detect your mockery?

And what do you mean by placing an exclamation point after the words "All of this pretentious prattle"? In this instance I am not referring to the opinions of the Orthodox, with whom I will not discuss what is Jewish and what isn't. With this sentence, which you discussed so extensively, I was not lodging a complaint against them. I was directing my words against the truly "modern" writers: those who philosophize about Judaism without being Orthodox and who, in their disbelief, pretend to know exactly what is or is not allowed within Judaism. As one who writes with tears in his eyes, I know absolutely nothing about such things. I regret my ignorance, though at the same time I rejoice in it.

My accusation against those pretentious modern windbags is that they do not know what they are talking about. They make judgments about what is Jewish and what is not Jewish without paying any attention to historical reality and to the boundless possibilities it opens to us. This is admittedly my own conviction, which I would by no means characterize as a dogmatic article of faith. I am completely mystified as to the basis of your arguments against me. My enormous respect for the many generations of Jewish tradition applies not only to what is on the surface but also to what is hidden. Your last sentence reads, "Essentially, Judaism wants nothing else but to cover over all abysses, and to flee from vertigo and the dangers it brings." If this is the part of your conclusion that deals with the legitimate content of Judaism, then I can only say it is news to me. I never knew that Judaism flees from abysses. Quite the contrary: so far as I know, Judaism has opened up history's main abysses. I also was not aware that you consider this definition decisive with respect to two thousand years of history which even before the Kabbalah, let alone before Sabbatianism, was full of abysses. I don't see what kind of value such a definition can have for the way in which our generation relates to the heritage of our forefathers. I have no interest whatsoever in definitions that so utterly contradict our historical and spiritual reality. [. . .]

Best greetings and Shalom

1959

TO BARUCH KURZWEIL[23]

Jerusalem, December 4, 1959

My honored opponent,

In the past few days I have read a large portion of your book, and I thank you for sending me this gift. I have also read your long polemic devoted to me—in part to things I have really said and written, in part to things you attribute to me. I have had to conclude with the greatest disappointment that the article of mine which I sent to you some time back (two years ago) has not sufficed to convince you of how wrong you are in attributing to me the motives you do, something you've done in your essays on the subject for some time. Not only do you ignore my carefully measured words in the article, which was not written in the tone you always seek to detect in my writing, but my words completely contradict the subjective interpretation you always ascribe to me whenever I write about these matters. This time you even added a new degree of polemical sharpness and misguided understanding. I gave my lecture on religious authority and mysticism in the weeks preceding the publication of your review of my book on Sabbatai Sevi. Your words were so foreign to my attitude and to my decades-long labors that I thought that if the large and detailed book *Major Trends* was not enough (in particular the chapter on the essence of mysticism and on the Lurianic Kabbalah and Hasidism), then sending you my latest pieces would succeed in freeing you of your error. [. . .]

Everything you accuse me of saying about the genealogical connection between secular nationalism and the Sabbatian movement is your own invention (or that of others who read what I say in the same inadequate fashion). Speaking for myself, I have never produced such nonsense. Nor do I have any secret intentions lurking behind my preoccupation with these phenomena. If there is a hidden dimension to my work (and one should have doubts on this score), then it's certainly of a very different type from what you wish to uncover. I believe it would be more appropriate to judge my scholarship according to its stated intentions, not some ostensibly secret ones. [. . .]

One could certainly argue about the connection between the

Frankists and the followers of the Enlightenment; the same goes for the dialectical nature of this connection. In the sequel to my book, I will go into this in detail. This is a subject open to scholarly consideration and clarification. The same by no means goes for your declarations on neo-mysticism and its apparent relationship to nihilism. I understand neither your presentation of these matters nor the justification you give. I won't allow myself to get into a discussion of this, for I found no logic in what you wrote, nor did I discover any relation to what I have written in my numerous essays. On the whole, it's difficult and ultimately useless to discuss general values, though at the same time I am certainly of the opinion that it's possible to interpret historical facts using methods different from mine. What surprised me in your comments is your obvious unwillingness to recognize facts that are inconvenient for your opinions—facts such as the spread and reach of the Sabbatian movement. [. . .]

Yours, Gershom Scholem

TO DORA BENJAMIN

December 30, 1959

My dear Dora,

Regardless of my sins and sloth, it would be unthinkable if I let your birthday pass without a heartfelt thought of you and for you. I have neither heard from you nor seen you in so long that, as the years pass, I am ashamed of myself. Meanwhile we've both become distinguished people of rank (which I grant you is hard to believe). Fanya and I both wish you health, rich days, happiness with your family, and rest from the burden of work and worries that have perpetually weighed down on you. Your life has always been the most turbulent of all, yet you have always stood your ground and braved the storms. I hope that now, sitting in the house you moved into the last time we saw you in London, you can reflect upon the past—all these years, from Czernowitz to Vienna, and all the way to London.

I cannot forget the years we spent together and the invincible youthfulness glowing within you. I don't know if you still travel or whether we will see each other again. I hope so, dearest Dora. May God grant you in old age the power and the vibrant heart you blessed us with in our youth.

Your old Gerhard

1960

FROM GOTTHARD KOSCHEL

June 10, 1960

Dear Herr Scholem,

[. . .] Your book[24] brought to mind the many Jews I once counted among my "acquaintances," those whose artistic and scientific power— or philosophic depth—remain etched in my memory. It filled me with comfort to know that what may appear to be "pointless" efforts and accomplishments can never be completely lost. Such efforts, eliminated without trace from the intellectual realm through a crazed maniacal hatred seeking to destroy these forms, will at some point take part, as forms from the past, in fashioning the future.

Now I've learned something! I have been driven from my home— and the horror aroused by this expulsion, when Russian *soldateska* invaded the Pomeranian, Schlesian, and East Prussia regions, can hardly be described. Many of the things the German people have been accused of committing pale (purely comparatively) beside the monstrous slaughter of women, children, and old people and the bestial acts of mass rape often accompanied by indescribable sadism. German guilt is, as such, not thereby removed. Guilt cannot be arithmetically balanced out against another guilt.

Sincerely yours, Dr. Gotthard Koschel

FROM GEORGE LICHTHEIM[25]

London, July 2, 1960

Cher maître,

Many thanks for the offprints, which just arrived. For personal reasons which will soon be clear to you, in recent days I've been inclined to ponder the supposed meaning of existence and, correspondingly, to occupy myself with studying it. I have the general impression that the ultimate foundation of our earthly pilgrimage remained just as hidden from the apocalyptic writers you cite as from later and lesser thinkers, yours truly included. The meaning of life and death, what happens to the soul before and after death, what kind of meaning to attach to suffering—before all these questions I remained just as helpless after I read your text as I did after perusing the leading Christian authors. At least one can say about the latter that they provided more substantial information—presumably originating from non-Jewish sources—about individual existence and its inexorable end than did the authorities you prefer. I don't say this as a criticism; as everyone knows, I can't claim membership in either of the two camps. I must also agree in principle with your rather carefully phrased criticism of a specifically Christian inwardness, insofar as this criticism rests upon a this-worldliness vis-à-vis earthly things, something I myself stubbornly cling to. The question I ask is simply whether humanity, with messianism and the belief in eternal life now behind it, will in the long run be able to endure the fact that life is of limited duration. As far as I can tell, the existentialists grapple with this problem. It occurs to me in this context that, to my mind, your assertion that the messianic idea is perhaps "the true anti-existentialism" lacks all clarity. I assume you said this against the thesis that man fulfills himself in action, *dans son projet.* But if the Jews had taken their messianism seriously—something which collectively they never did—they would have, as it were, fulfilled their project. No doubt the truly fatal flaw in messianism must have consisted in its being a compensation for real-life helplessness. [. . .]

Yours, George Lichtheim

TO GEORGE LICHTHEIM

Jerusalem, July 14, 1960

Dear George,

Your letter must have been written at the precise moment I was standing with others at your mother's grave. Your observations—and your mother's indescribable suffering in recent years gave ample stimulus for them—have my complete sympathy. But you can't deny that under your own assumptions of a so-called ultimate this-worldliness, your meditations are essentially hopeless. I am puzzled that you seem to feel more attraction to the pronouncements made by Christian sources than to those made by my preferred authors. Indeed, the abundance of such

Christian sources is as overwhelming as it is suspect. Your observations on my theologoumena as it relates to Jewish messianism betray what is to me an unexpected lack of sympathy for the attitude of traditional Jews. Moreover, there is nothing more baffling to me than the fact that you couldn't make sense of the statement (which was frankly written for you) concerning the true anti-existentialism of the messianic idea.

Rarely have I uttered something so clearly. So I must appeal to your rational ability—and previous experience gives me no reason to question it—to penetrate short statements as well. The opinion that the Jews would have fulfilled their own project had they taken the messianic idea seriously does not enlighten me in the least. The funny thing about this entire story is that the messianic idea devalued every historical action in its concrete execution. When the idea went beyond being a mere idea by entering into a messianic execution, it exploded in the course of this very execution, which then opened up abysses. World history has been forced to take more cognizance of these abysses through contemplating, or experiencing, Russian history. Your supposition that at the end of the day the Jews used the idea as a compensation for their own helplessness is unworthy of your own insight. This stale piece of Freud can't teach us a thing. [. . .]

> Your old—and unsuccessful—teacher and colleague

TO GOTTHARD KOSCHEL

Jerusalem, July 4, 1960

Dear Herr Dr. Koschel,

I read your letter from the tenth of June with great sympathy. It's the farthest thing from my mind to sit in judgment over the German people. I don't know who would be capable of doing so or whether he would get anywhere if he tried. I have also formulated the introductory remarks to the German edition of my book in such a way as to point out the self-evident fact (not what people could call a variable one) that scholarship, at least, cannot build a bridge over the bloody chasm that history has dug between Germans and Jews; and that Jews are the last people who should feel themselves called upon to undertake such a task. It touched me deeply to read your personal recollections of your own incidents and experiences, and I am certain that more than a few thought or felt as you did. These are all things so unimaginable that we today can no longer enter into their depths. The one thing that seems certain to me is that only the individual who has gone through these experiences and who is familiar with conditions in Germany has the calling to speak to Germans as a German. I do not claim to have any kind of mission or calling; I don't harbor the slightest illusion about the endless challenges to human behavior that are posed by terrorism; and I am enough of a Jew to bear in mind the old saying from the Mishna: don't judge your neighbor until you've been in his shoes.

I beg your forgiveness, but I must limit myself to these few words of thanks and explanation. I will be happy if you can glean from this that your words were in no way spoken into thin air.

Best regards, Gershom Scholem

TO ERNST SCHOEN[26]

Jerusalem, November 28, 1960

Dear Ernst Schoen,

I am most grateful for your detailed letter of November 16, and I'll answer it forthwith. I was very pleased to hear from you. The happy thought just dawned on me that, since you and your wife have moved to northern Italy, and seeing that for the past several years I have spent the latter half of August (from the fifteenth to the thirty-first) in Ascona, after all these years there may be a chance for us to see each other. In Ascona I have presented the fruits of my kabbalistic studies ten times now, in "High Swiss German." This is what one should perhaps call the language spoken by Jews who still speak the old German from before 1920 (after which the German language disappeared). This year my wife and I will most certainly be there. I would be delighted if we could meet somewhere in the region, be it in Ascona or elsewhere. Incidentally, next year (say, from April to April) I will spend my sabbatical year in London. From there I'll often be going to Switzerland.

Thank you very much for your willingness to make letters from Walter available to me for the sake of the edition. What you say about printing only one side of a correspondence may well be right, but you mustn't

forget that all of our letters to Walter were lost, so that a proper correspondence cannot be reconstructed. Of the hundreds of letters I wrote
to him, I have only four individual copies. [. . .] I urge you to send
more than the letters of so-called general interest. There are letters to
me of this sort from 1916 onward. Even for the selection, I believe there
are some from 1917 on. Dr. Unseld, the director of Suhrkamp Verlag,
has placed much importance (and in my opinion with total justice) on
including personal documents for Walter's biography and personality,
so that these may adequately balance the literary and philosophical statements. A large number of pieces of this latter kind can be included, as
well as, I hope, his letters to me. Now, we have nothing of this sort
from the years 1913–1917, which is particularly regrettable because this
was the time of *Der Anfang* and the youth movement.[27] Here your letters
will fill the lacuna. For the selection, I ask you kindly to give me everything you possess from these years. It's not so critically urgent for the
later years, since, as I explained, other materials exist. So please do not
place any limits on your generosity—give me whatever you have. The
most important letters from Benjamin's youth are all gone. None of his
friends have responded to my requests. [. . .] The letters to Dora were
lost in San Remo in the most unimaginable way. At some point Kraft,
in an attack of madness in the wake of some insult, burned Benjamin's
letters to him from these years, which is a particularly grievous loss. I
made myself a copy back then of the letter on Stifter, if it's the same
one you have.[28] The poem of his that you have must be the only surviving copy. The fifty sonnets he dedicated to the memory of Fritz Heinle
disappeared, along with the letters to Dora. I always wanted to make a
copy of them, but I could never get Walter to agree. This isn't the case
with his works such as "The Metaphysics of Youth," which I copied
during the early years of our friendship and which survived through me.

I am completely in the dark about the ownership rights to Klee's
Angelus Novus.[29] As far as I know, the picture was among Walter's effects
which were taken from Paris and given over to Adorno some time ago.
I can't say whether ownership of the picture is subject to Walter's last
instructions, which I have not seen.

Based on your biographical reflections, I realize I could have seen
you in 1957, when I was in Berlin for a week. Speaking for myself, I
have of course been sitting here in Jerusalem all these years and have

lived through all the local events and occurrences without taking any direct part in World History—which is scarcely surprising, given my life-long commitment to the exit of Jews from World History and a return to their own history. From this uncertain port I have made a number of forays into the big wide world, where, as is well known, it isn't any safer than here. Three years ago I was in America, and last year—don't laugh—in Poland. My scholarly reputation stood me in good stead there, and I was able to pursue studies that I've had on my mind for years. I have no family members or acquaintances left in Berlin. Speaking of which, I have heard that a young Hungarian Jew, now Swiss, whom I met in Zurich six weeks ago, wants to do his *Habilitation* on the history of literature at the Freie Universität Berlin with an essay or lecture on Walter Benjamin. His name is Peter Szondi, and he doesn't seem to be at all stupid.[30] The irony! A Jew does his *Habilitation* at a post-Hitler German university on an author whose own work failed to earn him a *Habilitation* from a German university.

With cordial greetings, to your wife as well. And with the hope of hearing from you soon.

My warmest wishes, Your old Scholem

TO HANNAH ARENDT

Jerusalem, November 28, 1960

Dear Hannah,

Your letter from the third of November, which you described as "disgusting," nevertheless provided me with a great deal of amusement. I flatter myself that my work on the messianic idea would hit the bull's eye with you and a number of others. I hope you will have the opportunity to cite me. I sent a copy of the essay to Nanda so that she can ascertain whether it is of interest to her and to her Christian and Jewish readers and their "universally human" concerns.[31] Once more I am "too Jewish," which of course does not bother me in the least. Meanwhile I hope that you have lovingly read your way through the Kabbalah volume, in particular the chapter on the meaning of the Torah. Its philosophical implications will not have escaped you. These thoughts were in fact the source of Walter Benjamin's attraction to the Kabbalah, insofar as I was in a position to explain them to him during my youth (when I was guided intuitively, rather than educated).

Yesterday a friend of mine received a copy of your *Vita activa;*[32] my own should be on its way. You'll have the opportunity to write me a personal dedication here in Jerusalem, as you in fact planned. This brings me to your travel plans. According to an official statement, the trial should begin on the sixth of March, if no new events create yet another delay.[33] This was announced here a week ago, so make your plans accordingly! It's also important for you to come in March if you want to see me. At the beginning of April, at the latest, I will be in London for about half a year. There I will finish writing a more or less immortal book on the development of the Kabbalah, something which I owe the world of scholarship and which will appear in both German and English.

The volume of Walter Benjamin's correspondence is coming together. Please check to see if you have any letters. If anything turns up, please send me the original or two copies. I would be most grateful if I could include his letters to you. Naturally, most letters have disappeared. Ernst Bloch finally explained that he had destroyed all letters from Walter Benjamin immediately after receiving them, and had done so "out of principle." This is what I call utopian principles.[34]

If you want to do me a favor, send me the issue of *Life* magazine containing Eichmann's confession. Strangely, they left it out of the international edition.

Yours, Gerhard

TO ALBERT SALOMON[35]

Jerusalem, December 20, 1960

Dear Herr Salomon,

Thank you for your letter of December 2. I am very sorry that I was unable to go to New York to discuss with you the text on Benjamin, and it's hardly possible to do so in a letter. So far as I can see, the problem with any attempt to present Benjamin's work consists in the fact that he, as a pure metaphysician—which he was, and which was the only capacity in which he could fulfill his true intuitions—attempted in his late work to speak through the language of Marxism. Not only this, but the way he orchestrated his work could give the impression that the results were the product of Marxist methodology. That this is an illusion can be demonstrated by any close analysis, which can easily lay bare the theological and metaphysical content of the questions asked and the answers given. This incongruity between his metaphysical genius and his regrettable attraction to an admittedly unorthodox Marxism was the topic of many debates between us. (What is orthodox Marxism today, anyway? It wasn't much different in his day.) If I can, I'll make a copy of a pertinent letter I wrote to him thirty years ago, after the publication of his essay on Karl Kraus. Benjamin was of course mostly aware of all this, even if he deliberately overlooked it in his literary works. He declared both in person and in writing that Marxism was, for him (and even this seems to me misleading, insofar as it relates to his way of thinking), a heuristic technique which, in its dialectic, had so many points of contact with his own intellectual concerns that he had to try and see how far he could get with it. [. . .] The best test cases of this are not the four essays you mentioned in *Die Gesellschaft*[36] (which are excellent, though scarcely Marxist in any sense), but the essays on Kraus and Baudelaire, and above all the Marxist aesthetic formulated in his fine article "The Work of Art in the Age of Its Technological Reproducibility." In this essay the artificiality of the connection between the magnificent metaphysical instruments in the first half, and the completely different orientation of the philosophy of film in the second, is particularly blatant. Benjamin had a superb feeling for dialectical processes; his conceptions, however, were that of a metaphysician and not a sociologist. Granted, it would perhaps be possible to write a metaphysics of the bourgeoisie's rise and fall from a Marxist perspective, as well; but this is not what Benjamin did. The seductive powers of Marxism never found a home in his extremely fertile and original thinking. I doubt whether Jewish factors played a large role. But they surely played an essential role to the extent that he believed he would find the true object of his thought in the realm of Judaism, even if he was ignorant of its sources. The complex nature of his relation to Jewish things, his endless efforts to learn Hebrew, and his failure to do so are important elements in his intellectual biography. He himself was wholly aware that his genius as a commentator on important texts was Jewish. He then declared that the texts of European literature which, due to ignorance, were the only ones he could turn to before arriving at Hebrew were in truth not the appropriate ones. To what extent we should take this statement seriously, or instead interpret it as somehow tongue-in-cheek, remains a matter of personal point of view. Be that as it may, he had an extraordinary fascination with Jewish concepts, a fascination which—as you rightly noted—is easily perceptible in his writings. His knowledge about these things was very underdeveloped. He always comforted himself by envisioning a time when he could fully devote himself to them: he would come to Palestine, learn Hebrew, and eventually teach literature at the university. That nothing came of these plans and that he repeatedly postponed his departure (doubtless because of his own inner reluctance) constitute the saddest chapters in Benjamin's biography. [. . .]

Yours, Gershom Scholem

1961

TO VICTOR GOLLANCZ[37]

London, June 13, 1961

Dear Mr. Gollancz,

I feel I should write to you to say how deeply distressed I am after having read your pamphlet on the Eichmann Case, which Leonard Montefiore gave me this morning. Being of those who have doubts as to the wisdom of putting Eichmann to death, I have never had any doubts as to the fundamental justice and dignity of this trial—the possibility of which, in contradiction to you, I consider one of the most redeeming aspects of the existence of the State of Israel. The somewhat perverse mixture of arguments adduced by you—judicial ones and essentially anarchist ones at the same time, canceling out each other—has done nothing to diminish this conviction. When I came to the last page, I just wept, overwhelmed by the sheer enormity of your "demands" in the face of the Jewish tragedy. I do not see why the Jews should become the only collective that ever followed "Christian" ethics, and I do not believe that to behave as you wish the Jewish people to behave would be in accordance with a higher code of values, as you imply. It is all very sublime—but it is also very cheap! How wonderful for a Jew to ask his fellow Jews not to try being what they are—which in this state of the world would be still more than difficult!—but being Christian angels as the History of Christianity has never known them. If it comes to this, I wish to stand up and be counted.

Yours sadly, Gershom Scholem

TO PETER SZONDI

Jerusalem, November 28, 1961

Dear Herr Szondi,

I am touched that you thought of me and sent a photocopy of Walter Benjamin's essay on Bachofen in the *Nouvelles Littéraires.* I was not familiar with the essay and previously had only glanced at it (I believe Werner Kraft has the issue of the journal). It's extraordinarily interesting to read these pages in a leisurely fashion now, after so many years. It is as if the author were conducting a sort of general inventory of all of his oldest themes, without identifying them as such. They pass by in a thoroughly uncanny incognito, and not without a bit of esotericism which, given the theme, is not in the least inappropriate. [. . .]

All the best to you and your work, Gershom Scholem

TO GEULA COHEN[38]

Jerusalem, December 15, 1961

Dear Ge'ula,

I have read to the end the *History of a Woman Warrior* you so kindly gave me. I wish to thank you not only for your testimony of days and deeds gone by, but also for the opportunity to reflect on the ideas from which you drew your strength. Your book was written with very great emotion. You articulate your vision and the things close to your heart during those years. In reading it, I thought much about my relation and attitude toward the *porshim*.[39] Again and again I asked the same question that troubled all of us at the time: What should we have done? Were your rhetoric and your deeds justified? At the time, we were outraged by your polemics. (And back then, who read *Ma'as* more often than I, seeing as it was plastered all over the walls of Keren Kayemet Street in our neighborhood?)[40] We were likewise incensed at your deeds. At the same time, the terrorism made us feel a deep sense of embarrassment, which was all the more profound because of our relationship with the people who practiced it. I recall a number of occasions when disputes broke out among friends over the question, "What would you have done if you had known those involved?" A number of people close to me spent many nights wrestling with this issue after they learned about some specific terrorist act and had to decide what to do. I was a pacifist not out of *principle,* but only in the very concrete case of our relations to the Arabs; I cannot deny that there may be circumstances which may justify a war or even an underground movement. Other people denied this a priori. To tell you the truth, I found the history of your ideology quite repugnant. Even today, after so many years, it's impossible for me to feel any enthusiasm for the citations you come up with. Especially problematic for me was the dream you discuss at many important junctures of your book. We each had our dreams, though these were not all the same. Even today my dreams do not conjure up the Kingdom and the heroism that enthralled you and your friends. But history makes equal fun of both your dream and mine, and this is a dreadful realization!

For the victory was not the one we had hoped to see. And there are many false notes in today's talk about what we have achieved. In this respect I share your feelings more than it may appear, though of course the falsity I perceive comes from the other side of the ideological coin. Hegel's "ruse of history" has done its work; your book, infused with so much purity of heart, confirms this ghastly dictum once again. The same thing happened with my dream. This victory is not the one I envisioned in my dreams. I never would have thought that the victors would so quickly forget the long years in which they themselves were the vanquished (and it was from those years that we drew our strength).

Many thanks both to you and to the angel hovering over your writing, your art. Fanya and I would be delighted to see you, so that we could express our gratitude in person.

Yours, Gershom Scholem

1962

TO LEO STRAUSS[41]

Jerusalem, December 13, 1962

Dear Strauss,

Since I fortunately have a secretary, I can reply at once to your letter (which I just received) and thus dispel the dark anxieties that have apparently spread over your soul concerning whether I approve of the publication of your autobiographical preface to the old heretic Spinoza.[42] Rest assured that you have my blessing. I will most probably be among the five or six people forming the only legitimate nucleus of readers for this *opusculum* (the number certainly won't reach the size of a Hessen *minjan*).[43] You can't harbor any great illusions about this; there is no doubt that American readers will find these pages as good as impenetrable. But if some institution is willing to print it, blessings be upon it. The very fact that you were prepared to put these thoughts on paper inspired me. But I understand everything now, because of your remark about Hobbes and the approach of old age. I'm going to put my own copy aside until the published version appears. I have plenty of time to write my own autobiography, and there should be a lot to say. The majority of German Jews now composing their memoirs and the like write completely godforsaken humbug. The two of us have something like a mission, though all of a sudden I have become skeptical about missions. In this I see eye to eye with you. It is in this spirit that I send Chanukka greetings to your entire family. I will spend it in Tiberias, the Palestinian Riviera.

Warmest greetings, G. Scholem

TO MANFRED SCHLOESSER

Jerusalem, December 18, 1962

Dear Herr Schloesser,

Your invitation to contribute to a memorial volume for Margarete Susman honors me while placing me in an undeniably embarrassing situation.[44] I see no way around declaring to you, and perhaps to the readers of your proposed festschrift, the substance of my embarrassment. According to the volume's prospectus, which you so kindly sent me, the festschrift is "intended not only as an homage but also as a document of the indestructible German-Jewish dialogue." No one could be more dismayed by such a statement than me. I am more than prepared to pay homage to a figure so worthy of honor as Margarete Susman, with whom I am connected by more than merely our views, but I must categorically turn down this invitation to foster what I see as the incomprehensible illusion of an "essentially indestructible German-Jewish dialogue." Allow me to explain myself in detail.

I deny that this German-Jewish dialogue, as a historical phenomenon, ever took place in any real sense. Having a discussion requires two parties that are willing to listen to each other, and to recognize and reply to what the other is and what he represents. There is nothing more misleading than to apply this concept to the conflicts between Germans and Jews over the past two hundred years. This dialogue died at birth and was never subsequently revived. It died when the successors to Moses Mendelssohn[45]—a man who still argued from a perspective of some kind of Jewish totality, albeit one that was determined by the concepts of the Enlightenment—agreed to sacrifice this totality and to salvage miserable fragments of it into an existence that itself betrays all the ambiguity of the recently fashionable characterization of a German-Jewish symbiosis. There is no question that Jews tried to enter into a dialogue with Germans, and from all possible perspectives and standpoints: now demanding, now pleading and imploring; now crawling on their hands and knees, now defiant; now with all possible compelling tones of dignity, now with a godforsaken lack of self-respect. Now that the symphony is over, it may be time to study its motifs and venture a critique of its harmonies. No one, not even someone who has long understood the hopelessness of this cry into the void, would belittle its passionate intensity and the notes of hope and sadness resonating from it. The attempt that Jews have made to explain themselves to Germans and to place at their disposal their own Jewish productivity, even to the point of complete self-abnegation, is an important phenomenon that has yet to be analyzed with adequate categories. Perhaps it can be done only now that the end has already come. Despite all this, I am unable to detect a dialogue. No one responded to this cry. And it was this simple yet vastly consequential realization that shocked many of us in our youth and led us to abandon the illusion of a German Jewry. When Germans—

from Wilhelm von Humboldt to Stefan George—entered with a humane spirit into a debate with Jews, they did so with the spoken and tacit assumption of the self-abnegation of Jews and their progressive atomization to the point of the dissolution of the Jewish community. In the best case, the individual—whether as a bearer of pure humanity or even as a bearer of a now historical heritage—could be accepted. The famous German solution from the period of emancipation, "Everything to Jews as individuals; nothing to them as a people" (that is, as Jews), prevented a German-Jewish dialogue from beginning. The only discussion partners who took Jews seriously as such were the anti-Semites, who somehow addressed the Jews, though not for their benefit. The boundless ecstasy of Jewish enthusiasm never earned a reply in any tone that could count as a productive response to Jews as Jews—that is, a tone that would have addressed what the Jews had to give and not only what they had to give up. To whom, then, did the Jews speak in this famous German-Jewish dialogue? They spoke to themselves, or rather they drowned each other out. Some did so with a feeling of uncanniness; most, though, acted as if everything were on the best path to be set right, as if the echo of their own voice would suddenly change into the voice of the others they so longed to hear. Jews have always been good listeners, a noble talent they brought with them from Mount Sinai. They have listened to all kinds of voices, but it can't be said that they've always heard correctly. When they thought they were speaking with Germans, they were speaking to themselves. No one as a Jew has ever been spoken to by the Jewish productivity of a thinker such as Simmel.[46] And Simmel is in fact symbolic of everything I have discussed here, because he illustrates a particular phenomenon: the way in which the substance of Judaism still reveals itself clearly in someone who has reached the nadir of complete alienation. I won't go into the disturbing chapter associated with the great name of Hermann Cohen and people's response to this unhappy lover, who was not reluctant to move from the sublime to the absurd.

The ostensibly indestructible spiritual community of Germans and Jews, which supposedly existed so long as the two parties really lived side by side, was composed solely of Jewish voices. As a historical reality, it was never anything more than a fiction—a fiction that, if I may say so, exacted too high a price. This fiction mostly irritated the Germans; at best they found it touching. To show this, I need cite only one of a rich array of sources. Jakob Wassermann's *My Life as German and Jew,*[47] no doubt one of the most profound documents of this fiction, appeared shortly before I left for Palestine. A true cry into the void, and he knew it. The response he received consisted of either embarrassment or sneers. In vain one looks for an answer on the level of discussion, which would have been a dialogue. [. . .] But what's the point in piling up examples when the entire ghostly German-Jewish dialogue played itself out in such an empty fictive space? I could go on forever discussing this, but I would remain standing in the same spot.

In the final analysis, it's true that Germans now acknowledge there was an enormous amount of Jewish creativity. This does not change the fact that you can't have a dialogue with the dead, and that to speak of the "indestructible German-Jewish dialogue" strikes me as blasphemy.

Yours, Gershom Scholem

1963

New York, April 17, 1963

Dear Scholem,

[. . .] In May of this year, at the meeting of the Hölderlin Society in Berlin, I will take it upon myself to give a keynote address on the philosophical problem of interpreting Hölderlin. In doing so I will of course pay due attention to Benjamin's text. It now strikes me that there are certain astounding, mostly linguistic, similarities between Benjamin and Heidegger, whose favorite expression vis-à-vis Hölderlin is "the poetized."[48] I intend to develop my critique of Heidegger precisely out of the differences pertaining to things so similar. As will be immediately evident to you, this involves the concept of the mythical. Heidegger holds that the mythical has the last word with Hölderlin; Benjamin shows that for Hölderlin it's the dialectical that counts. Not incidentally, I present certain of Benjamin's categories as having indisputable priority, though I'd like to leave the question open whether Heidegger knew Benjamin's work (which seems unlikely to me). I would be grateful if you could send me a quick comment.

Adorno

TO THEODOR ADORNO

Jerusalem, April 22, 1963

Dear Adorno,

I am responding to your letter of April 17, which arrived this afternoon by return post.

Walter Benjamin composed his essay on Hölderlin at the end of 1914 or at the very latest by the end of March 1915. It was the only essay he wrote at the beginning of the war. I received it as a birthday present in July 1915. The date appears in Podszus' biographical sketch.[49] Benjamin gave a few copies to friends and acquaintances (I doubt if it was more than half a dozen), and in the course of time he named some of those people to me. I have no reason to assume that Heidegger was among them or that he somehow got to know the essay second hand. The similarity in the use of the concept "the poeticized" occurred to me as well. [. . .]

I hope you will soon receive the copy of the lecture I gave last year at Eranos on the concept of tradition. It won't be hard for you to recognize me in it. I've also boasted a great deal in it, insofar as that is possible with the Kabbalah. Three weeks ago, in the *Neue Zürcher Zeitung,* old Buber published a rejoinder—the pathetic response of a helpless blabberer—to my criticism of his Hasidic interpretations. I'm wondering whether there is any sense at all in responding. [. . .]

With warmest regards, G. Scholem

TO ANIELA JAFFE[50]

Jerusalem, May 7, 1963

Dear Frau Jaffe,

I hope you've returned from Zurich and were able to convey our greetings to our friends. Seeing as you showed such an interest in the story of Baeck and Jung, I would like to set it down for your benefit. I have no objections if you quote me in this affair.

In midsummer 1947 Leo Baeck was in Jerusalem. I had just received an invitation to the Eranos conference in Ascona for the first time, obviously at Jung's initiative. I asked Baeck if he thought I should accept, for I had by then heard and read a number of criticisms of Jung's behavior during the Nazi period. "You must definitely go," Baeck said to me. In the course of our conversation, he recounted the following story. After he heard about Jung's reputation in the wake of his well-known articles of 1933–1934,[51] he felt extreme repugnance for him, in particular because he knew Jung from the days of the conferences at the Schule der Weisheit in Darmstadt and would never have expected to hear him utter National Socialist or anti-Semitic remarks. He therefore did not pay him a call during his first visit to Switzerland after his liberation from Theresienstadt. But Jung heard he was in town and requested a visit, which Baeck declined in view of those incidents. Jung then came to his hotel and they had a two-hour discussion, parts of which were quite heated. Baeck accused him of everything he had heard. Jung defended himself by referring to the special circumstances in Germany. At the same time he confessed that when the Nazis came to power, he had thought something great was under way. "Yes, I slipped up." I vividly recall the remark "I slipped up." Baeck repeated it several times. Baeck told me that in the conversation they clarified everything between them, and when they parted they were reconciled. On the weight of Baeck's explanation, I accepted the invitation to Eranos when it came for a second time in 1949.

Cordial greetings from my wife and me.

Yours, G. Scholem

P.S. The point of this brief account is neither to idealize nor to belittle C. G. Jung's image. Rather, it's intended to free his image from the "parties of hatred and prejudice." Generally, it's hard for people to exist side by side with great men, yet still maintain their own dignity. Such proximity leads either to uncritical hero worship or to an equally uncritical exaggeration of real faults. Even Goethe's image, considered so sacrosanct, wasn't immune to this. The recent history of literature has proved this. The reputations of Freud and Jung have been just as incapable of avoiding this fate.

Even more difficult than holding one's own and enduring the greatness of others is being fated to bear greatness yourself. Greatness acts like a sudden incursion of transcendence and becomes a life's calling pushed to the last extremity. As a result, the strongest personality is the one that can bind together greatness and humanity, the singular and the collective, spiritual light and wandering in the darkness. The suffering caused by this tension leads the greatest artists and researchers—the greatest human beings—to turn to the world with knowledge, understanding, and love.

TO HANNAH ARENDT

Jerusalem, June 23, 1963

Dear Hannah,

It's been six weeks since I received your book on the Eichmann trial.[52] I am just now writing because at first I couldn't concentrate on the book. I have only recently gotten to it. I won't concern myself here with whether you got all the objective or historical facts right. So far as

I can assess some of the details, the book is not lacking in misunderstandings and errors. A number of your critics—and there will be many—will take up the issue of factual accuracy; it isn't central to what I want to say.

Your book orbits around two centers: Jews and their behavior during the Catastrophe on the one hand, and Eichmann and his responsibility on the other. For many years I have given thought to the subject of the Jews and have studied no small amount of literature on the subject. It's utterly clear to me—and this probably goes for every reflective observer of these events—how bitterly serious, how complicated, how far from transparent and reducible this matter is. There are aspects of Jewish history (and this is what I have occupied myself with for the past fifty years) which are hardly free of abysses: a demonic decay in the midst of life; insecurity in the face of this world (in contrast to the security of the pious, whom your book, bafflingly, does not mention); and a weakness that is perpetually confounded and mingled with debasement and with lust for power. These have always existed, and it would be odd indeed if they didn't come to the fore in some form at times of catastrophe. This happened in 1291 and in the generation of disaster that followed, just as it has happened in our own day. The debate on this topic is for the most part legitimate and unavoidable, even if I don't think our generation can pass anything resembling a historical judgment. We lack, as we must, the true distance that could also inspire prudence. Still, the questions continue to press themselves on us. The query that young people in Israel are asking has real merit: "Why did they allow themselves to be killed?" The answer that one always starts to give cannot be reduced to a formula. In every important respect, particularly when it comes to your choice of focus, your book addresses only the weakness of Jewish existence. And to the degree that there really was weakness, your emphasis is, so far as I can tell, completely one-sided and leaves the reader with a feeling of rage and fury. Nevertheless, the problem you pose is genuine. Why, then, does your book evoke such a feeling of bitterness and shame for those who recognize this—indeed, not for the author's subject matter but for the author herself? Why does your account so dominate the events it records, which you rightly want people to reflect on? To the degree that I have an answer, I cannot hide it—if only because of my high regard for you. It will clarify what stands between us. It is the heartless, the downright *malicious* tone you employ in dealing with a topic that so profoundly concerns the center of our life. There is something in the Jewish language that is completely indefinable, yet fully concrete—what the Jews call *ahavath Israel,* or love for the Jewish people. With you, my dear Hannah, as with so many intellectuals coming from the German left, there is no trace of it. An exposition such as yours demands, if I may say so, the old-fashioned kind of objective and thorough treatment—especially where, as in the case of the murder of a third of our people, such deep emotions are necessarily at work and are so greatly aroused. And I see you as nothing other than a member of this people. I haven't the slightest sympathy for the light-hearted style, by which I mean the English flippancy, that you employ all too often in your book. It's inappropriate for your topic, and in the most unimaginable way. In treating such a theme, isn't there a place for the humble German expression "tact of the heart"?[53] You may laugh; I hope not, for I say this in earnest. Among the many passages in your book which have gnawed at me, I can point to no clearer example of what I mean than your description of the way in which residents of the Warsaw Ghetto bought and sold armbands bearing the Jewish symbol; also your comment on Leo Baeck, "who in the eyes of both Jews and Gentiles was the 'Jewish *Führer.*'" In this context your use in German of a Nazi term says a lot. For instance, you don't call him simply the Jewish leader, without quotation marks, which would have been sensible and free of any malicious aftertaste. You say the very thing that is most offensive and furthest from the truth. No one I have ever heard or read considered Leo Baeck, whom you and I both knew, a leader in the sense that your readers will be induced to adopt. Like you, I have read Adler's book on Theresienstadt.[54] A lot can be said about the work. But I have not found that the author, who speaks resentfully about people I have likewise read something about, has ever characterized or indirectly portrayed Baeck in such a way. What our people have gone through may be clouded on account of dark figures who earned or would have earned their bullets—and how could it be otherwise with a tragedy of this magnitude? But to discuss this in such a wholly inappropriate tone (to the benefit of those Germans whom your book mentions with stronger tones of disgust than those it uses to discuss the misfortune of the Jews) is not the way to lay out the true dimensions of this tragedy.

I don't find any balanced judgment in your discussion of Jewish behavior under extreme conditions—conditions that neither of us experienced; instead, it's more like demagogically twisted overstatement. Who of us today can say which decisions the "Elders," or whatever one wants to call them, should have made under those conditions? I don't know, and I have read no less on this issue than you have; nor do I get the impression from your analysis that your knowledge is any better grounded than my ignorance. Jewish Councils existed. Some of their members were scoundrels, others saints. I've read a great deal about both. There were also many average people, like the majority of us, forced to make decisions under conditions that will never recur and that are impossible to reconstruct. I have no idea if they did the right thing or the wrong thing. I don't presume to judge. I wasn't there. [. . .]

I won't say anything about the other central issue of your book, which is Eichmann's guilt, or the extent of guilt that should be allotted to him. I have read the judge's verdict against Eichmann, along with your substitute text. The judge's account strikes me as far more convincing than yours. Your verdict is a curious example of a massive non sequitur. Your justification holds true for hundreds of thousands, perhaps millions of people, and your last sentence could just as easily be applied to them. And only your last sentence provides justification for Eichmann's hanging, because in the earlier parts of the essay you explain in detail why, in your opinion (which I by no means share), the prosecution failed to prove what it should have proved, on all of the essential points. I would like to mention that, in addition to signing a letter to the president urging him not to carry out the execution, I wrote an essay in Hebrew explaining why I consider it historically misguided to carry out the death sentence (the primary reason being our position with regard to the Germans)—even if Eichmann has it coming to him in every way and in accord with the arguments of the prosecution. I don't want to burden this letter with a discussion of his sentence. I wish to say merely that your depiction of Eichmann as a convert to Zionism is conceivable only when it comes from someone like you, filled with *ressentiment* for everything connected to Zionism. I can't take these pages of your book seriously. They do nothing but mock Zionism—which is, I fear, the main point for you. I don't want to get into this.

After reading your book, I am not in the least convinced by the notion of the "banality of evil." If the book's subtitle can be believed, you strove to develop the theme. This banality seems rather more of a slogan than the result of the kind of in-depth analysis you presented far more convincingly under very different circumstances in your book on totalitarianism. Apparently, back then you had not yet discovered that evil is banal. The radical evil which your previous analysis testified to so elegantly and knowledgeably has disappeared without a trace into a slogan. If this is to be more than a slogan, it must be taken to a deeper plane of political morality and moral philosophy. I regret that, given my sincere and friendly feelings toward you, I have nothing positive to say about your theses in this work. I expected something else, especially after your first book.

Yours, Gerhard

FROM HANNAH ARENDT

New York, July 20, 1963

Dear Gerhard,

I found your letter waiting for me when I arrived back home eight days ago. You can easily imagine how things look after a five-month absence. I am truly writing at the first possible opportunity, though perhaps not with the detail I should.

Your letter contains a number of uncontroversial claims—uncontroversial because they are quite simply wrong. I'll begin with them so we can move on to the issues worth discussing.

I do not belong to the "intellectuals coming from the German left." This you couldn't have known, because we weren't acquainted in our youth. It's hardly a fact to boast of. In fact, I say so unwillingly, particularly since the McCarthy era descended upon this country. Only later did I learn something about Marx's importance. In my youth I was interested neither in history nor in politics. If I hailed from anywhere at all, it was from German philosophy.

Unfortunately, I can't say you couldn't have known a second point. I thought it peculiarly touching when you wrote, "I see you as nothing other than a member of this [namely, the Jewish] people." Not only have I never acted as if I were something else, but I have never even felt the temptation to do so. It's as if I were to say I am a man and not a woman. In other words, it would be sheer lunacy. Naturally I know this can be a Jewish problem, but it's never been mine. Not even in my youth. That I am a Jew is one of the unquestioned facts of my life, and I've never wanted to alter such brute facts. [. . .]

Let's get to the real issue. Tying in with what I just said, I'll begin with *ahavath Israel* (by the way, I would be extraordinarily grateful to you if you could tell me when this expression began to play a role in the Hebrew language and literature, when it appeared for the first time, and so on). How right you are that I have no such love, and for two reasons: first, I have never in my life "loved" some nation or collective—not the German, French, or American nation, or the working class, or whatever else might exist. The fact is that I love only my friends and am quite incapable of any other sort of love. Second, this kind of love for the Jews would seem suspect to me, since I am Jewish myself. I don't love myself or anything I know belongs to the substance of my being. To illustrate what I mean, let me tell you about a conversation I had with a leading political figure who defended what I consider a disastrous lack of separation between religion and state in Israel. She said more or less the following (I don't recall her exact words): "You understand, of course, that as a socialist I do not believe in God. I believe in the Jewish people." This is a horrible comment, in my view, and I was too shocked to offer a response. But I could have replied that the magnificence of this people once lay in its belief in God—that is, in the way its trust and love of God far outweighed its fear of God. And now this people believes only in itself? In this sense I don't love the Jews, nor do I "believe" in them. I *belong* to this people, in nature and in fact.

We could speak politically about this issue, and then we would discuss the question of patriotism. We would both agree that patriotism is impossible without constant opposition and critique. In this entire affair I can confess to you one thing: that injustice committed by my own people naturally provokes me more than injustice done by others. Furthermore, the role of the "heart" in politics in fact strikes me as highly dubious. You know as well as I do how often those who report the facts have been accused of lacking "tact of the heart." [. . .]

That you could form the opinion that my book is a "mockery of Zionism" would have struck me as completely incomprehensible if I didn't know the extent to which Zionist circles have forgotten that they should avoid listening to opinions set in stone and embraced by everyone from the start. A Zionist friend of mind told me quite naively that the last chapter (on the jurisdiction of the court and on the justification for the kidnapping)[55] is especially pro-Israel, which is of course true. But it threw you off because you didn't expect my arguments or my way of thinking—in other words, my independence. I mean on the one hand that I do not belong to any organization and speak only in my own name, and on the other that a person must think for himself and, whatever you may have against my results, you won't understand them unless you know that they are my results and no one else's. [. . .]

In conclusion, I come to the only point of agreement between us. I am happy you discovered it, and I wish to say a few words about it. You are completely right that I have changed my mind and now no longer speak of radical evil. We haven't seen each other for a long time; otherwise we would perhaps have gotten around to discussing this. It's unclear to me why you characterize the phrase "banality of evil" as a slogan. So far as I know, no one has ever used it before. But this isn't important. The fact is that today I think that evil in every instance is only extreme, never radical: it has no depth, and therefore has nothing demonic about it. Evil can lay waste the entire world, like a fungus growing rampant on the surface. Only the good is always deep and radical. As I said, however, I don't want to go into this here, since I intend to deal with these issues in a different context and in greater depth. [. . .]

Yours, Hannah

TO WERNER CONZE

Jerusalem, August 3, 1963

Most honorable Herr Colleague,

Thank you for your letter of July 23 inviting me to accept a visiting professorship in Jewish studies at Heidelberg. Solely because of timing— that is, other commitments—I cannot accept your invitation for the next two or three years. All other considerations aside, my response must be determined by these pragmatic constraints. But because you have asked for an answer that is not determined by scheduling alone, I wish to tell you frankly that my reflections on the specific conditions related to academic work in Germany make me feel extremely hesitant. It is impossible for me to accept an invitation in this field at Heidelberg, where my relations with my close scholarly colleagues—above all, those in Hebrew studies—would inevitably be shadowed and burdened by the darkest memories. This would render collegial relations impossible. Despite the pleasure it would give me to associate with the members of your faculty I esteem so highly, I don't think I could endure the perverse situations that would result. When I look into myself, I fear that my preparedness for such situations is insufficient for me to accept your faculty's honorable invitation.

Thank you once again, and best wishes.

Prof. G. Scholem

TO HANNAH ARENDT

Jerusalem, August 12, 1963

Dear Hannah,

[. . .] My comment and strong emphasis on your belonging to the Jewish people meant precisely the opposite of the sense you gave it. It was a riposte to all those who consider themselves (and, as you must have noticed, there are many) members of what has lately been characterized as a "post-Zionist assimilation"—that is, those who think they have cut themselves free from the Jewish people, or who would very much like to do so if it's at all possible, etc. By writing this, I showed that I don't count myself among the critics who accuse you of such a thing, but that on the contrary I am in full agreement with you here. You are so irritable and tense when it comes to anything related to this topic (which of course is understandable) that you want to write off your critics, myself included, as victims of an organized campaign, manipulated from above. You seem to take me for a more or less harmless victim of this campaign. I doubt very much whether such a campaign has been "set in motion" from the Israeli side (something I'm in a position to know about). The bitterness aroused by your book among so many readers hardly needed an organizational hand in order to find literary expression. [. . .]

My opinion on the execution of Eichmann is different from yours, though I know that under the present circumstances someone (or even you) could accuse me of unrealistic thinking in this case. My point was that we should not make it easier for the Germans to confront their past, as we in fact did with Eichmann's execution. A great sigh of relief swept through the forest of German newspapers (and not only there) when the Israelis hanged Eichmann. He now stands as a representative for everyone, and will remain so. This notion filled me with the deepest unease. No one who signed the letter thought about clemency; instead, they all thought of nonexecution.

One of these days the two of us will no doubt discuss evil and its banality through bureaucratization. Though you think you have proven it, I have not seen the proof. Maybe this kind of evil exists; but if so, philosophically it would have to be considered differently. I don't picture Eichmann, as he marched around in his SS uniform and relished how everyone shivered in fear before him, as the banal gentleman you now want to persuade us he was, ironically or not. I refuse to go along. I've read enough descriptions and interviews of Nazi functionaries and their conduct in front of Jews—while the going was good—to mistrust this innocuous *ex post facto* construction. The gentlemen enjoyed their evil, so long as there was something to enjoy. One behaves differently after the party's over, of course. So much for today. I hope you really will write something about my Kabbalah book. As you may have noticed, I have packed a lot into it.

Yours, Gerhard

FROM HANNAH ARENDT

New York, September 14, 1963

Dear Gerhard,

[. . .] Once again you've misunderstood the "banality of evil." The point isn't to turn evil into something banal or harmless. The opposite is true. Evil is a surface phenomenon, the decisive issue being that completely average people, neither good nor evil by nature, were able to bring about such immense ruin.

My last point: I consider it a fairy tale that the death of Eichmann could "make it easier for the Germans to confront their past." Even if it weren't a fairy tale, it wouldn't be a valid argument. After all is said and done, a trial was held in Jerusalem; and once a trial starts, the rules of the legal system must be followed. The real question was: How useful

are legal means in coming to grips with these issues? All political considerations, regardless of which side they relate to, could only be pernicious
here. A trial does not set out to make history; it pronounces justice.
Once the death sentence was read, it would have been impossible, in
the pursuit of justice, not to carry it out. The only reason would have
been a principled opposition to the death penalty, an argument that neither you nor the others made (even though Buber now gives this as his
reason).

With best wishes for your trip to Europe,

Hannah

1964

TO THEODOR ADORNO

Jerusalem, February 9, 1964

Dear Adorno,

Your letter arrived a few days before your latest book, *Quasi una Fantasia.*[56] Your writings have meanwhile taken on such impressive proportions that I will soon drop out of the competition. In any event, my reading in German has now been taken care of for a while. Many thanks for your dedication to the work of Arnold Schoenberg. I read your essay on him with the closest attention, especially the sections where my utter ignorance of the technical side of music didn't handicap me. One of these days I hope to hear his *Moses and Aaron,* so I can make some sense of it. Your reflections on this opera and on contemporary sacral music are very insightful. I can't say whether you have really managed to prove the impossibility of such music. For one cannot predict where and in which forms the tradition of sacral music will make its appearance in our present world. I don't want to concede its impossibility a priori. I must admit that the contradiction you pointed out between the dramatic and sacral element in drama made a lot of sense to me. Given my lack of knowledge, I also won't venture to say whether Schoenberg actually saw his opera as ritual music. The question still remains whether ritual still has enough life to engender authentic music. Jewish music strikes me as something downright inconceivable, which fits all too well with what you term the image-less image. Everything people call "Jewish music" carries a big question mark—that is, this is my view to the extent that I could follow you and have understood the discussion of these things. The Jewish element in it always boils down to something ritualistic. It's inevitably hiding somewhere. Regarding your observations on myth and music, I'm a bit doubtful about your conjecture on the subterranean mystical tradition among modern Jews. At the very most I can imagine it as one of Jung's hypotheses, which I don't find entirely convincing. This mystical tradition would more likely appear in the structured creative works of the Jews you named than in some historical thread, be it ever so thin. I can't belief in such a thread, especially

given what I know about the history of Moravian and Bohemian Jewry.
[. . .]

Gershom Scholem

FROM THEODOR ADORNO

New York, February 17, 1964

Dear Scholem,

[. . .] Rest assured that I am far from postulating any sort of Jungian
hypothesis on the question of a subterranean mystical tradition. The core
of Jung's teaching—archaic images—is still a Freudian motif. Freud, especially in his work on Moses, went so far as to postulate an inherited
memory, which necessarily implies the existence of a collective memory.
The falsity of Jung doesn't so much lie in his individual insights, which
are often quite fruitful. It's their isolation from the larger total framework
that lend these insights their reactionary and false features. But I intended
something far humbler when I wrote about this aspect of Jewish tradition. I simply reiterated my observation that an entire group of Jews
from this generation and from the Moravian-Bohemian region—Kraus,
Kafka, Schoenberg, and perhaps Freud—showed traces of a mystical tradition (God knows where they got it), just as they bore witness to the
tradition's radical secular metamorphosis. Heaven knows you're more
competent than I am to come up with an explanation.

Adorno

TO ANIELA JAFFE

Jerusalem, December 8, 1964

Dear Frau Jaffe,

Warmest thanks for sending the sketches of Jung during the Nazi
period. I've been unable to respond until now, and apologize for the
delay. You ask for my opinion; I'm very skeptical. I don't believe anyone
in either Israel or America will publish these notes in this form. You
might be able to publish them in a journal in Switzerland or Germany.

What's unsatisfactory about your commentary is its insufficient analysis of Jung's essays (insufficient to me, anyway), from which one could choose more piquant and far-reaching excerpts than the ones you offer. To do it right, there would have to be a thorough analysis of all these texts, or at the very least of the statements in his essays that are felt to be anti-Jewish, or that in fact are. In addition to Jung's statements in German periodicals, I assume there must be others on these matters—in published pieces, in letters, in oral sources—because he formally withdrew from the International Society and the editorship of the *Zentralblatt* only in 1940.[57] It seems to me that we have yet to get to the bottom of this entire riddle. The essay on Wotan you referred to is very ambivalent in tone. I know many people whose interpretation of it is very different from yours—who do not see it precisely as a criticism of National Socialism. This, too, requires closer analysis. [. . .]

With best wishes, G. Scholem

1965

TO HILDE SCHOLEM[58]

Jerusalem, February 26, 1965

Dear Hilde,

Yesterday a telegram arrived from Reinhold informing us that Erich has passed away. The news shook us to the core. We naturally knew how weak Erich's health had been in recent years and were aware that every additional year he wrung from his illness was something of a miracle. But still he enjoyed life greatly during this period. When I think back upon our time together in Europe, I can't forget how much pleasure he took in traveling. The two of you spent so many decades in close harmony with each other that the loss of your life's partner must be a terrible blow to you. As we have seen, though, you have so many inner resources that we can hope you will not succumb to such a difficult stroke of fate. How are Erich's children? We have lost all contact with them.

It's now been fifty years since Erich went into the military (until then I lived with him on Neue Grün Strasse, where for years we shared a room). After that I saw him only rarely, and at long intervals. So my picture of my brother is based almost entirely on impressions and experiences from our youth. He had a remarkably agile mind, which was inherently sure of itself. As far back as I can recall, he also had a healthy and abiding mistrust of the world. He was always rather inclined to keep to himself. You are surely the one who knew him the best, who knew him as he really was. These memories will certainly remain. Fanya and I are both aware of what you did for him all these years, what you meant to him, and how much he depended upon you. You gave him a good life, and for this, too, we thank you.

In this spirit we hold your hand.

Gerhard

TO PETER SZONDI

Jerusalem, March 3, 1965

Dear Herr Szondi,

Today I received your letter from Princeton. If I have understood you correctly, congratulations are in order for the professorship in comparative literature that the people in Berlin offered so that they could snap you up. Is this true? Didn't anything come of your plans to emigrate to a friendly foreign place? What will happen to your plans? What sorts of duties go along with making those literary comparisons? Enlighten me when you get a chance.

While you enter into academic offices, I am leaving mine. Two weeks from today I will deliver my last lecture as a professor. From then on, I will retreat into my science, my old and new love, and into its unofficial branches. I will become, as it were, master of my time. I'll be staying here for the summer, where I'll work and won't despair (because of the international congress on Judaica that is to take place here). In September I'll go to America for a few weeks to take part in a conference in California. I hope it's worth it. If in the meantime the volume of Benjamin's letters appears (I haven't yet seen a trace of it), I'll probably return via Frankfurt. By the way, has the discussion on W.B. you had with me and others found its way onto public radio? Is there a text of it? If I'm not mistaken, there's supposed to be an honorarium. I haven't received anything yet. Could you look into this sometime? I no longer recall who commissioned it. The *Neue Rundschau* wrote to me saying that they'd printed my talk. I assume the volume will arrive in a month. I wasn't exactly thrilled to hear that you found my article interesting. My considerable efforts should have brought better results. But perhaps I have exaggerated ideas on this and you are right about it. In any event I prefer my commentary to the insolent blabber of Herbert Marcuse, who recently wrote a postscript to Benjamin's "Critique of Violence" (in the Suhrkamp edition of his works). Marcuse's piece is a case of pure sleight-of-hand.

My soul really groans with pain at the fact that my letter to Herr Schloesser hasn't seen the light of day. Dr. Weber wanted to publish it in the *Neue Zürcher Zeitung*. He had my blessing to do so because it's very important to me that my judgment reach a wide audience. For reasons unclear to me, however, it doesn't seem to have appeared. It should have been included at the beginning of *Judaica,* which would have been the right place for it.[59]

I can't go to Eranos this year; I'll have to postpone it till next year.

We hope to hear from you. Until then, please accept warmest greetings from my wife and me.

Yours, G. Scholem

TO MANFRED SCHLOESSER

Jerusalem, April 6, 1965

Most esteemed Herr Schloesser,

A week ago I received five offprints of my contribution to the memorial volume for Margarete Susman, and today your letter from the twenty-ninth of March arrived. In view of the situation you described to me in your letter, I can do without additional offprints. I have no intention of causing difficulties for you or in any way increasing your deficit. I admire the idealistic project you've undertaken with this festschrift. I will make no more demands.

It's utterly impossible for me to say anything about the volume itself, and I assume you don't expect me to. Mostly I am interested in the letters you printed; often, they were more revealing than the four contributions.[60] But what's crucial in the end is that the person being celebrated derive some pleasure from it. I assume this is in fact the case.

We don't see at all eye to eye on the relationship between Germans and Jews, the issue you took up again in the main part of your letter. Obviously, our starting positions could not be more divergent, given our mutual hope of arriving at some common human factor, which I would never think to question. Moreover, I haven't the slightest interest in whether Benjamin declared himself a Jewish thinker or a German thinker. My essay in the *Neue Rundschau* did not touch on this question at all.[61] I allowed myself the liberty only to establish the simple fact that Benjamin considered himself a Jew *sans phrase,* and believed he had the manifest right to be a German writer without being a German. Whether this is right or not is a question we will scarcely agree on. I have become convinced that at present there's a belated tendency among Germans to lay claim to Jews who were killed for being Jews, as a kind of posthumous triumph. I know far too many Jews who are silent about this, and I

refuse to be among them. I see quite clearly the kind of precarious subjective situation that's typical of most people who come into question
here, which in turn makes their situation open to discussion. You can
see from this that I differentiate between those who hoodwinked themselves, as most did, and the few who had no illusions. Given the circumstances prevailing at the time, it took enormous spiritual power (which
you perhaps failed to take account of fully) to avoid self-delusion. The
opposite was easier, and brought with it more benefits—advantages for
people's so-called inner comfort. I am of course not speaking of those,
such as Simmel or Lukács, who came from baptized families and never
had any kind of ties to their Jewish background, yet who nevertheless
were considered by non-Jews to be in a certain sense "representatives
of Jewishness." This is a paradox, and only future generations will be capable of plumbing its depths. Why it was the Jews who were able to express
themselves with such influence and importance, particularly with regard
to Goethe, is a question you ask quite justifiably. But this is precisely the
question that was forbidden in the past. The answer remains open, just
like the answers to nearly all of the questions that deal with what happened
in this arena. Insightful people will still have a lot to think about.

[. . .] To be sure, I'll always maintain that we should leave open the
possibility for a dialogue, if this means a dialogue in the future and not
a pseudo-dialogue of the past, based on mendacious assumptions. I have
already expressed my support for this future dialogue through the simple
fact that I allowed my books to be published in Germany. No one can
predict whether this will lead to anything.

I wish you all the best with your work.

Sincerely yours, G. Scholem

FROM MICHAEL MACKEL

April 29, 1965

Dear Herr Scholem,

I am a student at the Technische Universität Berlin, and as a result
have nothing solid to stand on when it comes to making judgments—
just like the majority of my fellow students, I assume. When we want
to form an image of the Third Reich, we are dependent on statements
from people like you. Who has the time (or motivation) to read history

books in addition to so much coursework? We would rather speak to a Jew, a victim of that time, who is most likely to give us the true key to the source of the madness. We have all seen films and pictures from Auschwitz—often, in fact, with commentary by former prisoners who spoke at the Jewish community house. Our tears and sadness at this suffering gave rise to dread and to an abysmal mistrust in "human nature" and in the swamp on which our judgments grow. Moreover, I felt that I was a creature of this swamp, and that I was utterly helpless and deceitful when faced with these atrocities. We expect the Jews who speak to us to help us form sure-footed judgments by overcoming their feelings and by teaching us the clear—relentlessly clear—lessons they've drawn from those times. This is what we lack. Why shouldn't Jewish professors be guests in Germany? You must come here, otherwise many abstruse concepts such as collective guilt will go unexplained. People load us down even before we grow up; they demand that we become equal discussion partners. We speak with Jews who never want to go to Israel; who as former immigrants to Argentina return to Germany without commenting on the need and misery in Argentina; and who are outraged when they are not sufficiently compensated for having the teeth beaten out of them. Besides this, they have nothing to say. We need you here in Germany. We need to hear you in the media (especially on the radio), in the university, in the theater—everywhere that is open and accessible. [. . .]

Sincerely yours

TO GEORGES FRIEDMANN[62]

Jerusalem, May 3, 1965

Dear Herr Friedmann,

Please accept my thanks for sending me an inscribed copy of your book, *End of the Jewish People?*—and please forgive me for thanking you in German.[63] I was extremely pleased to receive it, and I hope we'll have another opportunity to discuss, in person, the questions raised by your book. If I understand you correctly, you say that the end of the Jewish people will come because the nation that has developed in Israel is no longer Jewish. While I understand perfectly well the reasons for such a prognosis, I still consider it totally mistaken. There is no doubt that the Israeli nation, which has separated itself from the Jewish people, is marching toward its ruin. Whatever weight you give assimilation—and naturally you're right to give it a lot—you underestimate the tremendous power of reconstituting historical memory through the dialectical swings of the pendulum. I find it difficult to agree with your eloquently expressed view that this consciousness will vanish in Israel. It would seem to me closer to the truth to say that a crisis will, and must, develop. Indeed, perhaps even a life-threatening crisis. But when we embarked on this journey, we knew perfectly well that the success of the Zionist enterprise would lead to such a crisis. We wanted it, for we believed in the creative power of the Jewish genius, however indefinable. That this crisis has erupted in earnest during our generation strikes me as a sign legitimizing the historical process we have witnessed. I am not saying that the Jewish people won't go under; yet a metamorphosis of tradition and of the forms its genius takes does not count as a disaster. It is this metamorphosis, its necessity, and its productive outcome which the best minds of the Zionist movement have believed in, and continue to do so. It is in this direction that our discussion would move if we were to take it up once again. In connection with your chapter entitled "Anguish and Happiness," allow me to cite a truly profound comment made by Hermann Cohen, a great Jew and philosopher, after Franz Rosenzweig asked him what he really thought about the Zionists. With all of the esoteric signs that accompany the revelation of a secret, Cohen replied: "These fellows just want to be happy." Good or bad, I have never heard so profound a comment on Zionism.

With cordial and friendly greetings, from both me and my wife.

G. Scholem

TO THEODOR ADORNO

Jerusalem, June 20, 1965

Dear Adorno,

Many thanks for your letter of June 10, which I received upon my return from Buber's funeral. It arrived at the same time as an invitation from the *Merkur* in Munich to say something about the deceased in a memorial essay. I declined straightaway and explained that unfortunately

I would be incapable of writing a piece for a German readership, discussing the issue of Buber's spiritual physiognomy and the reasons for his enormous success among the Germans and utter failure among the Jews. Just between us, this is a question for dialectical sociologists. By the way, I was asked to say a few words at his grave. I said to my wife, Fanya, "Give me three points I can make without telling a bald-faced lie." I have to pat myself on the back for my success, all thanks to Fanya! The news that Dora Benjamin died last year was something I did not know. It hit me hard. I saw her for the last time in May 1961, and was exceedingly disturbed—she was in total decline. After that, I could not bring myself to pay her another visit. [. . .]

Last year I gave my Eranos lecture on the concept of the tradition of commentary. The essay includes the most precise formulations of revelation and tradition I am capable of. They earned Walter Benjamin's unqualified agreement back in 1932, after I put them in writing for the first time in a debate with Herr Schoeps. [. . .]

Best wishes, Gerhard Scholem

TO MICHAEL MACKEL

Jerusalem, July 18, 1965

Esteemed Herr Mackel,

[. . .] I understand quite well that the Jews you speak with in Germany are not exactly people from whom you can expect the kind of elucidation mentioned in your letter. I readily admit this, nor can I think of any principled arguments in defense of the thesis that Jewish professors "shouldn't be guests in Germany." Unfortunately, my dear sir, these things entail very emphatic, nonprincipled considerations whose importance you may not be able to imagine. The expectation you have of Jews—that they are duty-bound to overcome their feelings—is hopeless. There is no one, including the author of these lines, capable of putting aside his feelings in these matters, even if he's prepared or even feels obliged to speak to Germans, in particular to young Germans. One can try to prevent these feelings from totally choking off one's speech. If anything more than this is demanded of us, I fear that we, of all people, cannot give it. I myself have given talks in Germany. Though I am a tolerably rational creature, I can testify to the enormous inhibitions this involves for a speaker who takes it seriously. Like you, I am of the opinion that it would be desirable if the number of those speaking as Jews to Germans were greater. Among us, though, there are many differences of opinion on this point. Those who question whether appearances in the German media should and can be promoted have good reasons for doing so. The decision whether one wants to go to Germany and is prepared to open one's mouth is profoundly determined by emotion. Sadly, in the majority of cases up to now, most have decided against it. Sometimes, too, Germans have charged me with being hostile toward Germany after I've resolutely and clearly mentioned the things that burden our two peoples. The person who doesn't need to hear something doesn't like being told the same thing twice. I would like to hope that, with the establishment of so-called normal relations, the number of those who think it makes sense to speak to the Germans will increase. At the same time, you are right to say that lightweights have an easier time finding opportunities to appear in Germany than do Jews with the "clear spirit" you seek. They don't allow themselves to be pressured. I still hope that in the course of time some person from this latter group will make his way to Germany, to engage with the new conditions and the recently developed state of affairs.

Cordially yours, G. Scholem

FROM REINHOLD SCHOLEM

Sydney, October 10, 1965

Dear Gerhard,

Since you last heard from me, I have read your article on Benjamin in the *Neue Rundschau* and the one in the *Zürcher Zeitung* that concerns his correspondence.[64] I have a couple questions for you, even though I know that my knowledge doesn't stretch far enough to enter into a well-founded conversation with you. I can only relay my personal impressions, which are not always logically grounded. In paragraph four (page 15) you defend the position that Schnitzler, Wassermann, and Stefan Zweig falsely looked upon themselves as belonging to *Deutschtum*.[65] You depict this as a tragic illusion. In the same breath, you declare that Kafka and Benjamin were German writers without being Germans. Finally, you cast doubt on whether they would have felt at home in Israel. Isn't this the weak point in your argument? If they felt as Jewish as you say, wouldn't the most immediate concomitant of this be a longing for Israel and a feeling of being at home there? Furthermore, if Benjamin was only barely grounded in Germanness (a topic which is hardly mentioned in your essay), how you do explain that the German *Neue Rundschau* printed your piece as a lead article? Someone once wrote somewhere that "the *Deutschtum* we seek is an ideal that has never existed." Should we view German poets with strong provincial backgrounds—Westphalian, Frisian, Low German—as non-Germans as well? And Thomas Mann, who did not feel at home in America, lives in Switzerland instead of returning to Germany. Even though Hitler and his comrades declared him to be non-German, he still remains a German writer. German Jews—the poets and writers, as well as common people like myself—all have this background. The question is to what extent the influence of the German culture in which we were raised has come to overshadow the inherited Jewish influence. But as Fontane's old Herr Briest says, that's too big a subject.[66] [. . .]

Your brother Reinhold

TO REINHOLD SCHOLEM

Jerusalem, November 16, 1965

Dear Reinhold,

I returned from my trip around the world two weeks ago, feeling uncommonly refreshed and alive and having no immediate academic duties. I will now devote myself to so-called minor immortality, to the degree that this is obtainable by writing more or less interesting works, in languages both holy and profane. I had some very pleasant weeks, especially in California and New York, where I combined a minimum of speaking with a maximum of rest and relaxation. Two or three people in Los Angeles pursued me after my lectures and asked what had happened to my brothers the printers, whom they'd known in the 1920s.

Fanya's condition has not yet improved. She suffers a lot from circulatory problems, mostly at night.

I cannot give a short answer to your questions about my remarks in the Walter Benjamin essay. Your questions show that things are not clear cut. Jewishness is not simply in every case naively synonymous with feeling at home in Israel. This is not even true today, and certainly wasn't true in the generation dealt with in my essay. The cautious statements I made in this direction were intended to counter the many overly simplistic portrayals I've seen in print (such as Brod's portrait of Kafka).[67] Regarding your question—If Benjamin was so Jewish, why then did the *Neue Rundschau* print my essay on the front page?—I think it is wrongly posed. The editor put my essay on the front page because he considered it outstanding—to date, the best piece written on the subject. Moreover, the Germans, or at least some of them, have become considerably more clear-sighted on the Jewish question. There's another point I consider totally absurd, an opinion you don't express directly but which I find defended from various angles: namely, that "Hitler and his comrades" were able to declare German Jews to be un-German only because there was a mechanical breakdown, so to speak, and that everything could actually have ended up just fine. We can't go into this in a letter. Some time ago I read an article in *Die Zeit* from Hamburg which was full of sentimental reflections (by a Jew, *nota bene*) in honor of the establishment of relations between Germany and Israel.[68] How lovely everything really was and how much people were able to give! Not surprisingly, I threw the author of the piece out of my home when he visited me in Jerusalem many years ago. [. . .]

Best wishes to you and Käthe

1966

TO LUCIEN ISRAEL

Jerusalem, February 1, 1966

Dear Herr Colleague,

[. . .] I can't say much about your specific question on whether Freud counted Frankists[69] among his ancestors, but there is no reason to assume so. The Freud family was a strict rabbinical family from Buczacz, with a traditional orientation. My own wife comes from the same family. In the last century (as I know from oral history) they still thought it quite important that no one from the family marry anyone who had the Frankish "shadow" on their background or even had roots in the Frankish center of East Galicia. By the way, there's a Freud family tree, even if Anna Freud hasn't thought fit to publish it. It was in Sigmund Freud's possession. To be sure, no one can be prevented from conjecturing that, say, one of Freud's ancestors had such a secret affinity in this direction, despite it all. By their very nature, such hypotheses cannot be disproved. [. . .]

With highest regards, G. Scholem

1967

TO THE EDITORS OF THE FREIBURGER RUNDBRIEF

Jerusalem, 1966 or 1967

Esteemed Herr and Frau Luckner,

Allow me to express my astonishment that you printed, without a word of disagreement or protest, the speech given by Herr Dr. Adolf Arndt, a member of parliament, on the occasion of the founding assembly of the German-Israel Society in Berlin, May 1966. As far back as I can recall, I have always read the *Rundbrief* with enormous attention, sympathy, and the highest respect for the spirit expressed in it. If I have understood correctly, it has always been our shared unquestioned assumption (yours and the Jews') that a Jewish people exists, however one may see its theological or secular history, view its unique place among the nations, or judge its future in light of a collective trust in God. These points allowed your Jewish readers to stand with you on common ground. Even more than this, they allowed Jews to follow with particular feeling your considerable efforts to create a sense of understanding for the Jewish people and to urge this understanding upon your readers. The conviction that there is a historical Jewish identity, which has entered into a new stage with the founding of the State of Israel (a problematic identity that no one who knows anything about it can deny), seems to me a fundamental assumption binding us together. Once this identity is subjected to scorn—and this is the upshot of Herr Dr. Arndt's self-declared "cautious" speech, in which he characterized the expression "Jewishness"[70] as being every bit as insulting and scandalous as a "racist vocabulary"—then you have abandoned the foundation that gives meaning to work such as yours. How is it possible that, through your silence, you could take even a neutral stance—which flies in the face of previous statements in your *Rundbrief*—toward juridical fictions that draw a line between the Jewish state and the Jewish people, who support the State of Israel and who will stand or fall with it? It's become fashionable in Germany to combine so-called sympathy for the State of Israel with a rejection of the Jewish people as a historically developed nation. The writer of the article has often taken such a stance—a position that continues to propagate the old, specifically social democratic blindness and lack of insight vis-à-vis the Jewish question, though now under new conditions. Let me be clear: I have no intention of protesting Herr Dr. Arndt's sympathy for the State of Israel. Moreover, if the article hadn't been published—without a word of dissent—in a forum such as yours, whose entire spirit runs counter to such claims, I would not take a position on his assertions about the existence or nonexistence of a Jewish people or on the membership of former German Jews in this nation. Such a debate requires common ground, which we lack. In the *Rundbrief,* more than in any other circle in Germany, one expected to hear protests against this divorce between the ostensibly "new Israeli people," which quite surprisingly came on the scene in 1948, and the Jewish people, whose history, past, and hopes for the future in themselves constituted the moral foundation of the state. For everything you say in your journal about the State of Israel makes sense only in light of this historical continuity and identity, and not in terms of the rejection of these things, as suggested by the speech I have mentioned. The legal categories mentioned in this speech are not decisively binding for us; historical ones are. From such a historical perspective, it can of course be debated whether the religious element can be severed from the Jews' nationality; what can't be doubted, however, is that in their consciousness, well into the nineteenth century and afterward, the overwhelming majority of Jews continued to think of themselves as members of the Jewish people, and were seen as such by others. That in Dr. Arndt's speech a supposed progressive conception of history *ad maiorem gloriam* calls this into question and celebrates the resurrection of ridiculous phrases such as "Mosaic faith" should not be silently tolerated by Catholics, whose sense of the existence of God's people, as indicated by the title of the *Rundbrief,* is surely still alive.

I would be grateful if you could bring my opposition to the attention of your readers.

Gershom Scholem

TO PETER SZONDI

Jerusalem, January 5, 1967

Dear Herr Szondi,

[. . .] What do you think of the Benjamin letters? Hartung broadcast a critique on West German Radio (I had them send a copy to me) that more than a little astonished me. It seems that I "recruited" Benjamin for Judaism or for Zionism, but that he "eluded the Judaic scholar's recruitment through the passive resistance of procrastination." This in view of the numerous letters—in particular, those addressed to people other than me—that provide very different information on his position! But I suppose this will become a popular reading of the story. [. . .]

G. Scholem

TO RUDOLF HARTUNG[71]

Jerusalem, February 14, 1967

Esteemed Herr Dr. Hartung,

A few days ago I received your essay on the Benjamin letters from a reader of *Die Zeit* who lives in Jerusalem.[72] I now recall your letter in which you expressed an earnest desire to hear my opinion of your review.

I read your essay very carefully and I am impressed with the energy you brought to this material and with the portrait you have sketched. Naturally, with something like Benjamin's letters, as with Benjamin's writings in general, everyone will form a different image. When it comes to Benjamin, as you quite rightly say—and the title of your essay touches upon a very crucial point—the picture one has is also a question of what one is prepared to ignore. While I was reading your piece, it dawned upon me that you, too, my dear Herr Hartung, are prepared to ignore many things.

In conveying my remarks, I am fully aware how easy it is to fall into the ridiculous position Max Brod did with Kafka. Personal intimacy and detailed knowledge of the life circumstances and character traits of a human being can never guarantee precise understanding of a cultural figure. None of us, least of all Adorno and myself, should claim any special privilege. At the same time, beyond the correctness or falsity of

Max Brod's commentaries or the tone of his hagiography, I have to give him credit for his scrupulous observation of Kafka's traits which, given today's fashion, don't fit into the framework employed by many of today's commentators and are hence readily dismissed or passed over in silence. I am not certain that the same thing won't happen to Benjamin (it was already painfully clear in Tiedemann's doctoral dissertation).[73]

In my view, you did an exceptional job in bringing out Benjamin's personality traits related to his distance from the world, his remoteness with people, his loneliness and melancholy. I have only a few small points to add. "Spiritually impoverished" would actually be the last thing one could associate with his presence. He was nothing of the sort. So far as I can tell, it is not really accurate to claim, as you did, that he was "the perfect archetype of the exclusively intellectual man" (which, to my surprise, you lifted approvingly from an essay by Jean Selz),[74] or to say, as you did in your own words, that his letters are devoid of any exuberant feeling. I consider this a strong overstatement. A very strong emotional intensity is evident in Benjamin's rather controlled mode of expression. I could refer here to a great many letters, whose emotional charge must have escaped you. This applies not only to his so-called early phase, but also to the letters he wrote after his emigration—not to mention the letters that he wrote to women and that were not included in the selection (or were not given to us), which would have been the most natural place for an open expression of such feelings. It's unclear how the letter he wrote to me on my twentieth birthday could be understood as anything other than an articulation of such sentiments.[75] In any event, Jean Selz's characterization strikes me as completely off the mark. Everyone who knew Benjamin personally can testify that he was a man with very intense feelings; and this intensity, being the foundation of countless pages of his writings, is the key to understanding them. The widely held opinion that Benjamin was an exclusively intellectual man is a view I've always considered singularly unperceptive. I've been hearing it now for forty years. Granted, he tried more than most people to harness his feelings and to infuse them with rationality; yet reason never determined his deeper impulses. [. . .]

Permit me a word of protest against the claim that "Scholem the Zionist and Judaic scholar overaccentuated these [Jewish] concerns." I don't understand how you can substantiate your assertion. That Benjamin felt he was not a German but a Jew is not Scholem's interpretation;

it's a brute fact evident to me through my years of association with him, and no less unequivocally borne out by his letters, both to me and to others. It *would* have been an overaccentuation had I made the claim—which I clearly repudiated in my essay in the *Neue Rundschau*—that he was a Zionist (he was neutral in this point) or that his engagement with Jewish thought or with the content of Judaism was anything more than an experiment. What I said—in a careful and measured way—and what can easily be proven was that his Jewish feeling was very deep; that he never denied this, and not solely as a favor to me (otherwise I wouldn't have been able to associate with him as I did—since, when all is said and done, I was not totally blind); that he had no illusions about his relation to *Deutschtum;* that I very much doubt he would have felt at home in Israel; and that later, in a secularized form, he maintained and defended Jewish theological categories which for him were self-evident. Even this seems to meet with resistance among German readers, as I have noticed from many comments on Benjamin which have appeared in print. I would have thought that in particular his letters to me referring to his Jewish efforts, and the letter you cited from me, show clearly how little one can speak of overaccentuation here. After all this, you will understand how surprised I was to read your comment that my "interpretation can by no means be completely dismissed." As if a different interpretation would be much closer to the truth but one that I, as a Zionist, would ostensibly refuse to acknowledge! I would like to know the basis for this interpretation. I would never maintain that Benjamin lived "directly" immersed in Jewish concerns. On the contrary, had he followed his reflections on Judaism he would have painted himself into a very troublesome corner. I would say that by distancing himself from Judaism he distanced himself from his own nature as well, and hence from the unfolding of Jewishness within him. At the same time, he experienced Jewishness as his "essence as a Jew" (and these words stem from him, not from me). [. . .]

His letters, more than any of his later writings, show most convincingly that in his so-called late period he scarcely denied anything from his earlier years and that, in his eyes, materialist and metaphysical statements could stand directly side by side without any attempts at mediation between them. Today Brecht would doubtless turn over in his grave if he could see the letter on Kafka that Benjamin wrote to me in 1938, which was long after he apparently went over completely, or not so completely, to the materialist camp.[76] It's without question the most magnificent of his surviving letters. The tensions in his life, and hence in his mind, could scarcely be more clearly demonstrated than through documents of this sort. If I have understood you correctly, the question you pose in the last sentence of your essay remains: What were the dark sources that actually served as the fertile soil for his work? The answer is neither Judaism nor materialism, but something that no one has yet succeeded in capturing conceptually. For those who knew him, it was something that resisted construction and formulation, yet stood before their eyes as very real indeed. [. . .]

With best wishes, G. Scholem

TO HENRI F. ELLENBERGER[77]

Jerusalem, March 29, 1967

Esteemed Herr Dr. Ellenberger,

I received your letter on the twenty-first of March, and am herewith responding briefly to your questions.

One can detect a certain influence of kabbalistic literature or a kabbalistic way of thinking in the writings of C. G. Jung, specifically in his later works and above all in his book on alchemical conjunctions.[78] The influence comes almost exclusively (before he discovered my own work) from a book he often draws upon: Christian Knorr von Rosenroth's extensive *Kabbala Denudata,* which appeared in Latin in 1677–1684. His concept of archetypes has nothing whatsoever to do with the ideas espoused by Eliezer of Worms,[79] which are based on neo-Platonic and Jewish doctrine and which he knew nothing about until he read my book. [. . .]

Sincerely yours, G. Scholem

TO THEODOR ADORNO

Jerusalem, Saturday, May 27, 1967

Dear Adorno,

My heartfelt thanks for the lines you wrote to me. They arrived Friday, in the midst of a very serious situation.[80] On Sunday I am supposed to fly to London to speak at the university. If shooting does not break out before my departure, I will make the trip because of the urgent wishes of the Israeli embassy. If this letter is postmarked from London it will mean that I am there, for a letter from Israel would arrive much later. If a war starts, heaven only knows whether I will fly back directly after my lecture (Tuesday evening) and cancel all other engagements, or whether, as planned, I will go on to Zurich (where Fanya will be as of the fifth of June). I am prepared for both. [. . .]

G. Scholem

Jerusalem, August 17, 1967

Dear Herr Kahler,

Thank you for sending me your book, *The Jews among the Nations.*[82] It was most kind of you to send it to me, with a dialectical dedication. [. . .]

It is deeply depressing to me that in 1967 a man such as yourself could publish a sentence like the one on page 112, which essentially echoes the anti-Zionist, cosmopolitan talk that all of the opponents of Zionism in my youth abandoned once they had their backs to the wall. I did not in fact expect to hear it from the mouth of Erich von Kahler. The sentence goes, "The Jews did not live . . . to end up within a tiny nationalistic framework." I don't know why the Jews have survived, but if this is the main point of the most decisive argument against the Jews' return home, then I can only be thankful. I did not imagine that a philosopher of history like yourself would employ this kind of critique on Zionism. But I still remain unruffled by our disagreement.

With cordial greetings.

FROM ERICH VON KAHLER

Princeton, New Jersey, Undated

Dear Herr Scholem,

Heartfelt thanks for your letter. I wish we could discuss your objections face to face in a long and satisfying conversation, with documents in hand. One would have to go much deeper than I was able to in my essay. I hope very much to see you again, either here or over there.

Today I wish merely to address, very briefly, the points in your letter that lend themselves to quick clarification, because it seems to me you skimmed over small details in my text or read them only "locally"— that is, apart from the wider context of the entire book. First, let's take the sentence that so "depressed" you: "It cannot be that the end of our endurance through thousands of years is our homecoming itself." The following passage explains what I was getting at—that is, a narrow nationalistic *sacro egoismo* which rivals, in this shameful world of ours, what others call their "national interests." My correspondence with Philip Hitti makes it clear that I did not support the Magnes plan, but that I believed there was a need for a completely autonomous and integral Israeli state.[83] Today, too, I take issue with many who condemn Israel's "preventive war," and I can understand how someone can demand guarantees of Israel's existence, along with extra territories including the entire city of Jerusalem. Nevertheless, I refuse to accept the State of Israel as an end in itself or as the final aim of Judaism, or that Judaism and Israel are now identical, pure and simple. The point I make has very important implications. Israelis must compensate for their battles by remaining Jews, and this means that, besides caring for and defending the country, they must remain conscious of belonging to a transnational, cultural, indeed spiritual faction of Judaism and all of the special responsibilities this entails (I trust it's obvious that I'm not referring to Orthodox religion). This means adopting a reflective, generous, and humane posture, which in turn implies a different attitude, less arrogant and less negligent, toward the Arabs—and in this regard I have heard from objective observers, Jews among them, that many wrongs have been committed (they say the Arabs have become the Negroes of Israel). I fully appreciate the difficulty of such an attitude and how terrible the problem with the Arabs is, especially given the present situation. I speak only of a general rule of thumb that must be obeyed—and not only because the State of Israel faces terrible danger, which has become blatantly clear of late, but precisely because we are Jews. For instance, was it absolutely necessary for the Israeli forces to drop napalm bombs? Unfortunately, Jews should not permit themselves to do what others are allowed. I repeat: it's not because of the external, practical consequences that Jews shouldn't be allowed it (our accomplishments and victories are what others find most unforgivable), but because it violates the meaning and dignity of the Jewish tradition I believe in. This is the last scrap of faith we have left, and I will cling to it until the end. [. . .]

Yours, Erich von Kahler

TO THEODOR ADORNO

Jerusalem, December 8, 1967

Dear Adorno,

Although the *Neue Zürcher Zeitung* has not dropped its old habit of sending me copies of your work via surface mail, Dr. Weber's secretary, who knows me and has learned to appreciate me, suddenly had second thoughts and sent me a copy airmail. So as of yesterday I am in possession of your essay, and I sincerely thank you for it.[84] I read your reflections with the greatest interest, both those from thirty years ago—which were not all that bad—and those from today. I was especially delighted to see how you celebrated my unpretentiousness, a quality that means a lot to me. It will resonate well with your dialectical sensibility when I tell you that my sympathies extend not only to the heterodox, but also to the orthodox. Much of my work has been an attempt to help establish connections between these two spheres. For you're correct in stating that I have something to say about the secularization of mysticism, and beyond that about religion. But besides this, it should be noted that I do not consider secularization as something final; I see it as one of those ever-changing forms. You know very well that I'm anything but an atheist and that my religious convictions are tightly bound up with my historical knowledge. [. . .]

Yesterday evening, to my great pleasure, I discovered that in a letter from 1916 Kafka said something very favorable about Herr Scholem and his radical views (he said this to his fiancée, who had written to him about me).[85] I had no idea that Kafka thought well of me as early as 1916. The editors, who can't tell heads from tails, identified me as the humorist Sholem Aleichem. How should I cash in on my honor?

Best wishes to you both, from your sentimental Leviathan[86]

1968

TO GEORGE LICHTHEIM

Jerusalem, January 4, 1968

Dear George,

I did not fail to set aside one of my copies of the *Neue Zürcher* from December third and to send it to you (probably with the outgoing mail) for your edification and as a contribution to the theme "Dialectic of Enlightenment" or "Scholem and the Hegelians." You'll be able to appreciate the prose more than other readers. I particularly liked the remark about my shabby grace. I would count this as one of my favorite qualities, if I really possessed such a trait. You don't have to send this important text back to me.

Along with other readers, I was not a little surprised to be told that in my essay I supposedly called Agnon a deep thinker. Not only is this absent from the English text, where I pile all profundity and intellectual superlatives before my own feet, but it's completely missing from the German text, which I prepared (together with an aging and attractive editorial assistant) from the English edition. Granted, there's no gainsaying my talent for bringing the tacit implications in Agnon's prose onto an articulated and dialectically presentable plane. It appeared as well in the *Neue Zürcher Zeitung.* Besides this, I would say that my opinions in all languages sound much more rational than they really are. Among those privy to my secrets, there is no difference of opinion here: this ability to deceive the world has been said to be one of my chief talents. In this regard, and for your collection, allow me to refer you to a letter from Kafka on September 22, 1916 (!!), where he says a few words about me. I've been waiting for something of this sort for a long time, and now I feel myself doubly proven right. Obviously you found the right master magician yourself.

Looking forward to your new editions. I remain a master magician emeritus.

G. Scholem

FROM GEORGE LICHTHEIM

London, January 11, 1968

Dear Scholem,

The interview you gave in the *Jerusalem Post* finally arrived a few days ago, and yesterday I got the monumental essay Adorno wrote for the *Neue Zürcher.* Somehow I'm tempted to imitate this man by writing you a truly memorable letter—with a carbon copy for my biographer. But this has to be left to someone like Adorno, who's aware of his own importance. It's already telling that he's able to recall his first discussion with you, in 1923 (when he himself was all of twenty). But it takes a really good filing system, probably managed by his wife, for him to be able to cite an entire letter he wrote to Benjamin in 1938. Be that as it may, his letter from that time is worth reading and gives the impression of having sprung from spontaneous inspiration rather than some *post facto* fabrication, as one might perhaps suppose. His description of you is accurate (according to my own memory of what you were like). The term "shabby grace" is quite enviable. He's also completely correct in emphasizing the Berliner in you (so closely related to the New Yorker). I'll have to read the letter by Kafka you mentioned, the one from 1916, in order to ascertain whether this thinker, as well, noticed the local shades of color (and the fact that he knew you has opened up entire new horizons for me). Incidentally, you've never struck me as a "Bedouin prince." I've known too many real Bedouins ever to think this. I assume Adorno was spinning a yarn here—inventing a trait by way of embellishment.

But whatever else he may wish to say, the article does not merely deal with an important topic; it's also readable and contains a few interesting observations. It confirms something I wrote in the *Times Literary Supplement:* that the cultural conflicts of the Weimar period, such as the one between you and the more or less Marxist-tinged thinkers, were an internal matter among the German-Jewish intelligentsia. This is naturally no longer the case today, which is why Adorno is a much greater figure now than he could ever have been in the old days. Circumstances have changed, and an entire cultural dimension has disappeared. Nor can Habermas (whom by the way I consider an important thinker) alter this.[87] If you leave his students out of the equation, he stands all alone. German Jewry was the cultural elite of the nation. And this is a fact that has not escaped today's reigning literary critic, Walter Jens. It's for this reason that some time ago he called Frankfurt and Berlin "the true cultural centers of the nation." As indeed they were, and you can see today that Hitler literally ruined Germany forever. I don't need to stress how much this present situation confirms me in my old anti-Zionist views, a perspective I probably share not only with Adorno but with Benjamin as well. The Catastrophe doesn't change this in the least. It only proves something we should have known earlier: that in our day the only way to turn the clock back on emancipation is through cultural and even political suicide. In a word, the Jews were and remain an integral part of so-called European Christian culture. In this regard, the internal differences among the disciples of Hess[88] (whom I have recently read through for my own purposes) and Marx prove secondary.

Apropos of Hess and Marx, it's striking when you read them today how much they had in common, not least in their relation to religion—even though everyone knows that Hess changed his mind again, though not before he provided Marx with a catch phrase (such as the remark he made in 1843, when he called the God of the Bible a Moloch who demands the sacrifice of his own son). This aspect of Christianity probably did not occur to Kierkegaard when he so enthusiastically gave his reading of the truly ghastly Abraham-Isaac story. The Jewish Hess, at least in his brief atheistic phase, had better instincts. It isn't that similar arguments could or must underpin atheism; one arrives at the nonexistence of the God-goblin by way of other means. But Hess saw with crystal clarity how the Old Testament God exhibits, let us say, numerous oriental features. Silberner *(Socialists and the Jewish Question)*[89] belabors the theme with all sorts of embarrassed phrases. When he reprimands Marx, he forgets to mention that Hess anticipated him—and not only in "Europäische Triarchie" (1837), where he dismisses Judaism as a "ghost," but even more unmistakably in "Philosophie der Tat" (1843), where highly significant things appear. For instance, "The absolute spirit that celebrates its reality in the state is an imitation of the Christian God, who had his first-born son crucified. . . . The Christian God is an imitation of the Jewish Moloch-Jehovah, whom the first-born was sacrificed to 'appease' and who was later bought off with a bit of cash during Judaism's period of law and order. The original sacrificial victim was a human." And so on. Instead of mentioning this, Silberner dedicated an entire chapter to *Rome and Jerusalem*.

I've had to devote time to such rubbish because (in connection with a short history of the beginnings of socialism, 1789–1848) I am writing an essay on anti-Semitism among the French. Once it appears, I'll send you a copy. Hess crept into my work in a different context and confirmed the Freudian thesis of the horror that emerges particularly from the Moloch-God, who fatally left significant traces of himself in the Bible. I know that all of this has been sublimated in Judaism; still, it doesn't change the fact that this Moloch aspect in particular must have strongly repelled even the worshipers of Wotan, not to mention others. That your instincts apparently fail you when it comes to such connections is one of the blind spots in your picture of history which Adorno has cited. To put it differently, if the God of the Bible (and I am now bracketing out problems of religion as such, just as Hess did in his own day) appeared as a horror-inspiring Moloch even to a well-meaning Rhineland Jew in 1843 (and it should be mentioned here that Hess was raised as an Orthodox [. . .]), why should it surprise anyone when millions of naive Europeans learned their lessons from this horror after reading such stories and looked upon the Jews in the same light? You once said to me that one should look for the deepest roots of Jew-bating in the conditions under which Christianity (that is, the prophetic ethical system) was forced upon the primitive barbarians of Europe, who were utterly unprepared for it. But the *ressentiment* springing from such roots is not murderous. The murderous element comes from somewhere else. Nor does it help in the least to blame the church for this. The church bears only half the responsibility; the other half belongs to old Moloch himself.

[. . .] A comment made by your former student Jacob Taubes comes to mind. When we met four years ago in Paris, he said proudly, "We have survived Christianity." "Judaism, too," I shot back. He didn't know how to respond. And there is no answer, if one takes "Judaism" to mean what the Jews themselves understood by it so long as they still found themselves in opposition to Christianity. The Reformed Jews silently gave this up, because they themselves are Christians but don't want to admit it. The others did too, because they believe in nothing, or at least they don't believe in a God. What's happening in this field in Israel is something you know better than I do.

At least for myself, I have solved the problem in the simplest possible way. If you should visit me one of these days, you'll see that old Marx (in Promethean or prophetic guise) hangs in my office, while the other

Jew—the one with the crown of thorns—is found in the next room. Both are there in the spirit of Feuerbach's adage: "What is hanging on the Cross is not a God; he is a man." Amen. We all stem from the same event at Sinai (whatever may have happened there), while a few of us have drawn the curious conclusion that the Carthaginian Moloch won't do as a representative of our conscience. Of course, you could justifiably claim that later forms of Judaism shed such barbarism long ago. Could be, though the naive man on the street who does not know the Gnostic neo Platonic literature of the Kabbalah (and who as a result knows the Bible all the better) sees it differently. And the so-called educated man, insofar as he has a tendency toward metaphysics, does not feel at home with old Jehovah. However you look at it, the old monster has become just as unbearable to the Catholic peasant as to the Viennese Jewish psychoanalyst, who once had to let out a curse because too much disgust had built up within him. I apologize for saying so, but Adorno's truly seminal essay stimulated precisely this same reaction in me. [. . .]

Yours, George Lichtheim

TO GEORGE LICHTHEIM

Jerusalem, January 28, 1968

Dear George,

I must sorely disappoint you if you thought you could rattle me (and I don't think I am too far off the mark) with your blasphemous letter and the identification of the biblical God with the Carthaginian Moloch and similar audacious remarks. It's true that, given your intelligence and education, I expected a bit less childish wisdom than what you offer on the "old monster." However much I dislike saying this, I must also confess that I can't take your philosophy of history any more seriously than your reflections on Judaism in the name of Moses Hess—or rather Daumer, from whom Hess took his foolish adolescent notions on Moloch (a fashionable theory that was of German-French provenance and that originated around 1840), only to subsequently abandon them again.[90] It's just as hard for me to take seriously your enthusiasm for Jewish intellectuals as the elite of the German nation. To my mind, this is all silly and baseless prattle. I don't agree with your conviction that you see eye to eye with Adorno on these insights of yours. The author's relevant statements on the Jewish God in Adorno and Horkheimer's *Dialectic of Enlightenment,* not to mention in other works, flatly contradict this. Given the choice between old Daumer's insights and Kierkegaard's on what you call the "truly ghastly Abraham-Isaac story," I'd still go with Kierkegaard, and with both eyes wide open. We will have less common ground to discuss Judaism now that you've realized that the blind spots in my picture of history include what you justly call a lack of instinct for the sort of preposterous associations you claim to have unearthed. You speak of blind spots and lack of instinct; as someone who has tried for fifty years, apparently in vain, to understand something of Judaism, I look upon your comments as totally frivolous. Here we won't find any common ground. I regret to say it, but my otherwise famous gift of gab will not be stirred when I see what comes to your mind in response to my stubborn silence on the theme of Jesus. That my former student Taubes is a good-for-nothing already follows from his inability to respond to your attempt to score points with the comment, "We have survived Judaism." You wouldn't find me such easy prey, Herr Director—that is, if the insight into the pointless nature of such a debate, on the level you prescribe, doesn't force me into silence. In my lifetime I have visited many Jews with pictures of Jesus hanging in their rooms. The first example that comes most clearly to mind was a visit to Martin Buber in Zehlendorf, in March 1916. Since then, if one may say this with such a fitting Yiddish phrase, I've *zugewehnt* myself to it.[91] [. . .]

God be praised! G.S.

TO THEODOR ADORNO

Jerusalem, February 29, 1968

Dear Adorno,

[. . .] I've sent Szondi your greetings. I don't think there's anything to the rumors that he's negotiating for a professorship here in Jerusalem. I of all people should know. There would be interest in him here, though I don't believe it would be mutual. He came here compelled by some dark drive at work within a wholly positive impelling force, which is otherwise highly unusual for him. But surrounding him is such an air of isolation and reluctance to break out of himself, such a tendency toward depression and a lack of interest in things, that it oppresses those of us who share a great deal with him. Others notice it, too. What seems to be surfacing is a terrible and deeply rooted feeling of guilt, particularly when he comes into contact with Jewish society. He feels guilty because he was saved on the infamous Kastner train of 1944—at the cost of others, he believes.[92] This gnaws at him more than one could imagine. It's hard for him to open up to others. Nearly the only time he speaks passionately with us is when discussing student affairs in Berlin. Next week I will travel with him to Tiberias, where I'll show him some kabbalistic holy sites. Some of that is bound to sink in. I have to admit it's impossible to come up with a more ambiguous formulation. In a nutshell, he's a highly gifted, complicated, and supremely unhappy man. This is just between the two of us.

> Warmest greetings to you both, Gerhard Scholem

TO HANS PAESCHKE[93]

Jerusalem, March 24, 1968, *Personal*

Esteemed Herr Paeschke,

In an open discussion regarding my reluctance to work with your journal, I believe it will do some good if I say something about a comment made in the sequel to Hannah Arendt's essay in *Merkur* (page 215), which you recently were kind enough to send me.[94] What led me to distance myself from her is the total indecency in tone that transforms rare and (often perhaps) exciting and moving events into banalities. This began with the Arendt-esque Eichmann book, where she employed arrogant and inquisitive insolence *ad nauseam.*

You surely know Benjamin's letters dealing with his years of struggle over the decision to learn Hebrew, which he never did. In spite of this, you printed in *Merkur* the author's truly shameful, not to say base, assertion that Benjamin was prepared, or thought he was prepared, "to learn Hebrew for 300 marks a month when the Zionists promised it to him; or to learn dialectical thinking, with all its mediated chicanery, for 1,000 French francs, if that was the only way the Marxists could speak intelligibly" (p. 215). What can I say about this view of his life—as someone who experienced the precise circumstances surrounding all these events and, where I was directly involved, in part documented them by publishing a volume of his letters? I won't hold back: I completely reject it. I knew Hannah Arendt when she was a socialist or half-Communist, and I knew her when she was a Zionist. It astonishes me to see the light-years of distance enabling her, from her sovereign height, to discuss movements that once meant so much to her. I don't have such sovereignty—and to tell you the truth, I don't think Arendt does either. Behind it lies a bitter *ressentiment* that is obviously disguised, yet appears in everything she has written. In this essay it also appears when she writes about Zionism and Zionists—when she says that Benjamin wanted to learn Hebrew and cultivate a Marxist way of thinking not because his own thoughts brought him to Hebrew and Marxism, in however problematic a manner, but because he was offered 300 marks a month or 1,000 (old) francs. Naturally, one *can* form such an interpretation of the letters; this much I've learned from the essay. But I despise the person who reads them like that.

A forum that nurtures such debates holds little attraction for me. Despite your positive opinion of my freedom, I can well understand Adorno when he wants to avoid this forum. You speak about an editor's limited possibilities. You are probably right. But I cannot fathom how your position could make you powerless to exclude this despicable trash. I write these lines with sadness.

Yours, Gershom Scholem

TO REINHOLD SCHOLEM

Jerusalem, May 24, 1968

Dear Reinhold,

Your letters from the fifth and twelfth of May were awaiting me when I returned from a short trip to Switzerland and Germany. [. . .]

All sorts of things took place on the occasion of my last birthday, some time back. Since you asked, there was, among other things, a reception at the president's house. You may know that I lived with him in 1917, after Father threw me out of the house.[95] A lot of speeches were made. Well, you can just imagine what they were about! In the meantime a festschrift has appeared in my honor, two-thirds in English and German, a third in Hebrew. The bindery just finished with it. I'll try to have a copy sent directly to you. Maybe it'll amuse you. It contains a complete bibliography of all my publications, put together by Fanya with some secret assistance. Nothing is missing, not even the Song of Songs (how horrible!) and the *Philosophical ABC,* which you printed in 1927 and which is still amusing. It's a list of five hundred items. Thank God you don't have to read them all, if only because most were written in Hebrew. My dissertation (which has now become a much sought-after rarity) is supposed to be republished as an offset reprint by the Wissenschaftlichen Buchgesellschaft in Darmstadt.

Fanya's doing better. She's feeling quite well, though she still walks with a cane. At the beginning of August I will travel to Switzerland with her, first to Sils and then to Ascona, where I'll deliver my lecture at the Eranos Conference. I just spent a couple of weeks in Zurich. Included here as a supplement are two documents related to my honorary doctorate. The text of the speech I gave for the occasion will interest you. The amusing part of the entire affair is that one must be elected unanimously, as if into an exclusive club. One dissenting vote in the faculty suffices to reject a candidate. Twenty-one years ago this in fact happened to Churchill, to the embarrassment and dismay of the university. Surprisingly enough, I won the race, even though in the past forty years the philosophy faculty in Zurich hasn't conferred the title of Ordinarius on a single Jew. The fact that I come from Israel certainly must have spoken in my favor, since we now command extraordinary respect in Switzerland. As a result, it was quite a lovely occasion. Twice I had a friendly meeting and open discussion with the philosopher who proposed and urged my candidacy. Pity that I'd never heard of him before. He has developed an astonishing knowledge of my work, and confessed to me that he won the support of his colleagues in German philology above all because of my German writing style. You see what such things are good for. Afterward I went to Heidelberg, Frankfurt, Tübingen, and Berlin, where once again I ran off at the mouth during various university panels. Sadly, you must admit that Berlin has the best climate of all these cities. I really don't mean this allegorically, but in terms of weather.

I hope you're tolerably well, Käthe especially.

Warm greetings, Gerhard

1969

TO GEORGE LEON[96]

Jerusalem, March 7, 1969

Dear Mr. Leon,

I received your letter of February 22, and I am very sorry to be unable to help you in your undertaking. The problem of Franz Kafka's relationship to Jewish mysticism has been very much on my mind for a long time. I have often been asked to write about it. I am not convinced that your approach promises positive results. [. . .] I do not believe that Kafka deliberately preserved a mystical side of his work for the small circle of those to whom kabbalistic allusions would set up an immediate train of associations. There were, precisely speaking, no people around to whom such associations would have made sense. Kafka's own explicit allusions to the Kabbalah are not a kind to suggest such a bent of mind. [. . .]

I hope you will excuse the expression of my basic skepticism as to your proposals. I do not deny at all the idea of Kafka's deep roots (mainly unconscious) in the tradition of Jewish mysticism. I have given testimony to this in a passage of my book *Zur Kabbala und ihrer Symbolik* (which you apparently don't know), 1960, p. 22–23. The book is now with Suhrkamp Verlag, Frankfurt am Main, and it may well be that you will find some stuff for reflection, especially in Chapter 2: "Der Sinn der Tora in der jüdischen Mystik." The book exists also in English if that suits you more (Schocken Books, New York, 1965).

I regret I have been unable to give you more encouragement.

Sincerely yours, G. Scholem

TO ERNA WEISS[97]

Jerusalem, December 14, 1969

Dear Erna,

[. . .] Do you have any idea where one could locate the notes Josef Weiss made of conversations with me and on me in general? All of us knew that he wanted to write a book about me—he said so often enough. For this purpose he gathered together information on discussions with me from all of his acquaintances. He often referred to this in conversations with me. Three years ago one of my students saw these sketches, arranged according to the distinctive types of paper they were written on. Do you perhaps know what happened to them? Did he destroy them? Were they among the personal papers that you destroyed after his death? Or do they exist somewhere?

Yours, G. Scholem

1972[98]

FROM JOSHUA SISKIN[99]

February 25, 1972

Dear Professor Scholem,

I thought you might be interested in seeing your name associated with American pop music. Are you really a Bob Dylan enthusiast? If so, please write me your opinion of his lyrics. You probably would not know my name without some kind of explanation. My father translated your article which appeared in *Ha'aretz* three years ago that dealt with Philip Roth's book *Portnoy's Complaint*. My father's name is Rabbi Siskin. I met you last winter one Shabbat afternoon at your house; I was studying in Jerusalem at the time.

Sincerely, Joshua Siskin

FROM REINHOLD SCHOLEM

Sydney, February 29, 1972

Dear Gerhard and Fanya,

I heard that Fanya was sick during Ernst's visit. Hopefully your last month in Switzerland will bring some improvement.[100] I've now been back home for four months. How time flies. The first thing I did was visit the children in Melbourne. Then the bibliophilic and typographic books arrived—some were gifts and some were purchases I had made. I have a lot on my hands with these now. But recently I've been more occupied with you than ever before. I told you in Zurich that I got hold of the Suhrkamp volume of your Brussels lectures and the books containing your basic ideas. Along with these comes the most important work, the second volume of your *Judaica*. I haven't yet gotten around to reading your basic ideas, though I've spent a great deal of time on *Judaica II*.[101] [. . .]

For me, the most interesting aspect of *Judaica II* consists of the personal details of your life that appear here and there throughout the book. On page 124 (on the Hebrew Club of Berlin, from May 1917): "A born and bred Berliner stood out like a sore thumb." Page 124: "We young Jews with a German education were dazzled by Agnon. Of course we spoke German. And then a genuine cult of the eastern Jews sprang up to counter the arrogance of the assimilated German Jews." And page 132: "How impressed I was, a young German Jew, by a conversation with [Agnon]! Of course, Hebrew was already spoken back then. (This must have been in Homburg in 1922.)" I have cited these passages— your own —in order to come to a surprising conclusion. After 1917 (or perhaps earlier) you turned your back on the feeling of being German. By the time you were speaking Hebrew "naturally," in 1922, you had consciously ceased being a German Jew; rather, you were 100 percent "Israeli," even if such a thing did not exist at the time. From this angle, it seems to me that your feelings and views are at odds with those of the majority of German Jews. You write that in the nineteenth century the German Jewish avant-garde raced into *Deutschtum,* but the masses did not want to follow. The precise opposite happened with you: you left us and made your way back to Judaism or "Israeliness," while the Jews, in the numbers you had hoped, did not follow. Not even Buber, much less the great Zionist rabbi Joachim Prinz and our own Rabbi Schenk. Golo Mann came closer to the mark with his comments. He says in his description of his grandfather's attempt to cross the border (see Gerstenmeier, p. 99): "If this is the law, it applies not only to German Jews but to all Germans."[102] I don't know anything about your worldwide status in the scholarship of the Kabbalah. Putting this aside, I see you, surprisingly, as a magnificent German writer. [. . .]

Reinhold

IO HANS-GEORG GADAMER[103]

Jerusalem, April 11, 1972

Dear Gadamer,

[. . .] I was in Zurich for a long time, interrupted by a visit to Berlin, where I was especially preoccupied with matters relating to the death of Peter Szondi.[104] I was also twice in Frankfurt, but regrettably I couldn't find the time to make a foray to Heidelberg. Only now does it strike me how wrong I was not to visit you from Zurich. After fifty years I wanted to spend a winter in Europe, but in this case winter never came. Instead, we had various difficulties concerning the health and illness of friends in Zurich, not to mention Peter Szondi's death. Over the past ten years he became very attached to us; I spent last summer with him. As you can surely judge better than anyone else, besides all his fine human qualities he was a hermeneutic philosopher of the first order.

I hope we can meet again soon. I'll gladly do my part.

Cordially yours, Gershom Scholem

TO MAURICE AND KATHY ZIGMOND[105]

Jerusalem, April 15, 1972

Dear Ziggy and Kathy,

[. . .] It was a great pity that we missed each other in Switzerland by one or two days, but I was under great pressure to return to Jerusalem and to prepare our longer sojourn in Zurich. We left on September 15 and took up residence in the most elegant and well-serviced guest house of the University of Zurich, which had been put at our disposal. We had a wonderful large room, a kitchen, a hall, and a large drawing room, with a library which some crazy millionaire is just transferring to this house after having bought the house itself as a gift to the university ten years ago. It had two more guest rooms of no special distinction which were occupied by varying types of scholars from Moscow and Japan and Spain and all the rest of the Gentiles, sprinkled richly with more or less surprising Jews, *meshoumodim*[106] and half-Jews, who opened up their hidden Jewish hearts to Fanya and to me. But these people only spent short periods in the Bodmer House, and most of them only a few days, so that we remained really *der ruhende Punkt* in the *erscheinungen Flucht,* if you will allow me poetic language. The house itself is just next to the main building of the university and considered a historical monument, having been the residence of one of Switzerland's literary glories more than two hundred years ago, the writer Johann Jakob Bodmer. The first visit to the house was very aptly described by Goethe, whose portrait hangs therefore most fittingly in the entrance. In the floor above our head the Thomas Mann Archives are housed, although they don't even belong to the university, Mann's widow having resented the personality of the professor of modern German literature at the University of Zurich, who obviously had written some malicious remarks about her illustrious husband. She therefore gave the archive paradoxically enough to the Eidgenössische Technische Hochschule,[107] which rented premises from the university to house them, instead of building itself a decent home for it. But we had the best of both worlds, being in friendly relations with the rector of the university and the president of the college. Fanya had a really good time because for the first time in over many years she had a housekeeper, a truly Swiss woman who took care of everything and we became very friendly with each other, and when Fanya had to go the hospital she felt obliged to "bemother" me, duly sustained by good tips. Never before had we had such service. The house being protected as a "historical monument," every room had a little very curious apparatus for alarm, and when you smoked five cigarettes or one cigar with the windows closed, after five minutes you had three cars from the fire brigade of Zurich at the door—which during our sojourn occurred twice. So we were very truly kept under good guard. [. . .]

In the meanwhile, your obedient servant also turned into a patient. The doctors discovered something of an "old age disease" called Pagets disease, which is something that nobody dies of, but in its various stages it is painful in various degrees, mine being rather moderate. I was subjected to all kinds of packings and infusions, which took up considerable time, but at least I did not have to go to hospital, as I would have been obliged to in Israel. I liked the doctors very much—more than can be said of Fanya, who has a natural disgust of physicians. "Was verstehen schon Ärzte?" ("What do the doctors understand, anyway?") being one of her favorite sayings. In the end, all the treatments administered to me proved of little help and the doctor said to me: You will have to live with it, but you can easily reach 120 years if nothing else interferes. Great comfort! [. . .]

With all our love and expecting another letter from you.

Gershom

TO WALTER KAUFMANN[108]

Jerusalem, April 24, 1972

Dear Kaufmann,

We have returned from Switzerland a month ago and it is lucky that you wrote to the University instead of taking a wrong turn. We are feeling relatively well, although my wife has not made any substantial progress in her ailments.

As to your question regarding a remark of mine concerning Erich Fromm's marriage. Your memory is at fault: I said in Dr. Jovel's house, when we talked about Fromm, that it was said in analytical circles at the time that Fromm was the first analysand who was now to have married his analyst (which was then considered as frowned upon by the master), but I did not ascribe the remark to Freud himself. I have no authority for that, and those who told the story did not ascribe the remark to Freud. In the only (long) talk I had with Fromm himself after his marriage (in 1927), no mention of this event was made, nor did we discuss Freud's attitude to Fromm, but Fromm tried to convince me of the compatibility of Marx and Freud, from whose union he expected then high things—after having left the Zionist "parochial" camp for broader human horizons, as he saw it. The gap that this opened up between us was the real subject matter of our talk.

With cordial regards from Fanya and me.

Yours, Gershom

TO JOSHUA SISKIN[109]

Jerusalem, April 24, 1972

Dear Mr. Siskin,

I was glad to hear from you and I remember your visit to our house. But I must disappoint you as far as your question is concerned. I do not know who has told you that I was a Bob Dylan enthusiast. I have not the slightest idea who Bob Dylan is and I have never read any of his lyrics. Perhaps you can tell me how my name became associated with American pop music. This would really be a new dimension of my rather checkered career.

Best wishes, sincerely yours, Gershom

TO GEORGE AND ZARA STEINER[110]

Jerusalem, April 30, 1972

Dear Steiner, dear Zara,

I'm delighted that you received my infamous essay on the theory of language in the Kabbalah and that you've returned from your adventures unscathed, not least by the fact that Ezra Pound attended your lecture in Venice. We are anxious to see what will come of the project in Zurich. Your silence on this point isn't exactly eloquent.

The first proofs of my *magnum opus* will now be completed in Jerusalem; I am supposed to receive the page proofs in late summer.[111] By then you should have it in typeset form. We're all hoping for the best.

I have not been able to ascertain whether people on Israeli radio in fact treated you as an anti-Semite in connection with, of all things, your reflections on Eliot. I tried to get some evidence, but no one knew anything with certainty! Could you tell me which broadcast supposedly said this?

It remains unclear whether I can go to Frankfurt. You'll hear about it in any event. I did not see your essay on Lévi-Strauss in the *Times Literary Supplement.* I really regret it; no one tells me anything.

Further plans will have to be made at a later date. Unfortunately, the theme of this year's Eranos conference won't be of much use to George Steiner the critic. You'll hopefully recover from the intellectual exhaustion you wrote about, through the influence of the related magical meetings. I trust this exhaustion won't have any effect on the essay that I— part master, part friend, but also part potential victim—expect from you on me.

Gershom Scholem

TO REINHOLD SCHOLEM

Jerusalem, May 29, 1972

Dear Reinhold,

[. . .] The dates you have pertaining to me and my Jewish decisions are interesting, and incomplete. You obviously don't know that I began to pick up the first elements of Hebrew in 1911 and then continued my studies for five years with such great intensity that as early as 1917 I appeared among the Hebrew-speaking Russians at the Hebrew Club as a well-known figure. I didn't intentionally turn my back on feeling German in 1917; I had already done so by 1913, at the latest. I still recall the torments I endured while listening to your speeches during your one-year military service in the fall of 1913. I believe you gave them before the Telegraph Regiment in Treptow during your furlough.[112] I held my tongue, just as I did about everything expressed at home on this theme, in particular from Father. Father was extraordinarily bitter about my silence, and about my Hebrew studies (performed with three pious rabbis early each Sunday, from seven in the morning to one in the afternoon). You weren't aware of any of this because you weren't at home, with the exception of the nine months between your release from the military and the outbreak of war. So unfortunately you missed the history of my youth and development. After the war, in 1920, you were astonished to meet me, as if I'd been someone from a different planet. I am of course not typical for most German Jews. In this you are completely right; and this, sadly, is why German Jews were so deceived in their feelings and opinions and why, from whatever complicated spiritual process, they deceived themselves. I have no respect for Golo Mann's remarks, and I don't agree in the least that he comes closer to the truth than me. The entire time, he speaks only about baptized Jews and people wholly alienated from Judaism. In reality, this does not come close to describing the majority of German Jews. Our own father, in whose house I never saw a non-Jewish couple in friendly social intercourse, refused even to see the non-Jewish wife of our brother Werner. And he was consciously an assimilated Jew. With us, things were very different from what they were with the "Famous Jews" or the literati Golo Mann speaks about so exuberantly. [. . .]

Your old but still quarrelsome brother (even if I've mellowed a bit),
Gerhard

TO MIRCEA ELIADE[113]

Jerusalem, June 6, 1972

Dear Eliade,

I am turning to you in a matter which concerns both of us personally. I enclose herewith photostats of several pages from a new journal on the history of the Jews in Romania, which started to appear in Jerusalem. These pages contain a personal attack on me and you. On me, because I am, as it were, "guilty" of having honored you by my contributions to your festschrift; on you, because the writer accuses you of having been a leading figure in the anti-Semitic organization "the Iron Guard" in Romania, and of having expressed anti-Semitic views in the course of your activities and continuing to do so during the Hitler period, including the years of the Second World War. [. . .]

I have read the Hebrew translation of his article—published in the same issue—and I am not quite clear as to what exactly it is all about. Does the writer whose diary he quotes—Mihail Sebastian, who tells of his personal contact with you and with your first wife in those years—accuse you of having been a Romanian nationalist, or has he had knowledge of specific activities of yours concerning the Jews in Romania and of views expressed by you as regards the Jews in general?

You will understand that I am most concerned about these things, and I would like you to react to these accusations, to state your attitude at those times and, if necessary, your reason for changing your mind. In those long years I have known you, I had no reason whatsoever to believe you to have been an anti-Semite, and even more so, an anti-Semitic leader. I consider you a sincere and upright man whom I regard with great respect. Therefore, it is only natural to ask you to tell me, and through me those concerned, the mere truth. If there is anything to be said on this score, let it be said, and let the atmosphere of general or specific accusations be cleared up. [. . .]

With cordial regards, Gershom Scholem

TO GEORGE LICHTHEIM

Jerusalem, November 16, 1972

Dear George,

I mustn't forget to thank you for the welcome arrival of your immortal work on European history, which was not slow to find its way to me. I thank you all the more because, in the nick of time and without your knowing it, I wrote a commentary on at least the first, yes the very first, page—namely, on Benjamin's motto from his "Theses on the Philosophy of History." To pay you back, if in a very small way, allow me to present to you my essay "Walter Benjamin and His Angel." I'm sending you the entire Suhrkamp volume, which is the only place it appears. You will see the kind of metamorphosis the angel went through, until it took on the form expressed in the citation you used. Your Highness will have to forgive me for the fact that my Rashi commentary, which goes deep into the circumstances of the case, has been held up for so long.

To my edification, yesterday I learned something during a meeting with Samuel Cramer, a Sumerologist from Philadelphia whom I greatly admire and who seems to be a faithful reader of your works. It came to his attention in London that you, unable to endure my chauvinism any longer, felt compelled to break off all contact with me. With full knowledge of and respect for the relationships, circumstances, and documents that come into play here, this piece of information amused me to no small extent. The same can be said of my colleagues, who were able to fully appreciate Cramer's information and to compare it to the facts.

Many thanks for your valuable gift. Regards from my chauvinistic corner.

Yours, Gershom Scholem

FROM GEORGE LICHTHEIM

London, November 21, 1972

Dear Scholem,

[. . .] Samuel Cramer is an amiable old man, though evidently a touch senile. I no longer recall exactly what I told him about our relationship, but it certainly was not what he said. Perhaps I said that I was no longer a Zionist when I left Jerusalem. [. . .]

FROM GEORGE LICHTHEIM

London, November 22, 1972

Dear Scholem,

When my father introduced me to Jabotinsky at the age of sixteen, I immediately and intuitively became both a Zionist and a Fascist. When around the same time I went over to the Marxist camp, I had to suppress this Zionism in me. My father never forgave me for doing that (and neither have you, it seems). This did not even change after I met Arthur Ruppin, who made the strongest moral impression upon me of anyone I have ever met. With regard to Zionism, I am and remain schizophrenic—something I shared with Benjamin (si licet parva componere magnis).[114] Of course I didn't notice this until years later. Out of this terminal schizophrenia grew my plan to begin my Marxist book on Europe with Benjamin's Angel of Death. The one thing I can add is that in 1932, when I was a twenty-year-old philosophy student in Heidelberg, I learned from reading Hegel that a state—even if be a Jewish one—can be founded and secured only through war. The former Brit Shalom people were obviously less clear about this. From 1934 to 1945, after Hitler solved my personal problems by forcing me to leave Germany, I enjoyed the best years of my life—all thanks to you, Sambursky, and above all Miriam Sambursky, to whom I dedicated my volume of essays published in 1973. Condemned to dilettantism by circumstances, I learned from you, Polotsky,[115] and Hans Jonas what scholarship is all about. The result is my book on Europe—my last and best book. I will never write anything else after this, for the simple reason that I have nothing left in my head. The book on Europe is my gravestone. [. . .]

George Lichtheim

1973

TO GEORGE LICHTHEIM

Jerusalem, January 3, 1973

Dear George,

I don't know if it's proper to congratulate you for surviving your departure from life, though we would like to.[116] From your perspective this probably isn't appropriate, which is understandable. We nevertheless hope that you'll rediscover the will to live. When I really think about it, however, no one has no right to meddle in such things.

I've given your announcement back to the dead Christ for critical review and analysis.[117] The first sentence, or rather the first paragraph, made such a dubious impression that at first I shrank back, speechless. Perhaps in the course of the coming year I'll succeed in establishing some kind of spiritual (which is not to say spiritist) connection with it.

We wish you and your psychophysics—along with their indelible metaphysical question marks—a speedy recovery.

Your loyal servant, Gershom Scholem

FROM REINHOLD SCHOLEM

Sydney, January 5, 1973

Dear Gerhard,

Enclosed you'll find the photograph of Zippora Scholem you asked for.[118] Eventually it will be handed on to Günter and his son Mark.[119] It took a long time for Kodak to produce a decent copy. I'm also sending you a shot of Marcus Scholem's grave in the Schönhauser Allee—a photo I took before my emigration in 1938. I can send you the negatives if you're interested. We had another heat wave, which didn't do me any good. Now I'm fit once again. *Time* (the issue of November 20, 1972) ran a story on Keter Publishing House's *Jewish Encyclopedia* and called your eighty-three-page article "the most lucid treatment of this complex subject." My copy of your article on the Kabbalah from the *Jüdisches Lexikon* has only fifty-one pages. How much progress have you made with the book on Sabbatai Sevi you mentioned to me in Zurich? [. . .]

Reinhold

FROM GEORGE LICHTHEIM

London, January 8, 1973

Dear Scholem,

This is just a brief note to tell you that the botched suicide attempt is now behind me and won't be repeated. I don't wish to go into the deep and lofty reasons for it. [. . .] Otherwise, I can only say that you, at seventy-five, have a lot more strength to live than I do at sixty. Maybe there's something to mysticism, after all. I'll keep going—that much is certain. My book on Europe, which has perhaps aroused your interest, is a success. The same goes for my literary essays published in New York. But I have no illusions about these things, and whatever I come up with next will be rather less ambitious. I must write to survive—or I have to throw everything overboard, and the experiment of doing so has given me a tremendous fright. Hopefully it didn't give you too much of one. Keep up your affection for me.

Yours, George Lichtheim

TO REINHOLD SCHOLEM

Jerusalem, January 30, 1973

Dear Reinhold,

Thank God your letter of January 5 came fairly punctually, meaning that I received the two photographs you included. The epitaph on Marcus Scholem's gravestone, with the exception of his name, is really undecipherable. Do you think it would be clearer in the negatives you have? It's also strange that the epitaph is only in German. Wasn't there supposed to be a Hebrew inscription on the other side of the stone? Did you by any chance photograph that side as well? The picture of our ancestor Zippora Scholem is excellent; she had typical Scholem features.

It's no wonder my present article on the Kabbalah is at least twice as long as the earlier essay in the first German-language *Encyclopedia Judaica,* volume 9, 1932 (and not the *Jüdisches Lexicon,* to which I didn't contribute). In reality, it's even much longer. For it's a summary of forty years of additional research. I wrote the first text in 1931; the other, in 1970. Moreover, these articles on Jewish mysticism will appear in a special book, which should be at least four or five hundred pages.

The book on Sabbatai Sevi you asked about is almost done. It'll be published in the spring by Princeton University Press. I have already read the final proofs. Other volumes of mine are piled up all around me: Hebrew, German, English, French, and Portuguese. The *Judaica* volumes you own have even come out in Japanese. [. . .]

Your Gerhard

FROM GEORGE STEINER

New York, February 3, 1973

Cher maître et ami,

Many warm thanks for your letter of January 28. Here is a small present in return for all the magnificence of *Judaica III.* My Deborah will be going to Israel in April and will live with a family in Tel Aviv. She's diligently learning Hebrew. I've taken the liberty of giving her the Scholem address in case of metaphysical necessity! The Israeli embassy in London has invited Koestler, Isaiah Berlin, and me—"the three leading Jewish personalities in the country"—to an official conference on "Jewish identity and Zionism." I hesitate to go—I really have no right to say anything about the topic (and neither do the other two gentlemen). [. . .]

Steiner

TO SIEGMUND HURWITZ

Jerusalem, February 11, 1973

Dear Dr. Hurwitz,

Now that I have rather carefully read through the second volume of Jung's letters you so kindly sent me, I can finally thank you from the bottom of my heart for your lovely birthday present. I am delighted to have this volume. Overall, it's of great interest to me insofar as it relates to the debate over the book *Answer to Job*.[120]

The first volume of letters made a deep impression on me because of Jung's relationship to the Nazis, even though after reading it I still have doubts about his behavior during the Nazi years. By contrast, I have to admit that the letters concerning *Answer to Job* left me almost devoid of all sympathy. After the vehemence of his initial outburst in this book, the letters that follow strike me as an uncommonly weak apologetic—he takes shelter behind psychological claims by saying that the book merely concerns the transformation of the image of God in the human unconscious. A careful reading of the book hardly supports this position. One has to ask: In whose unconscious was this image of God, found in the Jewish Bible, to be transformed—in the unconscious of Jews or of others? Both cases lead to senseless aporias. For in the most crucial issue of the entire book—namely, the Incarnation (be it first in the Trinity or later, thanks to our dear pope, in the Quaternity, preferred by Jung himself)—the image of God among Jews did not change at all.[121] The unconsciousness of non-Jews, on the other hand, never contained the image of God as the terrifying, wild, foolish Jewish creator and desert God described by Jung with Voltaire-like venom. In this way, Jung's apologia ends up playing games with psychological categories that I am unable to accept. The central point with Jung is precisely that the Jewish God, unable to rise to the challenge of Job's question—in other words, the question posed by his own creation—had to turn himself into a man. This was a completely new and in fact astonishing justification for the Incarnation. And if one were to view God as one of Jung's patients, this would have some logic. God would then partly leave the analysis after being released on probation and "integrated." But as a self-analysis on the part of the analysand, it's completely incredible. [. . .]

Putting Jung's question aside, the issue remains unresolved for me whether we Jews, as Jews, have ever really come to grips in our thinking or imagination with the biblical picture of God, if such a thing was really clearly given. As demonstrated by my many writings, I've occupied myself with this question for fifty years now, yet I still can't come up with an answer.

With cordial greetings.

Yours, Gershom Scholem

TO GEORGE STEINER

Jerusalem, March 13, 1973

Dear Steiner,

To my supposedly "only pupil" (which I really don't believe—in view of the fact that others also vie for this title, with no less right):

I'll begin with my greetings. I wish you lots of luck when you appear with Herr Koestler, of whom I don't have good memories. Judging from his books, I'm certain that you will express yourself somewhat less disdainfully on the topic of Jewishness in general and Israel in particular than can be expected from that writer.

Since you're traveling to California, I'm writing only a brief note to influence your further arrangements. We both, or at least I, intend to go to Ascona on the twentieth of August (though I won't be speaking at the conference this year). In case nothing else urgent comes up, I'll be in London sometime in September.

I read your chapter on the Jews with the greatest attention. To be honest, it touched me. It seems that those pages gave the goyim every opportunity to resent you, which I gathered from a number of nasty critiques that I came across in the university library and the reading room.

Should I congratulate you on this? If you ultimately decide to come to Israel, the goyish world will let out an audible sigh of relief.

In this spirit, I send my greetings to you and your wife.

Yours, Scholem

TO MIRCEA ELIADE[122]

Jerusalem, March 29, 1973

Dear Eliade,

I am very glad to have your letter of March 10, and I hope that if you come to Jerusalem, as our mutual friend Burton Feldman has told me you might, we shall meet and talk over those points in your letter of last June which are, I feel, in need of friendly and open-minded discussion and elucidation. When I read your letter (as I did several times), I did not know what to do about it. I understood the points you made; I used them in a long discussion with the man who had attacked me and you, and I tried to ascertain what exactly in your activities it was that he found objectionable. I could not find any definite statement about your personal biography, except a long harangue on the general background of what it meant in Romania in those years to be a member of the right. He said, to sum up, that one could not be a member of that political orientation without being anti–Semitic, even if the specific public activities of this type in which Eliade had participated could not be determined. It was a very long talk which left me feeling perplexed, since I could not judge the situation in Romania at the time. I did not know what to tell you, especially since you had not been specific about the Jewish point which interested me most. I would have liked to answer the attack on you by writing a documented article for the publication which had published the attack, but I was unable to do so because I lacked definite information of a positive nature. On the other hand, the man with whom I talked certainly was not somebody who would follow Communist slogans or propaganda, having been one of the main speakers of the Zionist movement in Romania. As I wrote in my earlier letter, I have always considered you an upright and honest friend, and if the conditions of those past years need to be cleared up, it should be done. My personal feelings toward you are the same as before, and I would be very pleased if you came for a visit here. [. . .]

Yours as ever, Gershom Scholem

TO JÜRGEN AND UTE HABERMAS

Jerusalem, April 23, 1973

Dear Herr and Frau Habermas,

This evening I received the wholly unexpected news of George Lichtheim's death, though at the moment we don't know the cause.[123] Three weeks ago he sent me an enthusiastic letter about his visit with you and said he had found a friend for life. I'm telling you this because I don't know if the news of his death will have already reached you before you learn how he felt about you.

Over the past several months he wrote many letters expressing a new-found will to live. Yet in recent years he truly did have a number of organic afflictions. What sad news! He wanted to dedicate his next book to you. He had already begun to think about it: it was to be on dialogues in political philosophy since Rousseau.

Yours, Gershom Scholem

TO ROBERT ALTER[124]

Jerusalem, May 15, 1973

Dear Professor Alter,

I owe you a word of cordial thanks for the highly perceptive essay you wrote about me.[125] It gave me much pleasure to have been subject to an analysis which comes so near to my own intentions. Of course, I would not subscribe to the view that I am a neo-Romantic historian, which appears to me misleading since the prime factors which stimulated my research were quite removed from Romanticism. But this qualification was invented by Gerson Cohn, and you gave it a twist which makes it more acceptable to me. As to Nietzsche, I must confess that I feel no kinship to him or to his heritage, and as a young man I turned away in disgust from those writings of Nietzsche which came into my hands. Unfortunately, those seem to have been the wrong ones, like *Zarathustra,* and they prevented me from delving deeper. I enjoyed very much your remarks on Agus' review of my book on the Messianic Idea.[126] He hates everything I stand for and said so in a roundabout way. His antipathy seems to me very legitimate, as it is obviously mutual. In fact, I despise the court Jew of Toynbee and the conservative variety of anti-Zionism.

Your remarks about paradox, dialectic, and abyss will serve as a warning against further usage. But what to do if my feeling is indeed turning towards the paradoxes of Jewish existence and all they imply? I cannot deny that I have a particularly vivid sense for these.

I hope you will enjoy the English edition of Sabbatai Sevi. May I mention *en passant* that I am likely to be in California (Santa Barbara) in the second week of September for some kind of symposium on Jewish theology in our times. Are you going to be among the audience? From there, I shall go to New York and Toronto for some weeks. I would very much like to see you again.

Yours cordially, Gershom Scholem

TO MIRIAM STRAUSS

Jerusalem, December 13, 1973

Dear Frau Strauss,

Fanya and I were both distressed to hear of the death of your husband, which we heard about only long afterward.[127] I have a letter he wrote to me the day before his death—even though it was barely legible, like so much of his late correspondence. I was delighted that he had received and had the chance to read my book on Sabbatai Sevi, after such a long publishing delay. He wrote me a wonderful letter about it. In Leo Strauss we have lost a man whose intellectual power I treasured above all others in this generation. Though our life trajectories and intellectual assumptions contrasted greatly, for years we had the secure feeling that we shared a deep fraternity far beyond intellectual differences. In my mind's eye I have the image of a thinker of immense depth, precision, and integrity who made an indelible impression on his pupils, many of whom I have met over the years. Shortly before he died we had dinner with Allan Bloom in Toronto, where an exclusive group of Strauss's former students and devoted admirers sat together and spoke about him. It was a noteworthy evening, four or five days before his death.

Have you decided what to do with his papers?

Fanya and I warmly offer you our hand.

Gershom Scholem

1974

FROM CYNTHIA OZICK[128]

January 28, 1974

Dear Professor Scholem,

My thanks to you and to Mrs. Scholem, on behalf of myself and Norma Rosen for the very great privilege of your hospitality. [. . .] I am enclosing, with a good deal of trepidation, a copy of my piece on *Sabbatai Sevi: The Mystical Messiah* (publication will be on February 10 in the *New York Times Book Review,* and I hope also to send along an early copy of that). As you and I agreed, there is no one in the world—except yourself!—qualified to review your work, and you are right to be astonished that the editors should choose a fiction-scribbler for that task. You recall that I asked (and now ask again) for advance forgiveness for any errors in understanding I am guilty of. May I tell you also how elated I am over receiving from your hands "The Name of God and the Linguistic Theory of the Kabbalah"? It was, in short, a treasure-visit, and I am more grateful than I am able to express to you for the privilege and the opportunity.

Very sincerely yours

TO CYNTHIA OZICK[129]

Jerusalem, February 11, 1974

Dear Ms. Ozick,

Thank you very much for the text of your review, which you so kindly have sent me. We very much enjoyed your visit, and I hope we may have another opportunity to meet again in New York or Jerusalem. I was no less curious to see how Cynthia Ozick would look than you may have been to find out how Gershom Scholem looks or behaves. It is good to know that both parties seem to have been satisfied. You should feel no trepidation about your review—there is no reason for that at all. I liked it very much, and the only sin with which I must charge you is a sin of omission. I would have thought it mandatory to mention that the book was originally written in Hebrew.

It was interesting news to me that you already in an early story had speculated about the paradoxes of my fascination with Jewish mysticism. I find the suggestion that the quarry may have been all the time in the pursuer not without plausibility. I have been asked this question so often that in the meanwhile I have invented at least twenty different answers, whereas the true one is hidden away between some of my lines.

With kind regards, Gershom Scholem

FROM REINHOLD SCHOLEM

Sydney, March 4, 1974

Dear Gerhard and Fanya,

We are back in Sydney, healthy and refreshed. The vacation in Tasmania was very lovely, though the weather could have been better. Once again I rented a car and we took a couple of nice excursions. I'm writing today because there's all sorts of family news. Esi will be seventy on Sunday, March 9. She continues to be downright depressed since Ernst's death. [. . .] Things are happening in the family of Ernst and Liesel (who are now divorced). A few weeks ago Liesel arrived back from Johannesburg, where she visited her father. Her oldest son, Peter, is going to marry a Catholic nurse in a Catholic ceremony on March 16. Phiechen, Ernst, and Liesel will all fly to Brisbane for the wedding. Phiechen, who otherwise never leaves home, will—of all things—be gone during the couple of days when Renee will be here. David, on the other hand, won't be at the wedding. He was at a camp for students, where he converted to strict Orthodox Judaism. Liesel says that he's decided to study in a Yeshiva for a year. In every generation, the Scholems pursue the most diverse interests.[130] [. . .]

TO REINHOLD SCHOLEM

Ragaz, Switzerland, March 25, 1974

Dear Reinhold,

Your letter from the fourth of March has arrived, together with the report on developments within the Scholem family—and in the most colorful forms, including the Catholic marriage of a Jewish relation. The fact that you all are so eager to fly to Brisbane surprises me less than the news that the brother of the bridegroom of a Catholic nurse has converted to strict Orthodox Judaism. I always thought the Scholem family had done its work fifty or sixty years ago. Now it turns out that I was mistaken and that, as you rightly said, the Scholems pursue the most varied interests in every generation. This goes for the London and Australian branches every bit as much as for the Israeli branch. Apropos of the latter, the old *Deutschnationaler* in you (as you described yourself to Fanya in Zurich)[131] will be astonished to hear that your Zionist-chauvinist brother, of all people, will receive the literary prize of the Bavarian Academy of Fine Arts in July. The reasons for granting it are eagerly awaited. I won't forget to send it to you once it gets that far. This was, needless to say, in no way envisioned when I left Munich fifty-two years ago. It's still secret, and officially you're not allowed to know it for six weeks. But I had to top one surprise with another. [. . .]

Gerhard

FROM REINHOLD SCHOLEM

Sydney, August 4, 1974

Dear Gerhard,

This was a "Gershom Scholem" week! Your thousand-page *Sabbatai Sevi* came on Tuesday, and on Friday your letter from Ragaz arrived with the astonishing news about the literary prize from the Bavarian (!!!) Academy of Fine Arts. You'll perhaps recall what I wrote in the context of our discussion on Judaism: that, despite everything, you are a fine writer of German. I never expected that a German academy would confirm my opinion with a literary prize. Sincerest congratulations! Besides a couple good pints of Bavarian beer, I hope the prize comes with a bit of cash. [. . .]

Who is Mr. Steiner, whom you obviously know very well? I have begun reading your *magnum opus.* My collection of reviews on Sabbatai begins with the May 1957 issue of *Scopus.* The *Jerusalem Post* from April 1959 (the article by D. Flusser) follows; next in line is the *Frankfurter Allgemeine Zeitung* from September 16, 1966 (the piece by Dr. Schoeps);

then C. Ozick's in the *New York Times* from February 24; and finally Steiner's long acknowledgment. My question for you is why you began *Sabbatai Sevi* with a German quotation as an epigraph. According to Knaur's *Lexicon,* Dilthey's dates are 1833–1911. Wasn't Yorck von Wartenburg a hero during the Wars of Liberation?[132] [. . .]

A new mixed marriage is in the works. Helga Major (born Kirschstein) has a daughter named Susan who will marry a Catholic on December 21. It'll be a garden wedding with a Baptist minister. I recently had dinner with Helga. The bridegroom is from Bombala, where Susan works as a teacher. He comes from a simple family; his mother raised four children after her husband left her, shortly after she gave birth to the last. He works for the Highway Department. Both of them want to move to Sydney, where he would like to enroll in a four-year evening program in civil engineering at the Technical College. Let us say, "Quod deus bene vertat."[133] [. . .]

Reinhold

TO REINHOLD SCHOLEM

Jerusalem, December 12, 1974

Dear Reinhold,

[. . .] If you began reading my *Sabbatai Sevi* in October, by now you've either despaired of the material or have finished it. I'd prefer the first alternative. You wouldn't really want to know in depth what it's all about. The long article by Steiner appeared in the *New Yorker* on October 22, 1973. Steiner is a very well known professor of comparative literature in Geneva. He grew up speaking English and French, though in an Austrian-Jewish-Zionist home; in short, he's an international Jew. If it's important to you to have an original copy, I'll get one to you. We became acquainted with him during the winter of 1971–1972 at Bodmer House in Zurich. He chattered away at me the whole time.

The German quotation, which is taken from the correspondence between Dilthey and Yorck von Wartenburg (and which you seem somewhat ambivalent about), comes from a very important mind. In my humble opinion, it's an incomparable quotation, since it relates to my own opinion on the nature of truth.

It seems that I collect prizes the way the Australian Scholem family does mixed marriages. On November 21 I received my third of the year here, and it came with the humble amount of a thousand dollars. It was awarded to me by the American chapter of B'nai B'rith. I believe your father-in-law belonged to it in Berlin. Be that as it may, my prizes are less problematic than your mixed marriages. A Baptist man of the cloth marrying a Catholic to a Jew!! [. . .]

Greetings from us both, Gerhard

1975

FROM REINHOLD SCHOLEM

Sydney, January 29, 1975

Dear Gerhard,

[. . .] Mixed marriages: Susan Major's wedding went without a hitch. The preacher was dressed in secular garb—no cassock—and I did not hear a word about Christ in his address. I must sadly report another mixed marriage. On Saturday, February 1, Lea Susman, who is the daughter of the late Gerd Sus (and who is already the product of a mixed marriage), will marry her boyfriend; she's already been living with him for some time. He's a Hungarian goy, a musician who plays for a jazz band. Until now he hasn't been able to get permission to stay in the country, but marriage to a native-born woman may help. [. . .] I would be thrilled if you could send me the *New Yorker* with the Steiner review. You've already seen Bodmer House a couple of times. Soon someone will hang up a plaque saying "Professor G. Scholem slept here." You sent me your Munich speech. Your credo. Together with the Steiner report, there were many things I did not know. The epigraph did not offend me; I simply saw it as confirmation of how German your background is, when you, despite all of your talmudic and kabbalistic wisdom, used a German citation on the "partial understanding" of truth. How would it be with a concealed picture of the goddess Thaïs? (In all my books, I haven't found anything about her.) Reading, or rather studying, *Sabbatai Sevi* goes very slowly, but I intend to keep at it. In the meantime I have read Cornelius Ryan's book *A Bridge Too Far*. It's the story of the Allies' failed attempt to break through the lines after Arnheim in September 1944. Ryan is the author of the famous book *The Longest Day*. [. . .]

Reinhold

1976

FROM REINHOLD SCHOLEM

Sydney, May 10, 1976

Dear Gerhard and Fanya,

Your letter from twenty-second of April arrived on the thirtieth. Exactly two days later your Benjamin book finally arrived here from Suhrkamp's distribution center in Munich.[134] [. . .] The book is as much about Scholem as it is about Benjamin. I began to write down notes about you even before your letter told me it contained information about your life. There are a lot of G's in the margins. Throughout the book you've scattered all sorts of small fragments for a future biographer. There are many things I had absolutely no idea about. I have a list of "questions for Gerhard." [. . .] As I recall, the four of us brothers were all together for the last time in Interlaken, when we stayed with our parents in the Hotel Jungfrau am Höhenweg. I believe it was 1908. I recall the impression we made when we marched behind our parents into the dining hall. Afterward I spent three years abroad; I believe the next time I saw you was in 1921, during my honeymoon in Munich. I'll have to write out for you my comments on what you said about the intervening period and the family (Werner, etc.). Benjamin gave me the impression of having a wishy-washy character. What are you going to speak about in your address to the Bavarian Academy? Warmest greetings to you both. [. . .]

Reinhold

TO REINHOLD SCHOLEM

Jerusalem, May 24, 1976

Dear Reinhold,

Thanks for your last letter. I'm pleased that you plan on studying my biography with my book on Benjamin as a guide, which in fact has no dearth of all kinds of information. I found it interesting that you can't recall exactly how long we went without seeing each other back then. My memory in these matters is very precise. Between 1909 (not 1908) and 1912 you were abroad for further training in various printing houses in England, France, and Italy. After your return, from October 1, 1912, to October 1913 you went to Treptow to do your one-year military training. From that point until mobilization at the end of July 1914, you spent the entire time at home. During your one-year service and the time spent in the room opposite our parents', we saw each other often enough, though we rarely discussed anything important. The age gap between us was too great, not to mention the differences in our opinions and our life plans. This must be the reason you thought you hadn't seen me until your honeymoon. Naturally, I saw you after I returned from Switzerland to Berlin in September 1919 and before I left for Munich. I remember particularly vividly our father's fiftieth birthday on March 5, 1913. You and your friends staged a grand spectacle and you sang a hit tune with the refrain, "We're selling our grandmother's little house," and "We don't need a mother-mother-mother-in-law. Shhh . . . Shhh . . . She's wearing a trico, trico, trico, tricot. Boots without soles and missing a heel." I remember your friends Freideberger, Preiss, and Bauchwitz who sang it with you. I was terribly irritated by this entire celebration, for I was forced to appear as a cherry salesman from Werder (also as a sausage salesman at a cherry festival, I believe).

Enough for now. With warmest greetings, as well, from Fanya.

Gerhard

FROM REINHOLD SCHOLEM

Sydney, June 20 and July 5, 1976

Dear Gerhard,

A couple answers to your letter from May 24, before I come to the notes I made on your book on Walter Benjamin. Your memory is considerably better than mine. At the time of father's fiftieth birthday on March 5, 1913, I was doing my one-year service in Treptow, just as you remember; but I don't have the foggiest memory of the great spectacle and the song. The tune "We're selling our grandmother's little house," and "trico, trico, tricot," now comes to me for the first time in sixty-three years. You mentioned my friends; only Paul Friedenberger is still alive. I'm in contact with his son in London. For about a year in 1919 we printed *Der Junggesellen,* which was a precursor of the modern sexual liberation movement. [. . .]

You mention a number of times the strong impression W. B. made when he spoke. According to page 175, he reached a magnificent high point in the speech he gave for Magnes in Paris: he "was obviously well prepared, and presented it in marvelous phrases." For nearly three pages you discuss the plans he elaborated, and he apparently made a great impression on Magnes. On page 191 you say that Magnes sent the "entire advance payment" to W. B. in Berlin, and that this greatly worried you. [. . .] You don't mention whether the university ever got the money back. At the top of page 201 W.B. says, "I have not known living Judaism in any form other than through you." To what degree are you the embodiment of "Judaism"? You are a particular scholar with many outside interests who is a product much more of the entire intellectual world than of the fact that you're an Israeli. [. . .] Who represents Judaism? You? The religious party? The Histadrut?[135] Or maybe the very lively city of Tel Aviv? A fool can ask more questions than the wise man can answer. [. . .]

Reinhold

TO ROBERT SILVERS[136]

Jerusalem, July 30, 1976

Dear Mr. Silvers,

Your communications from July 15 reached me only now, during my vacation in Switzerland.[137] I am not interested at all by Koestler's book, and even less in reviewing it.[138] It is, as you will allow me to say, sensationalist humbug. Why should I write about that?

Sigmund Freud told the Jews their religion was foisted upon them by an Egyptian, so that there was nothing for the Jews to be proud of. The Jews found it baseless but rather amusing. Some Gentiles loved it because it would tell those supercilious Jews a lesson. Arthur Koestler wants to give them the rest by telling them that they were not even Jews and that those damned Ashkenazim from Russia, Romania, and Hungary who had invented Zionism had not even the right to ask for

Israel as their homeland—which their Khazaric forefathers had never seen. *Quatsch.*[139] The whole thing is an old story, whose most learned (and still ridiculous) version was published in Hebrew by an Israeli Communist (later an ex-Communist like A.K. himself) more than thirty years ago.

I said an "old story." When I met Koestler's landsman Dr. Brody twenty-seven years ago in Ascona, a Hungarian Jew who published Joyce (in German), Broch, and yours truly in Switzerland, I asked him from which Jewish community his family came to Budapest—from Brody in Galicia or from Ungarish Brod in Moravia? He answered, "I am not a Jew; I am a Khazar." I said, "Das können Sie einem Goy erzählen."[140] Whereupon we became friends.

There is nothing more to be said by me about Koestler's scholarship and his courageous enterprises which, as far as I see from previews, many goyim will appreciate. Not so your obedient servant.

Gershom Scholem

TO REINHOLD SCHOLEM

Zurich, September 8, 1976

Dear Reinhold,

[. . .] To come back to your letter of May 24 containing your remarks on my Benjamin book, I would like to tell you that I read them with the greatest pleasure and interest. I have something to say on a number of your questions. It really is incontestable that my memory is much better than yours. The reason for this is that I forget all the important things I would like to remember, while my memory's sieve stores up all useless and secondary details with uncanny precision. This gives rise to the false impression, to which many people are prey, that I have a phenomenal memory. And how could I forget a scene such as Father's fiftieth birthday? To my displeasure and against my will, I was forced (in my fifteenth year of life) to appear dressed as a sausage salesman in a Werder Cherry Blossom Fair, and each one of you had to give me ten or twenty pfennigs for a couple of sausages. Because of my bad mood I naturally remember, and with great detail, the spectacle you and your friends made, accompanied by our cousin Trude Borchardt's sirens and those of a few similar young ladies. What I did not know and first learned from your letter was that the magazine *Der Junggeselle* was printed in our printing house! I'm completely flabbergasted. [. . .]

You would like to know whether the university ever got its money back. The answer is no. You also ask to what extent I embody Judaism. This is a good question and deserves to be answered with a confession: I embody nothing besides myself. Yesterday afternoon, however, I was visiting some friends of mine and watched a color TV film that was filmed six months ago in Jerusalem for Allgemeine Deutsche television. They broadcast forty-five minutes out of many hours of film. Based on the view presented in the clips they selected, I do embody Judaism. [. . .]

Your left-wing Israeli brother (but still known within the so-called New Left as a reactionary imperialist and Zionist aggressor)

1977

FROM JACOB TAUBES

Zurich, March 16, 1977

Esteemed Herr Dr. Scholem,

After twenty-five years, I am now considering going to Israel for Passover— but not without "fear and trembling." In Jerusalem I will visit my father's grave, and also the holy sites, though motivated more out of curiosity than natural instinct. As the saying goes, I'll see very few people, and only if it's intentional, with a purpose. I would be interested in speaking with you, for the following reasons: (1) A small circle of "ethnologists" (ethnologists of religion) and Benjamin experts (along with two Judaica scholars) would be interested in "honoring" the eightieth "birthday of Gershom Scholem." And *not* with Suhrkamp, which is afraid of bringing out anything "critical" of Scholem. Perhaps you would find it amusing, after so many festschrifts and prizes, to tolerate and even climb aboard a "critical discussion with Scholem"—*not* in the unbearably boring style of those worthless volumes, where Cassirer, Popper, Russell, Buber et al. have all been "buried alive"! I could imagine a first-rate discussion that would not only treat Scholem as a "monument," but grant him *new life* through the "mortification" of criticism. [. . .] My preference would be to "plan" along with you a quasi "anti-festschrift." The question is whether one should handle you with kid gloves, as many think (and then later, out of *boredom,* turn their attention to other topoi), or whether one should highlight controversial points in your work (both explicit and tacit). In order to work up a lively discussion, you should decide what you want. To what extent: (a) Suhrkamp comes into question as a publisher, or (b) you place yourself and your responses in the middle of the discussion. Scholem—not only as a historian of religion but as an author with a highly speculative mind—is not some private property to conceal by barring access to critical guests! The Scholem I knew and the man I honor—and wish to pay tribute to on his eightieth birthday—belongs under the second rubric. Friends who deny this would have to picture him as a little (intellectual) Caesar, someone who can dish it out but can't take it. [. . .]

What else is there to say? I might add that what came between us belongs to the vanity of academic life. Between and around us stand the dead: Susan Taubes, whom you traumatized to the end; Josef Weiss, for whom we both bear guilt; and Peter Szondi, Paul Celan, and George Lichtheim. Even though they knew that Scholem and Taubes were "enemies," they all remained bound to us in friendship to the very end. If we can meet each other with a purpose, beyond the abyss, let me know by March 29, c/o Edoes Postfach, Hauptbahnhof Zurich.

Always your pupil, Jacob Taubes

TO JACOB TAUBES

Jerusalem, March 24, 1977

Esteemed Herr Professor Taubes,

Only today did I receive your detailed airmail letter of March 16 (postmarked the eighteenth). You are completely mistaken in matters pertaining to me. What has irreparably separated us for twenty-five years hardly belongs to the "vanity of academic life." Rather, it belongs to the existential decisions of my life (and of *moral* rather than academic life, if I may use the word), along with experiences I have had in the course of my long years of effort to understand the Jewish people and Jewish phenomena.

I won't go into the contents of your letter. It's a free country, and you can write as many critiques of my propositions, essays, or books as you please. But I wish to state unequivocally that I will not participate in any book that deals with me critically, approvingly, or politely in which you, Herr Taubes, act as editor or contributor. You made your decisions twenty-five years ago, and I made mine.[141] I have no intention of changing this. "Look at each where he stands / and where he stands, that he does not fall."

In sad memory, and with best wishes for your health.

Gershom Scholem

1978

FROM KURT VON FRITZ[142]

February 15, 1978

Dear Herr Scholem,

A few weeks ago I read in the paper that you celebrated your eightieth birthday. I wanted to write immediately to offer you my warmest congratulations, but I was hampered by so many commitments that I couldn't get to it. [. . .] Now there is an additional reason for me to write, which is that I would like to ask a favor of you. In the conflict between the Arabs and the State of Israel, I have always, until now, stood on the side of the latter. But after the most recent events, it has become difficult for me to understand certain things. I would thus very much like to know how the situation appears from your perspective, and whether and for what reasons you are in complete agreement with current Israeli policy. There is of course no doubt that Sadat began his policy of peace not out of love for Israel, but because he finds himself in an extremely difficult situation. Nevertheless, the question arises whether it's clever to exploit this situation to the utmost and thus to potentially drive the Egyptians back into the camp of Israel's uncompromising enemies. The situation of Israeli settlements on the Sinai peninsula seems to me to bear a certain resemblance to that of the remaining German settlements in what is now Polish Upper Silesia. I don't believe that the Germans living there would gain anything if the Germans were allowed to have a few soldiers on Polish soil, which is what the Israeli government, if I understand it correctly, is demanding in case the settlements don't remain completely beyond the Egyptian borders. The opposite is the case. Though in the not so distant past the relationship between Poland and Germany has been considerably worse than that between Israel and Egypt, the present relationship between Germans and Poles, according to the reports from West German visitors to Polish Upper Silesia, is not so bad. In many respects, the Germans living in Polish Upper Silesia have it better than those in the "independent" German Democratic Republic, who don't approve of their dependence on the Soviet Union. It seems to me that it could only benefit Israel if a relationship developed between Israelis and Egyptians (who speak Arabic but

who are not Arabs) that was similar to that which exists between Poles
and Germans in Silesia—especially since both have to defend themselves
against the wild anti-Jewish Khaddafi. All the less can I understand, if
the reports are correct, why the Israelis create difficulties for Sadat by
supporting the Ethiopian government through arms shipments. My colleague, the Assyriologist D. O. Edzard, tries to explain this through the
ancient connection between Israel and the Negus, the "Lion of Judah."[143] But this, or rather the last of its representatives, was pushed
aside by the current military regime. These may all be "unenlightened
reflections." But they are close at hand and widespread. For this reason
I would be most grateful for expert enlightenment. [. . .]

Sincerely yours, Kurt von Fritz

TO KURT VON FRITZ

Jerusalem, April 12, 1978

Dear Herr von Fritz,

Cordial thanks for your letter of February 15 and for the birthday
congratulations. Even belated congratulations never hurt. You want to
know about my position on current Israeli policy. I can give you a rather
simple reply: by no means do I agree with this policy, which to my mind
is foolish and unstatesmanlike. I therefore can't give you a defense of
this policy, since on a number of important points I strongly take issue
with it. For some time a not insignificant number of people in Israel,
even those who did not vote for Begin,[144] expected him to come up
with a politically clever policy that could be defended with some success
before the world. As a result, his purely rhetorical posture which falsely
assessed important realities came as a disappointment. I must admit that
I never had a very high opinion of his dogmatic position. I was always
pessimistic about it. I don't want to imply by this that Israel could accept
the demands that Sadat formulated. I am very far from doing so, for he
thinks that his willingness to travel to Jerusalem and to recognize us as
a state (against the protests of most other Arab states) suffices to get him
everything without any concessions, along with everything else he otherwise demands. There is no government in Israel, irrespective of who's
running it, that could submit to such demands, presented as they are in

the form of an ultimatum. Like many other people, I would not hesitate to approve a government effort to show broad willingness to compromise and to push forward a wise policy, whose practical sense, given the current situation, can only be to move Egypt and possibly Jordan toward a separate peace (one cannot seriously expect most Arab states to demonstrate a willingness for peace—in particular Syria, which is, under the prevailing circumstances, Israel's most fanatical foe), not to mention the PLO.[145] Egypt needs this peace at least as much as Israel, and I could imagine conditions under which it will be concluded, provided the Egyptians are somewhat more careful in making demands outside the Sinai. I don't think much of these settlements in the Occupied Territories, and certainly not of forcing such installations even as one is trying to negotiate. I don't know whether Egypt would really be prepared for such a politics of peace based on mutual concessions; I even fear the opposite. In any case, this would be a clever policy that takes into account Israel's position and one that is also easier to defend politically. Unfortunately, there is no truth to the statement one so often hears: that border lines have become less important in the age of guided missiles. Given established borders and territorial conditions, anyone who lives here knows that this isn't true.

I can't say anything about Ethiopia. I can't make any sense of the situation there, which is certainly very complex. The present military dictatorship, which got rid of the king's dictatorship, has secretly maintained a far-reaching relationship with Israel. As far as I understand, both sides have done so for good reasons.

Perhaps these few comments will be of some help in clarifying my position on these matters.

With cordial greetings.

Yours, Gershom Scholem

FROM DANIEL MATT[146]

New York, June 18, 1978

Dear Professor Scholem,

[. . .] I decided to leave Delhi and headed up to the mountains to visit a friend of mine who was studying with a guru named Swamiji Jnanananda (meaning "the knowledge of bliss"). I stayed there for about a week. He was simply a mirror reflecting whoever I thought I was. Being with him, I was able to see a little more clearly who I really am and what I need to do. We discussed Kabbalah and Hinduism, scholarship and mystical experience, celibacy and Tantra. I found him a little dogmatic in his own way (he's very down on Buddhism, for example) but very clear and shining. A beautiful calm presence.

A quick look at the erotic temples of Khajuraho, a stop in Bombay, and then Goa—on the southwest coast. A taste of paradise—palm trees, papayas, sunsets over the Arabian Sea. Of course mixed in with Indian filth and squalor, but least 60 percent *Gan Eden*.[147] I stayed there for six weeks, just lying on the beach, doing yoga and breathing exercises, meditating, hanging out with a friend of mine, David, from the States.

I realized that if I wanted to start teaching next fall I'd have to head back and look for a job, so around the end of January I came back the quick way, flying from Bombay to London and New York. I've been around here since then. [. . .] Finally, just a few days ago, I heard from the University of Texas that they want me. I'm really happy and excited about this—sunshine, open spaces, away from the northeast Boston–New York syndromes. I won't get to teach much Kabbalah at first (the position is in Rabbinics and medieval Hebrew literature), but I'm eager to start and I'll have time to do *Zohar*. Speaking of which, I'm working on an anthology of *Zohar* translations for the Paulist Press. They're doing a series of classics of Western spirituality—Islam, Christianity, Judaism, American Indian. [. . .]

TO DANIEL MATT[148]

Jerusalem, July 20, 1978

Dear Dr. Matt,

[. . .] Your detailed account of your travels in the East and your experiences there with your several friends and some gurus I read with great interest. As a hitchhiker, you seem to be quite a success. My opinion of the swamis seems to be a little more reserved than yours. I smelled a rat in several of those whom I encountered. Actually, only two have left a real positive image on my mind. One of them I met years ago in Ascona, where he accompanied his pupil, a Jew from southern Germany, who had been a successful speculator in Swiss real estate and could therefore much later afford to finance the very valuable translation and English edition of the rather priceless *Gospel of Ramakrishna* by this swami of his, well known as Kikhilanda (1942). My wife, who likes to ask provocative questions, asked him, "Did you stand on your head long in order to see the light?" He answered very quietly and without showing any sign of being offended, "No, madam, I did not stand on my head, but I looked at a bare wall for ten years." I think he was quite serious. I certainly noted with envy that you seem to believe to have enjoyed at least 60 percent of *Gan Eden* in Goa. I wonder how you could manage not to go the short way from Goa to Pondicherry, to the ashram of the most famous Jewess after the Holy Virgin, or whatever title you want to give to Maria, who, according to the latest pronouncement of the previous pope (no, two steps removed from the present one) was bodily transfigured into Heaven. Has the ashram of Miss Miriam Mizrachi of Marseilles—later Mrs. Richards, and a great pupil of the famous former terrorist transformed into a saint, who one day recognized her as being an avatar of the goddess Kali—not attracted you, or at least your Jewish pride? Or were you perhaps prevented from being so by some vicious thought you heard from your former teacher Scholem? Since you asked whether I also am a Sagittarius—yes I am, but I never drew any consequences from this, in contradistinction to some of my astrologically minded acquaintances, who wanted to read into this fact all kinds of curious, possibly spurious, indications regarding my character, my past, and my future.

Reading your exposition of your plans regarding the preparations of your volumes on the *Zohar,* I wonder what material you noted on your card index about breath and breathing. You say you found some allusions by Moses de León to his own part in composing the *Zohar*. Does this go beyond the allusions which I noted in my book? That surely will be interesting. That there are "new discoveries every day" is only what I expect a young scholar of your age to find. Congratulations! And may I express the hope that they will stand up to critical scrutinizing. Who was, or is, Robert Zimmerman, called Bob Dylan? Being an old racist, please let me know if he is a Jew. The Zimmermans divide 50 percent into goyim and Jews. The book on him which you have sent has not yet arrived. The interview in the magazine *Rolling Stones* is not available to me and I have not found it in Jerusalem. My receptivity to music is, alas, nothing; therefore, I forgo the pleasure of listening to "Blonde on

Blonde" or even the more seducing "Desire." The title "Highway 61"
arouses no desire in me. Maybe I am too old for it.

I hope to write a book next winter. If I should finish it, it will appear.
Nothing more should be said at this time. I am superstitious enough to
dislike talking about my future plans. This should in no way discourage
you, since I suppose that your superstitions are on another line.

With kind regards.

Sincerely yours, Gershom Scholem

TO ROBERT ALTER[149]

Jerusalem, October 29, 1978

Dear Dr. Alter,

It is with great delay that I congratulate you on your strong remarks
on the book of Peter Gay which you published in *Commentary* last
March.[150] What you wrote intrigued me and led me to buy the book
in order to take real offense—as I actually did. It is a book written in
full knowledge of my stand in these matters and against me. You said
rightly that he makes no reference to my name in the whole book, but
he quotes verbally from my essay "On Jews and Germans" without naming me—right at the beginning of the book. He says that this is exactly
the position against which he will write. I envy your tact and generosity,
which I would have been unable to mobilize in writing about this rather
scandalous book. The title is really a perfect *chutzpah*. Freud all his life
considered himself a Jew and nothing else. I remember only one passage
in one of his letters, under the impact of the outbreak of the First World
War, that he used the phrase "wir Deutschen." But this has happened
to Martin Buber at the same time. If I have any occasion to do so, I
shall surely quote Peter Gay as a classic example showing to which length
glorifiers of Jewish assimilation in Germany are willing to go thirty-five
years after Auschwitz. The curious thing is that his wife, Mrs. Gay, has
written a most admiring letter about my stand on these questions to the
Leo Baeck Institute in New York, of which they sent me a copy.

Aren't we going to see you here in Jerusalem one of these days? I
would like very much to see you again, after more than three years.

Cordial greetings to you and your wife.

FROM EMIL FACKENHEIM[151]

Toronto, November 26, 1978

Dear Herr Scholem,

[. . .] I am now in the midst of grappling with Heidegger, the result of which is already clear to me: the main point is not what he did personally, but what he did philosophically; not his philosophical decisions in 1933, but above all everything that ensued. I think I can show how he failed to stand up to the real test. I have now read in the volume *Erinnerung an Martin Heidegger* (ed. Neske, 1977) that Buber spoke with Heidegger, which in turn led to vociferous debates in Jerusalem; that the "unmastered" past was not raised in their conversation; and that Buber did not continue the discussion—not because of this last point, but because he couldn't speak about religious matters. The article also mentions Marcel's stupid comment when he supposedly said that the people in Jerusalem were "Pharisees" who "want to forbid all understanding and forgiveness."[152] As you can imagine, I am of the opinion that you cannot speak with Heidegger if you cannot mention the past—even though it's obvious that talk of "mastering the past" is idiotic, to put it mildly. In this connection I clearly recall our conversation in Toronto in 1973, when you told me about your decision not to accept Gadamer's invitation to meet Heidegger. I think you were right. In case Buber really did speak with Heidegger, he did so only under the tacit agreement not to mention the past. Do you know anything more about Buber's visit? Is this report entirely correct? Do you want to add anything? I know that it would be better to discuss all of these issues in person, and I hope to visit you again this summer. But since I first of all don't know whether we can come, and since, second, I am now writing the book, I would be grateful for a written answer, even if only a few lines. Perhaps I should add that what is at stake for me here is not Heidegger but the philosophical concerns that he so profoundly stirred and that, in my opinion, he failed philosophically (not to mention personally) to carry out: namely, the historical-ness of Being and the question of truth in the Age of Technology. [. . .]

Sincerely, Fackenheim

TO EMIL FACKENHEIM

Jerusalem, December 7, 1978

Dear Herr Fackenheim,

[. . .] To your question on Heidegger: I don't know any details about Buber's meeting with H., which in fact did take place. What I know about the event comes from Ernst Simon, who told me about it at the time. I have not seen the volume *Erinnerung an M.H.*, from 1977. I know of no passionate debates in Jerusalem revolving around this meeting; I know only that Ernst Simon, who was closer to Buber than I, deeply disapproved of it and regretted that it took place. I can't say whether one of our acquaintances here ever had an exchange of views with Buber over this. I would consider it rather unlikely. I told you how Gadamer, in a discussion with me in 1969, used the encounter between Buber and H. as an encouraging precedent.

I can't say anything more than this. My refusal to accept Gadamer's invitation can be traced to the fact that I would have been incapable of conducting a discussion with H. without every second being reminded of his past, and of course without directly raising the issue. It should be clear to everyone that this would have been senseless and would have led to the immediate interruption of the discussion.

Yours, Gershom Scholem

1980[153]

FROM EDNA AIZENBERG[154]

New York, February 11, 1980

Dear Professor Scholem,

For some two years now I have been engaged in the researching and writing of a dissertation entitled "The Jewish Presence in Borges." This thesis is, I believe, the first comprehensive study of the factors which influenced Borges' interest in Judaism, and also of the ways in which this interest is manifested in his works. Earlier in the year I had the wonderful experience of speaking to Borges at length, and in the course of our conversation he mentioned that the "highlights" of his trips to Israel were his encounters with you. On those occasions, he claimed, you spoke and he listened and learned. I had, of course, known of your meetings from my research, but after hearing from Borges himself about them my enthusiasm was fired, and whatever trepidation I had about writing to you (would you answer?) disappeared. Mr. David Biale was kind enough to provide me with your address—and here is the letter.[155] From Borges' comments, I felt there was a rapport between the two of you which transcended the interest in the Kabbalah. This was confirmed by Biale's recent book, which I read with attention (after completing yours). It seems to me that Borges and you share such things as a celebrative view of irrationality and myth, an interest in the tension between tradition and innovation, a fascination with symbols and language as a major cognitive tool used by man to organize his chaotic sense perceptions, and a sympathy for anarchy and for Jung. More importantly, however, I think you share in the search for some form of spirituality meaningful in our secular, nonbelieving world (although Borges would never admit this). Having briefly expounded my project and my impressions of the affinities between Scholem and Borges, I would be honored if you could comment on your encounters with Borges, on his kabbalistic knowledge and his use of this knowledge, and on the affinities between the two of you. Do you think that both of you, one in the realm of historiography, the other in that of literature, are trying to answer the same impulses and achieve similar things? [. . .]

TO JUTTA BOHNKE-KOLLWITZ[156]

Jerusalem, March 19, 1980

Dear Jutta,

Hurrah, hurrah! I thank you from the bottom of my heart for your efforts. The information from Herr Schulte has indeed closed the circle. My conjecture that Benjamin's grandmother, Brunelle Meyer, was related through her mother to Heinrich Heine's aunt, Brunelle de Geldern, is clearly correct. All of this occurred by way of Siegburg, who married the first Brunelle. Now I have completely reconstructed the family tree. [. . .]

Hope to see you soon, Gerhard

TO EDNA AIZENBERG[157]

Jerusalem, June 22, 1980

Dear Mrs. Aizenberg,

I have the letter of June 2, 1980, regarding Borges. Your assumption about Borges and me sharing a similar interest in certain things which you mention is more or less correct. Only your remark about a common sympathy for anarchism and Jung needs correction. My sympathy for Jung is rather limited. I appreciate the uncommon and quite extraordinary personality of Jung, but I am not convinced that his theories, especially his doctrine of Archetypes and the Collective Unconscious expressing itself in myth, are true. I have also, like almost everybody Jewish, great reservations about his behavior in 1933–1934, and I find it difficult to accept his explanations. But I cannot comment, as you wish, on my very pleasant encounters with Borges and on his kabbalistic knowledge. I am not sure at what period or periods his kabbalistic stories have been written, and I cannot form a definite opinion whether he read my books before writing those stories or after it. What I can say is that they compare favorably with the mystical and partly kabbalistic stories written in German by Gustav Meyrink, whose imagination no doubt went in the same direction as Borges'. As to your last question, I must say that in the realm of historiography, I have not been trying to answer the same impulses as Borges and do not think that we have achieved similar things. Borges is a writer of considerable power of imagination and does not claim to represent historical reality, but rather an insight into what the Kabbalists could have stood for in his own imagination. What I did was to try to describe the world of the Kabbalists by analyzing their own works and ideas without overstepping, essentially, these limits. It is only here and now that very rarely I have made what I called "ahistorical" assumptions about what the Kabbalists may have meant beyond a historical analysis. You find an example of such tendency in Volume III of my German book *Judaica* (*Studien zur jüdischen Mystik*), pp. 264–271, which if you don't read German you may ask some friend to translate to you for your benefit.

With best wishes for your work.

Sincerely yours

FROM CYNTHIA OZICK[158]

New York, August 22, 1980

Dear Professor Scholem,

The pinnacle of our time abroad was the supernal hours spent with you and Mrs. Scholem. A foretaste of paradise! A thousand thanks. Having been appointed Ambassador by you, I have fulfilled all my tasks, some successfully, others less so. As follows: (1) Immediately after coming back to New York I wrote a letter to Irving Howe, based on what you dictated to me, which was: "Scholem wonders about your trustworthiness. This is the second time you have promised *Dissent* free of charge, and it has not come." No answer to my letter has arrived; but I heard Howe is traveling now and will be in Israel. Since you will be away, he will return to my waiting letter, with its severe admonishment. (2) I telephoned Kenneth Briggs. He is a very nice man, and his interview with you at the *Times* was a great event for him. It has not yet been published, and he still has hope that it will eventually appear in what he calls the "cultural pages." [. . .] (5) Also enclosed: the combination review-interview I wrote for the *Times Book Review*. Here my tone must necessarily darken. In two thousand words I had to: (a) render the interview; (b) review the book; (c) explain the work of Gershom Scholem. I did do all that. The editor, Harvey Shapiro, is, as it happens, away on vacation; Richard Locke, second in command, is in charge. Locke is not content with my work. He says I have not made Scholem accessible enough to the audience of the *Book Review;* I have aimed over their heads. For instance, I have not explained who Walter Benjamin is. We had this melancholy (on my side, at least) conversation only a few hours ago, earlier today, and I promised to rewrite portions, attempting to simplify. "You have to define the word Kabbalah; you just can't use it." I am going to try to please him. I had pleased myself in what I wrote; had enormously enjoyed the book, which I have now read three times; and came home to reread some of the essays in *Jews and Judaism in Crisis,* especially the spectacular one on the Jews of Germany. At any rate, the piece I am sending you now may not be the piece that will finally see print. On the other hand, the editor-in-chief will return from vacation in ten days; he may have a more favorable opinion. And there, at this writing, things stand.

After we were home a few days, having stopped in hedonistic London on the way, Lucy Dawidowicz telephoned. "Come and meet David Biale!" Ah, what a night that was! We spent four hours talking, nonstop, about Gershom Scholem. (I talked to Kenneth Briggs the next day and reported this. "Oh," he moaned, "if only I could have been there!" He explained that he needed an "outlet" for all his accumulated reflections.) To Lucy I said, "I think Professor Scholem offered us the chocolates you had brought him some time before." "Did they have soft centers?" she inquired. "No, they were caramel." "Then they were not mine," she said with much certainty. Then somehow I could not bear this. "Please say they were!" I entreated. "For the sake of continuity!" But she, meticulous historian that she is, remained adamant. "No, mine had soft centers." Despite this interlude, those were very serious, deeply speculative, exciting four hours. Ah, when all these unwritten novels about Professor Scholem begin to take shape! [. . .]

TO CYNTHIA OZICK[159]

Jerusalem, October 8, 1980

Dear Cynthia,

When I returned from abroad, where Fanya and I have enjoyed two months, I found your three letters between August 22 and September 15, plus the texts of your very moving review articles, and I have read

all of them with great attention and pleasure. I thank you for the understanding you showed of me and my work, but I weep about the discussion of my "shadow" which was forced upon you and Fanya. I would
rather have left the first paragraph which your censor struck out, and
censored this part, to which I have no reasonable answer. A man without
a shadow is a *saddik,* if I am understanding the old books correctly, and
I have no claim to this *madrega.*[160] It was news to me that Mr. Briggs's
article would be published in the *Times,* and I have not received any
other notice about this except yours. Has the piece indeed appeared? If
so, nobody seems to have noticed it. And if not, I am sorry for the two
hours of good talk which I spent with Mr. Briggs. [. . .]

That Cynthia Ozick, Lucy Dawidowicz, and David Biale should have
held a conference about me is good news, especially if I must take it for
granted that I was not torn to pieces that night. I like chocolates, whether
they have soft centers or not. Please, take notice of this state of affairs
in case you pay Fanya and me another visit. This we would welcome
very much. With many thanks and warm greetings.

Yours, Gershom Scholem

TO RUTH NANDA ANSHEN[161]

Jerusalem, October 15, 1980

Dear Nanda,

Many thanks for your letter of friendship, which arrived here just after
our return from Europe. I can make good use of your wishes and hopes
for my health, my work, and peace and justice in Israel. We have need
of all this, and the past year leaves a lot to wish in this field. I really do
not know whether the Jews have more chances to survive in a meta-
historical reality or in history itself, and I must admit that something can
be said for every side. Having convinced myself of the right diagnosis
of the Zionists, I have made some kind of choice and have thus expressed
my doubts about the meta-historians, of whom there is (to say the least)
no lack.

Fanya and I hope that the *milchigdige*[162] dinner (this is the right spelling,
if I may correct yours) with Cynthia and all the others was successful and
has led to the survival of the participants. Should there be a stenograph of

the talks, it will be received with pleasure. But Fanya says that we know, even without that, what could have been said—by which she seems to mean that a real critic of Scholem was missing.

The Jews are continuously persecuted, but they are also on the move even when they are not. This has convinced me of the utter falseness of my earlier definition of Zionism, which I used to give until 1950: Zionism is a movement against excess traveling of Jews. Could I have been more wrong? So now I have another definition, on which I hope to end my days: Zionism is the return of Jews into their own history. Of course, one can say (as Fanya does) that they don't seem to want it very much.

Since almost all the members of your board of editors under the letter-head "Religious Perspectives" are dead by now, it is high time that you change the list, or correct it to "Board of Editors, mostly in Heaven."

Cordial greetings for Ralph and you from both of us.

FROM IRMGARD AND ARTHUR SCHOLEM[163]

Sydney, October 29, 1980

Dear Gerhard, dear Fanya,

We have finally gotten back the various prints from the photographs we took and can pass them on to you. Maybe you heard from Eva about our excursion to Weissensee.[164] Ernst joined us, along with his companion (a very nice woman named Frau Schensig). We went there armed with spades, saws, assorted plastic bags, small garden tools, buckets, garden gloves, etc. We were lucky; it was a cloudy day, but free of rain. The back entrance, the one facing the factory, was closed, and so we used the main entrance. Everything was badly overgrown. We finally reached the rear of the cemetery, where we could pit our strength against nature. It was a good thing we'd brought African bush experience with us. It took us four straight hours of serious work. We even felled the trees to the right and left of the grave, and trimmed off a bit from the neighbor's trees. We were downright pleased with our efforts. We had no need for the black and gold paint we'd brought with us; the inscription on the marker was still very legible. It's good that it was chiseled into the stone, in contrast to the inscriptions on many other graves. On these, following the fashion of the 1920s, the letters were affixed to the stone with nails. Most of these nails had rusted and the letters had fallen off. Well, we hope the attached photos will make you happy. [. . .]

All the best, Irmgard and Arthur

FROM DAVID SCHOLEM[165]

Sydney, November 2, 1980

Dear Gerhard and Fanya,

In August I visited my father in Berlin, and at last actually sought out the graves of various forebears. Herewith I enclose photos of my great-grandparents, your, Gerhard's closer relatives. I was jolted to see that their gravestones, alone of those I saw, had bullet pockmarks, which show clearly in the photos. It was intriguing, to put it in a *pareve* way, to imagine how those crevices came into being. There was a lot of fighting in the Weissensee Cemetery at the advance of the Russian Army, aside from the periodic sweeps of German troops in search of Jewish fugitives, which could have inflicted the damage. However, as the graves are three substantial rows from the nearest path, there must have been a more specifically targeted *Aktion* than random vandalism.

You might be interested in how I found another set of graves—those of my grandmother Phiechen's parents. I stumbled and staggered my way through the undergrowth, around the coordinates that I had from my late cousin Harry Sussmann, who also determined the Scholem graves. You know how Amazonian the vegetation is in Weissensee. After about ten minutes of nearly blind "hunch-following," I looked up and there was the gravestone of my great-grandfather, Isidor Sussmann. At that moment, out of the blue, I was tangibly aware of a personality—invisible, but that was immaterial—standing there and saying what in American children's games they call "Tag"! That is, the end of one phase of a children's game of hide-and-seek. It was as tangible as any reality I have ever experienced. I had been in awe of the austere figure that Oma[166] had known—loving, but strict—and here was a boyish *Gestalt* playing children's games with someone from several generations later. It took me by surprise, to say the least, to experience such a reality-flavored encounter. I had my Tehillim[167] with me, despite being apprehensive about taking "literature from nonsocialist countries" over the checkpoint, and not being well-acquainted with the Tehillim at all. I "asked" which Psalm the ghost, which I took to be my great-grandfather, would like to hear after what I thought would have been many years of not being visited by a Tehillim-bearing descendent. "Psalm 43," came the answer. I was completely unfamiliar with it, but opening the book, I saw: "Plead my cause against an ungodly nation . . . Why must I walk around aggrieved, under the oppression of the enemy?" It was a truly riveting experience—I was in real communion with my ancestor. On the way to the cemetery, I had puzzled about the flags on a couple of official state cars parked at the Palazzo Protzo, opposite the Foreign Ministry, with full contingent of state apparatchiks, police, honor guards. When asked about the flags—as I couldn't put my finger on the country whose flag it was—the cautious guard answered politely, "PLO." "Why must I walk around aggrieved" indeed, I thought later, in reflection. [. . .]

David

TO REINHOLD SCHOLEM

Jerusalem, November 9, 1980

Dear Reinhold,

We've been back from Europe for a few weeks, where we visited Switzerland and Germany, Ascona, and a spa above Lugano. I then traveled alone back to Berlin and Frankfurt, as well as to Heidelberg and Zurich. As you can see, we're still more or less mobile. The weather was magnificent and I pursued detective work into the biography of a forgotten man, about whom I am now composing an essay. Though I've spent a lifetime writing exclusively about Jews and Judaism, he is the first goy I have pounced on with any success, and will most likely be the last. His name has been forgotten so completely that it won't mean a thing to you until I send you an offprint after the essay appears.[168] You'll throw up your hands in astonishment—to the extent you have such gestures left in you after ninety years of life.

Meanwhile, I hope you've finally received the volume of Benjamin-Scholem correspondence. The hero of my essay often shows up in it. There's been no dearth of reviews, whose authors, according to their political stance, are either deeply impressed or hostile (toward me). The Marxists don't like me very much. [. . .]

Wishing you good health, Gerhard

TO IRMGARD AND ARTHUR SCHOLEM

Jerusalem, November 12, 1980

Dear Irmgard and Arthur,

Warmest thanks for your letter from October 29 and the detailed report on the efforts that you and Ernst—along with this Frau Schensig whom I don't know—expended at the cemetery at Weissensee. Judging by the sweat on your faces, you all obviously did a wonderful job of proper hacking. It must have been a beautiful scene. You apparently don't know that the chiseled inscription was not the original. Arthur's father had it commissioned at the beginning of the 1960s, while he was in Berlin. The original, which was affixed to the stone with nails, had long since fallen off. Erich added the names of our mother and our brother Werner, names you also encountered there. The four photos gave us a great deal of pleasure, and we thank you enormously. I was unable to pay another visit to the grave during my brief stay in Berlin. [. . .]

Gerhard

TO HANNAH TILLICH[169]

Jerusalem, November 12, 1980

Honored Frau Hannah Tillich,

I received your letter from the sixteenth of October and will now allow myself to respond in German. I remember very clearly the visit Shalom Spiegel and I made to your home in New York in 1938. There is a noteworthy report of it on pages 259–260 in my correspondence between Benjamin and myself, which just came out. Later I visited you at Harvard in 1949 and 1956, and we had animated discussions in Ascona, when Tillich and I were among the speakers. A discussion also took place in the Hotel Tamaro. Tillich, Kurt Goldstein, and I debated the question whether Tillich, to judge by his lecture, was still a Christian. All of these are extremely vivid memories.

In light of my well-known record on the Zionist movement, I was speechless when I came to the passage in your letter where you say you didn't know that my wife and I are not only active in Israel, but even live here; and how you regret that my wife and I are not only militaristic, but have become something like Jewish "Nazis." On such a basis, you won't take offense if I don't discuss this any more. It makes me laugh that you considered Horkheimer's "Jewishness" in the 1930s to be the true, authentic Jewish spirit. Horkheimer later deeply regretted his earlier position and gave it up altogether. In my aforementioned correspondence with Benjamin (pp. 318–320), I said what I thought about "Die Juden und Europa," the essay Horkheimer wrote in 1939. As people say in English, it seems that the two of us are not on the same wavelength. [. . .]

Faithfully yours, Gershom Scholem

TO DAVID SCHOLEM[170]

Jerusalem, November 27, 1980

Thank you very much for your interesting letter of November 2, 1980. Your description of your adventures in Weissensee and of your discoveries and activities there was highly interesting. I went searching for Siegried Scholem's grave a year ago but was unable find it. The vegetation was too much for me, and I could find only Father's grave. The experience you had on the grave of your great-grandfather Sussmann is quite remarkable. These things happen, whatever the reasons may be. My brother's widow had such an experience the night he was murdered in Buchenwald in 1940: she saw her husband standing before her and dissolving into thin air. She could not forget it, and she had no explanation. [. . .]

You mention periodic sweeps of German troops at Weissensee Cemetery. It is, however, a fact that in the last days of Hitler, quite a number of Jews hid there and survived. In 1946 in Berlin, I spoke to one of them, who told me about it.

With kind regards from both of us.

FROM DANIEL BELL[171]

Cambridge, Massachusetts; December 5, 1980

Dear Gershom,

I write for several reasons. First, I have just finished your lovely book *From Berlin to Jerusalem,* a book that I read in one fell swoop, like taking a long drink down a parched throat. It had a magical effect (with apologies to Oskar Goldberg) of transporting me to a time and place that enveloped me completely. Not only was it like a letter from home— though it was not my home—in the sense that it filled in small details about dozens of individuals about whom I had read of before, but it gave me the vivid immediacy about the emotions and enthusiasms you had then, a feeling that could be conveyed so vividly because you still have those passions today. How remarkable. And then the small details, such as you roller skating across the asphalt streets of Berlin—an experience I could duplicate in the early 1930s: I roller skated in the streets of New York. And I never did, therefore, learn to ride a bicycle. And, after all, who could afford a bicycle? And where would one keep one? [. . .]

Dan Bell

TO DANIEL BELL[172]

Jerusalem, Undated (December 1980)

Dear Dan,

I owe you double thanks: for your book of essays *The Winding Passage,* which I have not acknowledged, I must confess, for a long time; and for your paper "First Love and Early Sorrow," which reached me this month. About the first book: the truth of the matter is that for quite some time I wanted to write you at length about your piece on Hannah Arendt and the Eichmann trial, which brought back to me one of the most bitter controversies of my life and caused me to break all and every connection with Hannah, up to the day of her death. I found it impossible to express, even to a friend like you, the bitterness of my feelings and thoughts in this matter. It has finished for me not only the question about the character of Hannah, but opened up a devastating new view of her own books. At the end, I said to myself: it is better not to renew this debate, which goes far beyond literature, and a discussion of the view you took at the time. Let us hope we could take up that at a time when we can sit together and talk freely. [. . .]

As ever yours, Gershom

1981

TO HELMUT BECKER[173]

Jerusalem, July 2, 1981

[. . .] In the past few days I've read another volume of *Transatlantik*. It contained an article on the Palestinians in which the author managed in a number of ways to leave one dumbfounded. Above all in the conclusion, where he fully concurs with Arafat's remark that we Zionists perpetrated and continue to perpetrate genocide on the Palestinian people. This despite the simple fact that in 1948 there were one and a half million Palestinians and that today, according to the claim of their spokesmen, there are supposedly up to four and a half million. [. . .]

It may well be that before these lines arrive you will already have heard the official announcement regarding the latest news from my life, and as a result you won't be as completely shocked as you should be: I have become a member of the order Pour le Mérite, naturally as a foreigner.[174] I have accepted. Herr Maier Leibnitz has not yet informed me what this actually entails. I will probably look quite grotesque wearing the ribbon of the order, which is made of silver together with a medal of pure gold. By the way, it remains the property of the Federal Republic of Germany and must be returned after my death! But otherwise I naturally feel distinguished. This is the latest thing to report—besides the sad news on the results of the Israeli elections, which all of us look upon with the greatest apprehension.[175] We'll discuss this more in person. The division of Israel into Ashkenazim and Asiatics gives reason for serious concern. [. . .]

Gershom Scholem

TO REINHOLD SCHOLEM

Jerusalem, July 8, 1981

Dear Reinhold,

A month from today you'll celebrate your ninetieth birthday. I want to send you my best wishes for you and your health, both mentally and physically (I do so on Fanya's behalf, too). I considered whether it would be possible for us to make a trip to Sydney to offer you our personal presence, but it's just not feasible. I must make do with a letter. You have an entire life behind you, which for the most part—of course with the interruption of a few bitter years—you've managed to fashion according to your will. You can certainly look back on rich memories and good times. I can picture the way you looked at twenty, when you were in the military in Treptow; and the way you looked at eighty, when we met in Zurich. I know little about what happened during the intervening years, but I think you experienced a lot. It must have been a shock to you that Hitler spoiled all of your plans. It's difficult for me to judge, since our lives took such different paths. Maybe sometime you should write about it, at least for your son; or you should dictate it to someone with a pen in hand. It would really be fitting, and I would wish you much happiness and strength in doing so. We're both delighted that you can enjoy your birthday in the company of an extended family. Not every ninety-year-old is granted this. [. . .]

Besides all this, you'll laugh when I tell you that I have been elected to the highest German order as a foreign member: the order Pour le Mérite for Science and the Arts. This is the pinnacle of irony, and something of an honor to boot, which is the reason I have accepted. Who would have thought that I would end up in such company? (Membership is limited to thirty.) With this cheerful news, we say goodbye. Cordial greetings and wishes to you, and also to the relatives who will be attending your birthday.

Your younger brother, Gerhard

TO DINA WASCHITZ[176]

Jerusalem, August 2, 1981

Dear Dina,

I received your letter of July 17, along with the article on Werner. It was news to me that during your time at Daliyyah[177] you worked with people who later became Trotskyites and who considered themselves Germans. [. . .]

So far as I can tell, whatever is new in the article—that is, where it goes beyond Kogon[178]—is exceptionally doubtful and is in great need of proof. The claim that my brother's true murderers were members of the German Communist party in Buchenwald contradicts everything I know about the subject. Emmy told me that Werner stood on rather good terms with the people in the concentration camp who had remained in the party—indeed, he was on good terms with them particularly in the concentration camp. She received a good deal of information about this from a trustworthy source. It's difficult to test the veracity of suspicions, such as those very often and very bitterly traded between Stalinists and Trotskyites after the war. I'll try to look into these things in Germany.

We'll be leaving here in two weeks, and wish you all the best.

Sincerely yours, Gerhard

TO REINHOLD SCHOLEM

Berlin, December 15, 1981

Dear Reinhold,

I haven't written for a long time. Thanks for the letter with the description of your ninetieth birthday. My own birthday has also passed and I now must get used to being eighty-five. I'll spend the greater part of next year, until the end of July, in Berlin. We'll have to see if my health will allow it. Your letter truly delighted us. It reached us in Zurich, where we spent the entire month of September (after two weeks in Sils-Maria) and where I underwent a series of tests. They removed two polyps from my intestines, which was really about time, and discovered that I am otherwise in good physical health. They told me that the stomach pains I have had for some time now, above all at night, mean nothing. But the pains grew and extended into the daytime. On October 6 we arrived in Berlin. Our apartment was not ready yet, so for almost a month we were put up in a nice two-room suite at the Kempinski Hotel. Then the stomach pains began to develop, first at night and then during the day. No one could explain it. Back in Zurich they had searched for weeks for the cause, without success. The organs are healthy, along with the polyp-free intestines. Only in Berlin were the specialists able to come up with a diagnosis: the so-called mobus Paget, which is a process in which certain bones thicken. With me it's happening in the pelvis. Most likely the right medicine can stop it within three months. [. . .]

Gerhard

1982

TO RUTH NANDA ANSHEN[179]

Jerusalem, January 24, 1982

I was very impressed by your so affectionate letter responding to the sad news of my yet undefined illness. It was very touching to read this testimony of love and friendship. Please forgive me for sending you a typed letter but I am too weak to write by hand. Nobody seems to know, at least presently, what has befallen me, but it is now quite some time that I do not feel well, although all the medical examinations have not brought any result. It is now almost six weeks that I am back in Jerusalem but the weakness that has come over me has not subsided and there must be something basically wrong with the functioning of my organism. Let us hope that they will get a result which would enable me to decide about my plans for the following months, which for the time being I cannot make. It is a state in which I have not been for many years, if at all. Your friendship and devotion are sustaining me. It is difficult for me to concentrate and I ask you to allow me to break off with cordial thanks and kind thoughts.

Ever yours, Gershom

TO RUDOLF ZUR LIPPE[180]

Jerusalem, January 31, 1982

Dear Herr zur Lippe,

To our great joy, today we received the news of the birth of Prince Friedrich zur Lippe. We cordially congratulate both parents. As for the circumstances surrounding the Scholem household, you'll find full information in a report to Helmut Becker, which will be sent out from here on the thirty-first of January and will clarify the difficulties under which we live and that preclude, for the time being, our return to Berlin. For this reason we dearly miss the continuation of our contact with you, begun as it was under such a good star. It belongs to the truly beautiful memories that we brought with us from Berlin. It's still uncertain whether we can return to Europe at some later time; it's out of the question for now.

I've been told that I missed a number of hellish winter days in Berlin, insofar as one speaks of "hellish" about the cold. We've not had anything similar to complain of until now. I suffer from other complaints, which mystify the doctors.

Forgive the brevity of this note; it's not easy for me to dictate letters. With warmest greetings from both of us.

Fanya and Gershom Scholem

Please don't be angry that I am not writing more. I am not doing especially well. Helmut Becker has an exact account. Enclosed is a copy of my letter to Peter Wapnewski. I hope someone will discover what's wrong with me. For the time being, I have to cancel all plans or at least postpone them a few months.

TO PETER WAPNEWSKI[181]

Jerusalem, January 31, 1982

Dear Herr Wapnewski,

I am writing to you with a heavy heart, for I owe you news of my condition and of whether I can return to Berlin in the middle of February, as we had planned. I have now been back in Jerusalem for more than six weeks. The condition of my hip, which is what in fact brought me back, has improved by itself, in a natural way. I no longer have any pains in that spot, and the doctors have stopped focusing on it. At the same time, my extraordinary weakness and my inability to concentrate on the work I had hoped to accomplish at the Wissenschaftskolleg have aroused my own doctor's concern, and in turn that of the physicians at the Department of Internal Medicine at Hadassah University Hospital. Owing to my inexplicable abdominal pain, I have been checked into this hospital, which is run by excellent doctors. I've now spent weeks here; only on weekends, when nothing can really be done, am I allowed to go home on furlough. To enable treatment, they've performed tests on every imaginable organ in order to locate the source of the pain. As with the earlier tests in Zurich and Berlin, none of the examinations have brought any results to date. The doctors [. . .] are still at a loss. With such clear symptoms of pain and fatigue, they advise me against returning to Berlin for the time being. I wouldn't be able to do any productive work there, and would most likely spend most of my time in a hospital—which is scarcely the purpose of the arrangement we made. [. . .] Given the circumstances, I think I must leave the decision up to you—whether you want to be patient with me for a while and await developments (perhaps a medical decision will be reached), or whether we should give up on the entire venture. For I am at present completely incapable of fulfilling the expectations you rightly have of me (above all, to write the book I have planned, for which all of the materials still remain in my office on Wallot Strasse). It could also happen that the pains might suddenly vanish the same way they appeared, though I cannot build my plans on such a happy outcome. At the moment I can scarcely send someone to pack up all my things and bring them back. My wife certainly could not go; I'm in great need of her here. There are complications. In any event, the doctors have ruled out all possibility of a serious illness, such as cancer. I therefore urge you to feel free to make the decision. Should my condition improve in the spring and I become strong and able to work, then we could always come to some agreement for a couple of months—and I will then be able to undertake a trip to Europe. I do not wish to commit myself, however. I ask you to pass on my cordial greetings and apologies to all of the colleagues in our group. Also, please give my warmest thanks to the co-workers of the Wissenschaftskolleg for all the kindness they showed me.

I am sending a copy of this letter to Helmut Becker, as well. [. . .]

Yours, Gershom Scholem

FROM HANS JONAS

New Rochelle, February 24, 1982

Dear Fanya,

The news of Gershom's death fills me with sadness for the loss we all have suffered—and you in particular. That this unique spirit is no longer with us, a spirit I was privileged to meet and for a time draw close to, means, for me personally, a gaping hole in what I see as my own world. This was a world I shared with him, despite the distance that grew between us. Memories stretching back over fifty years are now reviving. His image is indelible, vivid, singular; it is inseparable from both this century and from my own life, and it cannot be compared with that of any other person. For me, he was the essence of Jerusalem: the thoughts, the moods, the gestures, the din of passionate discussions, the electric high tension of each exchange, the lightning-quick statements and rebuttals, the inexhaustible originality, the tireless curiosity, the ever fresh interest, the aggressiveness joined with a generous recognition of his foe, a supreme self-confidence along with an open-handed kindness, humor in seriousness and seriousness in humor, humor amid a passion for knowing and naming; and in all this the palpably dark, uncanny, agitated depths behind the blinding brightness of the intellect. In this way he dominated our unforgettable circle, Pilegesch.[182] He was the focal point. Wherever *he* was, you found the center, the active force, a generator which constantly charged itself; he was what Goethe called an *Urphänomen*.[183] I don't need to mention his monumental body of work, which will guarantee his immortality in future generations and for which mortals can be grateful. And I don't need to add anything about the extraordinary recognition already bestowed on him by his contemporaries. For a time I was privileged to enjoy his friendship, and I would like to believe that he still felt a certain affection for me, despite our differences. My affection for him remained constant through all ups and downs. His passing marks the end of an era.

Yet I wish to recall not only memories of him, but memories of you too. I can still picture how he courted you, and I remember the stormy day before your wedding, when you came to visit me with Hans Lewy. And then the many years in which "Scholem" always meant "Gerhard and Fanya." With a personality equal in strength to his, you were never oppressed by his power. You were his lifelong partner, endowed with your own native wealth. I honor you at this sad moment, and I wish you inner strength as you face life without him, now and in the future. Please except this expression of my sympathy and devotion.

From your and Gershom's old friend, Hans Jonas

NOTES / SELECTED BIBLIOGRAPHY / CHRONOLOGY / INDEX

Letter from Gershom Scholem to his mother, Betty, written in Munich on October 20, 1919. Courtesy of the Jewish National and University Library, Jerusalem, Gershom Scholem Archive (Arc. 4o 1599).

NOTES

INTRODUCTION

1. Betty Scholem and Gershom Scholem, *Mutter und Sohn in Briefwechsel* (Munich: Beck Verlag, 1989), p. 223.

2. Josef Weiss, "Gershom Scholem: Fünfzig Jahre," *Yedioth Hayom,* December 5, 1947.

3. Gershom Scholem, *Judaica II* (Frankfurt am Main: Suhrkamp Verlag, 1970), p. 198.

4. Gershom Scholem, *"On the Possibility of Jewish Mysticism in Our Time" and Other Essays* (Philadelphia and Jerusalem: Jewish Publication Society, 1997), p. 80.

5. Gershom Scholem, *Briefe I* (Munich: Beck Verlag, 1994), p. 459.

6. Ibid., p. 332.

7. Ibid., p. ix.

PART I. A JEWISH ZARATHUSTRA

1. Gershom Scholem, *Briefe I* (Munich: Beck Verlag, 1994), p. 25.

2. Gershom Scholem, *From Berlin to Jerusalem,* trans. Harry Zohn (New York: Schocken Books, 1980), p. 8.

3. Walter Benjamin, *Berliner Kindheit um Neunzehnhundert,* in Benjamin, *Gesammelte Schriften,* ed. Rolf Tiedemann and Hermann Schweppenhäuser, vol. 4 (Frankfurt am Main: Suhrkamp Verlag, 1981), p. 258.

4. Scholem, *From Berlin to Jerusalem,* p. 8.

5. Martin Buber, *Drei Reden über das Judentum* (Frankfurt am Main: Rütten und Loening, 1911), p. 8.

6. Gershom Scholem, *Tagebücher* (Frankfurt am Main: Jüdischer Verlag, 1995), p. 158.

7. Scholem is quoting from Buber, *Drei Reden,* p. 141.

8. Scholem, *Tagebücher,* p. 9.

9. Scholem, *Briefe I,* p. 17.

10. Martin Buber, *Die Jüdische Bewegung* (Berlin: Jüdischer Verlag, 1916), p. 182.

11. See Scholem's letter to Salman Schocken, cited in David Biale, *Gershom Scholem: Kabbalah and Counter-History* (Cambridge, Mass.: Harvard University Press, 1979), p. 215.

12. Martin Buber, "Die Lösung," *Der Jude* (April 1916).

13. Heinrich Margulies, "Der Krieg der Zurückbleibenden," *Jüdische Rundschau*, February 5, 1916.

14. Scholem, *Tagebücher*, pp. 33–34.

15. Ibid., p. 210.

16. Ibid., p. 45.

17 Ibid., p. 52.

18. Ibid., p. 327.

19. Ibid., p. 213.

20. Gershom Scholem, "S. J. Agnon: Der letzte Hebräische Klassiker?" *Judaica II* (Frankfurt am Main: Suhrkamp Verlag, 1970), p. 124.

21. Scholem, *Briefe I*, p. 166.

22. Scholem, *From Berlin to Jerusalem*, p. 104.

23. Scholem, *Briefe I*, p. 95.

24. Gershom Scholem, *Walter Benjamin: The Story of a Friendship*, trans. Harry Zohn (Philadelphia: Jewish Publication Society of America, 1981), p. 58.

25. Ibid., p. 93.

26. Ibid., p. 76.

27. Scholem, *Tagebücher*, p. 472.

28. Scholem, *Briefe I*, p. 88.

29. Ibid., p. 168.

30. Scholem, *Walter Benjamin: The Story of a Friendship*, p. 83.

31. Walter Benjamin, "Das Leben der Studenten," *Gesammelte Schriften*, vol. 2 (Frankfurt am Main: Suhrkamp Verlag, 1977), p. 75. In English as "The Life of Students," in Benjamin, *Selected Writings, Volume 1: 1913–1926*, ed. Marcus Bullock and Michael W. Jennings (Cambridge, Mass.: Harvard University Press, 1996).

32. Walter Benjamin, "On Language as Such and on the Language of Man," in Benjamin, *Selected Writings, Volume 1*, p. 74.

33. Scholem, *Tagebücher*, p. 467.

34. Ibid., p. 468. On Scholem's adoption of the terms *Lehre* and *Ordnung* from Benjamin, see Gershom Scholem, *Walter Benjamin: The Story of a Friendship* (Philadelphia: Jewish Publication Society of America, 1981), p. 56.

35. Scholem, *Briefe I*, p. 86.

36. Ibid., p. 122.

37. Gershom Scholem, "Die Theologie des Sabbatianismus im Lichte Abraham Cardosos," *Judaica I* (Frankfurt am Main: Suhrkamp Verlag, 1963), p. 146.

38. Scholem, *Tagebücher*, p. 421.

39. Ibid., p. 406.

40. Ibid., p. 422.

41. See Scholem's letter to Theodor Adorno, *Briefe I,* p. 275.

42. The *Sefer ha-Zohar* (Book of Splendor) is the central text of the Kabbalah. Most of it was probably composed between 1270 and 1300 by the Spanish Kabbalist Moses de León, drawing on more ancient sources that may date back as far as the first century. Written largely in Aramaic, the *Zohar* consists of homilies, short discourses, and parables focusing on the religious leader Simeon ben Yohai (second century) and his disciples. It discusses the "inner" (mystical, symbolic) meaning of certain biblical texts, including the first five books of the Bible (the books known as the Torah) and the Song of Solomon. It also deals with the problem of evil, the cosmic significance of prayer and good deeds, and the meaning of the ten "divine emanations" (*sefirot,* or "numbers") of God the Creator, which are said to account for the universe.

LETTERS, 1914–1918

1. The Sozialdemokratische Partei Deutschlands (German Social Democratic Party) supported the war effort by casting its votes in the Reichstag in favor of war credits.

2. The Erfurt Program was the Social Democratic Party platform drawn up in 1891.

3. Pierre Proudhon (1809–1865), an early French socialist, countered Marx's vision of scientific socialism with his own "anarchistic" version.

4. Israel ben Eliezer (ca. 1700–1760), known as the Baal Shem Tov ("master of the Name of God"), was the founder of Hasidism, a renewal movement among eastern European Jews. In Buddhist teaching, "Arhat" means "the holy" or "perfection in spiritual life."

5. Karl Kautsky, *Ethik und materialistische Geschichtsauffassung: Ein Versuch* (Stuttgart: Dietz, 1906).

6. This was the address of the Scholem family.

7. Werner was going through basic training in Hannover.

8. Leopold von Ranke (1795–1886), Heinrich von Treitschke (1834–1896), and Friedrich Nietzsche (1844–1900) were all important figures in the discipline of historiography in Germany.

9. Wilhelm Wundt (1832–1920) attempted to reduce philosophical questions of truth to psychology.

10. In 1915 (which is not represented in this collection) Scholem composed relatively few letters. He was in Berlin the entire year, mostly occupied with his Zionist youth group and with debates surrounding the war. In cooperation with Erich Brauer, he brought out the Zionist newspaper *Blau-Weisse Brille* (Blue-White Spectacles). This was also the year he met Walter Benjamin.

11. Erich Brauer (1895–1942) was a Jewish ethnologist and cultural historian. His works include *Ethnologie der jemenitischen Juden* [Ethnology of the Jemenite Jews] (Heidelberg: C. Winter, 1934), and *The Jews of Kurdistan: An Ethnological Study,*

completed, edited, and translated by Raphael Patai (Jerusalem: Palestine Institute of Folklore and Ethnology, 1947; rpt. Detroit: Wayne State University Press, 1993).

12. Between June 20 and the end of July, Scholem underwent medical treatment in Oberstdorf.

13. The text of this letter is reproduced from *The Letters of Martin Buber: A Life of Dialogue*, by Martin Buber, ed. Nahum N. Glatzer and Paul Mendes-Flohr, trans. Richard and Clara Winston and Harry Zohn. Copyright © 1991 by Schocken Books, a division of Random House, Inc. Used by permission of Schocken Books, a division of Random House, Inc.

14. Buber had asked for Benjamin's assistance on *Der Jude,* a journal Buber had founded in 1915.

15. The text of this letter is reproduced from *The Letters of Martin Buber: A Life of Dialogue*, by Martin Buber, ed. Nahum N. Glatzer and Paul Mendes-Flohr, trans. Richard and Clara Winston and Harry Zohn. Copyright © 1991 by Schocken Books, a division of Random House, Inc. Used by permission of Schocken Books, a division of Random House, Inc.

16. Werner was wounded in a battle on the Western Front.

17. Hebrew for "my friend."

18. Aharon Heller (1899–1967) belonged to the Jung Juda group.

19. The reference is to their mutual friend Salo Pick.

20. Edgar Blum, a friend of Scholem's from school, died in battle in 1916.

21. Siegfried Lehmann (1892–1958) founded the Jüdisches Volksheim in 1916. This was a center for the children of eastern European Jewish refugees who had fled to Berlin because of the war.

22. The reference is to Toni Halle (1895–1964).

23. Scholem uses the word *Geschwätz* ("prattle"), alluding to Kierkegaard's essay "The Present Age."

24. "Moishe Rabbenu" ("Moses our teacher") is a reference to the Moses of the Old Testament. Israel Hildesheimer (1820–1899) was one of the few Orthodox rabbis of his time to support Zionism.

25. A number of Buber's closest followers, such as Robert Weltsch, Hugo Bergmann, and Hans Kohn, came from Prague.

26. The text of this letter is reproduced, with permission, from *The Correspondence of Walter Benjamin, 1910–1940,* ed. Gershom Scholem and Theodor W. Adorno, trans. Manfred R. Jacobson and Evelyn M. Jacobson (Chicago: University of Chicago Press, 1994). Copyright © 1994 by the University of Chicago.

27. This letter formed the basis for Benjamin's essay "On Language as Such and on the Language of Man." Benjamin, *Gesammelte Schriften,* ed. Rolf Tiedemann and Hermann Schweppenhäuser, vol. 2 (Frankfurt am Main: Suhrkamp Verlag, 1977), pp. 140–157. In English in Walter Benjamin, *Selected Writings, Volume 1: 1913–1926,* ed. Marcus Bullock and Michael W. Jennings (Cambridge, Mass.: Harvard University Press, 1996), pp. 62–74.

28. Harry Heymann (1900–1918). In the original letter, the date and the phrase "With God's help" are in Hebrew.

29. The reference is to Edgar Blum.

30. A traditional prayer for the dead.

31. Samson Raphael Hirsch (1808–1888) was the founder of the so-called Neo-Orthodox movement, which tried to modernize Orthodoxy without accepting the Reform movement. His book *Der Pentateuch* (The Torah) was published in Frankfurt in 1867–1868.

32. Isaac Bleichrode (1867–1954) was an Orthodox rabbi. Bab Mezia ("middle gate" in Aramaic) is the portion of the Talmud that deals with questions of civil and criminal law.

33. Käte Schiepan, a physician, was Betty Scholem's sister.

34. Benjamin here refers to Scholem's translation of the Song of Songs. See Gershom Scholem, *Walter Benjamin: The Story of a Friendship,* trans. Harry Zohn (Philadelphia: Jewish Publication Society of America, 1981), p. 39.

35. On June 18 Scholem was declared fit for service and sent to a military reserve camp in Allenstein for basic training.

36. Werner Kraft (1896–1991) was a German-Jewish writer and essayist. He had met Scholem through Benjamin, and eventually became one of Scholem's neighbors in Jerusalem.

37. Ricarda Huch, *Der Fall Deruga* (Berlin, 1917). Such phrases as "purity of spheres" and "the Spiritual Center" (see also letters of July 14, 1917; August 6, 1917; and August 19, 1917) relate to Scholem's extremely complex metaphysical system, which for reasons of space cannot be discussed here. The meanings of the terms come out in his diaries.

38. Jung Juda, a small and radical Zionist group in Berlin, was active between 1912 and 1920.

39. "Eretz Israel" is Hebrew for "the Land of Israel."

40. A *saddik* is a righteous man, a holy man.

41. The Hebrew word *galut* means "exile."

42. The closing to this letter was written in Hebrew.

43. The text of this letter is reproduced, with permission, from *The Correspondence of Walter Benjamin, 1910–1940,* ed. Gershom Scholem and Theodor W. Adorno, trans. Manfred R. Jacobson and Evelyn M. Jacobson (Chicago: University of Chicago Press, 1994). Copyright © 1994 by the University of Chicago.

44. The reference is to Benjamin's essay "On Language as Such and on the Language of Man."

45. Scholem is referring to an eighteen-page letter by Benjamin that evolved into the essay "On Language as Such and on the Language of Man." The letter is too long and dense to be reproduced here. See Benjamin's letter of November 11, 1916, above.

46. Gerda Goldberg (1898–1986) wrote to him on July 24, "I think we have communication problems because we make use of expressions without first defining them. For this reason I'd be very grateful if one of these days you would explain your philosophy to me. With definitions."

47. This is the way Scholem renders Harry Heymann's name into Hebrew.

48. *Stika* is Hebrew for "silence."

49. This letter was originally written in Hebrew.

50. The closing to this letter was written in Hebrew.

51. The text of this letter is reproduced, with permission, from *The Correspondence of Walter Benjamin, 1910–1940,* ed. Gershom Scholem and Theodor W. Adorno, trans. Manfred R. Jacobson and Evelyn M. Jacobson (Chicago: University of Chicago Press, 1994). Copyright © 1994 by the University of Chicago.

52. Werner was in prison, having been arrested for "insulting the majesty" of the kaiser during an antiwar demonstration.

53. Friedrich Hölderlin (1770–1843) was a German Romantic poet.

54. Johann Paul Richter (1763–1825), who used the pseudonym Jean Paul, was a German novelist whose writings are noted for their idealism, humor, and warm portrayals of simple life.

55. Between October 1917 and April 1918, Scholem studied mathematics in Jena.

56. The text of this letter is reproduced, with permission, from *The Correspondence of Walter Benjamin, 1910–1940,* ed. Gershom Scholem and Theodor W. Adorno, trans. Manfred R. Jacobson and Evelyn M. Jacobson (Chicago: University of Chicago Press, 1994). Copyright © 1994 by the University of Chicago.

57. This sentence is in Hebrew in the original.

58. II Samuel 1:17–27.

59. The reference is to Fritz Heinle, a poet who was a close friend of Walter Benjamin's. Heinle committed suicide soon after the outbreak of war. He was not Jewish.

60. This salutation is in Hebrew in the original.

61. Meta Jahr and Erna Michaelis.

62. In his letter, Heymann described university lectures by some of the leading German historians of the day. He also asked Scholem for "some good tips on useful introductory texts in philosophy."

63. Ernst Troeltsch was a Protestant theologian (1865–1923); Georg Simmel was a philosopher (1858–1918); Friedrich Gundolf was a literary historian. All taught at the University of Berlin.

64. Werner married Emmy Wiechelt.

65. Scholem refers to Heymann's military service using an image from apocalyptic literature. According to the Book of Daniel, Babylon represents a force opposing God's rule on earth. Heymann died of battle wounds on April 8, 1918.

66. Hebrew for "Germans."

67. That is, the Song of Solomon.

68. Ludwig Strauss (1892–1953) was a poet.

69. Scholem first met Escha Burchhardt (1896–1978) at the end of January, during a visit to Heidelberg.

70. The text of this letter is reproduced, with permission, from *The Correspondence of Walter Benjamin, 1910–1940,* ed. Gershom Scholem and Theodor W.

Adorno, trans. Manfred R. Jacobson and Evelyn M. Jacobson (Chicago: University of Chicago Press, 1994). Copyright © 1994 by the University of Chicago.

71. A reference to S. J. Agnon's short story "The Torah Scribe," written in Hebrew and published in German translation in *Der Jude*, 2 (1917–1918).

72. A reference to Benjamin's letter from December 3, 1917. See Scholem, *Walter Benjamin: The Story of a Friendship*, p. 49.

73. Muri was the name of the fictitious university that Benjamin and Scholem "founded."

74. Hermann Cohen (1842–1918) was a German philosopher and theologian.

75. Austria-Hungary agreed to a truce with the Allies on October 3, 1918.

76. Erich Brauer was in Switzerland at the time.

77. Scholem frequently moves back and forth between discussion of the Book of Lamentations and his interest in lamentations as a Jewish literary genre. Here he refers to his broader study of biblical and post-biblical lamentations.

78. Jakob Canan (1881–1960) was a translator and poet who wrote in Hebrew.

79. The Almohads were a Berber Muslim dynasty whose rule in North Africa and Spain (1120–1269) was marked by forced conversions to Islam.

80. Hermann Cohen also taught at the Akademie für die Wissenschaft des Judentums (Academy for the Science of Judaism) in Berlin.

81. Unlike the majority socialists, the independent socialists (or USPD) rejected the participation of any "bourgeois" party in the new government.

82. The Spartacans were a revolutionary group formed in 1917 by Rosa Luxemburg and Karl Liebknecht.

83. Reinhold and Erich Scholem were Gershom's two eldest brothers.

PART II. UNLOCKING THE GATES

1. On November 9, 1918, Philipp Scheidemann, a Social Democrat in the German cabinet, declared Germany a republic. The kaiser fled when the army failed to support him.

2. Betty Scholem and Gershom Scholem, *Mutter und Sohn in Briefwechsel* (Munich: Beck Verlag, 1989), p. 58.

3. Ibid.

4. The *Sefer ha-Bahir* (Book of Brightness), a twelfth-century commentary on the Old Testament, was written in Hebrew and Arabic and is based on ancient mystical ideas originating in Asia. Its emphasis on the mystical significance of the shapes and sounds of the Hebrew alphabet had great influence on the development of the Kabbalah.

5. *Der Jude*, 4, no. 2 (1921).

6. *Die jüdischen Studenten*, 19, no. 2 (1922).

7. Gershom Scholem, *From Berlin to Jerusalem* (New York: Schocken Books, 1980), p. 142.

8. Hans-Georg Gadamer, in Gershom Scholem, *Briefe I* (Munich: Beck Verlag, 1994), p. xv.

9. Gershom Scholem, "Lyrik der Kabbalah," quoted in Gary Smith, ed., *Gershom Scholem: Zwischen den Disziplinen* (Frankfurt am Main: Suhrkamp Verlag, 1995), p. 131.

10. Gershom Scholem, *Walter Benjamin: The Story of a Friendship,* trans. Harry Zohn (New York: Schocken Books, 1988), p. 173.

11. Scholem, *From Berlin to Jerusalem,* p. 169.

12. Quoted in David Myers, *Re-Inventing the Jewish Past* (Oxford: Oxford University Press, 1995), p. 159.

13. Robert Alter, "Sabbatai Zevi and the Jewish Imagination," *Commentary* (June 1967): 69.

14. The word *yekke* denotes someone with pampered European sensibilities and typical "German qualities," such as love of order, of good manners, and of cleanliness.

15. David Ohana and Robert Wistrich, *Mythos v-Zikron* (Jerusalem: Van Leer Institute, 1996), p. 142.

16. "Yishuv" is the Hebrew term for the Jewish settlements in Palestine. "Volapuek" is a kind of Esperanto.

17. See Scholem's open letter to Rosenzweig, cited in Walter Grab and J. Schoeps, eds., *Juden in der Weimarer Republik* (Stuttgart: Burg Verlag, 1986), p. 148. Scholem wrote this letter to be included in a packet of eulogies sent to Rosenzweig on the occasion of his fortieth birthday, in 1926.

18. Walter Laqueur, *A History of Zionism* (New York: Schocken Books, 1976), pp. 252–253.

LETTERS, 1919–1932

1. The Pflaums were Betty Scholem's relatives.

2. *Vorwärts* was a Social Democratic newspaper. Ullstein and Mosse were publishing houses that issued newspapers as well as books.

3. Julius Berger (1883–1948) was a Zionist leader.

4. Scholem is referring to rabbinical allowances designed to ease the burden of difficult commandments.

5. Werner Scholem.

6. Chaim Bialik, "Halachah and Aggada," *Der Jude* (1925): 82–107.

7. The socialist leader Rosa Luxemburg was murdered by the German police after her arrest on January 15, 1919.

8. Meta Jahr (1900–1992) belonged to Scholem's Zionist youth group. In 1922 she moved to Palestine, where she helped found the kibbutz Bet-Sara.

9. *Mida* = "quality"; *yira* = "veneration"; *chochma* = "wisdom."

10. "Kabbalist."

11. "Teacher."

12. "Jalkut" (which means "sack" in Hebrew) refers to various collections of ancient texts, in particular from the Midrash (literature consisting of commentaries on the underlying significance of biblical texts).

13. Scholem had translated Bialik's essay "Halachah and Aggada." The term "Halachah" (meaning "the way of going") refers to any text that deals with Jewish law. "Aggada" refers in a very broad sense to everything else—that is, to more narrative texts not dealing specifically with the law. These can be folktales, sermons, magical incantations, parables, and the like.

14. Scholem moved to Munich in September 1919 in order to pursue his studies.

15. The Council Republic was created after the fall of the Bavarian monarchy. It was overthrown by the German army before it could ever establish itself. A large number of the revolutionary leaders were Jews.

16. "M.d.V.L.d.R.X.Y.Z." stands for "Mitglied der Volkspartei, Leutnant der Reserve, X.Y.Z." (Member of the German Volkspartei, Lieutenant of Reserve Company X.Y.Z.).

17. Benjamin, in his letter to Scholem of January 13, had said that he was busy writing a detailed review of Bloch's *Spirit of Utopia* for a journal.

18. Scholem is misquoting the title of *Vom Judentum,* a book put out by a number of Buber's Prague disciples in 1913.

19. Scholem is referring to the Kapp Putsch, which took place March 13–17 in Berlin and which was an armed revolt aimed at restoring the German monarchy.

20. The text of this letter is reproduced, with permission, from *The Correspondence of Walter Benjamin, 1910–1940,* ed. Gershom Scholem and Theodor W. Adorno, trans. Manfred R. Jacobson and Evelyn M. Jacobson (Chicago: University of Chicago Press, 1994). Copyright © 1994 by the University of Chicago.

21. Hebrew for "getting down to business."

22. *Sepharim* = "books" in Hebrew.

23. "Guys."

24. A philosophical text by Moses Maimonides (1135–1204), originally written in Arabic.

25. The ten "divine emanations" of the *Sefer ha-Bahir* became widely known in the Kabbalah as the *sefirot,* the ten primordial or ideal "numbers."

26. Max Strauss's translation of Agnon's story appeared as "Der Verstossene" (The Outcast), in *Der Jude,* 5 (1920–1921).

27. The text of this letter is reproduced, with permission, from *The Correspondence of Walter Benjamin, 1910–1940,* ed. Gershom Scholem and Theodor W. Adorno, trans. Manfred R. Jacobson and Evelyn M. Jacobson (Chicago: University of Chicago Press, 1994). Copyright © 1994 by the University of Chicago.

28. Scholem had put pressure on Benjamin to make a decision "for Judaism."

29. Franz Rosenzweig (1886–1929) was a philosopher and theologian.

30. Rudolf Hallo (1896–1955) was an art historian and friend of Rosenzweig's.

31. "Humble and simple."

32. All three men enriched the German language through their translations. Notker Labeo (950–1022) translated sacred and secular Latin into Old High German. Martin Luther's translation of the Bible, done in the 1520s, established German as a literary language. Johann Friedrich Hölderlin (1770–1843) translated Sophocles' *Antigone* and *Oedipus Tyrannus*.

33. Arthur is referring to Gershom's essay "Lyrik der Kabbalah?"

34. Both Robert Weltsch (1891–1982) and Hans Kohn (1891–1971) belonged to the Prague circle that formed around Buber before World War I. Weltsch was also the editor of the *Jüdische Rundschau*.

35. *Vom Judentum* (which Scholem calls *Das Buch des Judentums*) was published in 1913.

36. "Teaching," or *Lehre*, was a word that took on great importance in Scholem's evolving project. It refers to truths handed down through tradition by scholars and teachers.

37. The text of this letter is reproduced, with permission, from *The Correspondence of Walter Benjamin, 1910–1940*, ed. Gershom Scholem and Theodor W. Adorno, trans. Manfred R. Jacobson and Evelyn M. Jacobson (Chicago: University of Chicago Press, 1994). Copyright © 1994 by the University of Chicago.

38. Benjamin is referring to Paul Klee's *Angelus Novus*, a hand-colored ink drawing done in 1920 which Benjamin owned and which is now in the Israel Museum, Jerusalem. He also used the name *Angelus Novus* for the literary journal he hoped to found.

39. The text of this letter is reproduced, with permission, from *The Correspondence of Walter Benjamin, 1910–1940*, ed. Gershom Scholem and Theodor W. Adorno, trans. Manfred R. Jacobson and Evelyn M. Jacobson (Chicago: University of Chicago Press, 1994). Copyright © 1994 by the University of Chicago.

40. Scholem had just finished his dissertation.

41. There are no letters from 1922 in this collection. After Scholem completed his doctorate in March 1922, he left Munich and went to Frankfurt, where he taught various courses at Franz Rosenzweig's Lehrhaus. In the fall, upon returning to Berlin, he worked on a number of translations and prepared for the oral defense of his dissertation.

42. Salman Schocken (1877–1959), a department-store magnate and philanthropist, was to become one of Scholem's premier patrons.

43. Unfortunately, Scholem's letter has been lost.

44. Edith was the daughter of Werner and Emmy Scholem. The "Erich" hosting the gathering was Erich Scholem.

45. Scholem had been offered a job at the National Library in Jerusalem.

46. This letter has been lost.

47. Scholem had met Ernst Simon (1899–1988) at Rosenzweig's Lehrhaus in Frankfurt.

48. Yiddish for "stepdaughter."

49. Arthur Hirsch (1860–1946) was Betty Scholem's cousin and a professor of mathematics in Zurich.

50. The wedding had taken place on December 5, 1923.

51. Martha was the family's maid.

52. Chancellor Bismarck's grandson, Otto von Bismarck, was also a member of the Reichstag. He represented the Deutschnationaler Volkspartei.

53. The text of this letter is reproduced, with permission, from *The Correspondence of Walter Benjamin, 1910–1940*, ed. Gershom Scholem and Theodor W. Adorno, trans. Manfred R. Jacobson and Evelyn M. Jacobson (Chicago: University of Chicago Press, 1994). Copyright © 1994 by the University of Chicago.

54. During the so-called Hitler Putsch in 1923, there were anti-Jewish demonstrations at the University of Munich.

55. The text of this letter is reproduced, with permission, from *The Correspondence of Walter Benjamin, 1910–1940*, ed. Gershom Scholem and Theodor W. Adorno, trans. Manfred R. Jacobson and Evelyn M. Jacobson (Chicago: University of Chicago Press, 1994). Copyright © 1994 by the University of Chicago.

56. Jacob de Haan, a Dutch Jew, was murdered by fellow Jews because of his strong anti-Zionism.

57. The rentenmark was the new currency introduced by the Federal Bank (Reichsbank) in November 1923. It brought an end to the hyperinflation.

58. The text of this letter is reproduced, with permission, from *The Correspondence of Walter Benjamin, 1910–1940*, ed. Gershom Scholem and Theodor W. Adorno, trans. Manfred R. Jacobson and Evelyn M. Jacobson (Chicago: University of Chicago Press, 1994). Copyright © 1994 by the University of Chicago.

59. This newspaper was the official organ of the Orthodox Zionist organization Agudat Israel.

60. *Der Israelit* was an Orthodox Jewish publication (1860–1938).

61. An allusion to a song cycle *(Songs for Dead Children)* by Gustav Mahler.

62. Landauer, an anarchist writer, was murdered in Munich in 1919. The phrase in parenthesis is in Hebrew in the original.

63. Simon was a Ba'al Tschva—that is, a secular Jew who converts to Orthodoxy.

64. Harry Levy (1893–1978) was a rabbi, and coeditor of the *Jüdisches Wochenblatt*.

65. "For no one who does this goes unpunished."

66. The founding ceremony for the Hebrew University in Jerusalem took place on April 1, 1925.

67. Paul von Hindenburg was the presidential candidate for the conservative parties, and Wilhelm Marx for the liberals. Hindenburg won the election.

68. The text of this letter is reproduced, with permission, from *The Correspondence of Walter Benjamin, 1910–1940*, ed. Gershom Scholem and Theodor W. Adorno, trans. Manfred R. Jacobson and Evelyn M. Jacobson (Chicago: University of Chicago Press, 1994). Copyright © 1994 by the University of Chicago.

69. Joseph Horowitz, a professor of Arabic culture at the University of Frankfurt, had attended the opening ceremonies for the Hebrew University.

70. See Scholem's open letter to Franz Rosenzweig, cited in Walter Grab and J. Schoeps, eds., *Juden in der Weimarer Republik* (Stuttgart: Burg Verlag, 1986), p. 148. In the letter, Scholem writes about the dialectical "revolt of the sacred language" against secular users. Despite efforts at secularization, he says, "archaic traces of the sacred tongue will reappear within the Palestinian 'Volapuek'" (that is, a kind of Esperanto). In "unforgettable, stigmatizing moments . . . Hebrew words that are not neologisms but that have been taken from the treasure house of our 'good old language' and are bursting with meaning" will "suddenly reveal all of the presumptuousness of our enterprise."

71. Gershom Scholem, "The Kabbalist R. Abraham ben Elieser Halevi" (written in Hebrew), *Kirjath Sepher*, 2 (1925–1926): 101–141.

72. Moritz Steinschneider (1816–1907) was a historian associated with the Wissenschaft des Judentums.

73. *Tikkun* means "repair."

74. This refers to the wave of immigration *(aliyah)* of middle-class Polish Jews that took place in the 1920s.

75. Isaiah 9:11. *Haluz* (plural *haluzim*) means "settler" and was the term used to designate the early immigrants from Russia—those who arrived in Palestine between 1900 and World War I. Inspired by Tolstoy and others, they set up the utopian agricultural communities that came to be known as *kibbutzim*. Immigrants from Lodz and other places in Poland and Ukraine came to Palestine after World War I, fleeing pogroms and economic hardship. There was a difference—at least for intellectuals such as Scholem—between "political" Zionism and "cultural" Zionism. The former was primarily directed at the colonization of Palestine, with the eventual aim of establishing a Jewish state. The latter was a movement within Jewish culture, the aim being the renewal of Jewish thought, religion, and tradition. For Scholem, "Zionism" meant the latter type.

76. *Natinut* is the Hebrew term for "citizenship." *Natin* means "citizen."

77. Gustav Noske (1868–1946) was a Social Democratic politician.

78. Hedwig Scholem ("Hete") was the wife of Theobald Scholem, Gershom's uncle.

79. Jeremiah 30:18.

80. *Toldut sifrut* is Hebrew for "history of literature." Joseph Klausner (1874–1958) was a historian and literary critic.

81. Oskar Goldberg (1885–1953), *Die Wirklichkeit der Hebräer: Einleitung in das System des Pentateuch* (Berlin: David, 1925).

82. Samson Raphael Hirsch (1808–1888) was the founder of Jewish neo-Orthodoxy.

83. *Xenia,* a Greek term, means a gift given to guests or strangers.

84. The text of this letter is reproduced, with permission, from *The Correspondence of Walter Benjamin, 1910–1940,* ed. Gershom Scholem and Theodor W. Adorno, trans. Manfred R. Jacobson and Evelyn M. Jacobson (Chicago:

University of Chicago Press, 1994). Copyright © 1994 by the University of Chicago.

85. Passover.

86. "Translation."

87. "You'll have to answer for this someday."

88. The text of this letter is reproduced from *The Letters of Martin Buber: A Life of Dialogue,* by Martin Buber, ed. Nahum N. Glatzer and Paul Mendes-Flohr, trans. Richard and Clara Winston and Harry Zohn. Copyright © 1991 by Schocken Books, a division of Random House, Inc. Used by permission of Schocken Books, a division of Random House, Inc.

89. "Harmony" or "tone."

90. In a letter written on April 6, Simon had praised Scholem for his opposition to the "legion." This was a reference to the Zionist leader Zev Jabotinsky's call for the creation of a "Jewish legion" to combat the British and the Arabs.

91. "May there be many more like them in Israel."

92. The text of this letter is reproduced, with permission, from *The Correspondence of Walter Benjamin, 1910–1940,* ed. Gershom Scholem and Theodor W. Adorno, trans. Manfred R. Jacobson and Evelyn M. Jacobson (Chicago: University of Chicago Press, 1994). Copyright © 1994 by the University of Chicago.

93. Letters from 1927 have been omitted. Scholem wrote relatively few because he spent much of the year in Europe, conducting research. During the spring and summer he was in Germany and France, and during August and September he was in London, studying Sabbatian texts for the first time. A number of his publications came out, including *Bibliographia kabbalistica* (Leipzig: W. Drugulin), a bibliography of all books published on the Kabbalah from the time of the German humanist Johann Reuchlin (1455–1522) to the 1920s.

94. The text of this letter is reproduced, with permission, from *The Correspondence of Walter Benjamin, 1910–1940,* ed. Gershom Scholem and Theodor W. Adorno, trans. Manfred R. Jacobson and Evelyn M. Jacobson (Chicago: University of Chicago Press, 1994). Copyright © 1994 by the University of Chicago.

95. Judah Magnes (1877–1949) was chancellor of the Hebrew University.

96. Gershom Scholem, *Kuntress ele schmot sifrei* [Pamphlet of Book Titles] (Jerusalem, 1928).

97. Scholem is referring to his Yemenite maid.

98. A "huppa" is a marriage canopy.

99. In 1923 Werner had been involved in organizing a general strike.

100. Max Brod (1884–1968) was a novelist and Zionist from Prague. He was a follower of Buber, and a lifelong friend of Franz Kafka's.

101. Betty visited Palestine from March to May 1928.

102. Novels by Franz Kafka.

103. A distant relative of Scholem's.

104. Scholem and Benjamin together wrote "Amtliches Lehrgedicht der Philosophischen Fakultät der Haupt- und Staatsuniversität Muri." The book was never published.

105. Gershom Scholem, "Über die Theologie des Sabbatianismus, im Lichte Abraham Cardozos" [On the Theology of Sabbatianism in Light of Abraham Cardozo], *Der Jude*, 9 (1928): 123–139.

106. The text of this letter is reproduced, with permission, from *The Correspondence of Walter Benjamin, 1910–1940,* ed. Gershom Scholem and Theodor W. Adorno, trans. Manfred R. Jacobson and Evelyn M. Jacobson (Chicago: University of Chicago Press, 1994). Copyright © 1994 by the University of Chicago.

107. Benjamin was compiling materials for the *Passagen-Werk,* his study of the arcades of Paris, which was incomplete at his death.

108. The text of this letter is reproduced, with permission, from *The Correspondence of Walter Benjamin, 1910–1940,* ed. Gershom Scholem and Theodor W. Adorno, trans. Manfred R. Jacobson and Evelyn M. Jacobson (Chicago: University of Chicago Press, 1994). Copyright © 1994 by the University of Chicago.

109. An ultra-Orthodox neighborhood in Jerusalem.

110. A traditional Hebrew greeting that means, "May you be granted a good year."

111. A name taken from the Kabbalah.

112. Scholem is referring to "Zur Frage der Entstehung der Kabbalah" (On the Question of the Development of the Kabbalah).

113. The text of this letter is reproduced, with permission, from *The Correspondence of Walter Benjamin, 1910–1940,* ed. Gershom Scholem and Theodor W. Adorno, trans. Manfred R. Jacobson and Evelyn M. Jacobson (Chicago: University of Chicago Press, 1994). Copyright © 1994 by the University of Chicago.

114. At the time, Arthur Koestler (1905–1983)—who later wrote *Darkness at Noon, Scum of the Earth,* and many other books—was working as a journalist for the *Vossische Zeitung* ("Aunt Voss"), a liberal Berlin daily.

115. Max Warburg (1867–1946) was a banker in Hamburg and an adviser to the Reichsbank.

116. The reference is to an Arab-Jewish clash at the Western Wall that triggered widespread rioting.

117. Wolfgang von Weisl was a foreign correspondent for the *Vossische Zeitung.*

118. Zernsdorf, a small town in a rural district outside Berlin, was the site of the family's summer home. Scholem's parents and brothers had first rented the house in 1924, and eventually bought it.

119. Julius Berger (1883–1948) was a Zionist leader in Germany.

120. A Jewish suburb of Jerusalem.

121. The Haganah ("defense") was an underground army established in 1920 to defend Jewish settlements.

122. Brit Shalom ("Covenant of Peace") was founded in 1925. The group urged greater cooperation between Arabs and Jews. Many of its members called for a binational, joint Jewish-Arab state in which Jews and Arabs would share sovereignty on a parity basis.

123. Yishuv was the name for the Jewish community in Palestine.

124. The reference is to policies adopted by the Revisionist party.

125. In a letter dated January 21, Werner sent "warm regards to the servant of English imperialism!"

126. Bergmann, one of the most active members of Brit Shalom, was widely attacked for his positions.

127. "Instruction."

128. The text of this letter is reproduced from *The Letters of Martin Buber: A Life of Dialogue,* by Martin Buber, ed. Nahum N. Glatzer and Paul Mendes-Flohr, trans. Richard and Clara Winston and Harry Zohn. Copyright © 1991 by Schocken Books, a division of Random House, Inc. Used by permission of Schocken Books, a division of Random House, Inc.

129. The text of this letter is reproduced, with permission, from *The Correspondence of Walter Benjamin, 1910–1940,* ed. Gershom Scholem and Theodor W. Adorno, trans. Manfred R. Jacobson and Evelyn M. Jacobson (Chicago: University of Chicago Press, 1994). Copyright © 1994 by the University of Chicago.

130. The text of this letter is reproduced from *The Letters of Martin Buber: A Life of Dialogue,* by Martin Buber, ed. Nahum N. Glatzer and Paul Mendes-Flohr, trans. Richard and Clara Winston and Harry Zohn. Copyright © 1991 by Schocken Books, a division of Random House, Inc. Used by permission of Schocken Books, a division of Random House, Inc.

131. Wilhelm Busch (1832–1908) was a satirist and cartoonist.

132. Scholem attached to the bottom of the letter a drawing of Hitler with his hand held high.

133. Jews were fearful of the election results, in which the Nazi party greatly increased its strength in the Reichstag.

134. Presumably in the Church of the Holy Sepulcher or in the Mosque of Omar.

135. Betty had been in Palestine from March to early May 1931.

136. Hermine was Erich's maid.

137. Benjamin had been in Moscow during the winter of 1926–1927.

138. From March to October Scholem was in Europe doing archival research, mostly in Italy.

139. "Das Pergament, ist das der heilge Bronnen, / Woraus ein Trunk den Durst auf ewig stillt?" *Faust, Part I,* lines 566–567 (trans. Walter Kaufmann).

140. The editor of the *Vossische Zeitung.*

141. The SA (Sturmabteilung, or Storm Troops) were groups controlled directly by the Nazi party to fight opponents.

142. The text of this letter is reproduced, with permission, from *The Correspondence of Walter Benjamin, 1910–1940,* ed. Gershom Scholem and Theodor W. Adorno, trans. Manfred R. Jacobson and Evelyn M. Jacobson (Chicago: University of Chicago Press, 1994). Copyright © 1994 by the University of Chicago.

143. Felix Noeggerath (1885–1960) was a friend of Benjamin's.

144. Hebrew for "blessing."

145. Franz von Papen (1879–1969) served as chancellor of Germany in 1932.

146. Ben Shemen was a youth village founded by Siegfried Lehmann in 1927.

PART III. REDEMPTION THROUGH SIN

1. Salman Schocken established his Jewish publishing house in 1931. It became an important institution only after 1933. The *Schocken Almanach,* an annual first published in 1933, contained articles and essays dealing with Jewish history, philosophy, literature, and religious thought.

2. Letter from August 26, 1936.

3. Elsa Lasker-Schüler, *Hebräerland* (Zurich, 1937), p. 2.

4. George Steiner, "A Friendship and Its Flaws," *Times Literary Supplement,* June 27, 1980, p. 723.

5. Ernst Simon, *Aufbau im Untergang: Jüdische Erwachsenenbildung im national-sozialistischen Deutschland* (Tübingen: J. C. B. Mohr, 1959), p. 76.

6. See, for example, Gershom Scholem, "Nach der Vertreibung aus Spanien" (On the Expulsion from Spain), *Schocken Almanach, 1933–1934,* pp. 55–70; and idem, "Zum Verständnis des Sabbatianismus: Zugleich ein Beitrag zur Geschichte der Aufklärung" (On Understanding Sabbatianism: Also an Essay on the History of the Enlightenment), *Schocken Almanach, 1936–1937,* pp. 30–42.

7. Gershom Scholem, "Mitzva ha-ba'ah be-avera" (Jerusalem, 1936).

8. Gershom Scholem, "Erlösung durch Sünde," *Judaica V* (Frankfurt am Main: Suhrkamp Verlag, 1995), p. 66.

9. Gershom Scholem, "Zum Verständnis der messianischen Idee im Judentum," *Judaica I* (Frankfurt am Main: Suhrkamp Verlag, 1963), p. 40.

10. Ibid., p. 114.

11. Gershom Scholem, *"On the Possibility of Jewish Mysticism in Our Time" and Other Essays* (Philadelphia and Jerusalem: Jewish Publication Society, 1997), p. 171.

12. Gershom Scholem, *Major Trends in Jewish Mysticism* (New York: Schocken Books, 1969), p. 248.

13. Gershom Scholem, *Walter Benjamin: The Story of a Friendship,* trans. Harry Zohn (Philadelphia: Jewish Publication Society of America, 1981), p. 226.

LETTERS, 1933–1947

1. The text of this letter is reproduced, with permission, from *The Correspondence of Walter Benjamin, 1910–1940,* ed. Gershom Scholem and Theodor W. Adorno, trans. Manfred R. Jacobson and Evelyn M. Jacobson (Chicago: University of Chicago Press, 1994). Copyright © 1994 by the University of Chicago.

2. Gershom Scholem, "Jüdischer Glaube in dieser Zeit," *Bayerischen israelitischen Gemeindezeitung,* 8 (1932).

3. Lambert Schneider (1900–1970) worked as an editor at Schocken Verlag in Berlin.

4. Hitler had been appointed chancellor of Germany in late January 1933.

5. Unter den Linden was the main shopping boulevard in Berlin.

6. The reference is to the popular author Emil Ludwig (1881–1948) and to his book *Am Mittelmeer,* which had been published in 1923.

7. Scholem strongly opposed his mother's plan to drive overland to Palestine.

8. This was the last free election, though accompanied by massive propaganda and intimidation.

9. The reference is to Betty's plan to drive from Hamburg to Palestine.

10. Arthur Ruppin (1876–1943) was a Zionist leader from Germany and a fellow member of Brit Shalom.

11. The printing shop established by Siegfried Scholem, Scholem's grandfather.

12. The Zentral Verein was an organization founded in 1893 in Berlin to defend Jewish civil rights.

13. The K.d.W. is the Kaufhaus des Westens, the most exclusive department store in Berlin at the time.

14. On April 1, 1933, the Nazis called for a national boycott of Jewish shops and businesses.

15. "Katen" was the nickname of Betty's sister Käte Schiepan.

16. The Spree is the river that flows through Berlin.

17. The Gaonic period (sixth century to eleventh century) was the time in which the Jewish academies in Babylon, located in the cities of Sura and Pumbedita, were the center of Jewish learning. *Gaon* (meaning "genius" or "excellency") was the title given to the sages who lived during this period.

18. Karl Meyer was a physician and family friend living in Switzerland.

19. Ulrich Gerhardt (1875–1950) was a German zoologist. He had met Scholem in 1931 while doing scholarly work in Jerusalem.

20. On March 31, 1492, the expulsion order from Spain was officially signed. It was made public on the first of April.

21. Dina was Scholem's cousin—the daughter of Theobald, Arthur's brother.

22. Martha was the Scholem family's maid.

23. The friend was Haim Arlozoroff (1899–1933), who was married to Meta Jahr, one of Scholem's close friends from his youth. The Jewish Executive was the local Palestinian organization representing the Jewish Agency, which was the main political body of the Zionist movement.

24. Ben Shemen was a children's village near Tel Aviv. See Scholem's letter to his mother dated December 28, 1932.

25. Benjamin was on Ibiza from April to the middle of July 1932, and then again from mid-April to October 1933.

26. This was the address of Erich and Edith Scholem.

27. In 1933 Buber was appointed director of an organization for Jewish adult education in Germany.

28. Money could be sent only if the sender had a passport.

29. The text of this letter is reproduced from *The Letters of Martin Buber: A Life of Dialogue,* by Martin Buber, ed. Nahum N. Glatzer and Paul Mendes-Flohr, trans. Richard and Clara Winston and Harry Zohn. Copyright © 1991 by Schocken

Books, a division of Random House, Inc. Used by permission of Schocken Books, a division of Random House, Inc.

30. The reference is to the woman who would become Scholem's second wife, Fanya Freud.

31. Scholem is referring to the pattern on the carpet Betty Scholem had sent him.

32. Scholem had been appointed full professor.

33. "No one will be spared."

34. The reference is to Werner Senator (1896–1953).

35. In a plebiscite, German voters massively supported the government's decision to withdraw from the League of Nations. German withdrew from the league on October 14, 1933.

36. The Arab National Council called for a one-day general strike to protest Jewish immigration.

37. Scholem is referring to the scholar Hermann Ibscher. The Persian prophet Mani (ca. 216–ca. 276), called Manes by the Greeks and Romans, founded the dualistic religion of Manichaeism. Major fragments of his writings were discovered in China in 1904–1905 and in Egypt in 1933.

38. The text of this letter is reproduced from *The Letters of Martin Buber: A Life of Dialogue,* by Martin Buber, ed. Nahum N. Glatzer and Paul Mendes-Flohr, trans. Richard and Clara Winston and Harry Zohn. Copyright © 1991 by Schocken Books, a division of Random House, Inc. Used by permission of Schocken Books, a division of Random House, Inc.

39. Scholem is referring to a book published in Hebrew entitled *Sichot ve-sepurim,* which contains the teachings of Rabbi Nachman and was compiled by Avramah Chazan (Jerusalem, 1933).

40. *Sheigetz* is the Yiddish word for *enfant terrible.*

41. Emmy fled Germany after her release from prison, taking her daughters with her.

42. Werner and Emmy had two children, Renate and Edith.

43. Plötzensee is a prison outside Berlin.

44. Moritz Spitzer (1900–1982), who worked as an editor at Schocken Books, had written to Scholem on June 16 with suggestions regarding a book of essays. He impressed upon Scholem the need "to make it understandable to the average reader."

45. Ernst Torgler was one of the Communists put on trial for burning down the Reichstag.

46. The Scholems tried to secure Werner's release through the intervention of the Quakers.

47. In her letter of May 22, Edith Rosenzweig had apologized to Scholem for including in a book of her husband's letters a comment which Scholem found objectionable. Rosenzweig had written to Joseph Prager on May 30, 1923, mentioning a course on the *Zohar* given by Scholem at Rosenzweig's Lehrhaus in Frankfurt. "Scholem is here and is behaving in his usual beastly fashion, but at the

same time he is as dazzling as always." Franz Rosenzweig, *Briefe* (Berlin: Schocken, 1935), p. 481.

48. Martin Buber, *Der grosse Maggid und seine Nachfolge* [The Great Maggid and His Succession] (Frankfurt: Literarische Anstalt, 1922).

49. The reference is to Hannah Arendt (1906–1975).

50. Among other things, the Nuremberg Laws forbade Jews from having "Aryan" domestic help under the age of forty-five.

51. *Die Rote Fahne* was a Communist periodical.

52. Betty was in Palestine in April and part of May.

53. In 1936, renewed rioting broke out over the issue of Jewish immigration from Europe.

54. Moza was a kibbutz located on a hillside outside Jerusalem.

55. Gershom Scholem, *Die Geheimnisse der Schöpfung* (Berlin: Schocken Books, 1936).

56. The colleague was Levi Billig.

57. Stephen Wise (1874–1949) was a rabbi, and president of the American Zionist Organization.

58. Scholem was a visiting professor at the Jewish Institute of Religion, in New York City, from February to September 1938.

59. Theodor Wiesengrund Adorno (1903–1969) was a philosopher and sociologist. Paul Tillich (1886–1965) was a German theologian associated with the Frankfurt School; he emigrated to the United States in 1933.

60. Scholem's embarrassment was probably due to the tensions that had arisen with the Institute of Social Research over the editing and publication of Benjamin's work. See also letter of March 20, 1939.

61. Renewed fighting between Jews and Arabs broke out in July and October 1938.

62. During the 1930s the Hilfsverein der Deutschen Juden, a relief organization, helped German Jews to emigrate from Germany.

63. Gershom Scholem had tried to obtain an immigration certificate for Werner in 1935.

64. On the night of October 9 the government had instigated a series of pogroms.

65. The reference is to Erich Scholem's wife, who (like the daughter of Werner and Emmy) was named Edith.

66. Scholem's birthday (December 5) was approaching.

67. Shalom Spiegel (1899–1984) was a professor of Hebrew literature at the Jewish Theological Seminary in New York. The salutation is a play on their names: "From [Gershom] Shalom to Shalom [Spiegel]." The Hebrew word *shalom* means "peace."

68. This was the book that would eventually be published as *Major Trends in Jewish Mysticism* (Jerusalem: Schocken Books, 1941). Written in English, it was based on the Hilda Strook Lectures that Scholem had given at the Jewish Institute of Religion, in New York.

69. On Benjamin's falling out with Horkheimer and Adorno, see Bernd Witte, *Walter Benjamin: An Intellectual Biography,* trans. James Rolleston (Detroit: Wayne State University Press, 1991), pp. 156ff. In the late 1930s, the most difficult years of his exile, Benjamin was almost entirely dependent on the Institute of Social Research for his livelihood—a situation that led to various conflicts. Adorno and Horkheimer often took the liberty of editing his articles, and disagreed with him on ideological matters. For Benjamin, the most painful blow came in 1938, when Adorno refused to publish his essay "The Paris of the Second Empire in Baudelaire."

70. Phiechen (or Sophia) was the wife of George Scholem, Arthur's brother. The identity of Hans is uncertain.

71. Günter was the son of Reinhold and Käthe Scholem.

72. Gershom Scholem, "Zur Frage nach der Entstehung der Kabbala," *Korrespondenzblatt des Vereins zur Gründung und Erhaltung einer Akademie für die Wissenschaft des Judentums,* 9 (1928): 4–26.

73. The British had proposed to settle Jews in Guyana.

74. The reference is to the Labor party, headed by David Ben-Gurion.

75. See letter of January 1, 1939, to Shalom Spiegel. Illegal immigrants had no official existence, since they were not counted or registered by the government.

76. With Scholem as its director, Salman Schocken opened a center for the study of Jewish mysticism within his private library.

77. Karl Kraus (1874–1926) was an Austrian essayist, poet, and satirist. His play *Die letzten Tage der Menschheit* (1919) is a monumental drama dealing with World War I. At the gathering in honor of Kraus, Scholem read from Benjamin's essay "The Work of Art in the Age of Its Technological Reproducibility." The person "whose impression is the only one that counts" was Salman Schocken, as Scholem wanted to persuade him to publish Benjamin's work.

78. The text of this letter is reproduced, with permission, from *The Correspondence of Walter Benjamin, 1910–1940,* ed. Gershom Scholem and Theodor W. Adorno, trans. Manfred R. Jacobson and Evelyn M. Jacobson (Chicago: University of Chicago Press, 1994). Copyright © 1994 by the University of Chicago.

79. The reference to "demons," here and in the previous letter, is an allusion to Max Brod, who was competing with Benjamin to win Salman Schocken's patronage. Benjamin wanted to write a book on Kafka, but Brod considered Kafka his own territory.

80. The *Zeitschrift für Sozialforschung* (Journal for Social Research) was the organ of the Frankfurt School. From 1932 to 1938 it was published in Germany, and from 1939 to 1941 in the United States (where it was titled *Studies in Philosophy and Social Science*).

81. Adorno wrote this letter in English.

82. Salman Schocken and his wife visited Australia on their way from Palestine to the United States.

83. Käthe is Reinhold's wife.

84. Scholem had been appointed dean of the Faculty of Humanities.

85. This letter was written in Hebrew.

86. In the summer of 1942 the British army defeated the German forces under Erwin Rommel near El Alamein, Egypt.

87. Gershom Scholem, "Sabbatai Sevi and Nathan of Gaza" (in Hebrew), *Luach ha'aretz* [Tel Aviv] (1940): 150–166.

88. Adorno wrote this letter in English.

89. The reference is to Werner Kraft and to Benjamin's essay on Carl Gustav Jochmann; see Benjamin, " 'Die Rückschritte der Poesie,' von Carl Gustav Jochmann, in Benjamin, *Gesammelte Schriften,* ed. Rolf Tiedemann and Hermann Schweppenhäuser, vol. 2 (Frankfurt am Main: Suhrkamp Verlag, 1977), pp. 572–585. In English as " 'The Regression of Poetry,' by Carl Gustav Jochmann," in Benjamin, *Selected Writings, Volume 3: 1935–1940* (Cambridge, Mass.: Harvard University Press, forthcoming). Jochmann was an obscure nineteenth-century writer; and according to Adorno, it was Kraft (not Benjamin) who had rediscovered him.

90. Walter Benjamin, "Zentralpark," in Benjamin, *Gesammelte Schriften,* vol. 1, pp. 657–690. For an English version, see Benjamin, "Central Park," trans. Lloyd Spencer (with Mark Harrington), *New German Critique,* 34 (Winter 1985). Also in Benjamin, *Selected Writings, Volume 3: 1935–1940* (Cambridge, Mass.: Harvard University Press, forthcoming).

91. "Über den Begriff der Geschichte." For an English translation, see Walter Benjamin, "Theses on the Philosophy of History," in Benjamin, *Illuminations,* ed. Hannah Arendt, trans. Harry Zohn (New York: Schocken Books, 1969), pp. 253–264.

92. The material was found and eventually published. See Walter Benjamin, *The Arcades Project,* trans. Howard Eiland and Kevin McLaughlin (Cambridge, Mass.: Harvard University Press, 1999).

93. Many of these letters have been published in English. See Gershom Scholem, ed., *The Correspondence of Walter Benjamin and Gershom Scholem, 1932–1940,* trans. Gary Smith and Andre Lefevere (Cambridge, Mass.: Harvard University Press, 1992). See also Scholem, *Walter Benjamin: The Story of a Friendship,* trans. Harry Zohn (New York: Schocken Books, 1988).

94. The marriage of Dora and Walter Benjamin collapsed in 1921. The divorce, finalized in 1930, was characterized by bitter accusations on both sides.

95. Dora never did write an account of Benjamin's life.

96. A German-language newspaper for central European immigrants in Palestine.

97. Ernst Simon, a professor of education at the Hebrew University, encountered great hostility owing to his moderate views on the Arab-Jewish conflict.

98. Leo Strauss (1899–1973) was a political philosopher who taught at the University of Chicago. Herbert Marcuse (1898–1979), also a political philosopher, taught at Harvard, Columbia, and Brandeis, before joining the faculty of the University of California at San Diego. Both were members of the institute's circle.

99. By *Anglicum* ("English thing"), Scholem means his book *Major Trends in Jewish Mysticism*.

100. Adolph S. Oko (1883–1944) was head librarian at the Hebrew Union College in Cincinnati, Ohio, associate editor of the *Menorah Journal* and the *Contemporary Jewish Record,* and a renowned Spinoza scholar. He wrote this letter in English.

101. Hans Kohn (1891–1971), "The Jewish Mystic," *Contemporary Jewish Record,* 6 (December 1943): 665–667. Kohn was an old acquaintance of Scholem's; he had belonged to Brit Shalom before leaving Palestine for the United States in 1931.

102. Scholem wrote this letter in English.

103. "Peerless babbler." In German in the original.

104. "The righteous man lives his aversions." In German in the original. Scholem may have made up this dictum.

105. The reference is to Hannah Arendt.

106. Oko wrote this letter in English.

107. The reference is to Henri, comte de Boulainvilliers (1658–1722), a philosopher and historian who translated Spinoza's works into French.

108. Käte Schiepan was deported to Theresienstadt (Terezin), in Czechoslovakia. She did not survive.

109. Scholem is referring to a rug that his mother had given him. See his letter of August 30, 1933.

110. Sholem Asch (1880–1957) was a novelist who wrote in Yiddish.

111. The reference is to Asch's novel *The Nazarene.*

112. World War II officially ended in Europe on May 8, 1945.

113. Psalms 83:2.

114. See Isaiah Sonne, "History of Sabbatianism in Italy," *Sefer ha-yovel* (1943): 89–103.

115. *Walter Benjamin zum Gedächtnis* [In Memory of Walter Benjamin] (Los Angeles: Institute of Social Research, 1942). This was a special mimeographed issue that came out one year after the institute ceased publishing its journal, *Studies in Philosophy and Social Science.* It thus did not carry a volume number.

116. The reference is to Stefan George and Hugo von Hofmannsthal.

117. Kurt Blumenfeld (1884–1963), a Zionist leader from Königsberg, was a close friend of Arendt's.

118. Hannah Arendt, "Concerning Minorities," *Contemporary Jewish Record* (August 14, 1944): 353–368.

119. The Jewish Brigade was a Jewish military unit within the British army during World War II. Hans Jonas (1903–1993) was a philosopher who had studied under Martin Heidegger and Rudolf Bultmann. In 1933 he had emigrated to Palestine, and had begun teaching at the Hebrew University in 1938.

120. Arthur Koestler, *Darkness at Noon* (New York: Macmillan, 1941).

121. Walter Benjamin, "Two Poems by Friedrich Hölderlin," in Benjamin,

Selected Writings, Volume 1: 1913–1926, ed. Marcus Bullock and Michael W. Jennings (Cambridge, Mass.: Harvard University Press, 1996), pp. 18–36; and "Franz Kafka," in Benjamin, *Selected Writings, Volume 2: 1927–1934,* ed. Michael W. Jennings, Howard Eiland, and Gary Smith (Cambridge, Mass.: Harvard University Press, 1999), pp. 794–818.

122. U.S. President Harry Truman had called for Britain to grant 100,000 Jewish refugees legal entrance to Palestine immediately.

123. Schocken's department store empire was based in Zwickau, Germany.

124. Hannah Arendt, "Zionism Reconsidered," *Menorah Journal,* 33, no. 2 (October–December 1945): 162–196.

125. The Zionist organization made a trade-and-transfer agreement with Nazi Germany that, said some, undermined the efforts of Jewish organizations to isolate Germany.

126. "Pardon the expression."

127. Buber's term is *Umkehr.*

128. This was Betty Scholem's final letter to her son. She died on May 5, 1946.

129. "Arthur" here refers to Scholem's nephew (Erich Scholem's son).

130. "Of the male species," "of the masculine kind."

131. Leo Baeck (1873–1956) was a rabbi who in 1933 had become president of the Reichsvertretung der deutschen Juden (National Council of German Jews). After 1945 he lived in London, where he continued to lead the organization.

132. Scholem was in Europe from April to October 1946.

133. Siegmund Hurwitz (1904–1994) was a Jungian psychiatrist.

134. Scholem wrote this letter in English.

135. Dr. Sharp was an American involved in the project to transfer Jewish libraries to Jerusalem. Scholem wrote to him in English.

136. Naharija, a town on Palestine's coast, was largely populated by German Jews, who were often called *yekkes* by the Russian and Polish Jews. See note 13 of the introduction to Part II.

137. A reference to the Eranos conference held yearly in Ascona, Switzerland.

138. "I fear the Greeks when they bring gifts." The line is from Virgil's *Aeneid* and refers to the Trojan Horse.

139. Scholem wrote this letter in Hebrew.

140. The reference is to the essay Bergmann wrote in honor of Scholem's fiftieth birthday, "Zum fünfzigsten Geburtstag," published in the Hebrew-language journal *Davar* on May 12, 1947. The essay discussed what Bergmann called "the greatest fallacy" in Scholem's scholarship. "In their present spiritual and physical state, the Jewish people cannot afford the dichotomy between 'professors' and 'prophets.' With all due respect to his enormous accomplishments as a scholar, we cannot allow that a man such as Gershom Scholem be only a historian and philologist and that his pupils be trained solely as historians and philologists. We feel that since he has passed his fiftieth year, a new and greater responsibility has fallen on him."

141. Micah 6:8.

142. Mapai (Mifleget Poalei Eretz Israel, or Workers' Party of the Land of Israel) was established in 1930 and became Israel's main labor party. "Declaration" refers to the United Nations' partition of Palestine, declared on May 15, 1947, and the subsequent announcement by the Arab Higher Committee that it would use force to prevent the partition.

143. "Prudence."

144. Josef Weiss, "Gershom Scholem: Fünfzig Jahre," *Yedioth Hayom,* December 5, 1947.

PART IV. MASTER MAGICIAN EMERITUS

1. Gershom Scholem, *Briefe III* (Munich: Beck Verlag, 1999), p. 462.

2. Gershom Scholem, *Briefe II* (Munich: Beck Verlag, 1995), p. 28.

3. See David Biale, "Scholem und der moderne Nationalismus," in Gary Smith, ed., *Gershom Scholem: Zwischen den Disziplinen* (Frankfurt am Main: Suhrkamp Verlag, 1995), p. 134.

4. Quoted in Robert Juette, *Die Emigration der deutschsprachigen Wissenschaft des Judentums* (Stuttgart: Franz Steiner, 1991), p. 35.

5. Gershom Scholem, *Sabbatai Sevi and the Sabbatian Movement during His Lifetime* [in Hebrew] (Tel Aviv: Am Oved, 1956). In English, *Sabbatai Sevi: The Mystical Messiah,* trans. R. J. Zwi Werblowsky (Princeton, N.J.: Princeton University Press, 1973). Sabbatai Sevi (1626–1676), a Jewish mystic born in Smyrna, believed in the link between earthly redemption and cosmic restoration, and declared himself the Messiah in 1648. His teachings gave rise to an underground movement that attracted an enormous number of followers, mostly in Turkey, Poland, and Italy.

6. *Briefe II,* p. 275.

7. *Briefe III,* p. 424.

8. Ibid., p. xiv.

9. Gershom Scholem, *Briefe I* (Munich: Beck Verlag, 1994), p. 444.

10. Gershom Scholem, "Walter Benjamin," *Neue Rundschau,* 76 (1965), reprinted in Scholem, *Judaica II* (Frankfurt am Main: Suhrkamp Verlag, 1970), p. 212.

11. *Briefe II,* p. 258.

12. "Wider den Mythos vom deutsch-jüdischen Gespräch," in Scholem, *Judaica II,* pp. 7–12.

13. *Briefe II,* p. 87–89.

14. *Briefe III,* pp. 463–464.

15. Cynthia Ozick, "The Fourth Sparrow: The Magisterial Reach of Gershom Scholem," in Ozick, *Art and Ardor: Essays* (New York: Knopf, 1983), p. 145, drawing on essays published in the *New York Times Book Review,* February 24, 1974, and September 21, 1980. See also Scholem, *Briefe III,* p. 344.

16. Scholem, *Briefe III,* p. 96.

LETTERS, 1948–1982

1. Isaac Seeligmann (1907–1982) was a Dutch historian of religion. After being released from a concentration camp, he worked as the chief librarian at the University of Amsterdam.

2. After the war, the U.S. military authorities set up a depot in Offenbach, Germany, to gather together Jewish books that had been stolen by the Nazis and scattered around various sites in Germany and Central Europe. According to the Offenbach Plan, the legal owners were to be located and their books returned to them. All Jewish books whose owners could not be found were to be transferred to Jerusalem.

3. General Lucius Clay was a U.S. army officer who served as the deputy military general of Germany after the American occupation in 1945.

4. After the Israeli declaration of statehood in May, Arab Armies attacked. The Jewish neighborhoods of Jerusalem were under siege.

5. Isaiah Tishby (1908–1992) had studied the Kabbalah with Scholem. Jacob Sasportas (1610–1698) was a rabbi who fiercely opposed Sabbatianism. Tishby brought out an edition of Sasportas' letters entitled *Zizat Novel Zevi* (Jerusalem: Mosad Byalik, 1954).

6. *Ha'aretz,* the leading daily Hebrew newspaper at the time, was owned by Salman Schocken and edited by his son Gershom.

7. Morton Smith (1915–1991) was a professor of ancient history at Columbia University. Scholem wrote this letter in English.

8. Samuel Sambursky (1900–1990), a physicist, presumably would have told the Arabs the truth.

9. Scholem wrote this letter in English.

10. Smith's doctoral thesis explored parallels between the Gospels and a number of first- and second-century Hebrew texts written by sages called the Tannaim.

11. Scholem wrote this letter in Hebrew.

12. An allusion to the Cairo Genisa, a cache of ancient books discovered in 1896 in the cellar of a Cairo synagogue. The Agnons were staying in the Scholem apartment because, during the War of Independence, heavy fighting had broken out in their neighborhood of Talpiot and their home had been damaged. Agnon's books were being stored in a secure building, at the Schocken library in Rehavia.

13. Scholem wrote this letter in English.

14. Jacob Taubes (1923–1987), a Judaic scholar, had studied with Scholem from 1949 to 1951.

15. "Things continuing thus"—that is, so long as conditions have not substantially changed.

16. Hans-Geert Falkenberg (1919–) is a German writer, editor, and producer who was active in German theater and television.

17. Scholem wrote relatively few letters in 1953. With the exception of a brief trip to Europe over the summer, he stayed in Jerusalem, where his heavy teaching responsibilities and work on his book on Sabbatai Sevi absorbed most of his ener-

gies. He nevertheless found time to publish more than a dozen articles, mostly in Hebrew.

18. Simcha Bonim Urbach (1913–) was a philosopher and rabbi. Scholem wrote this letter in Hebrew.

19. Scholem's life was uneventful in 1954, for which no letters are included here. He devoted his time that year to teaching, writing, and archival work.

20. The years 1956–1957 are not represented in this collection. In 1956 Scholem remained in Jerusalem most of the year. He wrote relatively few letters and only a handful of articles. Most of the year was taken up with teaching and with making the final corrections to his lifework, the two-volume biography *Shabtai Tsevi veha-tenu'ah ha-Shabta'it bi-yeme hayav* (Sabbatai Sevi and the Sabbatian Movement in Its Time). The signal event of 1957 was the publication of this book (Tel Aviv: Am Oved). *Major Trends in Jewish Mysticism* came out in German, under the title *Die Jüdische Mystik in ihren Hauptströmungen* (Frankfurt am Main: Metzner).

21. Zwi Werblowsky, who had studied with Scholem, later translated *Sabbatai Sevi* into English. Scholem wrote this letter in Hebrew.

22. Scholem's magnum opus, *Sabbatai Sevi: The Mystical Messiah,* was written in Hebrew and first appeared in 1956. Werblowsky's essay was entitled "Comments on G. Scholem's *Sabbatai Sevi*" (in Hebrew), *Molad,* 112 (1957): 539–546.

23. Baruch Kurzweil (1907–1972) was born in Czechoslovakia and raised in Germany. In 1939 he emigrated to Palestine, where he worked as a scholar and critic.

24. Koschel is referring to Scholem's *Major Trends in Jewish Mysticism.*

25. George Lichtheim (1912–1973) was a philosopher and critic. He translated Scholem's *Major Trends in Jewish Mysticism* into English.

26. Ernst Schoen (1894–1964) was a critic, a radio editor, and a close childhood friend of Walter Benjamin's.

27. *Der Anfang* was a journal of the radical left wing of the German youth movement.

28. For Benjamin's remarks on the Austrian novelist Adalbert Stifter (1805–1868), see Walter Benjamin, "Stifter," *Selected Writings, Volume 1: 1913–1926,* ed. Marcus Bullock and Michael W. Jennings (Cambridge, Mass.: Harvard University Press, 1996), pp. 111–113.

29. *Angelus Novus* is a hand-colored ink drawing that Paul Klee did in 1920 and that Benjamin had owned. Today it hangs in the Israel Museum in Jerusalem.

30. Peter Szondi (1929–1971) was a literary critic.

31. Ruth Nanda Anshen was the editor of *Encounter* magazine.

32. Hannah Arendt, *Vita activa oder vom tätigen Leben* (Stuttgart: Kohlhammer, 1960).

33. Gestapo officer Adolf Eichmann escaped to Argentina after the war. He was located by Israeli agents in 1960, abducted to Israel, and placed on trial for "crimes against humanity."

34. An ironic allusion to Bloch's book *The Spirit of Utopia* (1918).

35. Albert Salomon (1891–1966) was an émigré sociologist and the author of *The Tyranny of Progress: Reflections on the Origins of Sociology* (New York: Noonday, 1955). On December 2 he had written to Scholem raising some points about Benjamin's "unorthodox" Marxism.

36. *Die Gesellschaft*, a journal edited by Salomon in Weimar Germany, published a number of Benjamin's essays.

37. Sir Victor Gollancz (1893–1967) was an English publisher and writer. Scholem wrote this letter in English.

38. Geula Cohen (1925–) is an Israeli journalist and politician who supported extreme right-wing underground groups in the 1940s. She published her memoirs of that period, *Sipurah shel lohemet* (1961; trans. *Woman of Violence*, 1966) and served as a member of the Israeli Knesset. Scholem wrote this letter to her in Hebrew.

39. Porshim means "separatists." They consisted of a group of extreme nationalists who broke away from the right-wing underground group Ezel. Their official name was LEHI, a Hebrew acronym that stood for Fighters for the Freedom of Israel.

40. *Ma'as* ("Action") was an underground publication.

41. Leo Strauss (1899–1973) was a political philosopher who taught at the University of Chicago. On December 6 he had written to Scholem asking if he disapproved of the autobiographical elements in his preface to a book on Spinoza. He noted that Hobbes had published some daring things when he was close to death, because this condition fosters courage.

42. Leo Strauss, *Spinoza's Critique of Religion* (New York: Schocken Books, 1965); originally published as *Die Religionskritik Spinozas als Grundlage seiner Bibelwissenschaft* (1930).

43. Strauss came from Hessen, in Germany. A *minjan* is the number of men (ten) needed for an Orthodox service.

44. Margarete Susman (1872–1966) was a philosopher and essayist. Born in Hamburg, she studied with Georg Simmel in Berlin. In 1939 she emigrated to Switzerland. Among her works are *Frauen der Romantik* (1929) and a volume of memoirs (1964).

45. Moses Mendelssohn 1729–1786), a German-Jewish philosopher, was a symbol of Jewish emancipation and integration into German culture. He fought for tolerance and equality, yet remained an Orthodox Jew.

46. Georg Simmel (1858–1918) was a German-Jewish philosopher and sociologist.

47. Jakob Wassermann, *Mein Weg als Deutscher und Jude* (Berlin: Fischer Verlag, 1921). Wassermann (1873–1934) was a German-Jewish novelist.

48. In German, *das Gedichtete*. See Walter Benjamin, "Two Poems by Friedrich Hölderlin," in Benjamin, *Selected Writings, Volume 1: 1913–1926*, pp. 18–36.

49. The sketch appears in the introduction to Walter Benjamin, *Schriften*, ed. Theodor Adorno and Gretel Adorno, with Friedrich Podszus, 2 vols. (Frankfurt am Main: Suhrkamp Verlag, 1955).

50. Aniela Jaffe (1903–1991) was C. G. Jung's secretary.

51. C. G. Jung, "Zeitgenössisches," *Neue Zürcher Zeitung* (March 13, 1934); idem, "Geleitwort," in Gerhard Adler, *Entdeckung der Seele* (Zurich: Rasher, 1934); and idem, "Zur gegenwärtigen Lage der psychotherapie," *Zentralblatt für Psychotherapie und ihre Grenzgebiete* (Leipzig, 1934).

52. Hannah Arendt, *Eichmann in Jerusalem: A Report on the Banality of Evil* (New York: Viking, 1963).

53. *Herzenstakt.*

54. H. G. Adler, ed., *Die verheimlichte Wahrheit: Theresienstädter Dokumente* (Tübingen: Mohr, 1958).

55. Arendt is referring to Eichmann's abduction in Argentina by Israeli agents.

56. Theodor Adorno, *Quasi una Fantasia* (Frankfurt am Main: Suhrkamp Verlag, 1963). Translated as *Quasi una Fantasia: Essays on Modern Music,* trans. Rodney Livingstone (London: Verso, 1992).

57. Jung was president of the Allgemeine Ärztliche Gesellschaft für Psychotherapie from 1933 to 1940. The *Zantralblatt für Psychotherapie und ihre Grenzgebiete* was the organ of the society.

58. Hilde Scholem (d. 1982), née Samuel, was Erich's second wife.

59. The first volume of Scholem's *Judaica* series had appeared in 1963. The piece in question here was published as "Wider den Mythos vom deutsch-jüdischen Gespräch," *Judaica II* (Frankfurt am Main: Suhrkamp Verlag, 1970), pp. 7–11.

60. The volume included letters by, *inter alia,* Georg Lukács, Georg Simmel, Gustav Landauer, and Franz Rosenzweig.

61. Gershom Scholem, "Walter Benjamin," *Neue Rundschau,* 76 (1965), reprinted in Scholem, *Judaica II* (Frankfurt am Main: Suhrkamp Verlag, 1970), pp. 193–227.

62. Georges Friedmann (1902–1977) was a French sociologist.

63. Georges Friedmann, *Fin du peuple juif?* (Paris: Gallimard, 1965).

64. Gershom Scholem, "Walter Benjamin," *Neue Rundschau,* 76 (1965): 1–21; idem, "Walter Benjamin und Gerhard Scholem aus dem Jahr 1931," *Neue Zürcher Zeitung* (August 29, 1965): 4–5.

65. Arthur Schnitzler, Jakob Wassermann, and Stefan Zweig were all Jewish writers. *Deutschtum* means "Germanness."

66. This remark ("Das ist ein zu weites Feld") is a leitmotiv and the famous last sentence of *Effi Briest,* by Theodor Fontane (1819–1898), a German novelist of the realist school. It has become proverbial in German.

67. See Max Brod, *Franz Kafka: A Biography* (New York: Schocken Books, 1947); originally published in German in 1937.

68. Arnold Metzger, "Der Dialog zwischen Deutschen und Juden," *Die Zeit* (May 21, 1965): 32.

69. Followers of Jacob Frank (1726–1791), a Polish Jew who initiated a heretical movement that grew out of Sabbatai Sevi's teachings.

70. "Das Jüdische."

71. Rudolf Hartung (1914–1985) served as president of the German Academy of Science from 1958 to 1968.

72. Rudolf Hartung, "Der Mann, der von vielem absah: Die Briefe Walter Benjamins" (The Man Who Turned a Blind Eye to Many Things: The Letters of Walter Benjamin), *Die Zeit* (February 10, 1967): 27–28.

73. Rolf Tiedemann, *Studien zur Philosophie Walter Benjamins* (Frankfurt am Main: Europäische Verlagsanstalt, 1965).

74. Jean Selz, "Erinnerungen an Walter Benjamin," *Neue Zürcher Zeitung* (October 8, 1961).

75. See the letter Benjamin wrote on December 3, 1917.

76. See Benjamin's letter to Scholem dated June 12, 1938, in Walter Benjamin and Gershom Scholem, *Briefwechsel* (Frankfurt am Main: Suhrkamp Verlag, 1980), p. 266.

77. Henri F. Ellenberger (1905–1993), a psychiatrist, was born in Rhodesia, received his education in France, and for many years was a professor at the University of Montreal. Among his writings are *Beyond the Unconscious: Essays in the History of Psychiatry,* trans. Françoise Dubor and Mark S. Micale (Princeton, N.J.: Princeton University Press, 1993), and *The Discovery of the Unconscious: The History and Evolution of Dynamic Psychiatry* (New York: Basic Books, 1970).

78. C. G. Jung, *Mysterium coniunctionis: Untersuchung über die Trennung und Zusammensetzung der seelischen Gegensätze in der Alchemie* [Mysterium coniunctionis: An Inquiry into the Separation and Synthesis of Psychic Opposites in Alchemy] (Zurich, 1955–1957).

79. Eliezer of Worms was an eleventh-century German scholar of the Talmud.

80. Scholem is referring to the tensions leading up to the Six-Day War between the Arabs and Israelis in June 1967.

81. Erich von Kahler (1885–1970), a writer and literary scholar, was born in Prague and taught at Princeton.

82. Erich von Kahler, *The Jews among the Nations* (New York: Ungar, 1967).

83. That is, Kahler supported the plan for a binational state—a condition of shared sovereignty in which both populations would enjoy civic parity irrespective of their demographic strength. Philip K. Hitti (1886–1978), a scholar of Islam, was born in Lebanon, received his doctorate from Columbia University, became an American citizen in 1920, and taught for many years at Princeton. His numerous works on the history, literature, and culture of Islam include *History of the Arabs* (London: Macmillan, 1937; later republished in many editions and translations), *Islam and the West* (Princeton, N.J.: Van Nostrand, 1962), *Capital Cities of Arab Islam* (Minneapolis: University of Minnesota Press, 1973), and histories of Lebanon, Syria, and Palestine.

84. Theodor Adorno, "Gruss an Gershom Scholem zum 70. Geburtstag," *Neue Zürcher Zeitung* (December 2, 1967).

85. Franz Kafka, *Briefe an Felice* (Frankfurt: Fischer Verlag, 1967), pp. 703–704.

86. In "Gruß an Gershom Scholem zum 70. Geburtstag," Adorno cites a letter he wrote to Benjamin on May 4, 1938, in which he described his first meeting with Scholem: "It was fascinating. There was even some real contact, which in time developed into a certain sense of trust. It was comparable to an Ichthyosaurus

sitting down for a cup of coffee with a Brontosaurus, or, more to the point, a Leviathan with a Behemoth."

87. Jürgen Habermas (1927–) is a German philosopher and sociologist.

88. Moses Hess (1812–1875) was the author of many works, including *Rom und Jerusalem: Die letzte Nationalitätenfrage* [*Rome and Jerusalem: The Last Nationality Question*] (Leipzig: Wengler, 1862).

89. See Edmund Silberner, *Moses Hess* (Leiden: E. J. Brill, 1966), pp. 126–134; and idem, *Socialisten zur Judenfrage: Ein Beitrag zur Geschichte des Sozialismus vom Anfang des 19. Jahrhunderts bis 1914* (Berlin: Colloquium Verlag, 1962).

90. Georg Friedrich Daumer (1800–1875) was a philosopher of religion.

91. Zugewehnt is a Yiddish expression for "gotten accustomed to."

92. Rudolf Kastner negotiated with Eichmann for several thousand Hungarian Jews to travel by train to Switzerland.

93. Hans Paeschke (1911–1991), a German writer and publicist, was the editor of the periodical *Merkur*, which he founded in 1947.

94. Hannah Arendt, "Walter Benjamin: Die finsteren Zeiten" (Walter Benjamin: The Dark Times), *Merkur* 239 (March 1968): 209–233.

95. Zalman Shazar (1889–1974) was the third president of the State of Israel.

96. Scholem wrote this letter in English.

97. Erna was the wife of Josef Weiss. He committed suicide in 1969.

98. The years 1970–1971 are not represented in this collection. Scholem wrote few letters in 1970. With the exception of his annual trip to the Eranos conference (where he delivered his paper "The Name of God and the Theory of Language in the Kabbalah"), he stayed in Jerusalem most of the year. He published a large number of essays, in English, Hebrew, and German. Suhrkamp Verlag in Frankfurt brought out the second volume of his *Judaica* series. A bibliography of all of his writings, appropriately titled *Bibliography of the Writings of Gershom Scholem*, also appeared. Though relieved of his teaching duties, he remained deeply involved in the work and lives of his closest students. One, Josef Weiss, committed suicide in 1969. In 1971 Scholem divided the year between Jerusalem and Europe. During the summer he attended the Eranos conference. In September he began an extended visit to Bodmer House in Zurich. Schocken Books in New York published *"The Messianic Idea in Judaism" and Other Essays on Jewish Spirituality*.

99. This letter was written in English.

100. Scholem and Fanya were in Sils Maria (near Zurich) from September 1971 to March 1972.

101. *Judaica II* first appeared in 1970.

102. Golo Mann, the son of Thomas Mann and Katja Pringsheim, was Jewish.

103. Hans-Georg Gadamer (1900–) is a German philosopher.

104. Szondi committed suicide on April 23, 1971.

105. Scholem wrote this letter in English.

106. Converts to Christianity.

107. Federal Technical College.

108. Walter Kaufmann (1921–) taught philosophy at Princeton, and translated and edited the works of Nietzsche. Scholem wrote this letter in English.

109. Scholem wrote this letter in English.

110. George Steiner (1929–) is a literary critic.

111. Gershom Scholem, *Sabbatai Sevi: The Mystical Messiah* (Princeton, N.J.: Princeton University Press, 1973).

112. Treptow is a suburb of Berlin.

113. Mircea Eliade (1907–1986) was a Romanian-born historian of religion who taught at the University of Chicago. His profascist writings came to light in the 1970s. Scholem wrote this letter in English.

114. "If one may compare small things to great."

115. Hans Jacob Polotsky (1905–1991), an orientalist and linguist, taught at the Hebrew University.

116. Scholem is referring to Lichtheim's recent suicide attempt.

117. Scholem is alluding to a letter that Lichtheim had written to a mutual friend, Miriam Sambursky, informing her of his intention to take his life.

118. Zippora Scholem was Scholem's great-great-grandmother.

119. Reinhold's son and grandson, respectively.

120. Carl Gustav Jung, *Antwort auf Hiob* (Zurich: Rascher, 1952).

121. Jung believed that one of the most important archetypes was the principle of quaternity, reflected in fourfold structures like mandalas, squares, and crosses. He viewed such structures as symbols of balance, symmetry, and unbroken wholeness.

122. Eliade had written to Scholem on March 10, 1973, denying that he was an anti-Semite. He said that he had not collaborated on any Romanian publications since 1940, and that he had been subjected to harassment by the Romanian secret police. Scholem wrote this letter in English.

123. Lichtheim committed suicide on April 23, 1973.

124. Robert Alter (1935–) is professor of comparative literature at the University of California, Berkeley. Scholem wrote this letter in English.

125. Robert Alter, "The Achievement of Gershom Scholem," *Commentary* (April 1973): 66–77.

126. Gershom Scholem, *"The Messianic Idea in Judaism" and Other Essays on Jewish Spirituality* (New York: Schocken Books, 1971). The review in question is Jacob Agus, "Bringing Clarity into the Mystical," *Judaism,* 21 (Summer 1972): 376–383.

127. Leo Strauss died on October 19, 1973.

128. Cynthia Ozick (1928–) is an American novelist and essayist. This letter was written in English.

129. Scholem wrote this letter in English.

130. Esi was Scholem's cousin. Liesel was the ex-wife of Scholem's cousin Ernst, and David was Ernst's son.

131. *Deutschnationaler* = "German nationalist." The three Scholem brothers were reunited in Zurich in 1971.

132. See Scholem, *Sabbatai Sevi,* p. v. Wilhelm Dilthey (1833–1911) was a German philosopher. Paul Yorck von Wartenburg (1835–1897) was the nephew of a famous Prussian general, Ludwig Yorck von Wartenburg (1759–1830), who played a role in the Napoleonic wars.

133. "May God make this turn out well."

134. Suhrkamp Verlag published Scholem's books in Germany. The work in question here is *Walter Benjamin: Geschichte einer Freundschaft.*

135. The Histadrut is the main trade union organization in Israel.

136. Robert Silvers is the publisher of the *New York Review of Books.* Scholem wrote this letter in English.

137. Scholem spent the summer of 1976, from July to September, in Switzerland.

138. Arthur Koestler, *The Thirteenth Tribe: The Khazar Empire and Its Heritage* (London: Hutchinson, 1976).

139. "Nonsense."

140. "You can go tell that to a goy."

141. See letter dated October 7, 1951.

142. Kurt von Fritz (1900–1985) was a German professor of philosophy and history.

143. Ethiopian kings, who called themselves Negus, traced their origins back to Solomon. The Lion of Judah was the emblem of the Ethiopian royal house.

144. Menachem Begin was the prime minister of Israel from 1977 to 1983.

145. The PLO is the Palestinian Liberation Organization.

146. Daniel Matt (1950–) is a historian of religion. This letter was written in English.

147. Garden of Eden.

148. Scholem wrote this letter in English.

149. Scholem wrote this letter in English.

150. Robert Alter, "Modernism, the Germans, and the Jews," *Commentary,* 65 (March 1978): 61–67. Alter's essay discusses Peter Gay, *Freud, Jews, and Other Germans: Masters and Victims in Modern Culture* (New York: Oxford University Press, 1978).

151. Emil Fackenheim (1916–) was a rabbi and theologian.

152. The reference is to Marcel Dubois, professor of philosophy at the Hebrew University.

153. Letters from 1979 have been omitted from this collection. Scholem spent most of the spring and summer of that year in Europe, mainly in Germany and France. In August he delivered a paper entitled "Identification and Distance" at the Eranos conference. Harvard University Press brought out the first major study of his life and work in English, David Biale's *Gershom Scholem: Kabbalah and Counter-History.*

154. Edna Aizenberg is the author of *The Aleph Weaver* (1984). This letter was written in English.

155. David Biale is a professor of Jewish studies and author of *Gershom Scholem: Kabbalah and Counter-History* (Cambridge, Mass.: Harvard University Press, 1979).

156. Jutta Bohnke-Kollwitz (1923–) was the director of a library in Cologne dedicated to the history of German Jews.

157. Scholem wrote this letter in English.

158. Ozick wrote this letter in English.

159. Scholem wrote this letter in English.

160. A *saddik* is a holy man or religious leader. *Madrega* is the Hebrew word for "level" or "plane."

161. Ruth Nanda Anshen (1900–), born in Massachusetts, is a philosopher and the author of numerous works, including *Our Emergent Civilization* (1947), *Language: An Enquiry into Its Meaning* (1957), and *Anatomy of Evil* (1985). On September 24, 1980, she had written to Scholem sending greetings for the Jewish New Year and enclosing a copy of Cynthia Ozick's article "The Mystic Explorer," *New York Review of Books* (September 21, 1980). The article was originally titled "Gershom Scholem: His Memoirs, His Shadow." Scholem wrote this letter in English.

162. *Milchigdige,* a term relating to kosher laws, means a dairy meal—a meal with no meat.

163. Arthur Scholem (b. 1923) was Erich's son and Scholem's nephew.

164. The Friedhof Weissensee, the largest Jewish cemetery in Europe, is located in eastern Berlin. Their visit was to the grave of Scholem's father, Arthur. The names of Betty and Werner had also been inscribed on the marker after the war.

165. David was Scholem's nephew (Erich's son). This letter was written in English.

166. A reference to Betty ("Oma" means "Grandmother").

167. Book of Psalms.

168. The reference is to Felix Noeggerath (1885–1960). Noeggerath was born in New York, emigrated to Germany prior to World War I, and studied philosophy and linguistics in Munich, where he became friendly with Walter Benjamin. Scholem's essay was published as "Walter Benjamin und Felix Noeggerath," *Merkur,* 35 (February 1981): 134–169.

169. Hannah Tillich was a German Jew and the wife of the Christian theologian Paul Tillich. On October 16, 1980, she had written to Scholem in English, saying she had gotten the impression that certain attitudes in Israel were overly militaristic and nationalistic, that Scholem and his wife supported these views, and that the "real Jewish spirit" was expressed by Max Horkheimer and Friedrich Pollock, members of the Frankfurt School.

170. Scholem wrote this letter in English.

171. Daniel Bell (1919–) is an American sociologist. This letter was written in English.

172. Scholem wrote this letter in English.

173. Helmut Becker (1913–) was a professor of political science at the Freie Universität in Berlin.

174. The order Pour le Mérite is Germany's highest distinction.

175. Scholem is referring to the victory of Menachem Begin and his coalition in the 1981 elections.

176. Dina Waschitz was Scholem's cousin (daughter of his uncle Theobald).

177. Daliyyah is a kibbutz in northern Israel.

178. Eugen Kogon, *Der SS-Staat: Das System der deutschen Konzentrationslager* (Berlin: Verlag des Druckhauses Templehof, 1947).

179. On January 9, 1982, Anshen had written to Scholem in English, expressing concern about his health. Scholem wrote this response in English.

180. Rudolf zur Lippe was a fellow at the Wissenschaftskolleg in Berlin in 1981–1982, along with Scholem.

181. Peter Wapnewski (1922–), a historian, was the director of the Wissenschaftskolleg in Berlin.

182. Pilegesch ("Concubine") was a discussion circle that formed in Jerusalem during World War II.

183. "Primordial phenomenon."

SELECTED BIBLIOGRAPHY

Scholem's writings comprise more than six hundred individual books, articles, and review essays. All but a handful are in Hebrew or German. The short bibliography below includes the most important works that have appeared in English translation. The secondary sources dealing with Scholem are also quite numerous; those listed here are only the ones accessible to a general readership.

Works by Gershom Scholem

The Correspondence of Walter Benjamin and Gershom Scholem, 1932–1940. Trans. Gary Smith and Andre Lefevere. New York: Schocken Books, 1989. Reprint Cambridge, Mass.: Harvard University Press, 1992.

From Berlin to Jerusalem: Memories of My Youth. Trans. Harry Zohn. New York: Schocken Books, 1980. Reprint 1988.

Jewish Gnosticism, Merkabah Mysticism, and Talmudic Tradition. 2nd ed. New York: Jewish Theological Seminary of America, 1965.

Major Trends in Jewish Mysticism. 3rd ed. New York: Schocken Books, 1954. Reprint 1961, 1995.

"The Messianic Idea in Judaism" and Other Essays on Jewish Spirituality. New York: Schocken Books, 1971. Reprint 1974, 1995.

"The Name of God and the Linguistic Theory of the Kabbalah." *Diogenes,* 79 (1972): 59–80.

On Jews and Judaism in Crisis: Selected Essays. Ed. Werner J. Dannhauser. New York: Schocken Books, 1976.

On the Kabbalah and Its Symbolism. Trans. Ralph Manheim. New York: Schocken Books, 1965. Reprint 1969.

On the Mystical Shape of the Godhead: Basic Concepts in the Kabbalah. Ed. Jonathan Chipman. Trans. Joachim Neugroschel. New York: Schocken Books, 1991.

"On the Possibility of Jewish Mysticism in Our Time" and Other Essays. Ed. Avra-

ham Shapira. Trans. Jonathan Chipman. Philadelphia: Jewish Publication Society of America, 1997.

Origins of the Kabbalah. Ed. R. J. Zwi Werblowsky. Trans. Allan Arkush. Princeton, N.J.: Princeton University Press, 1987.

Sabbatai Sevi: The Mystical Messiah, 1626–1676. Trans. R. J. Zwi Werblowsky. Princeton, N.J.: Princeton University Press, 1973.

"Tradition and Commentary as Religious Categories in Judaism." *Judaism,* 15 (1966): 23–39.

Walter Benjamin: The Story of a Friendship. Trans. Harry Zohn. Philadelphia: Jewish Publication Society of America, 1981.

Zohar, the Book of Splendor: Basic Readings from the Kabbalah. New York: Schocken Books, 1995.

GENERAL WORKS

Alter, Robert. *Necessary Angels: Tradition and Modernity in Kafka, Benjamin, and Scholem.* Cambridge, Mass.: Harvard University Press, 1991.

Biale, David. *Gershom Scholem: Kabbalah and Counter-History.* Cambridge, Mass.: Harvard University Press, 1979. Reprint 1982.

Handelman, Susan A. *Fragments of Redemption: Jewish Thought and Literary Theory in Benjamin, Scholem, and Levinas.* Bloomington: Indiana University Press, 1991.

Mendes-Flohr, Paul, ed. *Gershom Scholem: The Man and His Work.* Albany: State University of New York Press, 1994.

Wasserstrom, Steven. *Religion after Religion: Gershom Scholem, Mircea Eliade, and Henry Corbin at Eranos.* Princeton, N.J.: Princeton University Press, 1999.

CHRONOLOGY

1897   December 5: Gerhard (Gershom) Scholem is born in Berlin.

1911   Celebrates his bar mitzvah in Berlin's Reformed synagogue.

1913   Begins his association with the Zionist group Jung Juda.

1914   Becomes a follower of Martin Buber.

1915   Leaves *Gymnasium* early and begins studying mathematics at the University of Jena.

       Meets Walter Benjamin.

1916   Breaks with Buber.

1917   January 27: Werner Scholem is arrested for participating in an anti-war demonstration on the kaiser's birthday.

       February 15: Gerhard is ordered out of the house by his father for opposing the war.

       May: Receives his draft papers.

       End of August: Released from the military for reasons of health.

       October: Begins studies at the University of Jena.

1918   January–April: Continues coursework at the University of Jena.

       End of January: Meets Escha Burchhardt.

       May: In Muri and Bern.

1919   January–September: In Muri.

       Fall: Begins studies in Munich, including mathematics, philosophy, and Semitic languages.

1921   Publishes his first essay on the Kabbalah, "Lyrik der Kabbala?" (in *Der Jude*).

1922   Teaches at Franz Rosenzweig's Lehrhaus in Frankfurt.

1923   End of January: Finishes dissertation on *Das Buch Bahir*.

       September 14: Emigrates to Palestine.

       Begins work as head of the Hebrew and Judaic Department of the National Library in Jerusalem.

       December 5: Marries Escha.

1924   May 4: Werner Scholem is elected to the Reichstag as a member
        of the German Communist Party.
        Gershom Scholem translates Agnon's short stories "Rise and Fall"
        and "Two Tales" for *Der Jude*.

1925   February 6: Arthur Scholem dies.
        April 1: The Hebrew University opens.
        October: Gershom Scholem begins teaching at the Hebrew Univer-
        sity.

1926   March–May: Betty visits her son in Palestine.

1927   Spring–summer: Scholem pursues research in Europe.

1928   Publishes "On the Theology of Sabbatianism in Light of Abraham
        Cardozo" (in German), in *Der Jude*.

1929   Arab-Jewish conflict in Palestine intensifies.
        Scholem actively supports Brit Shalom.

1931   March–May: Betty visits Jerusalem, accompanied by Scholem's
        brother Erich.
        Economic crisis in Germany worsens.

1932   March–October: Scholem conducts research in Italy and Germany.

1933   January: Hitler comes to power in Germany.
        February 23: Werner Scholem and his wife, Emmy, are arrested.
        September: Gershom Scholem appointed full professor in the field
        of Kabbalah studies.
        December: Emmy Scholem released from prison.
        Gershom Scholem's *Das Buch Bahir* published by Schocken Verlag
        in Berlin.

1935   March: Werner sent to concentration camp.
        Schocken Verlag publishes *The Secrets of Creation: Selections from the
        Zohar* (in German), edited by Scholem.

1936   April–May: Betty Scholem visits Jerusalem.
        Summer: Gershom Scholem and Escha are divorced.
        December 4: Scholem marries Fanya Freud.
        Publishes "Understanding Sabbatianism" (in German), in the
        Schocken Almanach.
        Publishes "Redemption through Sin" (in Hebrew).

1937   Werner Scholem is moved to Dachau.
        Gershom Scholem publishes "Kabbalah at the Hebrew University,"
        in *Reconstructionist*.

1938   February–July: Holds visiting professorship at the Jewish Institute of
        Religion in New York. On the way back to Palestine, sees Ben-
        jamin for the last time.

	Summer: Reinhold and Erich Scholem emigrate to Australia with their families.
	September: Werner is transferred to Buchenwald.
1939	March: Betty emigrates to Australia.
	March 28: Gershom and Betty meet for the last time in Port Said.
1940	July: Werner is murdered at Buchenwald.
	September: Benjamin commits suicide.
	December: Scholem publishes "Sabbatai Sevi and Nathan of Gaza" (in Hebrew), in the *Schocken Almanach*.
1941	Summer: Scholem is named dean of the humanities faculty at the Hebrew University.
	Publishes *Major Trends in Jewish Mysticism*.
1946	April–October: Travels to Europe on behalf of the Hebrew University to rescue and preserve Jewish libraries.
	May 5: Betty Scholem dies.
1948	May 14: State of Israel is founded.
1949	Scholem travels to New York to deliver the Hilda Stroock Lectures at the Jewish Institute of Religion.
	Summer: Participates in the Eranos conference in Ascona, Switzerland.
1957	Publishes *Sabbatai Sevi* (in Hebrew).
1959	Delivers lecture entitled "Understanding the Messianic Idea in Judaism," at the Eranos conference.
	Travels to Poland to conduct research.
1961	Pursues research at the Warburg Institute in London.
1963	The first volume of *Judaica* appears in Germany.
1964	Scholem delivers the Leo Baeck Memorial Lecture in New York, on Walter Benjamin.
1966	Edits Walter Benjamin's correspondence, in cooperation with Theodor Adorno.
1967	Six-Day War in Israel.
	Scholem celebrates his seventieth birthday.
1968	Receives honorary doctorate at the University of Zurich.
	Elected president of the Israeli Academy of Sciences and Humanities.
1970	Magnes Press, at the Hebrew University, publishes a complete bibliography of Scholem's writings.
1971	Scholem publishes *"The Messianic Idea in Judaism" and Other Essays on Jewish Spirituality*.
1972	September–March: In Switzerland.

1973   April 23: George Lichtheim commits suicide.

          Sabbatai Sevi is published in English.

          July–September: Scholem is in Sils Maria, Ascona, and Zurich.

          September–October: In the United States. Receives honorary doctorate at the Jewish Theological Seminary.

1974   Receives prize from the Bavarian Academy of Arts. Delivers address entitled "My Way to the Kabbalah."

1976   Publishes *On Jews and Judaism in Crisis: Selected Essays.*

1977   Publishes *From Berlin to Jerusalem: Memories of My Youth* (in German).

          December 5: Celebrates eightieth birthday.

1980   Edits *Walter Benjamin—Gershom Scholem: Correspondence, 1933–1940* (in German).

1981   February: Publishes "Walter Benjamin und Felix Noeggerath," in *Merkur.*

          Publishes *Walter Benjamin: The Story of a Friendship* in English.

          Summer: Honored with admission to the order Pour le Mérite by the German government.

          October–December: At the Wissenschaftskolleg in Berlin.

          Mid-December: Returns to Jerusalem for health reasons.

1982   February 21: Dies in Jerusalem.

          "Walter Benjamin's Ancestors and Relatives" (in German) is published in the *Bulletin des Leo Baeck Instituts.*

INDEX

Adler, H. G., 396

Adorno, Theodor Wiesengrund, 286, 300–301, 305, 404–405, 412–413, 423–424, 426, 432–433; and Benjamin, 215, 306, 312, 313, 314, 317, 325, 518n69; and GS, 215, 298–299, 325–326, 327, 349; and Heidegger, 392–393; and Judaism, 405; and Jung, 405; and Lichtheim, 428, 431, 432

Aggada, 107, 507n13

Agnon, Esther Marx, 106

Agnon, S. J., 15, 89, 90, 94, 106, 174, 323, 347, 360, 427; *Shira,* 210

Agus, Jacob, 454

Aizenberg, Edna, 478–479

Aliyah, 145–146, 510n74

Alter, Robert, 454, 474

Anshen, Ruth Nanda, 481–482, 492

Arendt, Hannah Stern, 215, 269, 305, 308, 319–320, 326–329, 330, 334, 352, 381–382, 394–400, 401–403, 433–434, 487–488; *Eichmann in Jerusalem,* 352, 394–398, 399–400, 433, 487–488; "Jewish History, Revised," 352; "Walter Benjamin: Die finsteren Zeiten," 433–434; "Zionism Reconsidered," 330–331, 333

Arlozoroff, Haim, 239, 515n23

Arndt, Adolf, 418, 419

Asch, Sholem, 323

Baal Shem Tov, 23, 501n4

Bab Mezia, 39, 114, 503n32

Baeck, Leo, 334–336, 393–394, 396

Bartinora: commentary on Mischna Bab Mezia, 114

Baudelaire, Charles, 383

Becker, Helmut, 489

Begin, Menachem, 470

Bell, Daniel, 487–488

Ben-Gurion, David, 95, 96, 332

Benjamin, Dora Kellner, 16, 74, 75, 76, 78, 314–315, 368, 375, 413

Benjamin, Stefan, 150, 311

Benjamin, Walter, 65, 76, 110–111, 277, 285–286, 294–295, 303–304, 480; and Adorno, 215, 306, 312, 313, 314, 317, 325, 518n69; and Arendt, 433; and Arthur Scholem, 112; and Baudelaire, 383; and Bloch, 507n17; and Brod, 518n79; and Buber, 16, 18, 28, 169, 502n14; and Capri, 133–134; and career, 92–93, 158; and Communism, 138, 139, 155; death of, 214, 308, 309, 311, 312, 313; and de Haan's murder, 136; and detective novels, 44–45; and Dora, 16, 314–315, 368; and education, 92, 102, 103, 144; estate of, 317; and experience, 18; and family, 478; as German, 409, 421–422; and German economy, 196–197; and GS, 15–16, 17, 18–19, 48–49, 61, 63–64, 70, 71, 73, 77, 78, 90, 92, 93, 102, 115, 121, 169, 180–181, 184, 201–202, 209, 215, 216, 243, 261, 265, 268, 296–297, 301, 304, 305–306, 308, 309, 311–312,

Benjamin, Walter *(continued)*
314–315, 317, 325, 327, 328, 349–
350, 351, 379–380, 382–383, 385–
386, 408, 409, 413, 415, 416, 420,
421–422, 433–434, 464, 484–485,
501n10, 507n28, 518n77; and Hartung, 421; and health, 16, 43, 50; and
Hebrew, 49, 92, 93, 116, 145, 158,
164, 166, 169, 433, 434; and Heidegger, 392–393; and history, 15, 18; and
Hölderlin, 392; and Horkheimer,
518n69; immigration, 306; and Institute of Social Research, 215, 517n60,
518n69; and Judaism, 29, 38, 57, 67,
74–75, 92, 93, 115–116, 150, 180–
181, 184, 351, 383–384, 416, 420,
421–422, 507n28; and Kabbalah, 382;
and Kafka, 209, 328, 422–423; and
Klee, 121, 380, 508n38; and Kraft,
44, 74, 75, 313; and Krauss, 383; and
language, 18, 38, 44, 49, 50, 51, 73,
74, 145, 502n27, 503nn44,45; literary
estate of, 215, 314, 327, 328, 349–
350, 368, 379–380, 382, 408, 420;
and literary exegesis, 138–139; and
Marxism, 383; and messianism, 15, 18;
and metaphysics, 382–383; and Palestine, 92, 93, 134, 136, 144, 164–166,
169, 243, 261, 263, 265, 268, 274,
278–279, 280, 295, 296–297, 301–
302, 384; and Paris, 207; and Paris arcades, 164, 512n107; and politics,
196–197; and Reinhold Scholem,
464; and Schocken, 305; and secret letters, 45–46; and Surrealism, 169; and
tradition, 18; and translation, 48–49;
and Zionism, 197, 433, 434, 447.
WORKS: "Franz Kafka," 328; "Johann
Jakob Bachofen," 385–386; *One-Way
Street,* 169; "On Language as Such
and on the Language of Man," 19,
50, 51, 502n27, 503nn44,45; "The
Role of Language in *Trauerspiel* and
Tragedy," 74; "Task of the Translator," 121; "Two Poems by Friedrich
Hölderlin," 328; "The Work of Art
in the Age of Its Technological Reproducibility," 383

Bergmann, Escha Burchhardt Scholem,
73, 75–76, 77–79, 81–82, 114, 166,
186–187, 247–248, 249, 340–341;
and GS, 77, 89, 91, 93, 101–102,
107, 128, 200, 273, 274, 504n69; and
health, 128, 257, 260, 271–272; and
Hugo Bergmann, 91, 211, 274, 277
Bergmann, Hugo, 10, 91, 93–94, 96,
136, 179, 210, 211, 255, 274, 277,
340–341, 364; "Zum fünfzigsten
Geburtstag," 521n140
Berlin, Isaiah, 450
Biale, David, 477, 480, 481
Bialik, Chaim Nachman, 94, 95, 507n13
Bleichrode, Isaac, 39
Bloch, Ernst: *Spirit of Utopia,* 89, 109,
507n17
Blum, Edgar, 14, 31, 32, 37–38, 39
Blumenfeld, Kurt, 326–327
Böhlich, Walter, 353–354
Bohnke-Kollwitz, Jutta, 478
Borges, Jorge Luis, 477, 478–479
Brauer, Erich, 14, 28, 30–32, 46–47,
99, 101, 102, 112–115, 126–127,
501nn10,11
Brauer, Grete, 14, 69–72, 89
Briggs, Kenneth, 479, 480, 481
Brod, Max, 10, 163, 168, 416, 420–421,
518n79
Buber, Martin, 28–30, 245; and Benja-
min, 16, 18, 28, 169, 502n14; and Bergmann, 91; and Bible translation, 151,
152, 153; death of, 412–413; and GS,
11–12, 18, 38, 57, 110, 149, 151–
152, 153, 160, 216–217, 227, 254,
255–256, 285, 341, 393, 412–413,
476; and Hebrew University, 247,
254, 255–256; and Heidegger, 475,
476; and Jesus, 432; and Judaism, 9–
10, 57; *Der Jude,* 90; and Palestine,
153, 184, 265–266, 285; *Three
Speeches,* 23; and World War I, 12
Burchhardt, Escha. *See* Bergmann, Escha
Burchhardt Scholem

Celan, Paul, 468
Chochma, 106, 506n9
Cohen, Gerson, 454

Cohen, Geula, 386–387
Cohen, Hermann, 77, 80, 390, 412
Cramer, Samuel, 446
Czaczkes. *See* Agnon, S. J.

Daumer, Georg Friedrich, 431, 432
Dawidowicz, Lucy, 480, 481
De Haan, Jacob, 136
Dylan, Bob, 473–474

Edman, Irwin, 320
Eichmann, Adolf, 397, 401–403
Eliade, Mircea, 351, 444–445, 452–453
Ellenberger, Henri F., 423

Fackenheim, Emil, 475–476
Falkenberg, Hans-Geert, 365–366
Frank, Jacob, 15, 212–213, 417
Freud, Fanya. *See* Scholem, Fanya Freud
Freud, Sigmund, 405, 417, 442, 464,
    474
Friedmann, Georges, 411–412
Fromm, Erich, 151, 442

Gadamer, Hans-Georg, 90, 439–440,
    476
Galut, 48, 503n41
Gaon, 515n17
Gay, Peter, 474
George, Stefan, 325
Gerhardt, Ulrich, 233–234
Goldberg, Gerda, 17, 53–55
Goldberg, Oskar, 148–149
Gollancz, Victor, 385
Grumach, Ernst, 334

Habermas, Jürgen, 428, 453–454
Habermas, Ute, 453–454
Halachah, 107, 507n13
Hallo, Rudolf, 117
Haluz / haluzim, 145–146, 510n75
Hartung, Rudolf, 420–423
Haznea lechet, 117, 508n31
Heidegger, Martin, 269, 392–393, 475,
    476
Heine, Heinrich, 312
Heller, Aharon, 14, 43, 44, 47–48, 49–
    50, 59, 76–77

Hess, Moses, 429, 430
Heymann, Harry, 14, 31, 39–40, 58–59,
    64, 65–66, 68–69, 504n65
Hildesheimer, Israel, 37
Hirsch, Arthur, 131, 306
Hirsch, Samson Raphael, 149; *Der Penta-
    teuch,* 39, 503n31
Hitler, Adolf, 89, 201, 208, 217, 218,
    219, 220, 221, 224
Hitti, Philip, 425
Hofmannsthal, Hugo von, 325
Hölderlin, Johann Friedrich, 49, 328,
    392
Hommel, Fritz, 134–135
Horkheimer, Max, 215, 286, 518n69
Horowitz, Joseph, 144
Hurwitz, Siegmund, 336–337, 338–339,
    340, 450–451

Israel, Lucien, 417
Israel ben Eliezer, 501n4

Jabotinsky, Zev, 95–96
Jaffe, Aniela, 393–394, 405–406
Jahr, Meta, 14, 106–107, 323, 324,
    515n23
Jalkut, 107, 507n12
Jens, Walter, 429
Jesus, 323, 431, 432
Jonas, Hans, 210, 327, 346, 494–495
Jung, C. G., 345, 347, 351, 361, 393–
    394, 404, 405, 406, 423, 450–451,
    477, 478, 529n121; *Answer to Job,* 451

Kafka, Franz, 10, 161, 163, 168, 201,
    209, 328, 414–415, 416, 420–421,
    422–423, 426, 427, 436
Kahler, Erich von, 424–425, 527n83
Kant, Immanuel, 66
Kaufmann, Walter, 442
Kiddush haschem, 111
Kierkegaard, Søren, 429, 432
Klee, Paul: *Angelus Novus,* 121, 380,
    508n38
Koestler, Arthur, 170, 327, 450, 452,
    464–465
Kohn, Hans, 10, 96, 119–121, 319, 320
Koschel, Gotthard, 351, 376, 378–379

Kraft, Werner, 44, 45–46, 50–52, 55–
    58, 59–60, 62–63, 65, 66–67, 74–75,
    101–102, 137–138, 162–163, 168,
    210, 261, 313
Kurzweil, Baruch, 374–375

Lacis, Asja, 93, 368
Lasker-Schüler, Elsa, 210
Lehmann, Siegfried, 32–37, 40
Leon, George, 436
Levy, Harry, 141
Lichtheim, George, 348, 376–378, 427–
    432, 445–448, 453, 468
Ludwig, Emil, 218
Luria, Isaac, 214
Luther, Martin, 118

Mackel, Michael, 410–411, 413–414
Madrega, 481, 531n160
Magnes, Judah, 92, 93, 94, 163, 164, 165,
    179, 180, 255, 335, 336, 341, 368
Maimonides, Moses: *Guide for the Per-
    plexed,* 89, 114
Mann, Golo, 444
Marcuse, Herbert, 317, 408
Margulies, Heinrich, 29
Marx, Karl, 442
Marxism, 34
Matt, Daniel, 471–474
Mendelssohn, Moses, 389
Meyer, Karl, 230
Mida, 106, 506n9
Midrash, 507n12
Moses de León: *Sefer ha-Zohar,* 21, 227,
    228, 262, 268, 272, 291, 292, 298–
    299, 473, 501n42

Nathan Benjamin of Gaza, 348, 349
Nietzsche, Friedrich, 14, 26, 454
Noeggerath, Felix, 201–202, 349–350
Notker Labeo, 118

Oko, Adolph S., 317–318, 319–320
Ozick, Cynthia, 354, 456–457, 479–481

Paeschke, Hans, 433–434
Paul, Jean. *See* Richter, Johann Paul
Plato, 66

Richter, Johann Paul, 88, 91, 504n54
Rosenzweig, Edith, 181–183, 267–268,
    516n47
Rosenzweig, Franz, 90–91, 96, 117–
    118, 148, 149, 151, 152, 153, 267–
    268, 368, 506n17, 508n41, 516n47;
    The Star of Redemption, 88, 181–183,
    184–185
Rubaschoff, Zalman, 15

Sabbatai Sevi, 15, 303, 312, 317, 345,
    348–349, 443, 522n5
Sadat, Anwar, 469, 470
Saddik, 48, 481, 503n40, 531n160
Salomon, Albert, 382–384
Scheerbart, Paul, 88, 91
Schiepan, Käte, 42–43, 161, 225, 269,
    321, 503n33
Schloesser, Manfred, 352, 388–391, 408,
    409–410
Schneider, Lambert, 216–217, 227–228
Schocken, Salman, 123, 212, 216, 261,
    262, 291, 302, 304, 305, 307–308,
    312, 329, 360, 514n1, 518nn76,77
Schoen, Ernst, 379–381
Schoenberg, Arnold, 404
Scholem, Arthur, 103–104, 108–109,
    113; and business, 91, 195; death of,
    92, 141–143; and Germany, 80, 81,
    97, 98, 104, 124–125; grave of, 217,
    482–483, 485, 486, 531n164; and GS,
    10, 15, 16, 41–43, 53, 58, 89, 90,
    101, 107, 111–112, 118–119, 128,
    347, 434, 444; and health, 88, 91,
    118, 125; and visit to Palestine, 130;
    and Werner Scholem, 10, 11, 13, 24,
    42, 143, 237–238; and will, 195
Scholem, Arthur (Erich's son), 333,
    482–483, 485
Scholem, Betty, 101, 103–104, 107–
    109, 111–112, 113, 168, 198,
    199–200, 201, 203–204; and anti-
    Semitism, 129, 133, 187–188, 219,
    222, 224, 225, 228, 229, 241–242,
    250, 297; and Arthur Scholem's death,
    141–143, 144, 217; and Australia,
    303, 310, 333; and Benjamin, 311;
    death of, 350; and emigration, 214,

228, 244, 282–283, 286–287, 288–
290, 292–293, 295, 296, 297; and
Emmy Scholem, 230–231, 232, 234,
235–236, 237, 242–243, 244–245,
250; and family conflicts, 10–11; and
finances, 194, 281, 283; and Fontana,
310; and Germany, 79, 80–81, 82–83,
87, 97–99, 104, 105, 123–124, 125–
126, 127, 129, 132, 143–144, 187–
188, 192–194, 202, 208–210, 217,
218–219, 221–223, 224–225, 228,
234–235, 241–242, 250; gifts from,
92, 108–109, 159, 161, 165, 273,
281, 323; and GS, 61, 62, 87, 92,
147–148, 229, 248, 282, 284, 295,
296, 310, 312; and health, 225–226,
229, 316; and Hebrew University,
143; and Heine, 312; and Jerusalem,
259; and Jewish-Arab conflict, 171,
173, 175–176, 177–178, 251; and
memoirs, 130, 136–137; and money
transfers, 246; and Palestine, 138, 147,
170, 177–178, 222, 273, 290, 320,
321; and politics, 81, 82–83, 132,
143–144, 202–203; and Schiepan,
321; and Stefan Benjamin, 311; under
surveillance, 246; and Theresienstadt,
321; and travel, 138, 147, 152, 154,
166, 167, 188–189, 190, 191–192,
273, 290, 320, 321; and Uncle Katz,
135–136; and Werner Scholem, 61,
132, 133, 156–157, 218, 219–220,
221, 230–231, 232, 234, 235–236,
237, 238–240, 242–243, 244–245,
250, 256–257, 258, 259–260, 264,
265, 266, 267, 270–271, 278, 279,
287–288, 290, 294, 295, 303, 306–
307; and World War I, 79; and Zionism, 140

Scholem, David, 483–484, 486

Scholem, Edith (daughter of Werner and
Emmy), 126, 232, 237, 240–241, 242,
245, 250, 508n44

Scholem, Edith (Erich's wife), 271, 290,
294

Scholem, Emmy Wiechelt (Werner's
wife), 67, 88, 132, 289; flight of, 256,
257; in prison, 230, 232, 234, 235–

236, 237, 240, 242–243, 244–245,
250; and Werner Scholem, 219, 220,
221, 264, 486, 491, 504n64

Scholem, Erich, 12, 83, 230–231, 237,
240, 294; and Arthur Scholem, 10,
143; and Australia, 214, 292, 297–
298, 299, 333; and business, 192–193;
death of, 407; and emigration, 282–
283; and Germany, 208–209, 221,
222

Scholem, Escha Burchhardt. *See* Bergmann, Escha Burchhardt Scholem

Scholem, Fanya Freud, 211, 247, 277,
310, 415, 435, 438, 441, 481, 482,
494–495

Scholem, Gershom: and Adorno, 215,
298–299, 325–326, 327, 349; and anarchism, 23, 26; and anti-Semitism,
47, 53, 111, 187, 201, 226–227, 233,
245, 317, 331, 346, 365, 366, 390,
445, 453; and Arendt, 269, 330–331,
332, 334, 352, 394–398, 433–434,
487–488; and Arthur Scholem, 10,
15, 16, 41–43, 53, 58, 89, 90, 101,
107, 111–112, 118–119, 347, 434,
444; autobiography of, 388; and Bavarian Academy of Fine Arts, 458; and
Ben-Gurion, 332; and Benjamin, 15–
16, 17, 18–19, 48–49, 61, 63–64, 70,
71, 73, 77, 78, 90, 92, 93, 102, 115,
121, 169, 180–181, 184, 201–202,
209, 215, 216, 243, 261, 265, 268,
296–297, 301, 304, 305–306, 308,
309, 311–312, 314–315, 317, 325,
327, 328, 349–350, 351, 379–380,
382–383, 385–386, 408, 409, 413,
415, 416, 420, 421–422, 433–434,
464, 484–485, 501n10, 507n28,
518n77; and Bergmann, 91, 93–94;
and Betty Scholem, 61, 62, 87, 92,
147–148, 229, 248, 282, 284, 295,
296, 310; and Bible, 16, 48–49, 51,
70, 71, 72–73, 74, 79, 80, 89–90, 95,
107, 152, 153, 503n34, 505n77; and
Blau-Weisse Brille, 14, 31; and Bloch,
89, 110; and Borges, 477, 478–479;
and Brauer, 14, 69–72, 89; and Brit
Shalom, 96, 176, 177, 185, 211, 331–

Scholem, Gershom *(continued)*
332, 512n122; and Brod, 163, 168;
and Buber, 11–12, 18, 38, 57, 110,
149, 152, 153, 160, 254, 255–256,
285, 341, 393, 412–413, 476; and career, 41, 89–90, 91, 94, 103, 111–
112, 119, 127, 135, 147–148, 151–
152, 159, 210, 213, 215, 223, 248,
280–281, 282, 284, 310–311, 345,
347–348, 381, 400–401, 408, 434–
435, 440–441, 508nn41,45; and Catastrophe, 395, 396, 397; and Christianity, 182, 323, 377–378, 385, 432; and
Cohen, 386–387; and community, 48,
100; criticism of, 467–468; and Czech
Jewry, 294, 296; death of, 353, 494–
495; and detective novels, 44–45; and
diary, 11; and education, 16, 25, 29–
30, 77–78, 89, 90, 103, 106–107,
112–114, 507n14; and Eichmann,
401–402; and Eliade, 452–453; and
emigration to Palestine, 146, 230, 231,
235, 239, 269, 276, 292, 329, 510n75;
and English-Italian crisis, 269; and Eranos conferences, 345, 347, 393, 394,
409, 413; and Erich, 407; and Escha
Scholem Bergmann, 77, 89, 91, 93,
101–102, 107, 128, 200, 273, 274,
504n69; eulogies for, 353–354; and
evil, 23, 55, 397–398, 402; and family, 10–11; and family business, 195–
196; and Fanya Scholem, 211, 247,
277, 415, 435, 441, 481, 482, 495;
and finances, 107, 159, 195, 200, 281;
and Frank, 15, 212–213, 417; and
Freies Jüdisches Lehrhaus, 90, 91; and
Freud, 417, 442, 464, 474; and German refugees, 223; and Germany, 8,
87, 89, 91, 111, 209, 226–227, 231,
233, 245, 252, 292; and Great Britain,
146, 269, 276, 294–295, 302, 329,
340, 341, 356; and greatness, 394; and
Haganah, 176–177, 356, 512n121;
and Hartung, 420, 421–422; and
Hasidim/Hasidism, 23, 25, 37; and
health, 16, 43, 44, 46, 47–48, 49, 50,
53, 59, 62, 73, 77, 106, 260, 291,
441, 491, 492, 493–494; and Hebrew,

12, 15, 16, 19, 20, 37, 39, 51, 52, 58,
78, 96, 106, 117, 145, 257, 443–444,
510n70; and Hebrew University, 94,
146, 147, 148, 153, 210, 215, 223,
248, 253–254, 255, 261, 304, 334–
338, 346, 355, 356, 358–359; and history, 2, 15, 26, 54, 80; and Hitler,
201, 220, 221; and holiness, 48, 55;
and inheritance, 193, 195; and Israel,
347, 412, 415, 418–419, 424, 469,
470–471, 486, 489; and Jesus, 323,
432; and Jewish-Arab conflict, 95–96,
171, 172–175, 176–177, 179, 211,
239, 251–252, 274, 275–276, 295,
331–332, 356–357, 386–387, 424;
and Jewish-German relationship, 28,
35, 58, 67, 351–352, 378–379, 389–
391, 400–401, 409–410, 411–412,
413–416, 439; and Jewish Institute of
Religion, 280–281, 282, 284, 517n68;
and Jewish legion, 154–155, 511n90;
and Jewish modernism, 88–89; and
Jewish National and University Library, 135; and Jewish state, 96, 278,
279–280, 292, 321, 340, 341; and
Job, 79, 451; and Judaism, 12, 15, 19,
20, 28, 30, 34, 35, 36, 37, 38, 39–40,
51, 52, 54, 55, 57, 58, 64, 67, 80,
110–111, 182, 227, 301, 331, 351–
352, 372–373, 378–379, 381, 385,
389–391, 395, 396, 400–401, 404–
405, 409–410, 411–412, 413–416,
418–419, 431–432, 439, 443–444,
451, 457, 464, 466; and *Jüdische Wochenblatt,* 140–141; and Jung, 351,
404, 405, 406, 423, 450–451, 477,
478; and Jung Juda, 14, 47; and Kabbalah, 1, 17, 18, 19, 20, 21, 36, 39,
89, 90, 93, 94, 107, 113, 114, 119,
155, 207–208, 212, 213–214, 227–
228, 252, 262, 263, 268, 272, 291–
292, 298–299, 300, 304, 308–309,
311, 325, 345, 349, 367, 393, 423,
436, 473, 478–479; and Kabbalah institute, 329; and Kafka, 163, 168, 201,
209, 414–415, 416, 420–421, 426,
427, 436; and Koestler, 452, 464–465;
and Kohn, 119–120; and language,

12, 15, 17, 18, 19, 20, 37, 39, 50, 51, 52, 54, 58, 63, 72, 73, 74, 78, 89, 96, 103, 104–105, 106, 117–118, 145, 152, 153, 183, 257–258, 272, 510n70; and libraries, 334–339, 346, 355, 361, 365–366; and Lichtheim, 428; and Luther, 152; and Magnes, 341; and Manichaeism, 252, 516n37; and mass murder, 328; and mathematics, 113–114, 504n55; and messianism, 15, 100, 101, 377, 378, 381; metaphysical system, 503n37; and the middle class, 7–8; and the military, 13, 16, 44, 45, 46–47, 48, 49–50, 53, 56–57, 58–59, 60, 65–66, 68; and morality, 23, 33, 47–48; and music, 404; and mysticism, 227, 257–258, 272, 404–405, 457; and myth, 7, 25, 26–27, 95, 367, 404; and Nietzsche, 14, 26, 454; and order Pour le Mérite, 353, 489, 490; and oriental religion, 361; and Palestine, 90, 91, 93, 94, 95, 96, 137–138, 145–146, 171, 172–175, 176–177, 179, 211, 230, 231, 235, 238, 239, 243, 251–252, 269, 274, 275–276, 278, 279–280, 292, 294–295, 302, 312, 323, 329, 331–332, 341, 346–347, 356–357, 386–387, 510n75; and philosophy, 51, 52, 53–55, 66; and politics, 22–23, 26, 95, 96, 109, 179, 187, 211, 469, 470–471; and psychology, 361, 371; and reactionaries, 332; and Rehavia house, 199, 200, 201–202, 210; and Reinhold, 350–351, 462–463, 489–490; reputation, 207, 319, 345; and Romanticism, 454; and Rosenzweig, 88, 148, 149, 152, 153, 181–183, 184–185, 267–268; and Sabbatai Sevi, 15, 303, 312, 345, 348–349, 443; and Sabbatianism, 304, 317, 325, 329, 349, 369–370, 371, 374, 375, 511n93; and Schlegel, 141; and Schocken Verlag, 212, 216–217; and Scholem school of research, 304, 518n76; and sectarianism, 331; and secularization, 96–97, 426, 510n70; and *Sefer ha-Bahir,* 89, 114, 252, 304; and *Sefer ha-Zohar,* 21, 227, 228, 262, 268,

272, 291, 292, 298–299, 473; and *Sefer ha-Zoreph,* 325; and Sefirot, 114; on self, 2, 89, 108, 162; and state, 331; and Strauss, 455; and Szondi, 432–433; and Talmud, 36, 39, 69, 503n32; and teaching, 19, 36, 121, 258, 508n36; and Tel Aviv, 203; and temperament, 159, 516n47; and terrorism, 321; and Theresienstadt, 322; and the Torah, 19, 34, 35, 36–37, 54, 55, 100–101; and tradition, 36, 54, 95, 121, 410–411, 508n36; and translation, 37, 48–49, 69, 70, 71, 72–73, 74, 79, 89–90, 96, 103, 104–105, 106, 117–118, 152, 153, 183, 212, 298–299, 503n34, 505n77; and travel, 198, 199–200; and University of Heidelberg, 400–401; and University of Munich, 135, 509n54; and University of Zurich, 440–441; and *Vom Judentum,* 111; and Wandervögel, 13–14; and Warburgs, 170; and Weltsch, 119–120; and Werner Scholem, 13, 31–32, 248–249, 266, 293, 353–354; and World War I, 12, 13, 14, 17, 22, 29, 37–38, 39, 40, 63, 64, 68–69, 81; and World War II, 312, 324, 328; and *Zeitschrift für Sozialforschung,* 305; and Zionism, 7, 12, 13, 14–15, 20, 27, 28, 29, 32, 33, 34, 35, 37, 38, 40, 42, 47–48, 52, 54, 55, 57, 60, 89, 90, 93, 94, 95, 96, 100, 120–121, 137, 140, 145–146, 182, 185, 197, 278, 279–280, 292, 321, 330–331, 332, 333–334, 340, 341, 397, 412, 418–419, 424, 425, 447, 481, 482, 489, 510n75; and Zionist Congress, 279, 280. WORKS, 163; "Against the Myth of a German-Jewish Dialogue," 352; *Alchemy and Kabbalah,* 167; Bible translations, 48–49, 69, 70, 71, 72–73, 74, 79, 89–90, 503n34, 505n77; *Bibliographia Kabbalistica,* 94, 511n93; *Das Buch Bahir,* 90, 94, 114; *The Correspondence of Walter Benjamin and Gershom Sholem,* 349–350; *From Berlin to Jerusalem: Memories of My Youth,* 346, 349, 487; *Die Geheimnisse der Schöpfung,*

Scholem, Gershom *(continued)*
212, 275; Hilda Stroock Lectures (Jewish Institute of Religion), 213–214, 517n68; "Jewish Faith in Our Time," 216; *Judaica,* 438–439, 479; "Lyric of the Kabbalah?" 90, 119, 121; *Major Trends in Jewish Mysticism,* 213, 215, 272, 291, 308–309, 317–318, 328, 345, 348, 351, 517n68; *"The Messianic Idea in Judaism" and Other Essays on Jewish Spirituality,* 454; "On the Question of the Origins of the Kabbalah," 167, 300, 512n112; Psalm 104 commentary, 77; "Redemption through Sin," 212–213, 369–370, 371; "A Reply to Mr. Lev on the Method of Studying the Hebrew Language," 90; *Sabbatai Sevi: The Mystical Messiah,* 345, 348–349, 369, 443, 450, 456–457, 458–459, 461; "Sabbatai Sevi and Nathan of Gaza," 519n87; *Schocken Almanach* articles, 212; *Walter Benjamin: The Story of a Friendship,* 346, 349, 462; *Zohar* dictionary, 291, 292; *Zohar* translation, 298–299
Scholem, Hedwig "Hete," 147, 177–178, 237, 510n78
Scholem, Hilde, 407
Scholem, Irmgard, 482–483, 485
Scholem, Käte, 310
Scholem, Marcus, 448, 449
Scholem, Reinhold, 83, 126, 270, 271, 434–435, 465–466, 484–485, 491; and Arthur Scholem, 10; and Australia, 214, 299–300, 303, 307, 310, 333; and Betty Scholem, 202, 203, 289, 290; and business, 92; and emigration, 214, 283–284, 292; and Germany, 87–88, 98, 104, 108, 208–209, 490; and GS's work, 350–351, 414–416, 438–439, 443–444, 448–449; and politics, 108; and Scholem family, 350–351, 457, 458, 459, 461, 462, 463–464; and temperment, 166; and Warburg, 170; and World War I, 12, 490
Scholem, Renate, 258
Scholem, Scholem (Siegfried), 10, 11, 515n11

Scholem, Theobald, 42, 147, 275, 510n78
Scholem, Werner, 224; and Arthur Scholem, 10, 11, 13, 24, 42, 143, 237–238; death of, 214, 306–307, 486, 490–491; and emigration, 287–288, 294, 299, 517n63; and Emmy Scholem, 67, 504n64; and GS, 13, 31–32, 248–249, 266, 293, 353–354; and Judaism, 30, 32; and politics, 7, 11, 13, 22, 23, 24, 25, 30, 88, 91–92, 102, 132, 133, 147, 150, 152, 156–157, 160–161, 218; and prison, 13, 61, 207, 209, 214, 219–220, 221, 230, 232, 234, 235–240, 242–243, 244–245, 250, 256–257, 258, 259–260, 264, 266, 267, 270–271, 278, 279, 287–288, 290, 293, 295, 303, 491, 504n52; on self, 249; and trial, 264–265; and Uncle Katz, 135–136; and Waschitz, 490–491; and World War I, 12–13, 23
Scholem, Zippora, 448, 449
Seeligmann, Isaac Leo, 355–357
Sefer ha-Bahir, 89, 114, 252, 304, 505n4, 507n25
Sefer ha-Zohar. See Moses de León
Sefirot, 114, 501n42, 507n25
Selz, Jean, 421
Senator, Werner, 249
Sepharim, 114, 507n22
Sharp, Dr., 338
Silberner, Edmund, 429
Silvers, Robert, 464–465
Simmel, George, 66, 390
Simon, Ernst, 90, 91, 96, 128, 140–141, 145–146, 148–149, 151–152, 154–155, 183, 185, 212, 476
Siskin, Joshua, 437, 442
Smith, Morton, 357–358
Sonne, Isaiah, 325, 351
Spiegel, Shalom, 291–292, 311–312, 324–325
Spitzer, Moritz, 262, 516n44
Steiner, George, 209, 443, 450, 459
Steiner, Zara, 443
Strauss, Eduard, 182
Strauss, Leo, 317, 347, 388, 455, 525n41

Strauss, Ludwig, 72–73, 79–80, 104–106
Strauss, Miriam, 455
Susman, Margarete, 388, 389, 409
Szondi, Peter, 348, 381, 385–386, 408–409, 420, 432–433, 439–440, 468

Taubes, Jacob, 348, 363–364, 430, 432, 467–468
Taubes, Susan, 468
Tikkun, 145, 510n73
Tillich, Hannah, 485–486
Tillich, Paul, 286, 485–486
Tishby, Isaiah, 348, 370

Von Fritz, Kurt, 469–471

Wapnewski, Peter, 493–494
Warburg, Felix, 170

Warburg, Max, 94, 170
Waschitz, Dina, 490–491
Wassermann, Jakob: *My Life as German and Jew,* 391
Weiss, Erna, 436–437
Weiss, Josef, 363–364, 436–437, 468
Weltsch, Robert, 10, 119–121, 169, 176–177
Werblowsky, Zwi, 369–373
Wise, Stephen, 282
Wolff, Kurt, 94

Yira, 106, 506n9

Zigmond, Kathy, 440–441
Zigmond, Maurice, 440–441
Zohar. See Moses de León
Zoreph, Heschel: *Sefer ha-Zoreph,* 325
Zur Lippe, Rudolf, 492–493